W9-CNX-939

Information Systems Today

Why IS Matters

Second Canadian Edition

Leonard M. Jessup
Washington State University

Joseph S. Valacich
Washington State University

Michael R. Wade
York University

Toronto

To Joy, Jamie, and David, for your love and support.
—Len

To Jackie, Jordan, and James, for your sacrifices, encouragement, and support.
—Joe

To Heidi, Christopher, and Benjamin, for your patience and encouragement.
—Mike

Library and Archives Canada Cataloguing in Publication

Jessup, Leonard M., 1961–
Information systems today: why IS matters/Leonard M. Jessup, Joseph S. Valacich, Michael R. Wade. — 2nd Canadian ed.
Includes bibliographical references and index.
ISBN-13: 978-0-13-174039-6
ISBN-10: 0-13-174039-3
1. Information technology—Textbooks. 2. Information storage and retrieval systems—Business—Textbooks. I. Valacich, Joseph S., 1959– II. Wade, Michael, 1968– III. Title.
T58.5.J48 2008 658.4'038011 C2007-900254-4

ISBN-13: 978-0-13-174039-6
ISBN-10: 0-13-174039-3

Editor-in-Chief: Gary Bennett
Acquisitions Editor: Don Thompson
Sponsoring Editor: Lori Will
Marketing Manager: Eileen Lasswell
Developmental Editor: Paul Donnelly
Production Editor: Cheryl Jackson
Copy Editor: Integra
Proofreader: Karen Alliston
Production Coordinator: Avinash Chandra
Composition: Integra
Permissions and Photo Research: Amanda McCormick
Art Director: Julia Hall
Interior Design: Miguel Acevedo
Cover Design: Julia Hall
Cover Image: Getty Images

1 2 3 4 5 12 11 10 09 08

Printed and bound in the United States.

About the Authors

Leonard M. Jessup is Dean of the College of Business and Economics and is the Philip L. Kays Distinguished Professor in Management Information Systems at Washington State University. Professor Jessup received his B.A. in Information and Communication Studies in 1983 and his M.B.A. in 1985 from California State University, Chico, where he was voted Outstanding M.B.A. Student. He received his Ph.D. in Organizational Behavior and Management Information Systems from the University of Arizona in 1989. He is a member of the Association for Information Systems and Alpha Iota Delta and was Associate Editor for the Management Information Systems Quarterly, a past member of the Editorial Board for Small Group Research, and Conference Co-Chair for the International Conference on Information Systems, hosted by WSU and held in Seattle in 2003.

He has taught in various areas of MIS and has published, presented, and consulted on electronic commerce, computer-supported collaborative work, technology-supported teaching and learning, and on related topics. He has earned numerous awards for teaching excellence and innovation. Jessup came to WSU from Indiana University in June 2000 as Coordinator of the Management Information Systems (MIS) program. While managing the MIS program he helped to implement a Web-based online version of the undergraduate MIS program and an "MIS Fellows" program that enabled top undergraduate MIS students to work side-by-side with MIS faculty on cutting edge research projects. After a national search in the 2001/02 school year, he was selected as Dean of the College of Business and Economics. As Dean he led a complete reengineering of the business program which recently resulted in the successful AACSB reaccreditation of the College and has helped to position the College among the best and most innovative in the country. He has also helped to focus the College on innovative approaches to teaching and learning and has guided the development of innovative new facilities such as the Boeing Wireless Classroom of the Future and the James C. Nelson Gallery of Excellence, a computer-based, interactive display of excellence throughout the business program.

Joseph S. Valacich, The Marian E. Smith Presidential Endowed Chair and The George and Carolyn Hubman Distinguished Professor in MIS, joined the faculty at Washington State University in 1996. He was previously an Associate Professor with tenure (early) at Indiana University, Bloomington, and was named the Sanjay Subhedar Faculty Fellow. He has had visiting faculty appointments at the University of Arizona, City University of Hong Kong, Buskerud College (Norway), and the Helsinki School of Economics and Business. He received his Ph.D. from the University of Arizona in 1989, and his M.B.A. and B.S. (computer science) from the University of Montana. His teaching interests include Systems Analysis and Design, Collaborative Computing, Project Management, and Management of Information Systems. Professor Valacich served on the national task forces to design *IS '97* and *IS 2002: The Model Curriculum and Guidelines for Undergraduate Degree Programs in Information Systems* as well as *MSIS 2000: The Master of Science in Information Systems Model Curriculum*. He is currently serving on the Executive Committees working to update both models. He also served on the Executive Committee, funded by the National Science Foundation, to define the *IS Program Accreditation Standards* and is currently on the Board of Directors for CSAB (formally, the Computing Sciences Accreditation Board), representing the Association for Information Systems (AIS). He was the general conference co-chair for the 2003 International Conference on Information Systems (ICIS) in Seattle and was the vice-chair of ICIS 1999 in Charlotte. He currently serves on the Executive Committee for the Association for Information Systems.

He has conducted numerous corporate training and executive development programs for organizations, including AT&T, Dow Chemical, EDS, Exxon, FedEx, General Motors, and Xerox. He previously served on the editorial boards of *MIS Quarterly* (two terms), and is currently serving on the boards at *Information Systems Research* and *Small Group*

Research. His primary research interests include technology-mediated collaboration, mobile and emerging technologies, e-business, and distance education. He has more than 50 referred journal articles in publications such as *MIS Quarterly, Information Systems Research, Management Science, Academy of Management Journal, Communication of the AIS, Journal of AIS, Communications of the ACM, Decision Science, Organizational Behavior and Human Decision Processes, Journal of Applied Psychology, Journal of Management Information Systems, Communications of the AIS, Database, Group Decision and Negotiation, European Journal of Operations Research, Communications Research, Small Group Research, Journal of Management, Information and Management, Decision Support Systems, IEEE Transactions on Systems, Man and Cybernetics,* and *International Journal of Man-Machine Studies*. He is a co-author of the best-selling *Modern Systems Analysis and Design*, 4th Edition, as well as *Essentials of Systems Analysis and Design,* 3rd Edition, and *Object-Oriented Systems Analysis and Design*; all are published by Prentice Hall.

Michael R. Wade is an Associate Professor of Operations Management and Information Systems at the Schulich School of Business, York University. He received his Ph.D. in Management Information Systems at the Richard Ivey School of Business, University of Western Ontario. Professor Wade is a co-author of the textbook *Cases in Electronic Commerce* (first and second edition), published by McGraw-Hill. His research has appeared in journals such as *MIS Quarterly, Strategic Management Journal,* the *Journal of MIS,* and *Communications of the ACM*. His current research and consulting focuses on the strategic use of information systems for sustainable competitive advantage. Professor Wade has worked extensively in the technology management field in the Americas, Europe, and Asia.

Brief Contents

Chapters:

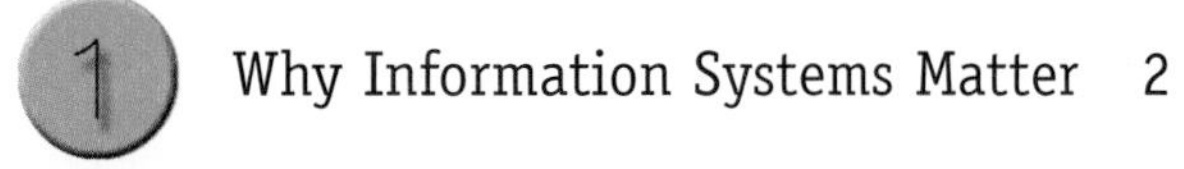

Contents

APPROACH

One of the greatest challenges that we face in teaching information systems courses is how to keep pace in the class with what is happening out in the real world. Hardware, software, telecommunications, and networking equipment—all of it continues to become faster, cheaper, and better, and business organizations continue to adopt and adapt these new technologies rapidly. Whereas a decade ago large businesses would spend two or three percent of their revenues on information technology, current spending on information technology for many large businesses can range from five to 10 percent of their revenue. Most important, organizations are now relying on that technology as a fundamental part of their business strategy and their competitiveness.

As a result of this pervasiveness and the fast pace of technology change and use in organizations, teaching people about information systems has never been more valuable or challenging.

Given the dynamic nature of information systems, and given that it is difficult to find introductory information systems textbooks that are both up-to-date and student-friendly, we wrote *Information Systems Today,* Second Canadian Edition, with four primary goals in mind. First, we want readers not only to learn about information systems, but to clearly understand ***why information systems matter*** to contemporary organizations and society. Second, we do not simply want to spoon-feed students with technical terms and the history of information systems. Instead, we want students to understand exactly what innovative organizations are doing with contemporary information systems and, more important, ***where things are headed.*** Third, we want to ***empower students with the essential knowledge they need to be successful*** in the use and understanding of information technology in their careers.

Finally, we want to present a uniquely Canadian perspective on the field of information systems (IS). When it comes to information systems, Canada shares a great deal with other countries of the world. After all, a computer works in much the same way in Kamloops as it does in Kuala Lumpur. However, there are a number of important factors that set Canada apart from other countries, particularly the United States. Canada relies much more heavily on the small- and medium-sized enterprise (SME) sector than the United States does. SMEs face a different set of challenges than large firms when it comes to the adoption and use of business information systems. As a large, sparsely populated nation, Canada must rely on a robust communications infrastructure. Partly for this reason, Canada has emerged as a world leader in networking technologies. Many of you reading this book will live and work in Canada, and so it is appropriate that you learn about information systems from a Canadian perspective.

To this end, we wrote *Information Systems Today,* Second Canadian Edition, so that it is contemporary, fun to read, and useful, and includes the essential body of knowledge regarding information systems in Canada.

AUDIENCE

Information Systems Today, Second Canadian Edition, is designed to be used in an undergraduate or graduate (MBA) introductory information systems course, as required by many schools of business. The introductory information systems course typically has a diverse audience of students majoring in many different areas, such as accounting, economics, finance, marketing, general management, human resource management, production and operations, international business, entrepreneurship, and information systems. Given the range of students taking this type of course, we have written this book so that it is a valuable guide to all business students and provides them with the essential information they need to know. Students majoring in areas outside of business may also attend the introductory information systems course. Therefore, this book has been written to appeal to a diverse audience.

WHAT'S NEW TO THE SECOND CANADIAN EDITION

Our primary goal for *Information Systems Today,* Second Canadian Edition, was to emphasize why information systems matter to all business students as the role of information technology and systems continues to expand within organizations and society. Given this clear focus, we are better able to identify those topics most critical to students and future business professionals. Consequently, we have made substantial revisions to the basic content of the chapters and pedagogical elements, as well as included several new elements that we believe achieve this goal. A sample of the new or expanded chapter topics include:

- Emerging technologies such as Bluetooth, PANs, WiFi, RFID, peer-to-peer networking, tablet PCs, and emerging mobile devices
- Technology management issues related to computer viruses and worms, as well as spam, cookies, and, spyware
- Disaster recovery planning, cyberwar, and cyberterrorism
- Enterprise-wide systems and the management of knowledge assets

In addition to the changes within the main chapter content, we have also added four new features to each chapter—"Canada Competes!," "Canadian NetStats," "SME Success," and "Ethical Dilemmas."

Canada Competes!: Canada Competes! opens each chapter with an example of a Canadian IT-related firm that has been successful on the international stage.

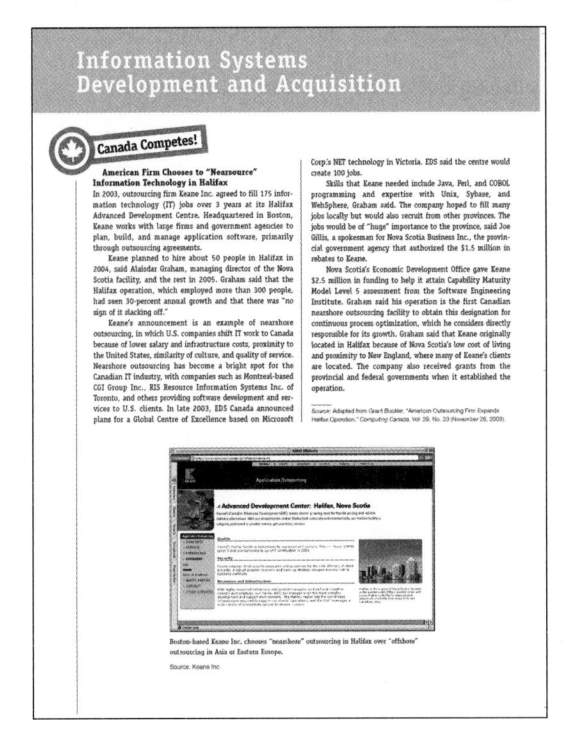

Information Systems Development and Acquisition

Canada Competes!

American Firm Chooses to "Nearsource" Information Technology in Halifax

In 2003, outsourcing firm Keane Inc. agreed to fill 175 information technology (IT) jobs over 3 years at its Halifax Advanced Development Centre. Headquartered in Boston, Keane works with large firms and government agencies to plan, build, and manage application software, primarily through outsourcing agreements.

Keane planned to hire about 50 people in Halifax in 2004, said Alaisdar Graham, managing director of the Nova Scotia facility, and the rest in 2005. Graham said that the Halifax operation, which employed more than 300 people, had seen 30-percent annual growth and that there was "no sign of it slacking off."

Keane's announcement is an example of nearshore outsourcing, in which U.S. companies shift IT work to Canada because of lower salary and infrastructure costs, proximity to the United States, similarity of culture, and quality of service. Nearshore outsourcing has become a bright spot for the Canadian IT industry, with companies such as Montreal-based CGI Group Inc., RIS Resource Information Systems Inc. of Toronto, and others providing software development and services to U.S. clients. In late 2003, EDS Canada announced plans for a Global Centre of Excellence based on Microsoft Corp.'s NET technology in Victoria. EDS said the centre would create 100 jobs.

Skills that Keane needed include Java, Perl, and COBOL programming and expertise with Unix, Sybase, and WebSphere, Graham said. The company hoped to fill many jobs locally but would also recruit from other provinces. The jobs would be of "huge" importance to the province, said Joe Gillis, a spokesman for Nova Scotia Business Inc., the provincial government agency that authorized the $1.5 million in rebates to Keane.

Nova Scotia's Economic Development Office gave Keane $2.5 million in funding to help it attain Capability Maturity Model Level 5 assessment from the Software Engineering Institute. Graham said his operation is the first Canadian nearshore outsourcing facility to obtain this designation for continuous process optimization, which he considers directly responsible for its growth. Graham said that Keane originally located in Halifax because of Nova Scotia's low cost of living and proximity to New England, where many of Keane's clients are located. The company also received grants from the provincial and federal governments when it established the operation.

Source: Adapted from Grant Buckler, "American Outsourcing Firm Expands Halifax Operation," Computing Canada, Vol. 29, No. 23 (November 28, 2003).

Boston-based Keane Inc. chooses "nearshore" outsourcing in Halifax over "offshore" outsourcing in Asia or Eastern Europe.

Source: Keane Inc.

Canadian NetStats: Canadian NetStats briefly examines topics related to the growing pervasiveness of the Internet within Canadian organizations and society.

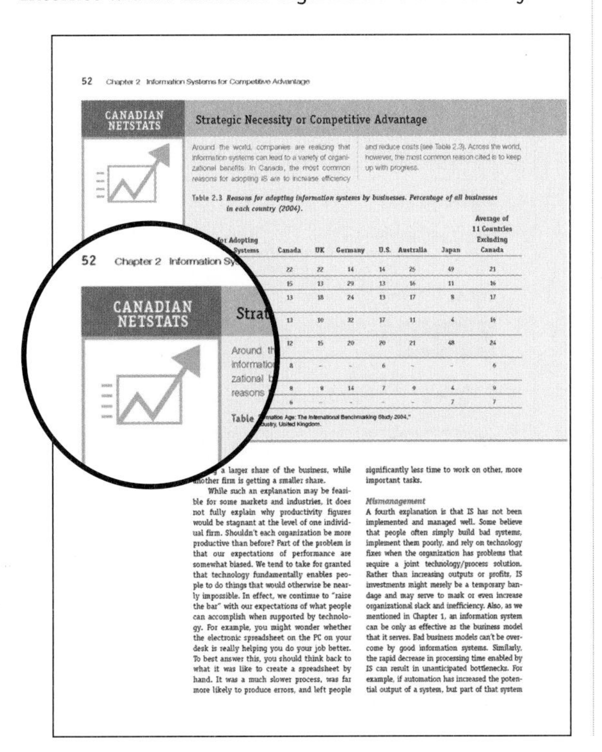

52 Chapter 2 Information Systems for Competitive Advantage

CANADIAN NETSTATS

Strategic Necessity or Competitive Advantage

Around the world, companies are realizing that information systems can lead to a variety of organizational benefits. In Canada, the most common reasons for adopting IS are to increase efficiency and reduce costs (see Table 2.3). Across the world, however, the most common reason cited is to keep up with progress.

Table 2.3 Reasons for adopting information systems by businesses. Percentage of all businesses in each country (2004).

[illegible] Adopting Systems	Canada	UK	Germany	U.S.	Australia	Japan	Average of 11 Countries Excluding Canada
[illegible]	22	22	14	14	25	49	21
[illegible]	15	13	29	13	16	11	16
[illegible]	15	15	24	13	17	8	17
[illegible]	13	10	12	17	11	4	16
[illegible]	12	15	20	20	21	48	24
[illegible]	8	–	–	–	6	–	6
[illegible]	8	8	14	7	9	6	9
[illegible]	6	–	–	–	–	7	7

[illegible] ation Age: The International Benchmarking Study 2004," [illegible] dustry, United Kingdom.

[illegible] a larger share of the business, while [illegible] other firm is getting a smaller share.

While such an explanation may be feasible for some markets and industries, it does not fully explain why productivity figures would be stagnant at the level of one individual firm. Shouldn't each organization be more productive than before? Part of the problem is that our expectations of performance are somewhat biased. We tend to take for granted that technology fundamentally enables people to do things that would otherwise be nearly impossible. In effect, we continue to "raise the bar" with our expectations of what people can accomplish when supported by technology. For example, you might wonder whether the electronic spreadsheet on the PC on your desk is really helping you do your job better. To best answer this, you should think back to what it was like to create a spreadsheet by hand. It was a much slower process, was far more likely to produce errors, and left people significantly less time to work on other, more important tasks.

Mismanagement

A fourth explanation is that IS has not been implemented and managed well. Some believe that people often simply build bad systems, implement them poorly, and rely on technology fixes when the organization has problems that require a joint technology/process solution. Rather than increasing outputs or profits, IS investments might merely be a temporary bandage and may serve to mask or even increase organizational slack and inefficiency. Also, as we mentioned in Chapter 1, an information system can be only as effective as the business model that it serves. Bad business models can't be overcome by good information systems. Similarly, the rapid decrease in processing time enabled by IS can result in unanticipated bottlenecks. For example, if automation has increased the potential output of a system, but part of that system

SME Success: SME Success profiles a successful Canadian small- or medium-sized enterprise in the IT sector.

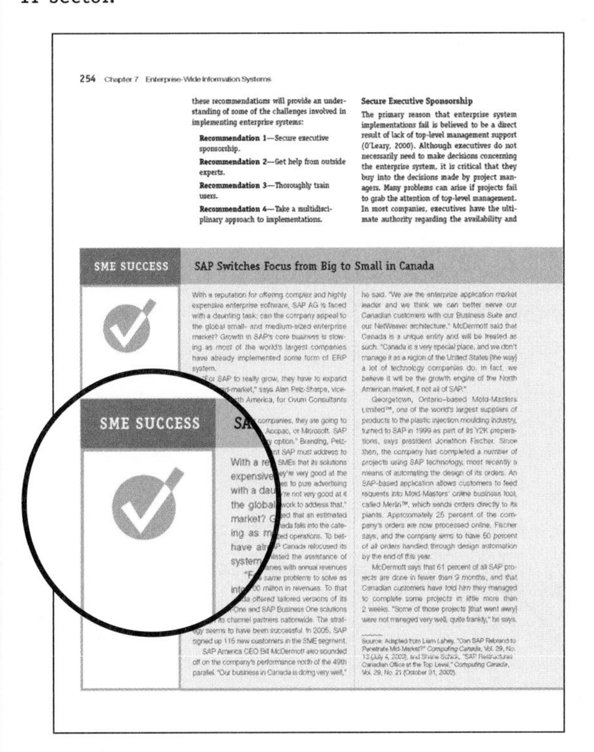

254 Chapter 7 Enterprise-Wide Information Systems

these recommendations will provide an understanding of some of the challenges involved in implementing enterprise systems:

Recommendation 1—Secure executive sponsorship.

Recommendation 2—Get help from outside experts.

Recommendation 3—Thoroughly train users.

Recommendation 4—Take a multidisciplinary approach to implementations.

Secure Executive Sponsorship

The primary reason that enterprise system implementations fail is believed to be a direct result of lack of top-level management support (O'Leary, 2000). Although executives do not necessarily need to make decisions concerning the enterprise system, it is critical that they buy into the decisions made by project managers. Many problems can arise if projects fail to grab the attention of top-level management. In most companies, executives have the ultimate authority regarding the availability and

SME SUCCESS

SAP Switches Focus from Big to Small in Canada

With a reputation for offering complex and highly expensive enterprise software, SAP AG is faced with a daunting task: can the company appeal to the global small- and medium-sized enterprise market? Growth in SAP's core business is slowing as most of the world's largest companies have already implemented some form of ERP system.

"For SAP to really grow, they have to expand [illegible] market," says Alan Pelz-Sharpe, vice- [illegible] America, for Ovum Consultants [illegible] companies, they are going to [illegible] Accpac, or Microsoft. SAP [illegible] option." Branding, Pelz- [illegible] SAP must address to [illegible] SMEs that its solutions [illegible] they're very good at the [illegible] to pure advertising [illegible] re not very good at it [illegible] work to address that." [illegible] that an estimated [illegible] nada falls into the cate- [illegible] operations. To bet- [illegible] P Canada refocused its [illegible] sted the assistance of [illegible] nies with annual revenues [illegible] same problems to solve as [illegible] 00 million in revenues. To that [illegible] da offered tailored versions of its [illegible] One and SAP Business One solutions [illegible] its channel partners nationwide. The strategy seems to have been successful. In 2005, SAP signed up 115 new customers in the SME segment.

SAP America CEO Bill McDermott also sounded off on the company's performance north of the 49th parallel. "Our business in Canada is doing very well," he said. "We are the enterprise application market leader and we think we can better serve our Canadian customers with our Business Suite and our NetWeaver architecture." McDermott said that Canada is a unique entity and will be treated as such. "Canada is a very special place, and we don't manage it as a region of the United States [the way] a lot of technology companies do. In fact, we believe it will be the growth engine of the North American market, if not all of SAP."

Georgetown, Ontario-based Mold-Masters Limited™, one of the world's largest suppliers of products to the plastic injection moulding industry, turned to SAP in 1999 as part of its Y2K preparations, says president Jonathon Fischer. Since then, the company has completed a number of projects using SAP technology, most recently a means of automating the design of its orders. An SAP-based application allows customers to feed requests into Mold-Masters' online business tool, called Merlin™, which sends orders directly to its plants. Approximately 25 percent of the company's orders are now processed online, Fischer says, and the company aims to have 50 percent of all orders handled through design automation by the end of this year.

McDermott says that 61 percent of all SAP projects are done in fewer than 9 months, and that Canadian customers have told him they managed to complete some projects in little more than 2 weeks. "Some of those projects [that went awry] were not managed very well, quite frankly," he says.

Source: Adapted from Liam Lahey, "Can SAP Rebrand to Penetrate Mid-Market?" Computing Canada, Vol. 29, No. 13 (July 4, 2003), and Shane Schick, "SAP Restructures Canadian Office at the Top Level," Computing Canada, Vol. 29, No. 21 (October 31, 2003).

Ethical Dilemma: Ethical Dilemmas provide opportunities for examining the growing dilemmas facing managers, organizations, and society as the role of information systems continues to expand.

Why Use Information Systems? 43

by certain types of people at certain times of the year (e.g., more auto loan applications in the fall, mostly from men in their twenties and thirties), the patterns of the loan decisions made, or the subsequent performance of those loans. This new system creates data about the underlying business process that can be used to better monitor, control, and change that process. In other words, you learn from this information system about loan applications and approvals; as a result, you can do a better job at evaluating loan applications.

A combined automating and learning approach, in the long run, is more effective than an automating approach alone. If the underlying business process supported by technology is inherently flawed, a learning use of the technology might help you detect the problems with the process and change it. For instance, in our loan-processing example, a learning use of technology may help us uncover a pattern among the accepted loans that enables us to distinguish between low- and high-performing loans over their lives and subsequently to change the criteria for loan acceptance.

If, however, the underlying business process is bad, and you are using technology only for automating (that is, you would not uncover the data that would tell you this process is bad), you are more likely to continue with a flawed or less-than-optimal business process. In fact, such an automating use of technology may mask the process problems.

With a bad underlying set of loan acceptance criteria (e.g., rules that would allow you to approve a loan for someone who had a high level of debt as long as they had not been late on any payments recently), a person might manually review four applications in a day and, because of the problematic criteria used, inadvertently accept two "bad" applications per week on average. If you automated the same faulty process, with no learning aspects built in, the system might help a person review 12 applications per day, with six "bad" applications accepted per week on average. The technology would serve only to magnify the existing business problems. Without learning, it is more difficult to uncover bad business processes underlying the information system.

Using Information Systems to Support Total Quality Management

Organizations that use information systems to support a ***total quality management (TQM)*** initiative are more than likely to be using these systems with a learning approach. As part of a TQM approach, people within the organization constantly monitor what they do to find ways to improve quality of operations, products, services, and everything else about the firm.

ETHICAL DILEMMA

Who Owns Your Address Book?

Information is power—if it's used in the right place, at the right time, and by the right people. For many people, information belonging to a previous employer can be a powerful aid in a new job. Sales employees often regard the contacts database as one of the most powerful information repositories; having this information enables them to maintain business contacts after changing to a new employer. Taking the contacts database with them to the new job greatly facilitates succeeding in the new job.

Today's networked workplaces facilitate this [illegible] information. Many employees simply transfer [illegible] needed" information to their own e-mail [illegible] others use storage devices such as [illegible] ROM, or flash key drive to take this [illegible] with them.

[illegible] ployees stealing pencils seem to [illegible] ys, employees are stealing [illegible] goods: information! From the organizations' standpoint, stealing information is not only more harmful than stealing a few pencils; it may be more harmful than stealing sophisticated computer hardware.

A recent survey has found that 70 percent of the respondents had stolen key information from an employer. Seventy-two percent of the people surveyed indicated that they had no ethical problems with taking proposals, presentations, contact databases, or e-mail address books when changing to a new employer. Often, employees justify these actions by their investment in preparing these resources. After all, hasn't their work helped to build that customer database and to create so many sales leads?

Source: Anonymous, "Workplace Data Theft Runs Rampant," BBC News (15 February, 2004), **http://news.bbc.co.uk/1/hi/technology/3486397.stm.**

Application Exercises: Beyond the chapter content and features, we have also made substantial additions and refinements to the end of each chapter. First, we have added a new feature called "Application Exercises" which provides students the opportunity to solve real-world business problems using contemporary desktop spreadsheet and database applications. Second, we have added a real-world business case called "Connexion by Boeing" which outlines the startup and struggles of a new technology business. Each installment of the case mirrors the primary content of its chapter to better emphasize its relevancy within the context of a real organization. All of these new elements are discussed more thoroughly below.

300 Chapter 8 Information Systems Development and Acquisition

APPLICATION EXERCISES

Note: The existing data files referenced in these exercises are available on the Companion Website: **www.pearsoned.ca/jessup**.

Spreadsheet Application: Outsourcing Information Systems at BlueSky

BlueSky Airlines wants to increase its consumer focus and wants to be able to better serve its most valued customers. Many members of the frequent flyer program have requested the ability to check on the status of their membership online; furthermore, the frequent flyers would welcome the opportunity to book reward flights online. As you know that there are many companies specializing in building such transactional systems, you have … to outsource the development of this system. The following … assigned to evaluate the different vendors' … formatting to highlight all vendors falling below 60 percent and above 85 percent to facilitate the vendor selection.

Database Application: Building a Movie Database

Since you and your roommates own a large number of DVD movies, you decide to create a database of the DVD collection to better locate individual movies. To make the system as useful as possible for all, you need to design reports for the users to retrieve information about the movies. Your roommates would like to have a system that contains the following information about the movies:

- Title.
- Copyright date.
- Category.
- Owner.

Each movie belongs to at least one category (e.g., comedy, action) but can also belong to multiple categories. Each category can contain multiple movies. Also, each movie belongs to one owner, but different people can own copies of the same movie. After designing the database, please design three professionally formatted reports that (1) list the movies in alphabetical order, (2) list all movies that belong to the different categories, and (3) list all movies that belong to a particular owner. Hint: In Microsoft Access, you can create queries before preparing the reports. Enter a few sample data sets and print out the reports.

4. B, p. 276 5. B, p. 281
9. D, p. 290 10. D, p. 287

Case *IT Outsourcing: A Mixed Blessing for Canada*

The offshore outsourcing of technology jobs will have a negative impact on the viability of the IT industry in Canada, according to most professionals surveyed by the Canadian Information Processing Society (CIPS). Of the 111 senior IT professionals polled, more than half told CIPS they have outsourced some IT functions or are considering it: 69.4 percent said they believed the trend does not bode well for the sector's overall health. Only 33 percent said they believed offshore outsourcing would help the Canadian economy.

The research reflects the growing fear among Canadian IT workers that their skills may be obsolete if lower-level programming work is moved to India, China, Romania, or elsewhere (see Table 8.12). From the employer's perspective, however, offshore outsourcing is simply a matter of dollars and sense. "What is the difference between sourcing a product offshore? We all have radios here, and I doubt many of them were made in Canada," said Gabor Takach, a lawyer who leads the technology group at Torys LLP. "This trend [offshore outsourcing] represents a concentration of expertise and a new and efficient way of delivering a service." Paul Harrington, a consultant for retail, small business, and marketing companies, says some IT workers may have reason to feel paranoid. "When an industry disappears—like buggy whips—they just disappear. Everybody in every industry has to take a look at what's happening in their industry. This is an industry that's in a great deal of turmoil at the moment."

Kevin Yan, CEO of global software development services firm Arackal Digital Solutions, says he looks at offshore outsourcing as a productivity tool because it allows companies to eliminate low-value coding tasks. "If you have a better way of doing business out there, why wouldn't you do it?" John Chettleburgh, a staffing industry consultant and former vice-president at CNC Global, points out that most offshore outsourcing is done by Canada's largest firms, which means some of the jobs may not disappear entirely. "It could mean a renaissance for these kinds of jobs in the SME market in Canada."

Our goal has always been to provide only the information that is relevant to all business students, nothing more and nothing less. We hope that we have again achieved this goal with *Information Systems Today, Second Canadian Edition*.

KEY FEATURES

As authors, teachers, developers, and managers of information systems, we understand that, in order for students to best learn about information systems with this book, they must be motivated to learn. To this end we have included a number of unique features to help students quickly and easily assess the true value of information systems and their impact on everyday life. We show how today's professionals are using information systems to help modern organizations become more efficient and competitive. Our focus is on the application of technology to real-world, contemporary situations in a Canadian context. Below, we describe each of the features that contribute to that focus.

A Multitiered Approach

Each chapter utilizes cases in a variety of ways to emphasize and highlight how contemporary organizations are utilizing information systems to gain competitive advantage, streamline organizational processes, or improve customer satisfaction.

Opening Scenario—Canada Competes!

All chapters begin with an opening scenario describing a real-world Canadian company that has been successful beyond our borders. These firms operate in IT-related sectors and include software companies, hardware companies, outsourcing providers, and even a video game designer. Firms described in Canada Competes! come from across the country including examples from British Columbia, Alberta, Ontario, Quebec, and Nova Scotia.

A photo or illustration is included with each scenario. Examples of Canada Competes! companies include Softchoice, Radialpoint, Redline Communications, 3LFilters, Beenox, Nordia, and Stantec Inc.

Brief Case

Each chapter also includes two brief cases that are taken directly from the news and that discuss contemporary Canadian and international companies and technologies. These are embedded in the text of the chapter and highlight concepts from the surrounding chapter material. Discussion questions are provided to seed critical thinking assignments or class discussions. Two or three 'bonus' brief cases for each chapter can be found on the Companion Website.

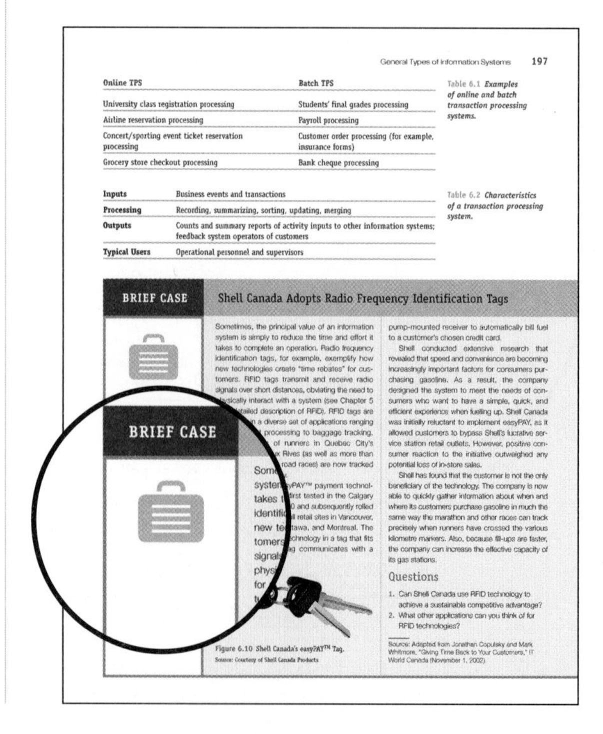
General Types of Information Systems 197

Online TPS	Batch TPS
University class registration processing	Students' final grades processing
Airline reservation processing	Payroll processing
Concert/sporting event ticket reservation processing	Customer order processing (for example, insurance forms)
Grocery store checkout processing	Bank cheque processing

Table 6.1 *Examples of online and batch transaction processing systems.*

Inputs	Business events and transactions
Processing	Recording, summarizing, sorting, updating, merging
Outputs	Counts and summary reports of activity inputs to other information systems; feedback system operators of customers
Typical Users	Operational personnel and supervisors

Table 6.2 *Characteristics of a transaction processing system.*

BRIEF CASE Shell Canada Adopts Radio Frequency Identification Tags

Sometimes, the principal value of an information system is simply to reduce the time and effort it takes to complete an operation. Radio frequency identification tags, for example, exemplify how new technologies create "time rebates" for customers. RFID tags transmit and receive radio signals over short distances, obviating the need to physically interact with a system (see Chapter 5 … detailed description of RFID). RFID tags are … a diverse set of applications ranging … processing to baggage tracking. … of runners in Quebec City's … Rives (as well as more than … road races) are now tracked … easyPAY™ payment technol… first tested in the Calgary … and subsequently rolled … retail sites in Vancouver, … tawa, and Montreal. The … technology in a tag that fits … tag communicates with a pump-mounted receiver to automatically bill fuel to a customer's chosen credit card.

Shell conducted extensive research that revealed that speed and convenience are becoming increasingly important factors for consumers purchasing gasoline. As a result, the company designed the system to meet the needs of consumers who want to have a simple, quick, and efficient experience when fuelling up. Shell Canada was initially reluctant to implement easyPAY, as it allowed customers to bypass Shell's lucrative service station retail outlets. However, positive consumer reaction to the initiative outweighed any potential loss of in-store sales.

Shell has found that the customer is not the only beneficiary of the technology. The company is now able to quickly gather information about when and where its customers purchase gasoline in much the same way the marathon and other races can track precisely when runners have crossed the various kilometre markers. Also, because fill-ups are faster, the company can increase the effective capacity of its gas stations.

Questions

1. Can Shell Canada use RFID technology to achieve a sustainable competitive advantage?
2. What other applications can you think of for RFID technologies?

Source: Adapted from Jonathan Copulsky and Mark Whitmore, "Giving Time Back to Your Customers," IT World Canada (November 1, 2002).

Figure 6.10 Shell Canada's easyPAY™ Tag.
Source: Courtesy of Shell Canada Products

SME Success

SME Success is a special example of a brief case in each chapter. It describes how small- or medium-sized Canadian firms have overcome challenges to achieve success in the IT sector. SME examples are drawn from across the country. This feature is relevant to students who are considering joining smaller organizations or who want to start their own businesses.

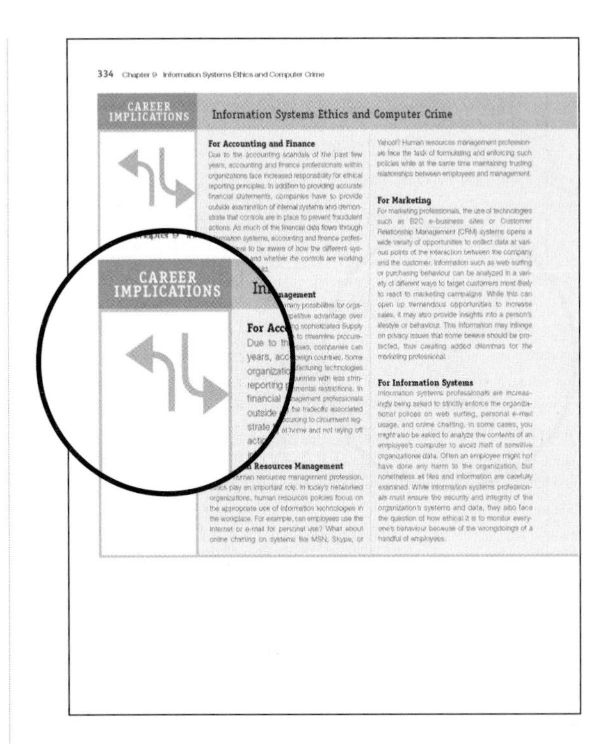

334 Chapter 9 Information Systems Ethics and Computer Crime

CAREER IMPLICATIONS — Information Systems Ethics and Computer Crime

For Accounting and Finance

Due to the accounting scandals of the past few years, accounting and finance professionals within organizations face increased responsibility for ethical reporting principles. In addition to providing accurate financial statements, companies have to provide outside examination of internal systems and demonstrate that controls are in place to prevent fraudulent actions. As much of the financial data flows through [illegible]ation systems, accounting and finance profes[illegible]ve to be aware of how the different sys[illegible] and whether the controls are working [illegible]

[illegible]nagement [illegible] many possibilities for orga[illegible]petitive advantage over [illegible]g sophisticated Supply [illegible] to streamline procure[illegible]sses, companies can [illegible]reign countries. Some [illegible]facturing technologies [illegible]untries with less strin[illegible]mental restrictions. In [illegible]nagement professionals [illegible] the tradeoffs associated [illegible]curing to circumvent reg[illegible] at home and not laying off [illegible]

[illegible] Resources Management

[illegible]uman resources management profession, [illegible]ics play an important role. In today's networked organizations, human resources policies focus on the appropriate use of information technologies in the workplace. For example, can employees use the Internet or e-mail for personal use? What about online chatting on systems like MSN, Skype, or Yahoo!? Human resources management professionals face the task of formulating and enforcing such policies while at the same time maintaining trusting relationships between employees and management.

For Marketing

For marketing professionals, the use of technologies such as B2C e-business sites or Customer Relationship Management (CRM) systems opens a wide variety of opportunities to collect data at various points of the interaction between the company and the customer. Information such as web surfing or purchasing behaviour can be analyzed in a variety of different ways to target customers most likely to react to marketing campaigns. While this can open up tremendous opportunities to increase sales, it may also provide insights into a person's lifestyle or behaviour. This information may infringe on privacy issues that some believe should be protected, thus creating added dilemmas for the marketing professional.

For Information Systems

Information systems professionals are increasingly being asked to strictly enforce the organizational polices on web surfing, personal e-mail usage, and online chatting. In some cases, you might also be asked to analyze the contents of an employee's computer to avoid theft of sensitive organizational data. Often an employee might not have done any harm to the organization, but nonetheless all files and information are carefully examined. While information systems professionals must ensure the security and integrity of the organization's systems and data, they also face the question of how ethical it is to monitor everyone's behaviour because of the wrongdoings of a handful of employees.

End of Chapter Case

To test and reinforce chapter content, we present a real-world case at the end of each chapter. Like the Brief Cases within the chapter, these are taken from the news and are contemporary. However, these are longer and more substantive than the Brief Cases and are followed by discussion questions that help the student apply and master the chapter. Two 'bonus' final cases for each chapter have been placed on the Companion Website.

Connexion by Boeing

This new, real-world business case is used throughout the book and follows each chapter in order to enable students to apply lessons from each chapter in the business world. The Boeing Company took a vision for providing high speed Internet connectivity within commercial airplanes and developed this concept into a company that will permanently transform the airline industry. Discussion questions are included with this running case after each chapter in order to promote critical thinking and class participation.

COMMON CHAPTER ELEMENTS

Throughout every chapter, a variety of short pedagogical elements are presented to highlight key information systems issues and concepts in a variety of contexts. These elements help to show students the broader organizational and societal implications of various topics.

In order to show students how the material applies to their individual career tracks, "Career Implications" maps the chapter material to the fields of accounting and finance, operations management, human resource management, marketing, and information systems. For example, an aspiring accountant or financial analyst will find an explanation within every chapter of how that chapter's material applies to their chosen fields. Similarly, this element will examine implications for a marketing major, for an operations management major, and so on. Chapter 1 includes a special section highlighting how knowledge about information systems can be useful for specific non-IS career paths.

We worked hard to ensure that this book is contemporary. We cover literally hundreds of different emerging technologies throughout the book. "Coming Attractions" describes some specific emerging technology that is likely to impact organizations or society. Topics include:

- Wearable computing and robots, electronic paper, portable lie detectors, and RFID
- Databases to store your entire digital life
- Turbo codes for revolutionizing data communication speeds
- The future of automated phone answering systems
- Using face and mouth movements to aid speech recognition systems

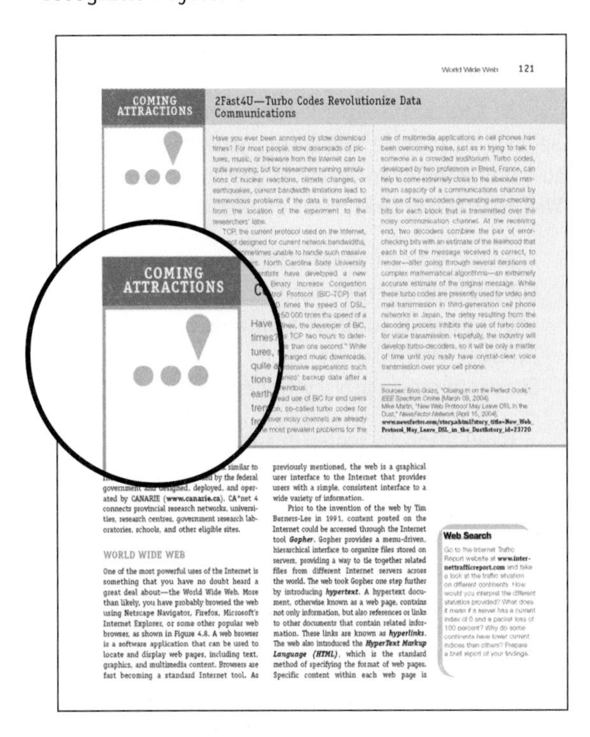

World Wide Web 121

COMING ATTRACTIONS — 2Fast4U—Turbo Codes Revolutionize Data Communications

Have you ever been annoyed by slow download times? For most people, slow downloads of pictures, music, or freeware from the Internet can be quite annoying, but for researchers running simulations of nuclear reactions, climate changes, or earthquakes, current bandwidth limitations lead to tremendous problems if the data is transferred from the location of the experiment to the researchers' labs.

TCP, the current protocol used on the Internet, [illegible]ot designed for current network bandwidths, [illegible]ometimes unable to handle such massive [illegible]s. North Carolina State University [illegible]ntists have developed a new [illegible] Binary Increase Congestion [illegible]rol Protocol (BIC-TCP) that [illegible] times the speed of DSL, [illegible]50 000 times the speed of a [illegible]nee, the developer of BIC, [illegible] TCP two hours to deter[illegible] than one second." While [illegible]harged music downloads, [illegible]tensive applications such [illegible]nies' backup data after a [illegible]endous. [illegible]ead use of BIC for end users [illegible]n, so-called turbo codes for [illegible]over noisy channels are already [illegible] most prevalent problems for the use of multimedia applications in cell phones has been overcoming noise, just as in trying to talk to someone in a crowded auditorium. Turbo codes, developed by two professors in Brest, France, can help to come extremely close to the absolute maximum capacity of a communications channel by the use of two encoders generating error-checking bits for each block that is transmitted over the noisy communication channel. At the receiving end, two decoders combine the pair of error-checking bits with an estimate of the likelihood that each bit of the message received is correct, to render—after going through several iterations of complex mathematical algorithms—an extremely accurate estimate of the original message. While these turbo codes are presently used for video and mail transmission in third-generation cell phone networks in Japan, the delay resulting from the decoding process inhibits the use of turbo codes for voice transmission. Hopefully, the industry will develop turbo-decoders, so it will be only a matter of time until you really have crystal-clear voice transmission over your cell phone.

Sources: Erico Guizo, "Closing in on the Perfect Code," *IEEE Spectrum Online* (March 09, 2004).
Mike Martin, "New Web Protocol May Leave DSL in the Dust," *NewsFactor Network* (April 15, 2004), **www.newsfactor.com/story.xhtml?story_title=New_Web_Protocol_May_Leave_DSL_in_the_Dust&story_id=23720**

[illegible] similar to [illegible] by the federal government [illegible], deployed, and operated by CANARIE (**www.canarie.ca**). CA*net 4 connects provincial research networks, universities, research centres, government research laboratories, schools, and other eligible sites.

WORLD WIDE WEB

One of the most powerful uses of the Internet is something that you have no doubt heard a great deal about—the World Wide Web. More than likely, you have probably browsed the web using Netscape Navigator, Firefox, Microsoft's Internet Explorer, or some other popular web browser, as shown in Figure 4.8. A web browser is a software application that can be used to locate and display web pages, including text, graphics, and multimedia content. Browsers are fast becoming a standard Internet tool. As previously mentioned, the web is a graphical user interface to the Internet that provides users with a simple, consistent interface to a wide variety of information.

Prior to the invention of the web by Tim Berners-Lee in 1991, content posted on the Internet could be accessed through the Internet tool ***Gopher***. Gopher provides a menu-driven, hierarchical interface to organize files stored on servers, providing a way to tie together related files from different Internet servers across the world. The web took Gopher one step further by introducing ***hypertext***. A hypertext document, otherwise known as a web page, contains not only information, but also references or links to other documents that contain related information. These links are known as ***hyperlinks***. The web also introduced the ***HyperText Markup Language (HTML)***, which is the standard method of specifying the format of web pages. Specific content within each web page is

Web Search

Go to the Internet Traffic Report website at **www.internettrafficreport.com** and take a look at the traffic situation on different continents. How would you interpret the different statistics provided? What does it mean if a server has a current index of 0 and a packet loss of 100 percent? Why do some continents have lower current indices than others? Prepare a brief report of your findings.

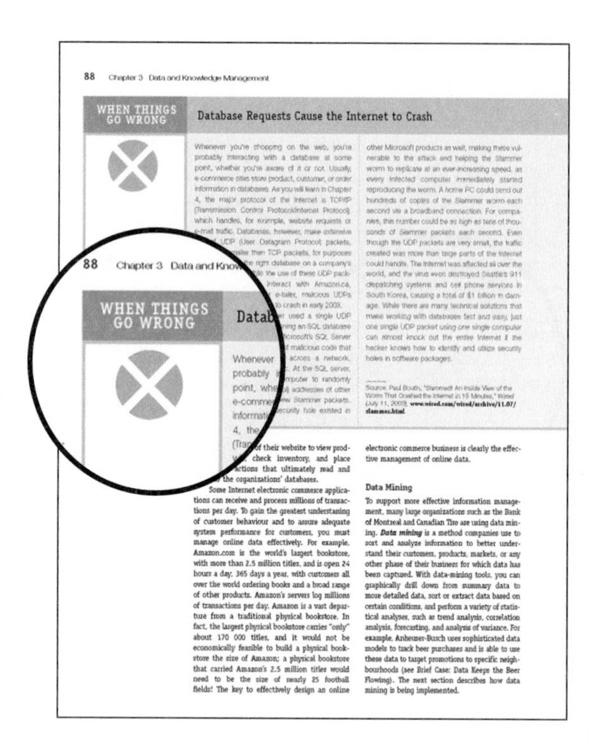
88 Chapter 3 Data and Knowledge Management

WHEN THINGS GO WRONG

Database Requests Cause the Internet to Crash

Whenever you're shopping on the web, you're probably interacting with a database at some point, whether you're aware of it or not. Usually, e-commerce sites store product, customer, or order information in databases. As you will learn in Chapter 4, the major protocol of the Internet is TCP/IP (Transmission Control Protocol/Internet Protocol), which handles, for example, website requests or e-mail traffic. Databases, however, make extensive [illegible] UDP (User Datagram Protocol) packets, [illegible] than TCP packets, for purposes [illegible] right database on a company's [illegible] the use of these UDP pack- [illegible] interact with Amazon.ca, [illegible] e-tailer, malicious UDPs [illegible] to crash in early 2003. [illegible] used a single UDP [illegible] an SQL database [illegible] Microsoft's SQL Server [illegible] malicious code that [illegible] across a network. [illegible] At the SQL server, [illegible] computer to randomly [illegible] addresses of other [illegible] Slammer packets. [illegible] security hole existed in other Microsoft products as well, making these vulnerable to the attack and helping the Slammer worm to replicate at an ever-increasing speed, as every infected computer immediately started reproducing the worm. A home PC could send out hundreds of copies of the Slammer worm each second via a broadband connection. For companies, this number could be as high as tens of thousands of Slammer packets each second. Even though the UDP packets are very small, the traffic created was more than large parts of the Internet could handle. The Internet was affected all over the world, and the virus even destroyed Seattle's 911 dispatching systems and cell phone services in South Korea, causing a total of $1 billion in damage. While there are many technical solutions that make working with databases fast and easy, just one single UDP packet using one single computer can almost knock out the entire Internet if the hacker knows how to identify and utilize security holes in software packages.

Source: Paul Boutin, "Slammed! An Inside View of the Worm That Crashed the Internet in 15 Minutes," Wired (July 11, 2003), **www.wired.com/wired/archive/11.07/slammer.html**.

[illegible] of their website to view prod[illegible], check inventory, and place [illegible]actions that ultimately read and [illegible] the organizations' databases.

Some Internet electronic commerce applications can receive and process millions of transactions per day. To gain the greatest understaning of customer behaviour and to assure adequate system performance for customers, you must manage online data effectively. For example, Amazon.com is the world's largest bookstore, with more than 2.5 million titles, and is open 24 hours a day, 365 days a year, with customers all over the world ordering books and a broad range of other products. Amazon's servers log millions of transactions per day. Amazon is a vast departure from a traditional physical bookstore. In fact, the largest physical bookstore carries "only" about 170 000 titles, and it would not be economically feasible to build a physical bookstore the size of Amazon; a physical bookstore that carried Amazon's 2.5 million titles would need to be the size of nearly 25 football fields! The key to effectively design an online electronic commerce business is clearly the effective management of online data.

Data Mining

To support more effective information management, many large organizations such as the Bank of Montreal and Canadian Tire are using data mining. ***Data mining*** is a method companies use to sort and analyze information to better understand their customers, products, markets, or any other phase of their business for which data has been captured. With data-mining tools, you can graphically drill down from summary data to more detailed data, sort or extract data based on certain conditions, and perform a variety of statistical analyses, such as trend analysis, correlation analysis, forecasting, and analysis of variance. For example, Anheuser-Busch uses sophisticated data models to track beer purchases and is able to use these data to target promotions to specific neighbourhoods (see Brief Case: Data Keeps the Beer Flowing). The next section describes how data mining is being implemented.

It is rare to find an information systems textbook that describes what not to do, but this can be very helpful to students. "When Things Go Wrong" enables students to learn about a real-world situation in which information systems did not work or were not built or used well. Topics include:

- Disaster recovery planning after 9/11 and other catastrophes
- Security vulnerabilities at Microsoft
- Slammer worm that brings the Internet to a halt and browser flaws that threaten electronic commerce security
- Data loss at the Canadian Revenue Agency
- An Enterprise Resource Planning disaster at Sobey's

In addition to end-of-chapter material (see below), we provide several opportunities for students to work alone or in teams to research topics on the Web that relate to chapter material. Topics include:

- Examining technology career opportunities
- Contrasting Internet business models
- Checking your Internet bandwidth and the Internet traffic report
- Examining your privacy rights

In addition to scores of international issues and examples throughout every chapter, "Global Perspective" examines how some aspect of the chapter applies to people, organizations, and technologies from around the world. Topics include:

- Global outsourcing of technology workers
- Using information systems to manage global organizations and transborder data security
- Global telecommunications standards and challenges

314 Chapter 9 Information Systems Ethics and Computer Crime

Web Search

Visit the Privacy Rights Clearinghouse, **www.privacyrights.org**, and learn more about how to protect your privacy. Review one of the site's numerous "fact sheets" on how to protect your privacy, and prepare a one-page report summarizing the fact sheet. Will reading these fact sheets influence your online shopping behaviour? If yes, what would you do differently? If not, how do you protect your privacy online?

Not only does each member state have its own method of administering the General Directive, but each may also have its own additional laws and regulatory schemes for personal information in the private sector. It is beyond the scope of this book to review data protection legislation in each of the EU member states. However, more information about privacy laws in the EU and around the world can be found at **www.epic.org/privacy** or **www.privacyrights.org**.

[illegible]oving on, it is important to distin[illegible] unethical behaviour and a crime. [illegible] clearly a crime. However, many [illegible]ters and information may [illegible] be considered unethical [illegible] technology moves forward [illegible] things not possible [illegible] do not apply to these [illegible] of the ongoing debates [illegible] innovations revolves [illegible] because it is not a [illegible] okay to do it?"

[illegible] *Privacy Online*

[illegible]chases in Canada, ven[illegible] to respect your privacy. [illegible] levels of privacy protection [illegible] jurisdictions. In the United [illegible], a vendor can track what [illegible] at, what products you examine, [illegible] which products you choose to buy, [illegible] method of payment you choose to use, and where you have the product delivered. After collecting all that information, unscrupulous vendors can sell it to others, resulting in more direct-mail advertising, electronic spam in your e-mail inbox, or calls from telemarketers.

When surveyed about concerns related to online shopping, most consumers list issues of information privacy as a top concern. As a result, governments have pressured vendors to post their privacy policies on their websites. Unfortunately, these policies do not often protect the privacy of consumers. To protect yourself, you should always review the privacy policy of all companies you do business with and refuse to do business with those that do not have a clear policy. According to the Consumer Protection Working Group of the American Bar Association at safeshopping.org, a seller's privacy policy should at least indicate:

- What information the seller is gathering from you
- How the seller will use this information
- Whether and how you can "opt out" of these practices

To make sure your shopping experience is a good one, you can take a few additional steps to maintain your privacy.

- *Choose sites that are monitored by independent organizations.* Several independent organizations monitor the privacy and business practices of websites. Organizations such as **www.epubliceye.com** and **www.openratings.com** provide a valuable service for consumers by monitoring the business practices of sellers and requiring conformance to standard guidelines or giving consumers a rating of a seller's practices. Choosing sites that are independently evaluated by a reputable rating company is a good way to ensure your privacy.
- *Avoid having "cookies" left on your machine.* Many commercial websites are designed to leave a small file on your hard drive so that the owner of the site can monitor where you go and what you do on the site. It is possible that the site owner could obtain your e-mail address from the visit, potentially sending you unsolicited e-mail spam. Fortunately, most web browsers provide the ability to turn off cookies or to warn you that the site is trying to deposit a cookie on your hard drive; when configured to warn you, your browser will prompt you with a notification and ask you if you want to accept the cookie. In addition to using settings within your web browser, you can get special "cookie management" software to help better maintain your privacy (go to **www.cookiecentral.com** for more on cookie management options).
- *Visit sites anonymously.* There are ways to visit websites anonymously. Using services provided by companies such as Anonymizer (**www.anonymizer.com**), you have total privacy from marketers, identity thieves, or even coworkers when surfing the web. Their software blocks cookies, Java, and other tracking methods from being left on your computer; for sites that require cookies to be left on your machine in order for you to visit, the software allows cookies to be encrypted so that no one can trace your activity. Similarly, URL addresses are also encrypted so that anyone monitoring your activity cannot log a meaningful address.
- *Use caution when requesting confirming e-mail.* When you buy products online, many companies will send you a confirming e-mail message to let you know that the

- Bridging the global digital divide in Africa
- Tackling global cybercrime

Information systems are now a significant part of every organization. "Canadian NetStats" provides interesting and important Canadian trends related to information systems within a variety of contexts. Topics include:

- Canadian Internet security issues
- The largest Canadian firms operating in the IT sector
- Up-and-coming Canadian IT firms
- Spam in Canada
- IT outsourcing in Canada

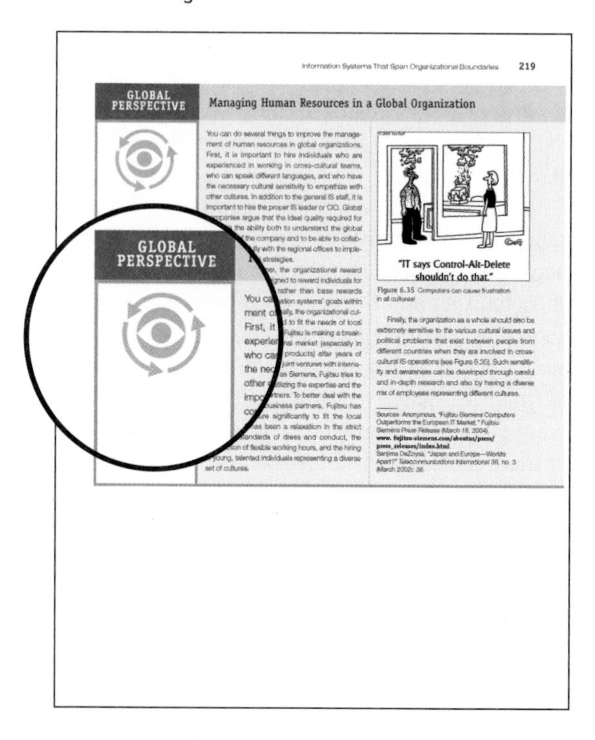
Information Systems That Span Organizational Boundaries 219

GLOBAL PERSPECTIVE

Managing Human Resources in a Global Organization

You can do several things to improve the management of human resources in global organizations. First, it is important to hire individuals who are experienced in working in cross-cultural teams, who can speak different languages, and who have the necessary cultural sensitivity to empathize with other cultures. [illegible]

Figure 6.35 Computers can cause frustration in all cultures!

Finally, the organization as a whole should also be extremely sensitive to the various cultural issues and political problems that exist between people from different countries when they are involved in cross-cultural IS operations (see Figure 6.35). Such sensitivity and awareness can be developed through careful and in-depth research and also by having a diverse mix of employees representing different cultures.

Sources: Anonymous, "Fujitsu Siemens Computers Outperforms the European IT Market," Fujitsu Siemens Press Release (March 18, 2004), **www.fujitsu-siemens.com/aboutus/press/press_releases/index.html**; Senjima DeZoysa, "Japan and Europe—Worlds Apart?" Telecommunications International 36, no. 3 (March 2002): 38.

Ethical business practices are now a predominate part of contemporary management education and practice. "Ethical Dilemmas" examines contemporary dilemmas related to the chapter content and highlights the implications of these dilemmas for managers, organizations, and society. Topics include:

- Global outsourcing of technology workers
- E-pending to build spam lists
- Spyware and employee monitoring
- Using CRM systems to target venerable customers
- System designs that eliminate jobs

Canadian Video Cases

The text is supported by three online video cases pertaining to Chapters 4, 5, and 9. Each case study focuses on a contemporary information systems–related issue faced by firms in Canada, and is accompanied by discussion questions. The cases are based on video segments from the CBC programs *The National*, *Venture*, and *Marketplace*. Students and instructors can read the cases and view the streaming video on our Video Central site, which is linked to the text's Companion Website (**www.pearsoned.ca/jessup**).

End-of-Chapter Material

Our end-of-chapter material is designed to accommodate various teaching and learning styles. It promotes learning beyond the book and the classroom. Elements include the following:

- **Key Terms**—Highlight key concepts within the chapter
- **Review Questions**—Test students' understanding of basic content
- **Self-Study Questions**—Enable students to assess whether they are ready for a test
- **Problems and Exercises**—Matching questions check quickly to see if students understand basic terms; problems push students deeper into the material and encourage them to synthesize and apply it
- **Application Exercises**—Challenge students to solve two real world management problems using spreadsheet and database applications. Student data files referenced within the exercises are available on the Companion Website: **www.pearsoned.ca/jessup**.

PEDAGOGY

In addition to the features described above, we provide a list of learning objectives to lay the foundation for each chapter. At the end of the chapter, the Key Points Review repeats these learning objectives and describes how each objective was achieved. A list of references is located at the end of the text, organized by chapter.

ORGANIZATION

The content and organization of this book are based on our own teaching, as well as on feedback from reviewers and colleagues throughout the field. Each chapter builds on the others to reinforce key concepts and allow for a seamless learning experience. Essentially, the book has been structured to answer three fundamental questions:

1. What are contemporary information systems, and how are they being used in innovative ways?
2. Why are information systems so important and interesting?
3. How best can we build, acquire, manage, and safeguard information systems?
4. How are information systems used in a Canadian business environment?

The ordering and content of our chapters was significantly influenced by a recent article, "What Every Business Student Needs to Know about Information Systems".[1] This article was written by 40 prominent information systems scholars to define the information systems core body of knowledge for all business students. By design, the content of *Information Systems Today,* Second Canadian Edition, carefully follows the guidance of this article. We are therefore very confident that our book provides a solid and widely agreed upon foundation for any introductory information systems course.

The chapters are organized as follows:

- **Chapter 1: Why Information Systems Matter**—This chapter helps you understand what information systems are and how they have become a vital part of modern organizations. We walk the student through the technology, people, and organizational components of an information system, and we lay out types of jobs and career opportunities in information systems and in related fields. We use a number of cases and examples to show the student the types of systems

[1] Ives, B., Valacich, J., Watson, R., Zmud, R. (2002). "What Every Business Student Needs to know about Information Systems. *Communications of the Association for Information Systems*, 9(30). Other contributing scholars to this article include: Maryam Alavi, Richard Baskerville, Jack J Baroudi, Cynthia Beath, Thomas Clark, Eric K. Clemons, Gordon B. Davis, Fred Davis, Alan R. Dennis, Omar A. El Sawy, Jane Fedorowicz, Robert D. Galliers, Joey George, Michael Ginzberg, Paul Gray, Rudy Hirschheim, Sirkka Jarvenpaa, Len Jessup, Chris F. Kemerer, John L. King, Benn Konsynski, Ken Kraemer, Jerry N. Luftman, Salvatore T. March, M. Lynne Markus, Richard O. Mason, F. Warren McFarlan, Ephraim R. McLean, Lorne Olfman, Margrethe H. Olson, John Rockart, V. Sambamurthy, Peter Todd, Michael Vitale, Ron Weber, and Andrew B. Whinston.

being used in Canada and to point out common "best practices" in systems use and management.

- **Chapter 2: Information Systems for Competitive Advantage**—In this chapter we provide a number of business examples to show how to use information systems to support organizational strategy and enable competitive advantage. We also show the student how to formulate and present the business case for a system, and we explain why and how companies are continually looking for new ways to use technology to achieve and sustain competitive advantage.
- **Chapter 3: Data and Knowledge Management**—The management of data and knowledge has become the engine running underneath all information systems and business processes. In this chapter, we use real world examples to describe what database and database management technologies are and to show why they have become very important for successful, modern organizations. The chapter also contrasts data and knowledge and explains how knowledge management systems are being rapidly deployed to enhance organizational performance.
- **Chapter 4: The Internet and Security**—Just as databases are the underlying engines, the Internet and other networks have become the artery and veins through which vital information flows in organizations. Here we use examples from a variety of organizations to provide an overview of the Internet and to examine how information security has become a paramount issue within the context of global information management.
- **Chapter 5: Electronic Business, Intranets, and Extranets**—Perhaps nothing has changed the landscape of business more than the use of the Internet for electronic business. In this chapter, we describe how a number of firms, such as Chapters.ca, are using the Internet and Web to do business with customers, building intranets to support internal processes, and building extranets to interact with other firms.
- **Chapter 6: Organizational Information Systems**—Given the many different types of information systems organizations use, in this chapter we use examples from Canadian firms to describe the various types of systems. We provide ways to categorize the systems so that you can better make sense of them all.
- **Chapter 7: Enterprise-Wide Information Systems**—In this chapter we focus on enterprise systems, which are a popular type of information system used to integrate information and span organizations' boundaries to better connect a firm with customers, suppliers, and other partners. We show you how firms use Enterprise Resource Planning, Customer Relationship Management, and other popular types of software packages to compete.
- **Chapter 8: Information Systems Development and Acquisition**—How are all these systems built? In this chapter we show you examples of how firms build and acquire new information systems. We walk you through the traditional systems development approach, as well as more contemporary approaches such as prototyping, rapid application development, and object-oriented analysis and design. We pay particular attention to global IT outsourcing and its possible impact on the Canadian economy.
- **Chapter 9: Information Systems Ethics and Computer Crime**—In this chapter we describe the ethical dilemmas associated with information systems, as well as common forms of computer crime. We show you how firms deal with hackers and ensure the safety and integrity of their critical systems. We also highlight the importance of personal privacy protection in Canada.

In addition to these nine chapters, we include three appendices focusing on basic hardware, software, and networking concepts. Although our market research found that many students have a solid understanding of these technological building blocks, this material is provided as a reference or can be used as a central part of the course. By delivering this material as appendices, we provide instructors the greatest flexibility in how and when they can apply it.

SUPPLEMENT SUPPORT

Instructor's Resource CD-ROM (ISBN: 0-13-241171-7)

The Instructor's Resource CD-ROM contains all of the text's supplements: Instructor's Manual, TestGen, PowerPoint Presentations, and Image Library (text art). The Instructor's Manual includes answers to all review and discussion questions, exercises, and case questions, including supplementary cases. The TestGen includes multiple-choice, true/false, short answer, and essay questions for each chapter. The PowerPoint Presentations highlight text learning objectives and key topics. They are also available on the text's Companion Website at **www.pearsoned.ca/jessup**. Finally, the Image Library is a collection of the figures and tables from the text for instructor use in PowerPoint slides and class lectures.

Companion Website

This text is supported by a Companion Website (**www.pearsoned.ca/jessup**) that features:

a. A link to the password-protected Video Central area where instructors and students can have access to streaming videos and the cases prepared to accompany them.
b. An Interactive Study Guide that includes multiple-choice, true-false, and essay questions for each chapter. Each question includes a hint and coaching tip for students' reference. Students receive automatic feedback upon submitting each quiz.
c. Web Search exercises. All of the Web Search exercises from the text margins appear on the Website for convenient student use.
d. PowerPoint lecture notes (as described above)
e. Bonus brief and end-of-chapter cases not included in the textbook

Videos

For in-class presentation, the CBC/Pearson Education Canada Video Library is available in both VHS (ISBN: 0-13-241173-3) and DVD (ISBN: 0-13-241172-5) formats.

REVIEWERS

We wish to thank the following faculty who participated in reviews for the Second Canadian Edition:

Michael Bliemel, Dalhousie University
James D. Clark, University of Lethbridge
Ward M. Eagen, Ryerson University
Robert C. Goldstein, University of British Columbia
Nija Hope, Rotman School of Management
Chitu Okoli, Concordia University
Robert Riordan, Carleton University
Ibrahim Sumrain, Grant MacEwan College

ACKNOWLEDGMENTS

Although only our names are listed as the authors for this book, this was truly a team effort that went well beyond the three of us. A particular debt of thanks is owed to Michael Rutherford for his help in compiling the information on PIPEDA and IP laws in Canada and elsewhere. Pearson Canada has been an outstanding publishing company to work with. They are innovative, have high standards, and are as competitive as we are.

Among the many amazingly helpful people at Pearson Canada, there are a few people we wish to thank specifically. Laura Forbes, Acquisitions Editor, and Lori Will, Sponsoring Editor, helped us to strategize well for this book throughout the project. Paul Donnelly, Senior Developmental Editor, helped to whip this book into shape and get the manuscript finished on time. Cheryl Jackson, Production Editor, skilfully oversaw the production of the text. Copy editing and composition were coordinated seamlessly with Integra in India for a nice example of real-world IT outsourcing. Finally, Eileen Lasswell and her exceptional team of marketing and sales professionals helped to get this book in the hands of students across the country.

Most important, we thank our families for their patience and assistance in helping us to complete this book.

The Pearson Education Canada **COMPANION WEBSITE**

A Great Way to Learn and Instruct Online

The Pearson Education Canada Companion Website is easy to navigate and is organized to correspond to the chapters in this textbook. Whether you are a student in the classroom or a distance learner you will discover helpful resources for in-depth study and research that empower you in your quest for greater knowledge and maximize your potential for success in the course.

PEARSON Prentice Hall

Jump to... http://www.pearsoned.ca/jessup | Home | Search | Help | Profile

Companion Website

Home >

Companion Website

Information Systems Today: Why IS Matters, Second Canadian Edition, by Jessup, Valacich, and Wade

Student Resources

This online study guide provides students with tools for learning course material. Each chapter includes:

- Chapter Objectives
- Chapter Overview
- Quizzes
- Bonus Cases
- Web Research Exercises
- Weblinks

In the quiz modules students can send answers to the grader and receive instant feedback on their progress through the Results Reporter. Coaching comments and references to the textbook may be available to ensure that students take advantage of all available resources to enhance their learning experience.

Instructor Resources

A link to this book on the Pearson Education Canada online catalogue (www.pearsoned.ca) provides instructors with additional teaching tools. Downloadable PowerPoint Presentations and an Instructor's Manual are just some of the materials that may be available. The catalogue is password protected. To get a password, simply contact your Pearson Education Canada Representative or call Faculty Sales and Services at 1-800-850-5813.

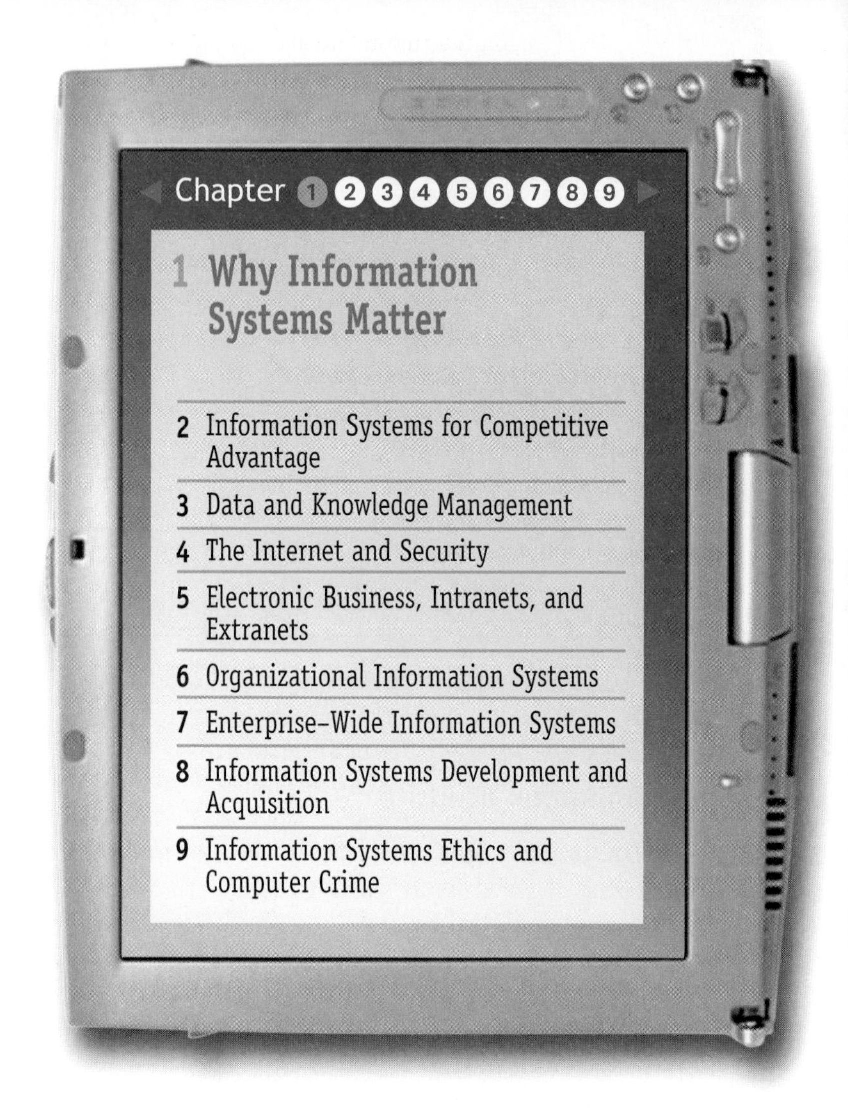

Preview

Organizations from Canadian Tire to Walt Disney use computer-based information systems to conduct business. These organizations use leading-edge information systems to provide high-quality goods and services to gain and sustain competitive advantage over rivals.

Our objective for Chapter 1 is to help you understand what information systems are, and how they have evolved to become a vital part of modern organizations. The chapter will also explain why information systems matter to you, whether you choose to pursue a career in information systems or in another area, such as finance, marketing, or accounting.

After reading this chapter, you will be able to do the following:

1. Define and understand the term "information systems" (IS).
2. Explain the technology, people, and organizational components of an information system.
3. Describe the types of jobs and career opportunities in IS and how knowledge of IS can help you in other career paths.
4. Describe the various types of IS.
5. Describe the dual nature of IS in the success and failure of modern organizations.
6. Understand and plan for the future of managing IS.

Why Information Systems Matter

SoftChoice Corp.

A flexible strategy has helped propel SoftChoice Corp. from a Canadian climber to a North American player. Formed in Toronto in 1989, SoftChoice began expanding into the Unites States 6 years later in 1995. The company now has 600 employees spread across 29 offices in the United States and 5 in Canada. SoftChoice is a systems value-added reseller (VAR), a firm that buys information technologies and systems from manufacturers and then resells them to individuals and businesses. The company also provides value-added services such as implementation assistance, leasing, and consulting. In 2004, Softchoice's revenues grew 24 percent, reaching $784 million, perhaps making it one of the largest firms in Canada that you have never heard of!

"It was a great year," says SoftChoice president Dave MacDonald, who credits the growth in part to a 61 percent jump in hardware sales, which totalled $142 million. "We're going to continue to grow our hardware business, which we think will grow to a very significant rate," he adds. "We believe we can take more share in the U.S. in the software licensing business, and then provide those customers with hardware products."

SoftChoice was recently ranked the number one VAR in Canada by the *Computer Dealer News*, and was listed as one of the top places to work in Canada by *Canadian Business* magazine. According to MacDonald, being a good employer is key in today's job market. Therefore, increasing employee retention by spending more on training is one of the company's key priorities. Getting the word out that SoftChoice is a good place to work will help that goal.

SoftChoice's roots are in corporate software sales, so there's no surprise that it's Microsoft's fastest-growing large account reseller in North America as well as the biggest in Canada. It has parlayed that record into becoming a North American player, carving out a niche in serving business markets, and partnering with systems integrators for installations. Sixty percent of its business now comes from south of the border, a figure MacDonald believes will rise to 65 percent in 2006.

Source: Adapted from Howard Solomon, "CDN Reveals the Top 100 Solution Providers," ITBusiness.ca (May 3, 2006), **www.itbusiness.ca/it/client/en/Home/News.asp?id=39256&bSearch=True**.

SoftChoice is one of Canada's leading IS firms.

Source: 2006 © Softchoice Corporation. www.softchoice.com.

WHAT YOU'LL FIND IN THIS BOOK

Figure 1.1 provides an overview of each of the components of this book. In this chapter we introduce you to what information systems are and how they are used, and we help to prepare you for what you will learn throughout the rest of this book. In Chapter 2 we talk about why information systems are critical to creating a successful organization and how to use information systems to support organizational strategy and enable competitive advantage, while also ensuring that they provide return on investment.

We then describe the essential elements of information systems. In Chapter 3 we describe databases and knowledge management. Next, in Chapter 4, we discuss the growing importance of the Internet and security. For those who want and need to learn more about these essential information technology building blocks, we provide more detailed briefings on hardware, software, and networking in appendixes at the end of this book.

We then describe information systems in practice in modern-day organizations. Building on what you learned in Chapter 4 about the Internet and security, in Chapter 5 we focus on electronic commerce and the use of intranets and extranets. In Chapter 6 we describe each of the various kinds of information systems that firms use. Then, in Chapter 7, we focus on enterprise-wide information systems, including Enterprise Resource Planning, Customer Relationship Management, and Supply Chain Management systems, all relatively new, special types of information systems that help integrate the entire organization and help connect the firm to customers, suppliers, and partners.

Next, in Chapter 8, we describe how information systems are developed and/or acquired. Then, in Chapter 9, we discuss key legal and ethical issues in managing information systems successfully. We will refer back to this "overview" figure at the beginning of every chapter. That way you will know exactly what we will be talking about in each chapter and how it fits within the book.

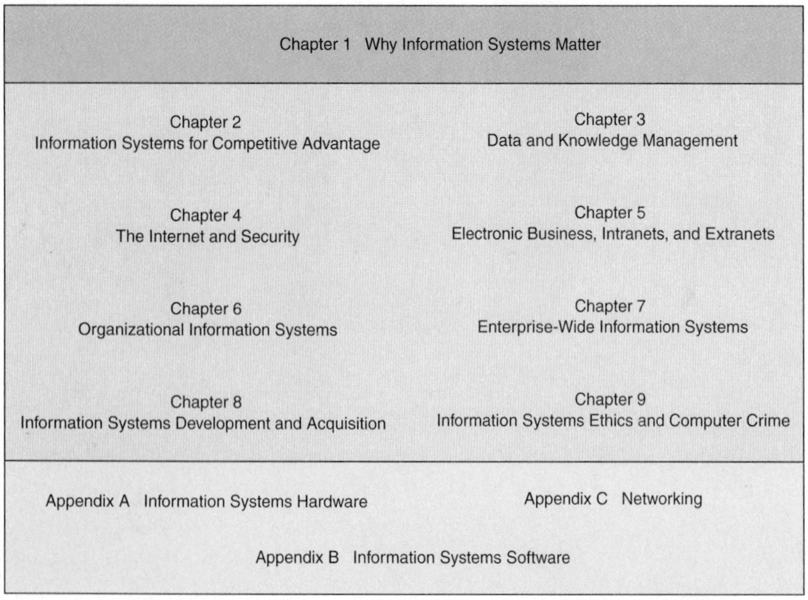

Chapter 1 Why Information Systems Matter

Chapter 2
Information Systems for Competitive Advantage

Chapter 3
Data and Knowledge Management

Chapter 4
The Internet and Security

Chapter 5
Electronic Business, Intranets, and Extranets

Chapter 6
Organizational Information Systems

Chapter 7
Enterprise-Wide Information Systems

Chapter 8
Information Systems Development and Acquisition

Chapter 9
Information Systems Ethics and Computer Crime

Appendix A Information Systems Hardware

Appendix C Networking

Appendix B Information Systems Software

Figure 1.1 The overview for this book, representing everything you need to know about using and managing computer-based information systems in organizations.

INFORMATION SYSTEMS DEFINED

Information systems (IS) are combinations of ***hardware***, ***software***, and ***telecommunications networks*** that people build and use to collect, create, and distribute useful data, typically in organizational settings. In Figure 1.2, we show the relationships among these IS components.

People in organizations use information systems to process sales transactions, manage loan applications, and help financial analysts decide where, when, and how to invest. Product managers also use them to help decide where, when, and how to market their products and related services, and production managers use them to help decide when and how to manufacture products. Information systems also enable us to get cash from ATMs, communicate by live video with people in other parts of the world, and buy concert or airplane tickets.

The term "information systems" is also used to describe the field comprising people who develop, use, manage, and study information systems in organizations. In Figure 1.3, we show the essential ingredients of the definition of IS.

Several terms are used to describe the field of information systems: "management information systems," "data processing management," "systems management," "business computer systems," "computer information systems," and simply "systems." People most commonly use the term "information systems"; therefore, we will stick with this term and its acronym IS. In the next section, we describe how the IS field has evolved into a dominant force in modern organizations and in the economy.

The Information Technology Revolution

Computers are the core component of information systems. Over the past decade, the advent of powerful, relatively inexpensive, easy-to-use computers has had a major impact on business. To see this impact, look around your school or place of work. At your school, you may register for classes online, use e-mail to communicate with fellow students and your instructors, and complete assignments on networked personal computers. At work, you may use a personal computer for e-mail and other tasks. Your paycheques are probably generated by computer and automatically deposited in your chequing account via high-speed networks. Chances are that each year you see more information technology than you did the year before, and this technology is a more fundamental and important part of your learning and work than ever before.

One characteristic of the computer industry is how fast computers change. More than 90 percent of the billions of dollars in revenue earned by computer chip manufacturing giant Intel comes from products that did not even exist just 2 or 3 years ago. Now, that is change. Even with the cyclic nature of the economy, Microsoft, Oracle, Cisco Systems, and many other companies in the computer industry often experience annual sales growth that is relatively high (as high as 30 percent) when compared to the median growth rate for all other industries (typically more like 5 to 10 percent). Just 20 or so years ago, the computer industry was a relatively minor player in the world's economy; today, it has become the 800 pound gorilla!

In Canada, the information and communications technologies (ICT) sector accounted for 5.6 percent of the domestic economy and 3.9 percent of total employment in 2004. Sector revenues grew at a compound average growth rate (CAGR) of 6.7 percent between 2004 and 2005, and employment grew at a 5.4 percent CAGR. The software and computer industries were particularly robust, with a CAGR of 10.5 percent. The Canadian NetStats box on page 9 shows the largest ICT firms in Canada. Of course, the relevance of information systems is not only restricted to those companies in the ICT industry. Information systems are used extensively by all firms in all industries.

The information technology revolution has been chronicled in the popular business press. For example, the cover stories in many issues of *Canadian Business, Fortune, Forbes,*

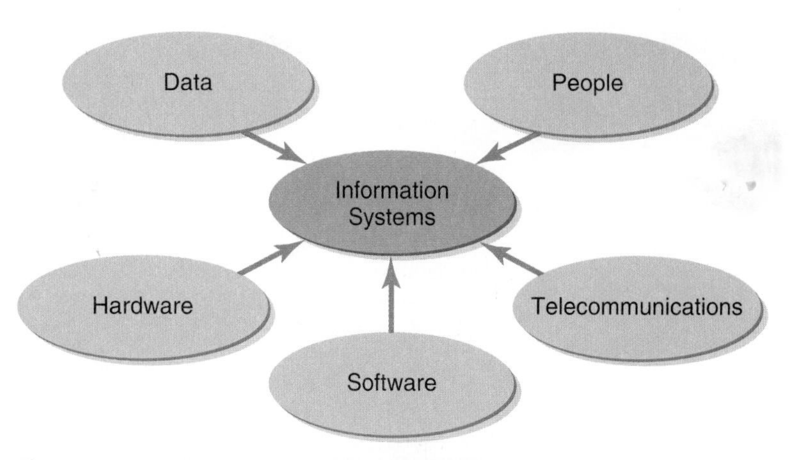

Figure 1.2 An information system is a combination of five key elements: people, hardware, software, data, and telecommunications networks.

Information systems are combinations of
hardware, software, and telecommunications networks
which
people build and use
to
collect, create, and distribute useful data,
typically in
organizational settings.

Figure 1.3 The essential ingredients of the definition of IS.

and other business magazines have focused on technology or a technology company or industry. Figure 1.4 shows a recent business magazine with a technology-related cover. In fact, the *Globe and Mail* now produces *TQ Magazine*, a quartely publication that focuses on IT strategies for business. These articles in the popular business press mirror what is happening in the real world. Information systems are pervasive in everything we do and represent the engine underlying business productivity and success. While stocks for technology companies are not as high as they were at their peak a few years ago, technology is still an important business and economic driver.

When you stop and think about it, it is easy to see why information systems are important. Increasing global competitiveness has forced companies to find ways to be better and to do things less expensively. The answer for many firms continues to be to use information systems to do things better, faster, and cheaper. With the economy improving, firms are again beginning to spend large amounts of money on IS projects, though they are much more concerned now that these projects provide a good return on investment. As Tom Murphy, CIO of pharmaceutical supply chain services provider AmerisourceBergen,

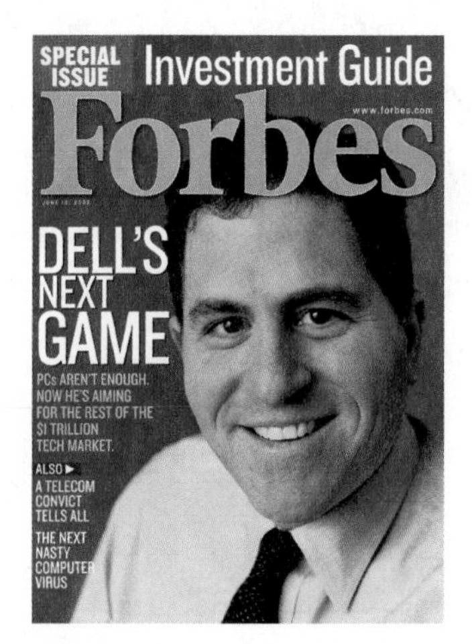

Figure 1.4 A popular business magazine featuring a cover story related to technology.

Source: *Forbes* Magazine

BRIEF CASE What Should Rule the Day: Theory or Practice?

Most IT professionals have known for years that hands-on experience counts when graduates head into the working world, but theoretical training is also important, particularly for the long-term development of graduates. Things are moving toward the practical at George Brown College in Toronto. "Everybody involved in this learning process, from the Ministry to college management to students to teachers, is pushing for hands-on experience," says Gerry Drappel, chair of the information technology department at George Brown. Stephen Mill, Toronto regional manager for recruiter Robert Half Technology, finds that a potential hire's practical experience outweighs his or her theoretical, classroom experience. "It's always skill-driven in IT," says Mill. "If someone has a [computer science] background, that's great! They will have way more in-depth knowledge than someone who doesn't have that. But if they've never done anything practical with that, or relevant, or current, it doesn't matter."

While colleges are trying to keep in step with industry, universities are finding themselves in a different sort of predicament. Kathryn Brohman, assistant professor of management information systems at Queen's University, says that at her school, theory remains the order of the day. "I think it's a challenge here in Canada because the university systems are very different [than in the U.S.]. And it comes down to the age-old argument of, 'Is a business school a practitioner school?' or are we more of a true philosophical discipline where we should be evaluated more like the true sciences?" Though Queen's recently joined NCR Corp.'s Teradata University Network, an international learning portal that allows students hands-on access to valuable resources in the fields of data warehousing and database administration, Brohman thinks that it won't find as much use at Queen's as it might at more technical schools. "There's a more fuzzy line in the university system between hands-on training and college-level training. If it's going to be hands-on, then a lot of those skills should be able to be offered in outside seminars," says Brohman. "There's not a lot of place for that in university education, especially in a business school—we're teaching a more conceptual understanding of MIS in business. But the recruiters are coming in and wanting [a] technical student for MIS jobs." Brohman says there is a fundamental disconnect between what schools are trying to achieve in academia, their whole pedagogical vision, and what recruiters are coming in and looking for. "It always comes down to the same thing: how can you be strategic about finance and strategic about marketing if you don't know the tools that you're dealing with? If you don't know how a database is structured, how could you use that tool strategically?"

Anthony Lucifero, a third-year student at George Brown, says that to him, theory and practice hold equal relevance toward his future. "I think that they're both essential to have; you need the theory part of the course as well as the hands-on, they're both very important."

Questions

1. Do you think business students need to learn about IS/IT? Why or why not?
2. What do you think is the right mix of theory and practice for an IS/IT course offered at a business school?

Source: Adapted from Liz Clayton, "IT Educators Grapple with Theory vs. Practice Debate," ITBusiness.ca (February 20, 2004), **www.itbusiness.ca/it/client/en/Home/News.asp?id=4966&bSearch=True**.

put it: "Information technology is everywhere; we touch almost every process in the firm. We must intimately understand operations to enable them; I have a complete view of the organization and its operations."

The Rise of the Knowledge Worker

In 1959, Peter Drucker predicted this rise in the importance of information and of information technology, and at that point over four decades ago he coined the term ***knowledge worker***. Knowledge workers are professionals who are relatively well educated and who create, modify, and/or synthesize knowledge as a fundamental part of their jobs.

Drucker's predictions about knowledge workers were very accurate. As he predicted, they are generally paid better than their prior agricultural and industrial counterparts; they rely on and are empowered by formal education, yet they often also possess valuable real-world skills; they are continually learning how to do their jobs better; they have much better career opportunities and far more bargaining power than workers ever had before; they make up about a quarter of the workforce in the United States and in other developed nations; and their numbers are rising quickly.

Drucker also predicted that, with the growth in the number of knowledge workers and with their rise in importance and leadership, a ***knowledge society*** would emerge. He reasoned that, given the importance of education and learning to knowledge workers and the firms that need them, education would become the cornerstone of the knowledge society. Possessing knowledge, he argued, would be as important as possessing property once was (if not more so). Indeed, research shows that people with a university education earn far more on average than people without a university education, and that gap is increasing.

People generally agree that Drucker was accurate about knowledge workers and the evolution of society. While people have settled on Drucker's term "knowledge worker," there are many alternatives to the term "knowledge society." For example, Manuel Castell has written that we now live in a network society. *Wired* magazine has declared that we now live in a ***new economy*** and described it as follows:

> So what is the new economy? When we talk about the new economy, we're talking about a world in which people work with their brains instead of their hands. A world in which communications technology creates global competition—not just for running shoes and laptop computers, but also for bank loans and other services that can't be packed into a crate and shipped. A world in which innovation is more important than mass production. A world in which investment buys new concepts or the means to create them, rather than new machines. A world in which rapid change is a constant. A world at least as different from what came before it as the industrial age was from its agricultural predecessor. A world so different its emergence can only be described as a revolution.[1]

Others have referred to this phenomenon as the digital society, the network era, the Internet era, and by other names. All of these ideas have in common the premise that information and related technologies and systems have become very important to us and that knowledge workers are vital.

Some have argued, however, that there is a downside to being a knowledge worker and to living in this new economy. For example, Sims-Taylor has argued that knowledge workers will be the first to be replaced by automation with information technology. Rifkin has argued that our over-reliance on information technology has caused us to think and act hastily and to lose our perspective. Others have argued that in the new economy there is a ***digital divide***, where those with access to information technology have great advantages over those without access to it.

To be sure, there is a downside to over-reliance on knowledge workers and information technology, but one thing is for certain: knowledge workers and information technologies are now critical to the success of modern organizations, economies, and societies.

Data: The Root and Purpose of Information Systems

Let us break down and discuss the definition of information systems. Earlier we defined IS as combinations of hardware, software, and telecommunications networks that people build and use to collect, create, and distribute useful data, typically in organizational settings. We will begin by talking about data, the most basic element of any information system.

Before you can understand how information systems work, it is important to distinguish between ***data*** and ***information***, terms that are often erroneously used interchangeably. Data is raw material—recorded, unformatted information, such as words and numbers. Data has no meaning in and of itself.

For example, if I asked you what 465889724 meant or stood for, you could not tell me. However, if I presented the same data as 465-889-724 and told you it was located in a certain database, in John Doe's file, in a field labelled "SIN," you might rightly surmise that the number was actually the social insurance number of someone named John Doe.

Data formatted with dashes or labels is more useful than unformatted data. It is transformed into information, which can be defined as a representation of reality. In the example just mentioned, 465–889–724 was used to represent and identify an individual person, John Doe. Contextual cues, such as a label, are needed to turn data into information that is familiar to the reader. Think about your experience with ATMs. A list of all the transactions at a bank's ATMs over the course of a month would be fairly useless data. However, a table that divided ATM users into two categories—bank customers and non-bank customers—and compared the two groups' use of the machine (their purpose for using the ATM machines and the times and days

[1] Excerpt from *Wired* magazine's "Encyclopedia of the New Economy," **http://hotwired.wired.com/special/ene**.

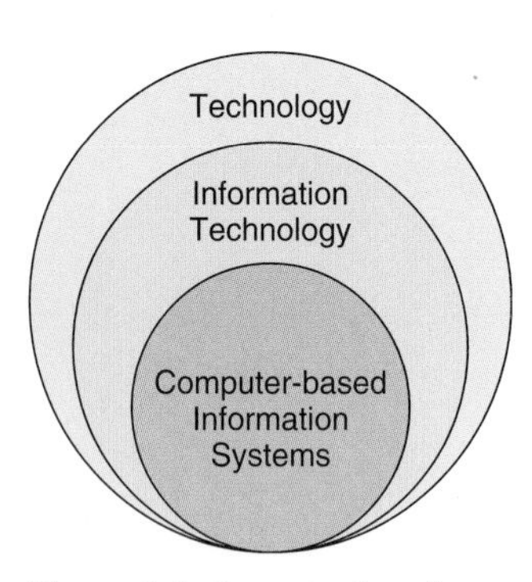

Figure 1.5 Computer-based information systems are a subset of information technologies and of technologies in general.

on which they use them) would be incredibly useful information. A bank manager could use this information to create marketing mailings to attract new customers. Without information systems, it would be difficult to make data useful by turning it into information.

In addition to data and information, knowledge and wisdom are also important. ***Knowledge*** is needed to understand relationships between different pieces of information. For example, you must have knowledge to be aware that only one social insurance number can uniquely identify each individual. Knowledge is a body of governing procedures, such as guidelines or rules, which are used to organize or manipulate data to make it suitable for a given task.

Finally, ***wisdom*** is accumulated knowledge. Wisdom goes beyond knowledge in that it represents broader, more generalized rules and schemas for understanding a specific domain or domains. Wisdom allows you to understand how to apply concepts from one domain to new situations or problems. Understanding that a unique individual identifier, such as a social insurance number, can be applied in certain programming situations to single out an individual record in a database is the result of accumulated knowledge. Wisdom can be gained through a combination of academic study and personal experience.

Understanding the distinctions among data, information, knowledge, and wisdom is important because all are used in the study, development, and use of information systems.

The Technology Side of Information Systems

When we use the term "information systems," we are talking about ***computer-based information systems***. Of course, not all information systems need to be computer-based. When Toronto's Royal York hotel opened in 1929 as the tallest building in the British Commonwealth, there were no terminals to check in weary travellers, and no data warehouses to store guest information. However, computer-based information systems form the basis of IS used in today's organizations. Computer-based information systems are a type of technology. ***Technology*** is any mechanical and/or electrical means to supplement, extend, or replace human, manual operations or devices. Sample machine technologies include the heating and cooling system for a building, the braking system for an automobile, and a laser used for surgery.

In Figure 1.5, we show the relationship between technologies and computer-based information systems.

The term ***information technology (IT)*** refers to machine technology that is controlled by or uses information. One type of information technology is a programmable robot on the shop floor of a manufacturing firm that receives component specifications and operational instructions from a computer-based database.

We could argue that any technology makes use of information in some fundamental way, as does each of the three examples of basic technology listed earlier (heating system, braking system, and a laser). However, information technologies, such as programmable manufacturing robots, use more information and in a more sophisticated way. It may appear that we are splitting hairs by distinguishing between technologies and information technologies. While the distinction is subtle, it is important. Information technologies use machine technologies as building blocks and then combine them with computing and networking technologies. A technology such as a mechanical drill press is useful, but it is more useful when combined with a computer database that instructs that drill press when and how to act.

Information technologies and information systems are also similar. Remember that we defined an information system as a combination of hardware, software, and telecommunications networks that people build and use to collect, create, and distribute data. The goal of an information system is to provide useful data to users.

An example of an information system is the use of specialized software on a computer-controlled, mechanical machine used to produce compact discs (CDs); combined with other shop-floor equipment it allows a person to monitor and control the production of each CD from a separate, possibly remote, computer.

Other examples of information systems include a series of integrated electronic spreadsheets used for a budget, an order-fulfillment system for managing customers' purchases, and a set of linked pages on the World Wide Web. You may be asking, "Does my PC at work or school count as part of the company's or university's overall information system?" Our answer is yes. An information system includes personal, group, organizational, interorganizational, and even global computing systems.

The People Side of Information Systems

The information systems field includes a vast collection of people who develop, maintain, manage, and study information systems. The career opportunities for a person with IS training are strong, and they are expected to continue to improve over the next 10 years. For example, *Business 2.0* magazine recently reported that information systems and related areas of hiring will be among the largest recruiters in the coming decade.

Even with lower-level technical jobs such as systems programmers being outsourced (i.e., performed by lower-paid workers in countries other than the country in which the host company resides), there continues to be a strong need for people with IS knowledge, skills, and abilities—in particular, people with advanced IS capabilities, as we will describe below.

However, knowledge about information systems is not just useful for people who want to pursue a career in IT. Just as the management

CANADIAN NETSTATS

Information and Communications Technology Firms in Canada

Canada has a rich tradition of excellence in the ICT sector. The sector is dominated by large hardware firms like Nortel and Celestica, and telecommunications companies like BCE and Telus (as shown in Table 1.1). However, the fastest growing areas of the ICT sector are software and professional services. Canada has a large number of dynamic and rapidly growing IT consulting and outsourcing companies. It also contains some of the world's leading film animation and video game design firms. In addition to home-grown firms, Canada is host to many of the world's leading ICT companies, like IBM, HP, and Microsoft.

Table 1.1 *Firms operating in Canada's ICT sector.*

Company	2005 Sales (C$ millions)	Company	2005 Sales (C$ millions)
Top 5 Canadian Hardware Companies		***Top 5 Canadian Professional Services and Consulting Companies***	
Nortel Networks	11 106	CGI Group	3 686
Celestica	10 057	MacDonald, Dettwiler and Assoc.	838
ATI Technologies	2 589	SoftChoice Corp.	784
Creo	800	Xwave, an Aliant Company	353
NexInnovations	520	Minacs Worldwide	293
Top 5 Canadian Software Companies		***Top Foreign IT-Sector Firms Operating in Canada***	
Cognos	962	IBM Canada	5 500
Geac Computer Corporation	518	Hewlett-Packard Canada	3 547
Open Text	483	Microsoft Canada	1 200
Hummingbird	275	Xerox Canada	1 167
Constellation Software	186	Cisco Systems	1 157
Top 5 Canadian Telecommunications Companies		EDS Canada	1 084
BCE (wireless and data)	7 076	Accenture	550
Rogers Wireless Communications	3 985	ADP Canada	481
TELUS (wireless and data)	3 225	Oracle Canada	365
Shaw Communications (Internet)	914	Computer Sciences	329
MTS Allstream	878		

Web Search

Visit Statistics Canada at **www.statscan.ca** and Industry Canada at **www.strategis.ic.gc.ca** to find information and publications about the effect of IT on the Canadian economy. Equivalent data from the United States can be found at the website of the Department of Commerce **www.commerce.gov.**

of organizational information is useful in all knowledge-based work, the study of information systems is relevant to all areas of the firm. All organizations gather, store, organize, analyze, and disseminate information. Information is the fuel that drives organizational change and growth, and information systems are the tools that make the engine work. So, even if you are not considering a technical career, a strong background in information systems is extremely valuable.

In this section, we examine the value of IS knowledge in different careers, and specifically how IS can be useful in the areas of accounting, finance, and marketing. We discuss which specific technical skills and abilities are useful for these careers in Canada. Then, we consider how IS knowledge can be useful for careers in general management. The focus of this section is less on specific technical abilities and more on skills related to the management of information and the role of IS in supporting strategic decision making. Finally, we look at potential careers in the IS field.

Careers in Accounting

Accounting is the process of recording, summarizing, classifying, interpreting, and communicating financial information. Accounting professionals create financial reports that are useful to managers, regulators, shareholders, creditors, and other relevant stakeholders.

In Canada, there are three official accounting designations: Chartered Accountant (CA), Certified General Accountant (CGA), and Management Accountant (CMA). The CA program is the most rigorous of the three, as candidates require auditing experience from a public accounting firm. The CGA program provides a more general approach to the accounting profession. Management accountants are specifically focused on providing management with the necessary financial information to make operating decisions. Each province has its own set of rules on what services individual accounting designations can, and cannot, provide. While CAs, CGAs, and CMAs form the basis of the accounting profession in Canada, there are many other career choices that draw on accounting knowledge.

Accountants use information systems perhaps more than any other non-IS field. In fact, the first organizational information systems were designed to support accounting work. Today, accountants continue to rely heavily on information systems in their jobs. In a recent Canadian survey by Robert Half Finance & Accounting, the world's largest recruitment firm specializing in the placement of accounting and finance professionals, chief financial officers (CFOs) said that the most sought-after skill (following accounting knowledge) was information technology proficiency (see Figure 1.6).

The report concluded that accounting graduates entering today's job market should be prepared to highlight their technical expertise as well as their proficiency for numbers. According to Max Messmer, CEO of Robert Half International Inc., "To improve efficiencies, organizations are automating many of their accounting functions or upgrading their financial information systems. As a result, recent accounting graduates with a demonstrated aptitude for technology-related projects are at an advantage in a competitive market."

Table 1.2 shows examples of accounting software packages commonly used in today's organizations. Students should focus on the applications that are relevant to the size of the firm they are planning to work for. In addition to accounting software, students wishing to pursue a career in accounting should also become familiar with database and spreadsheet software packages, such as Microsoft Excel, Microsoft Access, and Oracle.

Careers in Finance

Finance involves the management of funds within an organization. For smaller firms, the accounting and finance functions may overlap. An accountant, for example, may also oversee a company's financial affairs. In larger firms, however, the two functions differ considerably. Large firms have corporate finance departments whose job it is to provide funds for the corporation's activities. At the core of the finance function is the balance of risk and return. Financial managers ensure that sufficient funds are available for a firm's short- and long-term activities. Such funds may be provided by ongoing operations, or they may be

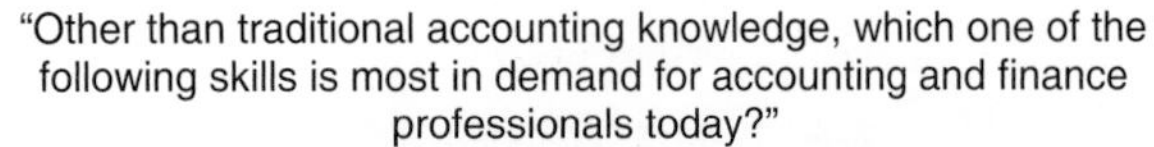

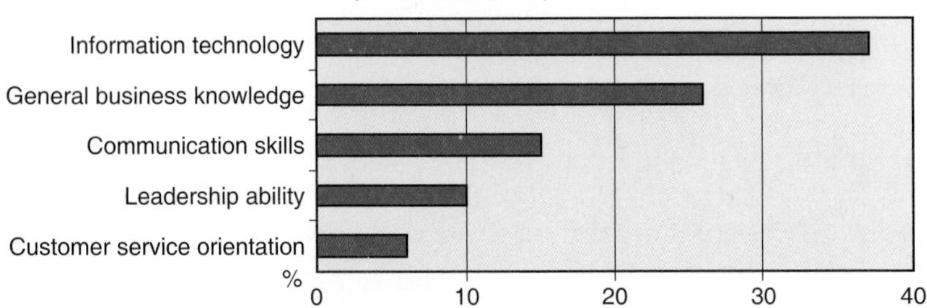

Figure 1.6 Canadian CFOs value information technology skills.

Source: Robert Half Finance and Accounting

Table 1.2 ***Common accounting software packages.***

Firm Size	Accounting Software
Very small firms (less than 10 employees)	Quicken Simply Accounting Quickbooks Microsoft Money
Medium-sized firms (11 to 250 employees)	ACCPAC Business Vision Blue Link Elite Microsoft Axapa Microsoft Great Plains
Large firms (more than 250 employees)	SAP Oracle Financials ACCPAC Executive

provided by loans (i.e., bonds, lines of credit) or equity (i.e., shares). These decisions lead to the company's capital structure.

Another business decision concerning finance is investment. Finance managers must decide where to place corporate funds to maximize returns while minimizing risk. It is also necessary to monitor those investments, and make adjustments in response to changes in the business environment.

Finance draws heavily on analytical sciences, such as mathematics, statistics, and economics. Financial managers use these areas to build financial models and to understand the implications of investment decisions. Since many of these decisions involve complex arrays of variables, information systems are widely employed.

For example, quantitative analysis software, such as Tradecision, TradeStation, and MATLAB, uses computerized artificial intelligence techniques to make decisions on the buying or selling of stocks, bonds, and other financial assets.

Finance managers should also become familiar with common accounting packages and database systems. These tools are the repositories in which financial data are stored. In today's integrated world, a firm's finances are also inextricably linked with external systems operated by banks, investment houses, and other financial institutions.

Finally, almost all financial managers need to be familiar with spreadsheet tools and statistical packages, such as Microsoft Excel and SAS. These tools are used to build financial models and conduct sophisticated financial analyses. While most students are familiar with spreadsheets, finance majors need to understand the advanced applications and functionality of such programs.

Careers in Marketing

The marketing field is concerned with the relationship between a firm and its customers. It encompasses areas such as product design, public relations, advertising, sales, pricing, customer service, and promotion. Two major aspects of marketing are the recruitment of new customers and the retention and expansion of relationships with existing customers.

Marketing draws on fields such as management science, organizational behaviour, strategy, economics, and the creative arts. Today's marketers must also rely extensively on a vast array of information systems. At one time, the sales function was based primarily on personal relationships and face-to-face meetings. The importance of relationships has not changed, but the medium through which these relationships develop has. Sales and marketing professionals now rely heavily on communications tools to develop and nurture contact with customers. Sales Force Automation (SFA) systems, for example, are now used extensively to manage the effectiveness of a field sales force. In addition, marketers are using Geographical Information Systems (GIS) to manage site locations and promotional programs.

Firms are also turning to large integrated marketing systems called Customer Relationship Management (CRM) systems to manage the complete customer relationship. These systems store a vast amount of information on customers and provide sophisticated tools designed to maximize lifetime customer value. The largest firm in the CRM marketplace is Siebel Systems, now part of Oracle. CRM systems can be integrated with Enterprise Resource Planning (ERP) systems, such as SAP, Oracle, and Baan.

Marketers also need to be familiar with tools to facilitate market research. For example, the design, and in many cases the delivery, of most consumer surveys is facilitated by computers. Internet search technologies and strategies are also useful in order to maximize the effectiveness of intelligence gathering. Information systems called Business Intelligence (BI) tools support market research activities.

Finally, a relatively new form of marketing uses the Internet as its primary channel. E-marketing extends the segmentation strategy used in traditional marketing to a one-to-one model, as opposed to a newspaper that is one-to-many. Thus, marketers can use e-marketing to target their customers more precisely.

The Importance of IS to Other Career Paths

Accounting, finance, and marketing are three areas that rely heavily on information systems, but they are not alone. Other career paths, like human resources, production and operations management, and media and communications, also use information systems extensively.

For example, many factories today are managed and operated by production systems and coordinated by supply chain management systems. The process of hiring and retaining employees relies on human resource management systems. Digital rights management systems are utilized by all media companies. In short, some familiarity with technology skills is important for practically all organizational careers. Table 1.3 shows examples of IS skills and solutions that are typically required for careers in human resources, production and operations management, and media and communications.

Human Resources and Skills Development Canada (HRSDC), a branch of the federal government, keeps track of the skills that employees are looking for. As part of its Workwaves program, the HRSDC monitors job postings in the *Toronto Star*, the *Toronto Sun*, and the *Globe and Mail*. Between January and October 2004, 692 job postings made note of the need for computer proficiency, which was more than language abilities, teamwork abilities, or customer service skills. A further 165 job advertisements called for

Table 1.3 ***IS skills relevant to different organizational areas.***

Organizational Area	Relevant IS Skills	Sample Solutions
Human Resources	Human resource management systems	Oracle HMRS
	Applicant tracking systems	RecruitTrack
	Payroll systems	Avanti Payroll
	Benefits administration tools	Ascentis HROffice
Production and Operations Management	Supply chain management systems (SCM)	Agile 9
	Inventory management systems	CoreIMS
	Production systems	SAP
	Scheduling systems	Microsoft Project
	Logistics systems	Manugistics
	Workflow and collaboration systems	Livelink
	CAD/CAM systems	DesignCAD 3D Max
Media and Communications	Digital rights management systems	Macrovision
	Intranets	Lotus Notes
	Desktop publishing software	QuarkXPress
	Web design software	Microsoft FrontPage
	Animation software	Macromedia Flash

analytical information-processing skills. It is perhaps not surprising that almost 600 advertisements called for experience with office automation software (i.e., Microsoft Office), but another 300 sought knowledge and experience in multimedia software, databases, and Internet technologies. Clearly, employers are seeking a more information technology–literate workforce. Yet, the field of information systems has more to offer than hard technical skills, as we will explore in the following section.

Information Systems to Support Strategic Decision Making

In our experience as IS managers, educators, and consultants, we have seen many millions of dollars wasted because of poor IS planning. Some estimates place IS at 45 percent of all commercial operating capital expenditures. That's a huge sum of money! Unfortunately, a large proportion of these funds is misallocated, or simply wasted. The marketplace has a large and recognized need for non-IS managers with a basic understanding of IS issues. There is a shortage of managers who even have enough IS knowledge to ask intelligent questions about IS-related organizational issues. Having this knowledge will provide you with a competitive advantage in the job marketplace.

As Trevor Zigelstein, Finance and Accounting manager at Robert Half, noted, "Entry-level professionals who have the ability to work collaboratively with their information technology counterparts are in a position to help bridge these two critical areas of operations, and in the process, add considerable value to their role."

Many managers are uncomfortable with their knowledge of IS, and thus tend to avoid IS-related decisions. Alternatively, they delegate these decisions to external consultants. These consultants may have a great deal of systems knowledge, but almost certainly do not know the firm as well as its managers. Thus, poor decision making in the IS area is disturbingly common. As Rob Solomon, senior vice president of sales & marketing at Outrigger Hotels and Resorts, points out, "Every manager must have an IT strategy. You can't delegate to technologists and only worry about your allocated cost or what training your employees need. You must understand how to be master of your own destiny and make IT work best for you. Too many managers still don't get that."

However, IS knowledge does not only influence decisions on hardware and software. Many strategic issues are related to information systems. Table 1.4 shows examples of strategic issues in various functional areas. In order to manage these issues, firms must draw on IS expertise. The solution to dealing with these issues is often a matter of choosing a correct system, aligning that system with the processes and culture of an organization, and putting the right people in place to manage it.

A 2004 study conducted by the HRSDC found that although *specific* technological skills will be increasingly important in the coming years, there will be an even greater need for *general* skills in the use of technology. The study emphasized that this is where basic literacy, numeracy, and electronic literacy are critical, because they provide the base on which to build skills in whatever technologies become prevalent in the next decades. Given the sheer volume of information that exists today, it is imperative that students develop the skills necessary to retrieve, catalogue, and manage information. The study further noted that those entering the marketplace will need stronger skills in analysis and critical thinking to enable them to use information more efficiently and effectively.

Another source that champions the importance of IS for students of all disciplines is the Conference Board of Canada, which publishes an annual report on job skills, attitudes, and behaviours entitled "Employability Skills 2000+." According to the report, three types of skills are most critical for job seekers (and popular with employers): fundamental skills, personnel management skills, and teamwork skills. While IS comes into play in each of these three areas, it is most prominent in the first category—fundamental skills, as illustrated in Table 1.5.

Information systems are much more than just the study of computers (although they do play a central role). At the core of IS is the ability to manage data, information, and knowledge in an organizational context. Technical skills are important, as all areas of a firm use computers and computer-based systems. However, the ability to use IS to solve organizational problems and enhance firm competitiveness is a more valuable skill. No matter what career choice you make, chances are you will be faced with decisions that require a fundamental knowledge of IS.

Careers in IS

The field of IS includes those people in organizations who design and build systems, those who use these systems, and those responsible for managing these systems. The people who help develop and manage systems in organizations include systems analysts, systems programmers,

Table 1.4 ***Strategic issues related to information systems by organizational area.***

Organizational Area	Strategic Issues Related to Information Systems
General Management	How can we use our unique and inimitable corporate knowledge to create a competitive edge? How can we find out what our competitors are doing? How can we ensure that our information is secure? Should we implement an Enterprise Resource Planning (ERP) system? If so, which ERP system is most appropriate for our business?
Accounting	Which accounting system should we adopt? Do our current systems comply with current legislation related to financial accountability and privacy rights?
Finance	How do we balance risk and reward in our financial decisions? How can we get the best information in the least amount of time?
Marketing	Should we adopt a Customer Relationship Management (CRM) system? If so, which one? How do we ensure that our sales force has full access to customer data in real time? How can we ensure that we fully understand the information we have about our customers?
Human Resources	How can we treat our employees fairly and equitably? How can we ensure that important information is not misplaced or lost? How can we ensure that we hire and retain the right people?
Production and Operations Management	How can we enhance the efficiency and effectiveness of our supply chain? How can we collaborate on product design, development, and testing? How can we reduce the number of defects in our production process?
Media and Communications	How can we protect our intellectual property? How can we create value from our intellectual property assets? How can we create and communicate the appropriate corporate image?

systems operators, network administrators, database administrators, systems designers, systems managers, and chief information officers.

Another significant part of the IS field is the group of people who work in IS consulting firms such as IBM, EDS, and Accenture. Experts in these consultant firms advise organizations on how to build and manage their systems and sometimes actually build and run those systems. Companies that have traditionally been hardware/software companies, such as IBM, are now doing a lot of systems consulting and related work. Similarly, companies that specialize in systems consulting, such as Accenture, are also very successful—hiring more people, opening new offices, taking on new business, and generating lots of revenue.

University professors are another group of people in IS. These professors conduct research on the development, use, and management of information systems. Nonacademic researchers who conduct research for agencies such as the Department of National Defence or for large corporations such as IBM, Xerox, Hewlett-Packard, and Bell Canada face almost unlimited opportunities. These professionals generally

Fundamental Skills Subcategory	Role of IS in Fundamental Skill
Communicate	Share information using a range of information and communication technologies (e.g., voice, e-mail, computers).
Manage Information	Locate, gather, and organize information using appropriate technology and information systems.
Use Numbers	Observe and record data using appropriate methods, tools, and technology.
Think and Solve Problems	Readily use science, technology, and mathematics as ways to think, gain, and share knowledge, solve problems, and make decisions.

Source: Conference Board of Canada

Table 1.5 ***Employability skills 2000+.***

conduct more applied research and development than academic researchers. For example, a researcher for a major computer manufacturer might be developing a new computer product or examining ways to extend the life of a current product by integrating leading-edge components with the older architecture.

The Advent of the Chief Information Officer

A number of important indicators show that organizations are trying hard to improve the management of information systems. Perhaps nothing better demonstrates the growing importance of information systems in organizations than the advent of the ***chief information officer*** (CIO) and related positions in contemporary organizations.

Today, most large organizations have a CIO or an equivalent position.[2] It is also now

[2] This is not to be confused with the Chief Technology Officer, a post usually held by a person within a technology company who helps to chart the course for the company's technology products.

Web Search

You can investigate issues relevant to CIOs in Canada at **www.itworldcanada.com/Pages/Docbase/BrowsePublication.aspx?Publication=CIO**. Another site that contains information on issues that are important to CIOs is **www.cio.com**.

SME SUCCESS Side Effects Software

When a massive flood crashed through Manhattan in the 2004 movie *The Day After Tomorrow,* the realistic visual effects were created with assistance from Houdini 3D Animation Tools from Side Effects Software (Sidefx). "A lot of those solutions for how water would react in a situation like that were directly related to the operators in that studio using Houdini," says Larry Bafia, who heads the Vancouver Film School's 3D Animation & Visual Effects Department.

Sidefx is a private company based in Toronto. Its Houdini software has been used in countless Hollywood films. For example, it was used to create the scene from 2005's *X-Men: The Last Stand,* where the Golden Gate bridge was uprooted and reattached to Alcatraz. Houdini was also instrumental in creating the chocolate river and multiple oompa loompas in the film *Charlie and the Chocolate Factory*.

"I don't know what we would have done in those shots without Houdini," says Peter Baldwin, founder of Myrtle Software. "In the sequence where the Candy boat goes over a chocolate waterfall and performs a 180° about turn we did some big fluid simulations entirely in Houdini of the boat going down the fall and used particles to create the waterfall itself. In those shots there are a load of elements that really worked well together."

The company is making quite a splash in the 3D animation industry. "Based on talking to a number of members of our advisory board, which includes some fairly big visual effects houses in Hollywood . . . as well as a number of employers in Canada, we've found that there's a demand for people that know and understand the program Houdini," Bafia says.

Source: Russ Francis, "Vancouver Film School Puts the Spotlight on Software Skills," ITBusiness.ca, (February 16, 2006), **www.itbusiness.ca/it/client/en/home/News.asp?id=38413**.

common for midsized and smaller organizations to have a CIO-like position within their organizations, although they may give this person a title such as Director of Information Systems.

IS Managerial Personnel

In large organizations, there are typically many other different management positions in addition to the CIO position within the IS function. In Table 1.6, we describe several such positions. This list is not exhaustive; rather, it is intended to provide a sampling of IS management positions. Furthermore, many firms will use the same job title, but each is likely to define it in a different way.

As you can see from Table 1.6, the range of career opportunities for IS managers is very broad.

What Makes IS Personnel So Valuable?

In addition to the growing importance of people in the IS field, there have been changes in the nature of this type of work. No longer are IS departments in organizations filled only with nerdy men with pocket protectors. Many more women are in IS positions now. Also, it is

Table 1.6 ***Some IS management job titles and brief job descriptions.***

Job Title	Job Description
CIO	Highest-ranking IS manager. Responsible for strategic planning and IS use throughout the firm.
IS Director	Responsible for managing all systems throughout the firm and the day-to-day operations of the entire IS unit.
Division or Account Executive	Responsible for managing the day-to-day operations of all aspects of IS within one particular division, plant, functional business area, or product unit.
Information Centre Manager	Responsible for managing IS services such as help desks, hotlines, training, consulting, and so on.
Development Manager	Responsible for coordinating and managing all new systems projects.
Project Manager	Responsible for managing a particular new systems project.
Maintenance Manager	Responsible for coordinating and managing all systems maintenance projects.
Systems Manager	Responsible for managing a particular existing system.
IS Planning Manager	Responsible for developing an enterprise-wide hardware, software, and networking architecture and for planning for systems growth and change.
Operations Manager	Responsible for supervising the day-to-day operations of the data and/or computer centre.
Programming Manager	Responsible for coordinating all applications programming efforts.
Systems Programming Manager	Responsible for coordinating support for maintenance of all systems software (e.g., operating systems, utilities, programming languages, and so on).
Manager of Emerging Technologies	Responsible for forecasting technology trends and for evaluating and experimenting with new technologies.
Telecommunications Manager	Responsible for coordinating and managing the entire voice and data network.
Network Manager	Responsible for managing one piece of the enterprise-wide network.
Database Administrator	Responsible for managing databases and database management software use.
Auditing or Computer Security Manager	Responsible for managing ethical and legal use of information systems within the firm.
Quality Assurance Manager	Responsible for developing and monitoring standards and procedures to ensure that systems within the firm are accurate and of good quality.
Webmaster	Responsible for managing the firm's World Wide website.

Table 1.7 *IS professionals' core competencies.*

Domain	Description
Technical Knowledge and Skills	
Hardware	Hardware platforms, peripherals
Software	Operating systems, application software, drivers
Networking	Networking operating systems, cabling and networking interface cards, LANs, WANs, Internet, security
Business Knowledge and Skills	
Business	Business processes, functional areas of business and their integration, industry
Management	Planning, organizing, leading, controlling, managing people and projects
Social	Interpersonal and group dynamics, political
Communication	Verbal, written, and technological communication and presentation
Systems Knowledge and Skills	
Systems integration	Connectivity, compatibility, integrating subsystems and systems
Development methodologies	Steps in systems analysis and design, systems development life cycle, alternative development methodologies
Critical thinking	Challenging one's and others' assumptions and ideas
Problem solving	Information gathering and synthesis, problem identification, solution formulation, comparison, and choice

now more common for an IS professional to be a polished, professional systems analyst who can talk fluently about both business and technology. IS personnel are now well-trained, highly skilled, valuable professionals who garner high wages and prestige and who play a pivotal role in helping firms be successful.

Many studies have been aimed at helping us understand what knowledge and skills are necessary for a person in the IS area to be successful (see, for example, Todd, McKeen, and Gallupe, 1995). Interestingly, these studies also point out just what it is about IS personnel that makes them so valuable to their organizations. In a nutshell, good IS personnel possess valuable, integrated knowledge and skills in three areas—technical, business, and systems—as outlined in Table 1.7.

Technical Competency

These three areas of knowledge and skills—technical, business, and systems—are the core competencies that make IS professionals valuable to organizations. The technical competency area includes knowledge and skills in hardware, software, networking, and security. In a sense, these are the "nuts and bolts" of IS. This is not to say that the IS professional must be a high-level technical expert in these areas. On the contrary, the IS professional must know just enough about these areas to understand how they work and how they can and should be applied. Typically, the IS professional manages or directs those who have deeper, more detailed technical knowledge.

The technical area of competency is, perhaps, the most difficult to maintain because the popularity of individual technologies is so fleeting. In Table 1.8, we list some technical skill areas that are currently popular. Many of these would not have appeared on this list a few years ago, and many will probably not appear on the list in a few years.

Business Competency

The business competency area is one that sets the IS professional apart from others who have only technical knowledge and skills, and in an era of increased outsourcing it may well save a person's job. For example, MSNBC.com recently reported (**www.msnbc.msn.com/id/5077435**) that information systems management is one of ten professions that is not likely to be outsourced. As a result, it is absolutely vital for IS professionals to understand the technical areas *and* the nature of the business as well. IS professionals must also be able to understand and

Table 1.8 ***What technical skills are hot?***

Office/E-mail	Languages and Data Formats	Applications
Microsoft Office	SmallTalk	Any ERP package (e.g., those from SAP or Oracle)
MS Internet Explorer	C, C++, and C#	
Mozilla/Mozilla Firefox	Java	Any CRM package
MS Project	JavaScript	Any SCM package (e.g., those from I2, Ariba, or Perfect Commerce)
Microsoft Exchange	HTML/CGI	
Lotus Notes	Perl	
Opera	ASP/VBScript	SAS Enterprise Miner
FrontPage	PHP	SPSS Clementine
POP and IMAP Mailers	Python	
	Visual Basic	
	XML	
	UML	
	JSP	
	Java Servlets	
	SOAP	
	UDDI	

RDBMS Administration	Development Tools	Operating Systems
Sybase	Oracle Developer 2000	Solaris
Oracle	Uniface	HP-UX
DB2	Lotus Domino/Designer	AIX
MS SQL Server	Microsoft Visual Studio	Variety of Windows platforms
MySQL	Microsoft.net platform	Variety of Linux platforms
	BEA Weblogic	Mac OS X Panther
	IBM WebSphere	
	Sun's J2EE	
	Tomcat	
	Eclipse and JBoss	

NOS LAN Administration	Networking	
Variety of Windows platforms	TCP/IP	
Variety of Linux platforms	SNMP	
SAMBA	IEEE 802.11 a, b, and g	
	Frame Relay	
	ATM	
	Voice over IP	
	VLANs	
	VPNs	
	Optical networking Add	
	MPLS	
	WiMax	
	IPSec	
	RFID Tags	

manage people and projects. These business skills propel IS professionals into project management and, ultimately, high-paying middle- and upper-level management positions.

Systems Competency

Systems competency is another area that sets the IS professional apart from others with only technical knowledge and skills. Those who understand how to build and integrate systems and how to solve problems will ultimately manage large, complex systems projects, as well as manage those in the firm who have only technical knowledge and skills.

Perhaps now you can see why IS professionals are so valuable to their organizations. These individuals have a solid, integrated foundation in technical, business, and systems knowledge and skills. Perhaps most important, they also have the social skills to understand how to work well with and motivate others. It is these core competencies that continue to make IS professionals valuable employees.

Given how important technology is, what does this mean for your career? Technology is being used to radically change how business is conducted—from the way products and services are produced, distributed, and accounted for, to the ways they are marketed and sold. Whether you are majoring in information systems, finance, accounting, operations management, human resource management, business law, or marketing, knowledge of technology is critical to a successful career in business.

The Organizational Side of Information Systems

We have talked about data versus information, the technology side of IS, and the people side of IS. The last part of our IS definition is the term "organization." People use information systems to help their organizations be more productive and profitable, gain competitive advantage, reach more customers, or improve services to their customers. This holds true for all types of organizations—professional, social, religious, educational, and governmental.

In Chapter 6 we will talk in detail about the basic types of information systems commonly used in organizations. It makes sense, however, for us to describe briefly here the various types of systems used so that you will know exactly what we mean by the term "information system" as we use it throughout the rest of the book. Table 1.9 provides a list of the major types of information systems used in organizations, and Figure 1.7 shows graphically how these systems fit within organizations.

The first three systems in Table 1.9—***transaction processing systems, management information systems,*** and ***executive information systems***—are some of the more traditional, major categories that are used to describe information systems. As depicted in Figure 1.7,

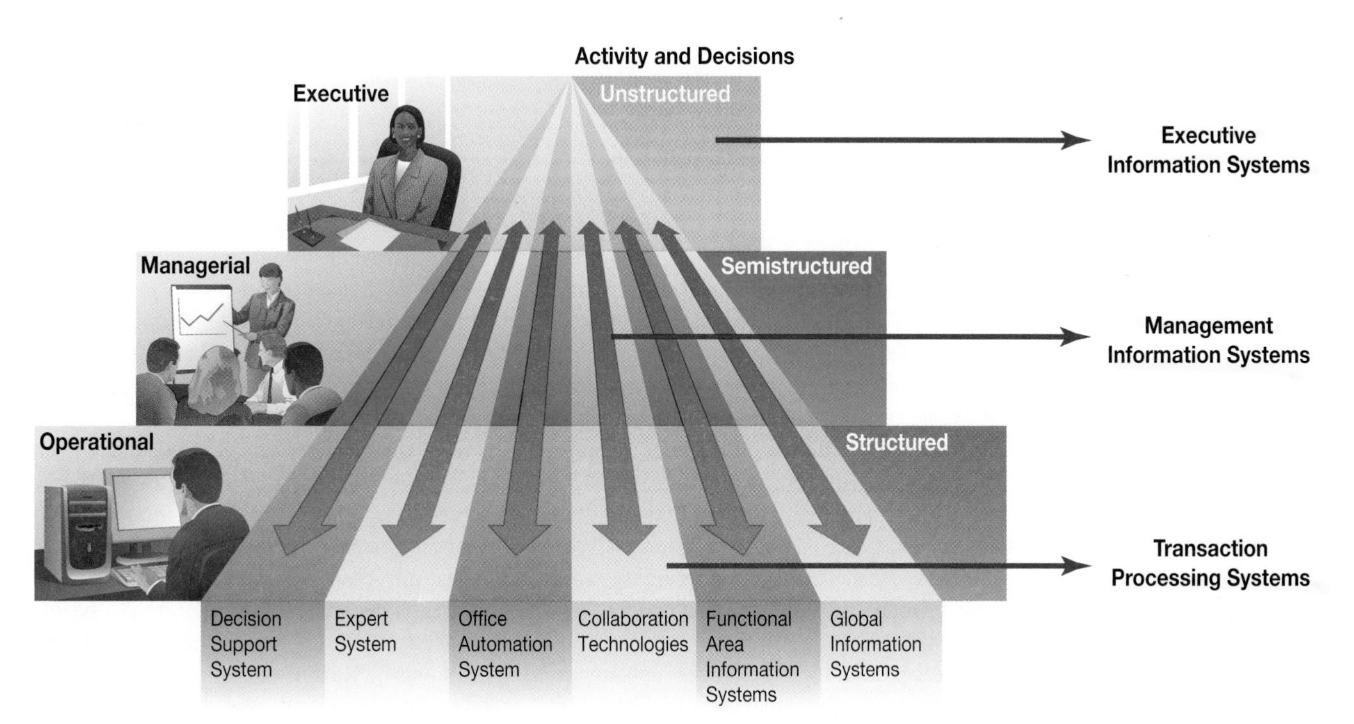

Figure 1.7 Information systems operate at all levels of the organization.

Table 1.9 ***Types of information systems used in organizations.***

Type of System	Designed To	Sample Application
Transaction Processing System	Process day-to-day business event data at the operational level of the organization	Grocery store checkout cash register with connection to network
Management Information System	Produce detailed information to help manage a firm or a part of a firm	Inventory management and planning system
Executive Information System	Provide very high-level, aggregate information to support executive-level decision making	News retrieval and stock update information system
Decision Support System	Provide analysis tools and access to databases in order to support quantitative decision making	Product demand forecasting system
Expert System	Mimic human expert in a particular area and provide answers or advice	Automated system for analyzing bank loan applications
Functional Area Information System	Support the activities within a specific functional area of the firm	System for planning for personnel training and assignments
Office Automation System (a.k.a. Personal Productivity Software)	Support a wide range of predefined, day-to-day work activities of individuals and small groups	Word processor
Collaboration System	Enable people to communicate, collaborate, and coordinate with each other	Electronic mail system with automated, shared calendar
Customer Relationship Management System	Support interaction between the firm and its customers	Siebel's suite of e-business software products, including Siebel Sales (now part of Oracle)
Electronic Commerce System	Enable customers to buy goods and services from a firm's website	**www.amazon.com**
Enterprise Resource Planning System	Support and integrate all facets of the business, including planning, manufacturing, sales, marketing, and so on	SAP R/3 (Systems, Applications, and Products in Data Processing, Release 3)

transaction processing systems exist to support the operational level of the organization. They use structured data like names, dates, and financial figures. Examples of transaction processing systems include accounts receivable systems, point of sale systems, and order entry systems.

Management information systems operate at the managerial level of the organization. They can process semistructured information and thus are more sophisticated than transaction processing systems. Management information systems are used to support decision making and for purposes of planning and control.

Executive information systems operate at the top levels of the organization. They can process structured and unstructured information. This information may come from within the firm, or it may be derived from external sources, such as competitive intelligence or recent economic news. Executive information systems are used to support key strategic decisions and long-range planning.

Five to ten years ago it would have been typical to see systems that fell cleanly into one of these categories. Today, with ***internetworking*** and ***systems integration***, it is difficult to say that any given information system fits into only one of these categories (e.g., that a system is a management information system only and nothing else). Modern-day information systems tend to span several of these categories of information systems, helping not only to collect data from throughout the firm and from customers, but also to integrate all that diverse data and present it to busy decision makers, along with tools to manipulate and analyze those data. Systems that span organizational levels include ***decision support systems, expert systems***, and ***functional area information systems***. Some systems in use by organizations today cut across levels and organizational functions. ***Customer Relationship Management (CRM) systems*** and ***Enterprise Resource Planning (ERP) systems*** are good examples of these types of systems that encompass many features and types of data and cannot easily be categorized.

Office automation systems and ***collaboration systems*** are typically bought "off-the-shelf" and enable people to (1) perform their own work and (2) work with others. A handful of software packages dominate this sector of the software industry and are commonly found on personal computers in people's homes and offices. Microsoft Office and OpenOffice are examples of popular office automation systems that provide word processing, spreadsheet, and other personal productivity tools. Microsoft's Exchange/Outlook and Lotus Notes are good examples of very popular collaboration systems that provide people with e-mail, automated calendaring, and online, threaded discussions.

Systems for ***electronic commerce***, such as corporate websites, are also very popular and important. These systems are typically Internet-based and enable (1) consumers to find information about, and purchase, goods and services from each other and from business firms and (2) business firms to electronically exchange products, services, and information. Given the pervasive use of the Internet to support electronic commerce, we devote a great deal of space to this topic in subsequent chapters. In Chapter 4 we talk about the nuts and bolts of how the Internet works. Then, in Chapter 5, we talk about how people are using the Internet to conduct electronic commerce.

While many modern-day information systems span several of these IS categories, it is still useful to understand these categories. Doing so enables you to better understand the myriad approaches, goals, features, and functions of modern information systems.

We have talked about each of the parts of our definition of IS, shown again in Figure 1.8, and we have talked about different types of information systems. In the next section, we focus on how information systems can be applied within organizations.

Information systems are combinations of
hardware, software, and telecommunications networks
which
people build and use
to
collect, create, and distribute useful data,
typically in
organizational settings.

Figure 1.8 A representation of the definition of IS, as shown in Figure 1.3.

THE DUAL NATURE OF INFORMATION SYSTEMS

Given how important and expensive information systems have become, information technology is like a sword—you can use it effectively as a competitive weapon, but as the old saying goes, those who live by the sword sometimes die by the sword. The two following cases illustrate this dual nature of information systems.

Case in Point: An Information System Gone Awry: The Denver International Airport

What happens when an information system is implemented poorly? Perhaps the best-known example of an information system gone wrong in recent years is the automated baggage-handling system for the new US$4.2 billion Denver International Airport (DIA), which is shown in Figure 1.9.

Like the newly constructed DIA, the new underground automated baggage-handling system for the airport was intended to be amazing. This information system would not only coordinate the automated check-in and routing of all luggage for all customers throughout the airport, but it would also enable airport employees to monitor the flow of baggage and literally locate bags anywhere in the airport. The system, which cost US$200 million, included the following features:

- 21 miles of steel track
- 4000 independent "telecars" that would route and deliver luggage among the counters, gates, and claim areas of 20 different airlines
- 100 networked computers
- 5000 electric eyes
- 400 radio receivers
- 56 bar-code scanners

Due to problems in the software, the system opened, damaged, and misrouted cargo, forcing airport authorities to leave the system sitting idle for nearly a year. Because of this

Figure 1.9 The US$4.2 billion Denver International Airport.

Source: Ron Coppock/Getty Images, Inc. Liaison

and other delays, the airport did not open and wasted $1.1 million a day in interest and operating costs for quite some time.

The DIA story has a happy ending, or beginning, as it were. They fixed the software, and the automated baggage system is now operational. The airport is now making money and winning awards. Indeed, the baggage-handling system is one of many ways in which this organization is attempting to be innovative and to outdo the competition. However, the airport is still useful as an example of how a problematic information system can adversely affect the performance of an organization.

Case in Point: An Information System That Works: FedEx

Just as there are examples of information systems that had gone wrong, there are many examples of information systems that are going right. For example, take the innovative use of information systems on the FedEx website.

FedEx, now a $25 billion family of companies, is the world's largest express transportation company and delivers millions of packages and millions of pounds of freight to 215 countries each business day. FedEx Express uses extensive, interconnected information systems to coordinate more than 245 000 employees, hundreds of aircraft, and tens of thousands of ground vehicles worldwide.

To improve its services and sustain a competitive advantage, FedEx now offers services on the Internet. Millions of customers visit the FedEx website to track FedEx Express and FedEx Ground shipments anywhere in the world, find out about FedEx's delivery options and costs, or use tools to prepare their own packages, verify them online, and print bar-coded shipping documents. These and other information systems assure FedEx a position of dominance in the shipping business for many years to come.

Information Systems for Competitive Advantage

The Denver International Airport and FedEx information systems are typical of those used in large, complex organizations. These systems are so large in scale and scope that they are difficult to build. It is important to handle the development of such systems the right way the first time around. These examples also show that as we rely more and more on information systems, the security of these systems is paramount to business success.

Not only were these systems large and complicated, but they were, and continue to be, critical to the success of the firms that built them. The choices made in developing the new systems at both DIA and FedEx were ***strategic*** in their intent. These systems were not developed solely because managers in these organizations wanted to do things faster or because they wanted to have the latest, greatest technology. These organizations developed these systems strategically to help gain or sustain some ***competitive advantage*** (Porter, 1985; Porter and Millar, 1985) over their rivals. Let us not let this notion slip by us—while the use of technology can enable efficiency, and while information systems must provide a return on investment, technology use can also be strategic and can be a powerful enabler of competitive advantage (see Chapter 2 for more on the strategic value of IS).

Although we described information systems' uses at two relatively large organizations, firms of all types and sizes can use information systems to gain or sustain a competitive advantage over their rivals. Whether it is a small mom-and-pop boutique or a large government agency, every organization can find a way to use information technology to beat its rivals. In the next chapter we will talk more about this opportunity to use information systems strategically.

Does IS Matter?

On May 1, 2003, Nicholas Carr published an article titled "IT Doesn't Matter" in *Harvard Business Review* that created quite a stir.

He argued that as IT becomes more pervasive it will become more standardized and

WHEN THINGS GO WRONG

Disaster Plans Found Lacking

While companies have had to rely more and more on their information systems, you would think that business executives would spend more time thinking about disaster recovery. Unfortunately, they have not, and two classic examples illustrate just how lacking these plans seem to be. First, apart from the tragic loss of human lives in the September 11 terrorist attacks, the destruction of the World Trade Center caused many telecommunications systems that were depending on the "densest fibre-optic network in the world" to break down. Furthermore, many companies who had offices in the World Trade Center found their important data processing equipment buried under piles of glass, steel, and concrete. Second, in summer 2003, a number of blackouts hit large parts of northeastern United States and Canada; during these power outages, companies that heavily depended on their information systems infrastructure were unable to conduct business, potentially losing millions of dollars.

In both cases, companies were ill prepared for these devastating events. For example, the blackouts negatively affected more than three-quarters of Canadian companies; this shows how important it is for business managers to make contingency plans for the information systems that are used to run their businesses. Surprisingly, according to a survey of more than 200 business/IT executives conducted by the Gartner group, 24 percent of the respondents mentioned that their company lacked disaster recovery plans due to lack of funding; 37 percent of the companies that had formal disaster recovery plans in place needed additional funds to make the plans fully functional.

Doran Boroski, a senior consultant with Compass Group, a Chicago-based management consulting firm, is not surprised by that. Boroski says cost is often a barrier to proper disaster recovery and testing. "Even if they have a plan, they don't test it, mostly for financial reasons," Boroski says. "Testing is the first thing to go out of the IT budget." The picture is no rosier in Canada. A study by *CIO Canada* magazine in 2003 found that 44 percent of the firms did not have a disaster recovery plan in place.

Bob Zimmerman, an analyst at Giga Information Group who specializes in storage management, says disaster recovery tests need to be random events, just like the disasters they are supposed to simulate. Too often, he says, companies schedule tests for a specific time, on a specific day, on a specific application, and when specific personnel are available. "Very few businesses could pass a rigorous disaster recovery test," Zimmerman says. In surveying 150 Compass Group clients over 12 to 18 months, Boroski found that one area where companies are sorely lacking in disaster readiness is their midrange data centres, which are likely to store information related to such things as payroll and HR. Just 25 percent of the companies had a disaster recovery plan for their midrange data centres, and only one-third of the companies with a disaster plan had actually tested it.

After the tragic events of September 11 and the blackouts of summer 2003, business leaders are thinking a lot more about how they might recover from similar disasters. Disaster recovery planning has taken on new meaning and importance since then.

Source: Adapted from Jon Surmacz, "Disaster Plans Lacking," *CIO* (September 26, 2001), **www2.cio.com/metrics/2001/metric269.html**.
Jon Surmacz, "Crash Crisis," *CIO* (March 12, 2003), **www2.cio.com/metrics/2003/metric515.html**.
Anonymous, "Blackouts Catch Businesses Off-Guard," *CIO* (August 28, 2003), **www2.cio.com/metrics/2003/metric598.html**.
Mark Hall & Lucas Mearius, "IT Focus Turns to Disaster Recovery," CNN.com (September 11, 2001), **www.cnn.com/2001/TECH/industry/09/11/disaster.recovery.idg**.

everywhere at same time -

ubiquitous, more of a commodity that is absolutely necessary for every company. He reasoned then that companies should focus IT strictly on cost reduction and risk mitigation and that investing in IT for differentiation or for competitive advantage is futile. Many experts in academia, in the popular press, and within technology companies not only disagreed with that argument but felt that, if taken literally, that line of thinking could hurt companies' competitiveness.

Given the debate that this article caused, on May 1, 2004, *CIO* magazine's editor in chief, Abbie Lundberg, published an interview with Carr on the subject, along with an invited counterpoint essay titled "The Engine That Drives Success: The Best Companies Have the Best Business Models Because They Have the Best IT

BRIEF CASE

A Service Department for a Service Organization: Marriott's IT Department

For global hospitality player Marriott, resourcefulness has often helped to weather crises in the hotel industry, and a culture of being resourceful is practised throughout the company. For example, after the global hospitality industry faced a slump in the aftermath of September 11, 2001, all of Marriott's departments had to cut costs by 20 percent; in addition to cutting their own costs, the members of Marriott's IT department had to help other departments reduce their budgets as well. One cost factor was the use of two different yield management systems, which help to sell the rooms at the best possible rates while at the same time selling as many rooms as possible, thus increasing both average daily rate and occupancy percentage. While the most obvious solution would have been to replace the different systems with a new one, Marriott's IT department reused the systems and integrated them with a new interface in a Web-based environment. In addition to being much cheaper than a new system, the "reused" system helped to significantly decrease support costs and improved forecasting accuracy, which in turn led to revenue increases of 20 percent.

In order to foster this resourcefulness, information technology has to be closely aligned with the company's overall business goals. At Marriott, this means that every IT employee receives a "hospitality crash course" so that employees of all departments can talk on the same terms. Furthermore, the term "IT project" does not exist in Marriott's language; instead, all employees are working on "business projects." As Marriott's CIO, Carl Wilson, believes that any technology can be quickly copied by competitors, he sees that having a culture of resourcefulness across the company is the only way for Marriott to sustain a competitive advantage.

Questions

1. How can being resourceful in the use of IT help other companies gain a competitive advantage?
2. Under which circumstances can resourceful use of IT hinder progress in an organization?

Source: Stephanie Overby, "The Keys to Marriott's Success," CIO.com (August 15, 2003), **www.cio.com/archive/081503/marriot.html**.

Strategies," by noted Canadian technology and business strategy author Don Tapscott. Tapscott argued that companies with bad business models tend to fail, regardless of whether they use information technology or not. On the other hand, companies that have good business models and use information technology successfully to carry out those business models tend to be very successful. He described many examples, across a variety of industries, where firms dominate their respective markets, have superior customer relationships, business designs, and differentiated offerings, and are well known for their superior use of IT in supporting a unique business strategy. His examples included Amazon.com, Best Buy, Citigroup, PepsiCo, Herman Miller, Cisco, Progressive Casualty Insurance, Marriott, FedEx, GE, Southwest Airlines, and Starbucks.

We tend to side with Tapscott on this one. We believe that information systems are a necessary part of doing business, that they can be used to create efficiencies, and that they can also be used as an enabler of competitive advantage. We do agree with Carr, however, that the competitive advantage from the use of information systems can be fleeting, as competitors can eventually do the same thing. Also, given how expensive information systems projects have become, and given how cost-conscious and competitive businesses now are, nearly every information system project today must show a clear return on investment. We'll talk more about the role of information systems in competitive advantage and return on investment in the following chapter.

THE FUTURE OF THE IS FUNCTION WITHIN THE FIRM

The current emphasis on the use of technology within businesses is not a fad. Indeed, all indicators point to the increased use of technology and to organizations' continued awareness of the importance of technology, both as a tool for productivity and as a vehicle for achieving competitive advantage and organizational change. In this section, we briefly discuss some likely future trends.

From Ownership and Control to a Consulting and Service Mentality

Early IS departments typically had huge project backlogs, and IS personnel would often deliver systems that were over budget, were completed much too late, were difficult to use, and did not always work well. In addition, many of these old-school IS personnel believed they owned and controlled the computing resources, that they knew better than users did, and that they should tell users what they could and could not do with the computing resources. Needless to say, this was not a recipe for success and good relationships. Indeed, relations between IS personnel and users within a firm were often sour and were sometimes bitter.

For a long time, users were forced to put up with the poor service and the poor attitude. Then technology started to become significantly better—faster, easier to build and use, and cheaper. As a result, end users began to develop their own computing applications. Disgruntled users simply said, "If the IS staff cannot or will not do this for us, then we will build our own systems." In many cases, they did just that, and they did it well, much to the dismay of some of the IS managers.

Business managers soon became more savvy about technology and the possibilities and opportunities that it offered, and they reasoned that the possibilities and opportunities were too great to let the IS function simply wither away as end-user development took over. In addition, smart, concerned IS personnel realized that they needed an attitude adjustment. Some people believe that the changes in the nature of technology forced people to cooperate more. For example, the shift from large "mainframe" computers to a "client–server" model (i.e., relatively powerful personal computers spread throughout the organization that share data, applications, or peripherals that are hosted by more powerful server computers—see Appendix A) may have forced people within the IS function to improve their operations and their relationships with people in other units of the firm. The client–server model required a new kind of relationship between IS and other people throughout the firm (Stevens, 1994). As a result of these forces, in modern IS units that do a good job, the atmosphere, attitude, and culture are very different and much more sensitive and responsive than they used to be (see Figure 1.10).

In these more responsive IS units, the personnel have taken on more of a consulting relationship with their users. The IS personnel believe that, fundamentally, they are there to help the users solve problems and be more productive. Indeed, in many cases, the IS personnel do not even refer to the users as "users." They are "clients" or "customers," or even better, they are "colleagues" within the organization. This new attitude is a major change from the old days, when IS personnel did not want to be bothered by users and thought that the techies knew better than users. It is unfortunate that this old-school mentality still exists in some organizations.

Figure 1.10 IS personnel are professional and helpful, and they add value to the organization.

Source: © Getty Images, Inc.

The new IS culture is much like that found in successful service organizations. Think of how customers are treated in service organizations, such as Royal Bank or Ernst & Young, or in product-based organizations where service is also important, such as McDonald's or Nordstrom. Great service to the customer is absolutely critical, and employees do everything they can to please customers. They often live by the credo that "the customer is always right."

The same holds for IS units that have taken on this new ***service mentality***. The IS personnel do everything they can to ensure that they are satisfying their systems customers within the firm. They reach out to customers and proactively seek their input and needs, rather than waiting for customers to come in with systems complaints. They modify the systems at a moment's notice just to meet customer needs quickly and effectively. They celebrate the customer's new systems ideas rather than putting up roadblocks and giving reasons why the new ideas cannot or will not work. They fundamentally believe that the customers own the technology and the information and that the technology and information are there for the customers, not for the systems personnel. They create help desks, hotlines, information centres, and training centres to support customers. These service-oriented IS units structure the IS function so that it can better serve the customer.

The implications of this new service mentality for the IS function are staggering. It is simply amazing how unproductive a company can be when the IS personnel and other people within the firm are at odds with one another. On the other hand, it is even more amazing how productive and enjoyable work can be when people in the IS function work hand in hand with people throughout the organization. Technology is, potentially, the great lever, but it works best when people work together, not against each other, to use it.

The Spread of Technology in Organizations

Another phenomenon that shows how integral and vital information systems and their proper management have become to organizations is the extent to which the technology is firmly integrated and entrenched within the various business units (accounting, sales, marketing).

In many organizations today, you will find that the builders and managers of a particular information system or subsystem spend most of their time out in the business unit, along with the users of that particular system. Many times, these systems personnel are permanently placed—with an office, desk, phone, and personal computer—in the business unit along with the users.

In addition, it is not uncommon for systems personnel to have formal education, training, and work experience in information systems as well as in the functional area that the system supports, such as finance. It is becoming increasingly difficult to separate the technology from the business or the systems staff from the other people in the organization (see Figure 1.11). For this reason, how information systems are managed is important to you, no matter what career option you pursue.

As information systems are used more broadly throughout organizations, IS personnel often have dual-reporting relationships—reporting to both the central IS group and the business function they serve. Therefore, at least some need for centralized IS planning, deployment, and management continues—particularly with respect to achieving economies of scale in systems acquisition and development and in optimizing systems integration, enterprise networking, and the like. Even in organizations that are decentralizing technology and related decisions, a need for technology and related decisions to be coordinated well across the firm still persists. This coordination is likely to continue to happen through some form of a centralized (or, at least, centrally coordinated) IS staff. Organizations are likely to continue to want to reap the benefits of IS decentralization (flexibility, adaptability, and systems responsiveness), but it is equally likely that they will not want to, and will not be able to, forgo the benefits of IS centralization (coordination, economies of scale, compatibility, and connectivity).

Figure 1.11 Information systems are indispensable to modern organizations.

Changing Skill Set and Human Resource Planning

Given the trend toward pushing people from the IS staff out into the various business units of the firm, and given the need for people within each of the functional areas of the business to have technology skills, there is clearly a need for people who know the technology side and the business side of the business well. We suspect that the need for people to play these boundary-spanning roles will continue. Many of these people will be hired into and located within the IS departments of firms, but they are likely to spend a lot of their time working out in the business unit with their clients (see Figure 1.13). Indeed, their work space is likely to be physically located out in the business unit. Staffing the IS group with these kinds of boundary spanners is and will continue to be critical to the success of the IS group and to the success of the organization.

Downsizing and Outsourcing

Many organizations that are ***downsizing***, or rightsizing as some call it, are looking toward the IS function and technology as the lever for simultaneously shrinking the organization by reducing personnel headcount and making the organization more productive (i.e., doing more with less). In short, they are using technology to streamline business functions and, in some cases, to slash costs and replace people. Although this approach may not be fair for the people who lose their jobs, many firms are forced to do this to remain competitive and, in some cases, to continue to exist. Such uses of information systems have interesting implications for the size and structure of organizations and for the size and structure of the IS function.

Similarly, ***outsourcing*** is on the rise for all aspects of business. In outsourcing, many of the more routine jobs are "outsourced": these jobs and/or tasks are being conducted by people in

COMING ATTRACTIONS

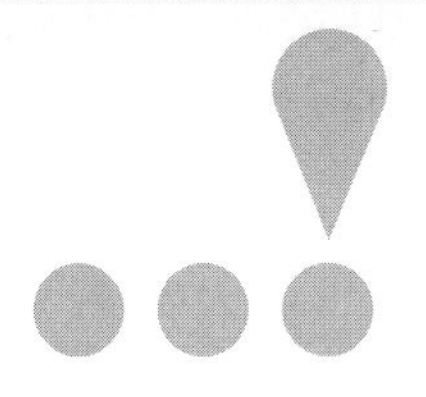

A Bright Future for Organic Displays

A group of University of Toronto researchers say they are the first Canadians to produce a display technology that is as flexible as paper. The experimental technology is called an organic light-emitting device (or OLED). It's flexible, so it could fit any form factor or even mould itself to the shape of your lap (see Figure 1.12). "What differentiates this device from conventional LEDs is that the molecules are very flexible. You can make any substrate you want," said Zheng-Hong Lu, the project's lead researcher at the University of Toronto. "That's really opened up a whole potential display media." Lu has been working with his team on the project for about five years and has developed OLEDs made on a number of flexible materials, like transparent plastic film and reflective metal foil. Lu said OLED could represent the next wave of display technology. In recent years, liquid crystal displays (LCD) have made substantial inroads against cathode ray tubes (CRT) in the monitor and display markets. "Many experts consider [OLED] the next major display device replacing LCD," said Lu.

Because of its flexible design, the OLED manufacturing process would be substantially different from the way conventional displays are produced today. "Like newspapers, you could print rolls and rolls of displays," said Lu. "With big companies willing to invest lots of money, I'm really optimistic about some sort of commercial device." Lu said he hopes to see commercially viable products in the market in five years. Further down the line, flexible laptops that could be rolled up and stuffed in a back pocket may be a reality. The commercial applications of OLED are very real and are already here, albeit in a much smaller-factor form. Kodak, which owns an OLED patent, has an Easy Share 633 digital camera with an embedded OLED display. Samsung is now shipping its E700 series cell phone with an external OLED screen. However, making the leap to full-size OLED for something the size of a computer monitor or TV is still a distant goal, according to IDC analyst Jennifer Gallo.

She conservatively estimates that it could be at least 2010 before such products are available. "It's been proven that it can be done, but not for large displays. There are a lot of people focusing on the production and the manufacturing process of OLED, such as DuPont, and they're still working on it. It's not easy," she said. The product has limitations that have yet to be overcome. Much like a break-and-shake glowstick that provides a light source only for a short time, OLED has some serious lifespan concerns, Gallo said. "It's a chemical and there's a lifetime to that chemical and how long it will emit light for." If that problem can be solved, the future for OLED looks bright. Aside from the inherent advantage of a flexible display, OLED produces an extremely clear image that can be viewed from multiple angles (an issue with colour-screen LCD is that the colour tends to fade when viewed from the side).

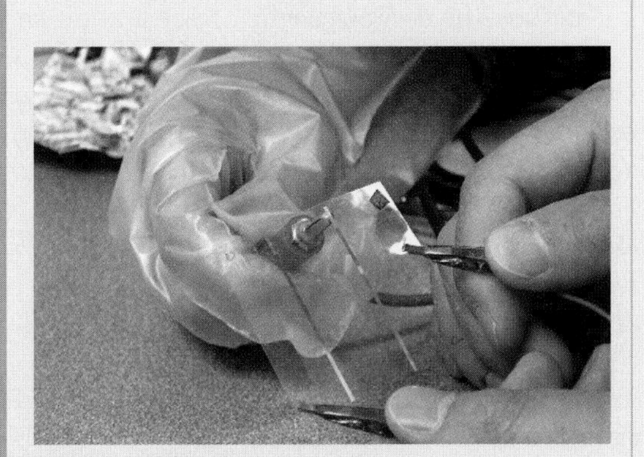

Figure 1.12 An organic light-emitting device.
Source: Zheng-Hong Lu, U of T, Department of Materials, Science and Engineering.

Source: Adapted from Neil Sutton, "U of T Lab Sees Potential in Organic Display Technology," ITBusiness.ca (January 20, 2004), **www.itbusiness.ca/index.asp?theaction=61&sid=54581#**.

another firm, in another part of the country or on another continent, at less cost. Some of these outsourced jobs are within the information systems function. For example, many computer programming tasks are now being completed by firms in India and China (see Chapter 8 for more information on IT outsourcing).

Career Prospects and Opportunities

Although technology at some levels continues to become easier to use, there is still and is likely to continue to be an acute need for people within the organization to have the responsibility of planning for, designing, developing, maintaining, and managing

Figure 1.13 IS personnel are likely to be put out in the business unit, working directly with the people who will use the system being implemented.

Source: © Getty Images, Inc.

technologies. Much of this will happen within the business units and will be done by those with primarily business duties and tasks, as opposed to systems duties and tasks. However, we are a long way from the day when technology is so easy to deploy that a need no longer exists for people with deep information systems knowledge and skills. In fact, many people in Canada and elsewhere believe that this day may never come. Although increasing numbers of people will incorporate systems responsibilities within their nonsystems jobs, there will continue to be a need for people with primarily systems responsibilities. In short, IS staffs and departments will likely continue to exist and play an important role in the foreseeable future.

While many organizations are downsizing, and while some are shrinking their IS staffs and/or sending the more routine jobs abroad, overall hiring within IS is back again and is expected to grow. Given that information systems continue to be a critical tool for business success, it is not likely that IS departments will go away or even shrink significantly. Indeed, all projections are for long-term growth of IS in both scale and scope. Also, as is the case in any area of business, those people who are continually learning, continuing to grow, continuing to find new ways to add value, and who have advanced and/or unique skills, will always be sought after, whether in information systems or in any area of the firm.

ETHICAL DILEMMA

Implications of Global Outsourcing

"It's considered a crime against humanity today, where for the last fifteen years, it was a sound business move." IBM spokesman John Bukovinsky recently stated what many companies think about global outsourcing. From software development to call centres, many companies have used outsourcing to get access to highly skilled but inexpensive labour in foreign countries, mainly India and China. Often, companies choose to outsource certain jobs because they are having a hard time finding the right workers in local markets; in many cases, however, outsourcing is mainly done to decrease costs, which has a positive impact on a company's bottom line.

While outsourcing can be beneficial for companies, it often means that comparable domestic jobs are cut—in cases where a worker costs a company more in current and future benefits than the worker will bring in current and future earnings, the companies often choose cutting that job. Frequently, the workers losing their jobs are employees in later stages of their lives; many of them end up having to work in low-paid, low-skilled jobs to be able to support their families and save for their retirements.

Recent studies claim that offshore outsourcing is not a zero-sum game; companies often use the cost reductions from outsourcing to move into new business segments or to invest in new products, thereby creating new jobs. Nevertheless, in the short run, "moving a job to India" can roughly be translated into laying off a domestic employee. Should this be viewed as a sound business move or a crime against humanity?

Source: Robert X. Cringely, "Body Count: Why Moving to India Won't Really Help," *PBS* (August 7, 2003), **www.pbs.org/cringely/pulpit/ pulpit20030807.html**.
Jason Lopez, "IBM Calls Daksh Buy Strategic Move," *Contact Center Today* (April 9, 2004), **http://contact-center-today.newsfactor.com/story.xhtml?story_id=23647**.
Erika Morphy, "Research: Outsourcing Risks and Rewards," *CRM Daily* (April 2, 2004), **http://crm-daily.newsfactor.com/story.xhtml?story_id=23600**.

GLOBAL PERSPECTIVE

North American Business Firms Look Overseas for IS Help

The growing demand for inexpensive yet competent programming talent is pushing the offshore-outsourcing market beyond its roots in India and encouraging North American IT service providers to increase their use of overseas workers. "The technology skills needed to program in languages such as C++, COBOL, and even Java are available in China, the Philippines, Russia, and other countries, but offshore outsourcing is most mature in India. The Indian government has been supportive of IT for decades and has continued to improve on the solid educational systems built by the British," says Mukesh Mehta, VP of corporate systems for Metropolitan Life Insurance Company, which has an offshore-outsourcing contract with Cognizant Technology Solutions Corp. For instance, the Indian Parliament granted the Indian Institute of Technology its charter in 1961, and the school has evolved into a centre for teaching, research, and industrial consulting.

While India is the biggest resource for offshore programmers and project managers, it is predicted that the demand for offshore workforce will soon outstrip the country's supply. A recent survey by India's National Association of Software and Services Companies (NASSCOM) has predicted that by 2008, 1 million IT workers will be needed in India, whereas India's IT workforce will only grow to 885 000 people.

North American executives are becoming increasingly comfortable with outsourcing projects to companies that do the work in remote locations at lower prices than can be found domestically. "A 25 percent cost savings on an outsourcing contract is a realistic goal when working with an offshore provider," according to Forrester analyst Christine Overby. However, as the labour costs in India continue to rise, companies might look to countries such as China when thinking about offshoring their work. To mitigate risk, many offshore companies have management personnel in North America who act as liaisons with overseas staff. The continued reliance on offshore talent by well-known service providers such as Accenture, CGI, and IBM Global Services also lends credence to the offshore model.

A recent study by the Information Technology Association of America and Global Insight has estimated that in 2008, U.S. companies will spend US$31 billion for global outsourcing of software and services, up from US$10 billion in 2003, which translates into an increase from 2.3 percent to 6.2 percent of total spending for software and services by the corporations. Interestingly, Canada is predicted to be the beneficiary of much of this spending. So-called "nearshore" projects can result in cost savings without some of the cultural and logistical challenges of working with firms on the other side of the world. According to the study, by 2008, the cost savings enabled by global outsourcing will help the U.S. real gross domestic product (GDP) to be over US$120 billion higher than it would be without global outsourcing.

What began more than a decade ago as a cheap way to supplement overworked internal application developers with workers from India has grown into a worldwide search for the right mixture of talent, resources, and cost savings to create and manage today's most complex IT environments.

Source: Anonymous, "Executive Summary: The Comprehensive Impact of Offshore IT Software and Services Outsourcing on the U.S. Economy and the IT Industry," *Global Insight* (March 2003), **www.itaa.org/itserv/docs/execsumm.pdf**.
W. Chai, "India Could Face IT Staff Drought," *CNet News.com* (February 19, 2003), **http://news.com.com/2100-1001-985118.html?tag=nl**.
L. Greenemeier, "Offshore Outsourcing Grows to Global Proportions," *InformationWeek* (February 11, 2002), **www.informationweek.com/showArticle.jhtml?articleID=6501137**.
M. Yamamoto, "Will India Price Itself Out of Offshore Market?" *CNet News.com* (March 29, 2004), **http://news.com.com/2100-1022_3-5180589.html**.

CAREER IMPLICATIONS

Why Information Systems Matter

For Accounting and Finance

In today's networked organizations, accounting and finance professionals rely heavily on information systems. Information systems are used to support various resource planning and control processes as well as to provide managers with up-to-date information. Accounting and finance professionals use a variety of information systems, networks, and databases to effectively perform their function. In addition to changing the ways internal processes are managed and performed, information systems have changed the ways organizations exchange financial information with suppliers, distributors, and customers. If you choose a career in accounting or finance, it is very likely that you will be working with various types of information systems every day.

For Operations Management

Information systems have greatly changed the operations management profession. In the past, orders for supplies had to be placed over the phone, production processes had to be optimized using tedious calculations, and forecasts were sometimes only educated guesses. Today, Enterprise Resource Planning (ERP) and Supply Chain Management (SCM) systems have eliminated much of the "busy work" associated with making production forecasts and placing orders. Additionally, with the use of corporate extranets, companies are connecting to their suppliers' and distributors' networks, helping to reduce costs in procurement and distribution processes. If you choose operations management as your profession, the use of information systems will likely be a big part of your workday.

For Human Resources Management

The human resources management profession has experienced widespread use of information systems for recruiting employees via Internet job sites, distributing information through corporate intranets, and analyzing employee data stored in databases. In addition to using information systems within your daily work activities, you will have to deal with other issues related to information systems use and misuse within your organization. For example, what are the best methods for motivating employees to use a system they do not want to use? What policies should you use regarding monitoring employee productivity or Internet misuse? For those who choose human resource management as a profession, information systems have become an invaluable addition to the recruitment and management of personnel.

For Marketing

Information systems have changed the way organizations promote and sell their products. For example, business-to-consumer electronic commerce, enabled by the Internet, allows companies to directly interact with their customers without the need for intermediaries; likewise, CRM systems facilitate the targeting of narrow market segments with highly personalized promotional campaigns. Marketing professionals must therefore be proficient in the use of various types of information systems in order to attract and retain loyal customers.

For Information Systems

Information systems have become a ubiquitous part of organizational life, where systems are used by all organizational levels and functions. Because of this, there is a growing need for professionals to develop and support these systems. To most effectively utilize the investment in information systems, professionals must be proficient in both business—management, marketing, finance, and accounting—and technology. In other words, information systems professionals must understand the business rationale for implementing a particular system, as well as how organizations can use various systems to obtain a competitive advantage. Being able to bridge the business needs of the organization to information systems-based solutions will provide you with a competitive advantage on the job market.

KEY POINTS REVIEW

1. **Define and understand the term "information systems" (IS).** Information systems are combinations of hardware, software, and telecommunications networks that people build and use to collect, create, and distribute useful data typically in organizational settings. When data are organized in a way that is useful to people, these data are defined as information. The term "information systems" is also used to represent the field in which people develop, use, manage, and study computer-based information systems in organizations. The field of IS is huge, diverse, and growing and encompasses many different people, purposes, systems, and technologies.
2. **Explain the technology, people, and organizational components of an information system.** The technology part of information systems is the hardware, software, and telecommunications networks. The people who build, manage, use, and study information systems make up the people component. They include systems analysts, systems programmers, information systems professors, and many others. Finally, information systems typically reside and are used within organizations, so they are said to have an organizational component. Together, these three aspects form an information system.
3. **Describe the types of jobs and career opportunities in information systems and how knowledge of information systems can help you in other career paths.** The people who help develop and manage systems in organizations include systems analysts, systems programmers, systems operators, network administrators, database administrators, systems designers, systems managers, and chief information officers. All of these types of people are in heavy demand; as a result, salaries are high and continue to rise. The field of IS has changed such that IS personnel are now thought of as valuable business professionals rather than as "nerds" or "techies." The need for technology-related knowledge and skills has spread to other careers as well as in fields such as finance, accounting, operations management, human resource management, business law, and marketing.
4. **Describe the various types of information systems.** Types of information systems include transaction processing systems, management information systems, executive information systems, decision support systems, expert systems, functional area information systems, customer relationship management systems, enterprise resource planning systems, office automation systems, collaboration systems, and systems for electronic commerce. While many modern-day information systems span several of these categories, it is still useful to understand these categories. Doing so enables you to better understand the myriad approaches, goals, features, and functions of modern information systems.
5. **Describe the dual nature of information systems in the success and failure of modern organizations.** If information systems are conceived, designed, used, and managed effectively and strategically, then together with a sound business model, they can enable organizations to be more effective, to be more productive, to expand their reach, and to gain or sustain competitive advantage over rivals. If information systems are not conceived, designed, used, or managed well, they can have negative effects on organizations, such as loss of money, loss of time, loss of customers' goodwill, and, ultimately, loss of customers. Modern organizations that embrace and manage information systems effectively and strategically, and combine that with sound business models, tend to be the organizations that are successful and competitive.
6. **Explain how you can plan for the future of the IS function.** The future is difficult to predict. Nonetheless, we can expect that there will be broad and continued growth for IS applications, spread of technology and IS personnel throughout organizations, a new service mentality toward technology and IS personnel, and continued downsizing supported by IS. The career opportunities for IS professionals will increase, particularly for jobs that require relatively high levels of skills and abilities, and the management of the IS function and IS human resources will continue to be an important part of managing all modern organizations.

KEY TERMS

chief information officer (CIO) 15
collaboration systems 21
competitive advantage 22
computer-based information systems 8
Customer Relationship Management Systems (CRMS) 21
data 7
decision support systems (DSS) 21
digital divide 7
downsizing 26
electronic commerce 21
Enterprise Resource Planning Systems (ERPS) 21
executive information systems (EIS) 19
expert systems (ES) 21
functional area information systems 21
hardware 4
information 7
information systems (IS) 4
information technology (IT) 8
internetworking 20
knowledge 8
knowledge society 7
knowledge worker 6
management information systems (MIS) 19
new economy 7
office automation system (OAS) 21
outsourcing 26
service mentality 25
software 4
strategic 22
systems integration 20
technology 8
telecommunications networks 4
transaction processing system (TPS) 19
wisdom 8

REVIEW QUESTIONS

1. Define and understand the term "information systems" (IS).
2. Explain the technology, people, and organizational components of an information system.
3. Define and list four business knowledge and/or skills core competencies.
4. Describe three or four types of jobs and career opportunities in information systems and in related fields.
5. What are some reasons that the position of CIO has grown in importance?
6. Define the term "knowledge worker." Who coined the term?
7. How does the textbook define "technology"? Give some basic examples.
8. List and define four of the systems knowledge and skills core competencies.
9. List and define five types of information systems used in organizations.
10. Describe key factors in the future of the IS function within the firm.

SELF-STUDY QUESTIONS

Visit the Companion Website for this text for additional Self-Study Questions: **www.pearsoned.ca/jessup.**

1. Information systems today are __________.
   A. slower than in the past
   B. continuing to evolve with improvements to the hardware and software
   C. utilized by only a few select individuals
   D. stable and should not change
2. Information systems are used in which of the following organizations?
   A. professional
   B. educational
   C. governmental
   D. all of the above
3. Whereas data are raw unformatted pieces or lists of words or numbers, information is __________.
   A. data that have been organized in a form that is useful
   B. accumulated knowledge
   C. what you put in your computer
   D. what your computer prints out for you
4. Computer-based information systems were described in this chapter as __________.
   A. any complicated technology that requires expert use
   B. a combination of hardware, software, and telecommunications networks that people build and use to collect, create, and distribute data
   C. any technology (mechanical or electronic) used to supplement, extend, or replace human/manual labour
   D. any technology used to leverage human capital
5. Which of the following is a popular title given to executives who are responsible for the information systems function?
   A. CFO
   B. CIO
   C. CEO
   D. CMA
6. Which of the following positions is typically the highest ranking in an IS department of a modern company?
   A. systems analyst
   B. systems programmers
   C. IS director
   D. networking professional
7. Which of the following IS job titles is used for a person whose primary responsibility is to direct the maintenance of an information system?
   A. IS director
   B. Webmaster
   C. systems analyst
   D. chief information officer
8. Which of the following is not classified as business knowledge and skills?
   A. management
   B. communication
   C. systems integration
   D. social
9. Which of the following was not discussed as a common type, or category, of information system used in organizations?
   A. transaction processing
   B. decision support
   C. enterprise resource planning
   D. Web graphics
10. Which of the following is not an example of an information system?
    A. an accounting system in a business
    B. a concession stand
    C. a combination of different software packages in a company
    D. a database of customers

PROBLEMS AND EXERCISES

1. Match the following terms with the appropriate definitions

_____ Transaction processing system

_____ Systems competency

_____ Information

_____ Knowledge society

_____ Electronic commerce

_____ Customer relationship management

_____ Systems analyst

_____ Chief information officer

_____ Information systems

_____ Service mentality

a. A society with a high proportion of knowledge workers who play an important leadership role

b. An executive-level individual who has overall responsibilities for the information systems component within the organization and is primarily concerned with the effective integration of technology and business strategy

c. The use of typically Internet-based systems to enable consumers to find information about, and purchase, goods and services from business firms

d. A system that processes day-to-day business event data at the operational level of the organization

e. Data that have been formatted in a way that is useful

f. Systems that enable employees to manage interaction with customers better

g. A job title for a person who helps to develop information systems

h. Ability to solve complex business problems and to build and integrate business systems

i. The mindset that your goal is to enable others to be successful and that the "customer is always right"

j. Combinations of hardware, software, and telecommunications networks that people build and use to collect, create, and distribute useful data, typically in organizational settings

2. How has Federal Express updated its information systems with current technology? Is the investment in technology a good one? How has this investment affected Federal Express's competitors? Visit their website and look at how to track a package.

3. Peter Drucker has defined the knowledge worker and knowledge society. What are his definitions? Do you agree with them? What examples can you give to support or disprove these concepts?

4. List three major IS professional core competencies or general areas from the textbook. Do you agree or disagree that all three are needed to become a professional? Why? What competencies do you currently possess, and what do you need to improve on or acquire? What is your strategy to acquire new skills? Where and when will you acquire them?

5. Of the 10 information systems listed in the chapter, how many do you have experience with? What systems would you like to work with? What types of systems do you encounter at the university you are attending? Read the Brief Cases in this chapter for application of information systems. The World Wide Web is also a good source for additional information.

6. Consider an organization that you are familiar with, perhaps one that you have worked for or have done business with in the past. Describe the type of information systems that organization uses and tell whether or not they are useful or up to date. List specific examples for updating or installing information systems that improve productivity or efficiency.

7. Identify someone who works within the field of information systems, as an information systems instructor, professor, or practitioner (e.g., as a systems analyst or systems manager). Find out why this individual got into this field and what this person likes and dislikes about working within the field of IS. What advice can this person offer to someone entering the field?

8. The case of the Denver International Airport provides insight into the resources used to build large information systems. Is this problem unique to airlines, or do you think other companies have experienced similar problems? What are the tangible or observable costs and the hidden costs when a system takes time to get working as planned?

9. What type of information system do you use at the university you attend to register and add or drop courses? Are course websites available? Are improvements to your current system planned?

10. Electronic commerce has changed purchasing over the Web. Have you bought anything over the Web yet? If you have not made any purchases, what is holding you back? Are you comfortable with the payment system of sending credit card information over the Internet?

11. What collaboration system are you using? Do you find e-mail a good communication method? What are the pros and cons of having one or more e-mail accounts? How often do you check your e-mail? Do you consider e-mail time effective? How comfortable are you with e-mail?

12. Based on your previous work and/or professional experiences, describe your relationships with the personnel in the IS department. Was the IS department easy to work with? Why or why not? Were projects and requests completed on time and correctly? What was the organizational structure of this IS department? How do your answers compare with those of other classmates?

13. As a small group, conduct a search on the World Wide Web for job placement services. Pick at least four of these services and find as many IS job titles as you can. You may want to try Monster.ca at **www.monster.ca**. How many did you find? Were any of them different from those presented in this chapter? Could you determine the responsibilities of these positions based on the information given to you?

14. What type of IT investment should Tim Hortons have and how would it be used in the corporate office and the individual stores? What would it need to track inventory and sales?

Search the Web or visit a Tim Hortons outlet in your city to determine whether you can see what technology is available in your local store.

15. The IS support group within the School of Business at Indiana University changed its name from "Business Computing Facility" to "Technology Services." Along with the change in name came an appropriate change in services and offerings to their clientele. Ford IT units are another example of an organization that changed its name and focus. Find an example of an organization that changed the external name of its IT or IS unit but did not change the internal structure or attitude. Why were these not changed as well? Was the name change merely to make it sound better to the outsider? Has anything been done to correct this problem?

APPLICATION EXERCISES

Note: The existing data files referenced in these exercises are available on the Companion Website: **www.pearsoned.ca/jessup.**

Spreadsheet Application: Ticket Sales at the Comedy Club

Last semester, you joined your university's comedy club, and you are now an assistant to the director of sales and marketing, who is trying to increase the comedy club's marketing efforts. Looking at the previous years' data, you realize that it is nearly impossible to perform a detailed analysis of ticket sales. While you recognize that you will not be able to sell tickets online, you nevertheless want to use information technology to analyze sales and help coordinate the club's sales efforts. The spreadsheet ComedyClub.csv contains the ticket sales data for Fall 2004. Your director has asked you for the following information:

- The total number of tickets sold for each event.
- The total number of tickets sold by each salesperson.
- A pie chart breaking down ticket sales by salesperson.
- A bar graph comparing ticket sales across the different events.

Modify the ComedyClub.csv spreadsheet to provide the information for your director.

Database Application: Tracking Season Ticket Holders at the Comedy Club

The director of sales and marketing of the comedy club would like to increase the efficiency of handling season ticket holders. Often, season ticket holders renew their reservations for the coming season or want to change their preferred seating area or price category. In the previous years, the data has been manually entered in a three-ring binder. In order to handle the season ticket holders' requests more efficiently, your director has asked you to build an Access database containing the following information:

- Customer Name (First and Last Name).
- Customer Address.
- Customer Phone Number.
- Season Ticket Holder Since (Year).
- Price category.
- Preferred seating area.

Create an empty database, import the data contained in the file SeasonTickets.txt into a new table, and save the database. Hint: Use tab delimiters when importing the data; note that the first row contains field names. After importing the data, create a report displaying the names and addresses of all season ticket holders.

ANSWERS TO THE SELF-STUDY QUESTIONS

1. B, p. 5	2. D, p. 5	3. A, p. 7	4. B, p. 4	5. B, p. 15
6. C, p. 16	7. B, p. 16	8. C, p. 17	9. D, p. 19	10. B, p. 4

Case *A Secure Channel to Better Government Services*

The Government of Canada's goal is to provide Canadians with access to its services anytime, anywhere. The vision underlying this goal was set out in 1999, when the government declared its intention to become the most connected government to its citizens in the world. Such a vision, however, required a strong technological infrastructure. A system to provide citizens and businesses with secure, private, and high-speed access to federal government online services and to provide an environment that enabled and encouraged departments to integrate with federated common services had to be built.

The project, named Secure Channel, was spearheaded by Public Works and Government Services Canada (PWGSC). Secure Channel was more than an IT project. It had to enable a transformation of the Canadian government - not only in how it operated, but in how it thought of itself. The project leader, Michael de Rosenroll, director general of the Strategic Infrastructure Services Sector of PWGSC's Information Technology Services Branch, says the project took a "Big Bang" approach to achieving the government's vision. "The government is moving to an enterprise model," de Rosenroll says. "It's a new way of doing business, more efficient and less labour-intensive."

"Rather than continue to exist as 130 independent agencies and departments, the government is now launching shared- and common-service initiatives—things like common travel, online procurement, human resources and financial systems. All such common systems depend on Secure Channel to operate because it ties them all together and provides access and authentication services."

From its inception shortly after the Speech from the Throne in 1999, Secure Channel was a project unmatched in size and scope. As of March 2005, $414 million had been spent on Secure Channel and its myriad sub-projects. The number of employees, full-time and part-time, within the government who contributed to the project was about 200, and the private-sector consortium working in partnership with PWGSC involved about 300 people, including many of Canada's leading IT strategists.

The magnitude and complexity of the project meant that it took two to three years for the government and the private-sector consortium led by Bell Canada to plan their strategy and approach, de Rosenroll says. "We had to learn how to work in a partnership arrangement with the private sector, when we didn't know what each other didn't know. We had to learn about each others' capabilities and how they came together. Everybody involved had to understand the policy issues – security, privacy, accessibility, a common look and feel – underlying the solution, and all of the departments and agencies had to harmonize their internal architecture with the common middleware."

Secure Channel is a portfolio of services built on a common infrastructure that provides authentication, communication, and security services for departments and programs of the Government of Canada. It authenticates individuals and businesses by means of a digital certificate, called an epass, which ensures that all transactions between the individual and the government program are encrypted and securely communicated.

By early 2006, more than one million epasses had been issued to the public. Seventy percent of departments that have access to the Internet go through Secure Channel to get their Internet services. By 2006, across 14 government departments, 26 programs were using Secure Channel's authentication services. For example, Secure Channel was used to manage the online version of the 2006 census. The system also operates "My Account," a system for Canadians to access a wide range of tax-related applications from the Canada Revenue Agency. If you want to apply for a passport, Secure Channel runs Passport On-Line, an interactive application that guides a citizen through all sections of the passport application form.

The Secure Channel project has placed Canada among the forefront of countries attempting to unify their governments and provide seamless service delivery to citizens anytime, anywhere. de Rosenroll says, "The privacy architecture we have devised is, as far as we know, unique to Canada and is being closely studied by other countries."

[Adapted from Public Works and Government Services Canada: Secure Channel, The Canadian Information Processing Awards, **http://www.cipa.com/award_winners/winners_05/PublicWorksGovServCanada.html**.]

Discussion Questions

1. Of the various categories of information systems described in this chapter, which types are talked about in this case?
2. What do you think of the Government of Canada's use of information systems? Is it on the right track?
3. How does the case illustrate the importance of combining technology skills with non-IS skills and competencies?
4. What advice would you give the Government of Canada for better utilizing information systems?

Log on to the Companion Website at www.pearsoned.ca/jessup for an additional case.

Running Case: Connexion by Boeing

Why Information Systems Matter

Over the past several years, there has been a tremendous downturn in worldwide travel, and this downturn has greatly impacted the airline industry. Several factors have led to this downturn, including the dot-com bust, the economic recession, the terrorist attack of late 2001, the SARS crisis in the Far East, and the ongoing war on terror. The poor economy affected many companies worldwide, resulting in layoffs and other cost-cutting measures such as reduced travel. A significant amount of the revenue generated within the airline industry is through the frequent business traveller. Thus, during this downturn, a large part of the lucrative business travel segment has collapsed, and several major international airlines, such as United Airlines and U.S. Air, were driven to the verge of bankruptcy; it was only through drastic cost-cutting measures and improved efficiencies that they were able to survive.

Information systems have played a major role in helping airlines reduce costs and improve efficiencies through streamlined crew, aircraft, and maintenance scheduling. While airlines all over the world continue to demand more from their sophisticated information systems, so too have the airlines' most valued customers, namely the business travellers. Over the past few years, most hotels that cater to business travellers have installed high-speed Internet access, to the point that it has now become a commodity. Likewise, most major airports provide wired kiosks and wireless access throughout the terminals so that busy travellers can access the Internet as they wait for a flight. However, one place where business travellers have been largely out of touch with their colleagues and customers while on the road has been when they were on a flight. Sometimes, a few hours of not being available online can be quite relaxing. At other times, however, it may be very beneficial to be online for processing e-mail messages, placing customer orders, or chatting with family and friends. Until recently, the only way for an airline traveller to communicate with the outside world was through a very expensive and very slow onboard telephone.

To address this need, the Boeing Company, headquartered in Chicago,

Connexion One Airplane

Illinois, is now offering solutions to help airlines meet their own, and their customers', need for real-time information. To better support the airlines, Boeing is developing the "e-enabled airplane" which integrates various airline operational processes using a variety of information systems and communication technologies. The e-enabled airplane will allow airlines to streamline operations and to better serve their various customer segments by providing sophisticated systems and real-time information to support various aspects of the airline's operations, including crew scheduling and aircraft maintenance. To support airline customers, in-flight broadband Internet access is available. The communication infrastructure to enable these capabilities is provided by a new Boeing company called Connexion by Boeing.

Connexion by Boeing is a mobile information services provider that is bringing high-speed Internet and data services to in-flight aircraft and maritime operators for the benefit of passengers, crew, and operations. Connexion was established in late 2000 as a business unit of Boeing and provides air travellers and the maritime industry with high-speed, satellite-based connectivity comparable to what they experience in a modern office environment. The Vision for Connexion is:

> People working together to revolutionize the way we work, communicate, entertain ourselves, and relax while mobile.

For the business traveller, the in-flight, high-speed Internet service allows travel time to be used more productively, eliminating the need for "catch-up" work that often accompanies travel and often comes at the expense of family, friends, entertainment, and recreation. The service also provides opportunities for entertainment, destination research, and learning while in flight. In sum, the service allows the traveller to choose work-related activities, socializing, entertainment, or any combination.

Although travellers have been able to place phone calls and connect to the Internet using existing seat-back phone technologies (and this service is not available unless over land) using services provided by competitors such as Tenzing, the performance of these connections is extremely sluggish, and the usage costs are quite high. In contrast, Connexion leases capacity on geostationary satellites, which enables transmission speeds of 5 mbps downstream and up to 1 mbps upstream, virtually anywhere in the world. In other words, users can connect to the Internet at speeds comparable to broadband connections at their homes or offices. The price of the service will be less than the cost of a 4-minute call using an in-flight phone.

After the development of the system and periods of extensive testing, Connexion received an FAA operating licence for in-flight broadband services in late 2001. Since then, the service has been available for corporate and government aircraft and was installed in early 2003 on both Lufthansa and British Airways flights between Europe and the United States. Although many airlines had initially indicated interest in this system, the crisis in the airline industry (discussed above) led many airlines to back off from their plans to deploy the system. Lufthansa became the first airline to install the service, putting it on several of its Airbus jets for use on transatlantic routes, and plans to have its entire fleet equipped with this system by early 2006. Given the success of Lufthansa, many other airlines quickly followed to become Connexion customers, including Scandinavian Airlines, ANA, China Airlines, and Singapore Airlines.

In addition to offering in-flight Internet services to their customers, airlines can use Connexion's systems for internal processes, such as crew members' access to the airline's reservation system or real-time transfer of maintenance requests to the destination airport. Furthermore, Connexion's systems can be used to receive satellite TV or the latest weather data so that the pilots can choose alternative routes, if necessary. Mitigating potential delays caused by adverse weather conditions can be a major factor leading to increased customer satisfaction. In the future, these systems can even be used for telemedicine applications, where the airline crew will be able to connect to specialists to remotely diagnose an ill passenger, thereby reducing the need for unplanned landings.

This broadband connectivity provides a foundation for Boeing's vision of the e-enabled airplane. In the past, many applications were not possible with older low-bandwidth connections, but that is no longer the case. For example, the airplane's central maintenance computer or the airplane crew can now automatically transmit alerts about potential service events to the airline's service centre. When they receive the transmission, maintenance staff can remotely research and diagnose a problem in order to reduce the time needed to solve the problem once the aircraft has landed. As soon as the problem has been diagnosed and a service plan has been established, the necessary parts can be automatically ordered and delivered to the gate so that the maintenance crew can begin working on the problem as soon as the airplane arrives.

Similarly, automatic alerts about thunderstorms looming behind the horizon can be generated and instantaneously transmitted to the airline's operations centre as well as to the flight crew. Sophisticated software systems can then calculate the possibility of the weather conditions' impacting the flight schedule and suggest alternatives to mitigate potential delays. The in-flight, high-speed capability also offers opportunities to improve customer service when it appears that an airplane's late arrival will cause some passengers to miss connecting flights. Operators could, for example, identify those passengers affected by a delay, arrange rebooking and check-in, and print new boarding passes while passengers are still in the air. Research shows that besides earning passenger loyalty (no more waiting in long standby lines), alleviating passenger anxiety about the possibility of a missed connection improves their opinion of every aspect of the flight, from seat comfort to food quality. For example, at the suggestion of Alaska Airlines during a demonstration flight in the spring of 2002, a Connexion by Boeing executive was able to expedite his boarding process for an Alaska Airlines flight later that day at a different airport by becoming the first person in history to use an airline website to check in for a flight—and print his boarding pass—while at 30 000 feet. These and many other applications can help to increase the airline's reliability and efficiency and also increase passenger satisfaction and loyalty (see table below).

Applications of Connexion by Boeing's broadband Internet service

Applications of Connexion by Boeing's broadband Internet service
In-flight video teleconference—of value to the executive services and maritime markets, which includes operators of private business jets and government VIP jets
Remote medical evaluations
Enhanced security, including audio/video cabin monitoring
Voice services
Streaming data
News and entertainment
Wireless cabin networks
Crew information services
In-flight reservations and check-in
Fleet management, operations, and maintenance data

In addition to providing in-flight services, Connexion has also added maritime communications to their portfolio. Connexion's satellite and ground-based network will enable broadband connectivity on all major shipping routes by early 2006. The high bandwidth available and the relatively low costs associated with installing and operating the systems aboard a maritime vessel promise to lure many customers away from Inmarsat, the current leader in maritime communications.

In most industries, organizations constantly have to evolve to stay in business. For example, just a few years ago, no coffee shop needed to provide wireless Internet access; today, however, it has become a necessity for keeping and attracting new customers. Connexion officials predict that the same will happen for airlines. If history is a good predictor of the future, all airlines will one day be "connected."

Source: Vicky Karantzavelou, "Connexion by Boeing and Lufthansa Offer Broadband Access for High-Flying Surfers," *Travel Daily News* (May 12, 2004), **www.connexionbyboeing.com.** Retrieved June 23, 2004, from **www.traveldailynews.com/new.asp?newid=16668&subcategory_id=53.**

Discussion Questions

1. Briefly outline how airlines can use Connexion's systems to stay ahead of their competition.
2. Do you think connectivity will be indispensable for travelers in the near future? Why or why not?
3. Under which conditions could a promising system like Connexion by Boeing become a success or failure?
4. Which factors can make a company like Connexion survive in times when their major customers face massive financial difficulties?

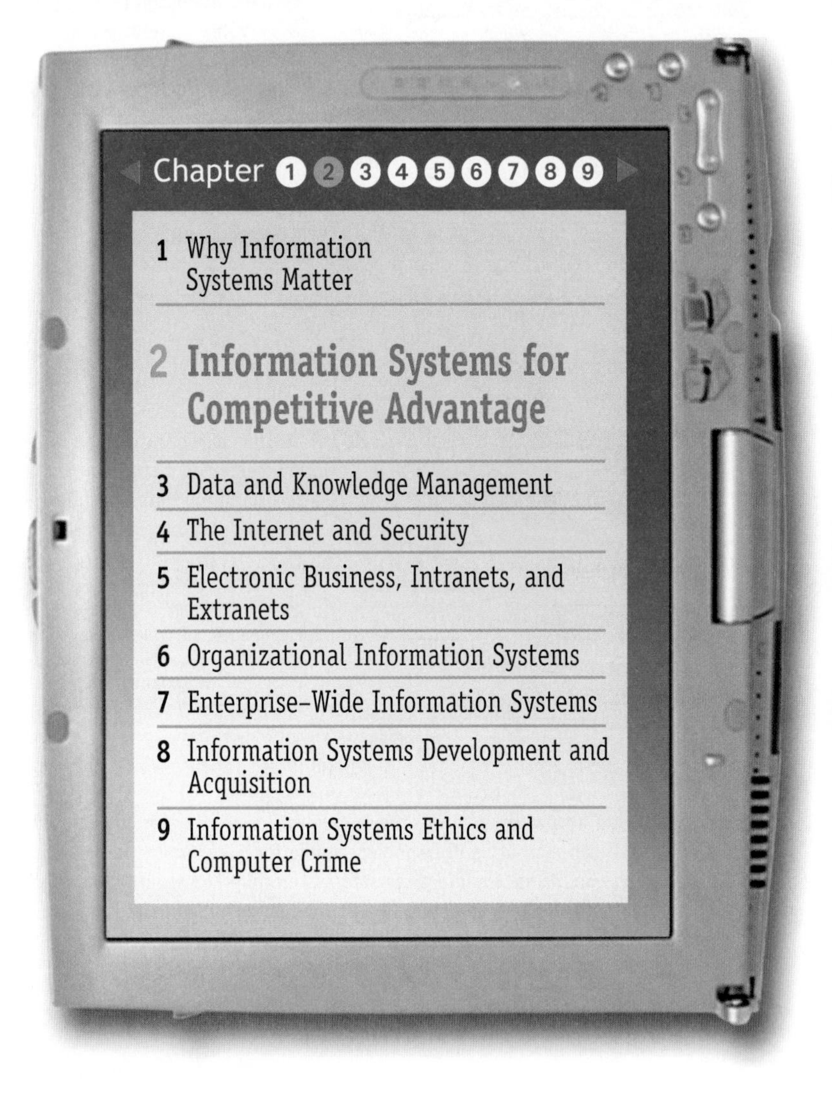

Preview

This chapter will show you how information systems can be used strategically to enable firms to gain or sustain ***competitive advantage*** over their rivals. As described in Chapter 1, a firm has competitive advantage over rival firms when it can do something better, faster, more economically, or uniquely when compared with its competitors. We will show why, in addition, it is vital, but sometimes difficult, for people to determine the value of a new system. The same difficulties face those evaluating an existing system that is being considered for modification, continued support, scaling back, or elimination. Presenting the "case" for an information system is necessary for making good investment decisions. After reading this chapter, you will be able to do the following:

1. Discuss how organizations can use information systems for automation, organizational learning, and strategic support.
2. Describe information systems' critical, strategic importance to the success of modern organizations.
3. Formulate and present the business case for a system and understand why it is sometimes difficult to do so.
4. Explain why and how companies are continually looking for new ways to use technology for competitive advantage.

Information Systems for Competitive Advantage

Canada Competes!

Stantec Inc. Improves Collaboration and Efficiency with Information Systems

Stantec Inc. provides professional design and consulting services in planning, engineering, architecture, surveying, and project management. The Edmonton-based company employs 5500 people in 60 locations across Canada, the United States, and the Caribbean. In 2005, Stantec had over $600 million in gross revenue. However, the company's strategic plan calls for continued growth to 10 000 employees and $1 billion in sales by 2008.

To meet this goal, the company had to change some of its more traditional, manual business methods. For example, its geographically dispersed offices needed current information on every competitive presentation, submission, and proposal, yet no common body of knowledge existed for reference or access. Standard company information resided in various versions on servers and desktops across the organization. This inefficient use of information technology translated into lost business.

Efforts were unnecessarily repeated when more than one office solicited a project of a similar nature without sharing information. Worse yet were the simultaneous pursuits, in which two or more offices unknowingly went after the same opportunity. It was clear that if the company expected to meet its growth targets, it would need to create an automated single source of truth for marketing support and business development.

In response to this challenge, the company built the Stantec Marketing Knowledge Centre (SMKC). The SMKC acted as a repository and clearinghouse for all marketing-related information in the company. As information was uploaded into the system, it became immediately available to staff through the company intranet. Employee confidence was improved as a result of the improved information-sharing, access, and capability. "Employees have reported a dramatic decrease in the time required to put together project and personnel profiles, and the numbers speak for themselves," explains Lara Masse, director of marketing. "The reduced amount of time required to produce these profiles saves Stantec approximately $1.2 million a year. With a single source of truth for all profiles, employees no longer have to spend large amounts of time searching for, or re-creating documents."

The company has digitized 20 000 images, more than 5000 project profiles, and personnel profiles for more than 4000 employees. "The information now included in our proposals is current, accurate, and relevant to the opportunity," Masse says. "In addition, it is far more strategic, with our focus shifting away from information gathering and toward meeting the business needs of our clients."

Source: Canadian Information Productivity Awards, "Stantec Inc.: Marketing Knowledge Centre," 2005, **www.cipa.com/award_winners/winners_05/StantecInc.html.**

Stantec improves collaboration and efficiency with information systems.

Source: © Stantec Incorporated. **www.stantec.com.**

Figure 2.1 Organizations today are figuring out clever ways to use information systems to support strategy and to gain or sustain competitive advantage over rivals.

Source: © Jon Feingersh/CORBIS

In this chapter, we begin by showing how and why a firm ought to use information systems to support its strategy and to enable it to gain or sustain competitive advantage over rivals (see Figure 2.1). We then describe what it means to make the business case for a system and discuss why it is important that the business case for technology-related projects be carefully developed. Next, we describe the factors you must identify and consider when building a successful business case. We then illustrate important factors to keep in mind when presenting the business case to executives and other decision makers. Finally, we talk about the continual need to find innovative ways to succeed with and through information systems.

WHY USE INFORMATION SYSTEMS?

In the first chapter, we introduced the notion that information systems can have strategic value to an organization. We described the strategic importance of information systems developed for the Denver International Airport and Federal Express. These systems were developed to help these organizations gain or sustain some competitive advantage over rivals. Next, in this chapter, we describe three ways to use an information system: for automating, for organizational learning, and for achieving strategy (see Figure 2.2). These three activities are not necessarily mutually exclusive, but we believe that each is progressively more useful to the firm and thus adds more value to the business. In the final category, strategizing, information systems are used to support a firm's strategy and to enable a firm to gain or sustain competitive advantage over rivals.

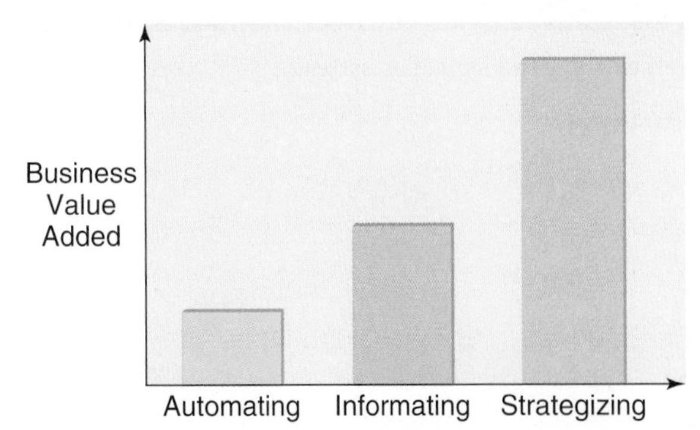

Figure 2.2 The business value added from automating, learning, and supporting strategy with IS.

Information Systems for Automating: Doing Things Faster

Someone with an ***automating*** perspective thinks of technology as a way to help complete a task within an organization faster, more cheaply, and perhaps with greater accuracy and/or consistency. Let us look at a typical example. A person with an automating mentality would take a loan application screening process and automate it by inputting the loan applications into a computer database so that those involved in decision making for the loans could process the applications faster, more easily, and with fewer errors. Such a system might also enable customers to complete the loan application online. A transition from a manual to an automated loan application process might enable the organization to deploy employees more efficiently, leading to further cost savings.

To illustrate the benefits of automating with an information system, in Table 2.1, we compare three different loan application processes. In the first example, everything is done by hand. In the second example, a technology-supported process, potential customers fill out applications by hand, and then an employee inputs them into a computer system. The third example is a completely automated process, in which potential customers input loan applications directly online via the web and then the system automatically receives and stores these applications into a database and processes them.

The real-time savings with the fully automated system come into play with the applications for loans under $250 000, which typically comprise the bulk of applications received. Conversely, one common thread across all three scenarios is that it takes the executive committee over 2 full weeks to make decisions on

Table 2.1 *Activities involved under three different loan application processes and the average time for each activity.*

Primary Activities of Loan Processing	Manual Loan Process (Time)	Technology-Supported Process (Time)	Fully Automated Process (Time)
1. Complete and submit loan application	Customer takes the application home, completes it, returns it (1.5 days)	Customer takes the application home, completes it, returns it (1.5 days)	Customer fills out application from home via the web (1 hour)
2. Check application for errors	Employee does this in batches (2.5 days)	Employee does this in batches (2.5 days)	Computer does this as it is being completed (3.5 seconds)
3. Input data from application into information system	Applications kept in paper form, although there is handling time involved (1 hour)	Employee does this in batches (2.5 days)	Done as part of the online application process (no extra time needed)
4. Assess loan applications under $250 000 to determine whether to fund them	Employee does this completely by hand (15 days)	Employee does with the help of the computer (1 hour)	Computer does this automatically (1 second)
5. Committee decides on any loan over $250 000	(15 days)	(15 days)	(15 days)
6. Applicant notified	Employee generates letters manually in batches (1 week)	Employee generates letters with the help of the computer (1 day)	System notifies applicant via e-mail (3.5 seconds)
Total Time:	Anywhere from **25 to 40 days**, depending on size of loan	Anywhere from **5 to 20 days**, depending on size of loan	Anywhere from **1 hour to 15 days**, depending on size of loan*

* Note that many online loan application services can now give you instant "tentative" approval pending verification of data you report in your online application.

applications for loans over $250 000. Automation can do only so much!

Although many significant gains from computing in organizations have come from automating previously manual processes, computing solely for automation is a bit shortsighted. In the next section, we will explain how technology can be used more effectively.

Information Systems for Organizational Learning: Doing Things Better

We can also use information systems to learn and improve. Shoshana Zuboff (1988) described this as ***informating***.[1] Zuboff explained that a technology informates when it provides information about its operation and the underlying work process that it supports. The system helps us not only to automate a business process but also to learn to improve the day-to-day activities within that process.

The learning mentality builds on the automating mentality because it recognizes that information systems can be used as a vehicle for ***organizational learning*** and change as well as for automation. In a 1993 *Harvard Business Review* article, David Garvin described a ***learning organization*** as one that is "skilled at creating, acquiring, and transferring knowledge, and at modifying its behaviour to reflect new knowledge and insights."

To illustrate a learning mentality, let us think again about our loan-processing example. Figure 2.3 shows how a computer-based loan-processing system tracks types of loan applications by date, month, and season. The manager easily sees the trends and can plan for the timely ordering of blank application forms and the staffing and training of personnel in the loan department. The manager can also more efficiently manage the funds used to fulfill loans.

A learning approach allows people to track and learn about the types of applications filed

Web Search

Visit the home page for the Society for Organizational Learning at **www.solonline.org** to further investigate the topic of organizational learning. How did this organization first begin? What is its purpose? Take a look at Peter Senge's answers to questions about organizational learning. Have you ever worked for a learning organization? If so, did you share Peter's excitement at being part of a learning organization?

[1] The concept of informating is also very closely related to Argyris's term, double-loop learning, in which individuals learn and as a result subsequently change their thinking and/or behaviour (C. Argyris. 1993. *On Organizational Learning.* Cambridge, MA: Blackwell).

WHEN THINGS GO WRONG

Ouch . . . ! A Small Mistake Proves Costly

When can a $100 mistake cost $5 million? The answer is when the $100 is the cost of a hard drive that contains information on nearly 1 million people . . . and it goes missing. IBM Canada learned the hard way that a simple blunder can lead to a mountain of direct and indirect costs.

Information Systems Management (ISM), a division of IBM, was fulfilling a contract to refurbish computers storing data for clients when a 30-GB hard drive went missing. ISM first thought that the hard drive contained information on about 100 000 clients of several agencies of the Government of Saskatchewan. While this was problematic, it was later discovered that the small storage device also contained information on about 170 000 customers of the Co-operators Life Insurance Company and 650 000 clients of Investors Group, a mutual fund company.

What happened to the hard drive? It was recovered by Regina city police at the home of an ISM employee. The employee had evidently brought the hard drive home and installed it in a personal computer to provide a little extra storage. Apparently, the employee had wiped the hard drive clean and none of the information had been compromised. The employee was charged with possession of stolen property under $5000 and the hard drive was recovered.

However, the cost to ISM will be significantly more than $5000. Direct costs, not including legal fees, have amounted to $500 000, and a class-action lawsuit has been launched claiming damages of $5 million. As the "lost" information included names, addresses, social insurance numbers, and bank account information, more litigation is likely. In addition, a number of firms and government agencies have put existing contracts with ISM under review and refused to renew expiring contracts until the firm can demonstrate that it has improved its security practices.

Figure 2.3 A computer-based loan-processing system tells the bank manager which types of loans are highest during each season.

by certain types of people at certain times of the year (e.g., more auto loan applications in the fall, mostly from men in their twenties and thirties), the patterns of the loan decisions made, or the subsequent performance of those loans. This new system creates data about the underlying business process that can be used to better monitor, control, and change that process. In other words, you learn from this information system about loan applications and approvals; as a result, you can do a better job at evaluating loan applications.

A combined automating and learning approach, in the long run, is more effective than an automating approach alone. If the underlying business process supported by technology is inherently flawed, a learning use of the technology might help you detect the problems with the process and change it. For instance, in our loan-processing example, a learning use of technology may help us uncover a pattern among the accepted loans that enables us to distinguish between low- and high-performing loans over their lives and subsequently to change the criteria for loan acceptance.

If, however, the underlying business process is bad, and you are using technology only for automating (that is, you would not uncover the data that would tell you this process is bad), you are more likely to continue with a flawed or less-than-optimal business process. In fact, such an automating use of technology may mask the process problems.

With a bad underlying set of loan acceptance criteria (e.g., rules that would allow you to approve a loan for someone who had a high level of debt as long as they had not been late on any payments recently), a person might manually review four applications in a day and, because of the problematic criteria used, inadvertently accept two "bad" applications per week on average. If you automated the same faulty process, with no learning aspects built in, the system might help a person review 12 applications per day, with six "bad" applications accepted per week on average. The technology would serve only to magnify the existing business problems. Without learning, it is more difficult to uncover bad business processes underlying the information system.

Using Information Systems to Support Total Quality Management

Organizations that use information systems to support a ***total quality management (TQM)*** initiative are more than likely to be using these systems with a learning approach. As part of a TQM approach, people within the organization constantly monitor what they do to find ways to improve quality of operations, products, services, and everything else about the firm.

ETHICAL DILEMMA

Who Owns Your Address Book?

Information is power—if it's used in the right place, at the right time, and by the right people. For many people, information belonging to a previous employer can be a powerful aid in a new job. Sales employees often regard the contacts database as one of the most powerful information repositories; having this information enables them to maintain business contacts after changing to a new employer. Taking the contacts database with them to the new job greatly facilitates succeeding in the new job.

Today's networked workplaces facilitate this theft of information. Many employees simply transfer the "needed" information to their own e-mail account, while others use storage devices such as floppy disk, CD-ROM, or flash key drive to take this intellectual property with them.

The days of employees stealing pencils seem to have gone; nowadays, employees are stealing much more valuable goods: information! From the organizations' standpoint, stealing information is not only more harmful than stealing a few pencils, it may be more harmful than stealing sophisticated computer hardware.

A recent survey has found that 70 percent of the respondents had stolen key information from an employer. Seventy-two percent of the people surveyed indicated that they had no ethical problems with taking proposals, presentations, contact databases, or e-mail address books when changing to a new employer. Often, employees justify these actions by their investment in preparing these resources. After all, hasn't their work helped to build that customer database and to create so many sales leads?

Source: Anonymous, "Workplace Data Theft Runs Rampant," *BBC News* (15 February, 2004), **http://news.bbc.co.uk/1/hi/technology/3486397.stm.**

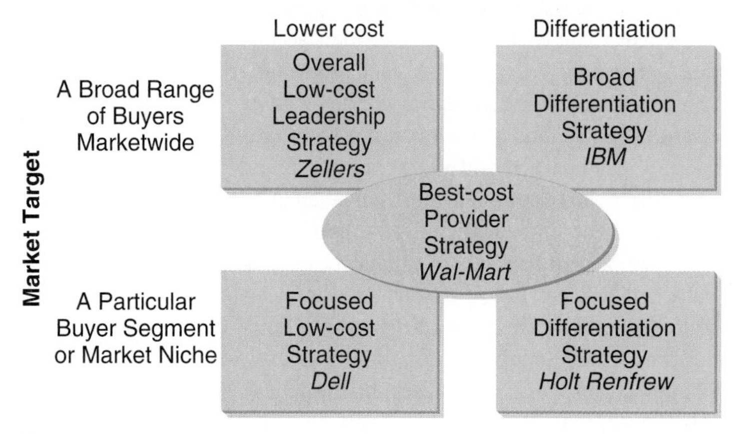

Figure 2.4 Five general types of organizational strategy: broad differentiation, focused differentiation, focused low-cost, overall low-cost leadership, and best-cost provider.

Courtesy Thompson, A. A. and Strickland, A. J. III, 1995. *Strategic Management: Concepts and Cases*, 8th Edition, Homewood: Richard D. Irwin, Inc.

Information systems can help with a computer-based statistical analysis, for example, to determine the exact procedures and materials that will achieve the highest levels of quality output in a manufacturing process. People use an information system to understand a business process better and, as a result, to make changes to improve that process.

Information Systems for Supporting Strategy: Doing Things Smarter

Using information systems to automate or improve processes has advantages, as described above. In most cases, however, the best way to use an information system is to support the organization's strategy in a way that enables the firm to gain or sustain competitive advantage over rivals. To understand why, think about ***organizational strategy*** and how it relates to information systems. When senior managers conduct ***strategic planning***, they form a vision of where the organization needs to head, convert that vision into measurable objectives and performance targets, and craft a strategy to achieve the desired results. In Figure 2.4, we show some common organizational strategies. An organization might decide to pursue a ***low-cost leadership strategy***, as does Zellers, by which it offers the best prices in its industry on its goods and/or services. Alternatively, an organization might decide to pursue a ***differentiation strategy***, as do Porsche, Holt Renfrew, and IBM, by which it tries to provide better products or services than its competitors. A company might aim that differentiation broadly at many different types of consumers, as IBM has done with a wide range of premium technology products and services. Alternatively, a firm might target a particular segment of consumers, as Holt Renfrew has done with designer clothing for professional women. Still other organizations might pursue a middle-of-the-road strategy of being the ***best-cost provider***, offering products or services of reasonably good quality at competitive prices, as does Wal-Mart.

A person with a strategic mentality toward information systems goes beyond mere automating and learning and instead tries to find ways to use information systems to achieve the organization's chosen strategy. This individual wants the benefits of automating and learning but also looks for some strategic, competitive advantage from the system. In fact, in today's business environment, if a proposed information system isn't going to clearly deliver some strategic value (i.e., help to improve the business so that it can compete better) while also helping people to work smarter AND saving money in the process, then it isn't likely to be funded (see Figure 2.5).

Figure 2.5 Not all organizations have effective strategies.

INFORMATION SYSTEMS FOR COMPETITIVE ADVANTAGE

Sources of Competitive Advantage

How do business firms typically get competitive advantage? An organization has competitive advantage whenever it has an edge over rivals in attracting customers and defending against competitive forces (Porter, 1985, 2001). To be successful, a business must have a clear vision, one that focuses investments in resources such as information systems and technologies to help achieve competitive advantage. Some sources of competitive advantage include the following:

- Having the best-made product on the market
- Delivering superior customer service
- Achieving lower costs than rivals
- Having a proprietary manufacturing technology
- Having shorter lead times in developing and testing new products
- Having a well-known brand name and reputation
- Giving customers more value for their money

Companies can gain or sustain each of these sources of competitive advantage by effectively using information systems. For example, rental car agencies compete fiercely with each other to provide the best cars, the best service, and the best rates. Companies find it difficult to differentiate themselves, so they discover innovative ways to use information systems to improve customer service.

For an information system to become the source of a competitive advantage, it must have two attributes: it must be valuable, and it must be rare. An automatic teller machine (ATM) network, for example, is a valuable asset for a bank; but, in Canada at least, it is not rare. Thus, an ATM network is unlikely to become a source of competitive advantage for a Canadian bank. Information technology assets are often valuable, but as they are not rare, they become fragile sources of advantage. Even if a technology is both valuable and rare, it must resist imitation and substitution if it is to sustain a competitive advantage. The Brief Case: Avis Rent a Car describes a technology-based system that enhances customer service in a very important way—it reduces the time that customers need to spend picking up and dropping off rental vehicles. For the moment, this resource is both valuable and rare. But, given time, other rental car firms will recognize Avis's advantage and seek to imitate it. If the system is based primarily on imitable technologies, then the advantage is likely to be short lived.

The key with information systems is to create a competitive advantage that is based on the *strategic use* of technology. The technology itself may be duplicated, but the usage of that technology may be much harder to copy. Think of Wal-Mart's logistics systems. The component parts of the systems, such as computers, networks, scanners, warehouses, and databases, are commercially available on open markets, but Wal-Mart's ability to combine and utilize those assets has been extremely hard for competitors, such as Kmart and Zellers, to duplicate.

Let us return to the computer-based loan application processing example. A person with a strategic view of information systems would choose a computer-based loan application process because it can help achieve the organization's strategic plan to process loan applications faster and better than rivals and to improve the selection criteria for loans. This process and the supporting information system

BRIEF CASE — Avis Rent a Car

Avis Rent a Car constantly uses technology to sustain a competitive advantage over its rivals; for example, to make the customers' lives easier while on the road, the drivers can get turn-by-turn "talking directions" (an extension of the Avis Assist services), an application that is enabled by the use of GPS, location-based services, and special software developed by Motorola. To obtain driving directions, the customer punches the destination information into a Motorola handset provided by Avis; at an Avis call centre, a route is calculated and subsequently downloaded to the handset, where the built-in speakerphone conveys it to the driver. If the driver makes a

Figure 2.6 Avis uses IT to reduce wait times.

Source: Courtesy of Avis.

wrong turn, the directions are automatically updated to reflect his change in route. Especially in big cities with heavy traffic, this technology can help customers find their destination and can help increase traffic safety, as the driver can focus on the road rather than on finding the correct turns to take. Because the system uses a handheld device, the customer can even take it along when leaving the car.

To make customers' lives easier when returning the cars, Avis Rent a Car customer service representatives wait for the customer out in the lot, armed with specially designed, handheld computers and printers either strapped around their waists or over their shoulders. With this "Avis Roving Rapid Return" service, the representative inputs the licence number of the car on the portable computer when he sees the customer driving in to return a car. Inputting this information brings up the customer's rental contract. As the customer gets out of the car, the representative inputs the mileage and the fuel level while a second attendant retrieves the customer's luggage and places it on the curb. By the time the customer has gotten out of the car and is standing next to her luggage, the representative has already printed her receipt. The service encounter for the customer is fast and pleasant. That is using technology for competitive advantage! In Table 2.2, we show how Avis's computer-supported process compares with the traditional rental car service encounter. Notice that the computer-based service encounter (in the right column) takes significantly less time than the traditional approach.

Questions

1. Would a service like Avis Assist make you consider choosing Avis over its rivals when going to a place you've never been to before?
2. Have you experienced something similar to Avis's system when returning a rental car? If yes, do you think this form of customer service would give the rental car company a competitive advantage? If no, would this use of technology entice you to try out Avis the next time you rent a car?

Source: Anonymous, "Avis and Motorola Make Busy Travel Season Easier with Mobile Navigation Service," Avis Press Release (December 9, 2003), **www.avis.com/AvisWeb/JSP/global/en/aboutavis/press_room/2003-044.jsp.**

Table 2.2 ***The Avis airport computer-supported service encounter versus the traditional airport rental car service encounter.***

	Traditional Rental Car Return Service Encounter	**Avis's Computer-Based Service Encounter**
	Return car to lot attendant, get bags from another attendant, walk inside and wait in line to settle contract with another attendant, walk out, and board a shuttle.	*Return car to lot attendant, grab receipt and bags, and board shuttle.*
Elapsed time	5–20 minutes	5–20 seconds
Number of people to interact with	2–3 people	1–2 people
Average number of footsteps customer takes	60–75 steps	5–10 steps
Relative efficiency	Low	High

Web Search

Visit the websites of Avis Canada **www.avis.ca** and Air Canada **www.aircanada.ca** and investigate ways that these companies are using technology to gain and sustain competitive advantages.

add value to the organization *and* match the organization's strategy. It is, therefore, essential to the long-term survival of the organization. If, on the other hand, managers determine that the organization's strategy is to grow and generate new products and services, the computer-based loan application process and underlying system might not be an efficient, effective use of resources, even though the system could provide automating and learning benefits.

Information Systems and Value Chain Analysis

Managers use ***value chain analysis*** to identify opportunities to use information systems for competitive advantage (Porter, 1985, 2001; Shank and Govindarajan, 1993). Think of an organization as a big input/output process. At one end, supplies are purchased and brought into the organization (see Figure 2.7). The organization integrates those supplies to create

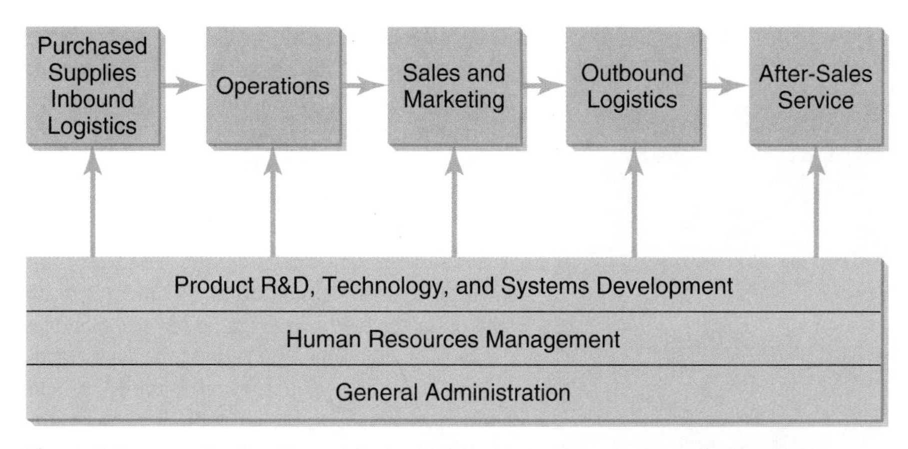

Figure 2.7 A sample generic organizational value chain.

products and services, which it markets, sells, and then distributes to customers. The organization provides customer service after the sale of these products and services. Throughout this process, opportunities arise for employees to add value to the organization by acquiring supplies in a more effective manner, improving products, and selling more products. This process of adding value throughout the organization is known as the ***value chain*** within an organization.

Value chain analysis is the process of analyzing an organization's activities to determine where value is added to products and/or services and what costs are incurred for doing so. Because IS can automate many activities along the value chain, value chain analysis has become a popular tool for applying IS for competitive advantage. In value chain analysis, you first draw the value chain for your organization by fleshing out each of the activities, functions, and processes where value is or should be added. Next, determine the costs—and the factors that drive costs or cause them to fluctuate—within each of the areas in your value chain diagram. You then benchmark (compare) your value chain and associated costs with those of your competitors. You can then make changes and improvements in your value chain to either gain or sustain competitive advantage. This advantage can be sustained by building in barriers to imitation, such as using proprietary technologies or locking partners into exclusive contracts.

The Role of Information Systems in Value Chain Analysis

The use of information systems has become one of the primary ways that organizations improve their value chains. In Figure 2.8, we show a sample value chain and some ways that use of information systems can improve productivity within it. For example, many organizations use the Internet to connect businesses with one another electronically so that they can exchange orders, invoices, and receipts online in real time. Using the Internet has become a popular method for

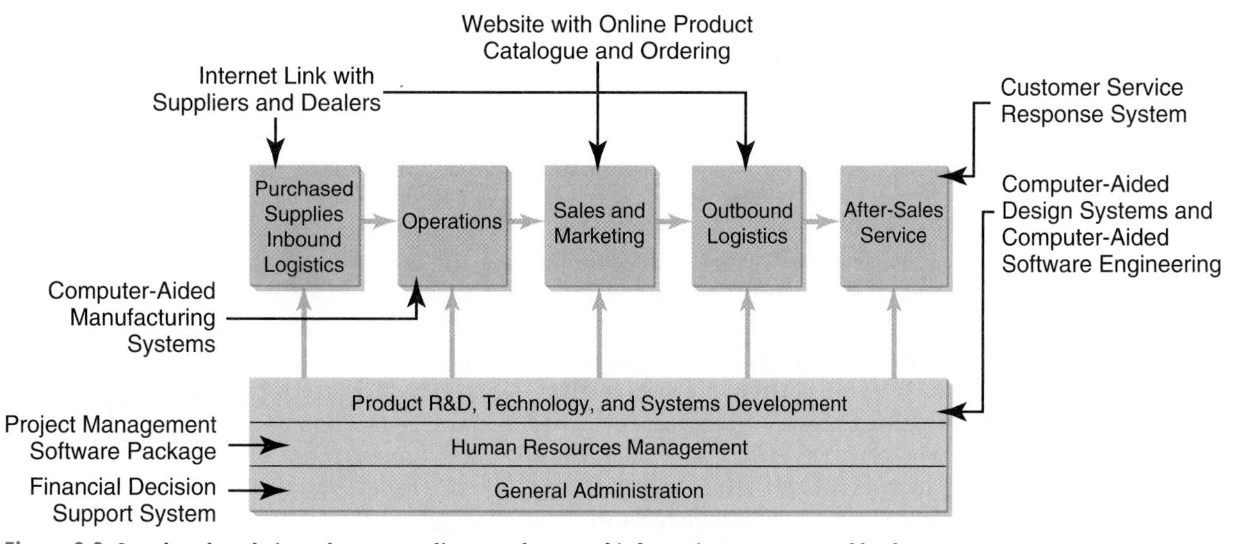

Figure 2.8 Sample value chain and corresponding sample uses of information systems to add value.

Figure 2.9 The McLaren F1 Supercar.

Source: © Getty Images, Inc.

improving the front end of the organizational value chain. In fact, many firms now use the Internet for such business-to-business interactions; these systems are called ***extranets*** (described in greater detail in Chapter 5).

An innovative way to use information systems to improve the back end of the value chain, the service after the sale, is to provide online customer service. For example, every one of McLaren's F1 Supercars (see Figure 2.9) is equipped with a modem that enables McLaren engineers to remotely diagnose the car and make adjustments to it over the phone lines in real time. That may sound exotic—and restricted to those few individuals who can afford a million-dollar automobile—but computer companies such as IBM and Sun also use this method to diagnose and maintain their customers' products remotely and, in some cases, to download new software products.

The Technology/Strategy Fit

You might be asking, if any information system helps do things faster and better and helps save money, who cares whether or not it matches the company's strategy? Good question. If money grew on trees, you probably would build and use just about every information system you could imagine. Organizations *could* build many different valuable systems, but they are constrained by time and money to build only those that add the most value: those that help automate and learn, as well as have strategic value. In most cases, you do not want systems that do not match the strategy, even if they offer automating and learning benefits. Furthermore, while spending on information systems is rising again, most companies are willing to spend money on projects only when they can see clear, significant value.

Given this focus on the value that the system will add, you probably do not want a system that helps differentiate your products based on high quality when the organizational strategy is to be the overall industry low-cost leader. For example, if managers of a firm were trying to make the firm a low-cost leader, would they want to buy or build an expensive ***computer-aided design system*** that enabled them to use high-powered computers to design very state-of-the-art, high-quality products? They probably would not choose that course, given that such a system would most likely add exorbitant costs to the design and manufacturing process and would likely defeat the strategy of spending less in the production of products and, subsequently, selling products at the lowest possible prices.

We should also caution that merely choosing and implementing an emerging information system is not sufficient to gain or sustain competitive advantage. In any significant information systems implementation, there must be commensurate, significant organizational change. This typically comes in the form of ***business process reengineering (BPR)*** and other similar methods of improving the functioning of the organization, as opposed to merely dropping in an information system with no attempts at changing and improving the organization. We will talk more in Chapter 7 about the role of BPR in enterprise-wide information systems implementations.

MAKING THE BUSINESS CASE FOR A SYSTEM

Given that money does not grow on trees, people in organizations are constantly trying to justify spending money on anything, especially information systems. Before people are willing to spend money to build a new information system or spend more money on an existing system, they want to be convinced that this will be a good investment. Will the system provide automating, learning, and/or strategic benefits? The phrase that is used to describe the process of identifying the value provided by an information system is ***making the business case***.

What does making the business case for an information system mean? Think for a moment about what defence lawyers do in court trials.

They carefully build a strong, integrated set of arguments and evidence to prove that their clients are innocent: they build and present their case to those who will pass judgment on their clients. In much the same way, people in business often have to build a strong, integrated set of arguments and evidence to prove that an information system is adding value to the organization or its constituents. This is, in business lingo, "making the business case" for a system.

As a business professional, you will be called on to make the business case for systems and other capital investments. As a finance, accounting, marketing, or management professional, you are likely to be involved in this process and will therefore need to know how to effectively make the business case for a system as well as to understand the relevant organizational issues involved. It will be in the organization's best interest, and in your own, to ferret out systems that are not adding value. In these cases, you will need to either improve the systems or replace them.

Making the business case is as important for proposed systems as it is for existing systems. For a proposed system, the case will be used to determine whether the new system is a "go" or a "no go." For an existing system, the case determines whether the company will continue to fund the system. Whether a new system or an existing one is being considered, your goal is to make sure that the system adds value, that it helps the firm to achieve its strategy and competitive advantage over its rivals, and that money is being spent wisely.

Hidden Gains and Elusive Returns

Unfortunately, while it is easy to quantify the costs associated with developing an information system, it is often difficult to quantify tangible productivity gains from the use of an information system. Recently, the press has given a lot of attention to computer systems' impact or lack of impact on worker productivity. In many cases, IS expenditures, salaries, and the number of people on the IS staff have all been rising, but results from these investments have been disappointing. For example, it is estimated that technology-related spending by organizations increased fivefold from the 1980s to the 1990s (Hagendorf, 1998). As a result, justifying the costs for information technology has been a hot topic among senior managers at many firms. In particular, "white-collar" productivity, especially in the service sector, has not increased at the rate one might expect, given the billions of dollars spent on office information systems (Leibs and Carrillo, 1997).

Why has it been difficult to show that these vast expenditures on information technology have led to productivity gains? Have information systems somehow failed us, promising increases in performance and productivity and then failing to deliver on that promise? Determining the answer is not easy. Information systems may have increased productivity, but other forces may have simultaneously worked to reduce it, the end result being no visible change. Factors such as government regulation, more complex tax codes and stricter financial reporting requirements, and more complex products can all have major impacts on a firm's productivity.

It is also true that information systems built with the best intentions may have had unintended consequences—employees spending excessive amounts of time surfing the web to check sports scores on the TSN website, volumes of electronic junk mail being sent by Internet marketing companies or from personal friends, and company PCs being used to download and play software games. In these situations, information technology can result in less efficient and effective communication among employees and less productive uses of employee time than before the IS was implemented. Does this kind of employee behaviour affect productivity figures? You bet it does. Still, in general, sound IS investments should increase organizational productivity. If this is so, why have organizations not been able to show this increased productivity? A number of reasons have been given for the apparent "productivity paradox" of IS investments.

Measurement Problems

In many cases, the benefits of information technology are difficult to pinpoint because firms may be measuring the wrong things. Often, the biggest increases in productivity result from increased ***system effectiveness***. Unfortunately, many business metrics focus on ***system efficiency***. Although information systems may have real benefits, those benefits may not be detected. Effectiveness improvements are sometimes difficult to measure. Also, expected benefits from IS are not always defined in advance, so they are never seen: to see something, you usually have to know what to look for. Measurement problems are not limited to traditional office information systems,

GLOBAL PERSPECTIVE

Managing Change at STS Training Inc.

STS Training Inc. is a training institute located in the southern region of Australia. The company was founded in the early 1980s. During the initial years, the company focused on providing various kinds of vocational training. At that time the company primarily had individual clients who were interested in furthering their careers or making changes in their current jobs through the use of these training classes. Later, the South Australian government decided to streamline its structure by reducing the number of training institutes, so STS needed to obtain a competitive advantage over the other institutes to survive this restructuring. While this was a threat to STS's survival, the growth of computers and the need for computer training offered a host of opportunities for STS Training Inc. to become the leading institute in this area. From vocational training classes, the company slowly moved toward training on various computer applications, architectures, and networks. In addition to continuing to work with individual clients, STS also signed annual contracts with many large companies to provide computer training to their employees and staff. At the same time, STS retained its entire range of vocational training classes, which continued to bring in the majority of its revenue.

In recent years, the company has gone through another major change. To attract clients not located in the same city, the company introduced online delivery, where communication and delivery occurred over the Internet. The online delivery method is being used not only by staff members who teach computer applications, but by others as well. This has led to a significant increase in the number of computers being used in the organization.

STS realized that to avoid chaos and breakdown within the company, it needed to take drastic measures to manage this change. The company initially conducted strategic planning to understand the organization's need for IS and other resources. The IS manager was closely involved in this process, and her foresight and knowledge regarding the changing computer environment proved valuable in making predictions regarding the organization's computer and other IS needs. Once the company conducted the strategic planning session and ascertained the IS needs of the organization, it established a formal asset management and support system. The goal was to provide more timely and reliable help to the ever-increasing and diverse group of users. The company hired additional support staff in the computer service department and installed new information systems to handle the increasing volume of users. The company realized that it needed open communication between the IS department and other staff members. Overall, STS Training spent a significant amount of time and resources to plan for the changes occurring in the external marketplace.

Source: Adapted from "A Scenario for Change: The Impact of Online Delivery on IT Managers in VET," **www.tafe.sa.edu.au/lsrsc/one/natproj/cm/itman.htm.**

either. All types of systems have potential measurement problems. Consider the following:

End-user development. Because end-user-developed systems are not designed by professional information systems developers, those individuals do not often meticulously track costs and benefits to measure system impact. In addition, end users in one business unit may be tracking and analyzing a system's benefits and costs in ways that are quite different from the methods used by end users in other units.

Decision support systems (DSSs). By definition, DSSs are designed to improve decision making. The problem is, how do you measure their impact? To quantify the results of a DSS, you would need to measure the differences between decisions made with the DSS and the decisions that would have been made if no DSS had been in place. This kind of comparison is difficult to make in a business setting. Furthermore, it is not clear what constitutes adding value in this context. Does adding value mean making decisions that result in better outcomes, improving the decision-making process, having the capability to make more decisions, being able to justify a decision more effectively, making people feel better about the decision outcomes and/or the decision-making process, or some combination of these and other factors? Until it becomes clearer how to measure the benefits of a DSS easily and effectively, making the business case for a DSS will continue to be difficult.

Strategic systems. Ideally, IS managers could point to strategic information systems as having a tremendous impact on the firm's financial performance. However, the intent of strategic systems is often to help the organization enter a new market, gain or maintain market share, better serve customers, and so on. As we have said, traditional financial measures of system benefits—time/money saved or return on investment—do not adequately indicate whether these strategic systems have been successful. Better serving customers may be vitally important in a competitive environment. However, this may not easily translate into impressive-looking productivity figures for an information system in the short run.

A good example of measurement problems associated with IS investment is the use of ATMs. How much have ATMs contributed to banking productivity? Traditional statistics might look at the number of transactions or output as some multiple of the labour input needed to produce that output (e.g., a transaction). However, such statistics do not work well for the ATM example. The number of checks written may actually decrease with ATMs, making productivity statistics appear lower. On the other hand, can you imagine a bank staying competitive without offering ATM services? The value added for the customer in terms of improved delivery of services almost dictates that banks offer a wide range of ATM services in today's competitive market. Deploying these information systems has become a strategic necessity.

Time Lags

A second explanation for why productivity is difficult to demonstrate for IS investment is that a significant time lag may occur from when a company makes the IS investment until that investment is translated into improvement in the bottom line. Brynjolfsson (1993) reports that lags of 2–3 years are typical before strong organizational impacts of IS investment are felt.

The explanation for lags is fairly simple. At one level, it takes time for people to become proficient at using new technologies. Remember the first time you ever used a computer? It probably seemed difficult and cryptic to use. It may have taken you more time to figure out how to use the computer than it would have to complete the task manually. Nonetheless, the computer probably became easier to use as you became more proficient with it. If you multiply this learning curve over everyone in an organization who may be using a given technology, you can see that until a firm has some experience in using a technology, the benefits associated with using it may be deferred. Everyone must become proficient with that technology to gain the benefits from its use.

It may also take some time before the tangible benefits of a new information system can be felt. Let us return to our ATM example. It may take years from the first implementation of this new system before the benefits may be felt. The system must first be implemented, which could take years in a large, widely distributed financial institution. Then the system must be fine-tuned to operate optimally and must be tied into all the necessary subsystems. Employees and customers must be trained in how to use the system properly, and it may take years before they become truly proficient and comfortable with using it.

When the system is working well and people are using it efficiently, productivity gains may be measured. It takes time for the system to produce any labour savings within the organization and for customers' satisfaction levels to rise. Given that the ATMs have become a strategic necessity, perhaps one of their benefits is that they enable banks to gain, or simply keep, customers. It can take years for a financial institution to feel the effects of its deployment of ATM machines.

If time lags are the reason IS investments do not show up in productivity figures, then eventually IS managers should be able to report some very good news about organizational return on IS investment. Still, for managers faced with the day-to-day pressures of coming up with a demonstrable impact on firm performance, the explanation of time lags may not be very helpful or comforting.

Redistribution

A third possible explanation for why IS productivity figures are not easy to find is that IS may be beneficial for individual firms, but not for a particular industry or the economy as a whole. Particularly in competitive situations, IS may be used to redistribute the pieces of the pie rather than making the whole pie bigger. In other words, strategic information systems may help one firm to increase its market share; however, this may come at the expense of another firm, which loses its market share as consumers transfer to the first firm.

The result for the industry or economy as a whole is a wash—that is, the same number of products are being sold and the same number of dollars are being spent across all the firms. The only difference is that now one firm is

CANADIAN NETSTATS

Strategic Necessity or Competitive Advantage

Around the world, companies are realizing that information systems can lead to a variety of organizational benefits. In Canada, the most common reasons for adopting IS are to increase efficiency and reduce costs (see Table 2.3). Across the world, however, the most common reason cited is to keep up with progress.

Table 2.3 ***Reasons for adopting information systems by businesses. Percentage of all businesses in each country (2004).***

Reason for Adopting Information Systems	Canada	UK	Germany	U.S.	Australia	Japan	Average of 11 Countries Excluding Canada
Increased efficiency	22	22	14	14	25	49	21
Reduced cost	15	13	29	13	16	11	16
Customer communication	13	18	24	13	17	8	17
Speed of access to information	13	10	32	17	11	4	16
Keep up with progress	12	15	20	20	21	48	24
Improve quality of service	8	–	–	6	–	–	6
Staff communication	8	8	14	7	9	4	9
Information sharing	6	–	–	–	–	7	7

Source: "Business in the Information Age: The International Benchmarking Study 2004," Department of Trade and Industry, United Kingdom.

getting a larger share of the business, while another firm is getting a smaller share.

While such an explanation may be feasible for some markets and industries, it does not fully explain why productivity figures would be stagnant at the level of one individual firm. Shouldn't each organization be more productive than before? Part of the problem is that our expectations of performance are somewhat biased. We tend to take for granted that technology fundamentally enables people to do things that would otherwise be nearly impossible. In effect, we continue to "raise the bar" with our expectations of what people can accomplish when supported by technology. For example, you might wonder whether the electronic spreadsheet on the PC on your desk is really helping you do your job better. To best answer this, you should think back to what it was like to create a spreadsheet by hand. It was a much slower process, was far more likely to produce errors, and left people significantly less time to work on other, more important tasks.

Mismanagement

A fourth explanation is that IS has not been implemented and managed well. Some believe that people often simply build bad systems, implement them poorly, and rely on technology fixes when the organization has problems that require a joint technology/process solution. Rather than increasing outputs or profits, IS investments might merely be a temporary bandage and may serve to mask or even increase organizational slack and inefficiency. Also, as we mentioned in Chapter 1, an information system can be only as effective as the business model that it serves. Bad business models can't be overcome by good information systems. Similarly, the rapid decrease in processing time enabled by IS can result in unanticipated bottlenecks. For example, if automation has increased the potential output of a system, but part of that system relies on human input, then the system can operate only as fast as the human can feed input into or through that system. Eli Goldratt very aptly showed how this happens in his best-selling book *The Goal*, in which he uses the format of a novel to show how people can think logically and consistently about organizational problems to determine true cause-and-effect relationships between their actions and the results. In the novel, the characters do this so well they save their manufacturing plant and make it successful. Spending money on IS does not help increase the firm's productivity until all the bottlenecks are addressed. From a management standpoint, this means that managers must be sure that they evaluate the entire process being automated, making changes to old processes as necessary, to truly benefit from IS investment. If managers simply overlay new technology on old processes, sometimes known as "paving the cow path," then they will likely be disappointed in the meagre productivity gains reaped from their investment.

If it is so difficult to quantify the benefits of information systems for individual firms and for entire industries, why do managers continue to invest in information systems? The answer is that competitive pressures force managers to invest in information systems whether they like it or not (see Canadian NetStats: Strategic Necessity or Competitive Advantage). You might ask, then, so why waste time making the business case for a system? Why not just build them? The answer: money doesn't grow on trees. These are typically expensive projects for companies, and a strong case must be made for investing in them.

Making a Successful Business Case

People make a number of types of arguments in their business cases for information systems. When managers make the business case for an information system, they typically base their arguments on **F**aith, **F**ear, and/or **F**acts (Wheeler, 2002a).[2] Table 2.4 shows examples of these three types of arguments.

Do not assume that you must base your business case on facts only. It is entirely appropriate to base the business case on faith, fear, or facts. Indeed, the strongest and most comprehensive business case will include a little of each type of argument. In the following

[2] Wheeler also adds a fourth F, for Fiction, and notes that, unfortunately, managers sometimes base their arguments on pure fiction, which is not only bad for their careers but also not at all healthy for their firms.

Table 2.4 ***Three types of arguments commonly made in the business case for an information system.***

Type of Argument	Description	Example
Faith	Arguments based on beliefs about organizational strategy, competitive advantage, industry forces, customer perceptions, market share, and so on.	"I know I don't have good data to back this up, but I'm convinced that having this customer relationship management system will enable us to serve our customers significantly better than do our competitors and, as a result, we'll beat the competition. . . . You just have to take it on faith."
Fear	Arguments based on the notion that if the system is not implemented, the firm will lose out to the competition or, worse, go out of business.	"If we don't implement this enterprise resource planning system we'll get killed by our competitors because they're all implementing these kinds of systems. . . . We either do this or we die."
Fact	Arguments based on data, quantitative analysis, and/or indisputable factors.	"This analysis shows that implementing the inventory control system will help us reduce errors by 50%, reduce operating costs by 15% a year, increase production by 5% a year, and will pay for itself within 18 months."

sections, we talk about each of these types of arguments for the business case.

Business Case Arguments Based on Faith

In some situations, arguments based on faith (or fear) can be the most compelling and can drive the decision to invest in an information system despite the lack of any hard data on system costs or even in the face of some data that say that the dollar costs for the system will be high. Arguments based on faith often hold that an information system must be implemented to achieve the organization's strategy effectively and to gain or sustain a competitive advantage over rivals, despite the dollar costs associated with that system. Given the power of modern information systems, their rapid evolution, and their pervasiveness in business today, information systems have become a common tool for enabling business strategy. Consequently, the business cases for systems are frequently grounded in strategic arguments.

In short, successful business case arguments based on faith should clearly describe the firm's mission and objectives, the strategy for achieving them, and the types of information systems that are needed to enact the strategy. A word of caution is warranted here. In today's business environment, cases based solely on strategic arguments, with no hard numbers demonstrating the value of the information system under consideration, are not likely to be funded.

For example, a firm has set as its strategy that it will be the dominant, global force in its industry. As a result, this firm must adopt a global telecommunications network and a variety of collaboration technologies such as e-mail, desktop video conferencing, and groupware tools to enable employees from different parts of the globe to work together effectively and efficiently. Similarly, a firm that has set as its strategy that it will have a broad scope—producing products and services across a wide range of consumer needs—must adopt some form of an enterprise resource planning system to coordinate business activities across its diverse product lines. For example, Procter & Gamble produces dozens of household products that are consumed under various brand names—Noxzema, Folgers Coffee, Tide laundry detergent, Cover Girl cosmetics, Crest toothpaste, and Pringles potato chips, to name a few. Integration across various product lines and divisions is a key goal for IS investments. Such integration allows Procter & Gamble to streamline inventory, thus improving efficiency.

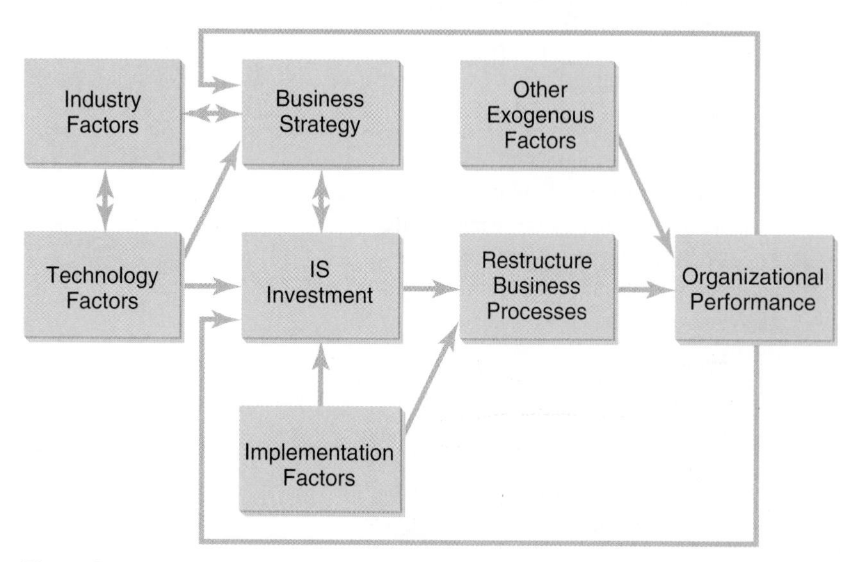

Figure 2.10 Factors in IS investment decisions.

Business Case Arguments Based on Fear

There are several different factors to take into account when making a business case in which you will provide arguments based on fear. These include a number of factors involving competition and other elements of the industry in which the firm operates, which are shown in Figure 2.10 (Harris and Katz, 1991).

Industry Factors

The nature of the industry can often determine what types of information systems would be most effective. Furthermore, many different types of industry factors can affect the business value of different systems. A system that may have a very positive impact on a firm in one industry may have little or no impact on a firm in another industry.

Stage of maturity. A given industry's stage of maturity can have an important influence on IS investment. For example, a mature and stable industry, such as the automotive industry, may need IS simply to maintain the current pace of operations. While having the newest IS available may be nice, it may not be needed to stay in business. However, a company in a newer, more volatile industry, such as the cellular phone industry, may find it more important to be on the leading edge of technology to compete effectively in the marketplace. In fact, it may be a strategic necessity in some industries to deploy newer technologies, even though the tangible benefits of deploying these technologies may be difficult to demonstrate.

Regulation. Some industries are more highly regulated than others. In some cases, companies can use IS to control processes and ensure compliance with appropriate regulations. For example, the aircraft industry is highly regulated. Information technology can provide sophisticated engineering and modelling tools to designers, who can test various designs for reactions to gravity forces (G-forces) and turbulence before aircraft prototypes are built. The designer can then understand which designs may not comply with regulatory requirements. Similar applications exist (and are often mandated) across other highly regulated industries, such as the radio and television broadcasting industries. The argument for the business case here would be something like, "If we do not implement this information system, we run the risk of being sued or, worse, being thrown in jail."

Nature of competition or rivalry. Probably the most important industry factor that can affect IS investment is the nature of competition or rivalry in the industry. For example, when competition in an industry is high and use of information systems is rampant, as it is in the personal computer industry, strategic necessity more than anything else forces firms to adopt information systems. Given how tight profit margins are in the PC industry, Dell and other manufacturers must use inventory control systems, web-based purchasing and customer service, and a host of other systems that help them to be more effective and efficient. If they do not adopt these information systems, they will likely go out of business. One framework often used to analyze the competition within an industry is Porter's notion of the five primary competitive forces (Porter, 1979): (1) the rivalry among competing sellers in your industry, (2) the threat of potential new entrants into your industry, (3) the bargaining power that customers have within your industry, (4) the bargaining power that suppliers have within your industry, and (5) the potential for substitute products from other industries. Table 2.5 provides examples of how IS can have an impact on the various competitive forces in an industry.

Porter's Five Forces model of competition can help you determine which specific technologies will be more or less useful, depending on the nature of your industry. You can then use these as the bases for your arguments as to whether or not to invest in new or existing information systems. This kind of industry-based business case might not enable you to attach specific monetary benefits to particular information systems, but it can show you and others that specific uses of particular systems are necessary to compete in your markets. Business case arguments formulated this way sound something like, "If we do not implement this information system, our competitors are going to beat us on price, we will lose market share, and we will go out of business."

Business Case Arguments Based on Fact

Many people, including most chief financial officers, want to see the business case for an information system be based on some convincing, quantitative analysis that proves beyond a shadow of doubt that the benefits of the system will outweigh the costs. The most common way to prove this is to provide a detailed cost-benefit analysis of the information system. Although this step is critical, the manager must remember that there are inherent difficulties in and limits to cost-benefit analysis for information systems, as described previously.

Cost-Benefit Analysis for a Web-Based System

In this section, we are going to discuss the cost-benefit analysis for an information system and show how that analysis would be part of a business case based on fact. Let us consider the development of a web-based order entry system for a relatively small firm.

In a cost-benefit analysis, costs can usually be divided into two categories, ***nonrecurring costs*** and ***recurring costs***. Nonrecurring costs are one-time costs that are not expected to continue after the system is implemented. These include costs for things such as the web server, telecommunications equipment, web server software, HTML editors, Java, Photoshop, and other tools. These one-time costs also include the costs of attracting and training a Webmaster, renovating some office space to serve as the location of the web server, and paying analysts and programmers to develop the system.

Recurring costs are ongoing costs that occur throughout the life cycle of systems development, implementation, and maintenance. Recurring costs include the salary and benefits of the Webmaster and any other personnel assigned to maintain the system, upgrades and maintenance for the system components, monthly fees paid to a local Internet service provider, and the continuing costs for the space in which the Webmaster works and the server resides. Personnel costs are usually the largest recurring costs, and the web-based system is no exception in this regard. These recurring expenses can go well beyond the Webmaster to include expenses for help desk personnel,

Table 2.5 ***IS impact on competitive forces.*** ***(Adapted from Applegate and McFarlan.* Corporate Information Systems Management: Text and Cases, *5th ed. [Columbus, Ohio: McGraw-Hill/Irwin, 1999].)***

Competitive Force	Implication for Firm	Potential Use of IS to Combat Competitive Force
Traditional rivals within your industry	Competition in price, product distribution, and service	Implement enterprise resource planning system to reduce costs and be able to act and react more quickly Implement website to offer better service to customers
Threat of new entrants into your market	Increased capacity in the industry Reduced prices Decreased market share	Better website to reach customers and differentiate product Inventory control system to lower costs and better manage excess capacity
Customers' bargaining power	Reduced prices Increased quality Demand for more services	Implement customer relationship management system to serve customers better Implement computer-aided design and/or computer-aided manufacturing system to improve product quality
Suppliers' bargaining power	Prices raised Reduced quality	Use Internet to establish closer electronic ties with suppliers and to create relationships with new suppliers located far away
Threat of substitute products from other industries	Potential returns on products Decreased market share Losing customers for life	Use decision support system and customer purchase database to assess trends and customer needs better Use computer-aided design systems to redefine products

maintenance programmers, IS management, and data entry personnel.

The sample costs described thus far have been fairly ***tangible costs***, which are easy to identify. Some ***intangible costs*** ought to be accounted for as well, even though they will not fit neatly into the quantitative analysis. These might include the costs of reducing traditional sales, losing some customers that are not "Web ready," or losing customers if the web application is poorly designed or not on par with competitors' sites. You can choose either to quantify these in some way (i.e., determine the cost of losing a customer) or simply to reserve these as important costs to consider outside of, but along with, the quantitative cost-benefit analysis.

Next you determine both ***tangible benefits*** and ***intangible benefits***. Some tangible benefits are relatively easy to determine. For example, you can estimate that the increased customer reach of the new web-based system will result in at least a modest increase in sales. Based on evidence from similar projects you might estimate, say, a 5 percent increase in sales the first year, a 10 percent increase the second year, and a 15 percent increase the third year. In addition, you might include as tangible benefits the reduction of order entry errors because orders will now be tracked electronically and shipped automatically. You could calculate the money previously lost on faulty and lost orders, along with the salaries and wages of personnel assigned to fix and find these orders, and then consider the reduction of these costs as a quantifiable benefit of the new system. Cost avoidance is a legitimate, quantifiable benefit of an information

BRIEF CASE

Competition and IS Investments: Domino's Pizza Delivers

Most of you have experienced the intense competition in the pizza restaurant industry, especially in and around college towns. This competition has forced many smaller companies to go out of business, although plenty are still around to compete with the big names of Pizza Hut, Domino's, Little Caesar's, and Pizza Pizza. As a result, even these large companies are using technology to stay ahead of the competition. Domino's Pizza Incorporated, headquartered in Ann Arbor, Michigan, is a prime example. Domino's inventory system automatically deducts the proper quantities of toppings (based on preset standards) from inventory files every time an order is placed. With the help of sophisticated supply-chain-management software, historical demand is calculated into the forecasts for the coming days, store inventories are checked, and orders are placed as necessary, so that the stores neither are overstocked nor run out of ingredients for their pizzas. For all this to happen, management does not have to intervene, except for approving the order. Similar advances are occurring in the delivery market. Domino's stores employ a custom software package that combines Caller ID with their order database to display to the employee the customer's name, address, phone number, and most recent order. The system can even display special delivery instructions to save time. All customers need to do is call up, say they want the same order as last time, and that is it. Some franchisees have even introduced automatic phone systems for customer orders. In both cases, the production and delivery processes are automatically set into motion, and the inventory system prepares the reorder report based on the order. So, although the pizza is made in 15 minutes and the driver reaches your home in another 10, a lot more is going on behind the scenes to make the process work and to keep the restaurant competitive.

Questions

1. In which ways does information technology help Domino's achieve a competitive advantage? If you have access to the Internet, try to find current information on Domino's systems to include in your discussion.
2. Sooner or later, Domino's competitors will follow and implement similar systems. What else could Domino's do in terms of information technology to stay ahead of its competitors?

Sources: Anonymous, "Prescient Systems Deliver for Domino's," *EA Library* (June 1, 2001), **http://ealibrary.bitpipe.com/detail/RES/992948190_335.html.**
Alice Dragoon, "Come and Get IT," CIO.com (April 15, 1998), **www.cio.com/archive/041598/ change.html.**
Jeremy White, "Tech Savvy: Chain of the Year Embraces Technology," *NTN Communications Press Release* (June 1, 2003), **www.ntn.com/about/ press_room/ publications/20030601- piztoday-dp.asp.**

system. Similarly, the new system may enable the company to use fewer order entry clerks or redeploy these personnel to other, more important functions within the company. You could consider these cost reductions as benefits of the new system.

A web-based system has intangible benefits as well. Some intangible benefits of this new system might include faster turnaround on fulfilling orders and resulting improvements in customer service. These are real benefits, but they might be hard to quantify with confidence. Perhaps an even more intangible benefit would be the overall improved perception of the firm. Customers might consider it more progressive and customer-service oriented than its rivals; in addition to attracting new customers, this might increase the value of the firm's stock if it were a publicly traded firm. Another intangible benefit might be simply that it was a strategic necessity to offer customers web-based ordering to keep pace with rivals. While these intangibles are difficult to quantify, they must be considered along with the more quantitative analysis of benefits. In fact, the intangible benefits of this web-based system might be so important that they could carry the day despite an inconclusive or even negative cost-benefit analysis.

An example of a simplified cost-benefit analysis with tangible costs and benefits is presented in Figure 2.11. Notice the fairly large investment up front, with another significant outlay in the fifth year for a system upgrade. You could now use the net costs/benefits for each year as the basis of your conclusion about this system. Alternatively, you could perform a break-even analysis (break-even occurs early in the second year of the system's life) or a more formal net-present-value analysis of the relevant cash flow streams associated with the system. In any event, this cost-benefit analysis helps you make the business case for this proposed

		2004	2005	2006	2007	2008
Costs						
Non-recurring						
Hardware		$ 20 000				
Software		$ 7 500				
Networking		$ 4 500				
Infrastructure		$ 7 500				
Personnel		$100 000				
Recurring						
Hardware			$ 500	$ 1 000	$ 2 500	$ 15 000
Software			$ 500	$ 500	$ 1 000	$ 2 500
Networking			$ 250	$ 250	$ 500	$ 1 000
Service Fees			$ 250	$ 250	$ 250	$ 500
Infrastructure				$ 250	$ 500	$ 1 500
Personnel			$ 60 000	$ 62 500	$ 70 000	$ 90 000
Total Costs		$139 500	$ 61 500	$ 64 750	$ 74 750	$110 500
Benefits						
Increased Sales		$ 20 000	$ 50 000	$ 80 000	$115 000	$175 000
Error Reduction		$ 15 000	$ 15 000	$ 15 000	$ 15 000	$ 15 000
Cost Reduction		$100 000	$100 000	$100 000	$100 000	$100 000
Total Benefits		$135 000	$165 000	$195 000	$230 000	$290 000
Net Costs/Benefit		$ (4 500)	$103 500	$130 250	$155 250	$179 500

Figure 2.11 Worksheet showing simplified cost-benefit analysis for the web-based order fulfillment system.

web-based order fulfillment system. It clearly shows that the investment for this system is relatively small, and the company can fairly quickly recapture the investment. In addition, there appear to be intangible strategic benefits to deploying this system. This analysis, and the accompanying arguments and evidence, go a long way toward convincing senior managers in the firm that this new system makes sense.

PRESENTING THE BUSINESS CASE

Up to this point, we have discussed the key issues to consider as you prepare to make the business case for a system. We have also shown you some tools for determining the value that a system adds to an organization. Now you are actually ready to make the case, to present your arguments and evidence to the decision makers in the firm. This task is much like that of a lawyer presenting a persuasive written and oral argument to win a judgment in the client's favour. Making a business case for IS really is not much different. You are simply trying to persuade the boss, steering committee, or board of directors to invest money in something you think is important to the business. Your job is to persuade them that you are right!

Know the Audience!

Depending on the firm, a number of people might be involved in the decision-making process. In the following sections, we describe the typical decision makers and their perspectives when evaluating a business case.

The IS Manager

Obviously, as the head of the information systems department, the IS manager has overall responsibility for managing IS development, implementation, and maintenance. They should be in the best position to make recommendations to decision makers, given their expertise in applying IS to business problems. The IS manager may also rely on experts in particular areas within IS to help analyze and present useful information to decision makers. For example, a networking expert may provide detailed technical information about cost, speed, and installation procedures.

Company Executives (Vice Presidents and Higher)

Often, executives act as the decision-making body for the firm's large investment projects. They typically represent various stakeholders or interest groups within the organization, and they may have their own agendas at stake when making decisions about expenses. For example, approving a large IS investment may mean that a new, expensive marketing idea gets delayed. Understanding the political implications of the approval process can be just as important as demonstrating a solid impact on the firm's bottom line. Also, these people will not be impressed with lots of technology jargon. Instead, use the language of business, the language they understand.

Convert Benefits to Monetary Terms

Try to translate all benefits into monetary terms. For example, if a new system saves department managers an hour per day, try to quantify that savings in terms of dollars.

SME SUCCESS New Partnerships Emerge to Counter old Threats

Major enterprise systems firms, such as SAP and Oracle, have traditionally made the majority of their money from software sales to very large firms. However, as the enterprise market becomes saturated, these companies have to look to smaller firms to sustain their growth. In recent years, enterprise systems vendors have aggressively targeted SMEs.

In response to this threat on their home market, smaller system vendors have started to form collaborative partnerships. Cisco Systems and Microsoft have already built two solutions that are ready for the SME channel. The first marries the Windows small business server with the Cisco router 831. The second combines Cisco IP communications with Microsoft's CRM software. Peter Alexander, vice-president of commercial marketing, said the products will reduce the integration burden on resellers working with SMEs: "This frees up resources for them to go after the higher-value services offerings for companies."

Dan McLean, lead networking analyst at IDC Canada, a technology research firm, agreed. "Both companies are being very strategic with SMEs. They want to be known as technology influencers. They are on the same page here. They want to be advisors of technology. They know more companies are interested in services and they want it to be on their products," McLean said. The upgraded program will be available only on the Cisco IP communications and Microsoft CRM package. Cisco and Microsoft will also create reference architecture blueprints for Microsoft's IT Solutions for SMEs. According to Alexander, this will enable resellers to provide Cisco-based secure networking infrastructures around Microsoft platforms.

Salesforce.com has built a partnership with Intacct to add enterprise resource planning capabilities to its customer relationship management software. Corel has entered into a partnership with Yahoo to provide office productivity tools for the SME market. McLean said he anticipates other vendors aligning themselves with collaborative partners. "Why not partner up with other vendors for SME solutions?" he asked.

Questions

1. Does this partnership between Microsoft and Cisco to target the SME sector make sense? Why or why not?
2. Why are more and more technology solution vendors targeting the SME sector?

Source: Adapted from Paolo Del Nibletto, "Cisco Constructs Programs around Partner Profitability," ITBusiness.ca (February 12, 2004), **www.itbusiness.ca/index.asp?theaction=61&sid=54799#**.

Figure 2.12 shows how you might convert time savings into dollar figures. While merely explaining this benefit as "saving managers time" makes it sound useful, managers may not consider it a substantial enough inducement to warrant spending a significant amount of money. Justifying a $50 000 system because it will "save time" may not be persuasive enough. However, an annual savings of $90 000 is more likely to capture the attention of firm managers and is more likely to result in project approval. Senior managers can easily rationalize a $50 000 expense for a $90 000 savings and can easily see why they should approve such a request. They can also more easily rationalize their decision later on if something goes wrong with the system.

Devise Proxy Variables

The situation presented in Figure 2.12 is fairly straightforward. Anyone can see that a $50 000 investment is a good idea because the return on that investment is $90 000 the first year. Unfortunately, not all cases are this clear-cut. In cases in which it is not as easy to quantify the impact of an investment, you can come up with proxy variables to help clarify what the impact on the firm will be. ***Proxy variables*** can be used to measure changes in terms of their perceived

Benefit:

New system saves at least one hour per day for 12 mid-level managers.

Quantified as:

Manager's Salary (per Hour)	$30.00
Number of Managers Affected	12
Daily Savings (One Hour Saved *12 Managers)	$360.00
Weekly Saving (Daily Saving *5)	$1 800.00
Annual Savings (Weekly Savings *50)	$90 000.00

Figure 2.12 Converting time savings into dollar figures.

value to the organization. For example, if mundane administrative tasks are seen as a low value (perhaps a 1 on a 5-point scale), while direct contact with customers is seen as a high value (a 5), you can use these perceptions to indicate how new systems will add value to the organization. In this example, you can show that a new system will allow personnel to have more contact with customers while at the same time reducing the administrative workload. Senior managers can quickly see that individual workload is being shifted from low-value to high-value activities.

Alternatively, you can create a customer contact scale from 1 to 5, with 1 representing very low customer contact and 5 representing very high customer contact. You can argue that currently your firm rates a 2 on the customer contact scale and that with the new information system your firm will rate a significantly higher number on the scale.

You can communicate these differences using percentages, increases or decreases, and so on—whatever best conveys the idea that the new system is creating changes in work, in performance, and in the way people think about their work. This gives senior firm management some relatively solid data upon which to base their decision. They typically like numbers. Why not make them happy?

Measure What Is Important to Management

One of the most important things you can do to show the benefits of a system is one of the simplest: Measure what senior managers think is important. You may think this is trivial advice, but you would be surprised how often people calculate impressive-looking statistics in terms of downtime, reliability, and so on, only to find that senior managers disregard or only briefly skim over those figures. You should concentrate on the issues senior business managers care about. The "hot button" issues with senior firm managers should be easy to discover, and they are not always financial reports. Hot issues with senior managers could include cycle time (how long it takes to process an order), customer feedback, or employee morale. By focusing on what senior business managers believe to be important, you can make the business case for systems in a way that is more meaningful for those managers, which makes selling systems to decision makers much easier. Managers are more likely to buy into the importance of systems if they can see the impact on areas that are important to them.

Web Search

Visit **www.3m.com/meetingnetwork/presentations/delivering.html** and find tips on giving presentations. How can this website help you find other ways to effectively make the business case for an information system? Think about how you deliver class presentations. What would you change when using a computer to display your presentation slides?

Assessing Value for IT Infrastructure

Howard Rubin, executive vice president of Meta Group, argued that we should take a more holistic view when assessing IT value (*CIO*, June 2004), particularly in areas such as IT infrastructure, where assessing tangible value may be difficult. IT infrastructure includes an organization's data centre, printers, network cabling, servers, and so on. While these things are important and expensive to maintain, they are often difficult to place a value on. Rubin reported that, on average, 41 percent of IT spending is associated with the infrastructure and the personnel needed to operate it. He reasoned that with the average company spending about 3.8 percent of its revenue on IT in 2004, this means that a typical company spends 1.6 percent of its revenue on IT infrastructure.

Rubin also suggested four categories for assessing the value of IT infrastructure. First, **economic value** is the contribution of the infrastructure to the profitability of the business. He recommended that we use important business metrics to gauge the economic value of the IT infrastructure. An airline, for example, might use a metric such as revenue per passenger per mile per year to determine effectiveness. That airline should calculate the IT infrastructure cost per passenger mile and observe how a change in the infrastructure cost over time has an impact on profitability.

Second, **architectural value** is derived from the infrastructure's capabilities to meet business needs today and in the future. It depends on infrastructure characteristics such as interoperability, portability, scalability, recoverability, and compatibility. Rubin recommended that for each area of the business, we should list the business requirements in terms of scalability, recoverability, and so on, and rate on a scale of 1 to 10 how well the infrastructure currently meets those needs.

Third, **operational value** is derived from assessing the actual performance the infrastructure provides to meet business processing requirements. Rubin recommended that we measure the cost to the business of outages or the unavailability of the systems it needs to function. For example, what would be the cost of a major data centre or network outage in terms of lost staff productivity, lost business revenue, or even lost customer base?

Fourth, **regulatory and compliance value** is derived from assessing the extent to which the infrastructure helps to meet requirements

COMING ATTRACTIONS

Ever Thought About Putting on Superman's Suit?

Wearable devices that are currently being developed by scientists at Nagasaki University might be close to offering Superman-like strength—unfortunately, without providing the ability to fly! Nonetheless, researchers in Japan have developed pants containing computerized sensors that detect what the human body is doing and artificial muscles that use compressed air to support the natural body movement in performing strenuous tasks. The next step for the scientists will be the development of a mechanical glove; by just tensing muscles in the upper arm, the user will be able to pick up objects with this glove. As these devices detect muscular movements thousands of times per second at multiple places, tremendous computing power is needed to calculate what the human body is trying to do and what is needed to support this task. According to researchers, a primary application of such devices is to help disabled people.

However, it is not only for these noble reasons that some agencies are interested in these technologies. Funded by the U.S. Defense Advanced Research Project Agency (DARPA), so-called exoskeletons have been developed by scientists at the University of California at Irvine; powered by rocket fuel, these wearable robots will help to increase payload, strength, speed, and endurance of soldiers to gain an advantage in the battlefield.

It is predicted that these devices will be ready for the market in 5 to 10 years; at that time, the possible applications will be nearly unlimited. Apart from uses for rehabilitation purposes or uses in the battlefield, one day these wearable robots might even help you jump higher or run faster when you're late for an appointment!

Sources: Gregory T. Huang, "Wearable Devices Add Strength," *Technology Review* 107, no. 1 (2004): 26. Bob Hirschfeld, "Deploying Exoskeletons," *TechTV* (October 11, 2002), **www.techtv.com/news/scitech/story/0,24195,3371422,00.html.**

for control, security, and integrity as required by a governing body or a key customer. What is the impact of, say, noncompliance with government reporting requirements or key service-level agreements with a key customer?

Rubin argued that, where possible, each of these measures should be compared with external benchmarks. In any event, these provide a useful framework for assessing value for something even as ubiquitous as IT infrastructure.

Changing Mindsets about Information Systems

Perhaps the most significant change in the information systems field has been in mindsets about technology rather than in technology itself. The old way for managers to think about information systems was that information systems are a necessary service, a necessary evil, and a necessary, distasteful expense that is to be minimized. Managers cannot afford to think this way any more. Successful managers now think of information systems as a competitive asset to be nurtured and invested in. Does this mean that managers should not require a sound business case for every information systems investment? No! Does this mean that managers do not need to have facts as part of a business case for a system? No! This means that managers have to stop thinking about systems as an expense and start thinking about systems as an asset to invest in wisely. Managers have to become strategic about information systems and think of them as an enabler of opportunities.

Canada's critical infrastructure (transportation; oil and gas; water; emergency services; continuity of government services; banking and finance; electrical power; and telecommunications) is largely operated through the use of computer networks, which makes protecting these networks increasingly a matter of national security. As a consequence of this concern, the Canadian Security Intelligence Service (CSIS) has applied a steadily increasing proportion of its resources to addressing this threat.

COMPETITIVE ADVANTAGE IN BEING AT THE CUTTING EDGE

To differentiate itself, an organization often must deploy new, state-of-the-art technologies to do things even better, faster, and more cheaply than rivals that are using older technologies. Although firms can choose to continually upgrade older systems rather than investing in new systems, these improvements can at best give only a short-lived competitive edge. To gain and sustain significant competitive advantage, firms must often deploy the latest technologies or redeploy and reinvest in existing technologies in clever, new ways.

Imagine, for example, that a manager decides to implement a wireless local area network (LAN) within a department store to automate the operations of the office workers, to enable them to share peripheral devices, such as laser printers, and to be more mobile throughout the store. To the delight of the office personnel, this wireless local area network is implemented using a relatively fast wireless access point. This may seem like state-of-the-art computing to the office workers, but it is likely that rival firms have already been doing this for years. Would this necessarily give the firm a clear advantage over rivals, and what would be the result of rivals' upgrading their own networks so that they are wireless?

Consider another example. A firm implements a relational database management system for sales and inventory, giving it an edge over rivals in fulfilling orders faster and more accurately. Competitors soon do the same thing, and it becomes necessary to improve to stay ahead. The firm could improve the system and gain a relatively small, short-lived advantage over rivals. Even better, the firm could extend this idea and implement similar database applications for all of its business processes and then integrate these applications with one another. Perhaps the firm could go one step further and enable customers and suppliers to access these systems directly. There is nearly always a better way to do things, along with new technologies to help you do these things better.

In our example above where the store owner implements a wireless network, consider a more radical use of technology. Instead, the owners of that store might consider implementing radio frequency identification (RFID) tags embedded in each of the products out on the floor of the store and then tracking each product through a store-wide wireless network connected to databases in the back office. That would likely enable them to gain a more significant, longer-lasting advantage over rivals. Clearly, if you choose to use information technology as a source of competitive advantage, you must choose to use emerging technologies in innovative ways. As they say, the best never rest.

But with the plethora of new information technologies and systems being developed, how can you possibly choose winners? Indeed, how can you even keep track of all the new breakthroughs, new products, new versions, and new ways of using technologies? For example, in Figure 2.13, we present a small subset of some new information technologies and systems, ranging from some that are here now and currently being used to some that are easily a decade away from being a reality. Which one is important for you? Which one will make or break your business? Does this list even include the one that you need to be concerned about?

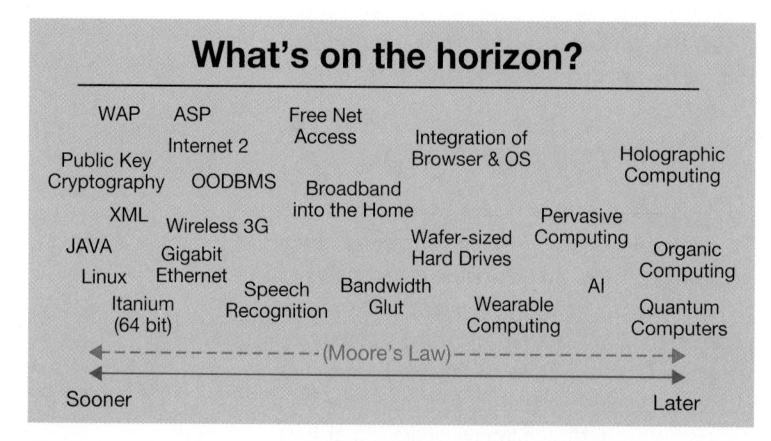

Figure 2.13 Some new information technologies on the horizon.

The Need for Constant IS Innovation

Sir John Maddox, a physicist and the editor of the influential scientific journal *Nature* for 22 years, was quoted in *Scientific American* in 1999 as saying, "The most important discoveries of the next 50 years are likely to be ones of which we cannot now even conceive." Think about that for a moment. Most of the important discoveries of the next 50 years are likely to be things that, at present, we have no clue about. To illustrate that point, think back to just over a short decade ago about what the state of the Internet was. That is difficult to do because the Internet as we now know it did not even exist then, and certainly the Internet was not on the radar screens of business organizations back at that point. Yet, look now at how the Internet has transformed modern business. How could something so transformational as the Internet not have been easier for businesses to imagine or predict a decade ago? Well, it is difficult to see these things coming. You have to work at it.

Executives today who are serious about using information technology in innovative ways have made it a point to have their people be continually on the lookout for new information technologies that will have a significant

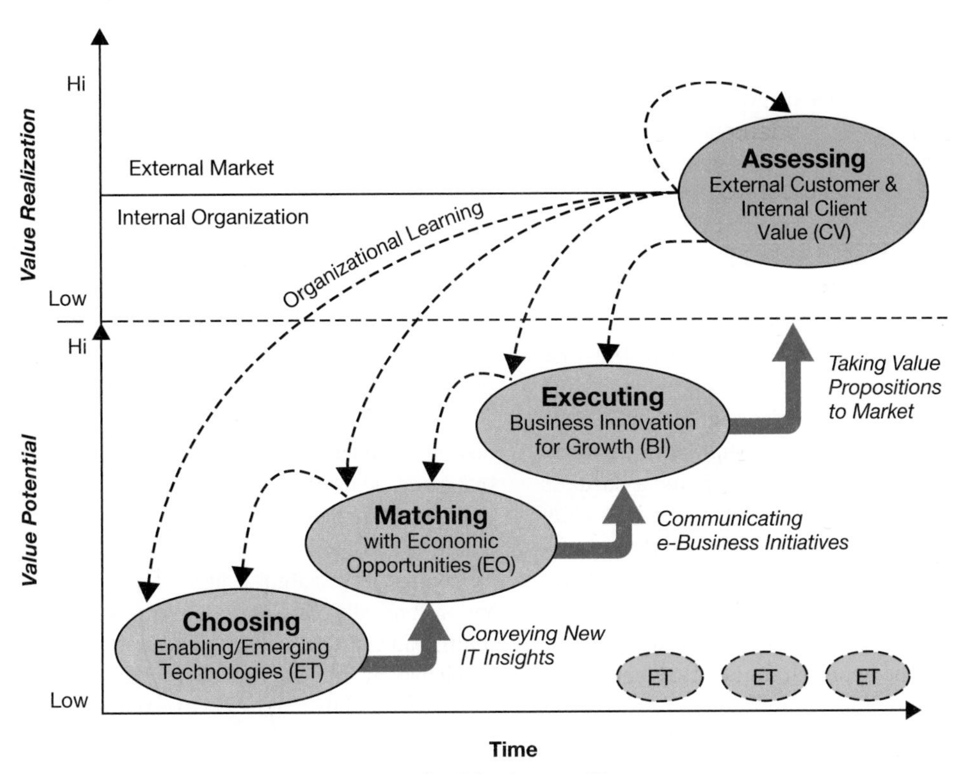

Figure 2.14 The E-Business Innovation Cycle. (Wheeler, 2002b)

impact on their business. Wheeler (2002b) has summarized this process nicely as the ***E-Business Innovation Cycle*** (see Figure 2.14). Like the term *electronic commerce*, *electronic business* refers to the use of information technologies and systems to support the business. Whereas the term *electronic commerce* is generally used to mean the use of the Internet and related technologies to support commerce, the term *electronic business* includes everything having to do with the application of ICTs to the conduct of business between organizations or from company to consumer. The model essentially holds that the key to success for modern organizations is the extent to which they use information technologies and systems in timely, innovative ways.

The vertical dimension of the E-Business Innovation Cycle shows the extent to which an organization derives value from a particular information technology, and the horizontal dimension shows time. The first bubble in the lower left of the graph shows that successful organizations first create jobs, groups, and processes that are all devoted to scanning the environment for new emerging and ***enabling technologies*** that appear to be relevant for the organization. For example, an organization might designate a small group within the MIS unit as the "Emerging Technologies" unit and charge them with looking out for new technologies that will have an impact on the business. As part of their job, this group will pore over current technology magazines, participate in Internet discussion forums on technology topics, go to technology conferences and conventions, and have strong, active relationships with technology researchers at universities and technology companies.

Next, in the second bubble, the organization matches the most promising new technologies with current ***economic opportunities***. For example, the Emerging Technologies group might have identified advances in database management systems (and a dramatic drop in data storage costs) as a key emerging technology that now enables a massive data warehouse to be feasible. In addition, managers within the marketing function of the firm have recognized that competitors have really dropped the ball in terms of customer service and that there is an opportunity to gain customers and market share by serving customers better.

The third bubble represents the process of selecting, among myriad opportunities, to take advantage of the database and data storage advances and addressing the current opportunity to grab customers and market share. The organization decides to implement an enterprise-wide data warehouse that enables them to have at their fingertips integrated corporate-wide data and an unparalleled capability to understand, react to, and better serve customers. The fourth bubble represents the process of assessing the value of that use of technology, not only to customers but to internal clients (i.e., sales representatives, marketing managers, the COO, and so on) as well.

So, what is new about this way of thinking about information technology? First, this approach says that technology is so important to strategy and to success that you have to begin with technology. Notice that the first bubble involves understanding, identifying, and choosing technologies that are important. The first bubble does not begin with strategy, as a traditional approach to running a business organization would suggest. In fact, many would argue that given how important technology is today and how fast it changes, if you start with a strategy and then try to retrofit technology into your aging strategy, you are doomed. This approach argues that you begin by understanding technology and develop a strategy from there. This approach is admittedly very uncomfortable for people who think in traditional ways and/or who are not comfortable with technology. We believe, however, that for many modern organizations, thinking about technology in this way is key.

The second way that this approach turns conventional wisdom on its head is that, like strategy, marketing takes a back seat to the technology. Think about it carefully and you will see that marketing does not come into play until later in this model. A very traditional marketing-oriented approach would be to go first to your customers and find out from them what their needs are and what you ought to be doing with technology. The trouble with this approach is that, given the rapid evolution of technology, your customers are not likely to know about new technologies and their capabilities. In some sense, they are the last place you ought to be looking for ideas about new technologies and their impact on your business. Indeed, if they know about the new technology, then chances are your competitors already do too, and that technology is not one to rest your competitive advantage on.

The third way that this approach is interesting, and potentially troubling, is that the process has to be ongoing. As shown along the time dimension along the bottom of the graph, the first bubble repeats over and over again as the Emerging Technologies group is constantly on the lookout for the "next new thing" that will revolutionize the business. The rate of information technology evolution is not likely to slow down, and innovative organizations truly cannot, and do not, ever rest.

Figure 2.15 Betamax tapes were shaped differently and required different technology inside the VCR than did VHS tapes.

Source: © Getty Images, Inc.

The Cutting Edge Versus the Bleeding Edge

As we hinted at above, there are limits to using emerging information systems to gain or sustain a competitive advantage. Information systems are often bought from, or built by, someone else. They are often either purchased from a vendor or developed by a consultant or outsourcing partner. In these situations, the information systems are usually not proprietary technologies owned by the organization. For example, although a soft drink company can patent the formula of a cola, or a pharmaceutical company can patent a new drug, an organization typically cannot patent its use of an information system, particularly if someone else developed it. The data in the system may be proprietary, but the information system typically is not.

Even in situations where an organization has developed an information system in-house, they usually do so with hardware, software, and networking components others can purchase. In short, rivals can copy emerging information systems, so this form of competitive advantage can be short-lived. Indeed, if use of the new system causes one organization to gain a significant advantage over others, smart rivals are quick to duplicate or improve on that use of the system.

Using emerging information systems always entails a risk. The classic example from consumer electronics is the choice of a VCR in the early days of that technology and the competing Betamax and VHS designs (see Figure 2.15). Most experts agreed that the Betamax had superior recording and playback quality, but VHS ultimately won the battle in the marketplace. People who made the "smart" choice at the time probably would have chosen a VCR with the Betamax design. Ultimately, however, that turned out to be an unfortunate choice. Other examples in the field of consumer electronics abound today. For example, when buying a stereo today, should you invest in traditional compact disc technology (such as the read-only CD-ROM), recordable compact discs, digital audiotape, an MP3 device, or some other technology? A situation very reminiscent of the Betamax versus VHS battle is brewing for the next generation of DVDs. Two groups have developed competing and non-compatible formats for high-capacity, high-definition (HD) DVDs: one group is led by Sony while the other is led by Toshiba. Both systems use Blu-ray laser technology to store between 30 and 50 GB of data, compared with 5 GB for current DVDs. It is likely that only one of these formats will survive. It is easy to make poor choices in consumer electronics, or to make choices that are good at the time but soon turn out to be poor.

Choosing among emerging information systems is just as difficult as choosing consumer electronics. In fact, choosing emerging systems may be far more difficult, given that the evolution of many consumer electronic technologies has stabilized, whereas the evolution of emerging information systems is just beginning to heat up. Furthermore, because of the size of the investment and the mission-critical nature of the system, it is far more devastating to choose a poor information system. Choosing a suboptimal home stereo, although disappointing, is usually not devastating.

Choosing new technologies in the information systems area is like trying to hit one of several equally attractive fast-moving targets. You can find examples of the difficulty of forecasting emerging technologies in the experiences that many organizations have had in forecasting the growth, use, and importance of the Internet. The 1994 Technology Forecast prepared by the major consulting firm Price Waterhouse mentioned the word "Internet" on only five pages of the 750-page document. The next year more than 75 pages addressed the Internet. In the 1997 briefing, the Internet is a pervasive topic throughout. Back in 1994 it would have been difficult, perhaps even foolish, to forecast such pervasive, rapidly growing business use of the Internet today. Table 2.6 illustrates how many people and organizations have had difficulty making technology-related predictions.

Given the pace of research and development in the information systems and components area, staying current has been nearly impossible. Probably one of the most famous metrics of computer evolution has been "Moore's Law." Intel founder Gordon Moore predicted that the number of transistors that could be squeezed onto a silicon chip would double every 18 months, and this prediction has proven itself over the past 20 years. In fact, some computer hardware and software firms roll out new versions of their products every 3 months. Keeping up with this pace of change can be difficult for any organization.

Requirements for Being at the Cutting Edge

Certain types of competitive environments require that organizations remain at the cutting edge in their use of information systems. For example, consider an organization that operates within an environment with strong competitive forces (Porter, 1979). The organization has competitive pressures coming from existing rival firms or from the threat of entry of new rivals. It is critical for these organizations to do things better, faster, and more cheaply than rivals. These organizations are driven to deploy emerging information systems.

These environmental characteristics alone, however, are not enough to determine whether an organization should deploy emerging information systems. Before an organization can deploy new systems well, its people, structure, and processes must be capable of adapting well to change. An organization that has, say, a 10-month approval process for new information systems will probably have difficulty

Table 2.6 ***Some predictions about technology that were not quite correct.*** **(*Source: "The Past Imperfect,"* Time Magazine [*July 15, 1996*]*: 54.*)**

Year	Source	Quote
1876	Western Union, internal memo	"This 'telephone' has too many shortcomings to be seriously considered as a means of communication. The device is inherently of no value to us."
1895	Lord Kelvin, president, Royal Society	"Heavier-than-air flying machines are impossible."
1899	C. H. Duell, commissioner, U.S. Office of Patents	"Everything that can be invented has been invented."
1927	H. M. Warner, Warner Brothers	"Who the hell wants to hear actors talk?"
1943	Thomas Watson, chairman, IBM	"I think there is a world market for maybe five computers."
1977	Ken Olsen, president, Digital Equipment Corporation	"There is no reason for any individuals to have a computer in their home."

keeping up in an environment that forces organizations to decide on and deploy emerging information systems within a matter of weeks.

To deploy emerging systems well, people in the organization must be willing to do whatever they can to bypass and eliminate internal bureaucracy, set aside political squabbles, and pull together for the common good. Can you imagine, for example, a firm trying to deploy a web-based order entry system that enables customers to access inventory information directly, when people in that firm do not even share such information with each other?

Organizations deploying emerging systems must also have the human capital necessary to deploy the new systems. The organization must have enough employees available with the proper systems knowledge, skills, time, and other resources to deploy these systems. Alternatively, the organization must have resources and able systems partners available to outsource the development of such systems.

The last characteristic of an organization ready for the deployment of emerging systems is that its members must have the appropriate tolerance of risk, uncertainty, and problems to be willing to deploy and use emerging information systems that may not be as proven and pervasive as more traditional technologies. If people within the organization desire low risk in their use of information systems, then gambling on cutting-edge systems will probably not be desirable or tolerable for them.

Predicting the New, New Thing

As you can see, using information systems toward a strategic end will be difficult to sustain. As Bakos and Treacy (1986) and others have argued, if you are using information systems to gain a competitive advantage in the area of operating efficiencies, it is likely that your rivals can just as easily adopt the same types of information systems and achieve the same gains. For example, you might set up a website that enables customers to check on the status of their order without requiring help from a customer service representative, and this might enable you to cut costs. Rivals could, however, easily copy this approach and match your cost reductions. The competitive advantage thus turns into strategic necessity for anyone in this industry.

On the other hand, there are ways to use information systems to gain a competitive advantage in a way that is easier to sustain. For example, Bakos and Treacy argued that if you can use information systems to make your products or services unique or to cause your customers to invest heavily in you so that their switching costs are high, then you are better able to develop competitive advantage that is sustainable over the long haul. For example, you might combine heavy investments in computer-aided design systems with very bright engineers to perfect your product and make it unique, something relatively difficult to copy. Alternatively, you might use a customer relationship management system to build an extensive database containing the entire history of your interaction with each of your customers and then use that system to provide very high-quality, intimate, rapid, customized service that would convince customers that if they switched to a rival it would take them years to build up that kind of relationship with the other firm.

How can you possibly predict the next wave of emerging information systems? Well, you have help. Michael Lewis wrote the bestselling *The New, New Thing: A Silicon Valley Story* (W. W. Norton & Co., 2000), which tells the story of Jim Clark, a noted high-tech entrepreneur who is famous for the unprecedented business "hat trick" of creating three separate billion-dollar technology companies—Silicon Graphics, Netscape, and Healtheon. As a result, Jim Clark is known as someone who is very good at knowing what the next, new, major information technology breakthrough will be. Most of us do not have that same level of business or technology acumen. Fortunately, there are Jim Clark and others like him to whom we can look and from whom we can take our cues.

In any event, while using information systems for competitive advantage has become a given for modern organizations, it can be difficult to achieve and sustain, and it can be expensive. Go forth and conquer, but do so with your eyes wide open!

CAREER IMPLICATIONS

Information Systems for Competitive Advantage

For Accounting and Finance

The effective management and control of financial resources has become a competitive advantage for many organizations. Therefore, the accounting and finance functions in most organizations rely heavily on information systems. Through the use of information systems, organizations can be much more efficient and effective in tracking costs and revenues. Furthermore, accounting and finance professionals use information systems for budgeting and forecasting future events. For example, when you introduce a new product line or acquire a company, gaining accurate estimates of costs and revenues over time is paramount to success for your organization and can provide it with a clear competitive advantage.

For Operations Management

In operations management, managing the supply chain—the processes associated with production and distribution of products—through the use of information systems has become a competitive advantage for many organizations. Information systems allow companies to obtain a competitive advantage by helping them to streamline processes such as forecasting optimal inventory levels, ordering, scheduling processes, and shipping the finished goods. If you are working in operations management, you will utilize information systems heavily for these tasks; therefore, being proficient in using different information systems will help you to also obtain a competitive advantage on the job market.

For Human Resources Management

Using information systems to assist in the management of human resources can provide a competitive advantage to many organizations. Today, most organizations rely on information systems to store employee records, to process payroll, and to communicate with current and future employees. In a growing number of organizations, virtual teams—work groups distributed potentially around the world—use information systems for their communication and collaboration on a broad range of work. For example, software companies that use virtual teams for new product development can obtain a competitive advantage by accelerating the development process by having teams work around the clock throughout the world. If you are working in human resource management, it is likely that you will not only use information systems to recruit and manage employees, but also apply systems to enable more effective work practices such as virtual teams.

For Marketing

Organizations need a clear marketing strategy to effectively communicate with potential customers. Today, information systems play an increasing role in executing this strategy. For example, information systems are used for analyzing sales data, planning for the future, and creating marketing material. Companies using information systems for data analysis and forecasting can quickly react to changes in demand, which can provide them with a competitive advantage over their rivals. For many companies, CRM systems (discussed in Chapter 7) have become indispensable where customer data are analyzed to better target customers with promotions or special offers. CRM enables organizations to increase marketing effectiveness while reducing costs. Additionally, websites have become a key part of virtually all organizations' marketing strategy. Understanding how information systems can be applied to the marketing function can provide you with a clear competitive advantage in the job market.

For Information Systems

As the need for information systems in organizations continues to grow, information systems professionals will become increasingly involved in making business cases for new systems. Given that the primary users of new systems are departments other than the information systems function, information systems personnel assist these departments in identifying which systems best fit their needs. Whenever a department is thinking about implementing a new system, information systems personnel act as consultants to the various departments throughout the organization. Therefore, being knowledgeable about both information systems and all business functional areas will help you to be most effective in this role.

KEY POINTS REVIEW

1. **Discuss how information systems can be used for automation, organizational learning, and strategic support of organizations.** Automating business activities occurs when information systems are used to do a business activity faster or more cheaply. IS can be used to help automate. It can also be used to improve aspects of an operation to gain dramatic improvements in the operation as a whole. When this occurs, technology is said to help us learn because it provides information about its operation and the underlying work process that it supports. Using information systems strategically occurs when the technology is used to enable organizational strategy and to help the firm gain or sustain competitive advantage over rivals.
2. **Describe information systems' critical strategic importance to the success of modern organizations.** Using information systems to automate and learn about business processes is a good start. However, information systems can add even more value to an organization if they are conceived, designed, used, and managed with a strategic approach. To apply information systems strategically, you must understand the organization's value chain and be able to identify opportunities in which you can use information systems to make changes or improvements in the value chain to gain or sustain a competitive advantage. This requires a change in mindset from thinking about information systems as an expense to be minimized to thinking of information systems as an asset to be invested in.
3. **Explain how you formulate and present the business case for a system and why it is sometimes difficult to do so.** Making the business case is the process of building and presenting the set of arguments that show that an information system is adding value to the organization and/or its constituents. It is often difficult to quantify the value that an information system provides. To formulate a business case for an information system, you must understand the nature of the industry—its stage of maturity, its regulation, and the nature of its competition or rivalry. You must also understand your organization's particular business strategy to make an effective business case for systems. In short, technology investments should be closely linked to the organization's business strategy because these investments are becoming one of the major vehicles by which organizations can achieve their strategy. After you gain an understanding of your organization's position in the marketplace, its strategy for investing in systems that add value, and firm-level implementation factors, you can quantify the relative costs and benefits of the system. Considering all of these factors simultaneously will help you formulate an effective business case. To make a convincing presentation, you should be specific about the benefits this investment will provide for the organization. To do this, you must convert the benefits into monetary terms, such as the amount of money saved or revenue generated. If you have difficulty identifying specific monetary measures, you should devise some proxy measures to demonstrate the benefits of the system. Finally, make sure that you measure things that are important to the decision makers of the organizations. Choosing the wrong measures can yield a negative decision about a beneficial system.
4. **Explain why and how companies are continually looking for new ways to use technology for competitive advantage.** Organizations are finding clever ways to use new technologies to help them do things faster, better, and more cost efficiently than rivals. Being at the technological cutting edge has its disadvantages. Given that new technologies are not as stable as traditional ones, relying on emerging systems can be problematic. Because constantly upgrading to newer and better systems is expensive, relying on emerging systems can hurt a firm financially. In addition, using emerging information systems for competitive advantage can provide short-lived advantages; competitors can quickly jump on the technological bandwagon and easily mimic the same system. As a result, many organizations find themselves on the technological bleeding edge rather than the cutting edge. Not every organization should deploy emerging information systems. Those organizations that find themselves in highly competitive environments probably most need to deploy new technologies to stay ahead of rivals. To best deploy these new technologies, organizations must be ready for the changes that will ensue, have the resources necessary to deploy new technologies successfully, and be tolerant of the risk and problems involved in being at the cutting edge. Deploying emerging information systems is essentially a risk/return gamble: The risks are relatively high, but the potential rewards are great. Firms today have people, and in some cases special units, that scan the environment, looking out for emerging and enabling technologies that can help their firm. They then narrow down the list to technologies that match with challenges the firm faces or create economic opportunities. Next, they choose a particular technology, or set of technologies, and implement them in a way that enables them to gain or sustain competitive advantage. Finally, they assess these technology projects in terms of their value not only to internal people and groups but to external clients and partners. This process is ongoing, as information technologies and systems continually evolve.

KEY TERMS

REVIEW QUESTIONS

1. Describe competitive advantage and list six sources.
2. Compare and contrast automating and learning.
3. Describe the attributes of a learning organization.
4. List five general types of organizational strategy.
5. What are some of the problems in measuring productivity changes?
6. List the three factors you should consider when making the business case for an information system.
7. Define a proxy variable and give an example.
8. Describe the productivity paradox.
9. Compare and contrast tangible and intangible benefits and costs.

SELF-STUDY QUESTIONS

Visit the Companion Website for this text for additional Self-Study Questions: **www.pearsoned.ca/jessup**.

1. __________ is using technology as a way to help complete a task within an organization faster and, perhaps, more cheaply.
   A. automating
   B. learning
   C. strategizing
   D. processing
2. Which of the following is an intangible benefit?
   A. negative benefits
   B. qualitative benefits
   C. quantitative costs
   D. positive cash flows
3. Which of the following is not improving the value chain?
   A. improving procurement processes
   B. increasing operating costs
   C. minimizing marketing expenditures
   D. selling more products
4. Which of the following is not one of the three types of arguments commonly made in the business case for an information system?
   A. fear
   B. fact
   C. faith
   D. fun
5. A company is said to have __________ when it has gained an edge over its rivals.
   A. monopoly
   B. profitability
   C. competitive advantage
   D. computer advantage
6. The IS manager has the overall responsibility for the __________ of the information systems.
   A. management, development, implementation, and maintenance
   B. development, implementation, and maintenance
   C. management, development, and maintenance
   D. management, development, and implementation
7. Many firms now use the Internet for business-to-business interactions, and these systems are called __________.
   A. Internets
   B. extranets
   C. intranets
   D. infonets
8. Each of the following was described in this chapter as a source of competitive advantage except for __________.
   A. delivering superior customer service
   B. achieving lower cost than rivals
   C. being the subject of a hostile takeover
   D. having shorter lead times in developing and testing new products
9. Making the __________ is the process of building and presenting the set of arguments that show that an information system is adding value to the organization.
   A. organizational chart
   B. organizational case
   C. law case
   D. business case
10. Besides business industry and strategic factors, other implementation-related factors must be considered when making the business case for systems, including the type of __________.
   A. organization
   B. culture
   C. political environment
   D. all of the above

PROBLEMS AND EXERCISES

1. Match the following terms with the appropriate definitions:

    _____ Value chain analysis

    _____ Tangible costs

    _____ Extranet

    _____ Competitive advantage

    _____ Business case

    _____ Learning organization

    _____ Total quality management

    _____ Value chain

    _____ E-Business Innovation Cycle

    _____ Proxy variable

    a. An approach in which people within an organization are constantly monitoring what they do to find ways to improve quality of operations, products, services, and everything else about the firm
    b. Costs that are quantifiable or have physical substance
    c. The set of arguments that illustrate that an information system is adding value to the organization and/or its constituents
    d. Firms' use of the Internet for business-to-business interactions
    e. A substitute variable (such as customer contact) expressed on a 5-point scale from low to high that is used in place of an information system's intangible benefit, which is difficult to quantify
    f. The edge a firm has over its rivals
    g. An organization that is able to learn, grow, and manage its knowledge well
    h. The extent to which an organization uses information technologies in innovative ways and derives value from these technologies over time
    i. Identification of opportunities to use information systems for competitive advantage
    j. The process of adding value to products/services throughout the organization

2. After reading this chapter, it should be fairly obvious why an IS professional should be able to make a business case for a given system. Why, however, is it just as important for non-IS professionals? How are they involved in this process? What is their role in information systems planning?

3. Search the World Wide Web for items related to end-user development. What information did you find? Why is end-user development difficult to track in terms of productivity? What are some of the measurement problems associated with end-user development? How can these problems be eliminated? Prepare a 10-minute presentation to the rest of the class of your findings.

4. Why is it important to look at industry factors when making a business case? What effect might strong competition have on IS investment and use? What effect might weak competition have on IS investment and use? Why?

5. Argue for or against the following statement: "When making the business case, you should concentrate on the decision makers' 'hot buttons' and gloss over some of the other details."

6. What role does the organizational culture play in IS investments? Is this something that can be easily adjusted when necessary? Why or why not? Who is in control of a firm's organizational culture? Do you have personal experiences with this issue?

7. Why can it be difficult to develop an accurate cost-benefit analysis? What factors may be difficult to quantify? How can this be handled? Is this something that should just be avoided altogether? What are the consequences of that approach?

8. Have you ever rented a car over the web? Research car rentals, including Avis Rent a Car, over the web, and then telephone the car agency to find the following answers: What types of vehicles are available for what price and for how long? Is there a minimum age required to rent a vehicle? Is insurance a consideration? Is it difficult to rent a car in a particular area of Canada, or is it easy? How do you make a car reservation?

9. Within a small group of classmates, describe any involvement you have had with making the business case for a system. To whom were you making the case? Was it a difficult sell? Why? Did you follow the guidelines set forth in this chapter? How did your business case differ from those of others in your group? Were you successful? Why or why not? Were they successful? Why or why not?

10. Consider an organization that is familiar to you or one of the Brief Cases in this chapter or in another chapter. Of the five industry factors presented in the chapter (Porter's model), which is the most significant for this organization in terms of IS investment and development? Why? Which is the least significant? Why?

11. Discuss the following in a small group of classmates or with a friend. Describe a situation from your own experience in which a system's cost-benefit analysis showed a negative result when based on tangible factors, but the system was still implemented. Was the implementation decision based on intangible factors? Have these intangible factors proven themselves to be worth the investment in this system? Was it a harder sell because of these intangible factors?

12. Choose one of the Brief Cases in this or another chapter or a firm that is familiar to you. Determine the length of time it has taken for various information systems to show their productivity improvements. Was it a long time? Why did it take so long? Was it longer than expected? Why or why not? Search the Internet to find additional anecdotes about IS productivity improvements. You may want to search through *CIO Canada* magazine online at **www.itworldcanada.com/Pages/Docbase/BrowsePublication.aspx?Publication=CIO** to get started. Summarize one of these articles for the rest of the class.

13. Why shouldn't every organization deploy cutting-edge emerging information systems? What are some of the recommended characteristics of an organization that are necessary for that organization to successfully deploy emerging information systems?

APPLICATION EXERCISES

Note: The existing data files referenced in these exercises are available on the Companion Website: **www.pearsoned.ca/jessup**.

Spreadsheet Application: Building a Business Case

Upon graduation, you were hired by FashionExpress, a nationwide fashion retailer, to assist in creating an infrastructure to sell products over the Internet. One aspect of this online system is a module to handle inventory requests so that the customers can see whether a particular product is available. You have determined that the current inventory management system cannot handle such ad hoc requests very well, as it was not designed for that purpose. In order to justify the introduction of a new inventory management system, the IS manager has asked you to prepare a thorough cost/benefit analysis including:

- A spreadsheet detailing the costs and benefits associated with the new system.
- A line graph showing the total costs, the total benefits, and the break-even point.

Use the data provided in CostBenefit.txt to set up the spreadsheet and the charts. Hint: use "import external data" to import the captions and values provided in the text file. Make sure to use formulas for all calculations. Once you have set up the spreadsheet, print out the results in both data and formula views. Hint: use ctrl + ´ (grave accent) to switch between formula and data views.

Database Application: Locating Stores for Fashionexpress

As FashionExpress is new to e-commerce, the management suggests following a stepwise approach for using the Internet to conduct business. Before using the Internet for conducting transactions, the managers recommend setting up a site that provides information to customers. Part of this informational site is a store locator for the three different types of FashionExpress stores. You have been asked to create a database containing the following information:

- Store locations.
- Type of store (FashionExpressForHer, FashionExpressForHim, and FashionExpressForKids).

Make sure that you create one table for location (including store ID, street address, city, state, ZIP code, and phone number) and a separate table for type of store (including store type ID and name). Once you have created the tables, connect the tables using a one-to-many relationship (multiple locations can be of the same store type) and print out the relationship. Hint: In the "Relationships" view, select "File>Print Relationships . . ." to print relationships in Microsoft Access.

ANSWERS TO THE SELF-STUDY QUESTIONS

1. A, p. 40 2. B, p. 57 3. B, p. 47 4. D, p. 53 5. C, p. 44
6. A, p. 58 7. C, p. 45 8. D, p. 48 9. D, p. 49

Case *Canada's First "Signatureless" Financing Solution Leads to a 200 Percent Revenue Increase*

Dell Financial Services Canada Limited (DFS) provides financial solutions and comprehensive asset services to Dell's Canadian customers. DFS has operated out of a single location in Canada since 1997 with approximately 80 staff. While DFS has been successful with equipment financing deals with large companies, the company has struggled in the small business segment.

Unlike the average retail sales outlet, the Dell sales team in this segment never sees the customer. Making the sale is essentially a two-part process: sales (which typically takes minutes) and financing (which typically takes days). Delays relating to the finance process impact customer/employee satisfaction and the successful closure of financed deals. This, in turn, reduces commissions and revenues.

The challenge for DFS was to profoundly change the financing process, while ensuring full business continuity. In particular, DFS needed to design a new sales process that would:

- Give the Dell sales team tools to sell financing during the initial sales call, without needing to transfer the call to a DFS representative.
- Reduce the turnaround time for credit approvals and fraud evaluation. DFS had previously been using a third-party service provider for this process.
- Streamline and simplify the exchange of information between the Dell sales team and DFS.

The DFS project team set out to build a new financial sales process initiative nicknamed "Helix." One of the key features of the new system was a "signatureless" capability (a first for financial products in Canada). Many technical and process challenges had to be addressed to gain acceptance and deliver a financial agreement to customers within seconds of an online or telesales transaction without a "wet signature."

DFS had a history of achieving modest technology-related improvements. Business expectations for the Helix project were, therefore, similarly modest. The successes delivered by the system, however, surpassed all expectations.

The Helix system resulted in a financial sales process that set new standards for the industry. Dell sales staff could sell financial products on the initial sales call and the process could be completed in minutes rather than days. As a result, customer/employee satisfaction and Dell/DFS revenues increased dramatically. Specific benefits included:

- Increased volume of annual consumer applications processed through Helix by 1200 percent.
- Increased revenue of 208 percent with the same staffing levels.
- Reduced the documentation process from 2–5 days to seconds with signatureless financing via e-mail and fax.
- Reduced the 4-hour turnaround time on over 60 percent of applications to less than 6 seconds for all applications with instant credit and fraud adjudication.
- Reduced DFS's costs by $150 000 annually.
- Ensured 100 percent automated adjudication in 5–8 seconds.
- Reduced financial sales cycle from 15 to 2 minutes due to radically simplified real-time interfaces between Dell and DFS.
- Enabled exception processing and reduced manual audits from 100 percent to below 40 percent with automated auditing processes.

According to Kevin Northrup, Director, Dell Change Management and IT, implementing Helix was like having a team of five people change all four tires on a car moving 50 km/h. "We have very knowledgeable people who run our business every day. But to grow our business and take it to a new level, we had to go beyond the familiar and attempt the extraordinary. We unleashed the imagination of our project team and created a solution that has transformed our business to the nth degree. We are now moving our business forward at over 200 km/h," says Northrup.

Source: Canadian Information Productivity Awards, "Dell Financial Services Canada Limited," 2005, **www.cipa.com/award_winners/winners_04/DellFinancialServices.html.**

Discussion Questions

1. Do the benefits to DFS described in the case constitute a competitive advantage? If so, can these benefits be appropriated by the company? Can they be sustained?
2. The benefits outlined in the case go beyond dollars and cents. What additional benefits are described? How important are these benefits?
3. When it comes to information systems, do you think it is a good strategy to "go beyond the familiar and attempt the extraordinary" as suggested in the case? Why or why not? Defend your position.

Log on to the Companion Website at www.pearsoned.ca/jessup for an additional case.

Running Case: Connexion by Boeing

Information Systems for Competitive Advantage

Over the past several years, most U.S. domestic and international airlines experienced a slump in ticket sales brought on by a global economic downturn. As described previously, many companies cut back their travel costs by choosing different carriers or by reducing business travel altogether. As a result, the airline industry found themselves in fierce competition for a shrinking number of passengers. Although a flight on one airline is not much different from that on another, airlines have been looking for ways to differentiate themselves from their competition by offering better service or having a better price structure. At the Boeing Company, executives believed they found an additional way for airlines to obtain a competitive advantage, an advantage that many airlines needed to stay alive.

According to recent studies, more than 600 million people worldwide have Internet access, and more than 40 million Americans have broadband Internet access (with a connection speed of 200 kbps or greater). Broadband connectivity is becoming increasingly popular, as the Internet is used for shopping, working, and communicating with colleagues, family, and friends. People expect to have broadband not only at work and school, but also at home and in many public places such as malls and restaurants. It is, therefore, quite reasonable to predict that broadband availability will expand into more and more locations, including airliners, boats, and trains. Market research supports the idea that consumers desire increased Internet access. For example, market research by the Boeing Company found that 50 percent of air travellers (in all classes) have a strong interest in in-flight e-mail and Internet access, with three in five saying they would be willing to pay for it. Half of those who were willing to pay said they would be willing to pay $20 or more for in-flight connectivity.

To get a better idea of the potential market for in-flight Internet service and to develop a solid business case, Connexion by Boeing conducted a more thorough market analysis and found the following:

- 75 percent of the business travellers carried laptops on flights
- 62 percent of U.S. frequent business travellers were either "extremely" or "very much" interested in in-flight broadband services
- about one-fifth of the different airlines' frequent fliers were willing to pay as much as $35 per flight for a

high-speed service offering (equal to the cost of about a 3.5 minute in-flight telephone call)

- 3 percent of the frequent fliers would be extremely likely to switch carriers for broadband Internet access
- 6 percent would even abandon frequent flier programs to obtain connectivity.

For an airline offering high-speed Internet service, such a service could attract and retain a large number of customers. An increase in a reasonable number of business travellers for an airline will translate into a huge increase in revenue. For example, an average increase of a single passenger per international flight for an international carrier equates to approximately $1 million in additional revenue annually. Consequently, Connexion believes that offering in-flight high-speed Internet access will provide an airline with a strong competitive advantage over its rivals.

In addition to our increasing dependence on the Internet for work and our personal lives, advances in aircraft technology are also expected to contribute to an increased demand for in-flight connectivity. For example, Singapore Airlines recently launched an 18-hour nonstop flight from New York to Singapore using Airbus's newest long-haul plane. While many passengers—especially business travellers—are choosing nonstop flights because it can save valuable time and reduce the risk of lost luggage and missed connections, being on a long flight also means not being able to connect to the office or not being able to answer important e-mail messages. For most business travellers, such extensive isolation from the rest of the world comes at a cost—ever-growing mountains of e-mail, missed opportunities, less productive time at the destination, and valuable hours or days lost in catch-up work upon return. In-flight Internet access could provide business travellers with a diversity of services to maintain connection with their clients or offices, making it much more likely that customers on long-haul flights will subscribe to in-flight service.

Being the first mover in this highly lucrative market will also provide Connexion with a clear competitive advantage. For example, the number of jetliners is expected to grow from 13 000 in 2002 to more than 21 000 by 2012. Connexion's market forecasts conservatively

Airline passengers using in-flight Internet service.

estimate that as many as 4000 aircraft will be equipped with Connexion's systems by 2012. Furthermore, while the primary near-term focus was on meeting the needs of the aviation industry and its customers, Connexion's medium-term focus is on providing services to the maritime market (which was estimated to be a $1 billion a year market) and on e-enabling airplanes—using the wireless capability of the Connexion by Boeing system and its tremendous bandwidth to reduce weight, power requirements, and complexity of the jetliners. Among other things, an e-enabled airplane might, for example, be able to distribute entertainment to passengers' seats through a wireless LAN. Less weight and complexity means the airplane can fly farther, haul more freight, and burn less fuel. In the cabin, an e-enabled airplane makes reconfiguring seating layouts simpler. Finally, longer term, Connexion sees opportunities to bring the benefits of high-speed connectivity to other mobile platforms, including trains and long-haul trucks. In terms of potential revenues, Connexion estimated the market for in-flight connectivity at about $8–10 billion a year by the year 2012 and expects to be able to serve about half of this market, thereby generating revenues in the range of $4 billion to $5 billion annually.

In addition to a promising revenue forecast, a thorough analysis of the competition revealed that there were no immediate direct competitors for high-speed in-flight connectivity that offered access to the Internet and company intranets—with both personal and VPN-secured company e-mail. While Boeing's fiercest competitor, Europe's Airbus, launched low-speed e-mail services together with Tenzing, Connexion's system could be installed on any commercial jetliner equal to or larger than a Gulfstream fuselage, regardless of manufacturer. In addition to commercial jets, Connexion also provides its services to a wide variety of business aircraft by delivering a turnkey system that can be installed on a mixed fleet of airliners regardless of size or manufacturer. The system has been designed to be extremely simple to use so that passengers are able to connect to the service via a laptop or PDA (personal digital assistant), with a standard Ethernet cable (RJ-45) or through wireless access points using a wireless-enabled computer. The system has been designed to be robust and stable; it must work the first time and every time. Nevertheless, Connexion provides 7-day, 24-hour Customer Care in case any questions arise. This centre handles billing and service inquiries as well as having direct access to the Network Control Centre, which is responsible for monitoring network and system performance.

Depending on external factors such as customer demand and a positive regulatory environment, Connexion is expected to cover transpacific routes in 2005, with South America and Africa coming online not long thereafter, in addition to the transatlantic routes already used by Connexion's first customers. Despite a shaky start due to the economic downturn, it appears that Connexion is far ahead of its competitors. Connexion has acquired a number of customers such as Lufthansa, which announced in 2003 that it had signed a definitive service agreement to equip its entire long-range fleet (80 Airbus and Boeing jetliners), and SAS, which announced the signing of a definitive service agreement for 11 of its long-range jetliners in July 2003. Additionally, Japan's leading carriers, Japan Airlines and ANA, announced definitive service agreements for their longer-range jetliners; Singapore Airlines, China Airlines, and Korean Air have also recently announced agreements with Connexion. Likewise, the U.S. government has chosen Connexion to provide service on military transport aircraft, as part of an overall communications upgrade, and on government VIP jets. Clearly, Connexion by Boeing has managed to obtain a competitive advantage over rivals using information technology.

Discussion Questions

1. How does Connexion help Boeing obtain a competitive advantage over its rivals?
2. Describe the competitive forces in Connexion's market and briefly outline how different information systems and technologies enhance or reduce these.
3. Do you believe Boeing's competitors can catch up with Connexion's services and technology? Why or why not?

Preview

In the last chapter, you learned how organizations are using information systems for competitive advantage. In this chapter, we focus on data and knowledge management systems, two types of information systems utilized by organizations to more easily store and manipulate their key information resources.

People in organizations rely on information about customers, products, invoices, suppliers, markets, transactions, and competitors. In large organizations, this information is stored in ***databases*** that can be billions (giga-) or trillions (tera-) of bytes in size. If an organization lost these data, it would have difficulty pricing and selling its products or services, cutting payroll cheques for its employees, and even sending out mail. More recently, knowledge management systems are being used to collect and share an organization's best practices to improve organizational efficiency and effectiveness for a broad range of activities. After reading this chapter, you will be able to do the following:

1. Describe why databases have become so important to modern organizations.
2. Describe what databases and database management systems (DBMSs) are and how they work.
3. Explain how organizations are getting the most from their investment in database technologies.
4. Describe what is meant by knowledge management and knowledge assets as well as the benefits and challenges of deploying a knowledge management system.

3L Filters Ltd.

3L Filters Ltd. is an engineer-to-order manufacturer of filtration pressure vessels used in nuclear power plants and other industrial settings. The company is based in Cambridge, Ontario, and sells to over 17 countries worldwide, including China, Korea, Romania, the United States, and Argentina. Filter vessels can be found anywhere gases and liquids at high pressures must be contained and filtered.

3L was growing very quickly and was having trouble keeping up with customer demand. For example, in order to prepare price quotations on new business, the sales staff typically required the engineering group to perform a technical evaluation of the customer's specifications and then provide a proposed design solution, along with the associated drawings. This process was time consuming and inefficient. As a result, 3L was losing some orders because it couldn't get the quotations to customers on time.

"More than 80 percent of our resources were being consumed to support only 50 percent of our business," says Kevin Cassells, engineering manager at 3L. "To increase our revenue in a market sector that has a growing need for engineering support, we needed to find a way to solve our resource-limitation problem."

3L adopted a web-based knowledge management system that enabled non-technical salespeople to design, price, and present engineering drawings for pressure vessels in just minutes—without engineering assistance. The system drew on proprietary internal and best practices–based external knowledge to generate 3D digital models, drawings, and quotations automatically. In consultation with a customer, a 3L sales representative could enter high-level specifications into the system, which then automatically generated detailed, full-scale digital prototypes and a price for the final product—without requiring involvement by engineering, purchasing, or estimating staff.

The system has enabled 3L salespeople to improve their quote conversion success ratio to 25 percent from 8, yielding a 28 percent increase in revenue for 3L over the past 2 years. "Our products are typically highly engineered, requiring very experienced people," says George Foss, owner of 3L. "By thinking a little outside the box, we found a way to capture engineering knowledge permanently, use it to increase revenues, and reduce the potential impact if there's any staff turnover."

Source: Adapted from the Canadian Information Productivity Awards, **www.cipa.com/award_winners/winners_05/3L-Filters.html**.

We begin by discussing the importance of database technology for the success of organizations. The chapter continues by describing the key activities involved in designing and using modern databases and is followed by an examination of how organizations are utilizing this stored information for competitive advantage. We conclude by providing an overview of how organizations are managing their knowledge to gain competitive advantage through the use of knowledge management systems.

DATABASE MANAGEMENT FOR STRATEGIC ADVANTAGE

Database technology, a collection of related data organized in a way that facilitates data searches, is vital to an organization's success. Increasingly, we are living in an information age. Information once taken for granted or never collected at all is now used to make organizations more productive and competitive.

Think about this book you are reading, which is in itself information. The publisher had to know available authors capable of writing this book. The publisher also had to have information on you, the target audience, to determine that writing this book was worthwhile and to suggest a writing style and collection of topics. The publisher had to use market information to set a price for the book, along with information on reliable wholesalers and distribution partners to get the books from the publisher to you, the consumer.

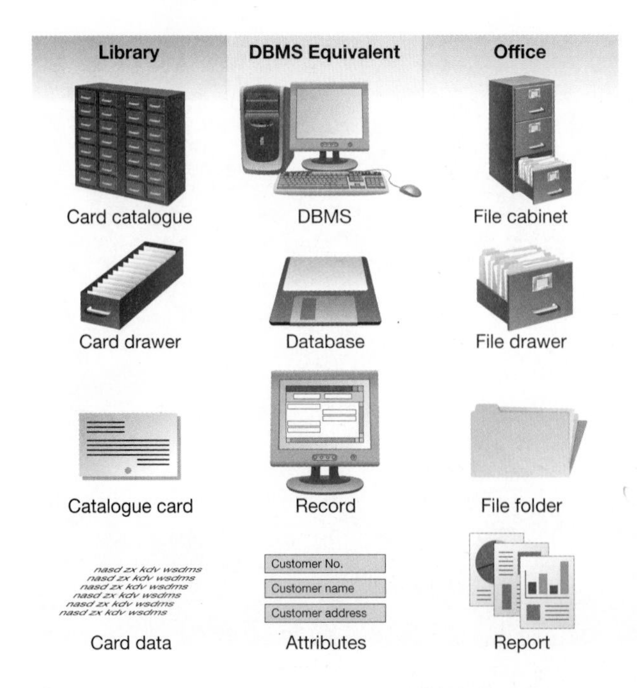

Figure 3.1 Computers make the process of storing and managing data much easier.

In addition to using databases to create this book, the publisher also uses databases to keep track of the book's sales, to determine royalties for the authors, to set salaries and wages for employees, to pay employees, to prospect for new book opportunities, to pay bills, and to perform nearly every other function in the business. For example, to determine authors' royalties on books sold, the publisher must collect information from hundreds of bookstores and consolidate it into a single report. Large publishers, such as Prentice Hall/Pearson Education, rely on computer databases to perform these tasks.

Other organizations also make use of the database process used to create and sell this book. For example, Lands' End uses databases to design and produce its clothing catalogue and to market and sell products. Companies such as Lands' End also use databases to gather and store information about customers and their purchasing behaviour. Companies such as The Bay and Eddie Bauer even produce tailor-made catalogues and other mailings for specific individuals, based on the purchasing information stored in corporate databases. FriendFinder, an online dating service, makes extensive use of databases to find perfect matches for its users (see Brief Case: Using Open Source Technology to Support FriendFinder). Additionally, database technology fuels electronic commerce on the web, from tracking available products for sale to providing customer service.

As these examples make clear, ***database management systems (DBMSs)*** have become an integral part of the total information systems solution for many organizations. DBMSs allow organizations to retrieve, store, and analyze information easily. Failure to properly build, populate, and manage databases can lead to organizational problems, such as increased costs or reduced levels of customer service. For example, difficulties with data incompatibility, database development, and technical administration contributed to the massive cost overruns with the Canadian Firearms Centre's gun registry.

Next we examine some basic concepts, advantages of the database approach, and database management.

The Database Approach: Foundation Concepts

The database approach now dominates nearly all of the computer-based information systems used today. To understand databases, we must familiarize ourselves with some terminology. In Figure 3.1, we compare database terminology (middle column) with equivalents in a library

ID Number	Last Name	First Name	Street Address	City	Province	Postal Code	Major
209345	Jung	Judy	1242 N. Maple	Kingston	Ontario	K7L 3N9	Recreation
213009	Beaubien	Louis	3400 E. Longvi	Kingston	Ontario	K7L 3P4	Business Management
345987	Fleury	Monika	367 Ridge Roa	Kingston	Ontario	K7L 4L1	Aeronautical Engineering
457838	Wade	Christopher	12 Long Lake	Kingston	Ontario	K7L 2S2	Computer Science
459987	Yim	Nathan	8009 Walnut	Kingston	Ontario	K7L 6N1	Sociology
466711	Park	Charles	234 Jamie Lan	Kingston	Ontario	K7L 2N7	Pre-Medicine
512678	Staples	Sandy	3837 Wood's E	Kingston	Ontario	K7L 1P6	Law
691112	Clark	Andrew	988 Woodbridg	Kingston	Ontario	K7L 1B0	Political Science
910234	Singh	Parv	1234 S. Grant	Kingston	Ontario	K7L 3P4	Civil Engineering
979776	Reich	Blaize	109 Hoosier Av	Kingston	Ontario	K7L 3N8	Psychology
983445	Huff	Sid	989 College	Kingston	Ontario	K7L 2N7	Sports Science

Figure 3.2 This sample data table for the entity Student includes 8 attributes and 11 records.

(left column) and a business office (right column). We use DBMSs to interact with the data in databases. A DBMS is a software application with which you create, store, organize, and retrieve data from a single database or several databases. Microsoft Access is an example of a popular DBMS for personal computers. In the DBMS, the individual database is a collection of related attributes about entities. An ***entity*** is something you collect data about, such as people or classes (see Figure 3.2). We often think of entities as ***tables***, where each row is a ***record*** and each column is an ***attribute*** (also referred to as a field). A record is a collection of related attributes about a single entity. Each record typically consists of many attributes, which are individual pieces of information. For example, a name and a social security number are attributes about a person.

Advantages of the Database Approach

In the 1960s, before there were DBMSs, organizations used the file processing approach to store and manipulate data electronically. Data were usually kept in a long, sequential computer file which was often stored on tape. Information about entities often appeared in several different places throughout the information system, and the data were often stored along with, and sometimes embedded within, the programming code that used the data. People had not yet envisioned the concept of separately storing information about entities in non-redundant databases, so files had repetitive data about a customer, a supplier, or another entity. When someone's address changed, it had to be changed in every file where that information occurred, a tedious and error-prone process. Similarly, if programmers changed the code, they typically had to change the corresponding data along with it. This was often no better than the pen-and-paper approach to storing data.

It is possible for a database to consist of only a single file or table. However, most databases managed under a DBMS consist of several files, tables, or entities. A DBMS can manage hundreds, or even thousands, of tables simultaneously by linking the tables as part of a single system. The DBMS helps us manage the tremendous volume and complexity of interrelated data so that we can be sure that a change is automatically made for every instance of that data. For example, if a student or customer address is changed, that change is made through all parts of the system where that data might occur. Using the DBMS prevents unnecessary and problematic redundancies of the data, and the data are kept separate from the programming code in applications. The database need not be changed if a change is made to the code in any of the applications. Consequently, there are numerous advantages to using a database approach to managing organizational data, and these are summarized in Table 3.1. Of course, moving to the database approach comes with some costs and risks that must be recognized and managed (see Table 3.2). Nonetheless, most organizations have embraced the database approach because most feel that the advantages far exceed the risks or costs.

Table 3.1 ***Advantages of the database approach.***

Advantages	Description
Program-data independence	Much easier to evolve and alter software to changing business needs when data and programs are independent.
Minimal data redundancy	Single copy of data assures that data storage is minimized.
Improved data consistency	Eliminating redundancy greatly reduces the opportunities for inconsistency.
Improved data sharing	Easier to deploy and control data access using a centralized system.
Increased productivity of application development	Data standards make it easier to build and modify applications.
Enforcement of standards	A centralized system makes it much easier to enforce standards and rules for data creation, modification, naming, and deletion.
Improved data quality	Centralized control, minimized redundancy, and improved data consistency help to enhance the quality of data.
Improved data accessibility	Centralized system makes it easier to provide access for new personnel within or outside organizational boundaries.
Reduced program maintenance	Information changed in the central database is replicated seamlessly throughout all applications.

Table 3.2 ***Costs and risks of the database approach.***

Cost or Risk	Description
New, specialized personnel	Conversion to the database approach may require hiring additional personnel.
Installation and management cost and complexity	Database approach has higher up-front costs and complexity in order to gain long-term benefits.
Conversion costs	Extensive costs are common when converting existing systems, often referred to as *legacy systems*, to the database approach.
Need for explicit backup and recovery	A shared corporate data resource must be accurate and available at all times.
Organizational conflict	Ownership—creation, naming, modification, and deletion—of data can cause organizational conflict.

Effective Management of Databases

Now that we have outlined why databases are important to organizations, we can talk about how organizational databases can be managed effectively. The ***database administrator (DBA)*** is responsible for the development and management of the organization's databases. The DBA works with the systems analysts (described in Chapter 8) and programmers to design and implement the database. The DBA must also work with users and managers of the firm to establish policies for managing an organization's databases. The DBA implements security features for the database, such as designating who can look at the database and who is authorized to make changes. The DBA should not make these

BRIEF CASE Using Open Source Technology to Support FriendFinder

Whenever you encounter dynamic content on a web page, the content is most likely drawn from some database; for example, online stores use databases to store information about products, prices, and about their customers' contact information. FriendFinder, the largest global online matchmaking network, with more than 20 million registered users, uses MySQL for its more than 2100 databases. These databases, ranging from several megabytes (MB) to many gigabytes (GB) in size, store user profiles and billing information, as well as information about the kind of person the user is looking for. Whenever someone tries to retrieve data about members in a certain region, of a certain gender, or in a certain age range, one or several of these databases are queried to display the member profiles that match the user's request. In addition to providing dynamic content, the databases help to generate information about revenues, sign-in statistics, and even information about how often an individual's profile has been viewed.

As the databases have to handle about 10 000 queries per second, FriendFinder views speed and reliability of the database applications as mission-critical. FriendFinder chose MySQL to deal with the massive amounts of data. While this open-source database software is exceptional in terms of performance and stability, FriendFinder directly benefits from MySQL's lower total cost of ownership, which is due to its lower installation and maintenance costs than for traditional off-the-shelf database products like those sold by software giant Oracle.

Questions

1. How can companies benefit from using database technologies for generating dynamic web content?
2. How does MySQL compare to traditional databases such as Oracle? If you have access to the Internet, compare several databases in terms of performance and total cost of ownership.

Source: Anonymous, "MySQL Database Tracks 20 Million Members of The FriendFinder Network, Saves $2 Million," *MySQL Success Stories* (May 4, 2004), **www.mysql.com/news-and-events/success-stories/friendfinder.html**.

decisions unilaterally; rather, the DBA implements the business decisions made by organizational managers. A good DBA is fundamental to adequately leveraging the investment in database technology.

KEY DATABASE ACTIVITIES

In this section, we describe the key activities involved in the design, creation, use, and management of databases (for more information, see Hoffer, Prescott, and McFadden, 2005). We start by describing how people use databases, beginning with the entry of data.

Entering and Querying Data

DBMS software enables end users to create and manage their own database applications. At some point, data must be entered into the database. A clerk or other data entry professional creates records in the database by entering data. These data may come from telephone conversations, preprinted forms that must be filled out, historical records, or electronic files (see Figure 3.3a). Most applications enable us to use a graphical user interface (GUI) (see Figure 3.3b) to create a ***form***, which typically has blanks where the user can enter the information or make choices, each of which represents an attribute within a database record. This form presents the information to the user in an intuitive way so that the user can easily see and enter the data. The form might be online or printed, and the data could even be entered directly by the customer rather than by a data entry clerk. Forms can be used to add, modify, and delete data from the database. The National Pardon Centre (NPC), based in Montreal, uses web forms to collect data on Canadians wishing to apply for criminal pardons. By using these forms, the firm has cut costs and increased operating efficiencies (see SME Success: NPC Streamlines Data Collection Using Web Forms).

To retrieve information from a database we use a ***query***. ***Structured Query Language (SQL)***

Web Search

Literally thousands of databases are available on the Internet for you to query to find information. Most of these databases are maintained by businesses trying to sell products; however, there are many other interesting databases that you might not be aware of. For example, if you go to **www.ga.gov.au/oracle/nukexp_form.jsp**, you can query nuclear explosions. The database includes information about the location, time, and size of explosions around the world since 1945. Another interesting database is CanLII **www.canlii.org**, maintained by the Federation of Law Societies of Canada. CanLII makes practically all federal and provincial statutes and regulations available in electronic format. Go to one of these sites and report back to your class on what you found when you queried the database.

Application For Employment — Pine Valley Furniture

Personal Information

Name: Date:

Social Insurance Number:

Home Address:

City, Province, Postal Code

Home Phone: Business Phone:

Citizenship:

Position Applying For

Title: Salary Desired:

Referred By: Date Available:

Education

High School (Name, City, Province):

Graduation Date:

Business or Technical School:

Dates Attended: Degree, Major:

Undergraduate University:

Dates Attended: Degree, Major:

Graduate University:

Dates Attended: Degree, Major:

Pine Valley Furniture

References

Form #2019
Last Revised:9/15/04

Figure 3.3a A preprinted form used for gathering information that could be stored in a database.

Source: Benjamin/Cummings Pub. [3.3A]

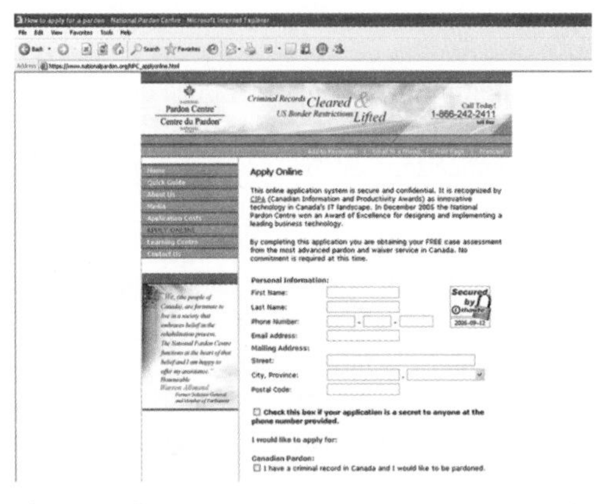

Figure 3.3b The National Pardon Centre uses web forms to collect data that are then saved to a database.

Source: © The National Pardon Centre. The National Pardon Centre provides pardons to remove criminal records. **www.nationalpardon.org/NPC_applyonline.html.**

is the most common language used to interface with databases. Figure 3.4 is an example of an SQL statement used to find students who earned an "A" in a particular course. These grades are sorted by student ID number. Writing SQL statements requires time and practice, especially

```
SELECT DISTINCTROW STUDENT_ID, GRADE
FROM GRADES
WHERE GRADE="A"
ORDER BY STUDENT_ID;
```

Figure 3.4 This sample SQL statement would be used to find students who earned an "A" in a particular course and to sort that information by student ID number.

when you are dealing with complex databases with many entities or when you are writing complex queries with multiple integrated criteria—such as adding numbers while sorting on two different attributes. Many DBMS packages have a simpler way of interfacing with the databases—using a concept called ***query by example (QBE)***. QBE capabilities in a database enable us to fill out a grid, or template, in order to construct a sample or description of the data we would like to see. Modern DBMS packages, such as Microsoft Access, let us take advantage of the drag-and-drop features of a GUI to create a query quickly and easily. Conducting queries in this manner is much easier than typing the corresponding SQL commands. In Figure 3.5 on page 82, we provide an example of the QBE grid from Microsoft Access's desktop DBMS package.

Creating Database Reports

DBMS packages include a report generation feature. A ***report*** is a compilation of data from the database that is organized and produced in printed format. Reports are typically produced on paper, but they can be presented to users on-screen as well. ***Report generators*** retrieve data from the database and manipulate (aggregate, transform, or group) and display it in a useful format (see Figure 3.6 on page 82).

An example of a report is a quarterly sales report for a restaurant. Adding the daily sales totals, grouping them into quarterly totals, and displaying the results in a table of totals creates a quarterly sales report. Reports are not limited to text and numbers. Report writers enable us to create reports using any data in the databases at whatever level we choose. For example, we could add to the restaurant report breakdowns of the data that show the average daily sales totals by days of the week. We could also show the quarterly sales totals in a bar chart, as shown in Figure 3.7 on page 82. Each of these reports could be presented to the user either on paper or online. We could create

SME SUCCESS

National Pardon Centre Streamlines Data Collection Using Web Forms

The NPC is a Montreal-based nonprofit organization that assists individuals with Canadian pardon applications. A pardon granted by the Canadian government removes the criminal record from an individual who has reformed his or her behaviour. In addition, the NPC processes U.S. entry waiver applications for people who wish to cross the U.S. border without risk of refusal.

Since 2001, the United States has tightened border restrictions and increased scrutiny of visitors attempting to enter the country. The F.B.I. can now legally gather information from R.C.M.P. databases without request. This means that U.S. border guards can type a name into their computer system to retrieve any criminal file the R.C.M.P. has in its database. Any individual with a record of a criminal offence is barred by law from entering the United States. Options are few: avoid the border completely or apply for a U.S. entry waiver.

Understandably, demand for the NPC's services greatly increased. Consequently, the company increased full-time staff to seven from the original two. Even with this increase, the NPC was having trouble keeping up with demand and decided to implement an interactive online system that closely conformed to the needs of users. The system collected all the required information from applicants using web-based forms on its site: **www.nationalpardon.org.** Administrators then completed and processed internal documents and sent instructions relevant to each client's needs. If a prospective client did not respond within the requisite time period, the system automatically generated e-mail reminders. Furthermore, all client-targeted features of the system were provided in both English and French.

The site resulted in a 400 percent a month increase in prospect inquiries, and client acquisitions increased to between 200 and 250 a month from 20 to 50. Furthermore, the web system resulted in a reduction in paper and stationery costs of 35 percent.

"Once we had established that the service could be offered so effectively with an IT solution, it was the people involved in the project that really made it work," explains Michael Ashby, co-director of NPC. "On the design side in Montreal, we had a very passionate group who believed that it was the right way to take the company. And on the technical side, we were able to find a very good web solutions provider who worked hard with us and provided excellent database and programming solutions. It was ultimately the result of a very good team effort."

Questions

1. The IT solution described in the case clearly improved the efficiency of the data collection process for the NPC, but can you think of any additional benefits for clients?
2. How could the NPC use database technologies to make its business processes even more efficient?

Source: Adapted from the Canadian Information Productivity Awards, 2005, **www.cipa.com/award_winners/winners_05/NationalPardonCentre.html**.

automatic links between the underlying sales data located in the database and the attributes on the report in which the underlying data is used so that the reports could be updated automatically.

Database Design

The best database in the world is no better than the data it holds. Conversely, all the data in the world will do you no good if they are not organized in a manner in which there are few or no redundancies and in which you can retrieve, analyze, and understand them. The two key elements of an organizational database are the data and the structure of that data. Let us refer back to the library example in Figure 3.1 to understand the structure of data. We know that we can find books in the library by using a card catalogue. A card catalogue is a structure for finding books. Each book has three cards, one each for the title, the author, and the subject. These classifications—title, author, and subject—are a model, or representation, of the data in this system. Likewise, we must have a data model for databases. A ***data model*** is a map or diagram that represents entities and their relationships.

Much of the work of creating an effective organizational database is in the modelling. If the model is not accurate, the database will not be effective. A poor data model will result in

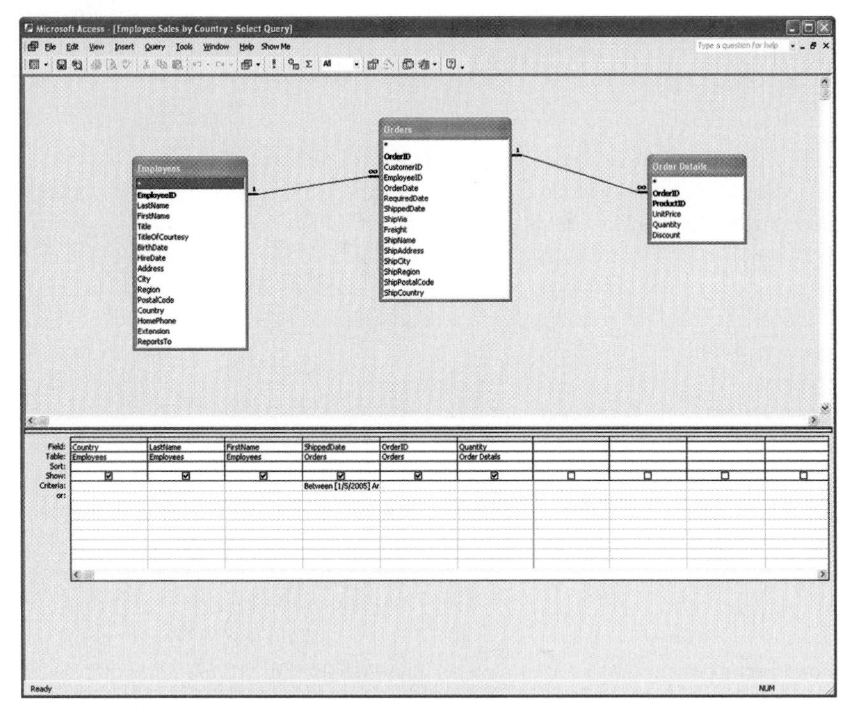

Figure 3.5 Query by example allows you to fill out a form to define what information you want to see.

Figure 3.6 Databases help to organize vast quantities of information.

data that are inaccurate, redundant, or difficult to search. If the database is relatively small, the effects of a poor design might not be too severe. A corporate database, however, contains many entities, perhaps hundreds or thousands. In this case, the implications of a poor data model can be catastrophic. A poorly organized database is difficult to maintain and process—thus defeating the purpose of having a database management system in the first place. Undoubtedly, your school maintains databases with a variety of entity types—for example, students and grades—with both of these entities having several attributes. Attributes of a Student entity might be Student ID, Name, Campus Address, Major, and Phone. Attributes of a Grades entity might include Student ID, Course ID, Section Number, Term, and Grade. (See Figure 3.8.)

For the DBMS to distinguish between records correctly, each instance of an entity must have one unique identifier. For example, each student has a unique Student ID. Note that using the student name, or most other attributes, would not be adequate because students may have the exact same name, live at the same address, or have the same phone number. Consequently, when designing a database, we must always create and use a unique identifier, called a ***primary key***, for each type of entity, to store and retrieve data accurately. In some instances, the primary key can also be a combination of two or more attributes, in which case it is called a ***combination primary key***. An example of this is the Grades entity shown in Figure 3.8, where the combination of Student ID, Course ID, Section Number, and Term uniquely refers to the grade of an individual student, in a particular class (section number), from a particular term. Attributes not used as the primary key can be referred to as ***secondary keys*** when they are used to identify one or more records within a table that share a common value. For example, a secondary key in the Student entity shown in Figure 3.8 would be Major when used to find all students who share a particular major.

Associations

To retrieve information from a database, it is necessary to associate or relate information

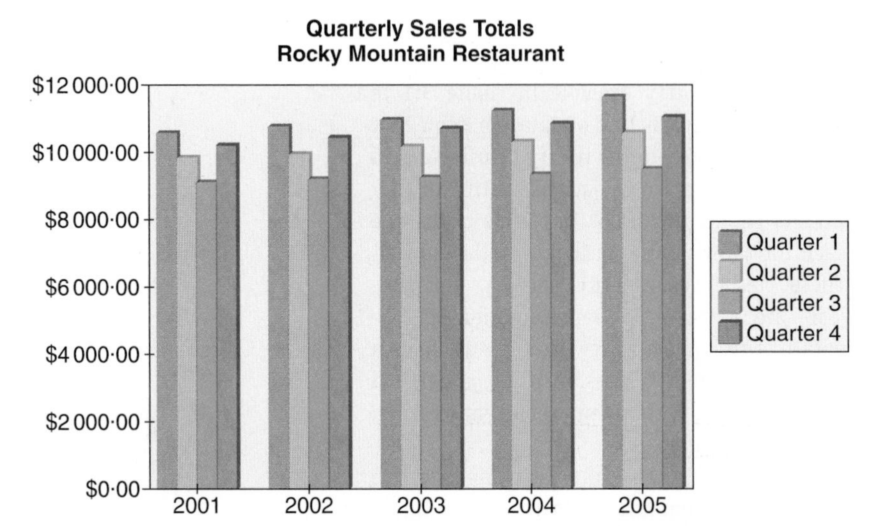

Figure 3.7 The quarterly sales report could show either text and numbers or a bar chart and could include the level of detail captured by the database data.

CANADIAN NETSTATS

Searching for the Next RIM

Who will be the next Nortel or Research in Motion in Canada? The following table lists some of the "up and coming" Canadian IT firms (Table 3.3). These companies operate in diverse markets including hardware, software, database, and telecommunications. Most of these firms are in high-tech clusters around Ottawa and Toronto, although a few are located in the west. If history is to be a guide, only a few of these firms will succeed, while most will fail. Some may even have disappeared by the time you read this chapter!

Table 3.3 *Top 15 "up and coming" Canadian IT firms.*

Company	Location	Year	Website	Area
Advanced IO Systems	Vancouver	2004	www.advancedio.com	Telecom
Apption Software	Ottawa	2004	www.apption.com	Software
Big Blue Bubble	London	2004	www.bigbluebubble.com	Video game
BlueC 802	Kitchner	2003	www.bluec802.com	Telecom
BOLDstreet	Ottawa	2002	www.boldstreet.com	Wireless
Clay Tablet Tech.	Toronto	2005	www.clay-tablet.com	Software
Eightfold Technologies	Ottawa	2003	www.eightfoldtech.com	Database
Elluminate	Calgary	2002	www.elluminate.com	Software
Fortiva	Toronto	2003	www.fortiva.com	Storage
Genex Systems	Toronto	2002	www.genexgroup.com	IS personnel
How2Share Tech.	Victoria	2002	www.pixpo.com	Publishing
Iotum	Ottawa	2003	www.iotum.com	Telecom
IPSS	Ottawa	2002	www.ipss.com	Security
Liquid Computing	Ottawa	2003	www.liquidcomputing.com	Hardware
MakePlain	Toronto	2003	www.makeplain.com	Database

Source: *Backbone* magazine (March/April, 2006).

from separate tables. The three types of associations among entities are one-to-one, one-to-many, and many-to-many. Table 3.4 summarizes each of these three associations and shows how they should be handled in database design for a hockey league.

To understand how associations work, consider Figure 3.9, which shows four tables—Home Rink, Team, Player, and Games—for keeping track of the information for a hockey league. The Home Rink table lists the Rink ID, Rink Name, Capacity, and Location, with the primary key underlined. The Team table contains two attributes, Team ID and Team Name, but nothing about the rink where the team plays. If we wanted to have such information, we could gain it only by making an association between the Home Rink and Team tables. For example, if each team has only one home rink, and each home Rink has only one team, we have a one-to-one relationship between the team and the home rink entities. In situations in which we have one-to-one relationships between entities, we place the primary key from one table in the table for the other entity and refer to this attribute as a ***foreign key***. In other words, a foreign key refers to an attribute that appears as a non-primary key attribute in one entity and as a primary key attribute (or part of a primary key) in another entity. By sharing this common—but unique—value, entities can be linked, or associated, together. We can choose in which of these tables to place the foreign key of the other. After adding the primary key of the Home Rink entity to the Team entity, we can

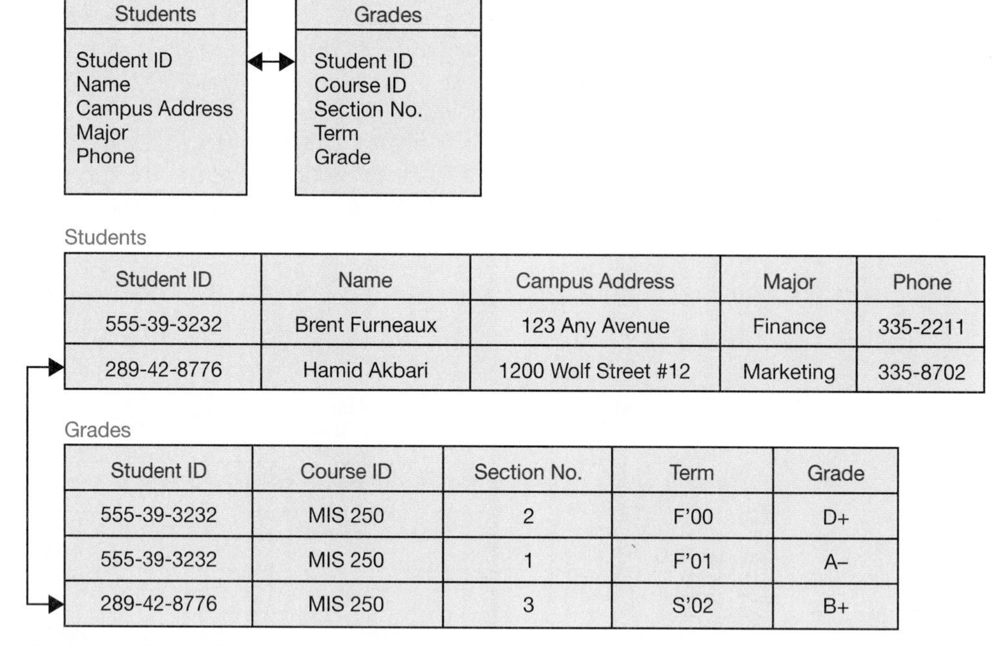

Students

Student ID	Name	Campus Address	Major	Phone
555-39-3232	Brent Furneaux	123 Any Avenue	Finance	335-2211
289-42-8776	Hamid Akbari	1200 Wolf Street #12	Marketing	335-8702

Grades

Student ID	Course ID	Section No.	Term	Grade
555-39-3232	MIS 250	2	F'00	D+
555-39-3232	MIS 250	1	F'01	A–
289-42-8776	MIS 250	3	S'02	B+

Figure 3.8 The attributes for and links between two entities—students and grades.

identify which rink is the home for a particular team and find all the details about that rink (see section A in Figure 3.10).

When we find a one-to-many relationship—for example, each player plays for only one team, but each team has many players—we place the primary key from the entity on the one side of the relationship, the Team entity, as a foreign key in the table for the entity on the many side of the relationship, the Player entity (see section B in Figure 3.10). In essence, we take from the one and give to the many, a Robin Hood strategy.

When we find a many-to-many relationship (e.g., each player plays in many games, and each game has many players), we create a third, new entity—in this case, the Player Statistics entity and corresponding table. We then place the primary keys from each of the original entities together into the third, new table as a new, combination primary key (see section C in Figure 3.10).

Home Rink

Rink ID	Rink Name	Capacity	Location

Team

Team ID	Team Name

Player

Player ID	Player Name	Position

Games

Team ID (1)	Team ID (2)	Date	Final Score

Figure 3.9 Tables used for storing information about several hockey teams, with no attributes added so that associations cannot be made.

You may have noticed that by placing the primary key from one entity in the table of another entity, we are creating a bit of redundancy. We are repeating the data in different places. We are willing to live with this bit of redundancy, however, because it enables us to keep track of the interrelationships among the many pieces of important organizational data that are stored in different tables. By keeping track of these relationships, we can quickly answer questions such as, "Which players on the Canucks played in the game on February 16 and scored more than 10 points?" In a business setting, the question might be, "Which customers purchased the 2007 forest green Ford Escape from Henry Kim at the Celtic Motors Ford dealership in Antigonish, Nova Scotia, during the first quarter of 2007, and how much did each pay?" This kind of question would be useful in calculating the bonus money Henry should receive for that quarter, or in the event of a manufacturer's recall of those specific vehicles.

Entity-Relationship Diagramming

A diagramming technique that creates an ***entity-relationship diagram (ERD)*** is commonly used when designing databases, especially when showing associations between entities. To create

Relationship	Example	Instructions
One-to-One	Each team has only one home, and each home has only one team.	Place the primary key from each table in the table for the other entity as a foreign key.
One-to-Many	Each player is on only one team, but each team has many players.	Place the primary key from the entity on the one side of the relationship as a foreign key in the table for the entity on the many side of the relationship.
Many-to-Many	Each player participates in games, and each game has many players.	Create a third entity/table and place the primary keys from each of the original entities together in the third table as a combination primary key.

Table 3.4 ***Rules for expressing associations among entities and their corresponding data structures.***

an ERD, you draw entities as boxes and draw lines between entities to show relationships. Each relationship can be labelled on the diagram to give additional meaning to the diagram. For example, Figure 3.11 shows an ERD for the hockey league data previously discussed. From this diagram, you can see the following associations:

- Each Home Rink has a Team.
- Each Team has Players.
- Each Team participates in Games.
- For each Player and Game there are Game Statistics.

When you are designing a complex database, with numerous entities and relationships, ERDs are very useful. They allow the designer to talk with people throughout the organization to make sure that all entities and relationships have been found.

The Relational Model

Now that we have discussed data, data models, and the storage of data, we need a mechanism for joining entities that have natural relationships with one another. For example, there are several relationships among the following four entities—students, instructors, classes, and grades. Students are enrolled in multiple classes. Likewise, instructors teach multiple classes and have many students in their classes in a semester. It is important to keep track of these relationships. We might, for example, want to know which courses a student is enrolled in so that we can notify her instructors that she will miss courses because of an illness. The primary DBMS approach, or model, for keeping track of these relationships among data entities is the relational model. Other models—the hierarchical, network, and object-oriented models—are also used to join entities with commercial DBMSs, but this is beyond the scope of our discussion (see Hoffer, Prescott, and McFadden, 2005).

The most common DBMS approach in use today is the ***relational database model***. A DBMS package using this approach is referred to as a relational DBMS, or RDBMS. With this approach, the DBMS views and presents entities as two-dimensional tables, with records as rows and attributes as columns. Tables can be joined when there are common columns in the tables. The uniqueness of the primary key, as mentioned earlier, tells the DBMS which records should be joined with others in the corresponding tables. This structure supports very powerful data manipulation capabilities and linking of interrelated data. Database files in the relational model are three-dimensional: a database has rows (one dimension) and columns (a second dimension) and can contain a row of data

Web Search

Using one or more search engines, research the origins of the entity-relationship diagramming notation. Who invented this notation and when? See if you can find an answer to this question at **www.csc.lsu.edu/~chen/chen.html**. How many different versions of the notation can you find? If you search an entity relationship or variations of it, you will likely find URLs to many class lecture notes. See how many different ways instructors draw ERDs. Why are there several notations rather than one international standard notation? Write a report of your findings to submit to your instructor.

A. One-to-one relationship: Each team has only one home rink, and each home rink has only one team.

Team

Team ID	Team Name	*Rink ID*

B. One-to-many relationship: Each player is on only one team, but each team has many players.

Player

Player ID	Player Name	Position	*Team ID*

C. Many-to-many relationship: Each player participates in many games, and each game has many players.

Player Statistics

Team 1	*Team 2*	*Date*	*Player ID*	Points	Minutes	Fouls

Figure 3.10 Tables used for storing information about several hockey teams, with attributes added in order to make associations.

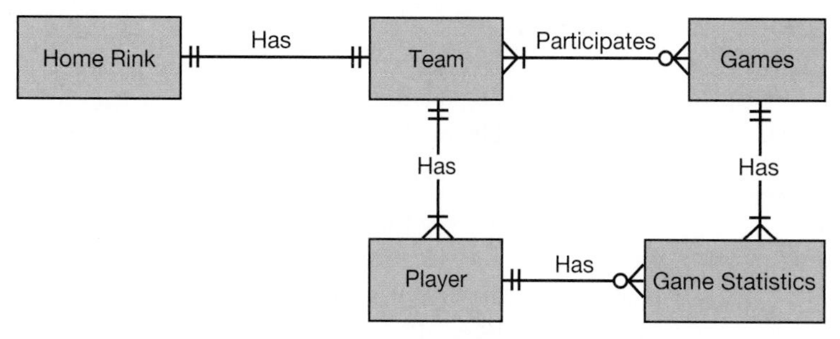

Figure 3.11 An entity-relationship diagram showing the relationships between entities in a hockey league database.

in common with another file (a third dimension). This three-dimensional database is potentially much more powerful and useful than traditional, two-dimensional, "flat file" databases (see Figure 3.12).

A good relational database design eliminates unnecessary data duplications and is easy to maintain. To design a database with clear, non-redundant relationships, you perform a process called normalization.

Normalization

To be effective, databases must be efficient. Developed in the 1970s, ***normalization*** is a technique to make complex databases more efficient and more easily handled by the DBMS (Date, 1995). To understand the normalization process, let us return to the scenario in the beginning of this chapter. Think about your report card. It looks like nearly any other form or invoice. Your personal information is usually at the top, and each of your classes is listed, along with an instructor, a class day and time, the number of credit hours, and a location. Now think about how these data are stored in a database. Imagine that this database is organized so that in each row of the database, the student's identification number is listed on the far left. To the right of the student ID are the student's name, local address, major, phone number, course and instructor information, and a final course grade (see Figure 3.13). Notice that there are redundant data for students, courses, and instructors in each row of this database. This redundancy means that this database is not well organized. If, for example, we want to change the phone number of an instructor who has hundreds of students, we have to change this number hundreds of times.

Elimination of data redundancy is a major goal and benefit of using data normalization techniques. After the normalization process, the student data is organized into five separate tables (see Figure 3.14). This reorganization helps simplify the ongoing use and maintenance of the database and any associated analysis programs.

Department Records

Department No	Dept Name	Location	Dean
Dept A			
Dept B			
Dept C			

Instructor Records

Instructor No	Inst Name	Title	Salary	Dept No
Inst 1				
Inst 2				
Inst 3				
Inst 4				

Figure 3.12 With the relational model, we represent these two entities, department and instructor, as two separate tables and capture the relationship between them with a common column in each table.

Data Dictionary

Each attribute in the database needs to be of a certain type. For example, an attribute may contain text, numbers, or dates. This ***data type*** helps the DBMS organize and sort the data, complete calculations, and allocate storage space.

Once the data model is created, a format is needed to enter the data in the database. A ***data dictionary*** is a document that database designers prepare to help individuals enter data. The data dictionary explains several pieces of information for each attribute, such as its name, whether or not it is a key or part of a key, the type of data expected (dates, alphanumeric, numbers, and so on), and valid values. Data dictionaries can include information such as why the data item is needed, how often it should be updated, and on which forms and reports the data appears.

Data dictionaries can be used to enforce business rules. ***Business rules***, such as who has authority to update a piece of data, are captured by the designers of the database and included in the data dictionary to prevent illegal or illogical entries from entering the database. For example, designers of a warehouse database could capture a rule in the data dictionary to prevent invalid ship dates from being entered into the database.

Microsoft Access - [Student_Course_Grades : Table]

ID	Student ID	Student Name	Campus Address	Major	Phone	Course ID	Course Title	Instructor Nar	Instructor Loc	Instructor Ph	Term	Grade
1	A121	Joy Egbert	100 N. State Street	MIS	555-7771	MIS 350	Intro. MIS	Hess	T240C	555-2222	F'04	A
2	A121	Joy Egbert	100 N. State Street	MIS	555-7771	MIS 372	Database	Sarker	T240F	555-2224	F'04	B
3	A121	Joy Egbert	100 N. State Street	MIS	555-7771	MIS 375	Elec. Comm.	Wells	T240D	555-2228	F'04	B+
4	A121	Joy Egbert	100 N. State Street	MIS	555-7771	MIS 426	Strategic MIS	Datta	T240E	555-2227	F'04	A-
5	A121	Joy Egbert	100 N. State Street	MIS	555-7771	MIS 374	Telecomm	Marrett	T240A	555-2221	F'04	C+
6	A123	Larry Mueller	123 S. State Street	MIS	555-1235	MIS 350	Intro. MIS	Hess	T240C	555-2222	F'04	A
7	A123	Larry Mueller	123 S. State Street	MIS	555-1235	MIS 372	Database	Sarker	T240F	555-2224	F'04	B-
8	A123	Larry Mueller	123 S. State Street	MIS	555-1235	MIS 375	Elec. Comm.	Wells	T240D	555-2228	F'04	A-
9	A123	Larry Mueller	123 S. State Street	MIS	555-1235	MIS 426	Strategic MIS	Datta	T240E	555-2227	F'04	C+
10	A124	Mike Guon	125 S. Elm	MGT	555-2214	MIS 350	Intro. MIS	Hess	T240C	555-2222	F'04	A-
11	A124	Mike Guon	125 S. Elm	MGT	555-2214	MIS 372	Database	Sarker	T240F	555-2224	F'04	A-
12	A124	Mike Guon	125 S. Elm	MGT	555-2214	MIS 375	Elec. Comm.	Wells	T240D	555-2228	F'04	B+
13	A124	Mike Guon	125 S. Elm	MGT	555-2214	MIS 374	Telecomm	Marrett	T240A	555-2221	F'04	B
14	A126	Jackie Judson	224 S. Sixth Street	MKT	555-1245	MIS 350	Intro. MIS	Hess	T240C	555-2222	F'04	A
15	A126	Jackie Judson	224 S. Sixth Street	MKT	555-1245	MIS 372	Database	Sarker	T240F	555-2224	F'04	B+
16	A126	Jackie Judson	224 S. Sixth Street	MKT	555-1245	MIS 375	Elec. Comm.	Wells	T240D	555-2228	F'04	B+
17	A126	Jackie Judson	224 S. Sixth Street	MKT	555-1245	MIS 374	Telecomm	Marrett	T240A	555-2221	F'04	A-
nber)												

Figure 3.13 Database of students, courses, instructors, and grades with redundant data.

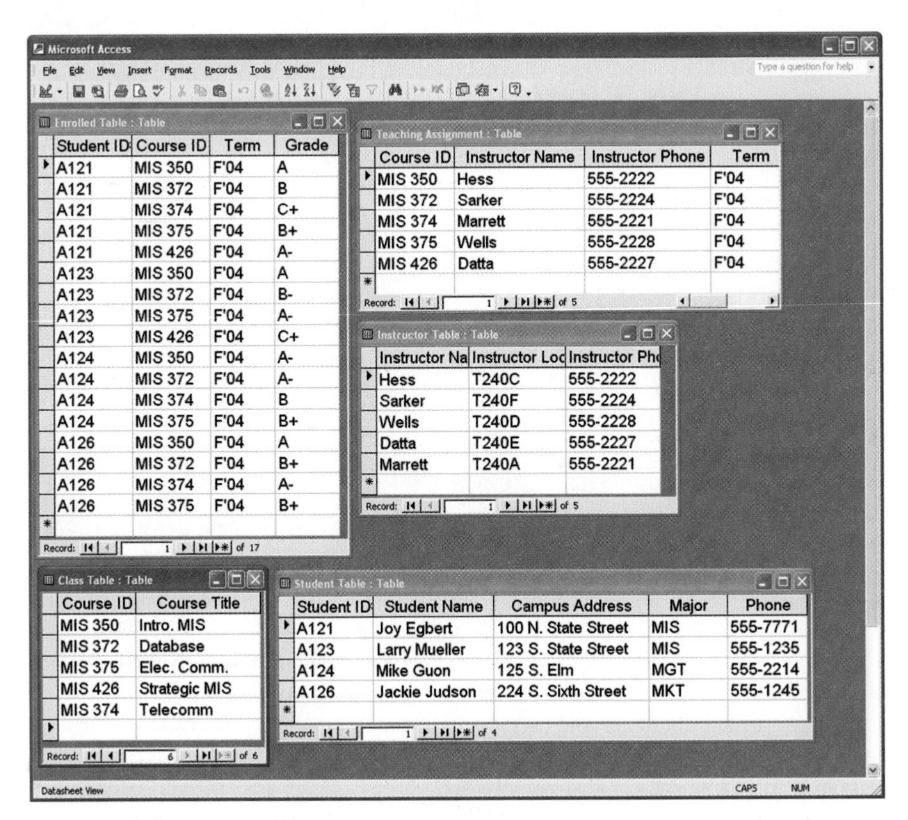

Enrolled Table : Table

Student ID	Course ID	Term	Grade
A121	MIS 350	F'04	A
A121	MIS 372	F'04	B
A121	MIS 374	F'04	C+
A121	MIS 375	F'04	B+
A121	MIS 426	F'04	A-
A123	MIS 350	F'04	A
A123	MIS 372	F'04	B-
A123	MIS 375	F'04	A-
A123	MIS 426	F'04	C+
A124	MIS 350	F'04	A-
A124	MIS 372	F'04	A-
A124	MIS 374	F'04	B
A124	MIS 375	F'04	B+
A126	MIS 350	F'04	A
A126	MIS 372	F'04	B+
A126	MIS 374	F'04	A-
A126	MIS 375	F'04	B+

Teaching Assignment : Table

Course ID	Instructor Name	Instructor Phone	Term
MIS 350	Hess	555-2222	F'04
MIS 372	Sarker	555-2224	F'04
MIS 374	Marrett	555-2221	F'04
MIS 375	Wells	555-2228	F'04
MIS 426	Datta	555-2227	F'04

Instructor Table : Table

Instructor Na	Instructor Loc	Instructor Ph
Hess	T240C	555-2222
Sarker	T240F	555-2224
Wells	T240D	555-2228
Datta	T240E	555-2227
Marrett	T240A	555-2221

Class Table : Table

Course ID	Course Title
MIS 350	Intro. MIS
MIS 372	Database
MIS 375	Elec. Comm.
MIS 426	Strategic MIS
MIS 374	Telecomm

Student Table : Table

Student ID	Student Name	Campus Address	Major	Phone
A121	Joy Egbert	100 N. State Street	MIS	555-7771
A123	Larry Mueller	123 S. State Street	MIS	555-1235
A124	Mike Guon	125 S. Elm	MGT	555-2214
A126	Jackie Judson	224 S. Sixth Street	MKT	555-1245

Figure 3.14 Organization of information on students, courses, instructors, and grades after normalization.

HOW ORGANIZATIONS GET THE MOST FROM THEIR DATA

Modern organizations are said to be drowning in data but starving for information. Despite being a mixed metaphor, this statement seems to portray quite accurately the situation in many organizations. The advent of Internet-based electronic commerce has resulted in the collection of an enormous amount of customer and transactional data. Some of these data are useful, while a large amount of them are not. For example, U.S. websites must be surprised to realize how many Canadians live in the 90210 zip code! Of course, Canadians frequently use this code as many web forms are not set up to accept Canadian postal codes, and it is the only zip code they are familiar with. How this data is collected, stored, and manipulated is a significant factor influencing the success of a commercial Internet website. In this section, we discuss how organizations are getting the most from their data.

Linking Website Applications to Organizational Databases

A recent database development is the creation of links between sites on the web and organizational databases. For example, many companies

WHEN THINGS GO WRONG

Database Requests Cause the Internet to Crash

Whenever you're shopping on the web, you're probably interacting with a database at some point, whether you're aware of it or not. Usually, e-commerce sites store product, customer, or order information in databases. As you will learn in Chapter 4, the major protocol of the Internet is TCP/IP (Transmission Control Protocol/Internet Protocol), which handles, for example, website requests or e-mail traffic. Databases, however, make extensive use of UDP (User Datagram Protocol) packets, which are smaller than TCP packets, for purposes such as finding the right database on a company's database server. While the use of these UDP packets enables you to interact with Amazon.ca, Gap.com, or any other e-tailer, malicious UDPs nearly caused the Internet to crash in early 2003.

A worm called Slammer used a single UDP packet to attack a server running an SQL database by using a security hole in Microsoft's SQL Server software. A worm is a piece of malicious code that replicates and sends itself across a network, crowding out legitimate traffic. At the SQL server, the code instructed the computer to randomly generate IP (Internet Protocol) addresses of other computers and send out new Slammer packets. Unfortunately, the same security hole existed in other Microsoft products as well, making these vulnerable to the attack and helping the Slammer worm to replicate at an ever-increasing speed, as every infected computer immediately started reproducing the worm. A home PC could send out hundreds of copies of the Slammer worm each second via a broadband connection. For companies, this number could be as high as tens of thousands of Slammer packets each second. Even though the UDP packets are very small, the traffic created was more than large parts of the Internet could handle. The Internet was affected all over the world, and the virus even destroyed Seattle's 911 dispatching systems and cell phone services in South Korea, causing a total of $1 billion in damage. While there are many technical solutions that make working with databases fast and easy, just one single UDP packet using one single computer can almost knock out the entire Internet if the hacker knows how to identify and utilize security holes in software packages.

Source: Paul Boutin, "Slammed! An Inside View of the Worm That Crashed the Internet in 15 Minutes," *Wired* (July 11, 2003), **www.wired.com/wired/archive/11.07/slammer.html**.

are enabling users of their website to view product catalogues, check inventory, and place orders—all actions that ultimately read and write to the organizations' databases.

Some Internet electronic commerce applications can receive and process millions of transactions per day. To gain the greatest understaning of customer behaviour and to assure adequate system performance for customers, you must manage online data effectively. For example, Amazon.com is the world's largest bookstore, with more than 2.5 million titles, and is open 24 hours a day, 365 days a year, with customers all over the world ordering books and a broad range of other products. Amazon's servers log millions of transactions per day. Amazon is a vast departure from a traditional physical bookstore. In fact, the largest physical bookstore carries "only" about 170 000 titles, and it would not be economically feasible to build a physical bookstore the size of Amazon; a physical bookstore that carried Amazon's 2.5 million titles would need to be the size of nearly 25 football fields! The key to effectively design an online electronic commerce business is clearly the effective management of online data.

Data Mining

To support more effective information management, many large organizations such as the Bank of Montreal and Canadian Tire are using data mining. ***Data mining*** is a method companies use to sort and analyze information to better understand their customers, products, markets, or any other phase of their business for which data has been captured. With data-mining tools, you can graphically drill down from summary data to more detailed data, sort or extract data based on certain conditions, and perform a variety of statistical analyses, such as trend analysis, correlation analysis, forecasting, and analysis of variance. For example, Anheuser-Busch uses sophisticated data models to track beer purchases and is able to use these data to target promotions to specific neighbourhoods (see Brief Case: Data Keeps the Beer Flowing). The next section describes how data mining is being implemented.

COMING ATTRACTIONS

Digital Handwriting

Scotiabank is using familiar technology in a new way to streamline data capture using digital pens, digital paper, and BlackBerry wireless handheld devices. The bank was looking to improve efficiency in the highly competitive residential mortgage business by improving the application process used by salespeople. Most applications are written using pen and paper, which is not conducive to electronic transfer and analysis. Therefore, Scotiabank developed a program to outfit its salespeople with digital pens and digital paper. Digital paper uses small black dots in mathematical patterns to map handwriting. Ink recognition software converts handwriting to text, while (Internet protocol) IP connectivity transmits the data to a computer.

Furthermore, the handwritten information can be forwarded real time to a Scotiabank server over a secure communications link using BlackBerry devices. "The business process doesn't change," said De Francesco, manager of business innovations with Scotiabank. "All we're doing is digitizing the capture of data." While it's still too early in the process to determine the return on investment, the real benefit will come from salespeople processing more deals than they would have in the past.

Other benefits include cost savings, as it eliminates redundant data entry and scanning, as well as streamlines workflow and automatic backup. Can you think of other applications for digital pens and paper?

Source: Vawn Himmelsbach, "Scotiabank Writes a New Chapter in Data Capture," ITBusiness.ca March (2006), **www.itbusiness.ca/it/client/en/home/News.asp?id=38578**.

Multi-Dimensional Analysis

Online Transaction Processing

Fast customer response is fundamental to having a successful Internet-based business. ***Online transaction processing (OLTP)*** refers to immediate automated responses to the requests of users. OLTP systems are designed specifically to handle multiple concurrent transactions from customers. Typically, these transactions have a fixed number of inputs, such as customer name and address, and a specified output, such as total order price or order tracking number. Common transactions include receiving user information, processing orders, and generating sales receipts. Consequently, OLTP is a big part of interactive electronic commerce applications on the Internet. As customers can be located virtually anywhere in the world, it is critical that transactions be processed efficiently (see Figure 3.15). The speed with which database management systems can process transactions is, therefore, an important design decision when building Internet systems. In addition to which technology is chosen to process the transactions, how the data are organized is a major factor in determining system performance. Although the database operations behind most transactions are relatively simple, designers often spend considerable time making adjustments to the database design in order to "tune" processing for optimal system performance. Once an organization has all these data, it must design ways to gain the greatest value from its collection; online analytical processing is one method being used to analyze these vast amounts of data. OLTP tools can be applied to non-commercial applications as well. For example, the Canadian and U.S. governments can process ID information at border-crossing points on a real-time basis for travellers using the NEXUS program (see Brief Case: How to Cross the U.S. Border in 15 Seconds).

Online Analytical Processing

Online analytical processing (OLAP) refers to graphical software tools that provide complex analysis of data stored in a database. The chief

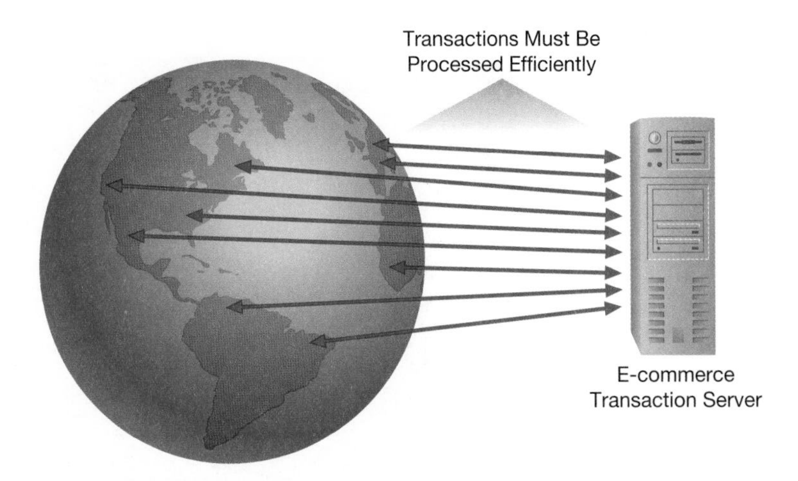

Figure 3.15 Global customers require that online transactions be processed efficiently.

BRIEF CASE

How to Cross the U.S. Border in 15 Seconds

A unified system for Canadian–U.S. commuters is one step closer, as the NEXUS program continues to grow—this time in Quebec. NEXUS, a fast-clearance crossing program operated jointly by the Canada Customs and Revenue Agency (CCRA), Citizenship and Immigration Canada (CIC), and the U.S. Bureau of Customs and Border Protection (CBP), has operated on the Ontario–Michigan and B.C.–Washington borders since mid-2001. New crossings between St.Bernard-de-Lacolle, Quebec, and Champlain, New York, and between Saint-Armand/Philipsburg, Quebec, and Highgate Springs, Vermont, opened in 2004, marking the first time the program has come to Quebec or Vermont.

NEXUS allows regular border-crossers express entry through customs checkpoints on both sides of the border via special lanes designated for cardholders only (see Figure 3.16). The program costs $80 for a 5-year membership. Admission to the program requires screening by both Canadian and U.S. authorities, as well as an in-person interview. "Once the client is really deemed by both countries to be low-risk, then the client is invited to an appointment for an interview. If the interview goes well, then a card is printed out right there on the spot," says Dominique McNeely of the CCRA. Fingerprints are also taken as part of the biometric screening process sometimes used at secondary border checkpoints.

At the moment, the card works somewhat differently on each side of the border. The cards themselves, manufactured by Intermec, contain radio frequency (RF) transmitters, which, in the United States, broadcast to proximity sensors as the cardholder's vehicle approaches a checkpoint. "The antenna captures the particular signal unique to that card, sends a search into the NEXUS database, and a digital photo of the person and various biographical data (citizenship, name, documents that are needed, etc.) are presented on a monitor in the inspection booth," says George St. Clair of the CBP. From that point, the U.S. inspector will make a visual identification between the driver and the cardholder's picture on the screen, ask if the individual has anything to declare, and release him or her. Should a further identification be required, the driver will be sent to secondary screening for a fingerprint ID check. Individuals entering Canada do not yet take advantage of the card's radio technology, and instead simply hand their card to an inspector as one might normally hand over a passport. However, the time saved for NEXUS cardholders is not so much in the actual interview process, but in their ability to utilize special NEXUS lanes that have far shorter lineups than the regular lanes. St. Clair notes that while border wait times are different at different crossings, the time saved by using a NEXUS lane can be significant, depending on where you are. "Waits at the Peace Arch [on the B.C.–Washington] border in the summertime can average 2 hours or more. Cars at the end of the line at 2:00 p.m. on a Wednesday were waiting an hour and 45 minutes. Cars in the NEXUS lane were waiting 15 seconds."

Construction of special approach lanes at sites such as the Peace Arch has further aided NEXUS commuters in staying out of checkpoint gridlock. At present, the NEXUS system is not nationally integrated in the United States, and each checkpoint draws on its own NEXUS member database for that specific site. In 2004, however, both the United States and Canada plan to

Figure 3.16

Source: Hugh Conroy—Whatcom Council of Governments.

launch national enrolment databases that will allow NEXUS members to cross with ease at any NEXUS lane, whether they signed up in Detroit, Michigan, or Fort Erie, Ontario. "NEXUS was designed originally as a commuter system. As a commuter lane, we figured everyone was local. We're realizing now they're not, and we're making amends," says St. Clair. On the Canadian side, plans to roll out a national NEXUS enrolment database will be paired with existing licence plate photography technology.

Questions

1. Does NEXUS sound to you like a good idea? Could it also work for cross-border air traffic?
2. Can you think of other examples of how IT-enabled solutions can facilitate international trade?

Source: Adapted from Liz Clayton, "All Roads Meet at the NEXUS," ITBusiness.ca (December 17, 2003), **www.itbusiness.ca/it/client/en/Home/News.asp?id=11058&bSearch=True.**

component of an OLAP system is the ***OLAP server***, which understands how data are organized in the database and has special functions for analyzing the data. OLAP tools enable users to analyze different dimensions of data, beyond data summary and data aggregations of normal database queries. For example, OLAP can provide time series and trend analysis views of data, data drill-downs to deeper levels of consolidation, and the ability to answer "what if" and "why" questions. An OLAP query for Amazon.com might be: "What would be the effect on profits if wholesale book prices increased by 10 percent and transportation costs decreased by 5 percent?" Managers use the complex query capabilities of an OLAP system to answer questions within executive information systems (EISs), decision support systems (DSSs), and Enterprise Resource Planning (ERP) systems (each of these systems is described in a later chapter). Given the high volume of transactions within Internet-based systems, analysts must

ETHICAL DILEMMA

E-Pending—Where Did They Get My E-mail Address?

You have recently purchased a new jacket from a traditional mail-order catalogue; in order to receive the merchandise, you have provided the store with your name and address. Suddenly, you receive promotional e-mails from that merchant, even though you have never given them your e-mail address.

This practice is known as e-pending, or e-mail appending, as it is sometimes called; companies purchase e-mail lists from third parties and connect them to their customer databases. This way, they are able to send e-mails to customers even though these have not given their addresses to the company. Anti-spam organizations claim that, too easily, companies can mismatch e-mail addresses purchased from questionable organizations with their own customer records; in this case, promotional or even confidential information is sent to the wrong people. In Canada, e-pending is illegal under the Personal Information Protection and Electronic Documents Act (see Chapter 9 for details). However, in the United States, the practice is legal. The U.S. Direct Marketing Association (DMA) has published a set of guidelines for e-pending. One recommendation includes taking "reasonable efforts" to append the "accurate e-mail addresses to the corresponding consumer records." By publishing these guidelines, the DMA effectively approves this practice, as long as marketers follow some basic rules. Although we are protected by law in Canada, we remain susceptible to the marketing practices of U.S. companies.

Many firms claim that because customers have entered into a relationship with the company, the company has the right to extend that relationship, be it via regular mail or via e-mail. How do you feel about receiving e-mails from a company even though you have chosen not to receive e-mails from them? How do you feel about the possibility of a fellow student, who happens to have the same name as you, receiving private information from a company you have purchased something from?

Sources: Anonymous, "The DMA Adopts New E-mail Append Guidelines," *DMA* (February 25, 2004), **www.the-dma.org/cgi/disppressrelease?article=552++++++.**
Amit Asaravala, "Buy Offline, Get Spammed Online," *Wired News* (March 1, 2004), **www.wired.com/news/infostructure/0,1377,62456,00.html**.

provide extensive OLAP capabilities to managers to gain the greatest business value.

Merging Transaction and Analytical Processing

The requirements for designing and supporting transactional and analytical systems are quite different. In a distributed online environment, performing real-time analytical processing diminishes the performance of transaction processing. For example, complex analytical queries from an OLAP system require the locking of data resources for extended periods of execution time, whereas transactional events—data insertions and simple queries from customers—are fast and can often occur simultaneously. Thus, a well-tuned and responsive transaction system may have uneven performance for customers while analytical processing occurs. As a result, many organizations replicate all transactions on a second database server so that analytical processing does not slow customer transaction processing performance. This replication typically occurs in batches during off-peak hours, when site traffic volumes are at a minimum.

Very few people enjoy receiving calls from telemarketers. As a result, the U.S. Congress implemented a "do not call" database that made it illegal for telemarketers to call anyone on the list. The database, which is administered by the Federal Communications Commission (FCC), was officially launched on October 1, 2003, at **www.donotcall.gov**. Not surprisingly, the telemarketing industry was (and is) greatly opposed to this plan because of the increased costs associated with maintaining accurate databases and the fear that a large part of the population would want to be listed in the database. Indeed, in the first 5 months of operation, 55 million Americans registered with the service, which is free of charge. In that same time period, the FCC received 10 000 complaints from consumers and issued eight citations.

Canada has yet to enact similar legislation. For the moment, the only recourse available to Canadians is to register with a "do not contact" service offered by the Canadian Marketing Association (CMA). The CMA is a trade organization for direct marketers in Canada, covering about 80 percent of the industry. Canadians can register for free with the service at **www.cmaconsumersense.org/marketing_lists.cfm**. The CMA distributes the list to its members, who are encouraged to remove registrants from their new-contact databases. The service works for telephone, fax, and mail solicitations. However, as there is no law in place, the effectiveness of this system in Canada is lower than in the United States. Canadian legislators are closely watching the development of the "do not call" list south of the border, so do not be surprised if similar legislation surfaces here.

The systems that are used to interact with customers and run a business in real time are called the ***operational systems***. Examples of operational systems are sales order processing and reservation systems. The systems designed to support decision making based on stable point-in-time or historical data are called ***informational systems***. The key differences between operational and informational systems are shown in Table 3.5. Increasingly, data from informational systems are being consolidated with other organizational data into a comprehensive data warehouse, where OLAP tools can be used to extract the greatest and broadest understanding from the data.

Data Warehousing

Large organizations such as Wal-Mart, The Bay, and Sears have built ***data warehouses***, which integrate multiple large databases and other information sources into a single repository.

Table 3.5 ***Comparison of operational and informational systems.***

Characteristic	Operational System	Informational System
Primary purpose	Run the business on a current basis	Support managerial decision making
Type of data	Current representation of state of the business	Historical or point-in-time (snapshot)
Primary users	Online customers, clerks, salespersons, administrators	Managers, business analysts, customers (checking status, history)
Scope of usage	Narrow vs. simple updates and queries	Broad vs. complex queries and analysis
Design goal	Performance	Ease of access and use

This repository is suitable for direct querying, analysis, or processing. Much like a physical warehouse for products and components, the data warehouse stores and distributes data on computer-based information systems. The data warehouse is a user's virtual storehouse of valuable data from the organization's disparate information systems and external sources. It supports the online analysis of sales, inventory, and other vital business data that have been culled from operational systems. The purpose of a data warehouse is to put key business information into the hands of decision makers. Table 3.6 lists sample industry uses of data warehouses. Data warehouses often take up terabytes of data and run on fairly powerful mainframe computers. The cost for a data warehouse can range from tens of thousands to millions of dollars. Data conversion costs can add significantly more to the overall cost of ownership.

Data warehouses represent more than just big databases. An organization that successfully deploys a data warehouse has committed to pulling together, integrating, and sharing critical corporate data throughout the firm.

Data Marts

Rather than storing all enterprise data in one data warehouse, many organizations have created multiple data marts, each containing a subset of the data for a single aspect of a company's business—for example, finance, inventory, or personnel. A ***data mart*** is a data warehouse that is limited in scope. It contains selected information from the data warehouse, such that each separate data mart is customized for the decision support applications of a particular end-user group. For example, an organization may have several data marts, such as a marketing data mart or a finance data mart, that are customized for a particular type of user. Data marts have been popular among small and medium-sized businesses and among departments within larger organizations, all of which were previously prohibited from developing their own data warehouses due to the high costs involved.

Table 3.6 ***Sample industry uses of data warehousing (adapted from Boar, 1998).***

Uses of Data Warehousing	Representative Companies
Retail	
Analysis of scanner checkout data	Loblaws
Tracking, analysis, and tuning of sales	Canadian Tire
promotions and coupons	Sears
Inventory analysis and redeployment	Osco/Savon Drugs
Price reduction modelling to "move" the product	Grocery Gateway
Negotiating leverage with suppliers	Chapters/Indigo
Frequent-buyer program management	Air Canada
Profitability analysis	Purolator
Product selections of granular market segmentation	Scotiabank
Telecommunications	
Analysis of the following:	AT&T
Call volumes	Telus
Equipment sales	Nortel
Customer profitability	Bell Canada
Costs	Microcell
Inventory	Telecom Ireland
Purchasing leverage with suppliers	Telecom Italia
Frequent-buyer program management	Primus
Banking and Financing	
Relationship banking	Royal Bank
Cross-segment marketing	Scotiabank
Risk and credit analysis	Bank of Montreal
Merger and acquisition analysis	CIBC
Customer profiles	TD Canada Trust
Branch performance	

Source: Copyright © 1998, NCR Corporation. Used with permission.

For example, Merck-Medco Managed Care is a mail-order business that sells drugs to hospitals and state governments in the United States. Using both data warehouses and data marts, Merck-Medco is mining its data to uncover hidden links between illnesses and known drug treatments, spotting trends that help pinpoint which drugs are the most effective for what types of patients. The results are more effective treatments that are also less costly. Merck-Medco's data-mining project has helped customers save an average of 10–15 percent on prescription costs.

Data marts typically contain tens of GBs of data, as opposed to the hundreds of GBs in data warehouses. Therefore, data marts can be deployed on less powerful hardware. The differences in costs between different types of data marts and data warehouses can be significant. The cost to develop a data mart is typically less than $1 million, while the cost for a data warehouse can exceed $10 million. Clearly, organizations committed to getting the most out of their data must make a large investment in database technology.

Database Challenges

This chapter has shown that databases are a key component of information systems. When utilized successfully, databases can propel a firm to a position of competitive advantage. However, databases can also present numerous challenges to firms. For example, firms often contain multiple databases and the data contained within these systems may be incompatible. This is often the case when new systems are connected to older, legacy systems. There are more than a few sophisticated websites where data has had to be re-entered manually behind the scenes! The problem of multiple systems and data incompatibility spurred the growth of enterprise systems in the 1990s. Enterprise systems will be discussed in depth in Chapter 7.

Another challenge with databases that has come to light recently is data security and privacy. Databases were developed primarily to ensure that data can be stored and retrieved accurately and efficiently. Recent legislation in Canada and elsewhere has placed a priority on keeping data secure and private (see Global Perspective: Transborder Data Security and Privacy). With many older systems, the process of redesigning the database to bring it into line with new standards and regulations is very complex, time consuming, and expensive. Even newer databases may require changes to ensure that the data contained within them is protected from unauthorized access, yet available

GLOBAL PERSPECTIVE

Transborder Data Security and Privacy

Apart from technical and human resource–related challenges, some cultural issues also pose significant challenges for organizations. The most important of these issues is that of the general rules and regulations existing in different nations regarding information systems and transborder data flow. One of the most prominent examples of rules and regulations on transborder data flow is the European Union Data Protection Directive, which went into effect in October 1998. The data protection laws according to this directive limit how personal data may be used within Europe. While some European countries, such as France, have had data protection laws for a long time, the laws passed by the directive are stricter. The Personal Information Protection and Electronic Documents Act (PIPEDA) in Canada contains a set of privacy standards similar to the European directive (see Chapter 9). However, regulations in the United States fall short of the European directive and PIPEDA in a number of respects. For example, unlike the United States, personal data collected in Europe and Canada may only be used for the purposes for which they were collected. For all other purposes, a consent form needs to be obtained from the consumer. Frequent-flyer rewards information, for example, can be associated with a passenger's name but cannot include other information about the passenger. This directive has had severe implications for the airline industry in Europe. Moreover, Article 25 of the directive argues that no personal data can be transferred from Europe to countries that have less stringent privacy policies, including the United States but not Canada. This article has posed challenges for U.S. organizations that conduct business with European companies. There is hope that a single unified treaty on data security and privacy might be developed. In the meantime, organizations will expend considerable resources complying with the different rules in different countries. Refer to Chapter 9 for more extensive coverage of this issue.

to legitimate users. The existence of multiple databases within some firms complicates this process considerably. Chapter 9 contains more information on data security and privacy.

KNOWLEDGE MANAGEMENT

In addition to effectively managing their data resources, organizations must effectively manage their knowledge. In Chapter 1, we outlined the rise of the knowledge worker-professionals who are relatively well educated and who create, modify, and/or synthesize knowledge—and the new economy where organizations must effectively utilize their knowledge to gain a competitive advantage. We also outlined the critical difference between data, information, and knowledge. In this section, we will provide a brief introduction to knowledge management and its significance to today's organizations.

What Is Knowledge Management?

There is no universal agreement on what exactly is meant by the term "knowledge management." In general, however, ***knowledge management*** refers to the processes an organization uses to gain the greatest value from its *knowledge assets.* In Chapter 1, we contrasted data and information as well as knowledge and wisdom. Recall that data are raw material—recorded, unformatted information, such as words or numbers. Information is data that have been formatted and organized in some way so that the result is useful to people. We need knowledge to understand relationships between different pieces of information; wisdom is accumulated knowledge. Consequently, what constitutes ***knowledge assets*** are all the underlying skills, routines, practices, principles, formulas, methods, heuristics, and intuitions, whether explicit or tacit. All databases, manuals, reference works, textbooks, diagrams, displays, computer files, proposals, plans, and any other artifacts in which both facts and procedures are recorded and stored are considered knowledge assets (Winter, 2001). From an organizational point of view, properly used knowledge assets enable an organization to improve its efficiency, effectiveness, and, of course, profitability.

Knowledge assets can be distinguished as being either explicit or tacit (Santosus and Surmacz, 2001). ***Explicit knowledge assets*** reflect anything that can be documented, archived, and codified, often with the help of information systems. Explicit knowledge assets reflect much of what is typically stored in a DBMS. Alternatively, ***tacit knowledge assets*** reflect the processes and procedures that are located in a person's mind on how to effectively perform a particular task. Identifying key tacit knowledge assets and managing these assets so that they are accurate and available to people throughout the organization remains a significant challenge. If employees change jobs or retire, then all those employees' tacit knowledge leaves with them. Organizations such as Halifax-based Coemergence (**www.coemergence.com**) produce software that captures the tacit knowledge resident in a firm's workforce, and makes it widely available as an intangible organizational resource.

Tacit knowledge assets often reflect an organization's ***best practices***—procedures and processes that are widely accepted as being among the most effective and/or efficient. Identifying how to recognize, generate, store, share, and manage this tacit knowledge is the primary objective for deploying a knowledge management system. Consequently, a ***knowledge management system*** is typically not a single technology but is instead a collection of technology-based tools that include communication technologies—for example, e-mail, groupware, instant messaging, and the like—as well as information storage and retrieval systems—for example, a database management system—to enable the generation, storage, sharing, and management of tacit knowledge assets (Malhotra, 2004).

Benefits and Challenges of Knowledge Management Systems

Many potential benefits can come from organizations' effective capturing and utilizing their tacit knowledge assets (Santosus and Surmacz, 2001). For example, innovation and creativity may be enhanced by the free flow of ideas throughout the organization. Also, by widely sharing best practices, organizations should realize improved customer service, shorter product development, and streamlined operations. Enhanced business operations not only will improve the overall organizational performance, but also will enhance employee retention rates by recognizing the value of employees' knowledge and rewarding them for sharing it. Thus, organizations can realize many benefits from the successful deployment of a knowledge management system (see Table 3.7).

Although there are many potential benefits for organizations that effectively deploy knowledge management systems, to do so requires that several substantial challenges be overcome

Table 3.7 ***Benefits and challenges of knowledge management systems.***

Benefits	Challenges
• Enhanced innovation and creativity • Improved customer service, shorter product development, and streamlined operations • Enhanced employee retention • Improved organizational performance	• Getting employee buy-in • Focusing too much on technology • Forgetting the goal • Dealing with knowledge overload and obsolescence

(Santosus and Surmacz, 2001). First, effective deployment requires employees to agree to share their personal tacit knowledge assets and to take extra steps to utilize the system for identifying best practices. Therefore, to encourage employee buy-in and also to enable the sharing of knowledge, organizations must create a culture that values and rewards widespread participation. Second, experience has shown that a successful deployment must first identify what knowledge is needed, why it is needed, and who is likely to have this knowledge. Once an organization understands "why, what, and who," identifying the best technologies for facilitating knowledge exchange is a much easier task. In other words, the best practices for deploying knowledge management systems suggest that organizations save the "how"—that is, what collaboration and storage technologies to use—for last. Third, the successful deployment of a knowledge management system must be linked to a specific business objective. By linking the system to a specific business objective and coupling that with the use of an assessment technique such as return on investment (ROI), an organization can then identify clear costs and benefits and also be sure that the system is providing value in an area that is indeed important to the organization. Fourth, the knowledge management system must be easy to use, not only for putting knowledge in but also for getting knowledge out. Similarly, the system cannot overload users with too much information or with information that is obsolete. Just as physical assets can erode over time, knowledge, too, can become stale and irrelevant. Therefore, an ongoing process of updating, amending, and removing obsolete or irrelevant knowledge must occur or the system will fall into disarray and will not be used. In sum, to gain the greatest benefits from an investment in a knowledge management system, the organization must take care to overcome various challenges (see Table 3.7).

How Organizations Utilize a Knowledge Management System

The people using a knowledge management system will be working in different departments within the organization, doing different functions, and likely be located in different locations around the building, city, or even around the world. Each person—or group of people—can be thought of as a separate island that is set apart from others by geography, job focus, expertise, age, and gender. Often, a person on one island tries to solve a problem that has already been solved by another person located on some other island. Finding this "other" person is often a significant challenge. The goal of a successful knowledge management system is to facilitate the exchange of needed knowledge between these separate islands.

The consultants at Accenture, one of the leading global consulting firms, depend on a knowledge management system on a regular basis. Unless knowledge is captured in a system, the learning of thousands of consultants from tens of thousands of projects worldwide would be lost to the rest of the organization. This system, known as Knowledge Xchange, is an online system, and consultants are required to be connected to the network to access it. From the system, they can access a wealth of information on past projects, processes, methodologies, and current research. Due to the fact that most of the consultants spend much of their time on planes and at hotels, they often run into difficulty in connecting and thus fail to access the knowledge management (KM) system. To add to the complexity, the KM system had grown to over 100 GBs of data, and accessing the database easily and quickly had become a problem. To ease these problems, Accenture's IT staff designed and developed a new application system called Pocket Xchange, which operates on a Microsoft SQL server database and is installed on Microsoft Windows NT server. Pocket Xchange accesses data from a Microsoft Access database using data access objects (DAO) and displays the data in a document view. The Access database is populated with data retrieved from a set of Lotus Notes databases. This application is loaded on the consultants' machines and enables them to access the data without being connected to the network. Some Accenture consultants have reported that the new software has saved them at least as much time as 1 day a week.

BRIEF CASE Data Keeps the Beer Flowing

Whenever you're out to buy some cold beverages, be it beer or bottled water, you might notice that some products are out of stock, whereas others are not. Anheuser-Busch, the market leader in the U.S. domestic beer market, is constantly trying to find out what the customers are buying; to take it a step further, their new data network, BudNET, allows them to find out when the customers are buying, where they are buying, and maybe even why they are buying what they are buying.

Whenever one of Anheuser-Busch's distributors enters a store to check on sales and inventory levels, all kinds of data are recorded into Anheuser-Busch's mobile computing platform. Every night, the data collected by the distributors is sent to Anheuser-Busch's servers, where it is aggregated and analyzed for sales patterns and trends. Equipped with these data, Anheuser-Busch knows exactly which beverages sell best in which packages, combined with which promotions in which areas. This information helps to distribute the products more efficiently and to create better targeted marketing campaigns. Using the store-level data, Anheuser-Busch can target specific neighbourhoods with their promotions or can even create targeted campaigns for individual stores.

Questions

1. How can Anheuser-Busch's data collection efforts help the company to obtain a competitive advantage?
2. Some companies are fairly secretive about their data collection and data-mining efforts, as customers might feel uncomfortable with the fact that their purchasing habits can be tracked. How can a company strike the balance between using these technologies to achieve an advantage over its rivals and not upsetting its customers?

Source: Kevin Kelleher, "66,207,896 Bottles of Beer on the Wall," CNN.com (February 25, 2004), **www.cnn.com/2004/TECH/ptech/02/25/bus2.feat.beer.network/index.html**.

An example of one organization that can be thought of as a group of separate islands is the U.S. Department of Commerce (DOC). The DOC consists of 100 offices in the United States, 150 additional offices in eighty countries worldwide, and a group of 1700 U.S. trade specialists located throughout the world. A key activity of the DOC is to provide counselling and advice to U.S. companies seeking to engage in international trade (Fox, 2004). Because each country has different regulations—as well as different regulations for different categories of products within the same country—finding the right information on how gain access to a particular market, with a particular product, in a particular place, at a particular time is an extremely complex and difficult process. To solve this problem, the DOC has developed a web-based knowledge management system connecting its worldwide offices and trade specialists with companies that desire to conduct international trade. Their knowledge management system facilitates the exchange of critical knowledge when, for example, a company needs to know exactly what paperwork must be filed, when, and with whom in order to do business in a particular country regarding a particular type of product.

Prior to the deployment of the knowledge management system, the DOC faced a challenge that many organizations face: relevant subject area experts are not well known and their knowledge is not well organized, making it extremely difficult for a company to identify whom to contact and what information is required to conduct business in a particular country or to do whatever the organization must do to survive and succeed. Today, companies or individuals seeking help from the DOC simply enter questions into the knowledge management system to retrieve documents on best practices or to direct specific questions to a particular subject area expert. The DOC believes that their knowledge management system is providing a competitive advantage to U.S.-based companies by helping to boost U.S. exports, reduce the current trade deficit, and sustain the United States as a global leader in business innovation. Similar kinds of positive results for deploying a knowledge management system that the DOC is experiencing are also found in countless other organizations, such as Ford Motor Company, Eli Lilly, Wal-Mart, and Dell Computers, who are also rapidly deploying knowledge management systems. We are learning from these deployments

Web Search

Visit MyBoeingFleet at **www.boeing.com/commercial/aviationservices/myboeingfleet/index.htm** and take the guest tour to explore how data and knowledge management technologies are used in the interaction between airplane owners/operators and Boeing. Prepare a presentation highlighting different ways in which databases are used to provide customized information for Boeing's customers.

that all organizations, whether for-profit or nonprofit, struggle to get the right information, to the right person, at the right time. Through the use of a comprehensive strategy for managing knowledge assets, organizations are much more likely to gain a competitive advantage and a positive return on their information systems investments.

CAREER IMPLICATIONS Data and Knowledge Management

For Accounting and Finance

Accounting and finance professionals interact with databases throughout their workday. For example, databases are used to store transactional data, which can be analyzed in a variety of ways to improve the management and control of the organization, such as in invoicing customers, tracking overdue bills, or preparing the necessary tax information at the end of the fiscal year. Managing cash flow and making investments to the most effective utilization of the organization's financial resources is a critically important activity that is largely supported by database systems. If you work in a financial company such as a bank or as an investment broker, you will use databases to speed up the process of determining which customers are credit worthy or to keep track of customers' investment portfolios.

For Operations Management

Operations management professionals utilize database systems for a variety of purposes, such as storing product information, controlling inventory levels, or managing information about suppliers. These databases can be linked to the company's Supply Chain Management (SCM) systems (discussed in Chapter 7) to determine reorder points or optimal inventory levels or to schedule just-in-time deliveries from suppliers. Often, suppliers can connect to companies' inventory databases via an extranet and can replenish the inventory as supplies reach a predetermined level; in this case, the company will not have to worry about the reorder process. It is clear that database management systems have become the heart of most key operations management systems.

For Human Resources Management

Databases are frequently used in human resources management to store pertinent information about employees. To satisfy the reporting requirements of governmental agencies, organizations must keep track of information about salaries and wages, age, gender, race, or job descriptions. Also, because most of the information stored about employees is confidential, human resource management professionals must be highly concerned about protecting these databases from unauthorized access. Furthermore, maintaining the integrity of the data is critical to ensure compliance with governmental reporting requirements, for example, in regard to Equal Employment Opportunity (EEO) regulations. Additionally, to most effectively develop fair and motivating reward systems for employees, organizations use database management systems to carefully track employee performance.

For Marketing

Marketing is an area in organizations where databases are heavily used. To better target individual customers, marketing professionals can use data mining techniques to find out which customers are primary targets for a particular product. Rather than sending out costly promotional material to a large number of potential customers, a company can personalize its promotional campaign to the needs of a particular customer or market segment. This targeting helps to increase the effectiveness and optimize the allotted budget of the marketing campaigns. Similarly, marketing professionals are increasingly using data-mining techniques to analyze which products sell best in which regions, to better identify new product opportunities, and to more effectively target broader marketing promotions.

For Information Systems

Because of the need for database management systems throughout many organizations, ability to apply these technologies is becoming an increasingly valuable skill for information systems professionals. Being able to set up databases in the most efficient and effective way is highly valued. Likewise, given the widespread use of database technologies, providing effective support to system users throughout the organization has become increasingly valuable. Because sometimes mission-critical data are stored in many databases, information systems professionals must be knowledgeable concerning how to merge these data using sophisticated queries or data-mining technologies as well as how to best secure and back up these systems in case of system failure or information loss.

KEY POINTS REVIEW

1. **Describe why databases have become so important to modern organizations.** Databases often house mission-critical organizational data, so proper design and management of the databases is critical. If they are designed and managed well, the databases can be used to transform raw data into information that helps people do their jobs faster, better, and more cheaply, which ultimately helps customers and makes the firm more competitive.
2. **Describe what databases and database management systems are and how they work.** A database is a collection of related data organized in a way that facilitates data searches. A database contains entities, attributes, records, and tables. Entities are things about which we collect data, such as people, courses, customers, or products. Attributes are the individual pieces of information about an entity, such as a person's last name or social security number, which are stored in a database record. A record is the collection of related attributes about an entity; usually, a record is displayed as a database row. A table is a collection of related records about an entity type; each row in the table is a record, and each column is an attribute. A database management system is a software application with which you create, store, organize, and retrieve data from a single database or several databases. Data is typically entered into a database through the use of a specially formatted form. Data is retrieved from a database through the use of queries and reports. The data within a database must be adequately organized so that it is possible to store and retrieve information effectively. The main approach for structuring the relationships among data entities is the relational database model. Normalization is a technique to transform complex databases into a more efficient form, allowing them to be more easily maintained and manipulated.
3. **Explain how organizations are getting the most from their investment in database technologies.** Many organizations are allowing employees and customers to access corporate database management systems via the web. This capability allows greater flexibility and innovative products and services. Data mining is a popular application of database technologies in which information stored in organizational databases, data warehouses, or data marts is sorted and analyzed to improve organizational decision making and performance. A data warehouse is the integration of multiple large databases and other information sources into a single repository or access point that is suitable for direct querying, analysis, or processing. A data mart is a small-scale data warehouse that contains a subset of the data for a single aspect of a company's business—for example, finance, inventory, or personnel.
4. **Describe what is meant by knowledge management and knowledge assets as well as the benefits and challenges of deploying a knowledge management system.** Knowledge management refers to the processes an organization uses to gain the greatest value from its knowledge assets. Knowledge assets include all the underlying skills, routines, practices, principles, formulas, methods, heuristics, and intuitions, whether explicit or tacit; all databases, manuals, reference works, textbooks, diagrams, displays, computer files, proposals, plans, and any other artifacts in which both facts and procedures are recorded and stored. Within a knowledge management context, tacit knowledge assets—those that reflect the processes and procedures that are often located in a person's mind on how to effectively perform a particular task—are what is commonly captured and shared by a knowledge management system. A knowledge management system is typically no single technology, but instead a collection of technology-based tools that include communication technologies as well as information storage and retrieval systems. Effective knowledge management can enhance organizational innovation and creativity, improve customer service, shorten product development, streamline operations, enhance employee retention, and improve organizational performance. To effectively deploy knowledge management systems, employees must support and utilize the system. Additionally, the organization must have a clear goal for the system and must focus on why it is needed. Lastly, the knowledge assets must be current and easy to access to be useful.

KEY TERMS

REVIEW QUESTIONS

1. Explain the difference between a database and a database management system.
2. List some reasons that record keeping with physical filing systems is less efficient than using a database on a computer.
3. Describe how the following terms are related: entity, attribute, record, and table.
4. Compare and contrast the primary key, combination key, and foreign key within an entity.
5. How do Structured Query Language (SQL) and query by example (QBE) relate to each other?
6. What is the purpose of normalization?
7. Explain how organizations are getting the most from their investment in database technologies.
8. How are databases used with a World Wide Web interface? Who has access to the database?
9. Compare and contrast a data warehouse and a data mart.
10. Describe why databases have become so important to modern organizations.
11. Describe what a knowledge management system is and how an organization would use it to be more effective or efficient.
12. Define and contrast what is meant by knowledge asset, explicit knowledge asset, and tacit knowledge asset.

SELF-STUDY QUESTIONS

Visit the Companion Website for this text for additional Self-Study Questions: **www.pearsoned.ca/jessup**.

1. A database comprises __________.
   A. attributes
   B. records
   C. organized data for querying
   D. all of the above
2. A database is used to collect, organize, and query information. Which of the following is least likely to use a database as a fundamental part of their job?
   A. airline reservations agent
   B. university registrar
   C. Social Security Administration
   D. security guard
3. A __________ is a unique identifier that can be a combination of two or more attributes.
   A. secondary key
   B. primary key
   C. tertiary key
   D. elementary key
4. Which of the following is not true in regard to the relational database model?
   A. Entities are viewed as tables, with records as rows and attributes as columns.
   B. Tables use keys and redundant data in different tables to link interrelated data.
   C. Entities are viewed as children of higher-level attributes.
   D. A properly designed table has a unique identifier that may be one or more attributes.
5. Each team has only one home rink, and each home rink has only one team. This is an example of which of the following relationships?
   A. one-to-one
   B. one-to-many
   C. many-to-many
   D. many-to-one
6. Data warehousing refers to __________.
   A. the secure storage of corporate data in a fireproof vault
   B. the integration of multiple large databases into a single repository
   C. a concept that is no longer practical due to the pace of technological change
   D. none of the above
7. Which of the following statements about databases is false?
   A. Databases are becoming more popular.
   B. Minimal planning is required since the software is so advanced.
   C. A data warehouse utilizes a database.
   D. A database administrator is responsible for the development and management of a database.
8. Databases are used for __________.
   A. data mining
   B. data marts
   C. expert systems
   D. all of the above
9. __________ is a technique to make a complex database more efficient by eliminating redundancy.
   A. Data depository
   B. Associating
   C. Normalization
   D. Standardization
10. Which of the following is a document, sometimes published as an online interactive application, prepared by the designers of the database to aid individuals in data entry?
    A. data dictionary
    B. database
    C. normalization
    D. data model

PROBLEMS AND EXERCISES

1. Match the following terms with the appropriate definitions:

_____ Database

_____ Database management system

_____ Data mart

_____ Query by example

_____ Data mining

_____ Data warehouse

_____ Data dictionary

_____ Relational model

_____ Normalization

_____ Knowledge management system

a. A data warehouse that is limited in scope and contains selected information that is customized for the decision support applications of a particular end-user group
b. A collection of technology-based tools that include communication technologies as well as information storage and retrieval systems to enable the generation, storage, sharing, and management of tacit knowledge assets
c. A collection of related data organized in a way that facilitates data searches
d. A method used to sort and analyze information to better understand data captured in normal business activities
e. A software application with which you can create, store, organize, and retrieve data for one or many databases
f. A technique used to simplify complex databases so that they are more efficient and easier to maintain
g. The capability of a DBMS to enable us to request data by simply providing a sample or a description of the types of data we would like to see
h. A DBMS approach in which entities are presented as two-dimensional tables that can be joined together with common columns
i. A single repository that integrates multiple large databases and other information sources
j. A document, sometimes published as an online interactive application, prepared by the designers of the database to aid individuals in data entry

2. You see an announcement for a job as a database administrator for a large corporation but are unclear about what this title means. Research this on the web and obtain a specific job announcement.

3. How and why are organizations without extensive databases falling behind in competitiveness and growth? Is this simply a database problem that can be fixed easily with some software purchases? Search the web for stories or news articles that deal with the issue of staying competitive by successfully managing data. How are these stories similar to each other? How are they different? Prepare a 10-minute presentation to the class on your findings.

4. What are six advantages of databases and three costs or risks of a database system? Why are databases becoming more popular?

5. Why would it matter what data type is used for the attributes within a database? How does this relate to programming? How does this relate to queries and calculations? Does the size of a database matter?

6. Discuss the issue of data accuracy based on what you have learned from this chapter. Does a computer database handle accuracy issues better than a filing system? Who (or what) is ultimately responsible for data accuracy?

7. List three different database software applications. Compare and contrast the advantages and disadvantages, including price, program size, and other pertinent factors.

8. Have several classmates interview database administrators within organizations with which they are familiar. To whom do these people report? How many employees report to these people? Is there a big variance in the responsibilities across organizations? Why or why not?

9. Go to the **ecampus.com** site on the web and search for a couple of textbooks that you either have bought or intend to purchase. What is the selection of books available, and what is the delivery time? Are shipping costs added to the cost of the books? How does this compare with the campus bookstore? Which process is more convenient?

10. Search the web to find examples of data warehouses and data marts. What companies are currently using them? How do they differ in size, implementation time, scope, cost, and so on?

11. Based on your understanding of a primary key and the information in the following sample grades table, determine the best choice of attribute(s) for a primary key.

STUDENT ID	COURSE	GRADE
100013	Visual Programming	A+
000117	Telesystems	A
000117	Introduction to MIS	A

12. Search the web for an organization with a homepage that utilizes a link between the home page and the organization's own database. Describe the data that the browser enters and the organization's possible uses for these data. Can you retrieve company information or can you only send information to the company? How are the data displayed on the home page?

13. Select an organization with which you are familiar that utilizes flat file databases for its database management. Determine whether the organization should move to a relational database. Why would you make this recommendation? Is it feasible to do so? Why or why not?

14. What databases are used at your educational institution? Have you filled out a lot of paperwork that was then entered by someone else? Did you actually do some of the data entry for your account? What kind of information were you able to retrieve about your account? From where was the database administered? Were you able to access it online?

15. For your university, identify several examples of explicit and tacit knowledge assets and rate these assets on their value to the university on a 10-point scale (1 = low value to 10 = high value).

16. Examine your university website to identify examples where a knowledge management system could be used (or is being used) to help provide improved services to students.

APPLICATION EXERCISES

Note: The existing data files referenced in these exercises are available on the Companion Website: **www.pearsoned.ca/jessup**.

Spreadsheet Application: Tracking Student Grades

You have recently landed a job as a teaching assistant for a professor. In your first meeting, the professor learned that you are taking an introductory MIS class. As the professor is not very proficient in using office software tools, he is doing all grade calculations with a calculator and records the students' current grades in a paper grade book. Being familiar with the possibilities of spreadsheet applications, you suggest setting up an electronic grade book to facilitate the grade calculations. Create formulas for 12 fictitious students and enter them into the spreadsheet StudentGrades.csv to calculate the following:

- Student's total points.
- Average points per assignment.
- Average total points.

Use conditional formatting to highlight all students who have less than 400 total points. Finally, sort the students by total points in descending order and print out the spreadsheet.

Database Application: Building a Knowledge Database

You have recently been hired by HospitalityConsult, a medium-sized firm that offers consulting services for the hotel industry. As the company has grown tremendously over the past few years, it has become increasingly difficult to keep track of the areas of expertise of each consultant; often, consultants on assignments waste valuable time trying to find out who in the company possesses the knowledge to solve a particular problem. The director of HospitalityConsult knows that you are proficient in using database software and has asked you to create a knowledge and skills database. The database should contain the following information:

- Employee name and ID.
- Current assignment (Client).
- Knowledge/skills possessed.

Note that multiple employees can be on one assignment, and one employee can be on multiple assignments; also, one employee can have multiple skills and multiple employees can possess the same skill. Once you have created the tables and relationships, (1) enter a few sample data sets, (2) create a query showing all employees together with their assignments, (3) create a query showing all employees along with the skills they possess, and (4) print out the results of the queries. Hint: If you are using Microsoft Access, use the wizard to generate the queries.

ANSWERS TO THE SELF-STUDY QUESTIONS

1. D, p. 77	2. D, p. 76	3. B, p. 82	4. C, p. 85	5. A, p. 83
6. B, p. 92	7. B, pp. 78, 93	8. D, pp. 88, 93	9. C, p. 86	10. A, p. 86

Case *Google Tackles the Enterprise*

Google wants to do for the enterprise what it has done for the Internet. The company has teamed up with the consultancy BearingPoint to make search a more relevant tool for businesses and allow enterprise data to be as accessible as Internet pages. Google's Enterprise division has developed the *Google Search Appliance (GSA)*—which is essentially "Google.com in a box"—and plans to customize it for use in specific vertical markets including pharmaceuticals, banking, brokerage, technology, and aerospace.

BearingPoint is "working with Google to build vertical and specific enterprise applications using the GSA as a platform through their APIs and XML feeds," says Chris Weitz, managing director of BearingPoint's search solutions practice. "We can extend the Google Search Appliance into different areas where the Google search engine cannot crawl . . . such as certain databases, document management systems, etc.," he adds.

The GSA would be able to work with several applications already in many enterprises, including Documentum, Oracle, PeopleSoft, and SAP. To the employees using the GSA, the results look similar to those they might see in an Internet search generated by Google.com. "We think companies ought to have 90-plus percent of their information searchable and accessible through a single search box, much akin to the way Google works on the Web," says Dave Girouard, general manager of Google Enterprise. He adds, "Google is attempting to cash in on its reputation as a starting point for a user session on the public Internet. In the corporate world, search can also be the entry point."

GSA could be a way for corporations to determine how effective they are at disseminating data or information, says Girouard. If the same search term is used over and over by employees but generates few results, managers may want to address why that's the case. GSA may also be able to unearth data that has become buried or lost in certain databases or applications, said Girouard. The degree to which GSA is able to accomplish those tasks "depends on the plug-ins that Google and BearingPoint are building," says Warren Shiau, analyst with the Toronto-based Strategic Counsel. "It's the same playing field for everyone. It depends on how well they have hooks into that data."

Weitz notes that GSA isn't designed to supplant existing data mining or business intelligence tools. But "people with these deep and complex software packages are going to have a lot of competitive pressure," he says. "Rather than expensive or time-consuming or lengthy project implementations, people are starting to use Google. It's considerably less traumatic to use this in the enterprise." At the moment, GSA is more of an adjunct to enterprise software, says Girouard. "I don't see it as a replacement for business intelligence—more like a front door."

Enterprise implementations of GSA are underway in the United States, says Weitz. There is nothing active in Canada currently, but BearingPoint has a presence here and will be offering this service to Canadian clients.

Source: Neil Sutton, "Google Makes a Play for Enterprise Data Management," ITBusiness.ca, February (2006), **www.itbusiness.ca/it/client/en/home/News.asp?id=38391.**

Discussion Questions

1. Why do you think Google is trying to enter the enterprise market?
2. The GSA lacks many of the advanced data analysis and manipulation features common in data mining and data warehousing systems. Why would firms be interested in purchasing the GSA?
3. Why is Google so successful? Does the GSA extend Google's competitive advantage? Is it a good fit with the company's core strengths?

Log on to the Companion Website at www.pearsoned.ca/jessup for an additional case.

Running Case: Connexion by Boeing

Data and Knowledge Management

The air transportation industry has always been about reaction time. Acquiring and utilizing the most accurate and timely information is a key to success. To be most effective, large amounts of data from a variety of sources must be collected, analyzed, and shared in real time, using a variety of data and knowledge management tools. To get the right information from the right person at the right time is a huge challenge, given the variety of people that need timely information to be most effective at their jobs.

For example, pilots must have the most up-to-date information about their aircraft, the weather, and the status of air traffic control to fly as efficiently and safely as possible. Mechanics need to know what condition the airplanes coming to their sites are in and how best to address the problems those airplanes might have. Airline flight operations centres need to know that they will have the aircraft and crew necessary in the right places at the right times for upcoming flights. Ground operations need to know where to bring fuel and catering items to service airplanes as they arrive at their gates. And passengers need to know what they are supposed to do if their flight is delayed or rerouted. The information technology revolution has gone a long way in helping bring all the information generated in the air transport enterprise to bear to increase safety, security, and efficiency. In fact, over the past several years, there have been vast improvements in the collection and dissemination of accurate and timely information throughout the various processes for supporting and operating an airplane. Nevertheless, the current systems and capabilities still have major shortcomings.

Specifically, the airplane itself, the prime generator of revenue and the prime consumer of operating funds, regularly unplugs from the rest of the information enterprise for as much as 14 hours at a time. Pilots have to navigate based on weather reports that are hours old.

Mechanics can't diagnose problems and implement solutions until the airplane is parked at the gate. Airline operations centres don't know whether an aircraft might have a mechanical problem or lack a crew for the next flight until it's time for that next flight. And passengers on delayed or rerouted flights have to scramble to locate new gates or rush to make connections.

Clearly, there are major gains to be made with improved data collection, analysis, and sharing. Because of this opportunity, the Boeing Company recently unveiled its e-Enabled Advantage, an effort to tie the entire air transport system into a seamless network that shares applications and data. As discussed in earlier chapters, e-enabling creates a common onboard information and communication infrastructure for the benefit of passengers, flight and cabin crews, airline operations, system performance, and the overall industry. Indeed, "e-enabled" is one of the concepts addressed in the "E" in the airplane's name. But customers don't have to wait for the 7E7 to take advantage of the e-enabled air transport system. Key e-enabling technologies, such as Connexion by Boeing, the Jeppesen Electronic Flight Bag (EFB), and Airplane Health Management (AHM), are in production today.

To make e-enablement possible, many different data needs have to be satisfied (see figure below). On the flight deck, for example, the Jeppesen EFB gives flight crews a sharper strategic picture of where they are, where they are going, and what waits over the horizon. The EFB offers the most up-to-date navigational information, live weather reports, instant access to flight and aircraft data, airport surface positional awareness, cabin-to-flight-deck surveillance, and more. In the airline operations centre, various systems and data can be integrated to give managers and planners advance knowledge of possible schedule disruptions and a wide range of options to mitigate any problems. For example, each airplane contains an onboard data server that can be coupled with Boeing's Communication Navigation Surveillance/Air Traffic Management applications, various simulation and analysis products, crew management applications, and Boeing's Integrated Airline Operations Center to produce forward-looking plans to maximize operational performance. Likewise, various systems provide flight attendants with access to detailed information on their customers' needs, helping to give passengers a more enjoyable flight. In addition, the airline cabin can be connected to the airline's credit-card verification systems on the ground, freeing flight attendants from having to carry thick wads of cash for beverage service, duty-free shopping, or other transactions. Catering and duty-free inventories will be updated automatically, assuring that airlines can keep control of their stocks, improve oversight and make sure every flight has the cabin items it needs.

The same Connexion technologies that link the airplane to the airline enterprise also deliver real-time, high-speed connectivity directly to the passenger. From the comfort of their seats, passengers can tune in their favourite radio and television programs, follow live sporting events, choose from a list of first-run movies, exchange e-mail and instant messages with family and associates, send and receive documents and files, play video games, or shop for gifts and souvenirs on the Internet. Travel plan alterations—whether due to flight delays or to simple changes in passenger plans—will become less of a disruption when onboard. For example, when disruptions occur, crews will access ground-based information systems to allow passenger service agents to arrange new itineraries and deliver new tickets (and boarding passes) to passengers while en route to a destination.

Boeing's Airplane Health Management (AHM) program takes advantage of high-bandwidth information flow to allow an airline to monitor airframe systems information across the entire fleet in real time. Engineers and maintenance personnel will be able to examine system behaviour while the airplane is in flight, quickly determine whether repairs can be deferred till the next scheduled maintenance, and inform the airline operations centre whether necessary repairs can be completed at the destination without disrupting the flight schedule. In fact, AHM will help determine if a problem is developing over time and allow the airline to fix critical systems before they break, avoiding costly delays and potential catastrophes.

On the ground, Boeing's Wireless Gatelink project will use wireless local area network technology to transmit data throughout an airport environment, enabling instant sharing of data among aircraft, passenger terminals, maintenance operations, baggage handling, ground-support equipment, and more. The e-enabled air transport system is Boeing's vision of a day when the airplane is just another node on an enterprise-wide information network, ensuring that everyone in the system has all the information they need to react at the very best moment.

To satisfy the variety of data requirements, Boeing depends on a variety of different software applications and databases. For example, Connexion uses a combination of systems that were purchased from outside vendors, developed in-house, or developed by outside companies. Connexion's CRM system was developed by one of the industry's leaders, PeopleSoft, while its data mining and data visualization were developed by Informatica and Cognos, both leaders in proving BI solutions (CRM systems are extensively discussed in Chapter 7). In addition to these systems purchased from outside vendors, the unique requirements of Connexion's application necessitated the use of systems developed by Boeing or by Connexion itself. For example, Autometric, a Boeing company, developed the flight visualization tools incorporated in the e-enabled airplane. Connexion also saw the need to develop content management tools, which were used to populate the portal site that airline passengers first see upon accessing the network aboard the airplane. This database-driven application was developed in-house by Connexion's systems developers. Other databases used by Connexion include one containing user information for Connexion's e-update newsletter, billing databases, marketing repositories for user surveys, and a database containing information published on Connexion's website.

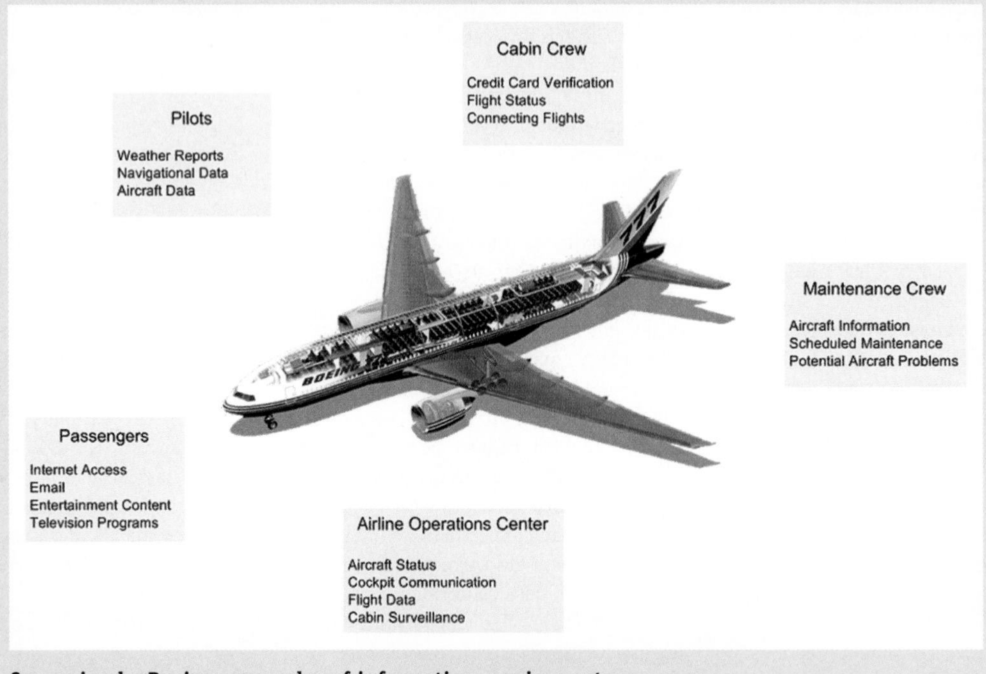

Connexion by Boeing—examples of information requirements.

To facilitate database installation, management, and maintenance, Connexion tried to minimize the number of different database management systems. However, the broad variety of applications from various vendors worked most effectively with different data management systems; therefore, it was not possible to choose a single system from a one vendor. Nonetheless, given the initial success of Connexion's systems to support the application and data needs of a vast number of individuals, the strategy of choosing the best available systems, regardless of the database vendor, appears to be successful.

Source: **www.boeing.com/news/frontiers/archive/2003/august/i_ca1.html**.

Discussion Questions

1. How does Connexion use databases for a competitive advantage?
2. Which other types of data might a company like Connexion want to collect and analyze?
3. How can a company solve the trade-off between trying to minimize the number of database management systems used and fulfilling the DBMS requirements of the different applications?

Preview

Organizations need to bring products to a global market quickly and to be closely integrated with their customers and suppliers. These and related demands have driven the rapid development of telecommunications technologies, particularly the Internet. These technologies enable people and enterprises to share information across time and distance, and they can lower boundaries between markets and cultures. The Internet revolution is changing how we live and work and how we communicate with each other. This chapter introduces key telecommunications applications, particularly how the Internet works and is being used in and across organizations. This discussion provides you with a solid foundation for understanding how organizations use the Internet to connect computers across a room or across the world. In addition, we explain how you can manage the security of computers, information systems, and the critical information they hold. After reading this chapter, you will be able to do the following:

1. Understand the role of telecommunications in organizations.
2. Describe the Internet and how it works.
3. Describe the basic Internet services and the use of the World Wide Web.
4. Explain what is meant by the term "information systems security" and describe various approaches for ensuring information systems security.
5. Describe and explain the differences between cyberwar and cyberterrorism.

Canada Competes!

Organizations and governments worldwide are increasing their spending on broadband wireless technologies. Broadband technologies are those that support the transfer of large amounts of data. The business case for broadband wireless networks is compelling. Wireless broadband networks are cheaper to install than landline networks, as there is no need to install wires on poles or under the ground. Further, network access (including Internet access) can be received anywhere within the coverage area of the wireless network. Firms operating in the wireless broadband sector stand to gain from this growing trend.

A world leader in this area is Redline Communications, based in the Toronto suburb of Markham. Redline designs and manufactures broadband wireless solutions that are based on the WiMax standard. WiMax (also known as 802.16) allows huge amounts of data to be transferred over a wireless network. Traditional WiMax networks have been "point-to-point," meaning that users can receive network access only through a fixed antenna. Emerging WiMax standards, however, support "point-to-multipoint" and mobile broadband network access.

In early 2006, Redline Communications became the first firm in the world to have its products certified by the standards body, the WiMax Forum. It was also named among the 2006 "Best of WiMax World" award program honourees, and the second fastest growing technology company in Canada by the Deloitte Canadian Technology Fast 50 Program. Redline's products have been installed in 75 countries across six continents. Examples of its products in use include the following:

- support for wireless Internet access in Brandon, Manitoba, with winter temperatures reaching –40°C
- support for a country-wide IP network in Saudi Arabia, robust enough to overcome frequent sandstorms
- support for mobile phone networks in mountainous regions of Taiwan and Croatia
- support for city-wide wireless network access in Krakow, Poland
- support for wireless communications links between off-shore Mediterranean oil rigs and on-shore base stations in Egypt

Source: Redline Communications.

Figure 4.1 Telecommunications technologies play a vital role in modern organizations.

Source: © Roger Allyn Lee/Superstock

Telecommunications technologies and the Internet are becoming more and more important in our lives. Understanding how these technologies work and how they can be used for competitive advantage is essential to the success of modern organizations (see Figure 4.1). This chapter begins with a discussion of the critical, expanding role that telecommunications plays in organizations.

THE ROLE OF TELECOMMUNICATIONS AND NETWORKS IN ORGANIZATIONS

People in organizations around the world are finding that telecommunications and networks are highly effective tools for communication, coordination, and collaboration across and among enterprises and people. ***Telecommunications*** refers to the transmission of all forms of information, including digital data, voice, fax, sound, and video, from one location to another over some type of network. A ***network*** is a group of computers and associated peripheral devices connected by a communication channel capable of sharing information and other resources (e.g., a printer) among users. ***Bandwidth***, or the carrying capacity of telecommunications networks, has increased to the point that any digitized data, from photographs, art, and movies to complicated business records, can be quickly transmitted via a network.

Powerful new technologies are giving networks the bandwidth needed to handle rich content, such as movies, medical records, or great works of art. These networks also work at speeds great enough to support interaction between users. The most remarkable feature of networking computers is not that computers can speak to each other, but that the people who use the computers can communicate with each other through their machines. For example, the Province of Ontario is using videoconferencing technology to reduce costs and enhance access to the justice system (see Brief Case: The Criminal Justice Video Network). Just as telephones let users communicate over long and short distances, networked computers allow users to send messages across the office, across town, across the country, or around the world. In Table 4.1 we offer some examples of how digital content and high-powered networks are changing interpersonal telecommunications applications (see Figure 4.2 for a sample interpersonal telecommunications application).

COMMON BUSINESS APPLICATIONS

Today, companies around the world consider networks to be an essential tool for daily business communication. In addition to supporting interpersonal communication, networks support other types of telecommunication used to exchange business information, including electronic business, electronic data interchange, telecommuting, and electronic

Figure 4.2 Telecommuting enables people to work from home, using computing and networking technologies.

Source: © Getty Images, Inc.

Table 4.1 ***Some sample interpersonal uses of telecommunications networks.***

Sample Interpersonal Telecommunications Uses	
E-mail	• The transmission of messages over telecommunications networks • Companies that are fully computerized make extensive use of e-mail because it is fast, flexible, and reliable • Nearly all online services and ISPs offer e-mail, and most also support ***gateways*** so that you can exchange mail with users of other systems • Eliminates "telephone tag" and enables widespread work groups to ignore time zones and office hours
Newsgroups (also called computer-based discussion groups)	• Allow individuals and organizations to participate in discussions on almost any subject • There are thousands of newsgroups, on every topic imaginable • Companies are using discussion groups as an easy way to share information with customers who want to discuss topics such as product applications or customer support
Mailing lists (also known as ***listservs***)	• Enable you to use e-mail to broadcast messages to groups on topics of special interest to you • Lists can be small and regional, or they can include participants from all over the world • Companies often create mailing lists for customers to send a single e-mail message to thousands of customers simultaneously
Instant Messaging (IM, also referred to as real-time messaging or ***Internet Relay Chat (IRC)***)	• Enables you to have conversations with others in real time on the Internet • The process is somewhat like talking on the telephone, although you must type your comments instead of speaking them • You can converse with others as long as they are online and using the same messaging service you are using • Companies are using IM as a way to have interactive conversations with colleagues and customers throughout the world
Facsimile (or "fax")	• Equipment that digitizes images, such as letters, memos, newspaper and magazine articles, photos, contracts, and even handwritten notes, so that they can be transmitted to other fax machines over telephone lines • Receiving fax machine translates the material from digital data back to the original image • Facsimile machines are stand-alone desktop peripherals that send and receive printed information • People often use a PC as a fax machine, where the fax is sent and received with specialized software
Voice mail	• Enables callers to leave voice messages in a voice mailbox, much like leaving a message on an answering machine • Unlike an answering machine, however, voice mail digitizes voice messages so that they can be stored and managed on computers
Videoconferencing	• A combination of software and hardware, including video cameras, microphones, and speakers, allows people in diverse locations to get together online to share information, discuss projects, and conduct business (for example, see Brief Case on the Criminal Justice Video Network) • Frees people from gathering together in one meeting room or travelling across the country to see one another in person • Some videoconferencing systems let remote participants share applications and data and jointly make changes to documents and other information shown on-screen

BRIEF CASE The Criminal Justice Video Network

If you are accused of a crime in Canada, you have the right to have your case heard before a court of law. However, in remote communities, transporting accused persons between correctional facilities and courtrooms for in-person hearings takes considerable time and police resources. There are also increased risks to the public, courts, and corrections personnel from potential escapes and assaults. In remote parts of Northern Ontario, for example, with limited highway access, the average cost of transporting an accused person by plane to a court hearing, accompanied by one or two police officers, is about $1500. In many cases, small communities must send their entire police force to accompany an arrestee. Transportation to and from the courthouse can be difficult on prisoners, too. Typically, a remand appearance before a judicial official takes only a few minutes to complete, but when the accused has to be transported to court to appear, it can take an entire day. The accused is awakened early, misses hot meals and programs, is strip-searched twice, and spends a majority of the day in a court-holding cell, which is often overcrowded.

Justice Technology Services, an IT division within the Ontario Provincial Government, commissioned Montreal-based CGI Group to look at reducing costs through the use of technology. CGI recommended the implementation of a province-wide videoconferencing network for court hearings to create efficiencies in the delivery of justice and improve public safety. Implementation and installation of the videoconferencing network was completed in 2005.

The Criminal Justice Video Network has brought all the justice partners together to create a province-wide network that uses videoconferencing technology to link correctional institutions and policing facilities with Ontario criminal courts. To date, the project has installed 57 videoconferencing units in criminal courts, 52 units in correctional facilities, and 23 units in policing facilities. About one in three transportations are being eliminated by the use of video conferencing technology.

The appearance via video usually takes 2 to 3 minutes to complete. At the scheduled court dial-in time, the accused is escorted to the video suite in the correctional facility. In the courtroom, the presiding judicial official addresses the accused, the Crown, and defence counsel in the usual manner. The accused can be viewed from one of several TV monitors in the courtroom. If a lawyer wishes to speak privately with the accused, he or she can enter a "privacy booth" located in a corner of the courtroom. The judicial official sets the next date to appear and the accused exits the video suite.

Questions

1. Can you foresee any problems or issues that the Criminal Justice Video Network may face? What are they and how could they be solved?
2. There may be limits to the usefulness of technology-mediated interaction, such as videoconferencing. For example, the Criminal Justice Video Network is used only for routine matters and not for more complex applications, such as criminal court cases. Do you think post-secondary education can be effectively delivered through videoconferencing? Would you like to take this course online? Why or why not?

Source: Adapted from the Canadian Information Processing Association, **www.cipa.com/award_winners/winners_05/OntarioMinCommSafetyCorrServ.html.**

funds transfer. In Table 4.2 we briefly describe these and other business examples. (In Chapter 5, "Electronic Business, Intranets, and Extranets," we describe in more detail how businesses use telecommunications networks to conduct business.)

In this section, our aim has been to help you understand how telecommunications and networks are commonly used. In Appendix C, we delve deeper into how underlying telecommunications and networking technologies work and how they have evolved. In the next section, we turn our attention to the Internet, the largest and perhaps most popular telecommunications network application in the world.

THE INTERNET

The name ***Internet*** is derived from the concept of ***internetworking***, which means connecting host computers and their networks together to form even larger networks. The Internet is a large worldwide collection of networks that use a common protocol to communicate with each other.

Table 4.2 ***Some sample business uses of telecommunications networks.***

Sample Business Telecommunications Uses	
Electronic business (EB or e-Business)	• Use the Internet and other computer networks to support a variety of business activities, such as streamlining operations, selling products and providing customer support, and connecting to suppliers • Nearly all business organizations—small and large—now have a presence on the World Wide Web and use the Internet to conduct day-to-day business • Business websites range from simple, just-the-facts pages that resemble printed brochures or data sheets to more sophisticated interactive sites where customers can do everything from ordering products to taking a virtual tour through manufacturing facilities
Electronic Data Interchange (EDI)	• A form of electronic commerce where organizations use telecommunications networks to transact business and thus cut down on paperwork and expenses • Sometimes conducted with private networks rather than on the public Internet • Myriad companies, such as General Motors, Dow Chemicals, and Canadian Tire, transact nearly all their business this way • Commonly used as a way for a company and its suppliers to conduct business
Telecommuting	• Working at home or from another remote location and "commuting" to the office via computing and networking technologies • Useful when the employee has children at home and desires to stay at home with the children yet continue to work • Can enable employees to live where they choose while being employed by a company in a distant location • Can be ideal for disabled and ill employees • Benefits for employers include increased worker satisfaction and productivity and decreased travel and on-site office maintenance costs
Electronic funds transfer (EFT)	• Transfer funds from one financial account to another via computer networks • Common application is sending paycheques electronically, directly from the company into the employee's bank account, thereby saving time and money and providing instant access to the funds • Also often includes authorizing the paying of bills electronically, directly from the bank accounts and/or from third-party bill-pay services • ATMs are another common example of electronic fund transfer; they allow ATM card users to make deposits or withdraw cash quickly from machines placed in handy locations • Companies, banks, and other financial institutions worldwide also use EFT to transfer funds among themselves
Distance learning	• Use telecommunications networks to provide instruction to students who are physically separated from instructors and perhaps from each other • Often includes use of videoconferencing, Internet chatting, and various web-based tools • As computer literacy and the availability of high-speed Internet access continue to increase, distance learning is gaining in popularity and teaching methods are rapidly improving
Telemedicine	• The exchange of medical information, or even the practice of caregiving, from one location to another via a telecommunications network • Enables remote patients to be examined by the best medical doctors, regardless of where the doctors are located

How Did the Internet Get Started?

You can trace the roots of the Internet back to the late 1960s, when the U.S. ***Defense Advanced Research Projects Agency (DARPA)*** began to study ways to interconnect networks of various kinds. This research effort produced ***ARPANET (Advanced Research Projects Agency Network)***, a large wide area network (WAN) that linked many universities and research centres. The first two nodes on ARPANET were the University of California at Los Angeles and the Stanford Research Institute, followed by the University of Utah.

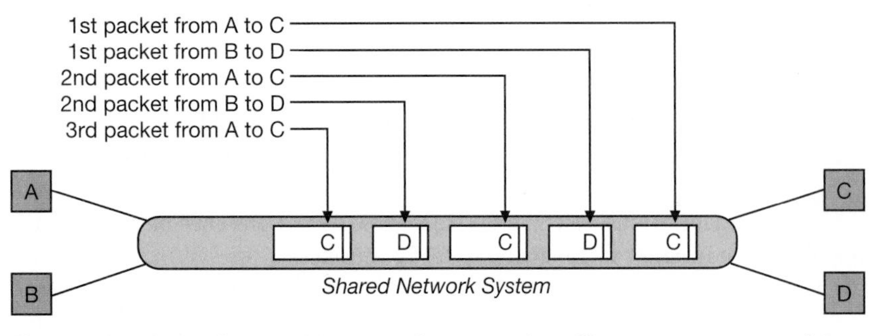

Figure 4.3 Using packet switching to send messages from files on computers A and B to computers C and D.

Comer, Douglas E. *The Internet Book*, 2nd ed. 1997; Prentice Hall.

ARPANET quickly evolved and was combined with other networks. For example, in 1986, the U.S. ***National Science Foundation (NSF)*** initiated the development of the ***National Science Foundation Network (NSFNET)***, which became a major component of the Internet. Other networks throughout the world were interconnected and/or morphed into the growing "Internet." Among these were BITNET, CSNET, NSINET, ESNET, and NORDUNET. Throughout the world, support for the Internet has come from a combination of governments, universities, national and international research organizations, and industry.

The Internet Uses Packet-Switching Technology

The Internet relies on packet-switching technology to deliver data and information across networks. ***Packet switching*** enables millions of users to send large and small chunks of data across the Internet concurrently. Packet switching is based on the concept of turn taking. To minimize delays, network technologies limit the amount of data that a computer can transfer on each turn. Consider a conveyor belt as a comparison. Suppose that the conveyor belt connects a warehouse and a retail store. When a customer places an order, it is sent from the store to the warehouse, where a clerk assembles the items in the order. The items are placed on the conveyor belt and delivered to the customer in the store. In most situations, clerks finish sending items from one order before proceeding to send items from another order. This process works well when orders are small, but when a large order with many items comes in, sharing a conveyor belt can introduce delays for others. Consider waiting in the store for your one item while another order with 50 items is being filled.

Local area networks (LANs), WANs, and the Internet all use packet-switching technologies so that users can share the communication channel and minimize delivery delays. Figure 4.3 illustrates how computers use packet switching. Computer A wants to send a message to computer C; similarly, computer B wants to send a message to computer D. For example, computer A is trying to send an e-mail message to computer C, while computer B is trying to send a word processing file to computer D. The outgoing messages are divided into smaller packets of data, and then each sending computer (A and B) takes turns sending the packets over the ***transmission media***. The incoming packets are reassembled at their respective destinations, using previously identified packet sequence numbers.

For packet switching to work, each packet being sent across a network must be labelled with a header. This header contains the network address of the source (sending computer) and the network address of the destination (receiving computer). Each computer attached to a network has a unique network address. As packets are sent, network hardware detects whether a particular packet is destined for a local machine. Packet-switching systems adapt instantly to changes in network traffic. If only one computer needs to use the network, it can send data continuously. As soon as another computer needs to send data, packet switching, or turn taking, begins. Now, let us see how the Internet handles this packet switching.

Transmission Control Protocol/ Internet Protocol (TCP/IP)

Organizations use diverse network technologies that may or may not be compatible with the technologies of other organizations. Because so many different networks are interconnected nowadays, they must have a common language, or ***protocol***, to communicate. The protocol of the Internet is called ***Transmission Control Protocol/Internet Protocol (TCP/IP)***. The first part, TCP, breaks information into small chunks called data packets and manages the transfer of those packets from computer to computer (via packet switching, as described above). For example, a single document may be broken into several packets, each containing several hundred characters, as well as a destination address, which is the IP part of the protocol. The IP defines how a data packet must be formed and to where a router must forward each packet. Packets travel independently to their destination, sometimes following different paths and arriving out of order. The destination computer reassembles all the packets based on their identification and sequencing information. Together, TCP and IP provide a reliable and efficient way to send data across the Internet.

A data packet that conforms to the IP specification is called an ***IP datagram***. Datagram routing and delivery are possible because, as previously mentioned, every computer and router connected to the Internet is assigned a unique IP address. When an organization connects to the Internet, it obtains a set of IP addresses that it can assign to its computers. TCP helps IP guarantee the delivery of datagrams by performing three main tasks. First, TCP automatically checks for datagrams that may have been lost en route from their source to their destination. Second, TCP collects the incoming datagrams and puts them in the correct order to recreate the original message. Finally, TCP discards any duplicate copies of datagrams that may have been created by network hardware.

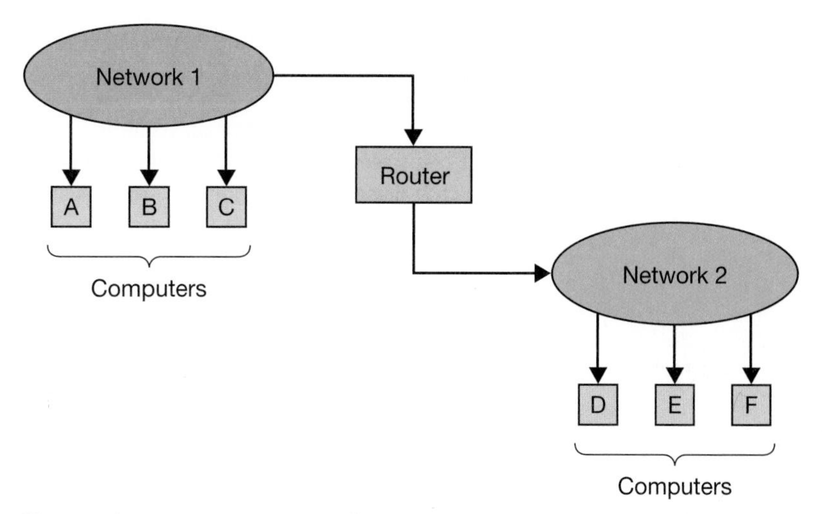

Figure 4.4 Routers connect networks.

Connecting Independent Networks

Now that you understand how computers share a transmission path, we can examine how packet-switching networks are interconnected to form the Internet. The Internet uses special-purpose computers, called ***routers***, to interconnect independent networks. For example, Figure 4.4 illustrates a router that connects Network 1 and Network 2. A router, like a conventional computer, has a central processor, memory, and network interfaces. However, routers do not use conventional software, nor are they used to run applications. Their only job is to interconnect networks and forward data packets from one network to another. For example, in Figure 4.4, computers A and F are connected to independent networks.

If computer A generates a data packet destined for computer F, the packet is sent to the router that interconnects the two networks. The router forwards the packet onto Network 2, where it is delivered to its destination at computer F.

Routers are the fundamental building blocks of the Internet because they connect thousands of LANs and WANs. LANs are connected to backbone WANs, as depicted in Figure 4.5. A ***backbone network*** manages the bulk of network traffic and typically uses a higher-speed protocol than the individual LAN segments. For example, a backbone network might use fibre-optic cabling, which can transfer data at a rate of 2 Gbps (gigabits per second), whereas a LAN connected to the backbone may use Ethernet cabling, transferring data at a rate of 10 or 100 MBps. To gain access to the Internet, an organization connects a router between one of its own networks and the closest Internet site. Business organizations typically connect to the Internet not only with personal computers but with web servers, or hosts, as well.

Web Domain Names and Addresses

Each of the hosts or ***websites*** that you visit on the Internet is assigned a ***domain name***. Domain names are used in ***Uniform Resource Locators (URLs)*** to identify particular ***web pages***.

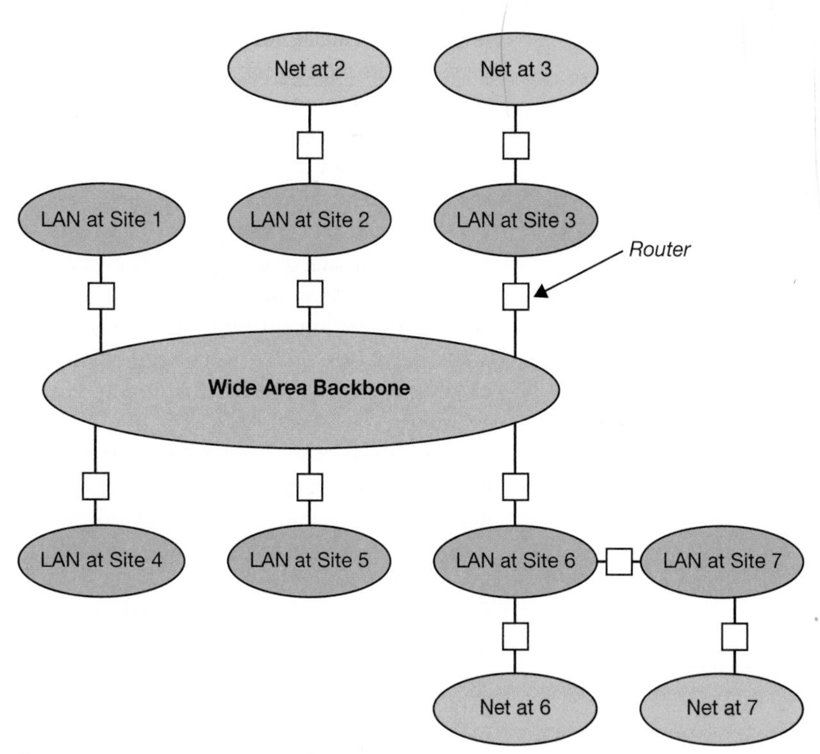

Figure 4.5 LANs connect to wide area backbones.

Comer, Douglas E. *The Internet Book*, 2nd ed., 1997; Prentice Hall.

For example, in the URL **www.pcWebopedia.com/index.html**, the domain name is pcWebopedia.com.

The prefix of every domain name is a term that helps people recognize the company or person that domain name represents. For example, Microsoft's domain name is microsoft.com. The prefix, microsoft, lets you know that it is very likely that this domain name will lead you to the website of Microsoft Corporation. Domain names also have a suffix that indicates which ***top-level domain*** they belong to. For example, the "com" suffix is reserved for commercial organizations. Some other popular suffixes are listed below.

- edu—educational institutions
- org—organizations (nonprofit)
- mil—military
- net—network organizations
- ca—Canada

Domain names ending with .com, .net, or .org can be registered through many different companies (known as "registrars") that compete with one another. An alphabetical listing of these registrars is provided in the InterNIC Registrar Directory on the InterNIC site at **www.internic.net/regist.html**. In Canada, the registration process for the "ca" domain is overseen by the Canadian Internet Registration Authority (CIRA) **www.cira.ca/en/register.html**. Organizations or individuals wishing to register a .ca domain must provide proof of residence in Canada. Once this proof has been provided, the registration process can be undertaken through a number of licensed registrars, including **www.internic.ca** and **www.domain. ca**. Over 650 000 .ca domains had been registered as of November 2006.

Each of these domain names is associated with one or more ***IP addresses***. For example, the domain name microsoft.com represents about a dozen underlying IP addresses. IP addresses serve to identify all the computers or devices on the Internet (or on any TCP/IP network). The IP address serves as the destination address of that computer or device and enables the network to route messages to the proper destination. The format of an IP address is a 32-bit numeric address written as four numbers separated by periods. Each of the four numbers can be any number between zero and 255. For example, 1.160.10.240 could be an IP address. You could set up a private network using the TCP/IP protocol and assign your own domain names and IP addresses for computers and other devices on that network. On the other hand, if you wish to connect to the Internet, you must use registered IP addresses.

Who Manages the Internet?

So, who keeps track of these IP addresses on the Internet? A number of national and international standing committees and task forces have been used to manage the development and use of the Internet. Among these is the Coordinating Committee for Intercontinental Research Networks (CCIRN) that has helped to coordinate government-sponsored research in this area. The Internet Society (ISOC) is a professional membership society with over 150 organizational and 16 000 individual members around the world, which helps to shape the future of the Internet and is home for the Internet Engineering Task Force (IETF) and the Internet Architecture Board (IAB). These groups help manage Internet standards. For example, the IAB has guided the evolution of the TCP/IP Protocol Suite. The Internet Assigned Numbers Authority (IANA) has provided the recording of system identifiers on the Internet and has helped to manage an ***Internet Registry*** that acts as a central repository for Internet-related information and that provides central allocation of network system identifiers. The Internet Registry also provides central maintenance of the ***Domain Name System (DNS)*** root database, which points to distributed DNS servers replicated throughout the Internet. This database is used to associate Internet host names with their Internet IP addresses.

In 1993 the NSF created ***InterNIC***, a government–industry collaboration, to manage directory and database services, domain registration services, and other information services on the Internet. In the late 1990s, this Internet oversight was transitioned more fully out into industry when InterNIC morphed into the ***Internet Corporation for Assigned Names and Numbers (ICANN)***, a nonprofit corporation that assumed responsibility for managing IP addresses, domain names, and root server system management. Specifically, the ***InterNIC Registration Service*** now assigns Internet addresses. The number of unassigned Internet addresses is running out, so new classes of addresses are being added as we adopt ***IPv6***, the latest version of the Internet Protocol.

How Do You Connect to the Internet?

Now you can see how the Internet works and how it is managed. How do you connect to the Internet? For personal use (i.e., from home) we typically connect to the Internet through

Internet service providers (ISPs). For a monthly fee, these ISPs will give you a username, password, and provide means to access the Internet. With your personal computer and a ***modem*** (either telephone dial-up, or an always-on technology such as a cable modem), you can then log on through the ISP's servers to access the Internet and browse the World Wide Web, and send and receive e-mail. ISPs not only serve individuals like you, but also serve large companies by providing them with a direct connection from the company's networks to the Internet.

ISPs connect to one another through ***network access points (NAPs)***. Much like railway stations, these NAPs serve as access points for ISPs and are an exchange point for Internet traffic. They determine how traffic is routed and are often the source of most of the Internet's congestion. NAPs are a key component of the ***Internet backbone***, which is the collection of main network connections and telecommunications lines that make up the Internet (see Figure 4.6).

The Internet follows a hierarchical structure, similar to the national highway system. High-speed central network lines are like provincial highways, enabling traffic from midlevel networks to get on and off. Think of midlevel networks as city streets, which in turn accept traffic from their neighbourhood streets or member networks. However, you cannot just get on a provincial highway or city street whenever you want to. You have to share the highway and follow traffic control signs to arrive safely at your destination. The same holds true for traffic on the Internet.

How Fast Is Your Connection to the Internet?

People can connect to the Internet in a number of ways. In addition to traditional connections through plain old telephones and modems, there are a number of high-speed alternatives. This section briefly describes several different ways that people connect to the Internet from home, office, and beyond.

Plain Old Telephone Service

Some of us still connect to the Internet through a telephone line at our home or work. The term we use for standard telephone lines is ***plain old telephone service (POTS)***. The speed, or bandwidth, of POTS is generally about 52 Kbps (52 000 bits per second). The POTS system is also called the ***public switched telephone network (PSTN)***.

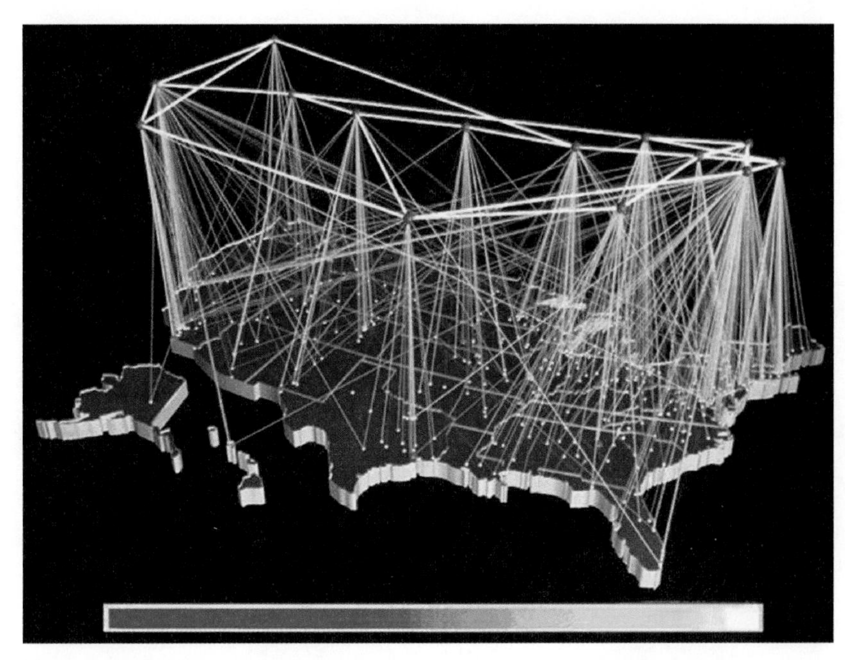

Figure 4.6 The Internet backbone.

Digital Subscriber Line (DSL)

One popular alternative now available from telephone service providers around the world is the use of ***digital subscriber lines (DSL)***. DSL uses special modulation schemes to fit more data onto copper wires. In Canada, DSL is quickly supplanting another digital telephone-based service called ISDN. DSL is referred to as a "last-mile" solution because it is used only for connections from a telephone switching station to a home or office, and is generally not used between telephone switching stations. DSL uses existing copper telephone lines and requires relatively short runs to a central telephone office (typically less than 5 km). DSL has relatively high speeds of up to 32 Mbps when receiving data (i.e., for downstream traffic) and from 32 Kbps to more than 1 Mbps when sending data (i.e., for upstream traffic).

The acronym DSL is used to refer collectively to ADSL, SDSL, and other forms of DSL. ADSL and SDSL enable more data to be sent over existing copper telephone lines. ADSL is short for ***asymmetric digital subscriber line*** and its speeds range from 1.5 to 9 Mbps downstream and from 16 to 640 Kbps upstream. ADSL requires a special ADSL modem-like device. SDSL is short for ***symmetric digital subscriber line*** and is said to be symmetric because it supports the same data rates for upstream and downstream traffic. SDSL supports data rates up to 3 Mbps and works by sending digital pulses in the high-frequency area of telephone wires.

Given that these high frequencies are not used by normal voice communications, SDSL enables your computer to operate simultaneously with voice connections over the same wires. Like ADSL, SDSL requires a special modem-like device. ADSL is most popular in North America, whereas SDSL is being developed primarily in Europe.

Cable Modems

In many parts of Canada, the company that provides cable television service also provides Internet service. With this type of service, a special ***cable modem*** is designed to operate over cable TV lines. Coaxial cable used for cable TV provides much greater bandwidth than telephone lines, and millions of homes in Canada are already wired for cable TV, so cable modems are a fast, popular method for accessing the Internet. Cable modems offer speeds up to 2 Mbps.

Satellite Connections

In many regions of the world, people can now access the Internet via ***satellite,*** referred to as ***Internet over Satellite (IoS)***. IoS technologies allow users to access the Internet via satellites that are placed in fixed positions above the Earth's surface in what is known as a ***geostationary*** or ***geosynchronous*** orbit (i.e., the satellite moves along with the Earth). With these services, your PC is connected to a satellite dish hanging out on the side of your home or placed out on a pole (much like satellite services for your television) and is able to maintain a reliable connection to the satellite in the sky because the satellite orbits the Earth at the exact speed of the Earth's rotation. Given the vast distance that signals must travel from the Earth up to the satellite and back again, IoS is slower than high-speed terrestrial (i.e., land-based) connections to the Internet over copper or fibre-optic cables. In remote regions of the world, IoS is the only option available because installing the cables necessary for Internet connection is not economically feasible or in many cases is just not physically possible. Download transmission rates are always much faster for satellite connections than upload rates. If fact, it is not uncommon to require a terrestrial link, like a phone line, to send information to an Internet server when using a satellite connection.

In addition to these ***fixed wireless*** approaches for connecting to the Internet, there are also many new ***mobile wireless*** approaches for connecting to the Internet. For example, there are Internet-enabled ***cellular phones*** from Telus and others, and small palm-top computers, like the BlackBerry from Research In Motion, that give you Internet access nearly anywhere. Redline Communications, described at the opening of this chapter, provides wireless connectivity for broadband networks. With a special network adapter card you can use your notebook computer, tablet PC, or personal digital assistant and enjoy the freedom of wireless mobility. The beauty of these ***wireless local area networks*** is that as long as you are in the coverage area you have access to the Internet (much like coverage with cellular phones). One other option for wireless access to the Internet is to use a wireless ethernet network adapter card in any of these computing devices, but with this type of equipment you have to be located near a transceiver on the network. You would be free to roam around your office or building, but that would be it. With these other technologies you would be able to wander freely around your network, or cellular, coverage area.

Up until now we have talked about ways that individuals rather than organizations access the Internet. In the following sections, we talk more about ways that organizations typically access the Internet—although an individual with high amounts of discretionary income could certainly access the Internet in these same ways!

T1 Lines

To gain adequate access to the Internet, organizations are turning to long-distance carriers to lease a dedicated ***T1 line*** for digital transmissions. The T1 line was developed by AT&T as a dedicated digital transmission line that can carry 1.544 Mbps of information. In the United States, companies such as BrandX that sell long-distance services are called ***interexchange carriers (IXCs)*** because their circuits carry service between major telephone exchanges. As previously mentioned, a T1 line can carry 1.544 Mbps and usually traverses hundreds or thousands of kilometres over leased long-distance facilities.

Bell Canada and other carriers charge anywhere from $500 to several thousands of dollars per month for a dedicated T1 circuit spanning 1000 kilometres. If you need an even faster link, you might choose a T3 line. T3 provides about 45 Mbps of service at about 10 times the cost of leasing a T1 line.

Web Search

Find a website offering tools to check your Internet connection speed. If you think your Internet connection is slower at certain times, check your speed at different times of the day. How is your Internet connection speed compared to the benchmarks provided (e.g., average speed for your connection type, or average speeds for other connection types)? Prepare a graph showing your connection speeds at 9 a.m., 12 noon, 3 p.m., 6 p.m., and 9 p.m.

Table 4.3 *Capacity of telecommunication lines.*

Type of Line	Data Rate
T1	1.544 Mbps
T3	44.736 Mbps
OC-1	51.85 Mbps
OC-3	155.52 Mbps
OC-12	622.08 Mbps
OC-24	1.244 Gbps
OC-48	2.488 Gbps

Alternatively, organizations often choose to use two or more T1 lines simultaneously rather than jump to the more expensive ***T3 line***. Higher speeds than the T3 are also available but are not typically used for normal business activity. See Table 4.3 for a summary of communication line capacities.

Asynchronous Transfer Mode (ATM)

Asynchronous Transfer Mode (ATM) is a method of transmitting voice, video, and data over high-speed LANs at speeds of up to 2.2 Gbps. ATM has found wide acceptance in the LAN and WAN arenas as a solution to integrating disparate networks over large geographic distances. ATM uses a form of packet transmission in which data is sent over a packet-switched network in a fixed-length, 53-byte cell. Although it is based on packet-switching technology, ATM has the potential to do away with routers, allocated bandwidth, and contention for communications media. Organizations in the movie and entertainment industries that need to deliver synchronized video and sound, for example, are particularly interested in ATM.

The Current State of Internet Usage

The Internet is now the most prominent ***global network***. NUA Internet Surveys reports that just over 600 million people worldwide use the Internet (NUA, 2002). Early in 2004, CNN reported on a UCLA-based study of Internet users across 14 countries that shattered the image of the typical Internet user as a computer "geek" (CNN, 2004). The results of that study suggest that the typical Internet user watches significantly less television than do others and more actively socializes with friends. The typical Internet user is an avid reader of

ETHICAL DILEMMA

Can't Get Rid of All Those Ads!

Have you ever downloaded "free" software that displayed banner advertising while you were using the program? In this case, the software you've just downloaded is not actually free, it's "adware"; the costs for developing and distributing the product are covered by advertising revenue. This helps to provide the software for a minimal fee or even for free; often you have the option of purchasing a registered version of the software where the ads are disabled.

So far, so good. Sometimes, so-called "spyware" is distributed as adware or freeware. Spyware programs run in the background and track your browsing or surfing habits and transmit this information to advertising or marketing companies, who either sell this information or use it themselves. In extreme cases, spyware disables its uninstall feature, scans your hard drive, or even logs your keystrokes. In extreme cases like this, the software is referred to as malware—or software than causes damage. Usually, when you install software containing spyware, you are not informed that some application will be running in the background, nor are you informed what data about you or your surfing habits will be transmitted to some other location!

Similar to adware (which is sometimes called spyware, too), spyware uses different sources to generate revenue for the producers. However, whereas adware usually informs you about what you're getting into, spyware uses deceptive practices to gain access to information you might not want to share. Many companies are walking a fine line between providing adware or spyware when offering "free" software; a disclaimer about the use of any personal information is hidden somewhere in lengthy end user license agreements. Is this an ethical way of obtaining your consent? After all, you've been informed . . .

Source: **http://simplythebest.net/info/spyware.html**

books and spends more time engaged in social activities than the nonuser. On the other hand, the study supported some long-established Internet usage trends, including the fact that the wealthiest segments of the population are the most avid users and that more men than women surf the web.

Use by men and women varied by country, however. For example, the gender gap is most pronounced in Italy, where 41.7 percent of Italian men are online, compared to only 21.5 percent of Italian women. By contrast, in Taiwan the difference is small: 25.1 percent for men and 23.5 percent for women.

One other way to measure the rapid growth of the Internet, in addition to the number of users, is to examine the growth in the number of Internet hosts, that is, computers working as servers on the Internet, as shown in Figure 4.7.

There is little doubt that Canadians have embraced the Internet like few other nations of the world. Ipsos-Insight found that Canadians are the leading users of the Internet in the world. More than 71 percent of Canadians accessed the Internet in 2003, compared with 70 percent in South Korea, 68 percent in the United States, and 65 percent in Japan.

What Are People Doing on the Internet?

The Internet enables people to access a wide range of data, including text, video, audio, graphics, databases, maps, and other data types. The Internet is more, however, than just access to data. The Internet also enables people to connect with each other. In the last couple of years, with increases in bandwidth and decreases in prices for computers and Internet access, there have been substantial changes in the ways people are using the Internet. For example, recent advancements in communication technologies and increasingly high transmission speeds have made interactivity—collaboration between people—possible over the Internet.

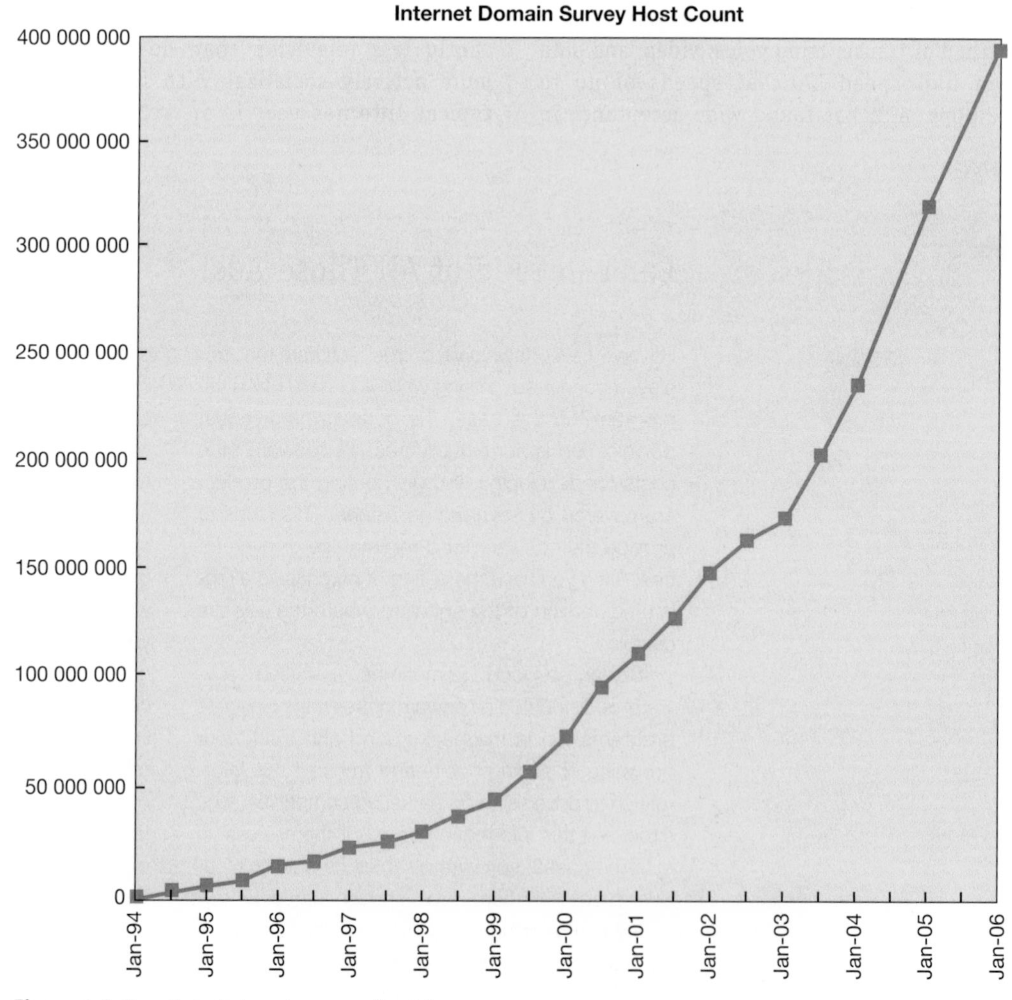

Figure 4.7 Growth in Internet servers (hosts).

This collaboration can occur in real time, or synchronous, two-way communication, via instant messaging, chat programs, or video and voice over IP. Collaboration can also happen through asynchronous channels, such as e-mail. Synchronous channels can generally support richer forms of communication. However, some experts have been surprised at the extent and richness of communication that can be supported by synchronous channels. It is not uncommon for colleagues to communicate on a daily basis over a period of months or even years without ever seeing or talking to one another.

A number of popular uses of the Internet are summarized in Table 4.4. Essentially, these involve ways to access information and to communicate with other people. For access to a variety of free software that will enable you to better use the Internet, visit one of the popular software download websites such as Canadian-based **www.tucows.com**.

While the Internet is an amazing collection of technologies, the real power of the Internet was not realized until the early 1990s, with the invention of the ***World Wide Web*** and the ***web browser***. The web and the web browser have essentially given us a graphical user interface with which to use the Internet and, as a result, have made the Internet much more accessible and easy to use, and opened the door for some very innovative uses of the Internet.

What Is Next for the Internet?

In the mid-1990s, many researchers at universities became frustrated with the increased personal and business use of the Internet. The Internet had previously been a network primarily for researchers from universities and other organizations, and all of a sudden, shortly after 1995 (note that this is the year Netscape went public and Microsoft turned its attention squarely to the Internet), the Internet was quickly being overrun with all types of non-research-oriented traffic. As a result, in 1996, 34 U.S. research universities began working on ***Internet2***, a faster, private alternative to the public Internet (**www.internet2.edu**). In 1997, the University

Table 4.4 ***Popular Internet uses and tools.***

Internet Use	Description	Popular Shareware/Freeware
E-mail	Enables users to send messages to each other.	Eudora, Outlook Express
Telnet	Enables users to connect, or log in, to any computer on the Internet.	Putty, TeraTerm Pro Web
File transfer	Enables users to connect to a remote computer in order to transfer files, either uploading (sending to the remote machine) or downloading (obtaining from the remote machine) files.	WSFTP LE
Web browsing	View and interact with web pages on the World Wide Web.	Internet Explorer, Firefox, Netscape, Opera
Chat messengers	Enables people to have real-time communication by entering text that appears on the other user's monitor.	MSN Messenger, Yahoo Messenger, mIRC
Newsreader	Enables people with common interests to post and read messages categorized by topic.	NewsPro
Voice over IP	A collection of hardware and software that enables the use of the Internet as the transmission medium for telephone calls.	Skype, PC Telephone, X-Lite Soft SIP VOIP Phone
Podcasting	A podcast is a web feed of audio or video files placed on the Internet and available for subscription or free download.	Shareware: Our media, iTunes, Pandera

WHEN THINGS GO WRONG

VoIP Users May Be Lost to Emergency Services

Flexibility and portability, the things that make Voice over Internet Protocol (VoIP) services attractive to enterprise users, are hindering efforts to track emergency 911 calls. VoIP devices are tracked back to an IP address rather than to a single physical location, which makes it hard for emergency services to locate callers. Providers of 911 solutions are holding their breath as industry and government bodies square off over how to regulate the transmission of voice over the Internet. "There's a great tug of war going on," says John Thompson, vice-president of marketing and product management at Gatineau, Quebec–based CML Emergency Services Inc. "One side is saying, 'Governments should mandate a solution so VoIP is carrier-grade, and as reliable as a legacy phone system,' while others believe private industry will solve the problem through the free market."

A big question regarding the use of residential VoIP is whether a 24/7, 911 service can be offered through an IP network. As IP phones are so mobile, it's possible that an emergency response team would not be able to locate a 911 caller, subsequently putting users' lives at risk. Yet companies aren't exactly "rushing forward with any radical new technology" to solve the problem until regulators decide whether to mandate a solution or to leave it up to industry, says Thompson. "You could push something forward, but if the regulatory body wins, your investment could be lost."

Nonetheless, it seems CML is prepared to take some chances. The company's lab is currently working on a solution that allows a VoIP user to send a call into an IT-enabled answering point through end-to-end IP calls. CML is ready to conduct trials with such technology and is prepared to release test products by the end of 2004, says Thompson. "We're looking to provide a bulletproof solution. We're pushing this forward as fast as we possibly can, but the market's going to take a while to mature."

Some solutions that already exist include an attempt by New Jersey–based Vonage Holdings Corp. The company introduced its residential VoIP plan last December and announced its 911 scheme last April. Vonage tries to solve the 911 problem by recording the location of all users in a database, giving them the option of changing their information if they move temporarily. However, that information becomes erroneous if the user moves for a day or 2 and doesn't provide an information update, says Thompson. Even a Vonage spokeswoman calls the system "very rudimentary." "If you need [traditional 911] capability, we encourage you to maintain a land line. We're . . . months away from a solution," says Brooke Schulz.

Source: Adapted from Scott Foster, "Do You Know Where Your VoIP User Is?," ITBusiness.ca (February 9, 2004), **www.itbusiness.ca/it/client/en/Home/News.asp?id=11112&bSearch=True.**

Corporation for Advanced Internet Development (UCAID) was created to help manage the Internet2 initiative. Internet2 is now a consortium being led by well over 200 universities working in partnership with industry and government to develop and deploy advanced network applications and technologies. Internet2 requires state-of-the-art infrastructure, so Internet2 universities are connected to the Abilene network backbone, which uses regional network aggregation points called gigaPoPs and very high-speed network equipment and facilities.

The term ***gigaPoP*** is short for gigabit Point of Presence, a network access point that supports data transfer rates of at least 1 Gbps. Each university that connects to Internet2 must do so through a gigaPoP, which connects the university's networks with Internet2. For comparison, the point-of-presence facilities maintained by regular ISPs are designed to allow low-speed modems to connect to the Internet, while these gigaPoPs are designed for fast access to a high-speed network like Internet2.

The cross-country ***Abilene network backbone*** now operates at 10 Gbps, with the goal of offering 100 Mbps of connectivity between all Abilene-connected desktops. Will you ever surf Internet2, as you now do the Internet? Not likely, unless you embark on a career in IS research! The good news is that Internet2 is now a fast, private place for researchers to come up with new Internet-related discoveries and technologies, and these will eventually migrate over onto the public Internet. Given this initiative and the tens of thousands of corporate and academic researchers pursuing new Internet technologies and applications, one thing is for sure: the Internet will continue to get better and faster!

COMING ATTRACTIONS

2Fast4U—Turbo Codes Revolutionize Data Communications

Have you ever been annoyed by slow download times? For most people, slow downloads of pictures, music, or freeware from the Internet can be quite annoying; but for researchers running simulations of nuclear reactions, climate changes, or earthquakes, current bandwidth limitations lead to tremendous problems if the data is transferred from the location of the experiment to the researchers' labs.

TCP, the current protocol used on the Internet, was not designed for current network bandwidths, and it is sometimes unable to handle such massive data transfers. North Carolina State University computer scientists have developed a new protocol called Binary Increase Congestion Transmission Control Protocol (BIC-TCP) that reaches about 6000 times the speed of DSL, which translates into 150 000 times the speed of a 56 k modem! Injong Rhee, the developer of BIC, stated that "What takes TCP two hours to determine, BIC can do in less than one second." While this may mean turbo-charged music downloads, the potential for data-intensive applications such as transferring companies' backup data after a natural disaster is tremendous.

While the widespread use of BIC for end users is still on the horizon, so-called turbo codes for transmitting data over noisy channels are already in use. One of the most prevalent problems for the use of multimedia applications in cell phones has been overcoming noise, just as in trying to talk to someone in a crowded auditorium. Turbo codes, developed by two professors in Brest, France, can help to come extremely close to the absolute maximum capacity of a communications channel by the use of two encoders generating error-checking bits for each block that is transmitted over the noisy communication channel. At the receiving end, two decoders combine the pair of error-checking bits with an estimate of the likelihood that each bit of the message received is correct, to render—after going through several iterations of complex mathematical algorithms—an extremely accurate estimate of the original message. While these turbo codes are presently used for video and mail transmission in third-generation cell phone networks in Japan, the delay resulting from the decoding process inhibits the use of turbo codes for voice transmission. Hopefully, the industry will develop turbo-decoders, so it will be only a matter of time until you really have crystal-clear voice transmission over your cell phone.

Sources: Erico Guizo, "Closing in on the Perfect Code," *IEEE Spectrum Online* (March 03, 2004).
Mike Martin, "New Web Protocol May Leave DSL in the Dust," *NewsFactor Network* (April 15, 2004), **www.newsfactor.com/story.xhtml?story_title=New_Web_Protocol_May_Leave_DSL_in_the_Dust&story_id=23720**.

Canada has a high-speed network similar to Internet2 called CA*net 4, funded by the federal government and designed, deployed, and operated by CANARIE (**www.canarie.ca**). CA*net 4 connects provincial research networks, universities, research centres, government research laboratories, schools, and other eligible sites.

WORLD WIDE WEB

One of the most powerful uses of the Internet is something that you have no doubt heard a great deal about—the World Wide Web. More than likely, you have probably browsed the web using Netscape Navigator, Firefox, Microsoft's Internet Explorer, or some other popular web browser, as shown in Figure 4.8. A web browser is a software application that can be used to locate and display web pages, including text, graphics, and multimedia content. Browsers are fast becoming a standard Internet tool. As previously mentioned, the web is a graphical user interface to the Internet that provides users with a simple, consistent interface to a wide variety of information.

Prior to the invention of the web by Tim Berners-Lee in 1991, content posted on the Internet could be accessed through the Internet tool ***Gopher***. Gopher provides a menu-driven, hierarchical interface to organize files stored on servers, providing a way to tie together related files from different Internet servers across the world. The web took Gopher one step further by introducing ***hypertext***. A hypertext document, otherwise known as a web page, contains not only information, but also references or links to other documents that contain related information. These links are known as ***hyperlinks***. The web also introduced the ***HyperText Markup Language (HTML)***, which is the standard method of specifying the format of web pages. Specific content within each web page is

Web Search

Go to the Internet Traffic Report website at **www.internettrafficreport.com** and take a look at the traffic situation on different continents. How would you interpret the different statistics provided? What does it mean if a server has a current index of 0 and a packet loss of 100 percent? Why do some continents have lower current indices than others? Prepare a brief report of your findings.

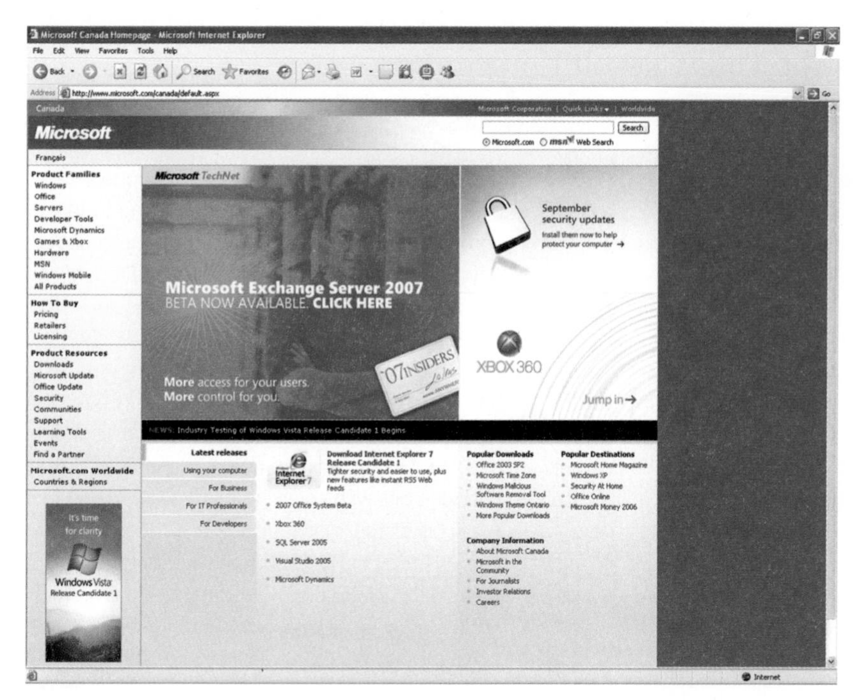

Figure 4.8 Microsoft's Internet Explorer web browser.

enclosed within codes, or markup tags, which stipulate how the content should appear to the user. Web pages are stored on ***web servers***, which process user requests for pages using the ***HyperText Transfer Protocol (HTTP)***. Web servers typically host a collection of interlinked web pages created by the same author, which is known as a website. Websites and specific web pages within those sites have a unique Internet URL address. A user who wants to access a website enters the URL, and the web server hosting the website retrieves the desired page and delivers it to the user.

The introduction of the web was the first of three events that led to its proliferation. The second event was the Information Infrastructure Act (Berghel, 1996), passed by the U.S. government in 1992, which opened the web for commercial purposes. Prior to this legislation, universities and governmental agencies were the web's predominant users. The third event was the arrival of a graphical web browser, Mosaic, which quickly transcended Gopher by adding a graphical front end to the web. Mosaic's graphical interface allowed web pages to be constructed to deliver an extended range of content, including images, audio, video, and other multimedia, all of which could be included and displayed within the same web page. Mosaic was the predecessor to Netscape's Navigator.

World Wide Web Architecture

The web uses web browsers, web servers, and the TCP/IP networking protocol to facilitate the transmission of web pages over the Internet. Figure 4.9 depicts the architecture of the web.

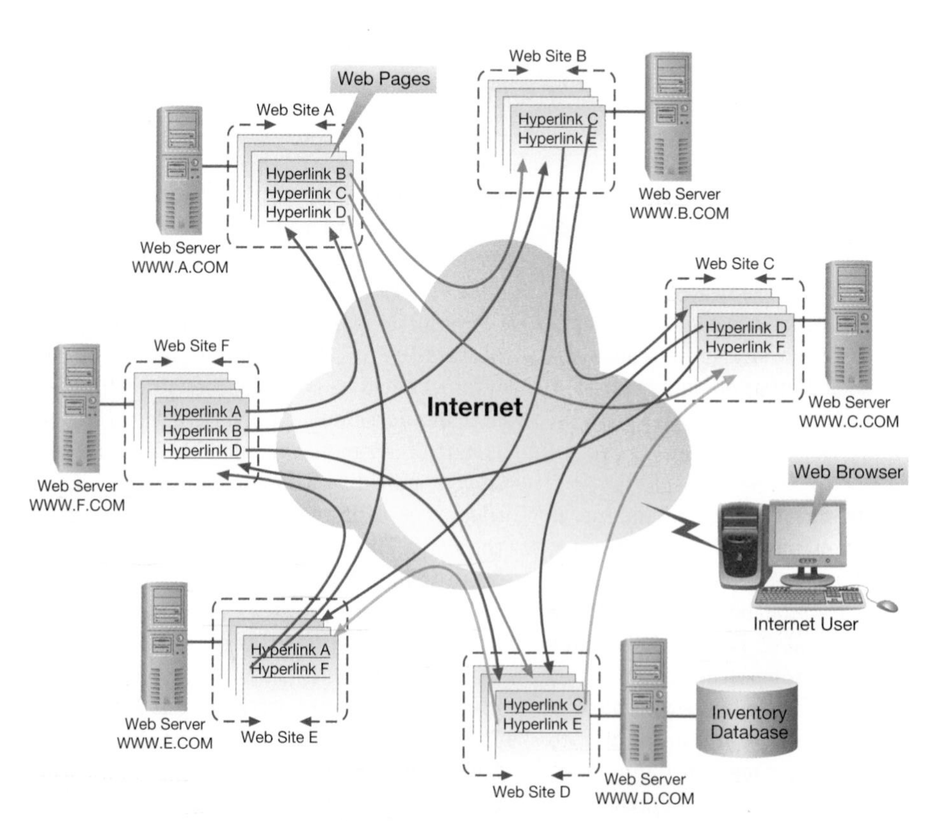

Figure 4.9 World Wide Web architecture.

To access information on the web, a web browser, as well as the TCP/IP protocol, must be installed on a user's computer. Users can access web pages by entering into their web browser the URL of the web page. Once the user enters the URL in the web browser, TCP/IP breaks the request into packets and routes them over the Internet to the web server where the requested web page is stored. When the packets reach their destination, TCP/IP reassembles them and passes the request to the web server.

The web server understands that the user is requesting a web page (indicated by the **http://** prefix in the URL) and retrieves the web page, which is formed into packets by TCP/IP and transmitted over the Internet back to the web browser. TCP/IP reassembles the packets at the destination and delivers the web page to the web browser. In turn, the web browser translates the HTML code contained in the web page, formats its physical appearance, and displays the results. If the web page contains a hyperlink, the user can click on it and the process repeats itself.

World Wide Web Applications

Because the powerful and relatively inexpensive web platform is extremely well suited for disseminating information on a global basis, organizations are constantly trying to devise innovative applications for the web. Over the years, many organizations have become very sophisticated users of web technologies. The first wave of web-based commerce occurred around 1994, when new businesses brought product marketing to the web, pioneering an explosion of commercial activity that will continue into the foreseeable future (Looney and Chatterjee, 2002).

Companies can utilize the web to support business activities in a number of ways. For example, many companies at least use the web to disseminate sales and marketing information—what is referred to as the ***electronic brochure***. Many companies also now use the web for ***online ordering***, which means that they enable customers to order, and in many cases to actually pay for, products and services online. Still other firms, such as eBay, create ***electronic marketplaces***, bringing multiple sellers and multiple buyers together and providing a vehicle for them to trade with each other online. Many firms also use the web to provide ***online customer service***, or at least to enhance their traditional customer service. (We will talk about each of these uses of the web in detail in Chapter 5, "Electronic Business, Intranets, and Extranets.")

MANAGING INFORMATION SYSTEMS SECURITY

How do you secure computers from viruses and other threats? The rule of thumb for deciding whether computer security is at risk is simple: All computers connected to networks are vulnerable to security violations from outsiders as well as insiders, and to virus infections and other forms of computer crime. Threats to information systems can come from a variety of places inside and external to an organization. ***Information systems security*** refers to precautions taken to keep all aspects of information systems (e.g., all hardware, software, network equipment, and data) safe from unauthorized use or access. That means that you have to secure not only the personal computers on people's desks but also the notebook computers, the handhelds, the servers, all levels of the network, and any gateways between the network and the outside world.

As the use of the Internet and related telecommunications technologies and systems has become more pervasive, the use of these networks now creates a new vulnerability for nations and organizations. For an example of the security risks associated with telecommunications technologies, see the Brief Case: Canada Confronts the Dark Side of Global Telecommunications. These networks can be infiltrated and/or subverted in a number of ways. As a result, the need for tight computer and network security has increased dramatically. Fortunately, there are a variety of managerial methods and security technologies that can be used to manage information systems security effectively. In the remaining sections of this chapter we address this new reality.

Assessing Risk

Any good approach to securing information systems begins first with a thorough ***audit*** of all aspects of those systems, including hardware, software, data, networks, and any business processes that involve them. By doing this, you can then decide which aspects of the various systems within the organization are most vulnerable to break-ins by unauthorized users and/or misuse by authorized users. After such an audit, you can then design and implement a security plan that makes the best use of the available resources in order to protect the systems and guard against (or at least minimize) any problems. People within the information systems department are usually responsible for implementing the security measures chosen,

GLOBAL PERSPECTIVE

Technology-Related Challenges for Global Telecommunications

The primary technological challenges faced by organizations when operating across national boundaries are related to telecommunications infrastructure. The price, quality, and speed of telecommunications support can vary from country to country. For example, in Greece only half of the telecommunication networks are digital, whereas the networks in Finland are 100 percent digital. You cannot assume you will find the same kind of telecommunications infrastructure and performance when you move from one country to the next. In some cases, the differences are merely in terms of performance (e.g., one country has a faster telecommunications infrastructure for businesses than does another country). Worse, however, are situations in which one country uses a different telecommunications standard than does another country; because of this, businesses may face compatibility and other problems as they move from one country to the next. For example, a company headquartered in Hong Kong recently expanded its operations to Thailand, only to realize that the manufacturing facilities were located in an area that had no telecommunications connections available using the X.25 standard. As a result, given the network infrastructure that the parent firm was using and assuming, the subsidiary was not easily able to interact electronically with its headquarters located in Hong Kong (Sarker and Sarker, 2000). Similarly, if you are travelling internationally with your Canadian cell phone, you may not be able to pick up a signal, as most countries have settled on the global standard for mobile communication (GSM), which is only one of the many different standards used in Canada.

Differences in telecommunications standards across the planet pose serious challenges for organizations, and these differences are more the norm than the exception. For example, in North America, most people prefer to use network standards produced by the American National Standards Institute (e.g., ANSI X.12), whereas in Europe people more commonly use network standards produced by the International Organization for Standardization (e.g., the OSI model for networks). Moreover, within Europe itself one can find a variety of different standards due to the lack of political unification (although things are slowly improving).

Similarly, the hardware platforms used in different countries are also different, causing further, significant integration problems. For example, Canada has seen a predominance of the use of IBM mainframes and Windows-based servers and PCs, whereas in Europe UNIX or its derivatives are much more popular. For example, many European universities and even government agencies use Linux-based servers or PCs. The preferences for software are also different. Some European nations prefer to use PDF—portable document format—files, whereas in Canada there is a predominance of files created using Microsoft Office software products. This, too, causes serious problems in data sharing and data transfer. The proliferation of the Internet and platform-independent programming languages such as Java has helped, but it is still very difficult to develop a seamless global telecommunications infrastructure for an organization.

Sources: Suprateek Sarker and Saonee Sarker, "Implementation Failure of an Integrated Software Package: A Case Study from the Far East," *Annals of Cases on Information Technology Applications and Management in Organizations* 2 (2000): 169–186. Jennifer L. Schenker, "Software Maker Wants Europe's Desktops," *International Herald Tribune,* May 4, 2004, p. 13.

though people from throughout the organization should participate in the systems security audit. Some organizations even go so far as to pay an external consulting firm to attempt to break in and breach their systems so that vulnerabilities will be uncovered and fixed.

It would not make sense to spend literally millions of dollars a year to protect an asset whose loss would cost the organization only a few thousand dollars. As a result, one critical component of a good information systems audit is also a thorough risk analysis. ***Risk analysis*** is a process in which you assess the value of the assets being protected, determine their likelihood of being comprised, and compare the probable costs of their being comprised with the estimated costs of whatever protections you might have to take. People in organizations often perform risk analysis for their systems to ensure that information systems security programs make sense economically (Panko, 2004).

Risk analysis then enables us to determine what steps, if any, to take to secure systems. There are basically three ways to react:

1. ***Risk reduction:*** Taking active countermeasures to protect your systems, such as installing firewalls like those described in the section "Firewalls."
2. ***Risk acceptance:*** Implementing no countermeasures and simply absorbing any damages that occur.
3. ***Risk transference:*** Having someone else absorb the risk, such as by investing in insurance.

Large organizations typically use a balance of all three approaches, taking steps in risk reduction for some systems, accepting risk and living with it in other cases, and insuring all or most of their systems activities as well.

Controlling Access

Organizations can prevent unauthorized access to computers by keeping stored information safe and allowing access only to those employees who need it to do their jobs. Passwords are one common form of ***authentication*** of appropriate

BRIEF CASE Canada Confronts the Dark Side of Global Telecommunications

Have you been promised millions of dollars by the ex-finance minister of an African country lately? Tens of thousands of Canadian e-mail recipients have. This type of scam is typical of the problem facing both Canadian Internet users and law enforcement officials, says Constable Patrick Boismenu, an investigator with the RCMP's Integrated Technological Crime Unit in Montreal. "Foreign fraud [artists] have been attacking Canada for a long time. There is little we can do about it. Why? Because they're not operating from within the country. They can bypass borders using the phone or letters or e-mail to [trick] people into giving money or bank account numbers. They can circumvent any security feature that we implement on the borders."

Similarly, many viruses, worms, and Trojans originate from the United States, Russia, China, and other Far Eastern countries. "You can't touch anybody outside the country for that type of offence," Boismenu says. "Viruses come from around the world. Unfortunately, developing countries such as China have weak legislation and sometimes not enough police expertise to enforce the legislation that does exist."

The very nature of technology guarantees a continuing battle, notes Gary Bouchard, head of the technology law group at Fogler, Rubinoff, Barristers and Solicitors, in Toronto. "You've got people from all over the world developing cutting-edge technology. It's the old one-upmanship problem—good guys keeping up with bad guys and bad guys keeping ahead of good guys—making for constant struggle."

For the international spy set, mi2g Ltd., a British security company, predicts an increase in politically motivated digital attacks, although this has not yet been a factor in Canada. "We don't see much of this as politically motivated," says Mark Fernandes, manager of the security services group at Deloitte & Touche in Toronto. Shortly after Fernandes predicted more attacks would come in the near future, Microsoft issued an alert about a new-found vulnerability in its Windows system, followed by dire warnings from security companies of possible damage.

Microsoft tacitly admitted the continuing struggle in a statement. "Microsoft understands that consumers are increasingly faced with a variety of cyber threats and [is] doing an unprecedented level of outreach to PC users with our 'Protect your PC' campaign to help raise awareness of the need for computer users to take steps, and ensure that those steps are as easy to understand and as easy to implement as possible."

Questions

1. Is your computer protected against viruses and other security threats? You can use freeware programs such as "Spybot Search and Destroy" to check whether your system is home to spyware, or is vulnerable to security threats.
2. Are spam, viruses, online fraud schemes and the like just facts of life on the Internet that must be endured? Or should governments and organizations take a more proactive approach to dealing with them? What advice would you give the federal government on how to deal with computer security threats that originate from outside the country?

Source: Adapted from Al Emid, "Cheats, Vandals, Spys and Villians," *Backbone* (January/February 2004).
[Figure 4.2 Global telecommunications link Canada to the world, but also threaten its security.]
Source: Courtesy of Amperion, Inc.

users, but passwords are effective only if chosen carefully and changed frequently. Besides passwords, employees may be asked to provide an ID combination, a security code sequence, or personal data such as a mother's maiden name. Employees authorized to use computer systems may also be issued keys to physically unlock a computer, photo ID cards, smart cards with digital ID, and other physical devices allowing computer access.

The point behind authenticating users is to then control their access appropriately. Managing ***information systems access*** is critical in securing systems, and organizations also often use special software to manage people's access to key computers, data, networks, and so on. Access-control software, for example, may allow computer users access only to certain networks, systems, files within those systems, or even certain areas within those files. The user might even be restricted to these resources only at certain times or for specified periods of time, and the user can be restricted to being able to only read a file, to read and edit the file, to add to the file, and/or to delete the file. Many common business systems applications now build in these kinds of security features so that you do not have to have additional, separate access-control software running on top of your applications software. Whether you are restricting user access within the application software or with the help of additional access-control software, the common approach is to authenticate that the user is indeed who they claim to be by requiring something that the user knows (e.g., a password) together with something that the user physically carries or has access to (e.g., an identification card or file).

Organizational Policies and Practices

Very often some of the best things that people can do to secure their information systems are not necessarily technical in nature. Instead, they may involve changes within the organization and/or better management of people's use of information systems. For example, one of the outcomes of the systems security audit described above may well be a set of computer and/or Internet use policies (sometimes referred to as ***acceptable use policies***) for people within the organization, with clearly spelled out penalties for non-compliance. More fundamental to security than management techniques such as these is that you make every effort to hire trustworthy employees and treat them well. Trustworthy employees who are treated well are less likely to commit offences associated with unauthorized access.

Backups and Disaster Recovery

Because of information systems' importance to modern organizations, in addition to implementing the systems security approaches described above, organizations also take great pains to create ***backups*** of their critical systems and data. Data backup software and hardware is a thriving industry in itself. In addition, organizations create ***disaster recovery plans***, which spell out detailed procedures for recovering from systems-related disasters such as virus infections and other disasters (e.g., fire) that might strike critical information systems. This way, even under the worst-case scenario, people will be able to replace or reconstruct critical files or data, or they will at least have readily available the contact information for people and organizations who can help. Some firms even go to the extreme of having completely redundant systems for key applications. This might seem expensive, but for a critical business application involving customers, it may be less expensive to run a redundant backup system in parallel than it would be to disrupt business or lose customers in the event of catastrophic system failure. Organizations should conduct a comprehensive risk assessment and cost-benefit analysis to determine the appropriate degree of disaster recovery planning.

On a more personal note, to protect work in progress on your personal computer, you should back up your own files regularly and keep the backup copies in a separate medium (e.g., a memory stick) in a separate, safe location. Also, while your personal computer software will periodically save the work you are doing, you should frequently save your work even while you are working within a document.

Resources for Information Systems Security

Our pervasive reliance on the Internet for both personal and professional uses has brought with it the disadvantage that the Internet, as a network of networks, has security weaknesses that must be aggressively managed. Securing the Internet is a huge endeavour, with participants from around the globe. For example, the Computer Emergency Response Team, Coordination Center (CERT/CC) was established by the U.S. federal government in 1988 as a major centre of Internet security expertise, located at the Software Engineering Institute (**www.sei.cmu.edu**), a federally funded research

SME SUCCESS NGRAIN

Let's say you're a Canadian soldier in Afghanistan and the armoured vehicle you're riding on breaks down in a dangerous territory. Facing the threat of hostile fire at any second, the last thing you want to do is to have to flip frantically through a manual for repair instructions. As Canadian soldiers are now on duty in dangerous environments like Afghanistan, getting the right information quickly can mean the difference between life and death.

Vancouver-based NGRAIN is an SME that provides interactive 3D training software that soldiers can use to access critical information. The information is delivered on "ruggedized" personal digital assistants (R-PDAs) in the field.

NGRAIN president and chief executive officer Paul Lindahl gives the example of a light armoured vehicle getting a flat tire in a war zone. Getting the tire fixed with minimal delay is crucial, and NGRAIN's 3D system is a fast way of teaching soldiers in the field how to do this. "3D is intuitively obvious," Lindahl says. "You're able to deliver the knowledge at the point it's required, at the time it's required. Whereas, if you have to read a manual, it takes forever. If you're actually doing it in a 3D format, the soldiers in the field are able to immediately grasp the concept." The military has discovered that in training its soldiers, they tend to remember only about 10 percent of what they read. However, they can recall 90 percent of what they actually do.

Master Warrant Officer Tom Stewart, of Canadian Forces J3 Engineer Operations, says that NGRAIN's system is the best on the market. "The ability to impart the knowledge and the logic of the actual internal components . . . of a landmine—nobody else can do it," Stewart says. "This is the next best thing to putting an actual mine in their hands." He adds that there is very little training material available that covers how to deal with landmines: "It's very difficult to buy realistic training aids." Suppose a soldier comes across a landmine in the field. With the NGRAIN system, details of each type of mine, including what it looks like, how it works, and how to deactivate or detonate it will be available in the field on the R-PDAs. As well, the NGRAIN system, also used by the U.S. military, allows critical updates to be quickly sent to the field.

Source: Adapted from Russ Francis, "NGRAIN Tool Used on Ruggedized PDAs for Real-time Access to Info," ITBusiness.ca (March 8, 2006), **www.itbusiness.ca/it/client/en/home/News.asp?id=38647**.

- ***Proxy server:*** A firewall can serve as, or create the appearance of, an alternative (or "proxy") server that intercepts all messages entering and leaving the network. The use of the "proxy" server thus effectively hides the true network addresses.

Firewall Architecture

In Figure 4.11, we show a variety of different ***firewall architectures*** that depict how firewalls can be used within a network. Figure 4.11a depicts a basic firewall for a home network, where the firewall is implemented as software on the single computer being used. Figure 4.11b depicts a firewall router being used either for a small office or a home office. Here the firewall consists of both hardware and software, but the firewall is limited to a fairly inexpensive router. Figure 4.11c depicts a firewall architecture for a larger organization that encompasses a single site (Panko, 2004).

The point here is not that you can decipher the details in these network architecture diagrams; rather, the point is to show you how the complexity and power of the firewall solution change as the situation gets more complex. At home, your firewall might simply be based on software. In the small office or home office, a router with firewall capabilities is used. For the larger organization at a single site you might have multiple layers and types of firewalls working in concert. For large, distributed organizations spanning multiple sites, you would have even more complex layers of defence.

Spyware, Spam, and Cookies

Firewalls have become very popular both within organizations and in private homes to keep unwanted traffic off networks. Three of the more prevalent forms of traffic that people want off their networks and computers are spyware, spam, and cookies. ***Spyware*** is any software that covertly gathers information about a user through an Internet connection without the user's knowledge (see the Ethical Dilemma box: Can't Get Rid of All Those Ads). Spyware is sometimes hidden within freeware or shareware programs. In other instances, it is embedded within

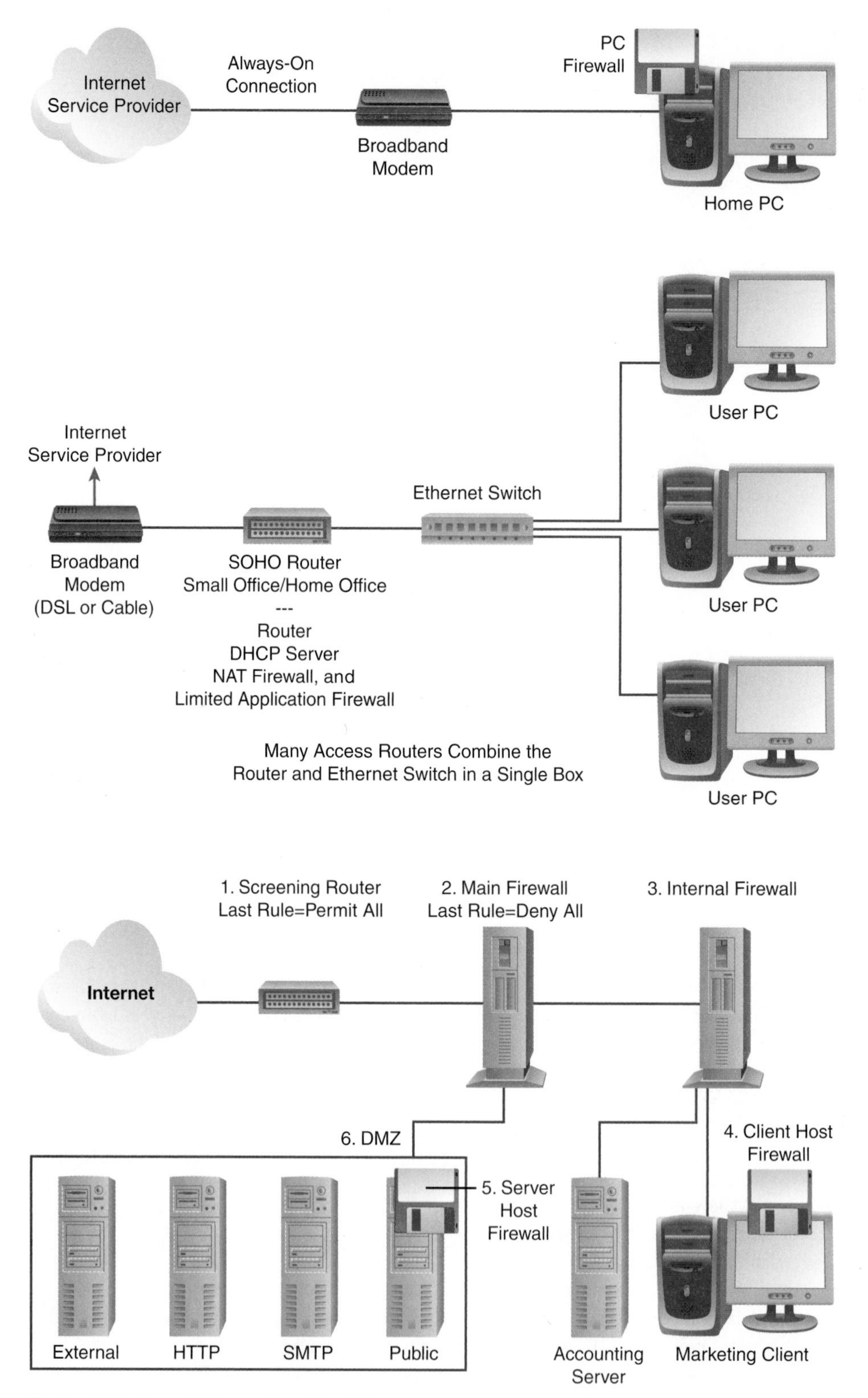

Figure 4.11 Three different firewall architectures.

a website and is downloaded to the user's computer, without the user's knowledge, to track data about the user for marketing and advertisement purposes. Spyware can monitor your activity and transmit that information in the background to someone else. E-mail addresses, passwords, credit card numbers, and websites you have visited are among the various types of information that spyware can gather. From a telecommunications perspective, spyware presents problems because it uses your computer's memory resources, eats network bandwidth as it sends information back to the spyware's home base via your Internet connection, and causes system instability or, worse, system crashes. Fortunately, firewalls and spyware protection software can be used to scan for and block spyware.

Another prevalent form of network traffic that invades our e-mail is spam. ***Spam*** is electronic junk mail or junk newsgroup postings, usually for the purpose of advertising for some product and/or service. In addition to being a nuisance and wasting our time, spam eats up huge amounts of storage space and network bandwidth. As a result, ISPs and those who manage e-mail within organizations often now use firewalls to fight spam. For example, Queen's and York universities recently began using the Barracuda Spam Firewall (see Figure 4.12), which filters for spam and helps reduce the amount of spam processed by the central e-mail servers and delivered to user inboxes. The Barracuda Spam Firewall can process over 10 million messages a day. Any e-mail identified as spam is placed in a quarantine folder that is managed by the e-mail owner through a web interface. Users are notified at regular intervals via e-mail if any e-mail has been placed in their quarantine. The user then visits their quarantine periodically and quickly marks and deletes spam messages. Because the spam firewall *learns* over time—through the process of users' marking messages as spam—any future messages from known sources of spam are automatically blocked by the firewall.

Another nuisance in Internet usage are cookies. A ***cookie*** is a message passed to a web browser on a user's computer by a web server. The browser then stores the message in a text file, and the message is sent back to the server each time the user's browser requests a page from that server.

Cookies are normally used for legitimate purposes, such as identifying a user to prepare a customized web page for them. For example, when you enter a website using cookies, you might be asked to fill out a form providing your name and interests or to simply provide your postal code. This information is packaged into a cookie, which is sent via your web browser to be stored on your computer for later use. The next time you go to the same website, your browser will send the cookie to the web server so that it can then present you with a custom-made web page based on your name and interests, or perhaps the web server triggers off your postal code and provides you with local news and weather forecasts. Firewalls can be used to manage cookies, but an even simpler way to manage

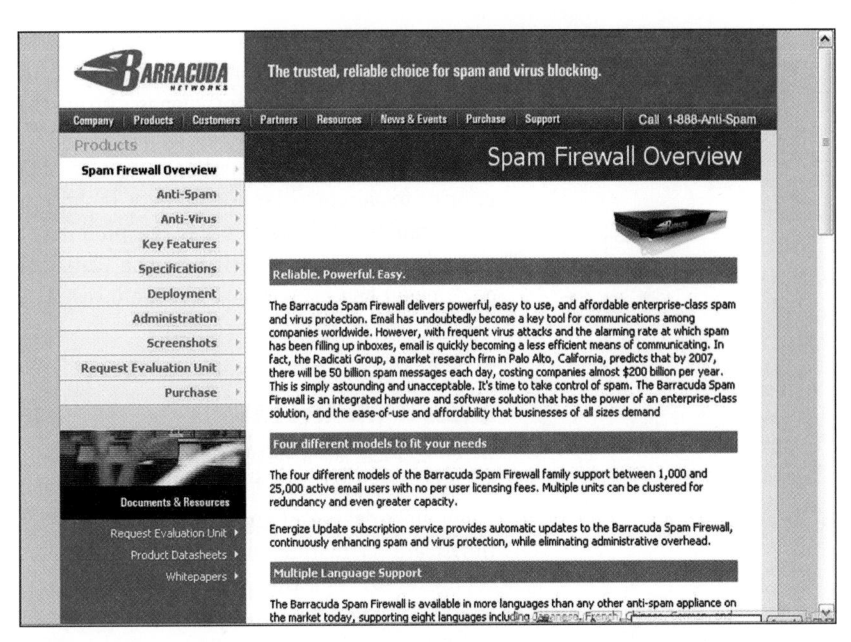

Figure 4.12 The Barracuda Spam Firewall handles over 10 million e-mail messages a day and blocks both spam and viruses.

cookies is through the settings in your web browser. In the settings of the Internet Explorer web browser, for example, you can set levels of restrictions on the use of cookies, you can stop the use of them altogether, and if you do allow them you can go in periodically and delete them from your computer. (In Chapter 9 we talk about the ethical concerns over spyware, spam, and cookies, particularly as an invasion of privacy.)

Biometrics

Biometrics is one of the most sophisticated forms of restricting computer user access. Biometrics is a form of authentication used to govern access to systems, data, and/or facilities. With biometrics, employees may be identified by fingerprints, retinal patterns in the eye, body weight, or other bodily characteristics before being granted access to use a computer (see Figure 4.13). Once the

Figure 4.13 Biometric devices are used to verify a person's identity.

Source: © AP/Wide World Photos

user has been authenticated, they are allowed to access certain systems, computers, data, and/or facilities with specified privileges. After the hijackings and attacks on September 11, 2001, the use of better security methods became a high priority for airports, large corporate buildings, and computers. Biometrics has the promise of providing very high security, so the Canadian government and many companies are investigating how best to use this technology.

Access to Wireless LANs

Wireless local area networks (LANs) are vulnerable to unauthorized access. Unfortunately, given how easy and inexpensive these networks are to install and use, their use has skyrocketed, and they leave many systems open to attack.

Whereas traditional LANs use physical transmission media such as copper wire and optical fibre, wireless local area networks use radio waves for transmission. As a result, while traditional LANs operate by sending signals through wires or fibres in cables, wireless LANs spread their signals widely over the airwaves, allowing attackers to access the network and intercept messages relatively easily. A new form of attack known as ***drive-by hacking*** has arisen, where an attacker accesses the network, intercepts data from it, and even uses network services and/or sends attack instructions to it, without entering the home, office, or organization that owns the network (Panko, 2004).

As described in more detail in Appendix C, the main standard for wireless LANs is the IEEE 802.11 family of standards. 802.11 signals can travel up to several hundred feet away from the wireless access point that generates the signals. These LANS can be extended to cover entire buildings by placing multiple access points around the premises. Unfortunately, covering great distances in this way can also give attackers easy access both within and external to the organization. When using wireless LANs, whether in the home or in the office, it is important to configure the wireless access points such that they do not allow open access. Many of these access points can be configured, for example, to allow access only to computers using preauthorized wireless network interface cards. Further, access passwords should be frequently changed. You may be surprised by how many wireless networks still use the default factory password!

Virtual Private Networks

A ***virtual private network (VPN)*** is a network connection that is constructed dynamically within an existing network—often called a secure *tunnel*—to connect users or nodes. For example, a number of companies and software solutions enable you to create virtual private networks within the Internet as the medium for transporting data. These systems use authentication and encryption (discussed next) and other security mechanisms to ensure that only authorized users can access the network and that the data cannot be intercepted and compromised.

Encryption

In any discussion of systems security, the problem of unauthorized eavesdroppers arises. Organizations can use secure channels not available to computer users outside their networks, but the Internet and public telephone lines and airwaves are not subject to the same restricted use. Most of us send e-mail around the globe, call friends, family, and colleagues on wireless telephones, and trust our desktop, notebook, and server computers with all manner of personal, financial, and corporate secrets. Until recent years, we may have felt secure in our activities. Now, however, news stories about corporate spies, malicious hackers, curious neighbours and coworkers, and suspicious government agencies have us wondering if every transfer of information is somehow subject to unseen eavesdroppers.

When you do not have access to a secure channel for sending information, encryption is the best bet for keeping snoopers out. ***Encryption*** is the process of encoding messages before they enter the network or airwaves, then decoding them at the receiving end of the transfer, so that recipients can read or hear them (see Figure 4.14). The process works because if you scramble messages before you send them, eavesdroppers who might intercept them cannot decipher them without the decoding key.

```
Ciphertext letters:
JOGPSNBUJPO TZTUFNT UPEBZ
Equivalent plaintext letters:
INFORMATION SYSTEMS TODAY
```

Figure 4.14 Encryption is used to encode information so that unauthorized people cannot understand it.

We now have access to encryption software that scrambles text and voice messages and also allows us to send digital signatures that guarantee we are who we say we are when we send a message. You can activate the encryption function from your browser.

How Encryption Works

All encryption systems use a key—the code that scrambles, then decodes, messages. When both sender and recipient use the same key, this is called a ***symmetric secret key system***. This method of encrypting messages was used for centuries. One problem with symmetric secret key encryption is that, as both sender and recipient must keep their key secret from others, key management can be a problem. If too many people use the same key, the system can soon become ineffective. If different keys are used for sending messages to different people, the number of keys can become unmanageable (see Brief Case: The Disappearing Key for some emerging approaches to encryption that may be able to solve some of these problems).

Key management problems of secret key encryption systems were eliminated with the development of public key technology. Public-key encryption is asymmetric, as it uses two keys—a private key and a ***public key*** (see Figure 4.15). An eccentric former MIT hacker and researcher named Whit Diffie is credited with first envisioning the possibility of using two keys—public and private—to encrypt and decode messages. He and two coworkers published their concept in 1976. Each person has his own key pair, a public key that is freely distributed and a private key that is kept secret. Say you want to send a message to Jane using this encryption system. First, you get Jane's public key, which is widely available, and you use it to scramble your message. Now even you cannot decode the encrypted message. When Jane receives the message she uses her private key, known only to her, to unscramble it. Public key systems also allow you to authenticate messages.

If you encrypt a message using your private key, you have "signed" it. A recipient can verify that the message came from you by using your public key to decode it.

To implement public-key encryption on a large scale, such as on a busy website, requires a more sophisticated solution. Here, a third party, called a ***certificate authority***, is used. The certificate authority acts as a trusted middleman between computers and verifies that a website is a trusted site. The certificate authority knows that each computer is who it says it is and provides the public keys to each computer. ***Secure Sockets Layer (SSL)***, developed by Netscape, is a popular public-key encryption method used on the Internet.

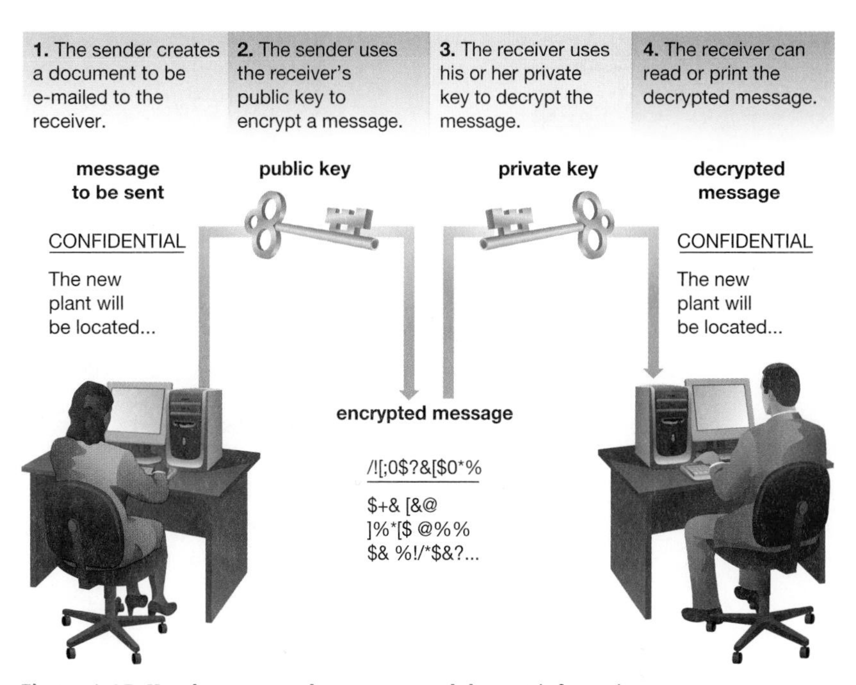

Figure 4.15 How keys are used to encrypt and decrypt information.

Other Encryption Approaches

Other encryption breakthroughs followed Diffie's public-private key revelation. In 1977, three MIT professors, Ron Rivest, Adi Shamir, and Len Adleman, created RSA (named for the surname initials of the inventors), a system based on the public-private key idea. They licensed the technology to several companies, including Lotus and Microsoft, but federal laws against exporting encryption technology kept companies from incorporating RSA into their software. In 1991, Phil Zimmermann devised PGP, a versatile encryption program that he gave away free to anyone who wanted to try it. It soon became the global favourite for encrypting messages.

While innovative encryption aficionados were mainstreaming the encryption concept, the government fought to keep control over keys that would allow its agents to decode communications deemed suspicious. In 1993, then President Bill Clinton endorsed the Clipper Chip, a chip that could generate uncrackable codes. The catch was that only the government would have the key to decode any messages scrambled via the Clipper Chip.

BRIEF CASE The Disappearing Key

If you're frequently sending log-in information, customer information, or your credit card data over "secure" connections over the Internet, you will be disappointed to hear that secure connections are in reality not perfectly secure. Current encryption technologies such as SSL or Pretty Good Privacy (PGP) use multiplications of very large prime numbers to generate keys, and cracking these keys would require tremendous computing power; however, given sufficient time and computing resources, these keys can actually be cracked, and the messages can be deciphered. Nevertheless, scientists claim that in the near future, it will be possible to create unbreakable code.

In March 2001, Harvard professor Michael Rabin announced that he may have devised a code that is absolutely guaranteed to be unbreakable. Rabin's "hyper-encryption" is based on the idea that codes can be formed at random each time a written or spoken message is sent. It works like this: A source, perhaps a satellite or a mainframe computer, generates a stream of random bits. Jane and John select bits from the stream in a secret, prearranged pattern. These selected bits help Jane encrypt a message to John. John uses the same bits to unscramble the message from Jane. Jane and John do not retain the random selected bits, and their computers delete them. No one else can break the code because the random stream is not stored; thus the "key" no longer exists. Rabin claimed to have proven that total secrecy is possible; however, using hyper-encryption is currently limited due to the requirement of sending massive amounts of high-speed data over crowded networks. Furthermore, as Rabin's primary interest is science, hyper-encryption has yet to be commercialized.

An encryption technology that is closer to the market is quantum encryption, which transmits data using photons. Whenever an eavesdropper intercepts the encrypted message, it causes changes in the orientation of the photons, which renders the message useless; furthermore, the receiving party will know that the message has been intercepted. Although quantum encryption is currently limited by a relatively short data-transmission range, scientists are making great progress in terms of speed. The start-up company MagiQ Technologies is already selling devices that use a combination of quantum and traditional encryption.

Source: © Denis Scott/CORBIS

Questions:

1. Given the technical requirements of hyper-encryption and quantum encryption, which companies/institutions could make use of this technology? What would be needed to use this technology on a large scale, given the current limitations?
2. What are the implications of having a technology that offers unbreakable encryption? How can it be ensured that the technology does not fall into the wrong hands?

Sources: John Edwards, "Emerging Technology," CIO.com (February 1, 2002), **www.cio.com/archive/020102/et_development.html.**
Michael Kanellos, "Quantum Encryption Inches Closer to Reality," CNet News.com (May 3, 2004), **http://news.com.com/2100-1029_3-5204725.html**.
Declan McCulagh, "Start-up Makes Quantum Leap into Cryptography," CNet News.com (November 6, 2003), **http://news.com.com/2100-1029_3-5103373.html.**

Opponents criticized the idea as a threat to personal liberty. But when a flaw was found in the chip, which under certain conditions would allow users to take advantage of the chip's strong encryption capabilities without giving the government the key, the Clipper Chip idea was scrapped before it could become reality.

The government finally loosened its control over encryption technology when, in 1999, federal regulations were written allowing the export of strong encryption programs. This paved the way for software developers to build encryption options into their products and made it easier for any computer user to take advantage of encryption technology.

While encryption cannot solve all privacy issues, such as the trading of consumer information collected on the web or deliberate leakage of e-mail messages the sender intended to be kept private, it is definitely effective in keeping snoopers out when both senders and receivers desire privacy. Perhaps eventually encryption will protect medical records, credit histories, credit card databases, and other information that should be marked "keep out" to unauthorized viewers.

Virus Prevention

Virus prevention, which is a set of activities for detecting and preventing computer viruses, has become a full-time, important task for information systems departments within organizations and for all of us with our personal computers. While viruses often have colourful names—Melissa, I Love You, Naked Wife—they can be catastrophic from a computing perspective. Below we describe some precautions you can take to ensure that your computer is protected:

- Purchase and install antivirus software, then update frequently—at least weekly—to be sure you are protected against new viruses. These programs can actively scan your computer, locate viruses, inform you of the presence of viruses, destroy and/or neutralize viruses, and keep your computer updated with the most up-to-date antiviral protection. This software is available relatively inexpensively from several software vendors and can be downloaded over the Internet from their websites, and updates are typically also available over the Internet as well.
- Do not use disks or shareware from unknown or suspect sources, and be equally careful when downloading material from the Internet, making sure that the source is reputable.
- Delete without opening any e-mail message received from an unknown source. Be especially wary of opening attachments. It is better to delete a legitimate message than to infect your computer system with a destructive germ.
- If your computer system contracts a virus, report the infection to your school or company's IT department so that appropriate measures can be taken, and inform people listed in your e-mail address book in case the virus has sent itself to everyone on your e-mail list. If forewarned, individuals listed in your address book can often delete the infectious message before it infects their computers.

Information systems security—especially issues of unauthorized computer access, sending spam e-mail, deploying spyware, or spreading computer viruses—is at minimum an ethical issue and at most a computer crime. (In Chapter 9, we will continue this discussion by exploring the ethical and legal implications of information systems security and use.)

Cyberwar and Cyberterrorism

Over the past several years, individual computer criminals have caused billions of dollars of losses through the use of viruses, worms, and unauthorized access to computers. In the future, many believe that coordinated efforts by national governments or terrorist groups have the potential to do hundreds of billions of dollars in damage as well as put the lives of countless people at stake (Panko, 2004). Most experts believe that cyberwar and cyberterrorism are imminent threats to the United States and other technologically advanced countries. A major attack that cripples a country's information infrastructure or power grid, or even the global Internet, could have devastating implications for a country's (or the world's) economic system, as well as make transportation systems, medical capabilities, and other key infrastructure extremely vulnerable to disaster.

Cyberwar

Cyberwar refers to an organized attempt by a country's military to disrupt or destroy the information and communication systems of another country. Cyberwar is often executed simultaneously with traditional methods to quickly dissipate the capabilities of an enemy. Given that the United States and the NATO alliance is the most technologically sophisticated war machine in the world—and also the most dependent upon its networking and computing infrastructure—it is also the most vulnerable to a cyberwar (or cyberterrorism) attack.

The goal of cyberwar is to turn the balance of information and knowledge in one's favour to diminish an opponent's capabilities and to also enhance those of the attacker. Cyberwar will utilize a diverse range of technologies, including software, hardware, and networking technologies, to gain an information advantage over an opponent. These technologies will be used to electronically blind, jam, deceive, overload, and intrude into an enemy's computing and networking capabilities to diminish various capabilities, including the following:

- Command and control systems
- Intelligence collection and distribution systems
- Information processing and distribution systems
- Tactical communication systems and methods
- Troop and weapon positioning systems
- Friend-or-foe identification systems
- Smart weapons systems

Additionally, controlling the content and distribution of propaganda and information to an opponent's civilians, troops, and government is a key part of a cyberwar strategy. One of the big challenges for governments moving forward will be to fully integrate a cyberwar strategy with overall fighting capabilities.

Cyberterrorism

Unlike cyberwar, cyberterrorism is not launched by governments, but by individuals and organized groups. ***Cyberterrorism*** is the use of computer and networking technologies against persons or property to intimidate or coerce governments, civilians, or any segment of society to attain political, religious, or ideological goals. One of the great fears about cyberterrorism is that an attack can be launched from a computer anywhere in the world—no borders have to be crossed, no bombs smuggled and placed, and no lives lost in making the attack. Because computers and networking systems control power plants, telephone systems, and transportation systems, as well as water and oil pipelines, any disruptions in these systems could cause loss of life or widespread chaos (Volonino and Robinson, 2004). Just as physical terrorist attacks have physical and psychological effects, so also do cyberattacks. Dealing with the unknown—where, when, and how—of an indiscriminant terrorist attack is what leads to "terror."

With the proliferation and dependence on technology increasing at an astronomical rate, the threat of cyberwar and cyberterrorism will continue to increase. To be adequately prepared, national governments along with industry partners must design coordinated responses to various attack scenarios. In addition to greater cooperation and preparedness, governments must improve their intelligence-gathering capabilities so that potential attacks are thwarted before they begin. Industry must also be given incentives to secure their information resources so that losses and disruptions in operations are minimized. International laws and treaties must rapidly evolve to reflect the realities of cyberterrorism, where attacks can be launched from anywhere in the world, to anywhere in the world. Fortunately, experts believe that the likelihood of a devastating attack that causes significant disruption in the major U.S. infrastructure systems is quite low because the attackers would need "$200 million, intelligence information, and years of preparation" to succeed (Volonino and Robinson, 2004). Nevertheless, small attacks have been occurring for years and are likely to increase in frequency and severity—and even a "small" attack, like an individual suicide bomber, can cause tremendous chaos to a society. Clearly, there are great challenges ahead.

CAREER IMPLICATIONS

The Internet and Security

For Accounting and Finance

In their need for information, accounting and finance departments depend heavily on communications networks. At an individual level, the computer of each accounting and finance professional is connected to organizational databases and systems through a network. More broadly, however, these professionals may be asked to determine the costs and the value (from an investment standpoint) of networks within the organization. While determining the costs is fairly easy, determining the value can be very complicated. Except for increases in productivity, the benefits of networks often cannot easily be quantified, but their value seems immeasurable at times.

For Operations Management

The Internet offers a host of new possibilities for operations management. While the Internet can be used to exchange data between a company and its suppliers, manufacturing companies can use telecommunications infrastructures for remote manufacturing. For instance, a factory can be located closer to the supply of raw materials or to a steady and low-priced energy source but away from the main centre of operations. If the company you are working for is using remote manufacturing, you might be controlling manufacturing processes from distant locations, so that only a few employees are responsible for the maintenance and troubleshooting at the factory location. Using a telecommunication network such as the Internet allows organizations to utilize a global manufacturing strategy without having to move operations management personnel to remote and less desirable locations.

For Human Resources Management

Telecommunication and the Internet open up a number of opportunities for human resources management. Facilitated by remote access to a company's information systems, more and more employees can telecommute and work from different locations, such as from their home office or from virtually any location around the world. To support these remote workers, many companies have introduced virtual offices, where several employees share a limited number of desks at a central office. To make this work, employees come into the central office only a few times a week at scheduled times. Organizations are able to save on expensive office space and equipment, as long as the employees have the necessary computer and Internet access. It should be evident that human resource managers have a much greater challenge monitoring, controlling, measuring, and motivating employees in these virtual environments.

For Marketing

The Internet allows employees in sales and marketing to be out on the road to visit potential customers and still have access to the company's information systems; for example, to access configuration information for a product, to enter, retrieve, or update customer data, or to input customer orders. In addition, remote access to corporate systems allows for real-time transmission of sales data from remote locations to a central system that allows sales and marketing managers to react more quickly to sales trends or potential problems such as product shortages.

For Information Systems

Telecommunications and the Internet open up vast opportunities for almost all departments in modern organizations. However, the heavy dependence on the Internet for both internal and external organizational communication and data exchange gives rise to many security issues. While telecommunications and the Internet facilitate the malicious work of outside intruders, theft of data and illegal access to systems can also occur from other sources; for example, data theft and remote system access frequently occur after a company laptop is stolen out of a car or at the airport. Given the strategic value of organizational systems and data, information systems professionals spend a considerable amount of effort on making these systems safe and secure.

KEY POINTS REVIEW

1. **Understand the role of telecommunications in organizations.** Interpersonal uses such as electronic mail, newsgroups, mailing lists, instant messaging, facsimile, and voice mail, as well as business uses such as electronic commerce, electronic data interchange, telecommuting, electronic fund transfer, distance learning, and telemedicine, are fundamentally and rapidly changing the ways we conduct business. Global computer networks allow organizations to streamline business operations in ways never before possible. Telecommunications technologies are becoming fundamental, not only for supporting day-to-day activities within most organizations, but also for playing a growing role in the competitive strategy of more and more organizations. More than ever before, managers must understand these technologies to apply the right solutions to the right problems.
2. **Describe the Internet and how it works.** The Internet is composed of networks that are developed and maintained by many different entities; it follows a hierarchical structure, similar to the national highway system. High-speed central networks called backbones are like provincial highways, enabling traffic from midlevel networks to get on and off. The Internet relies on packet-switching technology to deliver data and information across networks. Routers are used to interconnect independent networks. Because so many different networks are connected to the Internet, they use a common communication protocol (TCP/IP). TCP/IP is divided into two parts. TCP breaks information into small chunks, called data packets, which are transferred from computer to computer. IP defines how a data packet must be formed and how a router must forward each packet. All computers, including routers, are assigned unique IP addresses. Data routing and delivery are possible due to the unique addressing of every computer attached to the Internet. Together, TCP and IP provide a reliable and efficient way to send data across the Internet.
3. **Describe the basic Internet services and the use of the World Wide Web.** A collection of tools enables us to use the Internet to exchange messages, share information, or connect to remote computers. The many ways we can do this include e-mail, telnet, file transfer, chat messaging, newsreaders, voice over IP, and web browsing. Perhaps the most powerful application of the Internet is the World Wide Web, which binds together the various tools used on the Internet, providing users with a simple, consistent interface to a wide variety of information through the use of web browsers.
4. **Explain what is meant by the term "information systems security" and describe various approaches for ensuring information systems security.** Information systems security refers to precautions taken to keep all aspects of information systems (e.g., all hardware, software, network equipment, and data) safe from unauthorized use or access. Information security can be enhanced by auditing the state of systems security, by controlling user access through various authentication methods, and by developing clear organizational policies and practices. Because no system is 100 percent secure, organizations must also have backup and recovery plans and must utilize all available resources for implementing an effective information systems security plan. A number of organizations are available to help with systems security, including the Computer Emergency Response Team, Coordination Centre, and also the National Institute of Standards and Technology, Computer Security Division. They provide resources, solutions, alerts, research results, and training related to information systems security. In addition to improved management approaches, a variety of technologies can be deployed to enhance system security, including firewalls, biometrics, virtual private networks, encryption, and virus protection tools. Firewalls are hardware or software that is used to detect intrusion and prevent unauthorized access to or from a private network. Biometrics is a technology used to better authenticate users by matching fingerprints, retinal patterns in the eye, body weight, or other bodily characteristic before granting access to a computer. Virtual private networks use authentication and encryption to provide a secure tunnel within a public network such as the Internet so that information can pass securely between two computers. Encryption—the process of encoding messages before they enter the network or airwaves—is very useful for securing information when you do not have access to a secure telecommunications channel. Virus protection utilizes a set of hardware and software to detect and prevent computer viruses.
5. **Describe and explain the differences between cyberwar and cyberterrorism.** Cyberwar refers to an organized attempt by a country's military to disrupt or destroy the information and communication systems of another country. The goal of cyberwar is to turn the balance of information and knowledge in one's favour, to diminish an opponent's capabilities, and to enhance those of the attacker. Cyberterrorism is the use of computer and networking technologies by individuals and organized groups against persons or property to intimidate or coerce governments, civilians, or any segment of society to attain political, religious, or ideological goals. One of the great fears about cyberterrorism is that an attack can be launched from a computer anywhere in the world.

KEY TERMS

distance learning 111
domain name 113
Domain Name System (DNS) 114
drive-by hacking 132
electronic brochure 123
electronic business 111
electronic data interchange (EDI) 111
electronic funds transfer (EFT) 111
electronic marketplace 123
e-mail 109, 119
encryption 132
facsimile (fax) 109
file transfer 119
firewall 128
firewall architectures 129
fixed wireless 116
gateway 109
geostationary 116
geosynchronous 116
gigaPoP 120
global network 117
Gopher 121
hyperlinks 121
hypertext 121
HyperText Markup Language (HTML) 121
HyperText Transfer Protocol (HTTP) 122
identity theft 127
information systems access 126
information systems security 123
instant messaging (IM) 109
interexchange carriers (IXC) 116
Internet 110
Internet2 119
Internet backbone 115
Internet Corporation for Assigned Names and Numbers (ICANN) 114
Internet over Satellite (IoS) 116
Internet Registry 114
Internet relay chat (IRC) 109
Internet service provider (ISP) 115
internetworking 110
InterNIC 114
InterNIC Registration Service 114
IP addresses 114
IP datagram 113
IPv6 114
listserv 109
mailing lists 109
mobile wireless 116
modem 115
National Science Foundation (NSF) 112
National Science Foundation Network (NSFNET) 112
network 108
network access point (NAP) 115
newsgroups 109
newsreader 119
online customer service 123
online ordering 123
packet filter 128
packet switching 112
plain old telephone service (POTS) 115
podcasting 119
protocol 112
proxy server 129
public key 133
public switched telephone network (PSTN) 115
risk acceptance 125
risk analysis 124
risk reduction 125
risk transference 125
routers 113
satellite 116
Secure Sockets Layer (SSL) 133
spam 131
spyware 129
symmetric digital subscriber line (SDSL) 115
symmetric secret key system 133
T1 line 116
T3 line 117
telecommunications 108
telecommuting 111
telemedicine 111
telnet 119
top-level domain 114
Transmission Control Protocol/Internet Protocol (TCP/IP) 112
transmission media 112
Uniform Resource Locator (URL) 113
videoconferencing 109
virtual private network (VPN) 132
virus prevention 135
viruses 128
voice mail 109
voice over IP 119
web browser 119
web browsing 119
web page 113
web server 122
website 113
wireless local area networks (WLAN) 116
World Wide Web (WWW) 119

REVIEW QUESTIONS

1. List and describe three types of interpersonal communication uses for telecommunications.
2. List and describe three common business uses of telecommunications.
3. What is the Internet, and why was it created?
4. What are packet switching and TCP/IP?
5. Other than the telephone, what are three alternatives for connecting to the Internet?
6. List and describe five popular uses of the Internet.
7. What is the World Wide Web, and what is its relationship to the Internet?
8. List and describe several different approaches for ensuring information systems security.
9. Describe encryption and how it helps to secure information.
10. Describe risk analysis as it relates to information systems security and explain three ways to approach systems security risk.
11. Describe several methods for preventing and/or managing the spread of computer viruses.
12. Define and contrast cyberwar and cyberterrorism.

SELF-STUDY QUESTIONS

Visit the Companion Website for this text for additional Self-Study Questions: **www.pearsoned.ca/jessup**.

1. Telecommunications refers to the transmission of all forms of information, including __________, from one location to another over a network.
   A. data
   B. voice and sound
   C. fax and video
   D. all of the above
2. __________ allows typed conversations with others in real time on the Internet.
   A. Voice mail
   B. Newsgroups
   C. e-mail
   D. Instant Messaging
3. All of the following are applications of telecommunications except __________.
   A. electronic commerce
   B. telemedicine
   C. distance learning
   D. transmission media
4. All of the following are correct domain suffix pairs except __________.
   A. edu—educational institutions
   B. mil—military
   C. neo—network organizations
   D. com—commercial businesses
5. Which of the following is faster and becoming more popular than the standard telephone as a way to connect to the Internet?
   A. DSL
   B. Satellite
   C. Cable
   D. all of the above
6. Which of the following is the process of determining the true, accurate identity of a user of an information system?
   A. Audit
   B. Authentication
   C. Firewall
   D. Virtual private network
7. Websites and specific web pages within those sites have a unique Internet address called a URL, or __________.
   A. Universal Resource Login C. Uniform Resource Locator
   B. Universal Router Locator D. Uniform Resource Language
8. Which of the following approaches to information systems security is aimed at finding weaknesses in the systems and their use throughout the organization?
   A. Keeping stored information safe with passwords and allowing access only to those employees who need it to do their jobs
   B. Using biometrics that may include fingerprints and retinal scans or other bodily characteristics
   C. Making every effort to hire good employees and treat them well
   D. Conducting a systems security audit
9. A(n) __________ is a system composed of hardware, or software, or both, that is designed to detect intrusion and prevent unauthorized access to or from a private network.
   A. encryption
   B. firewall
   C. alarm
   D. logic bomb
10. __________ is the process of encoding messages before they enter the network or airwaves, then decoding them at the receiving end of the transfer, so that recipients can read or hear them.
    A. Encryption
    B. Biometrics
    C. Authentication
    D. Disaster recovery
11. The use of computer and networking technologies by individuals and organized groups against persons or property to intimidate or coerce governments, civilians, or any segment of society to attain political, religious, or ideological goals is know as __________.
    A. cyberwar
    B. cybercrime
    C. cyberterrorism
    D. none of the above

PROBLEMS AND EXERCISES

1. Match the following terms to the appropriate definitions:

____ Authentication

____ Instant messaging

____ Router

____ Internet service provider

____ Web browser

____ Telecommuting

____ Encryption

____ Domain name

____ Firewall

____ Hypertext

a. Specialized hardware and software that are used to keep unwanted users out of a system, or to let users in with restricted access and privileges

b. Used in Uniform Resource Locators (URLs) to identify a source or host entity on the Internet

c. Text in a web document that is highlighted and, when clicked on by the user, evokes an embedded command that goes to another specified file or location and brings up that file or location on the user's screen

d. A software application that can be used to locate and display web pages, including text, graphics, and multimedia content
e. The process of encoding messages before they enter the network or airwaves, then decoding them at the receiving end of the transfer, so that recipients can read or hear them
f. The process of working at home or at another remote location and "commuting" to the office via computing and networking technologies
g. An application that allows typed conversations with others in real time on the Internet
h. An intelligent device used to connect and route data traffic across two or more individual networks
i. The process of identifying that the user is indeed who they claim to be, typically by requiring something that the user knows (e.g., a password) together with something that the user carries with them or has access to (e.g., an identification card or file)
j. An individual or organization that enables other individuals and organizations to connect to the Internet

2. Have you taken a distance or online course at your university? What did you like and dislike? If you have not taken a course in this medium, investigate a course that you would be interested in taking. What are the pros and cons of a course without a regular classroom time?
3. How many types of communication tools do you use each day, such as e-mail, voice mail, fax, desktop videoconferencing, electronic fund transfers, instant messengers, pagers, and cellular phones? What are the strengths and weaknesses of each? For what tasks are each best suited? Are you better off having these tools available? Why or why not?
4. Have you ever, or do you know of anyone who has, telecommuted full-time or part-time? What types of technology were used to accomplish this? What are the positive and the negative aspects of this way of working?
5. Scan the popular press and search the World Wide Web for clues concerning emerging technologies for telecommunications. This may include new uses for current technologies or new technologies altogether. Discuss as a group the "hot" issues. Do you feel they will become a reality in the near future? Why or why not? Prepare a 10-minute presentation to the class of your findings.
6. Explain in simple language how the Internet works. Be sure to talk about backbones, packet switching, networks, routers, TCP/IP, and Internet services. What technologies, hardware, and software do you utilize when using the Internet? What would you like to use that isn't available to you?
7. How long, on average, are you willing to wait for a web page to load in your browser on your computer? Under what conditions would you be willing to wait longer for a page to come up in your browser? Based on your answers, what are the implications for website design? Do you wait longer if you know what you will be seeing, that is, if you are loading a page at a site you have been to in the past?
8. Search through recent articles in your favourite IS publication—whether print or online. What are some of the issues being discussed that relate to the Internet and/or the World Wide Web in particular? Have you experienced any of these technologies, applications, and/or issues? What is your opinion about them? How will they affect your life and career? Prepare a 10-minute presentation to the class of your findings.
9. Research projects can now be accomplished by using the Internet as the sole source of information. Conduct such a research project using solely the Internet for source information, and answer the following questions: (1) what is the history of the Internet, (2) what are the demographics of the users of the Internet, and (3) what are the historic growth and the projected growth of the Internet? Remember, use only the Internet itself to research and write this short paper, and reference all of your sources completely and accurately.
10. There are many brands of software firewalls, with Zone Labs's Security Suite, Norton's Personal Firewall, McAfee's Firewall, and BlackICE PC Protection being four popular choices. Search for these products on the web and learn more about how a firewall works and what it costs to give you this needed protection; prepare a one-page report that outlines what you have learned.
11. What is the difference between 128-bit and 40-bit encryption? What level of encryption is used in your web browser? Why has the U.S. government been reluctant to release software to other countries with higher levels of encryption?
12. What levels of user authentication are used at your school and/or place of work? Do they seem to be effective? What if a higher level of authentication were necessary? Would it be worth it, or would the added steps cause you to be less productive?
13. Search for more information on the Computer Emergency Response Team, Coordination Center (CERT/CC), and the Computer Security Division (CSD) of the U.S. National Institute of Standards and Technology's Information Technology Laboratory. What role do you envision they will continue to play in the development of better information systems security? Do either of these seem to be organizations you might want to work for? Are they hiring?
14. What laws should be enacted to combat cyberterrorism? How could such laws be enforced?

APPLICATION EXERCISES

Note: The existing data files referenced in these exercises are available on the Companion Website: **www.pearsoned.ca/jessup**.

Spreadsheet Application: Analyzing Server Traffic

Recently, the employees of the company you're working for have started complaining about slow Internet connections, especially during certain periods of the day. Therefore, the IS manager has proposed to increase the capacity of the company's network; in a few days, he has to present the business case for this proposal at the weekly meeting of the department heads. You are asked to prepare graphs for the presentation to support the IS manager's business case. In the file ServerLogs.csv you will find information about the network traffic for a 1-week period. Please prepare the following graphs:

- Total bandwidth used for each day (line graph)
- Bandwidth used per day, by time period (line graph)
- Average bandwidth used in each 2-hour period (line graph)

Format the graphs in a professional manner, and print out each graph on a separate page. Hint: if you are using Microsoft Excel's Chart Wizard, select "Place chart: As New Sheet" in Step 4.

Database Application: Tracking Network Hardware

Due to your background in information technology, the director of HospitalityConsult has put you in charge of the company's network. On the first day of this assignment, you realize that there is no clear system in place to let you know which computer is installed in which office, where the routers/hubs are located, or which IP addresses are assigned to which computer. You know that you will need to have this information stored in a way that you can quickly access it in case something malfunctions. Therefore, you decide to create a database to store this information. The database needs to contain the following information:

- Equipment (Equipment_ID, description, and assigned IP address, if any)
- Location (Location_ID, description)

Note: there can be multiple pieces of equipment in one location. Please import the data provided in the files Locations.txt and Equipment.txt into the database you have created, assign a Location_ID to every piece of equipment, and create a report of all pieces of equipment that have an IP address assigned, including the locations and the IP addresses. Hint: Set up a query to use as a basis for creating the report. In the query, make sure to add a criterion to ensure that only equipment having an IP address is selected. Make sure to include the appropriate title, headers, and footers, and print out the report.

ANSWERS TO THE SELF-STUDY QUESTIONS

1. D, p. 108 2. D, p. 109 3. D, p. 111 4. C, p. 114 5. D, pp. 115–116
6. B, p. 125 7. C, p. 113 8. D, p. 123 9. B, p. 128 10. A, p. 132 11. C, 136

Case *Convergence in Canada*

Depending on whom you talk to, telecommunications competition in Canada either needs regulatory first aid or is unfolding as intended. Not surprisingly, many competitors take the first view, while major incumbent carriers tend toward the second. In either case, the 90s buzzword "convergence" is becoming a reality in many Canadian communities, as the distinction between telephone, TV, and Internet services is becoming blurred. The latest battleground is local telephone service.

"The incumbents are still leveraging their position," says Michael Stephens, vice-president of marketing for competitive local carrier Group Telecom Inc. "The regulatory system the Canadian Radio-television and Telecommunications Commission [CRTC] has adopted is the right model to promote sustained long-term competition," says Lawson Hunter, executive vice-president of Bell Canada parent BCE Inc. Local telephone service has been open to competition for more than 5 years, but most of the competitive local exchange carriers (CLECs) that sprang up in the late 1990s are history now. One significant survivor, Group Telecom, emerged from bankruptcy in early 2003 to be bought by Vancouver-based 360networks Corp.

Along with Group Telecom, competitors in local business telephony include the major competitive long-distance carriers Allstream Corp. (formerly AT&T Canada), Rogers Communications (formerly Call-Net Enterprises Inc. operating as Sprint Canada), and Telus Corp. Residential local service is even less competitive. Rogers is the only sizeable nonincumbent in the market; Allstream abandoned it several years ago, and most CLECs have focused on business customers.

A few cable companies and electrical utilities have taken advantage of existing networks and rights-of-way to get into local service. For instance, the Halifax-based Eastlink group of companies competes with incumbent Aliant Inc. in parts of Nova Scotia and Prince Edward Island. Some local hydro companies have subsidiaries offering phone service. Yet the incumbents—Aliant, Bell Canada, MTS, SaskTel, and Telus—carry well over 90 percent of local traffic.

Competitive startups in the telecom field have had a rough time in the years since local competition began, admits Lawrence Surtees, senior telecom and Internet research analyst at IDC Canada Ltd. in Toronto. "If we think that those are the only competitors, we get a pretty horrific picture in our minds." But Surtees contends that the real competition in local service will come from companies that are new entrants in telecom but well-heeled incumbents in their own industries. Those would be cable companies, electrical utilities, and possibly IT service firms. Commercial service based on Internet protocol (IP) could be a reality by 2006. Add to that the fact that the largest incumbents—Bell Canada and Telus—are making cautious forays into each other's home territories, and some say you have a recipe for healthy competition in time.

Incumbents like to add that wireless service already competes with traditional local service. "In the not-too-distant future, perhaps a year or a little bit longer, there will be more wireless phones in Alberta and B.C. than there are wireline phones," predicts Willie Grieve, vice-president of public policy and regulatory affairs at Telus. Most Canadians have a choice of wireless carriers. As their volumes rise and their costs decline, Grieve says, wireless carriers will become more competitive.

The telecom ventures of electrical utilities, while small potatoes so far, could lead to bigger things. "You can laugh off little local companies," Surtees says, but municipal operations in Quebec are banding together, buying in bulk, and targeting the telecom market. Such alliances could become significant competitors with the incumbent telcos.

The major cable companies are clearly interested in the local market, and would probably play primarily in residential service. Ken Engelhart, vice-president of regulatory at Rogers Communications Inc., says a few technological pieces still need to be put in place for his company to compete in telephony, but they will be there soon. Rogers has raised regulatory issues the company feels would put it at a disadvantage, and Engelhart says its future plans depend partly on the CRTC's response to those concerns.

While electrical utilities and cable companies are widely talked about as potential local phone competitors, Surtees suggests there is another dark horse in the race. Major computer services companies like IBM Canada Ltd. and Electronic Data Systems Corp. are increasingly providing communications services to large corporate customers.

Analysts and some competitors say that the CRTC is moving to promote competition more aggressively. For years, the commission made rules but paid little attention to policing them, says Robert Yates, co-president of Montreal-based LeMay-Yates Associates Inc. Recently, the CRTC has taken a more activist role in enforcing its rules, but competitors want more. "We need more change, and we would like that change faster," says Chris Peirce, senior vice-president of regulatory and government affairs at Allstream. In particular, CLECs have asked for restrictions on bundling services, limits on the steps incumbents can take to lure back customers, and a better deal on facilities the competitors lease from incumbents.

Competitive carriers won a victory in July 2003 when the CRTC ordered incumbent carriers to unbundle digital subscriber line (DSL) Internet access from residential phone service. Both Rogers and Eastlink have asked the commission to stop incumbents from bundling local service with other services, arguing that such bundles hurt competition in both local service and other areas. With three or four services bundled together, says Engelhart, "it just gets more complicated if you want to go to another competitor."

Rogers alleged that incumbent carriers are not equitable in handling cutovers from their services to the competitors. For instance, incumbent carriers will do residential installations for their own customers on Saturdays but won't do the same for customers switching to Rogers. And cutovers don't always happen as quickly and smoothly as they might—for which the customer inevitably blames the competitive carrier. Ted Chislett, president of competitive carrier Primus Canada, adds that charges for cutovers vary widely across the country.

Rogers also wants a 2-year reduction in charges for services CLECs must buy from incumbents and for a public education campaign to make consumers more aware that competitive local service exists. Recently, Rogers has been trying to move local telephone subscribers from using phone cables, owned by the telcos, to using cable TV cables, which they own. With this change, in some markets, the company can offer local and long distance phone service, cable TV service, and Internet access, all through cable lines.

With all these claims and counterclaims, one could forgive regulators for feeling overwhelmed. The solution, Yates says, is to look at the whole picture and develop a blueprint for making competition work. "The reaction of the CRTC should be to have a proceeding on competition," he says. A very Canadian solution.

Sourcce: Adapted from Grant Buckler, "Can You See the Difference?" *Communications & Networking*, Vol. 6, No. 9 (September 2003).

Discussion Questions

1. Have you ever switched local phone companies? Have you ever switched long distance phone companies or wireless phone companies? If you answered yes to one question and no to the other, how do you explain the difference?
2. Do incumbents have an unfair advantage in local telephone services? Why or why not?
3. Who do you think will be the winners in the battle for the telecommunications market in Canada?
4. How far can information technology convergence go? Predict how a home or business will send and receive information in 2015.

Log on to the Companion Website at www.pearsoned.ca/jessup for an additional case.

Running Case: Connexion by Boeing

Telecommunications and the Internet

Over the past few years, adoption of broadband Internet access has increased at a tremendous rate. It has been estimated that more than 40 million Americans had access to broadband Internet services from home in 2004, an increase of 36 million in just 4 years. Likewise, global revenues for providing broadband services are expected to increase by more than $136 billion between 2002 and 2008. Broadband Internet access in homes or offices can be set up in a variety of ways, including digital subscriber lines (DSL), cable modems, fixed wireless, or even satellite connections. The technologies for providing ground-based Internet access are mature and well established, but prior to the development of the Connexion by Boeing network, there was no existing way for accessing the Internet using broadband speeds from an in-flight airplane.

Even though developing a system to enable broadband Internet access in airplanes was not easy, Connexion realized the business potential associated with providing these services. While traditional seatback phones could be used for sending and receiving e-mails at rather slow connection speeds, Connexion envisioned Internet access at DSL-like speeds, enabling applications such as teleconferencing, which would be especially valuable to operators of private business jets and government VIP jets, maritime markets, and remote medical evaluations, as well as enhancing onboard security (including audio/video cabin monitoring). In addition to video, broadband in-flight Internet access could be used for voice services, streaming data, delivery of news and entertainment content, wireless cabin networks, crew information services, in-flight reservations and check-in, as well as transmission of fleet management, operations, and maintenance data. Clearly, there are countless applications that could benefit from this high-speed Internet service.

To provide these services, Connexion's engineers devised a system capable of transmitting data at broadband speeds between an aircraft and a satellite. To make this system work, an antenna mounted atop the aircraft fuselage locks onto a signal relayed from a geosynchronous satellite, which relays transmissions to and from the plane while the aircraft soars through the air at subsonic speeds. The satellite communicates with ground stations, from which the signal is carried securely through Connexion's Network Control Centers and to the Internet (see figure below). To achieve coverage of the major flight routes between America and Europe as well as between America and East Asia, Connexion decided to rely on leased capacity on different satellites. For flights above the United States, capacity on Loral Skynet's Telstar 6 satellite, which relays transmissions between the plane and the ground station in Littleton, Colorado, was leased. From the ground station in Colorado, the signal is then carried to Connexion's Network Control Center. Connexion also leased transponders from Intelsat and Eutelsat for data transmission across the North Atlantic and in Europe. In 2004, SES Americom was selected to provide North Pacific region coverage. Additionally, Connexion set up operational ground stations in the United States and Switzerland, and additional ground stations were to be developed in Japan and Russia.

While Connexion could easily lease capacity on the different satellites, great care had to be taken to comply with regulations when choosing frequencies for data transmission. For example, in July 2003, the member states of the International Telecommunication Union (ITU) approved a secondary allocation for aeronautical mobile satellite service in the 14.0–14.5 GHz frequency band at the ITU's World Radiocommunication Conference (WRC-03), which enables two-way high-speed communications in flight. This action set the regulatory framework for the provision of Connexion's global network strategy. Before approving the frequency for the use of in-flight communications, seven ITU technical working groups studied the feasibility of providing this service without interfering with other spectrum users. Each technical group concluded that there was no technical reason preventing a service from operating in that spectrum without causing harmful interference with other users; therefore, Connexion had the green light for using these frequencies for building its network. Within 6 months of the ITU's allocation of frequency for aeronautical services, Connexion's regulatory team had received licences from more than 30 countries and had filed applications with many more. It was decided to obtain additional individual country authorizations in accordance with the global rollout schedule.

Connexion clearly benefited from its parent, the Boeing Company, during the R&D phases of the network development. Boeing is a global leader in the development of telecommunications and aviation equipment standards, not only helping to build various components, but also assisting in the authorization and certification processes as well as system installation within new and existing aircraft. In April 2002, the U.S. Federal Aviation Administration (FAA) certified Connexion's system with the First-Generation array antenna for use on the Boeing 737–400 model. This system consisted of two low-profile antennas—one for transmission, one for reception—that were installed atop the crown of the airplane. The relatively small footprint of the antennas ensured that this configuration would also work well for executive jet platforms in both the private and the governmental markets. The certification for the system with the Second-Generation antenna and associated subsystems was completed in 2004. This Second-Generation antenna, supplied by Mitsubishi Electric Corporation, was important for Connexion in order to make global in-flight connectivity possible. It will support connectivity up to 75 degrees latitude, such as across northern Greenland, and significantly farther north than the northernmost reaches of Siberia and Alaska. In contrast to the two antennas used in the First-Generation system, it was decided to use a single aperture antenna in the Second-Generation, to handle both transmission and reception, thus improving the aerodynamics and reducing time and effort needed for the installation on the aircraft.

In addition to the data transmission between the airplane and the ground stations via satellites, Connexion had to find a way for the users of the system to be able to connect with minimal effort, while at the same time ensuring that the system would not interfere with the aircraft's internal systems. Due to its great popularity, standard wireless networking technologies were chosen so that travellers carrying a wirelessly enabled laptop or PDA could easily connect to the network. Additionally, operators of commercial jetliners were very interested in wireless cabin configurations, as wireless promised the benefits of reduced complexity, ease of configuration management, and less weight, resulting in better

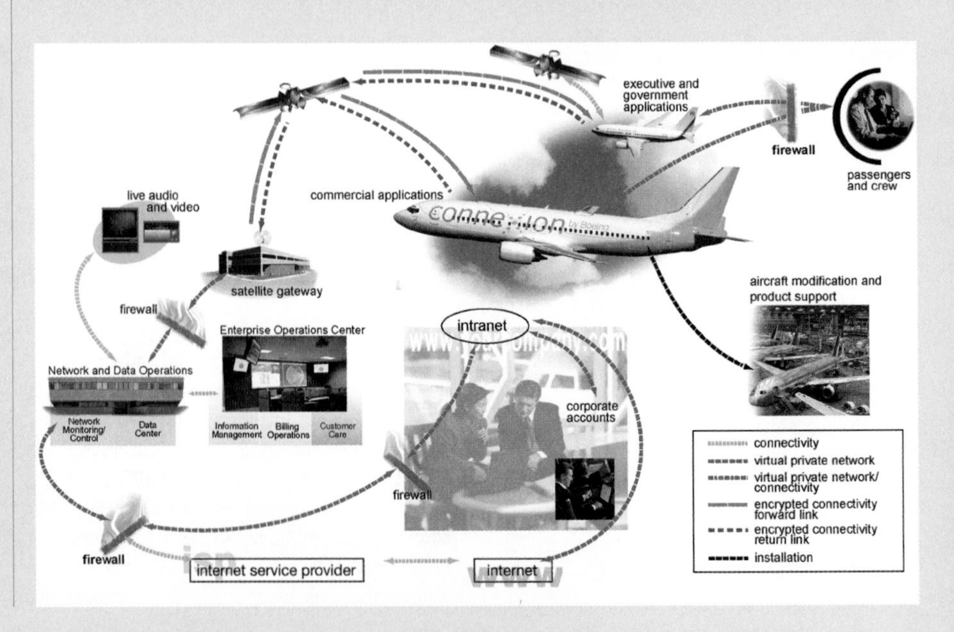

fuel burn and range. In May 2003, regulatory authorities in the United Kingdom (CAA) and Germany (LDB) granted certifications to Connexion and Lufthansa Technik (the world market leader in the maintenance, repair, and overhaul of commercial aircraft [Lufthansa Technik, 2004]) that paved the way for passengers to connect to the Internet in flight wirelessly with their 802.11b-equipped "Wi-Fi" laptops and PDAs. Lufthansa and British Airways became the first airlines to make wireless in-flight connectivity available to their passengers in 2003. Depending on the configuration of Connexion's system, passengers may also be able to connect to the service via a laptop or PDA using a standard Ethernet cable (RJ-45) (although most airlines are opting for a completely wireless system due to concerns over the added weight for the network cabling).

While wireless connectivity offers many benefits for aircraft operators and travellers, Connexion also focused extensively on network security when designing their system. To solve network security concerns inherent in any wireless data transmission, Connexion chose to provide passengers with virtual private network—secured access to business intranets and e-mail accounts. This solution not only helps to provide greater security to passengers' data, it also helped Connexion gain a competitive advantage, as their system was the only one offering this level of security for in-flight data communications.

To ease airlines' installation concerns, Connexion also made sure that the installation of the system could be accomplished during regularly scheduled maintenance, regardless of the aircraft size or manufacturer. Experience with the first commercial jetliner installation (Lufthansa) in 2002 demonstrated that it could be accommodated readily during scheduled maintenance with no impact on the return-to-service schedule. Additionally, the installation into new airplanes was designed to meet the needs of both Boeing and Airbus.

Source: Lufthansa Technik, Company Profile. Retrieved June 28, 2004, from **www.lufthansa-technik.com**.

Discussion Questions

1. What were the major obstacles Connexion faced in establishing its "broadband in the sky" service?
2. If you were to decide, would you rent transmission capacity on satellites or use your own satellites? Explain.
3. Do you think Connexion could have set up the service without the backing of its parent company, the Boeing Company? Why or why not?

Preview

This chapter focuses on how companies are conducting business electronically with their customers, business partners, and suppliers, which is referred to as ***electronic business*** (e-business, or EB). The Internet and World Wide Web are extremely well suited for conducting business electronically on a global basis. Web-based e-business has introduced unprecedented opportunities for the marketing of products, accompanied by features, functionality, and innovative methods to serve and support consumers. After reading this chapter, you will be able to do the following:

1. Describe e-business and how it has evolved.
2. Describe the strategies that companies are adopting to compete in the online marketplace.
3. Explain the differences between extranets and intranets and show how organizations utilize these environments.
4. Describe the stages of business-to-consumer e-business and the key drivers for the emergence of mobile commerce.
5. Understand the keys to successful e-business applications.

Electronic Business, Intranets, and Extranets

Canadian e-Business Firms Battle with Larger Rivals

Since the dot-com bubble burst more than 6 years ago, competition on the Internet has become more fierce and unforgiving. Canadian firms have had to battle hard to keep pace with their international rivals. While 69 percent of all Canadian household Internet spending in 2003 was from Canadian websites, foreign websites have been gaining ground quickly. Many Canadian firms have chosen to focus on niche markets that have been underserved by larger competitors.

One such provider is Points.com. The site acts as a central management tool for people who subscribe to multiple loyalty programs from Air Canada to American Eagle. Airlines have strongly supported the site, said its CEO Robert MacLean, as they welcome any opportunity that helps lift the travel industry out of its post-9/11 slump. MacLean claims that the key ingredient to dot-com success is focus.

Google and eBay "are not unbeatable if you maintain your focus," said Denis Gadbois, CEO of Quebec-based Mediagrif Interactive Technologies. The company operates 12 industry-specific B2B exchanges, as well as the Merx e-tendering service, which handles contract tenders for the Canadian federal government.

Chapters.Indigo.ca has chosen to focus on Canadian book lovers. Initially, the company had a built-in advantage over U.S.-based rivals like Amazon.com and Barnesandnoble.com, as Canadian shoppers were faced with shipping delays, import duties, and shifting exchange rates. However, in June 2002, Amazon.com "officially" entered the Canadian marketplace with Amazon.ca. Canadians could order in Canadian dollars, and shipping was provided by Canada Post. Almost immediately, Amazon.ca cut the prices of its 40 best sellers by 40 percent in a bid to topple Chapters.Indigo.ca as Canada's dominant online book retailer. "We run our business based on what customers tell us they want. We have yet to meet a customer who doesn't like lower prices," Amazon's Kristin Schaefer said in an interview with the *Toronto Star*. "That's our corporate strategy." Chapters.Indigo.ca countered with a 30-percent discount on its best-selling books. Both firms offered free shipping on orders greater than $39.

Chapters.Indigo.ca then lodged a complaint with the Canadian Heritage Department arguing that Amazon.ca was violating rules that prohibited foreign-owned bookstores from setting up in Canada. However, Amazon.ca replied that the company had no Canadian place of business and the complaint was dismissed.

In 2003, Amazon.ca teamed up with HMV Canada to relaunch HMV.com. Then, in mid-2005, it agreed to manage one of the leading Canadian retail websites, Sears.ca. The company also unveiled a program with Canada Post to place its logo on mail delivery trucks.

In response, Chapters.Indigo.ca increased its sponsorship of Canadian literary festivals and broadened its product offerings to include gifts, DVDs, lifestyle products, and jewellery. The firm also increased the integration between the online store and traditional Indigo retail stores.

The Canadian e-business marketplace has grown steadily, and Canadian firms are capitalizing on this growth. However, the pressure to stay ahead of foreign rivals is intense.

Figure 5.1 e-Business continues to grow rapidly.

Source: Phil Degginger/Color-Pic, Inc.

Web Search

Have you ever wondered about starting your own e-business? The Government of Canada has created a website designed to help Internet entrepreneurs get started. The site is called ebiz.enable and can be found at **http://strategis.ic.gc.ca/epic/internet/inee-ef.nsf/en/Home**.

While the financial markets have risen and fallen over the last 10 years, online consumer and business spending have grown steadily in Canada and elsewhere. According to Statistics Canada, average annual online purchases jumped to $956 in 2003, up from $146 in 2000. People with e-business skills are in high demand in the marketplace, and therefore, the more you know about EB, the more valuable you will become (see Figure 5.1)!

ELECTRONIC BUSINESS DEFINED

The growth of electronic business has given rise to a plethora of new terminology. Figure 5.2 illustrates the relationship among a number of the new economy terms. The largest oval is labelled electronic business. Simply put, this includes everything having to do with the application of information and communication technologies (ICT) to the conduct of business between organizations or from company to consumer. Within the EB oval is a smaller oval labelled ***electronic commerce***. This placement highlights the fact that there are numerous forms of business-related ICT-based interactions that can occur between businesses, or between a business and an end consumer, which do not directly concern buying and selling (i.e., "commerce"). Only those forms of interaction having to do with commerce are included in the electronic commerce oval. This includes advertising of products or services, electronic shopping, and direct after-sales support. It would not include such things as interorganizational collaboration using ICT-based collaboration systems for the development of a new product.

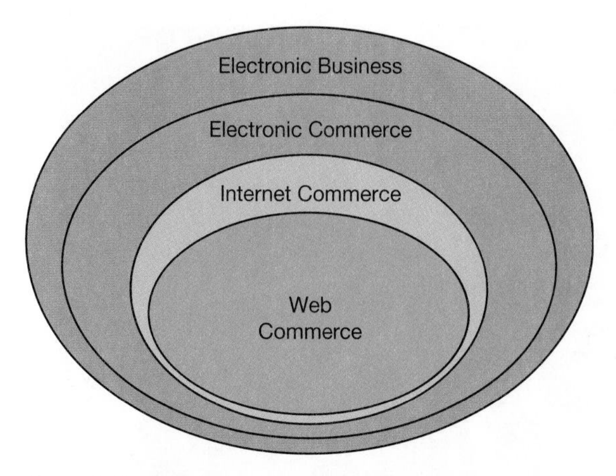

Figure 5.2 The relationship among e-business terms and concepts.

Source: S. L. Huff, M. Wade, and S. Schneberger, *Cases in Electronic Commerce*, 2nd ed. (Irwin/McGraw-Hill, 2002).

Within the electronic commerce oval is a smaller oval labelled ***Internet commerce***. This reflects the fact that electronic commerce need not be conducted only over the Internet. In fact, a great deal of business-to-business electronic commerce today is still conducted over private networks, using primarily traditional electronic data interchange (EDI) channels and value-added network (VAN) service providers. This is changing, as more and more companies adopt the Internet for some or all of their business-to-business electronic commerce, but it will be many years before the Internet totally displaces the VANs.

Within the Internet commerce domain lies an even smaller subset, termed ***web commerce***. This is the component of Internet commerce conducted strictly over the World Wide Web. The WWW is not the only way of using the Internet for commercial interactions. Electronic mail, for example, serves well for certain forms of commerce. As another example, software may be conveniently sold over the Internet using the file transfer protocol (FTP) for product distribution. Nevertheless, the web is clearly the dominant medium for the large majority of Internet commerce today. Furthermore, as modern web browsers incorporate other Internet applications, including electronic mail and file transfer via FTP, all under one "hood," users today have the perception that they are relying solely on the web even as they send and receive e-mail, transfer files, and conduct other forms of Internet applications that used to be conducted using separate application programs.

Contrary to popular belief, EB goes beyond merely buying and selling products online. EB can involve the events leading up to the purchase

Table 5.1 *Types of electronic commerce.*

Type of EC	Description	Example
Business-to-Consumer (B2C)	Transactions between businesses and their customers	A person buys a book from Amazon.ca
Business-to-Business (B2B)	Transactions among businesses	A manufacturer conducts business over the web with its suppliers
Business-to-Employee (B2E)	Transactions between businesses and their employees	An employee uses the web to make a change in his/her health benefits
Consumer-to-Consumer (C2C)	Transactions between people not necessarily working together	A person purchases some memorabilia from another person via eBay.ca

of a product, as well as customer service after the sale. Furthermore, EB is not limited to transactions between businesses and consumers, which is known as ***business-to-consumer (B2C)*** EB and vice versa. EB is also used to conduct business with business partners such as suppliers and intermediaries. This form of EB is commonly referred to as ***business-to-business (B2B)*** EB. Some companies choose to operate in both arenas, such as the clothing and home furnishing retailer Eddie Bauer, while other firms concentrate solely in B2C or B2B. Some forms of EB happen between businesses and their employees and are referred to as ***business-to-employee (B2E)***. Some forms of EB do not even involve business firms, as would be the case with an online textbook exchange service for students at a university or an online trading website such as eBay.ca; these forms of EB are referred to as ***consumer-to-consumer (C2C)***. These four basic types of EB are summarized in Table 5.1.

Furthermore, there is a wide variety of ways to conduct business in each arena. In the following section, we examine the reasons that web-based EB is revolutionizing the way business is being done. This is followed by an in-depth analysis of how companies are utilizing EB in their daily operations.

Internet and World Wide Web Capabilities

Technological forces are driving business, and the Internet and web have emerged as strong new agents of change. The resulting technological revolution has essentially broken down the barriers to entry, levelled the playing field, and propelled commerce into the electronic domain. Companies are exploiting one or more of the capabilities of the web to reach a wider customer base, offer a broader range of products, and develop closer relationships with customers by striving to meet their unique needs. These wide-ranging capabilities include global information dissemination, integration, mass customization, interactive communication, collaboration, and transactional support (Looney and Chatterjee, 2002; Chatterjee and Sambamurthy, 1999).

Information Dissemination

The powerful combination of Internet and web technologies has given rise to a global platform where firms from across the world can effectively compete for customers and gain access to new markets. EB has wide geographical potential, given that many countries have at least some type of Internet access. The worldwide connectivity of the Internet enables ***global information dissemination***, a relatively economical medium for firms to market their products and services over vast distances. This increased geographical reach has been facilitated by storefronts located on every web-enabled computer in the world. Unlike the situation with traditional storefronts, time limitations are not a factor, which allows firms to sell and service products 7 days a week, 24 hours a day, 365 days a year to anyone, anywhere. A larger customer base creates increased sales volumes, which ultimately saves consumers money, as firms can offer their products at lower prices. In addition, parking for customers is no problem, and firms can deliver the goods right to the customer's door.

Integration

Web technologies also allow ***integration*** of information via websites, which can be linked to corporate databases to provide real-time access to information. No longer must customers rely on old information from printed catalogues or account statements that arrive in the mail once a month. For example, when Air

CANADIAN NETSTATS

E-Business Is BIG Business

Do you shop online? If you do, you're not alone (see Table 5.2). Besides offering the capacity to shop online, the Internet provides an opportunity for consumers to research products prior to making purchase decisions. While some people have resisted online shopping, they nevertheless use the web to gather information. Although still a minor part of total retail sales, the number of people actually purchasing goods and services on the Internet is rapidly increasing. The trend is clear: e-business is here to stay. How do you feel about purchasing goods and services online?

Table 5.2 ***Electronic business average expenditures (Cdn$).***

	2001	2002	2003
Average Expenditures			
Canada	803	876	956
Quebec	566	536	633
Ontario	853	982	1037
Manitoba and Saskatchewan	731	875	930
Alberta	891	930	1101
British Columbia	915	951	1011
Average Expenditures Per Order			
Canada	135	146	144
Quebec	123	113	122
Ontario	127	149	146
Manitoba and Saskatchewan	148	156	124
Alberta	168	165	173
British Columbia	162	167	149
Average Number of Orders			
Canada	5.9	6.0	6.7
Quebec	4.6	4.7	5.2
Ontario	6.7	6.6	7.1
Manitoba and Saskatchewan	4.9	5.6	7.5
Alberta	5.3	5.6	6.4
British Columbia	5.6	5.7	6.8

Source: Statistics Canada, **www40.statcan.ca/l01/cst01/comm04a.htm**

Canada (**www.aircanada.ca**) updates fare information in its corporate database, customers can access the revisions as they occur simply by browsing the company's website. As with nearly every other major airline, the web allows Air Canada to disseminate real-time fare pricing. This is particularly important for companies operating in highly competitive environments such as the airline industry. Furthermore, Aeroplan offers Air Canada's valued customers the ability to check the balances of their frequent-flyer accounts at its site, **www.aeroplan.com** (see Figure 5.3). Customers do not have to wait for monthly statements to see if they are eligible for travel benefits and awards.

Mass Customization

Web technologies are also helping firms realize their goal of ***mass customization***. Mass customization helps firms tailor their products and services to meet a customer's particular needs. For instance, clothing retailer Lands' End (**www.landsend.com**) has developed an application called My Virtual Model™, which allows customers to create a virtual person to model clothing for them (see Figure 5.4). Customers can configure the virtual model based on a number of criteria such as gender, height, weight, build, complexion, and hair colour. Once customers have created a virtual model, they can dress the model in clothing to see how it will look on them. The virtual model application also assists Lands' End in tracking customers' preferred clothing styles and colours, allowing them to target marketing efforts to individual customers.

Interactive Communication

Interactive communication via the web enables firms to build customer loyalty by providing immediate communication and feedback to and from customers, which can dramatically improve the firm's image through demonstrated responsiveness. Many firms are augmenting telephone-based ordering and customer support with web-based applications and electronic mail. In some cases, online chat applications are provided to allow customers to communicate with a customer service representative in real time through the corporate website. The online brokerage firm E*Trade Canada (**www.etrade.ca**) has implemented such a feature. Should a question arise during the placing of an order, customers can click a button that opens a chat application, connecting them in real time to a customer service representative. The customer can type questions into a window and receive immediate responses from the representative. This feature allows the customer service agent to walk the customer through the ordering process step by step while the customer is entering the transaction. Customers never have to leave E*Trade Canada's website or terminate their Internet connection to get their business done. This customer-driven approach far outdistances traditional, nonelectronic means in terms of tailoring and timeliness.

Collaboration

Web technologies can also enable ***collaboration***. As an example, E*Trade Canada maintains a community for investors, who regularly share opinions concerning companies, news, rumours, and investment strategies through an E*Trade Canada–sponsored forum. The community exposes investors to a wide array of information that would otherwise be unavailable through traditional channels. IBM Microelectronics uses the web to collaborate with its custom-logic chip customers. A Java-enabled web browser allows users to share product information, access design specifications, and download software tools from the website. The application provides interactive, or two-way, communications, helping IBM engineers to pinpoint design issues and provide personalized support to better serve customers (Alexander, 2001).

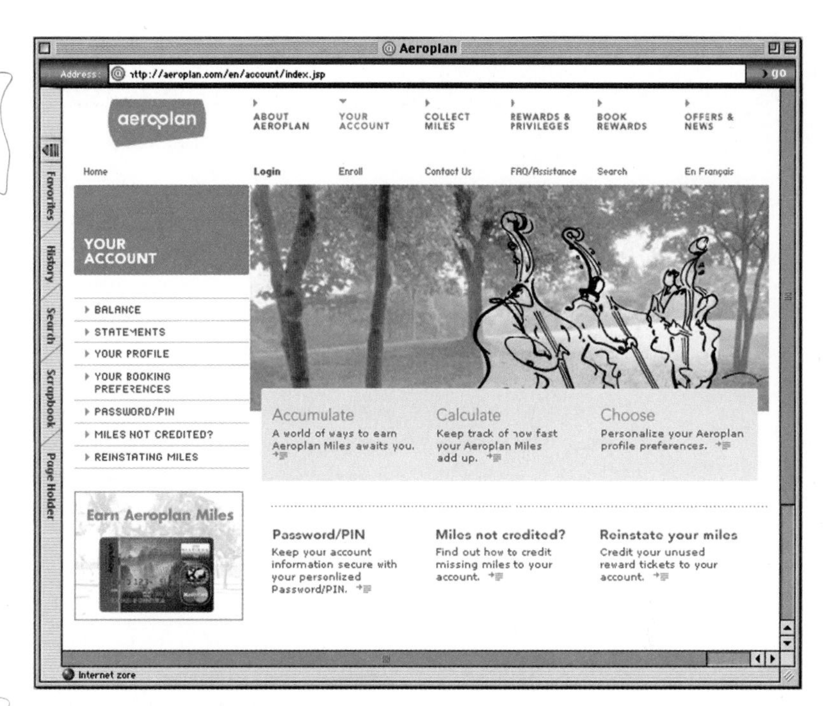

Figure 5.3 Aeroplan's rewards website.

Source: Courtesy of Aeroplan.

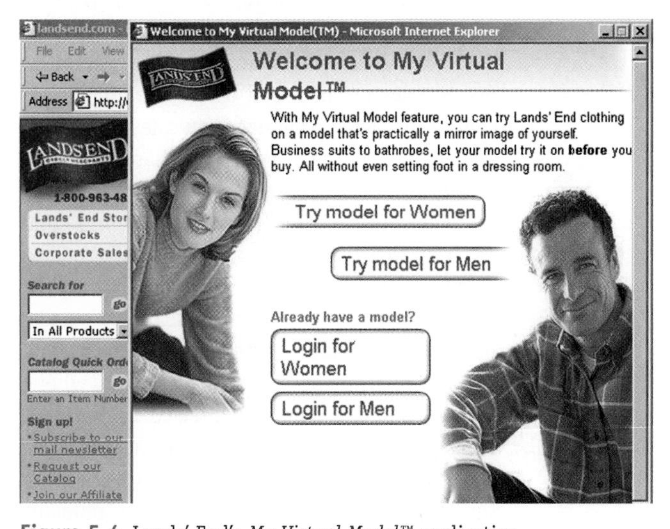

Figure 5.4 Lands' End's *My Virtual Model*™ application.

Source: **www.landsend.com**

WHEN THINGS GO WRONG

Software Flaws Can Threaten Electronic Business

An Internet user who goes by the name ThePull reported an alleged flaw in Internet Explorer to Microsoft Corporation. ThePull is an example of a "White Hat," a hacker who uncovers problems in software and then reports those problems to the software's manufacturer. White Hats are the "good" version of Black Hats, who exploit software vulnerabilities for malicious purposes. The alleged flaw in Internet Explorer could potentially allow hackers to enter websites undercover and steal cookies and related information from those websites, or even from the computers of individual browser users. Rain Forest Puppy, another White Hat, found a vulnerability in Microsoft's Internet Information Services (IIS) server. If unchecked, hackers could use the vulnerability to gain access to the computers running IIS software and make any changes they wanted, including modifying or stealing content and erasing the hard drive. Every few weeks, it seems, another critical security flaw is uncovered in a piece of widely used software.

Microsoft has responded to these threats by launching the Microsoft Security Response Center (MSRC). The goal of the MSRC is to protect users by eliminating security vulnerabilities whenever they are found in a Microsoft product or service. Since its creation, the MSRC has eliminated more than 1000 vulnerabilities affecting roughly 100 Microsoft products. In 2005, the MSRC replied to over 12 000 e-mails. Most of these potential problems, it turned out, were not security vulnerabilities at all but occurred as a result of user error. According to Scott Culp, ex-manager of the MSRC and now senior security strategist for Microsoft's Trustworthy Computing Team, fewer than 1 percent of potential vulnerabilities actually turn out to be verified problems requiring action from Microsoft. Culp adds that software security vulnerabilities occur at about the same rate in software from all manufacturers. The economic consequence of software security vulnerabilities is hard to measure, but one can assume that it is significant.

For up-to-date information on security issues at Microsoft, check TechNet at **http://technet.microsoft.com/en-us/default.aspx**.

Transaction Support

By providing ways for clients and firms to conduct business online without human assistance, the Internet and web have greatly reduced transaction costs while enhancing operational efficiency. Many companies, such as Dell Computer Corporation, are utilizing the web to provide automated ***transaction support***. Dell began selling computers on the web in mid-1996. By early 1998, Dell was making around US$3 million in online sales per day. Dell derives about 90 percent of its overall revenues from sales to medium and large businesses, yet more than half of its web-based sales have been to individuals and small businesses, who typically buy one computer at a time. As a result, Dell is experiencing significant cost savings per sale by reducing the demand for phone representatives on the smaller purchases. Individual customers can access product information at any time from anywhere, empowering customers to service themselves. This benefits not only the end consumer but Dell as well. Customer service representatives can focus on lucrative corporate customers, reducing labour costs involved in servicing small-ticket items. By streamlining operations and greatly increasing sales through both online and traditional channels, Dell has grown into one of the world's largest personal computer manufacturers, with sales in excess of US$41 billion in 2005. This phenomenon of cutting out the intermediary and reaching customers more directly and efficiently is known as ***disintermediation***.

Nearly Unlimited Selection

Since the Internet is so large, and relatively unconstrained by geographic and economic boundaries, it can provide a ***nearly unlimited selection*** of merchandise. Consumers can purchase practically anything online, from the ubiquitous bestseller to the extremely rare first edition. Canadian bookstore Abe Books (**www.abebooks.com**) battles Internet giants like Amazon.com by selling products that larger firms are not able to offer, such as out-of-print books, rarities, and first editions. The company has partnered with 13 000 booksellers to gain access to a massive inventory of rare merchandise.

Abe Books is able to compete with Amazon.com because of an interesting characteristic of the Internet increasingly being referred to

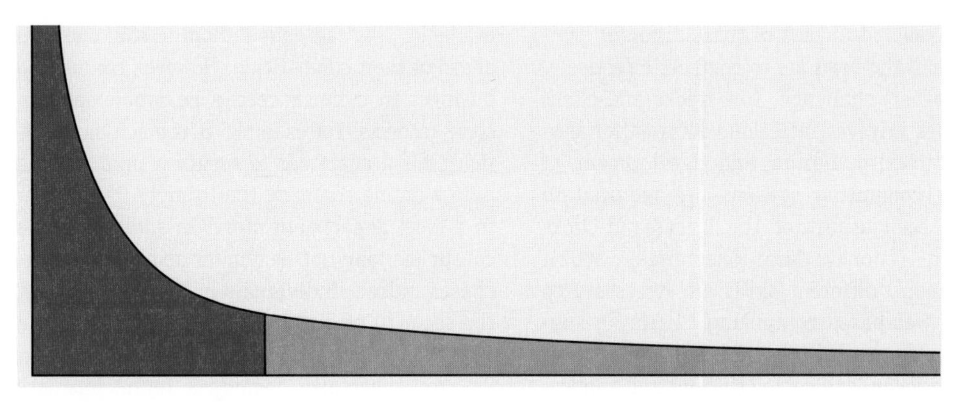

Figure 5.5 A large number of uncommon items in the "tail" can collectively outsell the few common items.

as the "Long Tail" phenomenon. The Long Tail was first coined by Chris Anderson in a 2004 *Wired* magazine article (**www.wired.com/wired/archive/12.10/tail.html**). The argument notes that products that are in low demand or have low sales volumes can collectively make up a market share that rivals or exceeds high-demand products. Most firms focus on popular, high-demand items, but there is also money to be made selling low-volume products. A former Amazon.com employee exemplified the Long Tail phenomenon as follows: "We sold more books today that didn't sell at all yesterday than we sold today of all the books that did sell yesterday." The relationship between high- and low-volume products can be seen in Figure 5.5. High-volume products are shown in the blue area, while low-volume items are shown in yellow. Successfully tapping into a Long Tail market can be lucrative, and doing so was not possible prior to distribution and sales channel opportunities made possible by the Internet.

ELECTRONIC BUSINESS STRATEGIES

The web has transformed traditional business operations into a hyper-competitive electronic marketplace. Companies must strategically position themselves to compete in the EB environment. At one extreme, companies following a ***bricks-and-mortar*** approach choose to operate solely in the traditional, physical markets. These companies approach business activities in a traditional manner by operating physical locations such as department stores, business offices, and manufacturing plants. In other words, the bricks-and-mortar business strategy does not include EB. In contrast, ***clicks-only companies*** (also referred to as ***virtual companies,*** or "pure play" companies) conduct business electronically in cyberspace. These firms have no physical locations, allowing them to focus purely on EB. One of the few remaining examples of a clicks-only company is the popular eBay trading and exchange website, which does not have a physical storefront in the classic sense. Other firms choose to straddle the two environments, operating in both physical and virtual arenas. These firms operate under the ***bricks-and-clicks*** business model. The three general business models are depicted in Figure 5.6.

The Bricks-and-Clicks Strategy

The greatest impact of the web-based EB revolution has occurred in companies adopting the bricks-and-clicks approach. Bricks-and-clicks companies continue to operate their physical locations and have added the EB component to their business activities. With transactions occurring in both physical and virtual environments, it is imperative that bricks-and-clicks companies learn how to fully maximize commercial opportunities in both domains. Conducting physical and virtual operations presents special challenges for these firms, as business activities

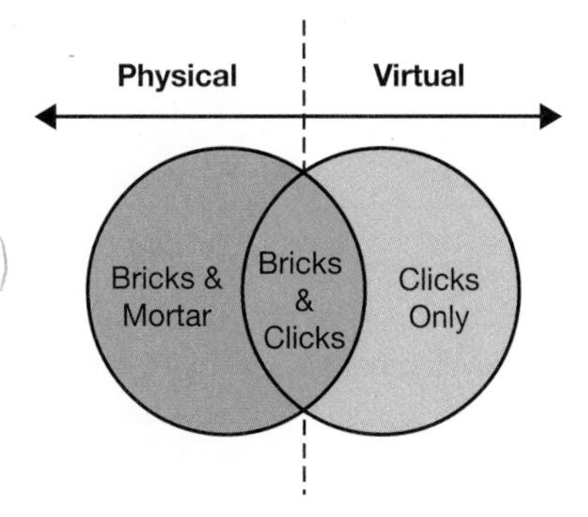

Figure 5.6 General approaches to electronic business.

Source: Modified from Looney and Chatterjee, 2002.

must be tailored to each of these different environments if the firms are to compete effectively.

Another challenge for bricks-and-clicks companies involves increasing information system complexity. Design and development of complex computing systems are required to support each aspect of the bricks-and-clicks approach (Looney and Chatterjee, 2002). Furthermore, different skills are necessary to support web-based computing, requiring substantial resource investments. Companies must design, develop, and deploy systems and applications to accommodate an open computing architecture that must be globally and persistently available. For instance, with total client assets of approximately US$985 billion, hundreds of thousands of daily trades by customers, a variety of ways that customers use their website, and a dynamic, fast-changing set of online products and services, the bricks-and-clicks brokerage firm Charles Schwab has a large, complex information systems staff and set of interrelated information systems.

The Clicks-Only Strategy

Clicks-only companies often have a price advantage, as they do not need to support the physical aspects of the bricks-and-clicks approach. Thus, these companies can reduce prices to rock-bottom levels. On the other hand, a relatively small clicks-only firm may not sell enough products and/or may not order enough from suppliers to be able to realize economies of scale and thus reduce prices. Clicks-only firms also tend to be highly adept with technology and can innovate very rapidly as new technologies become available. This can enable them to stay one step ahead of their competition. However, conducting business in cyberspace can be problematic in some respects. For example, it is much more difficult for a customer to return a product to a purely online company than simply to return it to a local department store. In addition, some consumers may not be comfortable making purchases online. Individuals may be leery about the security of giving credit card numbers to a virtual company.

You must also develop a sound business model to be successful with e-business. A ***business model*** is a summary of how a company will generate revenue, identifying its product offering, value-added services, revenue sources, and target customers (Prenhall Web site, 2004). In other words, a business model reflects the following (Changewave Web site, 2004):

1. What does a company do?
2. How does a company uniquely do it?
3. In what way (ways) does the company get paid for doing it?
4. How much gross margin does the company earn per average unit sale?

Laudon and Guercio-Traver (2003) identified eight ingredients of a business model (see Table 5.3). Perhaps the most important ingredient for e-business is a firm's revenue model. A ***revenue model*** describes how the firm will earn revenue, generate profits, and produce a superior return on invested capital (Laudon and Guercio-Traver, 2003). Table 5.4 describes five common revenue models for e-business, including advertising, subscription, transaction

Table 5.3 ***Eight ingredients of a business model.***

Components	Key Questions
Value proposition	Why should the customer buy from you?
Revenue model	How will you earn money?
Market opportunity	What marketspace do you intend to serve, and what is its size?
Competitive environment	Who else occupies your intended marketspace?
Competitive advantage	What special advantages does your firm bring to the marketspace?
Market strategy	How do you plan to promote your products or services to attract your target audience?
Organizational development	What types of organizational structures within the firm are necessary to carry out the business plan?
Management team	What kinds of experiences and background are important for the company's leaders to have?

Laudon/Traver, *E-Commerce: Business, Technology, Society*, Table 2.1 (p. 62), Table 2.2 (p. 66),

Table 5.4 ***Five common revenue models for e-business.***

Revenue Model	Examples	Revenue Source
Advertising	Yahoo.com	Fees from advertisers in exchange for advertisements
Subscription	WSJ.com, Consumerreports.org, Sportsline.com	Fees from subscribers in exchange for access to content or services
Transaction Fee	eBay.com, E-Trade.com	Fees (commissions) for enabling or executing a transaction
Sales	Amazon.com, LLBean.com, Gap.com, Sears.com, JCPenney.com	Sales of goods, information, or services
Affiliate	MyPoints.com	Fees for business referrals

Laudon/Traver, *E-Commerce: Business, Technology, Society*, Table 2.1 (p. 62), Table 2.2 (p. 66), © 2004. Reprinted by permission of Pearson Education, Inc. Publishing as Pearson Addison Wesley.

fee, sales, and affiliate. Many firms use more than one revenue model to compete.

As you can see, firms can conduct e-business in a variety of ways. In the next sections, we describe in greater detail how firms have evolved toward using the Internet and web to conduct business with their customers and to interact with each other.

BUSINESS-TO-CONSUMER ELECTRONIC BUSINESS

The Internet and web have evolved with mind-boggling quickness, achieving mass acceptance faster than any other technology in modern history. The widespread availability and adoption of the Internet and web, which are based on an economical, open, ubiquitous computing platform, have made Internet access affordable and practical, allowing consumers to participate in web-based commerce. In addition, a great number of businesses have similarly benefited from the revolution and have implemented web-based systems in their daily operations. This heightened level of participation by both consumers and producers has made the emergence of business-to-consumer (B2C) e-business economically feasible. Unlike business-to-business (B2B) e-business, which uses extranets to facilitate transactions between firms, or business-to-employee (B2E) e-business, which focuses on the use of intranets to support internal organizational communication and process, B2C focuses on retail transactions on the Internet between a company and end consumers. Table 5.5 provides a high-level comparison between these three approaches to conducting electronic business. We will expand our discussion of intranets and extranets later in the chapter.

The Evolution of Electronic Retailing

The major portion of B2C focuses on electronic retailing, or ***e-tailing***, which provides many advantages over brick-and-mortar retailing in terms of product, place, and price. Websites can offer a virtually unlimited number and variety of products because e-tailing is not limited by physical space restrictions. For instance, e-tailer Amazon.ca offers millions of book titles on the web, compared with a local bricks-and-mortar-only book retailer, which can offer "only" a few thousand titles in a store due to the restricted

Table 5.5 ***Characteristics of the Internet, intranet, and extranet.***

Focus	Type of Information	Users	Access	
The Internet	External communications	General, public, and "advertorial"	Any user with an Internet connection	Public and not restricted
Intranet	Internal communications	Specific, corporate, and proprietary	Authorized employees	Private and restricted
Extranet	External communications	Communications between business partners	Authorized business partners	Private and restricted

Szuprowicz, 1998; Turban et al., 2004.

physical space. Place proves advantageous in the e-tailing environment because company storefronts exist on every computer that is connected to the web, enabling e-tailers to compete more effectively for customers. Whereas traditional retailing can be accessed only at physical store locations during open hours, e-tailers can conduct business anywhere, at any time. E-tailers can also compete on price effectively, as they can turn their inventory more often due to the sheer volume of products and customers who purchase them. Companies can sell more products, reducing prices for consumers while at the same time enhancing profits for the company (Christensen and Tedlow, 2000).

Despite all the recent hype associated with e-tailing, there are some downsides to this approach. Excepting products that you can download directly, such as music or an electronic magazine, e-tailing requires additional time for products to be delivered. If you have run out of ink for your printer and your research paper is due this afternoon, chances are that you will drive to your local office supply store to purchase a new ink cartridge rather than ordering it online. The ink cartridge purchased electronically needs to be packaged and shipped, delaying use of the product until it is delivered. Other issues can also arise. The credit card information that you provided online may not be approved, or the shipper may try to deliver the package when you are not home.

Another problem associated with e-tailing relates to a lack of sensory information such as taste, smell, and feel. When trying on clothes with your virtual model at Lands' End, how can you be sure that you will like the feel of the material? Or what if you discover that the pair of size 9 EE in-line skates you just purchased online fits you like an 8 D? Products such as fragrances and foods can also be difficult for consumers to assess via the web. Does the strawberry cheesecake offered online actually taste as good as it looks? How do you know if you will really like the smell of a perfume without actually sampling it? Finally, e-tailing eliminates the social aspects of the purchase. Some e-tailers are having a hard time competing with shopping malls because going to the mall with some friends is a lot more fun for most people than buying online! As with B2B procurement, comparison shopping can be difficult since vendors provide product information in different ways. However, a number of comparison shopping services that focus on aggregating content are available to consumers. Some companies fulfilling this niche are BestBookBuys (**www.bestwebbuys.com/books**), BizRate (**www.bizrate.com**), and mySimon (**www.mysimon.com**). These comparison shopping sites can literally force sellers to focus on relatively low prices in order to be successful. If sellers do not have the lowest price, they must be able to offer better quality, better service, or some other advantage. These comparison shopping sites generate revenue by charging a small commission on transactions, by charging usage fees to sellers, and/or through advertising on their site.

E-Information → E-Integration → E-Transaction

Figure 5.7 Stages of business-to-consumer electronic commerce.

Stages of Business-to-Consumer Electronic Business

With thousands of B2C-oriented websites in existence, websites range from passive to active. At one extreme are the relatively simple, passive websites that provide only product information and the company address and phone number, much like a traditional brochure would do. At the other extreme are the relatively sophisticated, active websites that enable customers to see products, services, and related real-time information and actually make purchases online. As shown in some early, pioneering research on EB (Kalakota, Olivia, and Donath, 1999; Quelch and Klein, 1996), companies usually start out with an electronic brochure and pass through a series of stages as depicted in Figure 5.7, adding additional capabilities as they become more comfortable with EB. These stages can be classified as ***e-information***, ***e-integration***, and ***e-transaction***. The Brief Case on page 159 describes how courier-giant FedEx developed its EB strategy by gradually enhancing the complexity and functionality of its website.

E-Information

One of the first ways corporations utilize the web is to promote sales and marketing information via an **electronic brochure**, or ***e-brochure***. Figure 5.8 provides an example of an e-brochure developed by Italian car manufacturer Ferrari (**www.ferrariworld.com/FWorld/fw/index.jsp**). The e-information stage achieves the goal of global information dissemination, allowing potential customers to access information about the company and its products. The company can disseminate this information globally in the sense that e-information can be accessed by any Internet user with access to a web browser. Furthermore, the information is available

Figure 5.8 An e-information website operated by Ferrari.

Source: **www.Ferrari.com**

24 hours a day, 7 days a week, 365 days a year. No matter where on earth the user is located and regardless of the time, the e-brochure is available for their review.

E-information is more flexible than traditional promotional methods such as hard-copy catalogues and print advertisements. When information needs updating, e-information can be modified and posted very quickly, whereas traditional methods require typesetting, printing, and/or distribution, depending on the medium. Eliminating these manual processes not only shortens cycle times but also reduces the associated labour expenses. In the process, users are provided with the timeliest information possible. E-information may ultimately lead to a purchase. However, the e-information stage is limited because it merely provides company and product information, not the capability to customize information dynamically, which leads to the next stage of B2C: e-integration.

E-Integration

Once companies have mastered the e-information stage, they become more comfortable with EB and want to enhance their websites by adding additional features and functionality. The e-information stage provides a mechanism to distribute information to the general public, yet cannot accommodate requests for customized information. Customized information is dynamic, meaning that web pages are created on-the-fly to produce tailored information that addresses the particular needs of the consumer. For instance, a banking customer may want more than information related to the bank and its products. This customer would like to access information related to her accounts, such as the balance in her chequing account or the amount of interest credited to her savings account last month. In other words, customers may want information that is relevant to them rather than the general public (see Figure 5.9).

To facilitate this type of customer request, websites must be integrated with corporate databases to extract and display the appropriate information. This integration process characterizes the e-integration phase of B2C. The e-integration stage helps companies fulfill their goals of integration and mass customization. Firms such as the insurance and financial services company Allstate (**www.allstate.ca**) provide a useful example of the e-integration approach to EB. Customers register their identity through an online form to gain access to their account. Once registered, customers can access detailed, personalized information about their auto, home, and life insurance policies online. Allstate can also identify specific groups of customers, such as those holding home insurance policies, and target marketing efforts to those individuals.

The Burlington Northern Santa Fe Railway (BNSF) (**www.bnsf.com**), one of North America's largest railroads, utilizes the e-integration approach to assist with transactional support. Using a web-based application called Custom Tracing, customers enter their shipment number and receive information about the status of their shipment. In addition, customers can use the website to calculate shipping rates by simply entering the source and destination locations. Companies that provide e-integration services have enabled customers to find the information they need when they want it, without having to call a customer service representative for assistance.

Figure 5.9 Most B2C eBusiness is safe, but it pays to be cautious!

One drawback of the e-integration stage lies in its inability to accommodate online ordering. Although companies such as Allstate and Burlington Northern Santa Fe enable access to customized information, when customers want to conduct a transaction, they must resort to calling the company. For instance, when Allstate customers need to update their life insurance policies, they must contact their agents through other means. Similarly, BNSF customers must call the railroad to schedule shipments. In the cases of Allstate and BNSF, there are strategic business reasons not to enable online ordering, although the ability to place orders online can prove beneficial in many cases. The ability to conduct transactions online leads us to the next stage of B2C: e-transaction.

E-Transaction

E-transaction takes the e-integration stage one step further by adding the ability for customers to enter orders and payments online. The e-transaction stage helps companies fulfill their goals of collaboration, interactive communication, and transactional support. Many of the most well-known B2C websites fall into the e-transaction category, such as the clicks-only e-tailer Amazon.ca (see Figure 5.10). Customers not only find out product information but may also make purchases, enter payments, and track the status of their orders once the sale has been made. The Amazon.ca website has been so successful that the company has branched out from selling books to offering other products such as electronic equipment, home decor, pharmaceuticals, and even cars!

Figure 5.10 Amazon.ca website.

Source: © 2004 Amazon.com, Inc. All Rights Reserved.

E-transaction can take many forms. Virtual companies such as Priceline.com and eBay have developed innovative ways of generating revenue. Priceline.com offers consumers discounts on airline tickets, hotel rooms, rental cars, new cars, home financing, and long-distance telephone service. The revolutionary aspect of the Priceline.com website lies in its ***reverse pricing*** system called Name Your Own Price. Customers specify the product they are looking for and how much they are willing to pay for it. This pricing scheme transcends traditional ***menu-driven pricing***, in which companies set the prices that consumers pay for products. After a user enters the product and price, the system routes the information to appropriate brand-name companies such as United Airlines and Avis Rent a Car, which either accept or reject the consumer's offer. In a recent business quarter, Priceline.com sold 1.7 million hotel room nights and 1.2 million rental car days (Priceline.com, 2004).

eBay has transformed e-tailing into an ***electronic marketplace***. Unlike e-tailers such as Lands' End and Amazon.ca, where one seller services many buyers, an electronic marketplace services many buyers and sellers, who can come together to sell and purchase a wide variety of products. Items sold on eBay range from rare coins to antiques and fine art. Looking for that hard-to-find concert ticket? eBay may be the place to find it. However, you must outbid other consumers in an auction-style format to get what you want. The bidding starts at a price set by the seller and continues until a predetermined time, when the auction ends.

If you are the top bidder, you are the proud owner of your prized concert ticket. But be careful, and know what you are purchasing and from whom you are purchasing it! In 1997, a series of forged signatures on baseballs, bats, and pieces of paper appeared on the eBay auction block. These included signed memorabilia from baseball greats Mickey Mantle, Joe DiMaggio, and Babe Ruth, all of whom attract high prices for their autographs (Couzin, 2000). Although the FBI eventually caught the perpetrators, electronic marketplaces are not immune to improprieties.

E-transactions may not necessarily use the web. Radio frequency identification systems (RFID) present great opportunities for B2C EC. For example, over 1 million Canadian consumers buy gasoline using RFID tags on their key chains linked directly to a credit or debit card.

BRIEF CASE

Evolution of Business-to-Consumer Electronic Commerce at FedEx

Innovative, aggressive firms such as package shipper FedEx are finding ways to use technology to sell goods and services. FedEx generates approximately $22 billion in revenues annually in overnight package shipping and related activities. The company understands the importance of doing EB on the web and created a long-range goal of generating 100 percent of its business online. With the multibillion-dollar overnight shipping market at stake and technologically savvy competitors such as UPS right on their heels, FedEx's financial future depended on the development of a world-class website that allows customers to do all their business online.

Rather than jumping into the unfamiliar web environment, FedEx chose to implement its website in a step-by-step fashion. The company's website has undergone a series of developmental stages, starting with an e-brochure and evolving into a sophisticated website where customers can track shipments and arrange online for pickups. Recently, wireless PowerPad PDAs have been introduced to the FedEx couriers. Using Bluetooth, the delivery information is immediately transferred to the delivery van, where the status is updated so that customers can see the latest tracking information even faster on the FedEx website. Table 5.6 shows the stages of the development of the FedEx website (**www.fedex.com**). The staged approach has allowed the company to be continually innovative with its online business, mastering one facet of EC before progressing to the next. The website has evolved into a venue where all the necessary features are available, allowing customers to conduct business with FedEx via the corporate website. FedEx has become a B2C pioneer, continually inventing new ways of using web-based EC to achieve competitive advantage.

Questions

1. How have FedEx's competitors reacted to the online services offered? Do you think the competitors have done an equally thorough job in setting up their services? Provide examples, if possible.
2. Will systems such as FedEx's tracking system always lead to improved customer service, or can there be instances in which the information provided can lead to customer dissatisfaction? How can a company such as FedEx handle such problems?

Sources: John A. Klein and Lisa R. Welch, "The Internet and International Marketing," Sloan *Management* Review 37, no. 3 (1996): 60–75.
Ken Schles, "FedEx Success Doesn't Come with Big IT Budget Increase," InformationWeek (January 12, 2004), **www.informationweek.com/story/showArticle.jhtml?articleID=17300234**.

Table 5.6 ***The stages of website deployment for FedEx.***

Stage	Focus	Activities
E-Information	Establishment of a corporate image and dissemination of product information	Registered a domain name and created a website that provides information about the company and its products.
E-Integration	Information collection, market research	The company created electronic forms with which customers can register their identity and be assigned account numbers. FedEx uses customer information as a tool for conducting market research, enabling the company to get to know its customers.
	Customer support and service	Linked website to the company's corporate database, which allows customers to enter shipment numbers and view up-to-date information on package delivery or location.
E-Transaction	Online order entry	Created facilities that allow customers to request pickups and arrange payment options.

Source: Quelch and Klein, 1996.

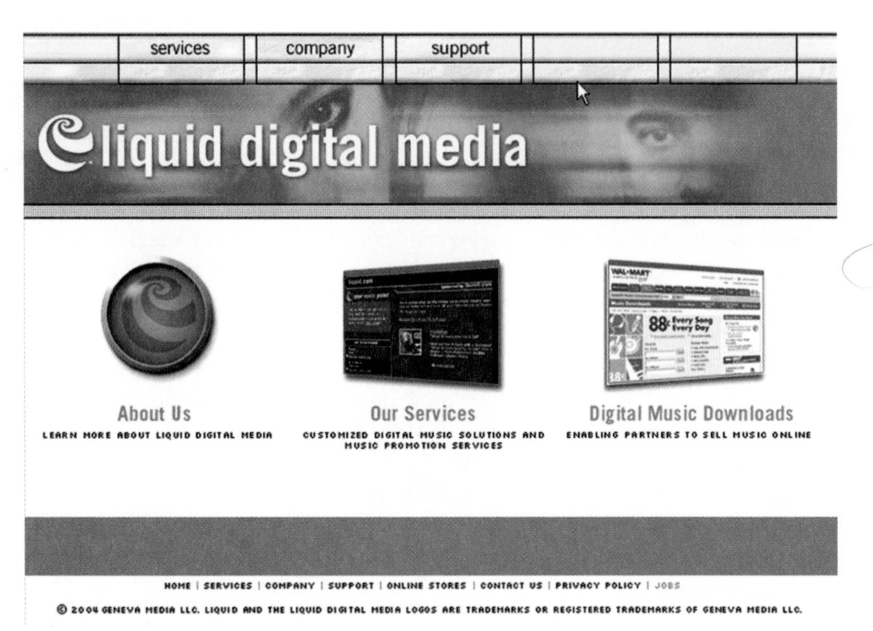

Figure 5.11 Liquid Digital Media's website.

Source: **www.liquidaudio.com**

Also, a variety of retail stores now prevent theft by using RFID-tagged merchandise that set off alarms when shoplifters walk out the store exits. RFID clearly presents all kinds of interesting new opportunities. Later in this chapter, we will talk about the further use of RFID systems for intranets and extranets.

The e-transaction stage can also include electronic distribution of virtual products and services. If the product or service can be digitized, it can be delivered online, as in the case of information-based products, videos, and software. ***Digitization*** creates products without tangible features, which are commonly referred to as ***virtual products***. Liquid Digital Media's web-based music distribution system (see Figure 5.11) is changing how music is being purchased and delivered. The company's technology enables the music industry to use the web as another distribution channel without fear of piracy. The system enables users to download CD-quality music that can be played only on the computer to which it was downloaded.

The music is ***watermarked*** so that any illegal copy—even on cassette tapes—can be traced to the original purchaser. Electronic watermarking is similar in concept to watermarks placed on paper currency to prevent counterfeiting. Such technology works for the distribution of any type of information-based product. Orders of tangible products such as electronic equipment can be fulfilled by more traditional brick-and-mortar or click-and-mortar methods, but any information-based components of these products or services—such as an owner's manual—can be digitized and delivered online. It is a certainty that you will see more and more virtual products such as music, art, video, and software delivered over the web in the near future.

The Rise in M-Commerce

One exciting new form of EB is mobile electronic commerce, or ***m-commerce***.

M-commerce is defined as any electronic transaction or information interaction conducted using a wireless mobile device and mobile networks (wireless or switched public network) that leads to transfer of real or perceived value in exchange for information, services, or goods (MobileInfo, 2004).

Common wireless mobile devices used for m-commerce include "smart" mobile phones, personal digital assistants, and pagers. In Appendix A, we describe these and other handheld devices. In Table 5.7 we list some popular devices, operating systems data presentation formats,

Table 5.7 ***Some popular technologies for m-commerce.***

Popular Handheld Product Lines

- RIM BlackBerry
- Handspring Treo
- HP iPaq
- Samsung SCH
- Motorola MP

Operating Systems

- Symbian (EPOC)
- PalmOS
- Pocket PC

Data Presentation Standards

- SMS
- WML
- HDML
- i-Mode
- SyncML
- XTML

Browsers

- Phone.com UP.Browser
- Nokia browser
- MS Mobile Explorer

Bearer Networks

- GSM
- GSM/GPRS
- TDMA
- CDMA
- CDPD

browsers, and networks for m-commerce. One of the more common platforms for m-commerce is the use of powerful ***smartphones*** with colour display screens, high-speed data transfer, and "always-on" connectivity over high-speed cellular networks that provide a wide variety of services and capabilities in addition to voice communication, such as multimedia data transfer, video streaming, video telephony, and full Internet access. In Table 5.8 we list some sample m-commerce applications.

Table 5.8 ***Some m-commerce applications.***

Purchasing and Other Financially Related Transactions

- Online Purchasing of Goods or Services
- In-Store Purchases
- Directory/Store-Finder Services
- M-Wallets
- Vending Machine Purchases
- Stock Trading and Other Investments
- Paying Bills
- Online Banking

Reserving and/or Booking

- Reserving and/or Purchasing Tickets for Airlines, Movies, Concerts, or Sporting Events
- Reservations for Restaurants or Hotels

Entertainment and Information

- Downloading and Playing Games
- Streaming Media for Movies or Music
- General Information such as News and Weather

Key Drivers for M-Commerce

Several factors have led to the rapid rise of m-commerce. First, there is an exponential growth of consumer interest and adoption of the Internet and EB generally. Second, there is now development and deployment of real-time transfer of data over 2.5G and 3G cellular networks that has enabled faster data transmission and "always-on" connectivity, resulting in tremendous growth in mobile telephony and availability of powerful wireless handheld devices. We describe these types of networks in greater detail in Appendix C.

Through a convergence of Internet and wireless technologies, m-commerce promises to propel business into the new millennium by enabling the electronic exchange of capital, goods, and commercial information via mobile, untethered computing devices (Stafford and Gillensen, 2003; Looney, Jessup, and Valacich, 2004). Indeed, the m-commerce market is predicted to grow to over $220 billion by 2007 (Ovum, 2004).

While the more general term *EB* is meant to include all forms of electronic exchanges of value, including those over wireless handheld devices, m-commerce is a specialized form of EB. In Table 5.9 we describe several critical

Table 5.9 ***Critical issues in m-commerce.***

Issues in M-Commerce	Explanation
Mobility	Has ability to connect to a network anywhere.
Ubiquity	Computing is spread unobtrusively throughout the physical environment, in kiosks, phones, personal digital assistants, and so on.
Embedding	Computing is embedded within everyday artifacts such as automobiles, toys, appliances, etc., and they are network enabled.
Accessibility	Mobile devices enable the user to be contacted at virtually any time and place.
Convenience	The wireless device and its functions, from storing data to access to information or persons, have ease-of-use and portability.
Localization	Location-specific based applications enable the user to receive relevant information on which to act.
Instant Connectivity	Has easy, fast, or "always on" connectivity.
Personalization	Customized information for and about the user enables faster, easier access and transactions.
Time Sensitivity	Has access to real-time information such as a stock quote that can be acted upon immediately or a sale at a local boutique.

aspects of m-commerce applications that differentiate it from general EB (derived from MobileInfo Web site, 2004).

EXTRANETS: BUSINESS-TO-BUSINESS ELECTRONIC BUSINESS

In order to communicate proprietary information with authorized users outside organizational boundaries, a company can implement an ***extranet***. An extranet enables two or more firms to use the Internet to do business together. Using the Internet to support business-to-business (B2B) activities has become one of the best ways for organizations to gain a positive return on their technology-based investments. For example, aerospace giant Boeing launched an extranet that can be accessed by over 1000 authorized business partners. One of Boeing's business partners, aluminium supplier Alcoa, accesses the extranet to coordinate its shipments to Boeing, as well as to check Boeing's raw materials supply to ensure appropriate inventory levels. Customers, such as the U.S. Department of Defense, log in to Boeing's extranet to receive status updates on the projects Boeing is working on for them. Overall, countless organizations are gaining benefits from B2B electronic commerce, with nearly all Fortune 1000 companies deploying some type of B2B application.

Interestingly, there is a long history of organizations using proprietary networks to share business information. In this section, we will examine the evolution to the present-day extranet and review how organizations are utilizing extranets to improve organizational performance and gain competitive advantage.

The Need for Organizations to Exchange Data

Prior to the introduction of the Internet and web, B2B EB was facilitated using ***Electronic Data Interchange (EDI)***. These systems are generally limited to large corporations that can afford the associated expenses. The Internet and web have provided an economical medium over which information can be transmitted, enabling small to midsized enterprises to participate in B2B markets. Companies have devised a number of innovative ways to facilitate B2B transactions using these technologies. Web-based B2B systems range from simple extranet applications to complex trading exchanges where multiple buyers and sellers come together to conduct business. In the following sections, we examine the stages under which modern B2B EC is done, shedding light on the different approaches and their suitability for different business requirements. Figure 5.12 provides a high-level overview of how B2B architectures typically evolve.

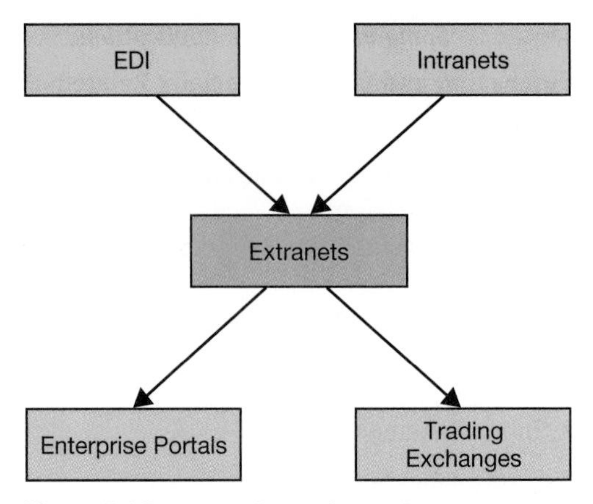

Figure 5.12 Stages of B2B electronic commerce.

How Electronic Data Interchange Works

Electronic data interchange is the forefather of modern B2B EB and continues to maintain a stronghold in B2B computing. Giga Information Group estimates that Canadian and U.S. companies buy about $500 billion worth of goods and services electronically each year via EDI networks. EDI refers to the digital, or electronic, transmission of business documents and related data between organizations via telecommunications networks. More specifically, these telecommunications networks commonly take the form of ***value-added networks (VANs)***, which provide a direct link over which data can be transmitted. VANs are telephone lines that are leased from telecommunications providers, creating a secure, dedicated circuit between a company and its business partners. Figure 5.13 depicts a typical EDI system architecture using VANs to connect a company with its suppliers and customers.

Companies use EDI to exchange a wide variety of business documents, including purchase orders, invoices, shipping manifests, delivery schedules, and electronic payments. Currently, over 100 000 U.S. and Canadian companies conduct business via EDI. EDI began in the mid-1960s as an initiative to reduce paperwork. Although EDI has never totally eliminated paper, it does help reduce the number of times business documents need to be handled. EDI provides many efficiencies because it helps to streamline business processes.

EDI enabled RJR Nabisco to reduce the cost of processing a paper-based purchase order from $70 to less than $1. However, the cost associated with EDI-based systems has limited its usefulness to large companies. EDI is costly to implement and maintain. Software and hardware required to enable EDI can cost upwards of $100 000, and monthly telecommunications charges associated with VANs can approach several thousand dollars per month, depending upon the number of communication lines necessary to connect the company with its business partners.

Large enterprises can afford the costs associated with EDI. They can justify the costs since EDI has created such dramatic efficiencies for their organizations. Yet EDI has proved to be beyond the reach of SMEs. Before the introduction of the Internet and web, a viable, economical alternative to EDI was unavailable, preventing small to midsized firms from participating in B2B markets. To make matters worse, some large corporations and government agencies had gone so far as to refuse business to companies that were not EDI enabled. What small and midsized companies needed was a technology that would level the playing field, making B2B affordable and accessible. This leads us to the next generation of Internet-based B2B architectures.

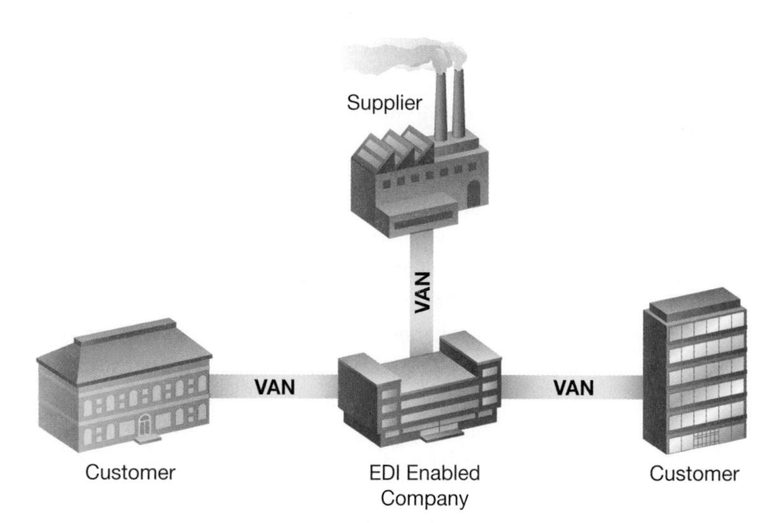

Figure 5.13 A typical EDI system architecture.

How the Internet Changed Everything: The Evolution from EDI to Extranets

EDI has been used for more than four decades to conduct business between organizations. However, the trend in business today is to use the public Internet and web as the vehicle for B2B EB. The global accessibility and economics afforded by the Internet and web have enabled SMEs to participate in B2B markets once reserved for large corporations. With the entrance of buyers and suppliers of all shapes and sizes, the mass adoption of these technologies has propelled B2B into the forefront of modern commerce. Mesotec, a parts supplier to the aeronautics and electronics industries based in Sherbrooke, Quebec, adopted a web-based EDI solution to tap into the supply chains of its major customers. The company found web-based EDI to be cheaper and easier to use, compared with traditional EDI. Interestingly enough, Mesotec decided against developing a unique presence on the web, so while the company is a heavy user of e-business, through the use of web-based EDI, it doesn't have its own website!

By late 1997, Cisco Systems, a leading producer of networking technologies such as routers, had shifted nearly 40 percent of its B2B sales from bricks-and-mortar markets to the web. That amounts to almost $9 million per day, or more than $3 billion per year. Cisco has continued its trend toward a clicks-only approach, selling more than 50 percent of its products online in 1998 and 60 percent in 1999. Additionally, Cisco is letting its biggest customers, such as Qwest Communications and Sprint, connect directly into its online inventory and product ordering system through web-based applications. Cisco's B2B initiatives have enabled customers to service themselves, resulting in a redeployment of customer service representatives to other critical areas within the company. As a result, Cisco is saving about $20 million per year related to sales transactions. These cost savings are being invested into the company's research and development (R&D) program—far exceeding the R&D investment of Cisco's nearest competitors, such as Nortel Networks and Foundry Networks. Cisco's savings are passed on to its customers. For example, a six-person department at Sprint Communications buys approximately 40 routers per week for its customers. Using Cisco's B2B applications, Sprint estimates it will save as much as $200 000 per year in order processing costs.

Benefits of Extranets

Extranets, as well as intranets (which will be discussed in the "Intranets: Business-to-Employee Commerce" section), benefit corporations in a number of ways, so it is no surprise that firms have readily and rapidly adopted these technologies. First and foremost, extranets can dramatically improve the timeliness and accuracy of communications, reducing the number of misunderstandings within the organization as well as with business partners and customers. In the business world, very little information is static; therefore, information must be continually updated and disseminated as it changes. Extranets facilitate this process by providing a cost-effective, global medium over which proprietary information can be distributed. Furthermore, they allow central management of documents, thus reducing the number of versions and amount of out-of-date information that may be stored throughout the organization. While security is still thought to be better on proprietary networks, the Internet can be made to be a relatively secure medium for business.

Web-based technologies are cross-platform, meaning that disparate computing systems can communicate with each other, provided that standard web protocols have been implemented. For example, an Apple Macintosh can request web pages from a UNIX web server. Even though the computers are running under different operating systems, they can communicate with each other over the Internet, provided that TCP/IP is being used by each machine. The cross-platform nature of the web makes implementing extranets extremely attractive as a way to connect disparate computing environments.

In addition, extranets do not require large expenditures to train users on the technologies. As many employees, customers, and business partners are familiar with the tools associated with the Internet and web, they do not require special training to familiarize them with extranet interfaces. In other words, extranets look and act just like public websites and web pages. As long as users are familiar with a web browser, they can utilize extranets with little difficulty.

Above all, extranets impact the company's bottom line. A company can use them to automate business transactions, reducing processing costs and achieving shortened cycle times. Extranets can also reduce errors by providing a single point of data entry from which the information can be updated on disparate corporate computing platforms without having to rekey the data. Management can then obtain real-time information to track and analyze business activities. Extranets are incredibly powerful and intensely popular. We describe in the following sections how they work and how they are being effectively utilized.

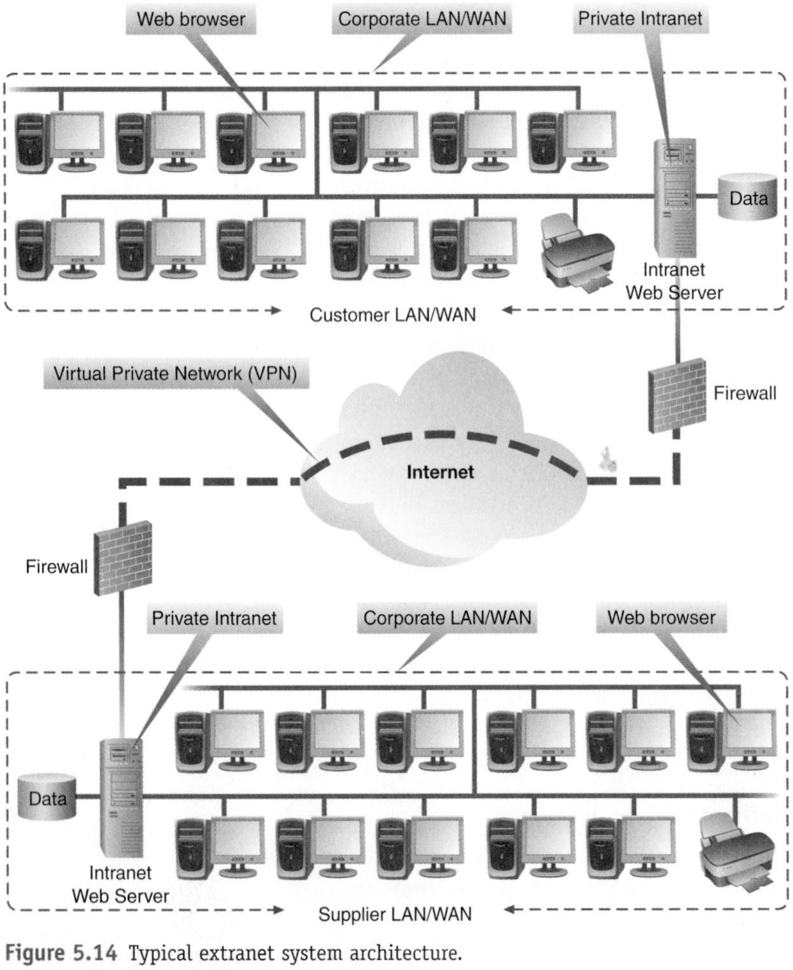

Figure 5.14 Typical extranet system architecture.

Extranet System Architecture

An extranet looks and acts just like a typical Internet-based application, using the same software, hardware, and networking technologies to communicate information (see Figure 5.14). However, an extranet connects the Internet infrastructure of two or more business partners and thus requires an additional component. Organizations can connect their internal intranet infrastructure (see discussion of intranets to follow) together using a ***virtual private network***, or ***VPN***, to facilitate the secured transmission of proprietary information between business partners. As described in Chapter 4, VPNs take advantage of the public nature of the Internet and its standardized protocols to communicate information by combining the global connectivity of the Internet with the security of a closed, private network. When partners are connected via a VPN, they act as if they are directly connected as a single LAN/WAN, but in reality they are not. As the name implies, VPNs are virtual in the sense that a connection is created between the separate organizations when a transmission needs to take place and terminated once the transmission has been completed. In other words, the VPN exists only when it is needed. Furthermore, a VPN is backed by the telephone service provider, which adds an increased level of trust in the network. In addition, this approach enables you to scale bandwidth up and down as needed.

To access information on an extranet, web browsers are installed on the workstations within each organization, and the TCP/IP protocol must be implemented on top of existing network protocols. Authorized business partners can access extranet content through a web browser by entering the URL of their business partner's main extranet web page. Once the user enters the URL in the web browser, TCP/IP breaks the request into packets and routes the packets over the internal LAN/WAN to the firewall.

VPNs use a technology known as ***tunnelling*** to encapsulate, encrypt, and transmit data over the Internet infrastructure, enabling business partners to exchange information in a secured, private manner between organizational firewalls. Before information can be transmitted from one organization to the other, the VPN connecting the two firewalls is established, and a secured tunnel is created over the VPN. TCP/IP routes the encrypted packets through the firewall and through the tunnel en route to their destination. When the packets reach the business partner's firewall, each packet is verified to ensure it has been sent from an authorized business partner. After packet verification, the packets are decrypted, and TCP/IP reassembles the packets and delivers them to the organization's web server for processing.

Extranet web servers perform an additional security measure through a process called ***authentication***. As described in Chapter 4, authentication confirms the identity of the remote user who is attempting to access information from the web server. The authentication process forces the remote user to supply a valid username and password before the web server fulfills requests. Great-West Life has implemented authentication through the web page depicted in Figure 5.15.

After the remote user has been authenticated, the web server retrieves the requested information, which is packetized by TCP/IP and sent back to the firewall. At the firewall, the packets are encapsulated and encrypted and sent via TCP/IP through the tunnel across the VPN. When the packets reach the business partner's firewall, each packet is verified to ensure it has been sent from an authorized business partner. After verification, the packets are decrypted, and TCP/IP reassembles the packets and delivers them to the web browser that originally requested the information. The web browser processes the HTML code, formats the physical appearance of the web page, and displays the results in the web browser. Once the transmission has been completed, the tunnel is discarded and the VPN is disconnected.

Extranet Applications

As the use of extranets has increased, a common set of applications has been found to be particularly beneficial to organizations. In this section, we highlight those that are having a substantial impact on how organizations work more effectively with external partners, including supply chain management, real-time access to information, and collaboration.

Supply Chain Management

The big three U.S. automobile manufacturers, Ford, General Motors, and Chrysler, teamed up in 1997 to implement an industry-wide

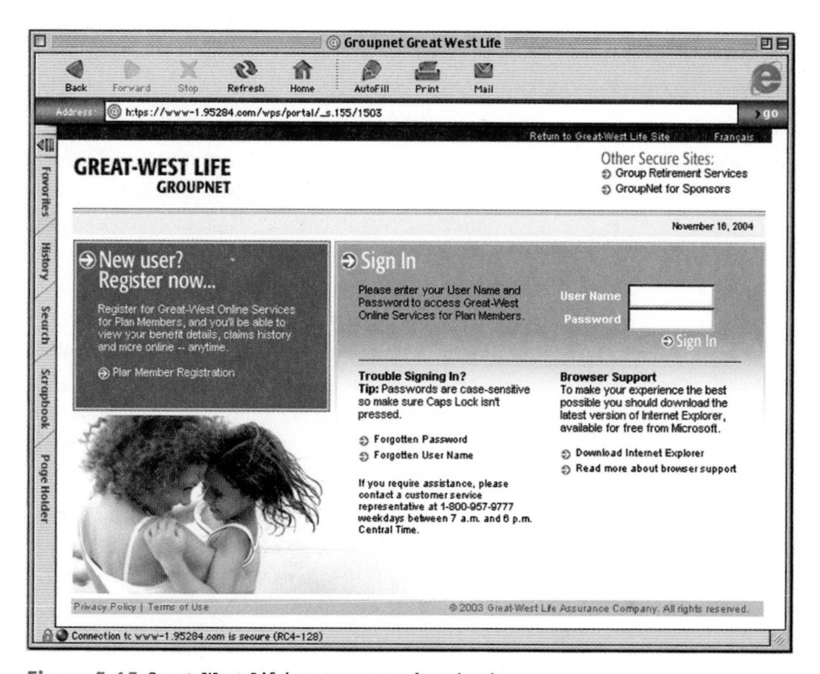

Figure 5.15 Great-West Life's extranet authentication page.

Source: Great-West Life

extranet to exchange supply and manufacturing information between customers and suppliers. Although it may seem outlandish that major competitors within an industry are teaming up for ***supply chain management***, the results have benefited everyone in the industry (Turban et al., 2004). The extranet includes features that allow participants to make online purchases, check supplier inventory levels, and transfer design specifications, as well as perform a variety of related tasks involved in business transactions. The extranet has helped reduce product manufacturing time, enabled inventory to arrive on a just-in-time basis, and compressed the turnaround time on work orders from 3 weeks to as little as 5 minutes. Overall, the extranet has achieved an industry-wide savings in the billions of dollars per year.

Dell has used an extranet to streamline its supply chain, reducing its number of suppliers from more than 1000 to approximately 100. Dell's suppliers are able to predict upcoming demands by accessing data from the extranet and can pass these forecasts and orders along to their suppliers, in turn, to ensure they can meet Dell's orders. This trickle-down effect introduced by Dell's use of extranet technologies has resulted in operational efficiencies throughout its supply chain (McDougall, 2000).

Real-Time Access to Information

CSX, one of the largest railroad companies in the United States, leverages extranet technologies to facilitate real-time information access by customers and business partners. CSX developed an application, originally implemented as an intranet-based tool for the company's customer service agents (see below for a discussion of intranets), that can track train shipments from coast to coast, providing real-time status updates. CSX now offers this service to its customers and business partners through an extranet. CSX has connected its extranet with over 200 business partners,

GLOBAL PERSPECTIVE

Using B2B Electronic Commerce to Support the Global Fashion Industry

If you are into following the latest fashion trends, have you ever taken a careful look at the labels inside the garments you purchase? If you do, you will most likely find that many of the tags say "Made in India," "Made in Bangladesh," or "Made in Mauritius." Even if the label says "Made in Canada," at least some of the raw materials, such as fabrics, fibres, dyes, trims, or yarns, have probably been imported. As the fashion industry is operating at an ever increasing speed, the manufacturers constantly have to be able to purchase the required raw materials in the right quality and quantity; similarly, the fashion retail chains have to be able to purchase huge quantities of the latest models as soon as they become available. Recently, Zara, a Spanish clothing chain, has been compared to computer manufacturer Dell due to its superior ability to change fashion lines at an incredibly fast pace.

In trying to stay ahead of their competitors by offering the newest fashion lines or clothing at the best prices, the international fashion industry heavily relies on B2B electronic commerce portals such as **fibre2fashion.com** or **FashionUnited.com.** Fibre2fashion's "Marketplace" offers companies a place to buy or sell raw materials, completed garments, equipment, or even machines. Recently, a buyer from China wanted to purchase rabbit skins, a manufacturer from Vietnam offered to sell large lots of jackets, pants, and knitwear, and a buyer from Turkey posted a buying offer for a shoe-sole manufacturing machine.

The European B2B portal **FashionUnited.com** provides a platform for brand name clothing manufacturers such as Levi Strauss, Hugo Boss, Triumph, and Adidas to conduct transactions with Europe's large department stores such as Kaufhof, Metro, Wal-Mart (Europe), and Otto Versand, the world's second largest online retailer. To integrate the interactions between manufacturers and retailers, **FashionUnited.com** supports a wide variety of different EDI formats such as EDIFACT, EANCOM, Tradacoms, VICS, and XML. The next time you're standing in the apparel department at The Bay or in a GAP store, think about the technology supporting the global fashion industry.

Sources: John Tagliabue, "A Rival to Gap That Operates Like Dell," New York Times (May 30, 2003), **www.fibre2fashion.com**, **www.fashionunited.com**. Nicola Schleicher, "Otto im Online-Handel weiter auf Erfolgskurs," Otto Versand Press Release (July 21, 2003).

including freight shippers and forwarders, who act as intermediaries between CSX and its customers. These business partners deliver customer shipments to the railroad and deliver arriving shipments to customers on the company's behalf. CSX's business partners use the extranet's real-time information to streamline their business operations, enabling them to pick up and deliver goods at the yard on a just-in-time basis.

CSX customers can log in to see where their shipments are in transit (down to the individual package level), allowing them to identify unanticipated delays and respond to them in a timely manner. Customers also use the extranet to calculate expected shipping rates, which CSX keeps updated on a regular basis. Customers can enter purchase orders online and receive confirmations nearly instantaneously, creating great efficiencies in the order-processing cycle for both companies (Turban et al., 2004).

Collaboration

Collaboration via extranets allows companies to respond proactively to the changing marketplace by working directly with their business partners, suppliers, and customers. These applications provide companies with the ability to develop products that will soon be in demand, giving them an understanding of what will be needed and when. Through extranet-based collaboration, the product development cycle can be initiated and completed faster. Companies can plan for the necessary components and communicate information with suppliers well in advance of the product's coming to market. Companies can also deploy purchasing resources more effectively, transforming traditional procurement personnel into supplier relationship managers rather than transaction processors.

Caterpillar, a global manufacturer of heavy machinery, implemented an extranet to assist with customer requests for customizations to their products. Prior to the extranet, salespeople, managers, and technical staff needed to wade through a plethora of paperwork to process a request, resulting in poor response times and unsatisfactory customer service levels. With the extranet, customers can request customized components online, and the request can be forwarded to Caterpillar's product engineers and component suppliers, who can securely share the required information, such as CAD/CAM drawings. In some cases, Caterpillar gains process efficiencies by acting as an intermediary between the end customer and supplier. Caterpillar can redirect requests directly to the supplier, who builds the custom component and delivers it directly to the customer (Turban et al., 2004).

ENTERPRISE PORTALS

Many companies operate multiple extranets, each designed to service particular business partners with particular business requirements. A desire to integrate these stand-alone extranets has prompted the evolution of a more powerful class of extranets known as ***enterprise portals. Portals,*** in the context of B2B EB, can be defined as access points (or front doors) through which a business partner accesses secured, proprietary information from an organization. Enterprise portals provide a single point of access to this type of information, which may be dispersed throughout an organization. Enterprise portals can provide substantial productivity gains by combining multiple extranet applications to create a single point of access where the company can conduct business with any number of business partners. This can help reduce the maintenance costs associated with supporting multiple extranets and can simplify the process for end users, as all the information they need to carry out business is available from a single source.

Enterprise portals come in two basic forms, distribution portals and procurement portals. Distribution portals automate the business processes involved in selling, or distributing, products from a single supplier to multiple buyers. On the other end of the spectrum, procurement portals automate the business processes involved in purchasing, or procuring, products between a single buyer and multiple suppliers (see Figure 5.16). Distribution and

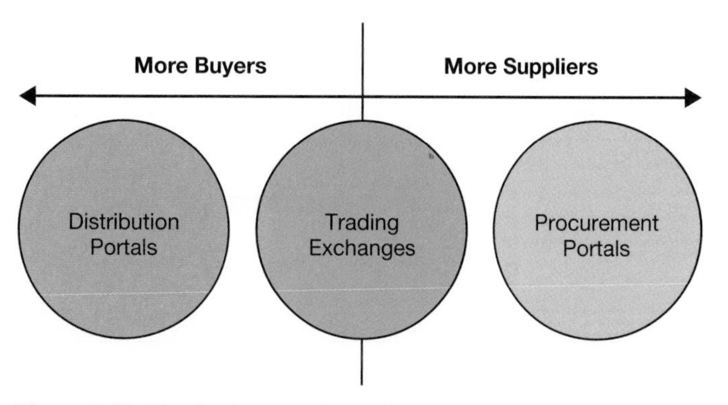

Figure 5.16 Distribution portals, trading exchanges, and procurement portals.

procurement portals can vary based on the number of buyers and suppliers that utilize the portal. For example, automotive industry giants Ford Motor Company, DaimlerChrysler, and General Motors have teamed up to create a procurement portal that suppliers to the big three can access. Similarly, a few companies can share distribution portals to purchase products from many suppliers. When the balance between buyers and sellers nears a point of equilibrium, these systems are classified as ***trading exchanges***.

Distribution portals, procurement portals, and trading exchanges commonly service specific industries or groups of firms that rely on similar products or services. Tailoring products and services to particular companies creates a ***vertical market***, or a market that services the needs of a specific sector. Vertical markets can create tremendous efficiencies for companies as they can take advantage of existing applications that already meet the requirements of other companies in their industry, eliminating the need to develop proprietary systems of their own.

Distribution Portals

Distribution portals are designed to automate the business processes that occur before, during, and after sales have been transacted between a supplier and multiple customers. In other words, distribution portals provide efficient tools for customers to manage all phases of the purchasing cycle, including product information, order entry, and customer service. Dell Computers services business customers through its distribution portal **Premier.Dell.com** (see Figure 5.17).

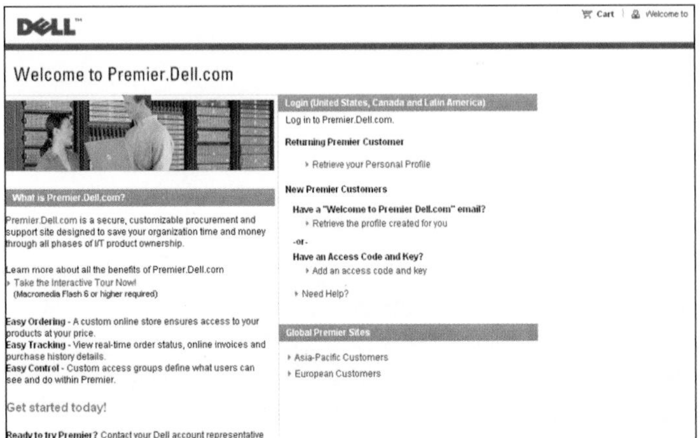

Figure 5.17 Distribution portal Premier.Dell.com.

Source: **www.dell.ca**

Premier.Dell.com goes well beyond providing its business customers with order entry and status updates. The distribution portal helps companies keep track of and manage their computing equipment through a series of online reporting tools. Need to know when a particular piece of equipment was ordered? **Premier.Dell.com** can search Dell's corporate database and produce a report tracing the equipment purchase to a particular transaction, purchase order, and/or order number.

Customers can also obtain customized, system-specific technical information about the products they have purchased. **Premier.Dell.com** provides help-desk personnel with the same information available to Dell technicians. This information includes a troubleshooting toolkit, a library of documents containing manuals and technical specifications, and a knowledge base containing searchable documentation from technicians and end users.

When placing orders, customers are taken to a personalized storefront, where discounted prices are calculated depending upon rates negotiated with Dell. The system immediately informs customers exactly how much an order will cost. Customers can build a purchase order online and send a copy of the quote via e-mail to a purchasing manager for approval. Once the customer's purchasing department receives the quote, a purchasing agent reviews the quote, approves it, and places the order with one click of the mouse. There is also an option to have Dell keep customers abreast of technological trends and changes before they impact Dell's products. This enables customers to make more educated purchasing decisions and plan ahead for technical innovations that can benefit them. Premier.Dell.com allows Dell's business customers to take control of business needs, saving them time and money while creating management efficiencies (Dell, 2004).

Procurement Portals

Procurement portals are designed to automate the business processes that occur before, during, and after sales have been transacted between a buyer and multiple suppliers. Procurement portals provide efficient tools for suppliers to manage all phases of the distribution cycle, including dissemination of product information, purchase order processing, and customer service. Ford Motor Company has implemented a procurement portal called Ford Supplier Portal **(portal.covisint.com/wps/public/?pan=fsp.everyone.page.Home)**, where suppliers come to share information and conduct business with Ford (see Figure 5.18).

The Ford Supplier Network (FSN) portal consists of a variety of applications addressing such issues as customer support, quality control, purchase order management, and product development. Distribution, Export, and Logistics Information System (DEALIS) is a real-time tracking application built for FSN that provides up-to-the-minute sales and shipping information to suppliers and shippers. These business partners use DEALIS to receive updates on shipments in transit and allow users to view information based on containers or packages, or even down to specific parts. If you are a Ford supplier and need to know where that shipment of bumpers is located, DEALIS can help you find out.

The Master Part Number Registry (MPNR) is an application designed to standardize part numbers and descriptions. In an environment in which a company makes purchases from multiple suppliers, each supplier may use different nomenclature to describe the same part. Implementing a common set of part numbers and descriptions allows Ford to make more efficient purchasing decisions, as product comparisons can be based on a common set of standards. Suppliers use MPNR to verify that the product information given to Ford adheres to the company's standards. MPNR is linked to Ford's corporate databases to ensure the accuracy and consistency of part numbers and descriptions used within Ford and throughout its supply chain.

FSN is also a learning and information site. Included in the portal are applications that enable suppliers to take courses online. The FORDSTAR program helps Ford certify its dealerships, employees, and suppliers. Here, users can access training materials, online courses, and developmental resources that will help Ford and its suppliers remain competitive in the ever-changing automotive industry. The interactive system helps suppliers determine which learning opportunities would be most beneficial to the organization.

FSN also provides suppliers with information concerning Ford's key business processes and plans for the future, as well as an online

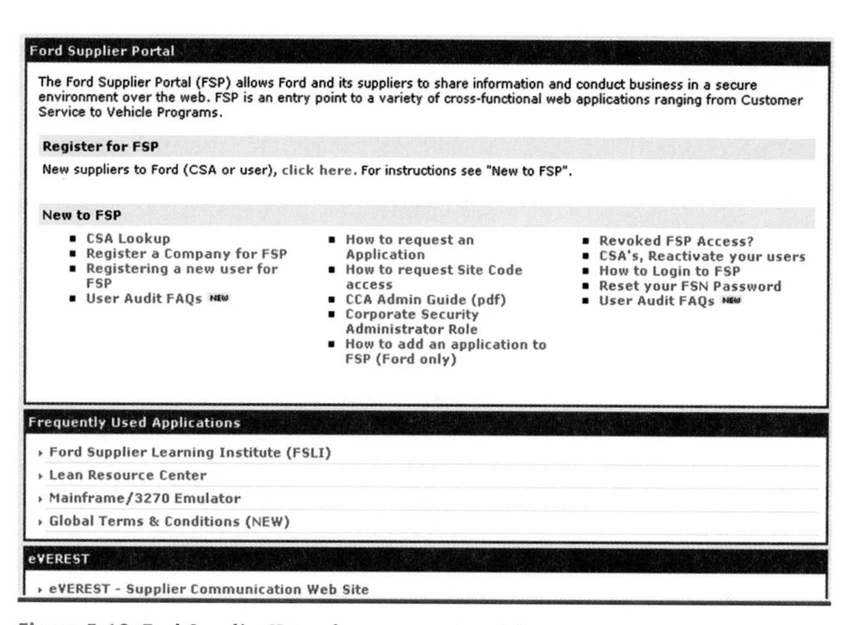

Figure 5.18 Ford Supplier Network procurement portal.

Source: **www.Ford.com**

tutorial to teach suppliers how to conduct business with Ford. From a supplier perspective, one of the key attractions of FSN lies in its distribution of competitive intelligence. Being aware of market trends and the activities of competitors enables Ford's suppliers to stay one step ahead of the competition.

The Ford procurement portal has created a win-win situation for the company, its suppliers, and end consumers. Ford has been able to streamline its business operations with suppliers, leading to dramatic process efficiencies and cost reductions. By using FSN, suppliers have direct access to a large company that can produce a substantial revenue stream. Suppliers also benefit from the information provided on FSN, which enables them to operate more efficiently, access Ford-sponsored training, and remain competitive in their markets. End consumers also profit from the distribution portal. When products can be manufactured more cheaply and efficiently, consumers ultimately benefit through reduced prices and faster delivery.

TRADING EXCHANGES

Enterprise portals tend to be beyond the reach of small to midsize businesses due to the costs involved in designing, developing, and maintaining this type of system. Many of these firms do not have the necessary monetary resources or skilled personnel to develop

Web Search

Visit the home page for Strategis, the federal government's electronic business portal, **www.strategis.gc.ca**, to see what types of information and services can be found there.

EB applications on their own. To service this market niche, a number of trading exchanges, or electronic marketplaces, have sprung up. Trading exchanges are operated by third-party vendors, meaning that they are built and maintained by a particular company. These companies generate revenue by taking a small commission for each transaction that occurs, by charging usage fees, by charging association fees, and/or by generating advertising revenues. Unlike distribution and procurement portals, trading exchanges allow many buyers and many sellers to come together, offering firms access to real-time trading with other companies in their vertical markets. This can be accomplished at a reasonable cost, making trading exchanges a competitive reality.

There are hundreds of public trading exchanges in operation, though the majority of this type of online trading now happens within private trading exchanges (Bowman, 2003). Trading exchanges provide companies with not only transaction processing, but also information pertinent to their industries, procurement resources to compare products from various sellers, and invoicing services. Some of the most popular trading exchanges include **www.e-steel.com** and **www.scrapsite.com** (steel), **www.paperspace.com** (paper), and **www.neoforma.com** (medical equipment).

An example of a successful trading exchange is SciQuest Inc. (www.SciQuest.com), which provides services to the $36 billion laboratory products and scientific supply industry (SciQuest, 2001). With industry globalization rapidly occurring, the industry had become increasingly fragmented, producing inefficiencies in the distribution and procurement processes. Many customers purchased products from a multitude of suppliers, based on outdated information in paper-based catalogues. As a result, firms were wasting time in product/supplier research and managing relationships with many more suppliers than necessary. To exacerbate matters, outside influences were exerting pressure on the industry to become more cost conscious, bring new products to market at a faster pace, and adhere to environmental legislation mandated by government agencies. To address this situation, SciQuest supports the particular needs of the laboratory products and scientific supply industry in six ways, as depicted in Figure 5.19.

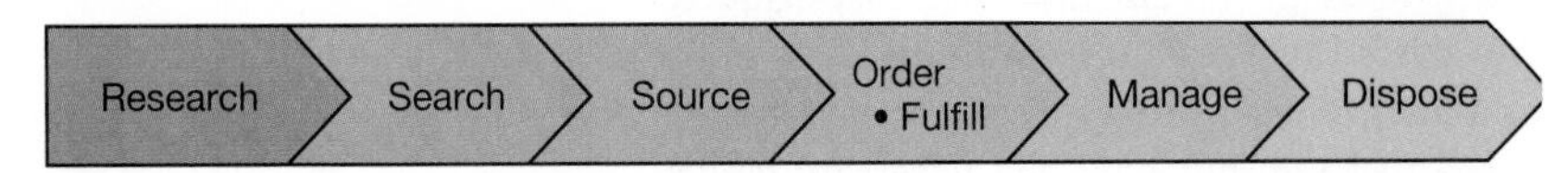

Figure 5.19 SciQuest supports its vertical market in six ways.

Source: **www.SciQuest.com**

SciQuest's SciCentral application provides a centralized repository for research articles relevant to the industry. SciCentral allows users to search thousands of scientific journals by keyword and also offers the capability to order and download research online. Trading exchange participants can also search for innovations that assist in the development of new products such as pharmaceuticals. Once customers locate the product they are interested in, they need to source the product. "Sourcing" means finding the supplier that can provide the highest quality product at the lowest price. SciQuest's SelectSite procurement application takes the customer's request and matches it with the most appropriate supplier. This eliminates the time customers spend in searching for the best supplier, as the application does it for them. Customers review the results from the sourcing application and choose to place the order automatically with one mouse click or reject the transaction.

SciQuest also supports the customer service aspects of the transaction by providing functions for coordinating shipping, receiving products, and tracking customer and supplier inventory levels. Furthermore, transactions in the laboratory products and scientific supply industry can involve a great deal of managerial overhead. For example, certain chemical compounds, because they can be used in the manufacture of illicit drugs, must be cleared through government agencies. SciQuest can assist companies in coordinating government approvals. Other chemicals must be tracked and monitored as they move throughout an organization, and SciQuest's applications can perform bar-code tracking functions to locate sensitive materials. Some products used in the industry, such as chemicals that can potentially harm the environment, need to be disposed of properly once they are used. SciQuest can guide customers through the disposal process by helping them locate an approved materials disposer and coordinating pickup between the two companies.

SciQuest's customers include Dow Chemical, DuPont, Glaxo Wellcome, McGill University, and Monsanto, while suppliers include Alltech Associates, Ambion Inc., Endogen, PerkinElmer Inc., Pierce Chemical, QIAGEN, and Shimadzu. In other words, if you are a small company in this industry, by using SciQuest you can conduct business as if you were an industry heavyweight.

NEW TECHNOLOGIES FOR B2B ELECTRONIC BUSINESS

Several new technologies are now available to companies that enable them to take even greater advantage of the Internet and web for their B2B systems. In this section, we briefly review two that hold significant promise for transforming organizational performance.

Extensible Markup Language (XML)

Extensible Markup Language (XML) is a data presentation standard first specified by the World Wide Web Consortium (W3C), an international consortium of companies whose purpose is to develop open standards for the web. XML allows designers of web documents to create their own customized tags, enabling the definition, transmission, validation, and interpretation of data between applications and between organizations (see Appendix B for more on XML).

XML does not specify any particular *formatting*; rather it specifies the rules for tagging elements. A ***tag*** is a command that is inserted in a document to specify how the document, or a portion of the document, should be formatted and/or used. As a result, XML is a powerful, tailorable information tagging system that can be used for sharing similar data across applications over the web (CIO, 2004).

You'll recall our discussion of the hypertext markup language (HTML) back in Chapter 4. HTML instructs a web browser how data on a web page should be laid out cosmetically on a user's screen. XML are also used as tags in web documents much like HTML, but they go well beyond HTML. XML instructs systems as to how information should be interpreted and used. For example, by using XML, you can tag a string of numbers and text on a web page as an invoice or a set of images in a product catalogue. With these advanced data definition characteristics built into the web applications, you can then use the web as the worldwide network for B2C and B2B EB.

Many people think that XML is on its way to becoming the standard for automating data exchange between business information systems and may well replace all other formats for EDI. Companies can, for example, use XML to create an application for doing web-based ordering, for checking on and managing inventory, for signalling to a supplier that more parts are needed, for alerting a third-party logistics company that a delivery is needed, and so on and then can have all these various applications working together using the common language of XML.

XML is customizable, and a number of variations of XML have been developed. For example, ***Extensible Business Reporting Language (XBRL)*** is an XML-based specification for publishing financial information. XBRL makes it easier for public and private companies to share information with each other, with industry analysts, and with shareholders. The TSX Group, owner of the Toronto Stock Exchange, is a heavy user of XBRL. The company is one of more than 40 Canadian organizations, including Export Development Canada, Royal Bank, and Public Works Canada, to join an international consortium working to bring the language to market.

XML is not, however, a panacea for EB. Support for, and use of, XML is growing rapidly, but all the necessary standards and agreements are not yet in place to enable XML-based applications to work seamlessly with all other applications and systems. Furthermore, while nearly anyone can learn to use a text editor to create a basic HTML document, XML is far more complex and requires not only knowledge of XML but expertise in distributed database design and management.

Radio Frequency Identification

Another exciting new technology now being used for extranets and other forms of EB is ***radio frequency identification (RFID)***. RFID is a way to identify objects, somewhat like a barcode that you might find on a grocery product. A key difference between barcodes and RFID tags is that RFID tags, because they use radio waves, can be read from a distance. Items can quite literally be identified as they drive by, as in car toll transceivers (a transmitter and receiver in one device). The range of an RFID tag can be as short as a few centimetres to as long as hundreds of metres, depending on the design of the device. RFIDs can also carry a great deal more information than barcodes. Some RFIDs can contain pages and pages of information, such as information on the contents of a shipping container.

RFID uses the electromagnetic or electrostatic coupling in the RF portion of the electromagnetic spectrum to transmit signals.

An RFID system uses a transceiver and antenna to transfer information to a special device, or ***RFID tag.***

RFID tags can be used just about anywhere that a unique identification system might be needed, such as on clothing, pets, cars, keys, missiles, or manufacturing parts. RFID tags can range in size from being a fraction of an inch and inserted beneath an animal's skin up to several inches across and fixed on a shipping container. The tag can carry information as simple as the name of the owner of the pet or as complex as how a product is to be manufactured on the shop floor. Some casinos have even embedded RFID tags into gambling chips. Using mobile readers, these casinos can keep close track of where all the chips are, as well as the value of a particular pile of chips, or of all the outstanding chips at any point in time.

RFID systems offer advantages over standard bar-code technologies in that RFID eliminates the need for line-of-sight reading. RFID also does not require time-consuming hand scanning, and RFID information is readable regardless of the entity's position or whether or not the tag is plainly visible. RFID tags can also contain more information than bar codes. It is possible to retrieve information about an entity's version, origin, location, maintenance history, and other important information, and to manipulate that information on the tag. RFID scanning can also be done at greater distances than can bar-code scanning. Passive tags are small and relatively inexpensive (less than a dollar) and typically have a range up to a few feet. Active tags, on the other hand, cost upward of $5, include a battery, and can transmit hundreds of feet (Edwards, 2003).

RFID systems offer great opportunities for extranet and other EB applications. For example, airlines are strapped for cash and think a lot about those metal, rolling serving carts that are used on airplanes and can cost as much as $1000 each. "We've heard horrific stories of airlines losing up to 1500 of these things in three months," says Tony Naylor, vice president of in-flight solutions for eLSG.SkyChefs, a technology provider for the airline catering industry, based in Irving, Texas (Edwards, 2003). To keep tabs on their vanishing carts, eLSG.SkyChefs now uses an RFID system with a RFID tag on each cart.

Montreal's ePoly, the e-business arm of Ecole Polytechnique, has been working closely with HP to build a business case for using RFID for a variety of applications for clients such as Hydro Quebec, Bombardier, and even a casino that has contemplated putting RFID tags in poker chips. Using RFID systems across the web enables power extranet applications as well. For example, the U.S. Wal-Mart Stores division now requires its 137 top suppliers to affix RFID tags to cases and pallets of goods. Wal-Mart began the roll-out RFID in the Texas region in early 2006 and is now expanding to the rest of North America, including its 235 Canadian locations. Wal-Mart expects RFID to lower distribution costs, reduce theft, and improve inventory management.

While RFID's deployment is growing rapidly, the systems are still relatively expensive, there isn't yet a clear set of data standards, and global radio frequencies differ between countries. Fortunately, these hurdles are being overcome by cooperation between vendors. In any event, RFID is clearly a valuable new technology for EB.

INTRANETS: BUSINESS-TO-EMPLOYEE COMMERCE

Once organizations realize the advantage of using the Internet and web to communicate public information outside corporate boundaries, web-based technologies can also be leveraged to support proprietary, internal communications within an organization through the implementation of an ***intranet,***[1] or B2E electronic commerce. An intranet consists of an internal, private network using web technologies to facilitate the secured transmission of proprietary information within the organization. An intranet can be considered a private, internal web, which limits viewing access to authorized users within the organization. Intranets take advantage of standard Internet and web protocols to communicate information to and from authorized employees. As they do on the web, employees access information on the intranet through a web browser. However, this information cannot be viewed by users outside the organization and thus is separated from the visible, publicly accessible web. Like extranets, intranets provide many benefits to

[1] It can be argued that, on a technological level, intranets and extranets are variants of the same thing in that both employ firewalls to cordon off a select group of users. However, given that intranets and extranets have very different purposes from a business point of view, we choose to distinguish between the two.

ETHICAL DILEMMA

RFID: Is It Safe?

RFID technology has proven to be a great means to improve supply chain efficiency; however, a technology that can not only tell you what goods you're carrying but also where you're headed has some people worried. If it can be used to scan cargo, can it not also be used to scan an individual? Could it be used to determine someone's whereabouts, blood type, or bank account number?

The Electronic Frontier Foundation (EFF) has spent several years investigating the potentially damaging impact a technology like RFID could have on society. Because RFID tags do not require line-of-site scanning technology, as barcodes do, they can be read from a distance. Tags also contain a great deal more information than barcodes. The worry may not immediately be identity theft, says Seth Schoen, staff technologist for the EFF, but could be a problem in the future if RFID is used to store personal data as part of a passport or other form of ID.

RFID tags can be copied, claims Schoen, and cost pressures may cause businesses to cut corners when they're rolling out RFID for various business applications. "You might say that these threats derive from the fact that the RFID industry wants things to be as cheap as possible," says Schoen. "And people haven't necessarily thought through the implications of deploying a lot of tags without any security measures for a particular application."

Several libraries are rolling out RFID as a means to track books, he says, but they haven't considered the possibility that the people carrying the books could also be tracked. Bartek Muszynski, president of Vancouver-based RFID consulting firm NJE Consulting Inc., says that most of the concerns about the technology are "significantly overblown." But that isn't to say they don't exist.

The level of detail that can be applied to an RFID chip is far beyond conventional barcoding means. "When you buy a can of Coke with a barcode on there, all that will tell is that it's a can of Coke. With an RFID tag, if you bought a sweater, it would not just tell that it's a certain kind of sweater, it will tell you it's sweater No. 2 000 456," he says.

GS1, the international standards body that governs RFID requirements, has considered the potential for abuse and built in safeguards to prevent such abuse, according to GS1 Canada CEO Arthur Smith. There is a "kill switch" built right into an RFID tag that would render it virtually useless after it leaves a store, for example.

Last year, IBM Canada opened the first RFID centre in Canada with the cooperation of GS1 Canada and several interested groups like the Canadian Council of Grocery Distributors. The centre was designed to showcase RFID as a means to supply chain efficiency, initially for agricultural products.

Source: Adapted from Neil Sutton, ITBusiness.ca, **www.itbusiness.ca/it/client/en/home/News.asp?id=38300.**

the organization, including improved information timeliness and accuracy, global reach, cross-platform integration, low-cost deployment, and a positive return on investment.

As with the use of the Internet to support B2B activities, using the Internet to support internal organizational communication and processes—B2E—is also rapidly expanding. For example, like the use of the Internet to support B2B activities, the Boeing Company also operates an intranet with more than 1 million pages registered with its internal search engine, serving nearly 200 000 employees. The intranet has become pervasive, impacting every department within the organization. Employees rely on the intranet to assist them in their daily business activities, ranging from tracking vacation benefits to monitoring aircraft production. In the remainder of this section, we examine the characteristics of an organizational intranet as well as the types of applications being deployed.

Intranet System Architecture

An intranet looks and acts just like a publicly accessible website and uses the same software, hardware, and networking technologies to communicate information. However, intranets use ***firewalls*** to secure proprietary information stored within the corporate LAN and/or WAN. As described in Chapter 4, hardware firewalls with specialized software are placed between the organization's LAN/WAN and the Internet, preventing unauthorized access to the proprietary information stored on the intranet. In the simplest form of an intranet, communications take place within the confines of organizational boundaries and do not travel across the Internet.

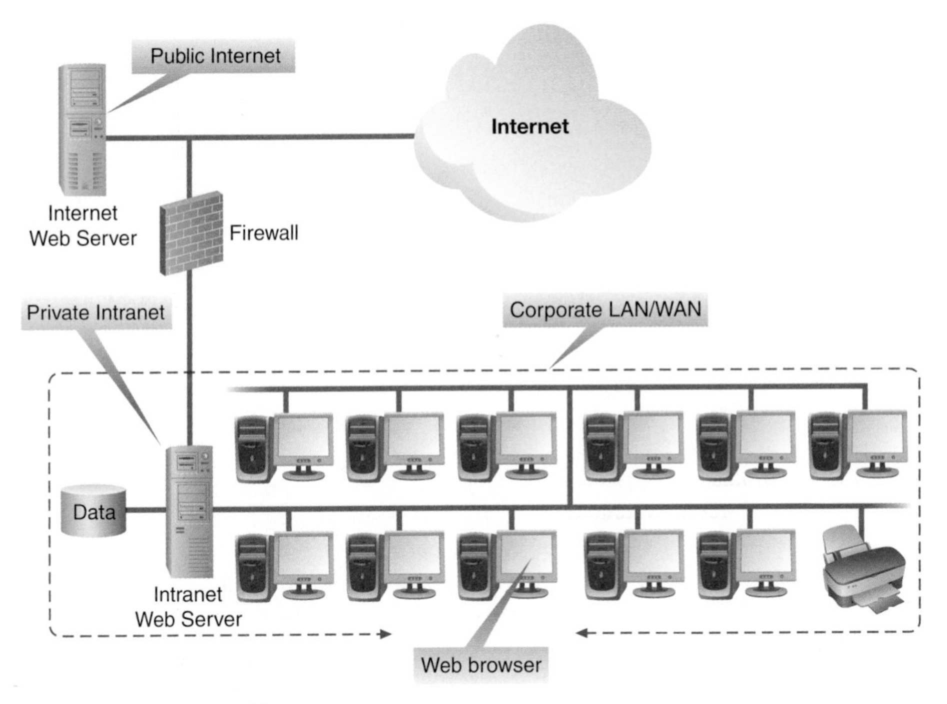

Figure 5.20 Intranet architecture.

Figure 5.20 depicts a typical intranet system architecture.

To enable access to an intranet, web browsers are installed on each employee's workstation, and the TCP/IP protocol must be implemented on top of the protocols existing on the corporate LAN/WAN. An intranet web server is placed behind the firewall and connected to the LAN/WAN to facilitate user requests for information. Employees may access intranet content through a web browser by entering the URL of the main intranet web page. Once the user enters the URL in the web browser, TCP/IP breaks the request into data packets and routes the transmission over the LAN/WAN to the intranet web server. When the packets reach their destination, they are reassembled and passed to the web server. The web server understands that the user is requesting a web page and retrieves the information, which TCP/IP breaks into packets and transmits back to the web browser. TCP/IP reassembles the web page at the destination and delivers it to the web browser. In turn, the web browser processes the HTML code, formats the physical appearance of the web page, and displays the results in the web browser. It should be noted that during the intranet transaction, packets are never routed outside the corporate firewall. All transmissions travel within the bounds of the organization's private network rather than over the public Internet, eliminating potential security risks such as unauthorized access to corporate information.

Web Search

Visit the Intranet Journal online at **www.intranetjournal.com** and find three collaboration tools that you would like to see used in the company you're going to work for after graduation. Why would these tools be useful to you? Can you think of innovative ways to extend the use of these technologies to enhance productivity or job satisfaction?

Intranet Applications

Organizations are deploying a variety of common intranet applications to leverage their EB investments. In this section, we briefly review a few of the most significant: training, application integration, online entry of information, real-time access to information, and collaboration.

Training

The Boeing Company offers nearly 200 000 employees training via the Center for Leadership and Training (CLT) intranet site. The training being delivered over Boeing's intranet opens up courses and training opportunities for employees worldwide. By using the CLT intranet, employees can choose from a wide range of course offerings, including educational programs, supervisor training, and techniques to improve quality control. CLT contains an online catalogue summarizing course offerings and provides a feature that allows employees to register for courses using their web browsers. Once registered for a course, users can access multimedia content, including video lectures, presentation slides, and other course materials, directly from their desktops.

Boeing's intranet-based training initiative has led to dramatic business improvements and cost reductions. The intranet helped eliminate redundant courses and standardize course material. It virtually eliminated travel costs associated with sending employees to training sites. In addition, employees can take courses on a time-permitting basis, meaning that they can learn at a pace that accommodates their work schedule. At Boeing, employee training is no longer subject to the physical and time constraints associated with traditional forms of education.

Application Integration

Many organizations have invested substantial sums of money and resources in a variety of software applications such as Enterprise Resource Planning (ERP), Customer Relationship Management (CRM), Sales Force Automation (SFA), and various other packages to support internal operations. Often these disparate applications are installed on different computing platforms, where each may be running under a different operating system, using a different database management system, and/or providing a different user interface. Due to these disparate environments, it may be difficult for a user to consolidate information from these different systems into a single screen that can display all the information the user needs to make a business decision. Intranets can be used to alleviate this problem by providing application integration.

For example, salespeople may need information about the sales calls they need to make for the upcoming day, as well as information related to customers that they currently support. Data related to sales calls may be located in an SFA application running on a UNIX server, whereas the CRM application may be running on an IBM mainframe. Prior to the emergence of intranets, the workstation that a salesperson used to access the information would need to be loaded with the appropriate network operating systems and user interfaces necessary to retrieve the information from each of the disparate systems. In addition, the salesperson would need to toggle back and forth between the applications to access all the necessary information from the SFA and CRM systems.

By installing a product such as Netegrity's SiteMinder on the intranet web server, information from the SFA and CRM applications can be consolidated and presented to the user through a single web browser interface (Figure 5.21). Now, when the salesperson needs information related to sales calls and customer support activities, the request is routed to the intranet web server running EIP, which accesses the relevant data

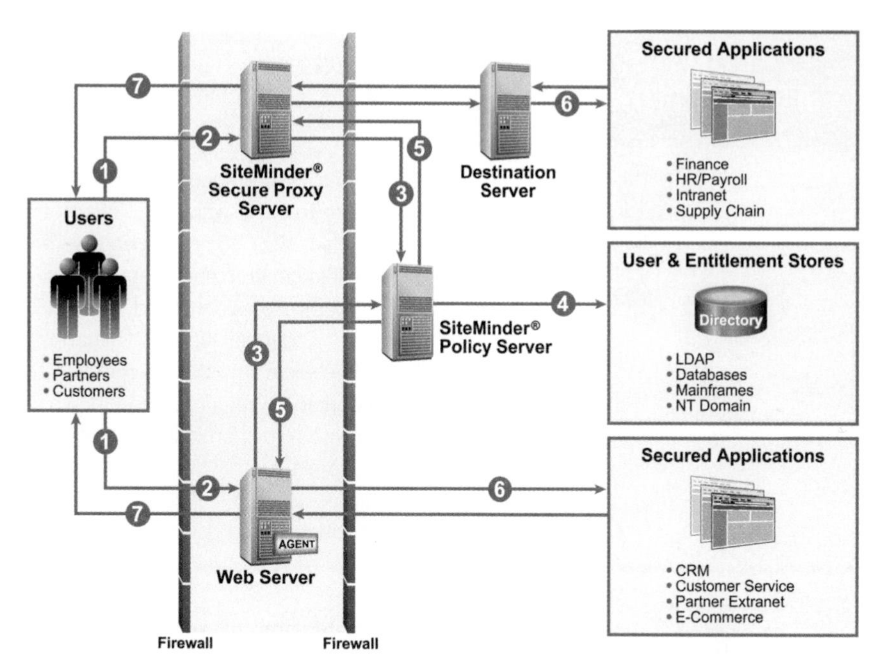

Figure 5.21 Application integration using Netegrity SiteMinder.

Source: **www.netegrity.com**

from the SFA and CRM applications. The intranet server consolidates the information and delivers it to the salesperson, displaying all the information necessary to make business decisions in a single web page.

Online Entry of Information

Companies can use intranets to streamline routine business processes because an intranet provides a web browser interface to facilitate online entry of information. Microsoft has implemented an intranet-based expense reporting application, called MSExpense, that allows employees from across the world to submit expense reports online, dramatically reducing the inefficiencies and expenses associated with paper-based expense report processing.

Prior to MSExpense, 136 different expense report templates existed within the corporation, and information such as mileage rates was often outdated. These issues cost Microsoft employees precious time and effort in locating the appropriate template and ensuring that the expenses they were submitting were accurate. With MSExpense, expense report templates and expense rates are centrally managed on the intranet web server, where modifications can be made instantaneously as conditions change. Now, Microsoft employees submit the appropriate template electronically with the assurance that they have used the correct version and up-to-date expense rates.

COMING ATTRACTIONS

Urban WiFi

In early 2006, Toronto Hydro announced plans to blanket downtown Toronto with WiFi Internet access. Starting in mid-2006, computer users were able to access the Internet from any location within the city's core. Similar systems are already in place in San Francisco, Philadelphia, and London, England, as well as in some smaller Canadian communities like Fredericton, Waterloo, and Ottawa. However, the Toronto Hydro project is Canada's largest by a wide margin.

Toronto Hydro installed WiFi equipment on company-owned street lighting poles to eventually cover a 6 square kilometre section of the city. The first zone of the network was installed in the city's financial district. Four additional zones were added one by one until the entire network became operational in early 2007. For the first 6 months, the service was offered to users free of charge, after which time access charges would be assessed. Toronto Hydro is hoping that there will be a demand for its wireless service despite the widespread availability of landline alternatives.

The implementation of the MSExpense intranet application reduced the cost of processing employee expense reports by over $3.3 million per year, shortened expense reimbursements from 3 weeks to 3 days, and dramatically reduced error rates by providing a single point of entry (Microsoft, 2001). Furthermore, applications such as MSExpense provide management with accurate, up-to-date information to track and analyze the costs associated with key business activities, as well as a way to enforce business policies to take advantage of reduced corporate rates offered by airlines, rental car companies, and hotels.

Real-Time Access to Information

Unlike paper-based documents, which need to be continually updated and distributed to employees when changes occur, intranets make it less complicated to manage, update, distribute, and access corporate information. U.S. Steel, the United States' largest manufacturer of steel products, developed a sophisticated intranet solution to provide employees access to up-to-date personal benefits information, allowing them to make more informed decisions related to health and financial benefits offered by the company. The intranet reduces employee reliance on human resources personnel, freeing them up for other tasks.

Labatt disseminates corporate news using multimedia files distributed over the company's intranet, called The Pub (see Brief Case: Labatt's Puts The Pub on Tap). Formerly, news releases were printed, duplicated, and distributed via surface mail to each corporate location around the country. With the intranet-based solution, the company allows employees to monitor company news releases as they occur. Labatt is now able to disseminate news in a more timely fashion while, in the process, saving millions annually in distribution costs.

With intranet-based solutions such as those deployed at U.S. Steel and Labatt's, up-to-date, accurate information can be easily accessed on a company-wide basis from a single source that is both efficient and user friendly. Companies can become more flexible with resources required to create, maintain, and distribute corporate documents, while in the process, employees become more knowledgeable and current about the information that is important to them. Employees develop a sense of confidence and become self-reliant, reducing time spent dealing with employment-related issues, which allows them to focus on their work responsibilities.

Collaboration

One of the most common problems occurring in large corporations relates to the communication of business activities in a timely fashion across divisional areas of the organizations. For instance, a product engineer located at a branch office in Sydney, Australia, may need to access information from product marketing personnel located in Vancouver, to ensure the product will meet the needs of the market. These individuals may need to share technical information such as CAD/CAM drawings, project management reports, and information related to prevailing industry and market conditions. In other words, employees must be able to collaborate across departmental and geographical boundaries to complete project requirements in an efficient and timely manner.

Boeing uses its intranet to facilitate these collaborative efforts. Project managers disseminate daily project progress reports over the intranet to members of the project team, who

BRIEF CASE Labatt's Puts The Pub on Tap

In 2001, Labatt launched an ambitious corporate intranet project called The Pub (See Figure 5.22). Since its debut, The Pub has changed the beer company's approach to business intelligence and knowledge management and made it possible for teams to effectively collaborate online. Labatt implemented an enterprise portal that improved overall communications between employees and eliminated silos of information between business units. Early on, Labatt was faced with the problem of convincing 3800 employees, from Newfoundland to British Columbia—many of whom did not own computers—that The Pub was a better source of corporate information than traditional meetings, newsletters, and bulletin boards. To overcome this problem, Labatt installed information kiosks to give employees easy access to The Pub, and it ran the intranet like a news wire. "We provide national, regional, and local news," says Sharon Mackay, director of public affairs at Labatt. "We provide frequent updates, sometimes twice a day." Those frequent updates were the key to The Pub's early acceptance.

Figure 5.22 Labatt's intranet changes its approach to collaboration.

Source: Labatt Breweries of Canada

Over time, the intranet's ability to break down information silos and create an open business intelligence environment has been at least as important. For example, if anyone in marketing wanted to review brand positioning data, a recent presentation made to a corporate client, or a particular Blue commercial from the 1960s, they could find what they were searching for in The Pub's multidimensional database.

In terms of online collaboration, The Pub reduced confusion over document versions and eliminated instances where two people were working on the same document at the same time. Once used primarily as communication and knowledge management tools, intranets are now used to improve workforce performance and link that performance to business value. To improve performance, intranets must align with processes and roles in specific industries and ensure that knowledge can support decision making—factors that have become critical in the competitive brewing industry.

Questions

1. A primary function of an intranet is to spread knowledge across the firm, as the above example illustrates. What are other functions of corporate intranets?
2. One problem with data repositories like The Pub is that employees do not tend to use them. Can you think of approaches that firms can take to improve the usage of corporate intranets?

Source: Adapted from "Heard It at The Pub," EDGE Magazine, Vol. 2, No. 12 (December 2003/January 2004).

may be located in any of its offices in 60 countries. Companies can also use multimedia technologies such as videoconferencing or Microsoft NetMeeting to facilitate team meetings over the intranet. Intranet-based collaboration alleviates the need for costly travel and use of less user-friendly media such as conference calling. Furthermore, three-dimensional modelling of aircraft designs can be shared between aerospace engineers. For example, an engineer can send a drawing across the intranet to another engineer at a remote location; the second engineer revises the drawing as necessary and returns the updated drawing using the intranet. The Labatt intranet provides the company with the capability of reducing product development cycles, as well as the ability to stay abreast of current project, corporate, and market conditions.

THE FORMULA FOR ELECTRONIC BUSINESS SUCCESS

The basic rules of commerce are to offer valuable products and services at fair prices. These rules apply to EB as well as to any business endeavour. However, having a good product at a fair price may not be enough to compete in the EB arena. Companies that were traditionally successful in the old markets will not necessarily dominate the new electronic markets. Successful companies are found to follow a basic set of principles, or rules, related to web-based EB.[2] These rules are:

- Rule 1—The website should offer something unique.
- Rule 2—The website must be aesthetically pleasing.
- Rule 3—The website must be easy to use and FAST!
- Rule 4—The website must motivate people to visit, to stay, and to return.
- Rule 5—You must advertise your presence on the web.
- Rule 6—You should learn from your website.

Rule 1. The website should offer something unique. Providing visitors with information or products that they can find nowhere else leads to EB profitability. Many small firms have found success on the web by offering hard-to-find goods to a global audience at reasonable prices. For example, Eastern Meat Farms (**www.salami.com**), an Italian market in New York, sells hard-to-find pasta, meats, cheeses, and breads over the Internet at its website (Figure 5.23). Their first order came in 1995 from a customer in Japan. Although the Japanese customer paid $69 in shipping costs for the $87 order of pasta, he did not mind; he was saving $150 by not buying the Italian delicacies locally (Rebello, 1996). Scantran, an online translation agency based in Ontario, offers localization services between English and the languages of Scandinavia and Finland. Competing sites may offer one or two of these languages, but not all of them together. Webview 360, a real-estate imaging company from Winnipeg, has successfully used the web to expand its business internationally (see SME Success: Steady Growth for Webview 360.com).

Figure 5.23 The Salami.com website.

Source: **www.salami.com**

Rule 2. The website must be aesthetically pleasing. Successful firms on the web have sites that are nice to look at. People are more likely to visit, stay at, and return to a website that looks good! Creating a unique look and feel can separate a website from its competition. Aesthetics can include the use of colour schemes, backgrounds, and high-quality images (but not too many!). Furthermore, websites should have a clear, concise, and consistent layout, taking care to avoid unnecessary clutter—an approach perfected by Google.

Rule 3. The website must be easy to use and FAST! As with nearly all software, websites that are easy to use are more popular. If web surfers have trouble finding things at the site or navigating through the site's links, or have to wait for screens to download, they are not apt to stay at the site long or to return. In fact, some early studies suggest that the average length of time that a web surfer will wait for a web page to download on his screen is only a couple of seconds. Rather than presenting a lot of information on a single page, successful websites present a brief summary of the

[2] Note that these rules apply mainly to how to make a website more successful. Realize that the underlying business model must be sound and that there are a host of similar rules that information systems personnel must follow to ensure that (1) the website works well, (2) it interacts properly with back-end business information systems, and (3) the site is secure.

information with hyperlinks, allowing users to "drill down" to locate the details they are interested in.

Rule 4. The website must motivate people to visit, to stay, and to return. People visit websites that provide useful information and links or free goods and services. One of the reasons why Microsoft's website is popular is that users can download free software. Other firms motivate visitors to visit their websites by enabling them to interact with other users who share common interests. These firms establish an online community where members can build relationships, help each other, and feel at home. For example, at GardenWeb (**www.gardenweb.com**), visitors can share suggestions and ideas with other gardeners, post requests for seeds and other items, and follow electronic links to other gardening resources. At this website, the participants communicate and carry out transactions with one another, returning over and over for more (see Figure 5.24).

Rule 5. You must advertise your presence on the web. Like any other business, a website cannot be successful without customers. Companies must draw, or pull, visitors to their websites. This strategy is known as ***pull marketing.*** Unlike ***push marketing,*** which actively pushes information at the consumer whether it is wanted or not (e.g., television commercials), pull marketing is a passive method used to attract visitors to your site and away from the thousands of other sites they could be visiting. The predominant method of pull marketing involves advertising the website. The first way to advertise your firm's presence on the web is to include the website address on all company materials, from business cards and letterheads to advertising copy. It is now common to see a company's URL listed at the end of its television commercials.

Another strategy is to register the website with the more popular search engines, such as Google and Yahoo. In most cases, registering with these sites is free and fast and can be done online. Many search engines provide context-sensitive advertising, meaning that your ad will be shown only when a related keyword is entered into the search engine. For example, if you are selling sporting goods, you can have your advertisement appear when certain terms such as baseball, football, basketball, and so on are entered in the search.

In addition to registering with the many search engines, a firm can advertise its website on other commercial sites or websites containing related information. Companies have made a great deal of money by enabling other companies to advertise on their websites. For example, Yahoo recently posted a quarterly net profit of $112.5 million, double that of the previous year, driven by rising revenue in its acquired Overture Services Web advertising unit (**www.abcnews.go.com/wire/SciTech/reuters 20040707_385.html**). Advertising your presence on other popular websites, such as CNN.com (**www.cnn.com**), can cost as much as $20 000–$30 000 per month, but they can promise that more than a million users a day will visit their sites. Given the high cost of advertising on these sites, and the fact that many of those web surfers do not even look at the online ad, the trend in web advertising is moving away from high, fixed monthly charges

Figure 5.24 The GardenWeb website.

Source: **www.GardenWeb.com**

SME SUCCESS Steady Growth for Webview 360.com

Webview 360.com is a Manitoba-based company that provides a tool to view homes, condominiums, and commercial property through the web. Webview 360 allows viewers to take a virtual tour of a property with the ability to zoom in and out of specific areas. Searching for a house can be done by location, style, size, or price, as well as numerous other searching preferences.

Paul Schmitt, a real-estate agent and Webview 360.com's founder, saw something in 1998 at a technical conference that caught his eye. An insurance company was using 360-degree digital imaging technology for insurance purchases. Schmitt returned to Winnipeg in February of 1999 to explore how this technology could be applied to the real estate industry.

Schmitt's goal was to provide listings of properties complete with 360-degree images of all important areas. Webview recognized the need to raise capital to get the business started. Initial thoughts were to go public; however, advice from close friends and business acquaintances encouraged Schmitt to obtain funds from private parties. In fact, Webview 360 experienced a lot of frustration as a result of the varied opinions and suggestions received from lawyers, accountants, financial advisers, and business people. However, after a few months, Schmitt met an interested "angel" from the United States who agreed to provide the company with sufficient funds to get started. He was then also encouraged to set up the company by way of franchises and offer franchise-licensing agreements to individuals across North America. It was at this time, Schmitt claims, that the stress started.

The guidelines for franchising law are extremely onerous and very time consuming. The legal fees for franchisee agreements alone amounted to thousands of dollars. Once again, Webview 360.com was faced with having to raise more money. Many people approached Schmitt with the intent to invest; however, he thought it would be best to have one to two large investors versus numerous small ones. Schmitt approached a large investment fund and was successful in obtaining additional capital. As of early 2006, he had sold franchises in six provinces and three U.S. states.

Lessons learned from the experience, according to Schmitt, were to listen carefully to what others tell you and always use a lawyer for any type of contract regardless of the size. Furthermore, dot-coms should be ready for reluctance and hesitancy from the marketplace (initially for capital, later for product and service offerings). Be patient and persistent.

Questions

1. SMEs can use the Internet to "sell to the world," yet most small firms are merely needles in a giant haystack. How can small firms enhance their exposure on the Internet to increase sales?
2. The founder of Webview 360.com cautions Internet entrepreneurs to be "patient and persistent," yet others have claimed that the key to success is to "go big, go fast, or go home." In your opinion, which of these strategies is the most correct?

Source: Adapted from Canada/Manitoba Business Service Centre, Document No. 6315 (2001).

to a "pay by the click" scheme. Under this type of pricing scheme, known as ***hypermediation,*** the firm running the advertisement pays only when a web surfer actually clicks on the advertisement (Carr, 2000).

Rule 6. You should learn from your website. Smart companies learn from their websites. A firm can track the path that visitors take through the many pages of its site and record the time of day, day of the week, or times throughout the year that people visit these sites. It can then use this information to improve its website. If 75 percent of the visitors follow links to check the company's online posting of job opportunities within the firm, or check on current pricing for a particular product, then that firm can redesign its website to provide that information quickly and easily for visitors. Similarly, pages that go unused can be eliminated from the site, reducing maintenance and upkeep.

CAREER IMPLICATIONS

Electronic Commerce, Intranets, and Extranets

For Accounting and Finance

For accounting and finance departments, intranets and extranets have created many opportunities for streamlining business processes. For example, using extranets for EDI, companies can instantaneously and seamlessly exchange inventory, sales, and payment data with suppliers, customers, and financial institutions. Corporate intranets allow employees to view and modify up-to-date financial information such as health plans, vacation schedules, paycheque deposits, or travel reimbursement. Financial institutions can reach new customer segments by providing opportunities for online banking or stock trading; interested customers can view the financial institution's terms and conditions and access a wide variety of different resources. Electronic commerce, intranets, and extranets have become pervasive in the world of accounting and finance.

For Operations Management

Operations management relies heavily on both intranets and extranets. For example, operations management professionals use intranets to obtain access to databases containing information about inventories of raw materials or finished goods, and to manage automated production processes. Interaction with outside suppliers or distributors can be accomplished using the organization's extranet to schedule production processes or order raw materials. In just-in-time production processes, outside suppliers can access a company's extranet to check on inventory levels of raw materials to replenish stock levels. Similarly, extranets can be used to check on the order status for products or to access detailed specifications for raw materials.

For Human Resources Management

The use of company intranets facilitates many aspects of human resources management. In addition to enabling employees to access HR-related information, such as employee manuals, and services, such as enrolling in health care plans, corporate intranets can help to deliver educational content to employees. Using multimedia technologies, human resource professionals can provide training material that employees can access at any time and from any place; the interactive content can increase the employees' retention of the relevant material, and at the same time, the company can reduce expenses for training delivered by expensive trainers during scheduled training sessions.

For Marketing

The advent of the Internet makes marketing professionals increasingly important. B2C electronic commerce allows organizations to sell a wide variety of products and services to customers in almost every corner of the world with the elimination of intermediaries such as distributors or retail outlets. This disintermediation results in an increase in the amount of direct interaction with customers from around the world, requiring greater skill and sophistication of the marketing and sales functions.

For Information Systems

The opportunities created by intranets, extranets, and electronic commerce have led to increased demand for skilled information systems professionals. Managing an organization's electronic commerce infrastructure can be a highly complex task, and information systems professionals must be aware of the implications of network downtime due to maintenance or disruption. For organizations engaging in B2C electronic commerce, where just 1 hour of downtime can lead to losses of tens of thousands of dollars and customer goodwill, reliable network connections are essential for generating revenue. Therefore, information systems professionals have the demanding tasks of choosing reliable networking infrastructures and managing the networks to maximize system performance and reliability.

KEY POINTS REVIEW

1. **Describe e-business and how it has evolved.** EB is the online exchange of goods, services, and money between firms, and between firms and their customers. Although EB was being used as far back as 1948 during the Berlin Airlift, the emergence of the Internet and World Wide Web has fuelled a revolution in the manner in which products and services are marketed and sold. Their far-reaching effects have led to the creation of an electronic marketplace that offers a virtually limitless array of new services, features, and functionality. As a result, a presence on the Internet and web has become a strategic necessity for companies. The powerful combination of Internet and web technologies has given rise to a global platform where firms from across the world can effectively compete for customers and gain access to new markets. EB has no geographical limitations. The global connectivity of the Internet provides a relatively economical medium for marketing products over vast distances. This increased geographical reach has been facilitated by storefronts located on every web-enabled computer in the world. Unlike the situation with traditional storefronts, time limitations are not a factor, which allows firms to sell and service products 7 days a week, 24 hours a day, 365 days a year to anyone, anywhere. A larger customer base creates increased sales volumes, which ultimately saves consumers money, as firms can offer their products at lower prices. Companies are exploiting one or more of the capabilities of the web to reach a wider customer base, offer a broader range of product offerings, and develop closer relationships with customers by striving to meet their unique needs. These wide-ranging capabilities include global information dissemination, integration, mass customization, interactive communication, collaboration, and transactional support.
2. **Describe the strategies that companies are adopting to compete in cyberspace.** The web has transformed the traditional business operation into a hyper-competitive electronic marketplace. Companies must strategically position themselves to compete in the new EB environment. At one extreme, companies known as brick-and-mortars choose to operate solely in the traditional, physical markets. These companies approach business activities in a traditional manner by operating physical locations such as department stores, business offices, and manufacturing plants. In other words, the brick-and-mortar business strategy does not include EB. In contrast, clicks-only (or virtual) companies conduct business electronically in cyberspace. These firms have no physical locations, allowing them to focus purely on EB. Other firms choose to straddle the two environments, operating in both physical and virtual arenas. These firms operate under the bricks-and-clicks business approach. Companies must also select a specific business model, which defines how they will earn money, which markets they intend to serve, whom they will compete with, what competitive advantage they will have, how they will market themselves, and so on. Firms in cyberspace must also define a revenue model, which can be based on advertising revenue, subscription revenue, transaction fee revenue, sales revenue, or some combination.
3. **Explain the differences between extranets and intranets and show how organizations utilize these environments.** An extranet, which enables two or more firms to use the Internet to do business together, is also referred to as B2B EB. Extranets use virtual private networks to connect the internal Internet infrastructure of organizations so that the data transmissions are secure. Organizations are utilizing extranets to facilitate supply chain management, real-time information access, and collaboration. Many organizations are integrating their unique extranets with various partners into comprehensive enterprise portals that support the distribution of goods (distribution portals) or the procurement of resources (procurement portals). Additionally, third-party vendors are creating trading exchange portals where smaller companies can utilize a full-featured extranet without bearing the costs of construction and ongoing operation and maintenance. An intranet refers to the use of the Internet within an organization to support internal business processes and activities. Examples of the types of processes or activities that might be supported include things such as training, application integration, online entry of information, real-time access to information, and employee collaboration. Both extranets and intranets provide significant benefits to organizations and are being very widely adopted by firms both big and small.
4. **Describe the stages of business-to-consumer e-business and the key drivers for the emergence of mobile commerce.** B2C EB focuses on retail transactions between a company and end consumers. Business websites can be relatively simple or very sophisticated and can be classified as e-information, e-integration, or e-transaction-type sites. E-information-type sites simply provide electronic brochures and other types of information for customers. E-integration-type sites provide the customers with the ability to gain personalized information by querying corporate databases and other information sources.

   E-transaction-type sites allow customers to place orders and make payments. Mobile electronic commerce, or m-commerce, enables people to take full advantage of the Internet on portable, wireless devices such as smartphones. M-commerce is rapidly expanding with the continuing expansion of worldwide Internet adoption as well as the continued evolution of faster cellular networks, more powerful handheld devices, and more sophisticated applications.
5. **Understand the keys to successful e-business applications.** The basic rules of commerce are to offer valuable products and services at fair prices. These rules apply to EB as well as to any business endeavor. However, having a good product at a fair price may not be enough to compete in the EB arena. Companies that were traditionally successful in the old markets will not necessarily dominate the new electronic markets. In addition to having a sound business model and plan for generating revenue, successful companies are found to follow a basic set of principles, or rules, related to web-based EB. These rules include having a website that offers something unique, is aesthetically pleasing, is easy to use, and is fast and that motivates people to visit, to stay, and to return. A company should also advertise its presence on the web and should try to learn from its website.

KEY TERMS

authentication 165
bricks-and-clicks 153
bricks-and-mortar 153
business model 154
business-to-business (B2B) 149
business-to-consumer (B2C) 149
business-to-employee (B2E) 149
clicks-only companies 153
collaboration 151
consumer-to-consumer (C2C) 149
digitization 160
disintermediation 152
distribution portals 168
e-brochure 156
e-information 156
e-integration 156
e-tailing 155
e-transaction 156
electronic business (EB) 146
electronic commerce 148
Electronic Data Interchange (EDI) 162
electronic marketplace 158
enterprise portals 167
Extensible Business Reporting Language (XBRL) 171
Extensible Markup Language (XML) 171
extranet 162
firewall 173
global information dissemination 149
hypermediation 180
integration 149
interactive communication 151
Internet commerce 148
intranet 172
m-commerce 160
mass customization 151
menu-driven pricing 158
nearly unlimited selection 152
portal 167
procurement portals 168
pull marketing 179
push marketing 179
radio frequency identification (RFID) 171
revenue model 154
reverse pricing 158
RFID tag 172
smartphones 161
supply chain management 166
tag 171
trading exchanges 168
transaction support 152
tunnelling 165
value-added network (VAN) 162
vertical market 168
virtual companies 153
virtual private network (VPN) 164
virtual products 160
watermarked 160
web commerce 148

REVIEW QUESTIONS

1. What is EB, and how has it evolved?
2. How have the web and other technologies given rise to a global platform?
3. Compare and contrast two EB strategies.
4. What are the key elements of a business model?
5. Explain the differences between the Internet, an intranet, and an extranet. What is the common bond among all the three?
6. Describe two types of portals and several applications.
7. Define trading exchanges, and give a couple of examples.
8. What are the three stages of B2C EB?
9. Compare and contrast reverse pricing and menu-driven pricing.
10. What is an electronic marketplace? Give an example.
11. Describe m-commerce and explain how it is different from regular e-business.
12. List and describe six elements of or rules for a good website.

SELF-STUDY QUESTIONS

Visit the Companion Website for this text for additional Self-Study Questions: **www.pearsoned.ca/jessup.**

1. Electronic business is the online exchange of __________ between firms, and between firms and their customers.

   A. goods
   B. services
   C. money
   D. all of the above

2. __________ allow many buyers and many sellers to come together, offering firms access to real-time trading with other companies in their vertical markets.

   A. Distribution portals
   B. Procurement portals
   C. Trading exchanges
   D. E-exchanges

3. __________ are those companies that operate in the traditional, physical markets and do not conduct business electronically in cyberspace.

   A. Bricks-and-mortar
   B. Clicks-only
   C. Both A and B
   D. Dot-coms

4. A __________ is a summary of how a company will generate revenue, identifying its product offering, value-added services, revenue sources, and target customers.

   A. profit and loss statement
   B. revenue model
   C. business model
   D. annual report

5. __________ automate the business processes involved in purchasing, or procuring, products between a single buyer and multiple suppliers.

   A. Distribution portals
   B. Procurement portals
   C. Enterprise portals
   D. Resource portals

6. According to the text, the three stages of websites include all of the following except __________.
   A. e-tailing
   B. e-integration
   C. e-transaction
   D. e-information

7. The revolutionary aspect of the Priceline.com website lies in its system of __________ called Name Your Own Price. Customers specify the product they are looking for and how much they are willing to pay for it.
   A. immediate pricing
   B. menu-driven pricing
   C. forward pricing
   D. reverse pricing

8. Under this type of pricing scheme, known as __________, a firm running an advertisement pays only when a web surfer actually clicks on the advertisement.
   A. cost-effective
   B. hypermediation
   C. cost-plus
   D. pay-plus

9. __________ creates electronic forms with which customers can register their identity and be assigned account numbers. Customer information is used as a tool for conducting market research, enabling the company to get to know its customers.
   A. E-business
   B. E-integration
   C. E-transaction
   D. E-information

10. A website should __________.
   A. be easy to use and fast
   B. offer something unique and be aesthetically pleasing
   C. motivate people to visit, to stay, and to return
   D. all of the above

PROBLEMS AND EXERCISES

1. Match the following terms with the appropriate definitions:

   _____ Electronic business

   _____ Hypermediation

   _____ Value-added networks

   _____ E-transaction

   _____ Electronic market

   _____ Electronic Data Interchange

   _____ Distribution portals

   _____ Vertical markets

   _____ E-integration

   _____ Digitization

   a. The online exchange of goods, services, and money between firms, and between firms and their customers
   b. The online sale of goods and services between firms with proprietary networks that the firms have developed and paid for entirely themselves
   c. A process that creates products without tangible features, which are commonly referred to as virtual products
   d. A class of extranets that automate the business processes involved in selling, or distributing, products from a single supplier to multiple buyers
   e. A pricing scheme whereby a firm running an advertisement pays only when a web surfer actually clicks on the advertisement
   f. Telephone lines that are leased from telecommunications providers, creating a secure, dedicated circuit between a company and its business partners
   g. Markets that service the needs of a specific sector, creating tremendous efficiencies for companies, as they can take advantage of existing applications that already meet the requirements of other companies in their industry, eliminating the need to develop proprietary systems of their own
   h. A stage that takes the e-integration stage one step further by adding the ability for customers to enter orders and payments online
   i. A market that allows many buyers and many sellers to come together, offering firms access to real-time trading with other companies in their vertical markets
   j. A stage in which web pages are created on the fly to produce tailored information that addresses the particular needs of a consumer

2. How did FedEx implement the development of the FedEx website (**www.fedex.com**)? Who is the company's primary competitor? How has the website improved FedEx's competitive advantage?

3. Visit Air Canada's website (**www.aircanada.ca**) for real-time pricing, and test the clothing model at the clothing retailer Lands' End (**www.landsend.com**). How have Internet technologies improved over the years?

4. Search the World Wide Web for the website of a company that is purely web-based. Next find the website of a company that is a hybrid (i.e., it has a traditional "brick-and-mortar" business plus a presence on the web). What are the pros and cons of dealing with each type of company?

5. Choose a company doing business on the web and, as best you can, identify for that firm the eight ingredients of a business model outlined in Table 5.3. Does the business model for this firm appear to be sound? How is it positioned relative to competitors?

6. Choose a company doing business on the web and, as best you can, identify that firm's revenue model. Which of the five common revenue models outlined in Table 5.4 does that firm employ? Now visit that firm's website and read its most recent annual report. Is it successfully earning revenue, generating profits, and producing a superior return on invested capital?

7. Search on the web for recent stories about the adoption of XML for web-based intranets, extranets, or other applications. To what extent does it appear that XML is becoming the standard? Based on your analysis, would you say that XML will be the de facto standard for intranet and extranet applications in 5 years? Why or why not?

8. What applications other than those mentioned in the chapter are there for RFID tags? What must happen in order for the use of RFID to become more widespread?
9. Do you feel that e-business will help or hurt shipping companies such as FedEx and UPS? Have you purchased anything over the Internet? If so, how was it delivered?
10. Do you receive advertisements through e-mail? Are they directed toward any specific audience or product category? Do you pay much attention or just delete them? How much work is it to get off an advertising list?
11. What is it about a company's website that draws you to it, keeps you there on the site longer, and keeps you coming back for more? If you could summarize these answers into a set of criteria for websites, what would those criteria be?
12. Consider an organization with which you are familiar that maintains an e-business website. Determine the types of information and processes available on the system. Do the employees make good use of the system and its capabilities? Why or why not?
13. Visit the following services for comparison shopping: BestBookBuys (**www.bestwebbuys.com/books**), Bizrate (**www.bizrate.com**), and mySimon (**www.mysimon.com**). These companies focus on aggregating content for consumers. What are the advantages of these websites?
14. Look at the list of your favourite bookmarks on the World Wide Web. Why have you saved these addresses? How often do you visit some of these websites? Is it faster to bookmark an address than to look it up again?
15. Have you ever used a mobile, wireless device such as a smartphone? If so, what do you like or dislike about it? In what ways could your use of that device be made better? If you are not using one, what is preventing you from using one? What would have to happen before you would begin using such a device?

APPLICATION EXERCISES

Note: The existing data files referenced in these exercises are available on the Companion Website: **www.pearsoned.ca/jessup**.

Spreadsheet Application: Tracking Website Visits

FashionExpress has recently started selling products on the Internet; the managers are eager to know how the company's website is accepted by the customers. The file FashionExpress.csv contains transaction information for the past 3 days, generated from the company's web server, including IP addresses of the visitors, whether or not a transaction was completed, and the transaction amount. You are asked to present the current status of the e-commerce initiative. Use your spreadsheet program to prepare the following graphs:

- A graph highlighting the total number of site visits and the total number of transactions per day.
- A graph highlighting the total sales per day.

Make sure to format the graphs in a professional manner, including headers, footers, and the appropriate labels, and print each graph on a separate page. Hint: to calculate the total number of site visits and the total number of transactions, assign the values 1 to "yes" and 0 to "no" using the "IF worksheet function" and count the number of 1s.

Database Application: Creating a Product Database at MountainSports

After helping FashionExpress get a good start in the e-commerce world, you are hired by MountainSports, a sportswear company, to help it with its new e-commerce project. From your experience at FashionExpress you know that customers want to be able to browse products by category and sort products by price or name. As this can be implemented using a database, you decide to set up a database containing MountainSports' offerings. The database should include the following entities:

- Products (including name and prices)
- Product Categories (including descriptions)

One product can be in only one category, but one category can have multiple products. Create a form to enter/modify products and product categories; if you are using Microsoft Access, use the form wizard. Hint: Create a query containing product names, prices, and categories before creating the form. Submit a file containing the database as well as a printout of the form.

ANSWERS TO THE SELF-STUDY QUESTIONS

1. D, p. 146
2. C, p. 168
3. A, p. 153
4. C, p. 154
5. B, p. 168
6. A, p. 156
7. D, p. 158
8. B, p. 180
9. B, p. 157
10. D, p. 178

Case *Can Canada Lead and Trail the World at the Same Time?*

A number of international studies have shown that Canada is among the global elite in terms of economic competitiveness and productivity. Canada has also ranked well internationally on factors relating to Internet infrastructure and e-business. Yet, while Canada is very strong on an aggregate level, it is not strong in all areas. In particular, the data suggests that Canadian businesses lag behind their counterparts in the United States and the European Union in areas such as Net readiness and Internet commerce.

Canada has been an international leader in terms of information and communication technologies (ICT), Internet infrastructure, and innovation. One recently published example of Canada's high standing came from INSEAD, a French business school. The INSEAD study aggregated data from a wide variety of sources to come up with a measure of national new economy performance, which they named the Network Readiness Index (NRI). The NRI was used to rank 82 nations on a variety of variables including Internet usage, e-commerce, technology infrastructure, and regulatory structure, among others. Many of the variables were broken down into individual, business, and government categories. Overall, Canada ranked sixth among the 82 nations on the full 2002 NRI. This rank represented a jump from 12th place in 2001. Canada ranked second behind the United States among nations with populations greater than 10 million. The study made explicit mention of Canada's significant policy initiatives and public/private partnerships as contributing factors to its high ranking.

Data produced by the OECD showed Canada to be among global leaders in terms of investment in ICT. Canada lagged behind the United States on these dimensions but was on par with the United Kingdom and ahead of other large European economies. Canada was also well positioned globally on a variety of measures of Internet infrastructure. Canada was second only to the United States in both Internet hosts per capita and websites per capita. Canada led the United States and European nations in terms of broadband connectivity, reflecting perhaps the concerted effort by various levels of government in Canada to promote infrastructure development. Finally, Canada led the United States and Europe in the proportion of patents allocated to ICT. This suggests that Canada has pursued an innovation agenda in technologies relating to net enablement and infrastructure development.

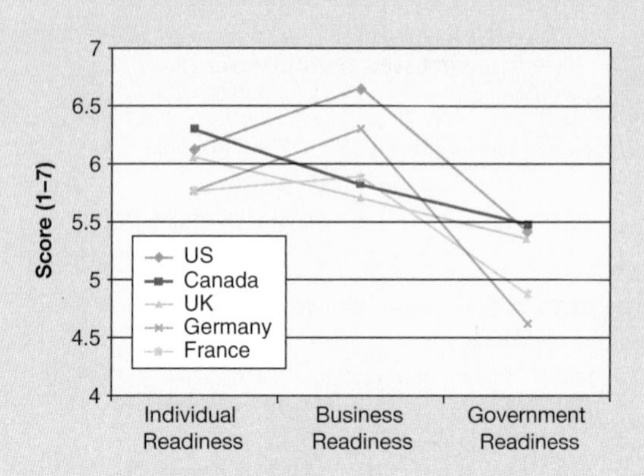

Figure 5.25

Despite these positive indicators, there is some evidence to suggest that, in the case of e-business, Canada has not attained the same level as the United States or some European nations. The evidence further shows that while Canadians and the Canadian government have embraced the Internet, the commercial sector has been slower to adopt e-business.

A closer examination of the Net Readiness study from INSEAD shows that while Canada had very advanced infrastructure and regulatory support for e-business, Net readiness in the business sectors lagged behind other nations. For example, while individual (fourth place) and government readiness (sixth place) were high, business readiness in Canada was relatively low (12th place). Figure 5.25 shows that Canada was first among key trading partners in both individual and government readiness, but second to last in business readiness. The opposite was found in the United States, where individual readiness was seventh, while business readiness ranked first among nations.

Data from the OECD appears to corroborate this evidence. For example, Internet commerce as a percentage of total commerce in Canada, at 0.5 percent, lagged behind many other OECD nations (see Figure 5.26). Internet commerce in the United States was proportionally double that of Canada, and Canadian Internet commerce was only a quarter of that of Scandinavian countries. Other data suggests that Canadian businesses were less likely than their United States or European counterparts to buy and sell over the Internet, even though their connection rates were similar. The OECD data shows that despite having similarly high rates of connectivity, Canadian firms were less likely to purchase online and substantially less likely to sell online than European firms.

Another indication of Canada's global economic position came from the Growth

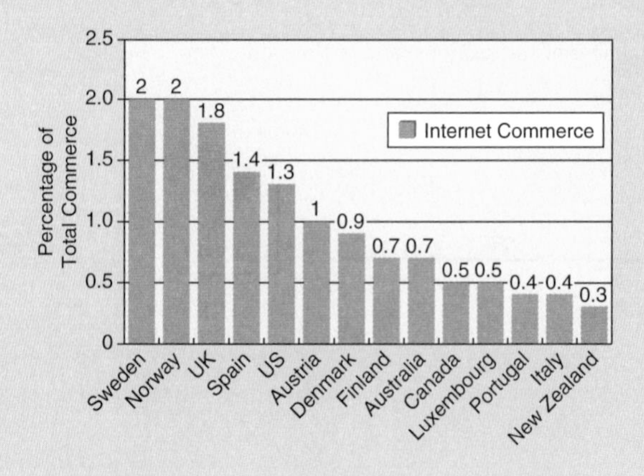

Figure 5.26

Competitiveness Index (GCI), produced annually by the World Economic Forum. In 2002, Canada's GCI placed it in eighth place among the 74 nations measured, down from third place in 2001. Canada actually improved its placing for public institutions and macroeconomic environment categories (from 11th to 9th and 13th to 12th, respectively). However, Canada dropped from second to eighth place in the technology ranking category, causing the fall in the overall ranking. The drop in the technology rank appears to be linked to a slippage in national performance in innovation and ICT. Canada's fall in the rankings may also be due to another factor measured in the report: Canada's rank in government expenditure was 52nd among the 74 nations in the study. The results show that while Canada is still high among nations on measures of productivity and competitiveness, other nations are catching up, and in some cases passing Canada when it comes to e-business.

Source: Adapted from McClean, Johnston, and Wade, "Net Impact Canada: The International Experience," *The Canadian eBusiness Initiative* (May, 2003), **www.cebi.ca**.

Discussion Questions

1. Why do you think Canada is falling behind some key trading partners in e-business?
2. Place yourself in the shoes of the federal government. What could you do to increase the adoption of e-business in Canada?
3. What do you see as the future of e-business in Canada?

Log on to the Companion Website at www.pearsoned.ca/jessup for an additional case.

Running Case: Connexion by Boeing

Electronic Commerce, Intranets, and Extranets

As Connexion by Boeing is in the business of providing broadband in-flight Internet access, telecommunications is at the heart of its business. Without the vast opportunities telecommunication technology provides, Connexion would not be able to deliver the services it has developed. Using wireless technologies for communications onboard the aircraft and satellite technologies for the communication between the aircraft and Connexion's ground stations (see Chapter 4 for a more detailed description), airline passengers can surf the Internet at broadband speeds, access corporate networks, hold videoconferences, or even view movies and live television. The airlines can also utilize Connexion's technology to streamline day-to-day operations by enabling better maintenance and crew scheduling, and by providing extended customer services to in-flight passengers. As typical for any net-enabled organization, Connexion depends heavily on intranets and extranets to manage internal operations and conduct business with its customers and suppliers.

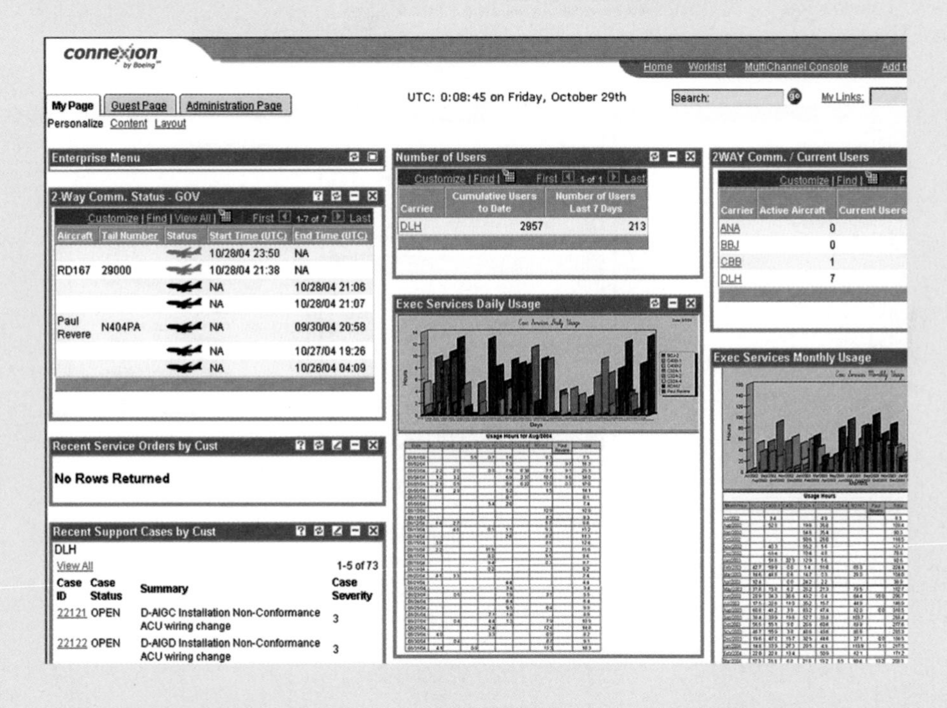

Regarding intranet usage, Connexion's employees rely heavily on its secure internal networks to access all relevant corporate data. Because of the broad range of internal Connexion employees that access these internal systems and data, steps were taken to ensure that individuals had access only to the information necessary to do their job. To control data access, profiles were created for different types of employees such that each user must log in to the intranet, and the system controls what information can be created, read, updated, or deleted. For example, employees from the systems development team have access to the technical specifications of the system but are not able to access any customer-related data. Likewise, members of the sales group have access to customer information but are blocked from accessing technical system specifications.

To maximize productivity and provide confidence that information was secure, Connexion utilized standard virtual private network (VPN) software to grant access to the corporate intranet. Using a VPN, Connexion's employees can access the intranet from any Internet connection in the world. Additionally, Connexion's corporate customers can also access their own companies' intranets while in-flight, using standard web browsers and VPN software. To guarantee hassle-free connectivity to these networks prior to operation, Connexion uses a portable simulator of its in-flight Internet service. This simulator is taken to each corporate client to verify that their VPN software and systems are compatible with Connexion's network and firewalls.

The heart of the Connexion intranet is its Customer Relationship Management (CRM) system. Using this system, Connexion personnel can access features such as event management, problem management, or system status to determine the performance of Connexion's network and systems. In addition to this information, internal stakeholders can access profiles or history of their customers. Connexion's sales force can utilize the system to manage correspondence or track sales leads. Likewise, Connexion's executive team can access a variety of reports to analyze the business's performance or to guide their strategic planning efforts (see figures below).

Regarding extranet access, Connexion also decided to use a standard VPN technology. Within the extranet, customers can access services such as CRM or aircraft configuration management within a standard web browser. Upon logging in, airlines employees can access data about the performance of their portal site (which an aircraft passenger first sees when connecting to the Internet aboard the airplane), usage statistics such as service acceptance by the customers, or the current status of Connexion's systems. Depending on the user's access permissions within the extranet, the user gets a custom-tailored startup screen providing different links to the information he or she has permission to retrieve from the extranet.

Airlines can also access Connexion's CRM system via this extranet. For example, the airlines' operations centres can access Connexion's most up-to-date system status, a number of different reports, and problem management status. As the CRM system also stores aircraft configuration data, the airlines' operations and maintenance facilities can access the system to get the most current information on their aircrafts' configurations. A link to Connexion's inventory management system informs the maintenance facilities about the availability of replacement parts, which can then be ordered via the integrated parts shipment module while the aircraft is in-flight. This real-time communication with the aircrafts' central computer system can help to speed up any maintenance-related activities. Not only can the airlines reap the benefits from accessing Connexion's extranet, they are also gaining benefits from real-time management of their day-to-day operations. For example, crew scheduling, weather and maintenance updates, and real-time performance monitoring of key system thresholds for safety and end of equipment life can greatly enhance the efficiency of operating, provisioning, and repairing an overall fleet. Digital data communications offer better quality than analog transmission and

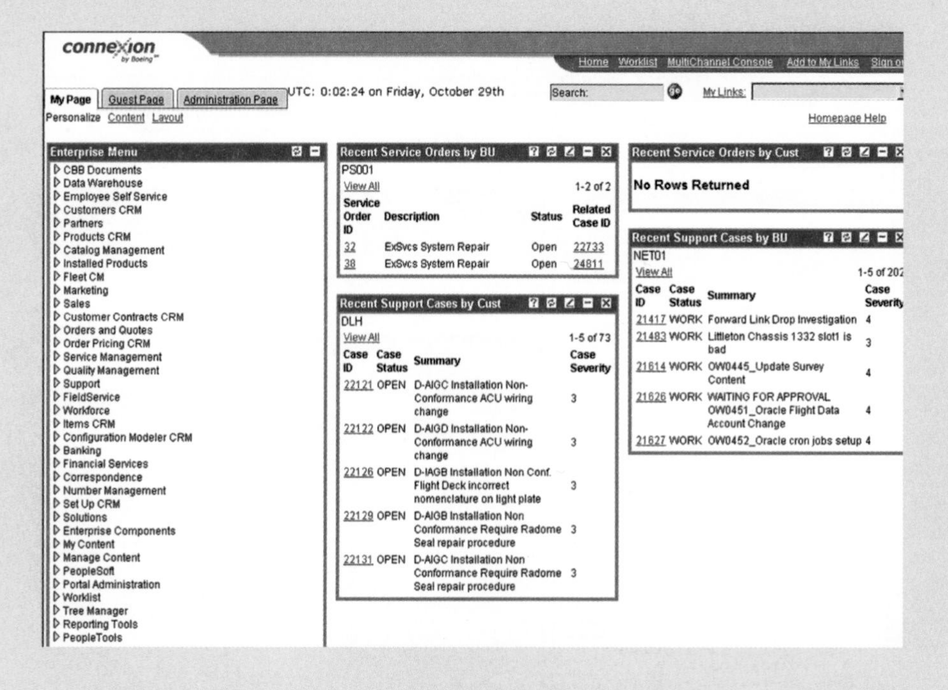

furthermore offer remote capabilities to aid the air crew in the operation of the aircraft.

To secure the transmission of sensitive flight information and internal airline information, it is transmitted separately from airline operational data through the use of VPN technology. The decision to utilize open industry standards for computing, network access, routing, and interfacing has eased implementation complexity as well as increased customer adoption and satisfaction.

Discussion Questions

1. How can Connexion's employees and customers benefit from Connexion's intranet and extranet infrastructure? Provide examples.
2. Why did Connexion choose to use Internet technologies for providing access to the corporate intranet and extranet?
3. Which other services could Connexion offer to its customers using the corporate extranet?

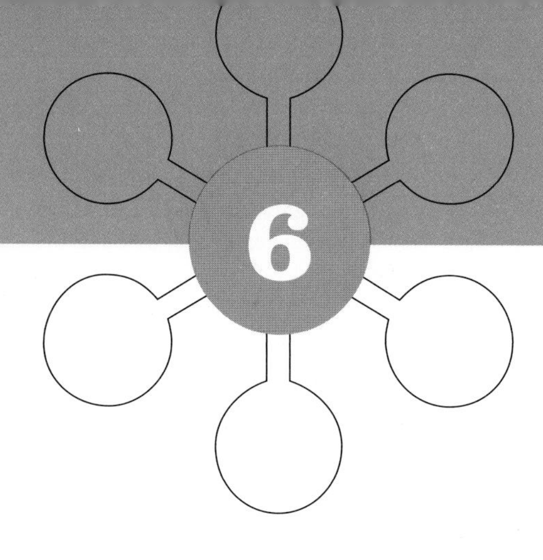

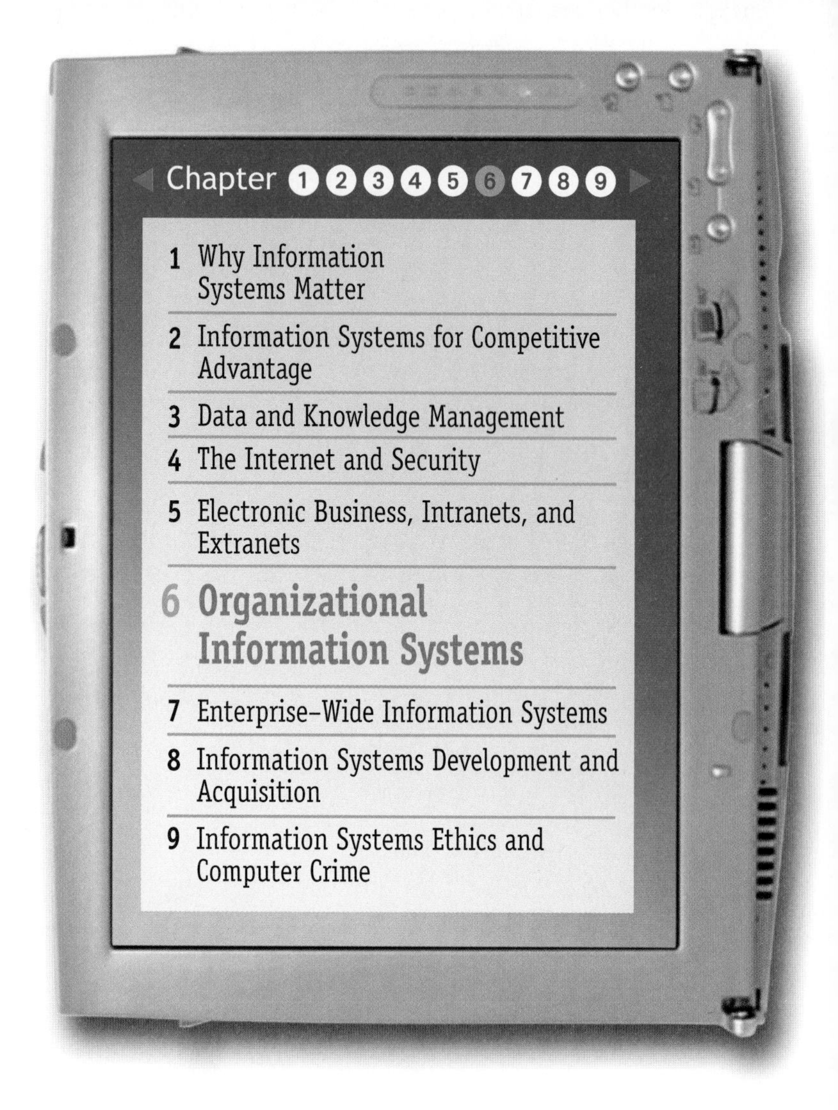

Preview

Every day, the capabilities of many organizational systems are expanding, making it difficult to make clear-cut distinctions between the capabilities and the focus of some systems. Nevertheless, it is important to understand that organizations comprise different levels and functions. Additionally, these different levels and functions require different types of information system capabilities and information to be effectively managed. Consequently, this chapter describes several types of information systems and where and how each is used in organizations. Some of the systems described are relatively new, while others have been mainstays in organizations since the 1960s. After reading this chapter, you will be able to do the following:

1. Describe the characteristics that differentiate the operational, managerial, and executive levels of an organization.
2. Explain the characteristics of the three information systems designed to support each unique level of an organization: transaction processing systems (TPSs), management information systems (MISs), and executive information systems (EISs).
3. Describe the characteristics of six information systems that span the organizational, managerial, and executive levels: decision support systems (DSSs), expert systems (ESs), office automation systems (OASs), collaboration technologies, functional area information systems, and global information systems.

Organizational Information Systems

Canada Competes!

Quebec has one of the fastest growing video game development talent pools in North America, and Beenox Inc. of Quebec City is one of its leading companies. Beenox has built a reputation for being able to "port" games developed for console-based systems, such as Xbox and PlayStation, to Windows-based personal computer (PC) and Mac platforms. Cross-platform game development of this kind is becoming increasingly expensive and complex.

Two challenges have historically made it difficult for game publishers to make money from games running on Windows-based PCs and Macs. The first challenge is the complexity of porting console games to PCs because of the vast array of hardware combinations that need to be supported. "New graphics cards, memory, input devices and other hardware components are continuously being added to PCs, offering more and more features," says Paul Gadbois, game producer at Beenox. "This makes the game developer's task far more complicated—like trying to hit and keep up with a moving target. By contrast, most game consoles stay the same for 4 or 5 years."

The other challenge facing game publishers is to release PC versions of games in time to take advantage of the huge investment in advertising and promotion that usually accompanies the release of the original console-based games. A development group may need to add 10–15 developers to handle the porting of the console-based game to a PC platform and still not complete the task for an additional 6 months—too late to ride the wave of hype and sales energy created for the original console game release.

Beenox developed a simultaneous cross-platform game development expert system that allows much of the porting work to be done automatically. The primary benefit of the Beenox porting solution is that it does not require the original game code to be touched, so the porting can be done while the base console game is still under development. It takes only two or three Beenox software engineers to port a console game at a fraction of the traditional production cost, and they can have it ready within 2 weeks following the release of the base console game.

By pairing up world-class game developers with Beenox's porting system, game publishers can release their biggest titles simultaneously on multiple platforms. For example, Beenox's port of The Incredibles required an average of only four people to produce the 25 versions of the game in 13 different languages. "Where the biggest publishers saw a problem, we saw an opportunity—and seized it," exclaims Gadbois.

Source: Activision Canada/Beenox: Simultaneous Cross-Platform Game Development, Canadian Information Productivity Awards, 2005.

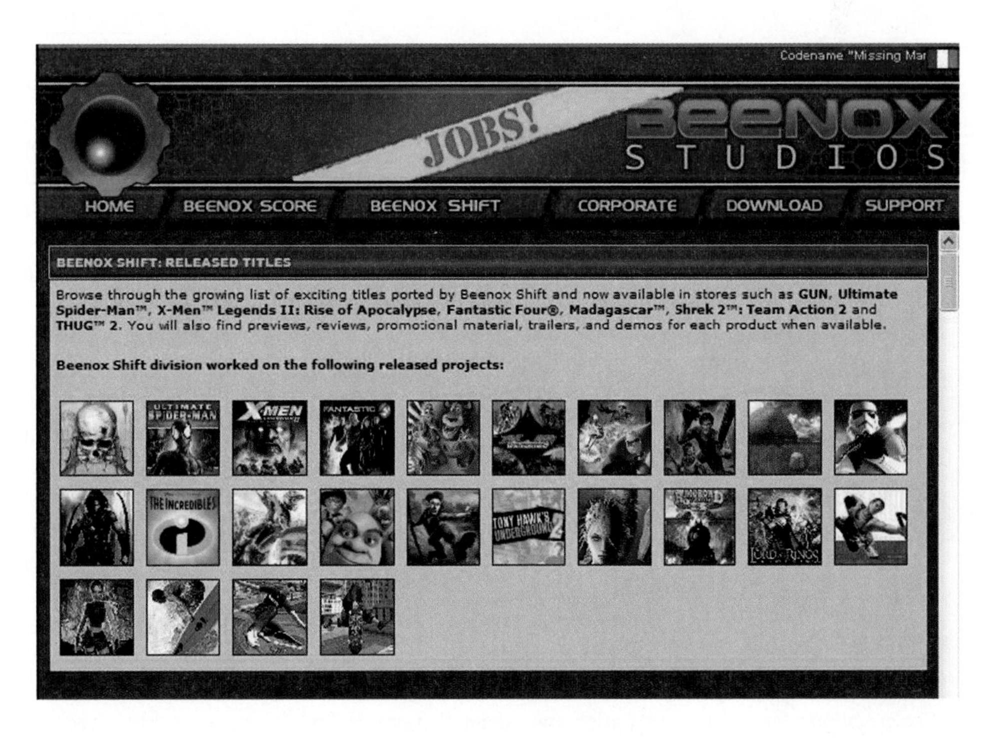

This chapter focuses on how organizations are using and applying information systems. The first section describes the different types of information required at various levels of organizations. This is followed by a discussion of the general types of information systems used to span organizational boundaries. We will discuss an additional class of organizational information system, the enterprise-wide information system, in Chapter 7.

DECISION-MAKING LEVELS OF AN ORGANIZATION

Every organization is composed of decision-making levels, as illustrated in Figure 6.1. Each level of an organization has different responsibilities and, therefore, different informational needs. In this section, we describe each of these levels.

Figure 6.1 Organizations are composed of levels, with each using information technology to automate activities or assist in decision making.

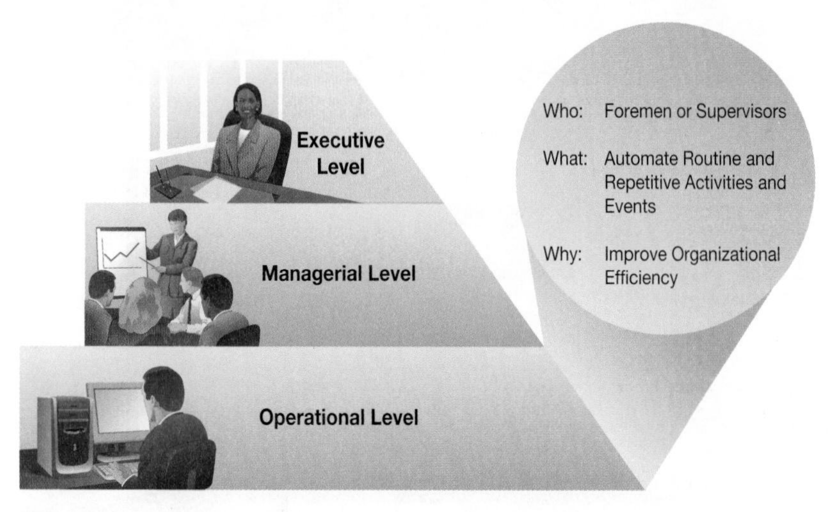

Figure 6.2 The operational level of an organization uses information systems to improve efficiency by automating routine and repetitive activities.

Operational Level

At the ***operational level*** of a firm, the routine, day-to-day business processes and interaction with customers occur. Information systems at this level are designed to automate repetitive activities, such as sales transaction processing, and improve the efficiency of business processes and the customer interface. Managers at the operational level, such as foremen or supervisors, make day-to-day decisions that are highly structured and recurring. ***Structured decisions*** are those in which the procedures to follow for a given situation can be specified in advance. For example, a supervisor may decide when to reorder supplies or how best to allocate personnel for the completion of a project. As structured decisions are relatively straightforward, they can be programmed directly into operational information systems so that they can be made with little or no human intervention. For example, an inventory management system for a shoe store in the mall could keep track of inventory and issue an order for additional inventory when levels drop below a specified level. Operational managers within the store would simply need to confirm with the inventory management system that the order for additional shoes was needed. Figure 6.2 shows the general characteristics of the operational level.

Managerial Level

At the ***managerial level*** of the organization, functional managers (e.g., marketing, finance, manufacturing, and human resources) focus on monitoring and controlling operational-level activities and providing information to higher levels of the organization. Managers at this level, referred to as *midlevel managers*, focus on effectively utilizing and deploying organizational resources to achieve the strategic objectives of the organization. Midlevel managers typically focus on problems within a specific business function, such as marketing or finance. Here, the scope of the decision usually is contained within the business function, is moderately complex, and has a time horizon of a few days to a few months. For example, a marketing manager at Canadian Tire may decide how to allocate the advertising budget for the next business quarter or some other fixed time.

Managerial-level decision making is not nearly as structured or routine as operational-level decision making. Managerial-level decision making is referred to as semistructured decision making because solutions and problems are not clear-cut and often require judgment and

WHEN THINGS GO WRONG

Computer Problems Ground Airplane Travellers

In today's highly competitive airline industry, having integrated computer systems is a necessity. To process passengers' reservation requests, change flight dates, or conduct check-ins at the airport, all major airlines use sophisticated transaction processing systems. Unfortunately, these integrated systems can be particularly vulnerable to failures of certain parts of the system. In August 2003, MSBlast, a widespread worm using a vulnerability in Microsoft's operating systems, clogged wide parts of the Internet. Shortly after this attack, "Welchia," another worm, made its rounds, targeting computers infected with the MSBlast. Although Welchia's creator intended the worm to patch computers infected by the earlier worm, the traffic created by Welchia led to the overloading of many networks. In the case of Air Canada, Welchia interrupted services at the main call centre in Toronto and check-in counters all over North America, leading to flight delays and cancellations.

While you might think that it should not be too hard to protect such systems from breaking down, a host of factors have the potential to cause extreme damage to globally interconnected computer systems; even something as trivial as a power outage in one part of the system can have implications on a global scale. In late 2003, a 2-hour power outage at British Airways' hub near London led to a breakdown of British Airways' airport check-in systems all over the world, causing major delays and the cancellation of 11 flights. If your company's systems are highly interrelated, then you had better think of backup plans, because it is almost a certainty that more worms and viruses are on the way.

Sources: Anonymous, "Computer Failure Hits BA Flights," *BreakingNews.ie* (September 6, 2003), **http://archives.tcm.ie/breakingnews/2003/09/06/story112440.asp**.
Anonymous, "Worm That Targets 'Blaster' Hinders Air Canada Operations," CNN.com (August 19, 2003), **www.cnn.com/2003/TECH/internet/08/19/internet.worm.ap**.
Lemon, Robert, "'Good' Worm, New Bug Mean Double Trouble," News.com (August 19, 2003), **http://news.com.com/2100-1002_3-5065644.html**.

expertise. For ***semistructured decisions***, some procedures to follow for a given situation can be specified in advance but not to the extent where a specific recommendation can be made. For example, an information system could provide a production manager at Canadian Tire with summary information about sales forecasts for multiple product lines, inventory levels, and overall production capacity. The manager could use this information to create multiple production schedules. With these schedules, the manager could examine inventory levels and potential sales profitability, depending upon the order in which manufacturing resources were used to produce each type of product. Figure 6.3 shows the general characteristics of the managerial level.

Executive Level

At the ***executive level*** of the organization, managers focus on long-term strategic issues facing the organization, such as which products to produce, which countries to compete in, and what organizational strategy to follow. Managers at this level include the president and chief executive officer (CEO), vice presidents, and possibly the board of directors, and are referred to as "executives." Executive-level decisions deal with complex problems with broad- and long-term ramifications for the organization. Executive-level decisions are referred to as *unstructured decision making* because the problems are relatively complex and nonroutine. In addition, executives must consider the ramifications of their decisions in terms of the overall organization. For ***unstructured decisions***, few or no procedures to follow for a given situation can be specified in advance. For example, top managers may decide to develop a new product or discontinue an

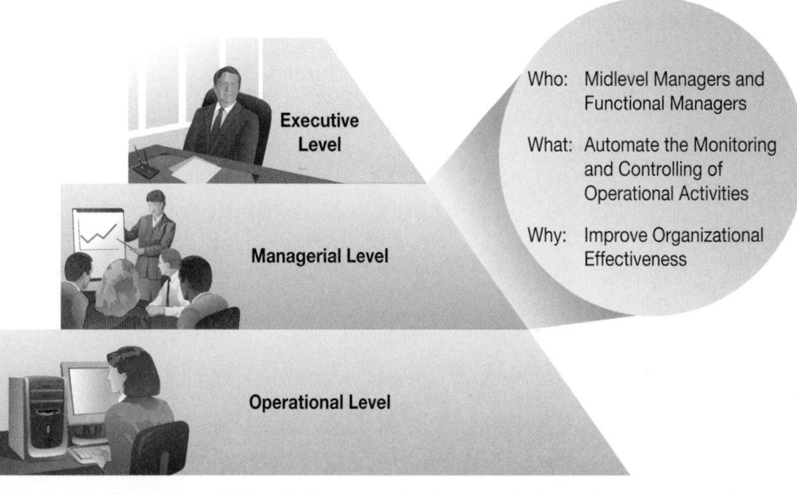

Figure 6.3 The managerial level of an organization uses information systems to improve effectiveness by automating the monitoring and control of organizational activities.

existing one. Such a decision may have vast, long-term effects on the organization's levels of employment and profitability. To assist executive-level decision making, we use information systems to obtain aggregate summaries of trends and projections of the future. Figure 6.4 shows the general characteristics of the executive level.

In summary, most organizations have three general levels: operational, managerial, and executive. Each level has unique activities, and each requires different types of information. The next section examines various types of information systems designed to support each organizational level.

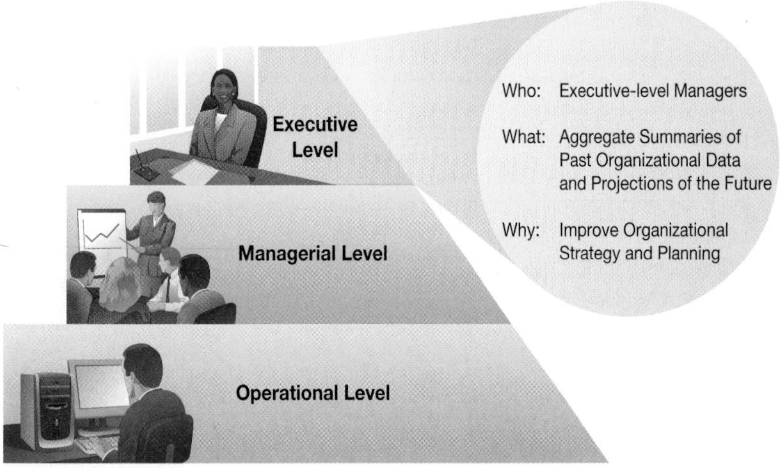

Executive Level
Managerial Level
Operational Level
Who: Executive-level Managers
What: Aggregate Summaries of Past Organizational Data and Projections of the Future
Why: Improve Organizational Strategy and Planning

Figure 6.4 The executive level of an organization uses information systems to improve strategy and planning by providing summaries of past data and projections of the future.

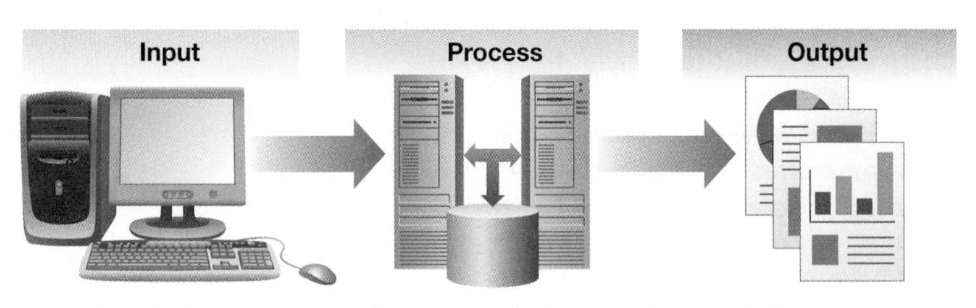

Figure 6.5 The basic systems model can be used to describe all types of information systems.

GENERAL TYPES OF INFORMATION SYSTEMS

An easy way to understand how all information systems work is to use an input, process, and output model—the basic systems model (see Checkland, 1981, for a thorough discussion). Figure 6.5 shows the basic systems model that can be used to describe virtually all types of systems. As an example, Figure 6.6 shows elements of a payroll system decomposed into input, process, and output elements. The inputs to a payroll system include time cards and employee lists as well as wage and salary information. Processing transforms the inputs into outputs that include paycheques, management reports, and updated account balances. The remainder of this section uses the basic systems model to describe various information systems.

Transaction Processing Systems

Many organizations deal with repetitive activities. Grocery stores scan groceries at the check-out counter. Banks process cheques drawn on customer accounts. Fast-food restaurants process customer orders. All these repetitive activities are examples of ***transactions*** that occur as a regular part of a business's day-to-day operations.

Transaction processing systems (TPSs) are a special class of information system designed to process business events and transactions. Consequently, TPSs often reside close to customers, at the operational level of the organization, as illustrated in Figure 6.8. The goal of TPSs is to automate repetitive information- processing activities within organizations to increase speed and accuracy and to lower the cost of processing each transaction—that is, to

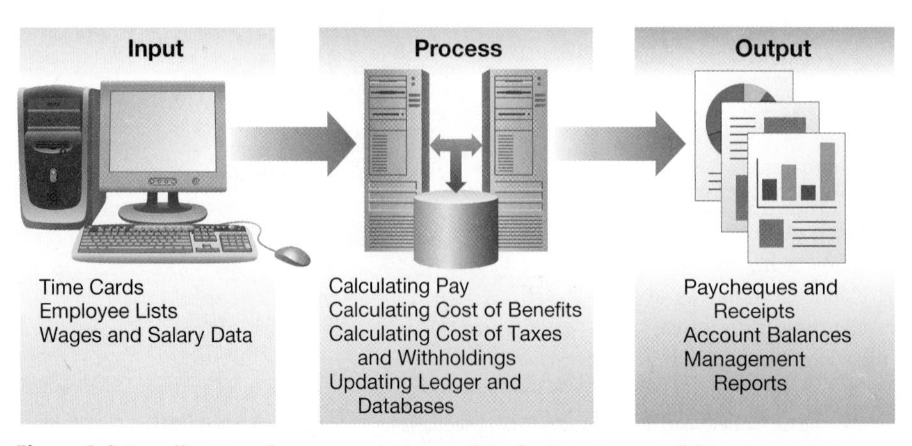

Figure 6.6 Payroll system shown as an instance of the basic systems model.

ETHICAL DILEMMA

Is Big Brother Watching You?

If you think you are the only one reading your private e-mail, then we have some bad news for you. Ever since the inception of employer–employee relationships, employers have been trying to control whether the employees are doing their jobs. Traditionally, offices have been equipped with surveillance equipment, which was mostly used for security purposes. Information technology has taken employee monitoring to a whole new level. Using the right software, your employer can read your e-mails, monitor your web-surfing behaviour, and even log the keystrokes on your computer.

In addition to this, technologies such as radio frequency identification (RFID) tags can be used to track employee movements throughout the company's buildings, through the tracking of access or ID cards (for an extensive discussion of RFID, see Chapter 5). Someone using the global positioning system (GPS) technology could locate you virtually anywhere in the world if you are using your company's vehicle (see Figure 6.7). With the current legal environment in Canada, your company has the right to collect almost any information about what you are doing. Often, companies use this freedom to collect sensitive data under the disguise of attempting to safeguard the companies' data or equipment. While this certainly can help to avoid potential wrongdoings of a few malicious employees, many privacy rights groups complain about the intrusion of the employees' privacy (see Chapter 9 for an extensive discussion of privacy issues).

You might think that you are not affected by this. If you are sitting at a computer in your university's library and are using the computer for private activities that are not directly related to your studies, then you might already be violating your university's appropriate use policies. And as you are using your university's (organization's) resources, they have a complete right to monitor what you are doing.

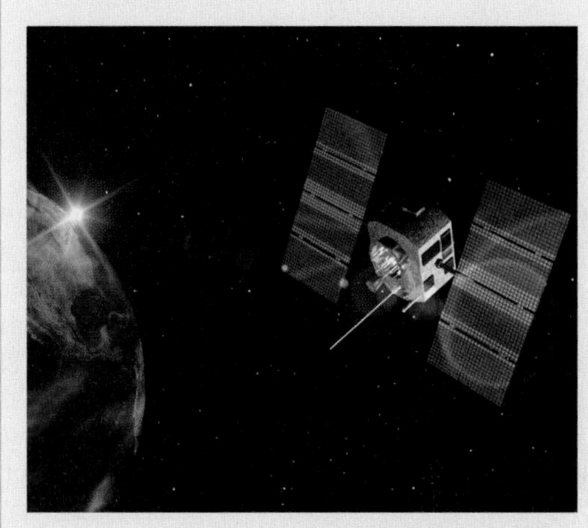

Figure 6.7 A global positioning system (GPS) uses a series of satellites to track something anywhere in the world.

Source: © T. Kevin Smyth/CORBIS

Figure 6.8 Transaction processing systems are used to improve operational-level decision making.

make the organization more efficient. As TPSs are used to process large volumes of information, organizations have spent considerable resources designing them. A TPS can reduce or eliminate people from the process, thereby reducing transaction costs and reducing the likelihood of data entry errors. Examples of the types of activities supported by TPS include

- Payroll processing
- Sales and order processing
- Inventory management
- Product purchasing, receiving, and shipping
- Accounts payable and receivable

Architecture of a Transaction Processing System

The basic model of a TPS is shown in Figure 6.9. When a business transaction occurs, source documents describing the transaction are created.

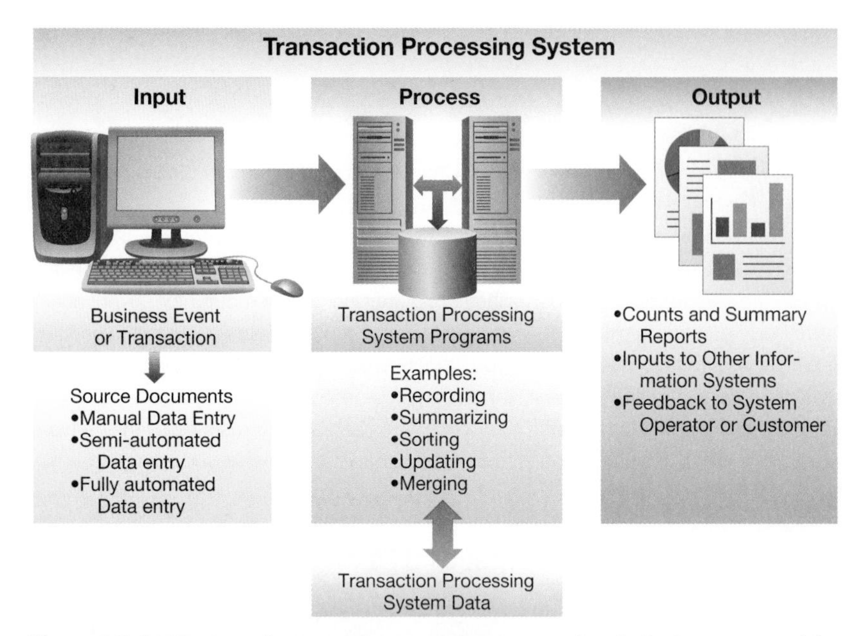

Figure 6.9 Architecture of a transaction processing system using the basic systems model.

Source documents, paper or electronic, serve as a stimulus to a TPS from some external source. For example, when you fill out a driver's license application, it serves as a source document for a TPS that records and stores all licensed drivers in a province. Source documents can be processed as they are created—referred to as *online processing*—or they can be processed in batches—referred to as *batch processing*. ***Online processing*** of transactions provides immediate results to the system operator or customer. For example, an interactive class registration system that immediately notifies you of your success or failure to register for a class is an example of an online TPS. ***Batch processing*** of transactions occurs when transactions are collected and then processed together as a "batch" at some time later. Banks often use batch processing when reconciling cheques drawn on customer accounts. Likewise, your university uses batch processing to process end-of-term grade reports—all inputs must be periodically processed in batches to calculate your grade point average. Online processing is used when customers need immediate notification of the success or failure of a transaction. Batch processing is used when immediate notification is not needed or is not practical. Table 6.1 lists several examples of online and batch TPSs.

Information can be entered into a TPS in one of the three ways: manually, semiautomated, or fully automated. ***Manual data entry*** refers to having a person enter the source document information by hand into the TPS. For example, when you apply for a new driver's licence, a clerk manually enters information about you into a Driver's Licence Recording System, often copying the information from a form that you filled out.

In a ***semiautomated data entry*** system, a data capture device such as a grocery store checkout scanner speeds the entry and processing of the transaction. The checkout scanner speeds the checkout for the customer and also provides accurate and detailed data directly to many types of information systems. Another example of a semiautomated TPS is an electronic shopping mall on the web. In this mall, customers enter their purchase requests, which go directly to an order fulfillment system without any additional human intervention.

Fully automated data entry does not require any human intervention. Two computers "talk" to each other through a computer network. For example, for automobiles built at Ford Motor Company, each part used in the manufacturing process represents a transaction in the inventory management system. When the inventory of windshields runs low, the inventory management system automatically contacts the supplier's computer system through a computer network to request more windshields. Electronic Data Interchange (EDI), an electronic link between computers to share data related to business operations, was discussed in detail in Chapter 4. Many organizations spend considerable effort with their suppliers and customers working on EDI standards—both how to communicate over the network and how data is to be formatted—so that more and more information can be exchanged without human intervention. Shell Canada uses a fully automated data entry system in conjunction with its easyPAY key fob. Drivers can pay for gasoline, snacks, and other items automatically without any intervention from a sales clerk (see the Brief Case: Shell Canada Adopts Radio Frequency Identification Tags).

The characteristics of a TPS are summarized in Table 6.2. Inputs to a TPS are business events or transactions. The processing activities of a TPS include recording, summarizing, sorting, updating, and merging transaction information with organizational databases. Outputs from a TPS include summary reports, inputs to other systems, and operator notification of processing completion. People who are very close to day-to-day operations most often use TPSs. For example, a checkout clerk at the grocery store uses a TPS to record your purchases. Supervisors may review transaction summary reports to control inventory, to manage operations personnel, or to provide customer service.

Online TPS	Batch TPS
University class registration processing	Students' final grades processing
Airline reservation processing	Payroll processing
Concert/sporting event ticket reservation processing	Customer order processing (for example, insurance forms)
Grocery store checkout processing	Bank cheque processing

Table 6.1 ***Examples of online and batch transaction processing systems.***

Inputs	Business events and transactions
Processing	Recording, summarizing, sorting, updating, merging
Outputs	Counts and summary reports of activity inputs to other information systems; feedback system operators of customers
Typical Users	Operational personnel and supervisors

Table 6.2 ***Characteristics of a transaction processing system.***

BRIEF CASE

Shell Canada Adopts Radio Frequency Identification Tags

Sometimes, the principal value of an information system is simply to reduce the time and effort it takes to complete an operation. Radio frequency identification tags, for example, exemplify how new technologies create "time rebates" for customers. RFID tags transmit and receive radio signals over short distances, obviating the need to physically interact with a system (see Chapter 5 for a detailed description of RFID). RFID tags are turning up in a diverse set of applications ranging from payment processing to baggage tracking. Even the times of runners in Quebec City's Marathon Des Deux Rives (as well as more than 120 other Canadian road races) are now tracked using RFID technology.

Shell Canada's easyPAY™ payment technology (Figure 6.10) was first tested in the Calgary market in the fall of 2000 and subsequently rolled out in 2001 to other Shell retail sites in Vancouver, Edmonton, Toronto, Ottawa, and Montreal. The system embeds RFID technology in a tag that fits on a key ring. The tag communicates with a pump-mounted receiver to automatically bill fuel to a customer's chosen credit card.

Figure 6.10 Shell Canada's easyPAY™ Tag.
Source: Courtesy of Shell Canada Products

Shell conducted extensive research that revealed that speed and convenience are becoming increasingly important factors for consumers purchasing gasoline. As a result, the company designed the system to meet the needs of consumers who want to have a simple, quick, and efficient experience when fuelling up. Shell Canada was initially reluctant to implement easyPAY, as it allowed customers to bypass Shell's lucrative service station retail outlets. However, positive consumer reaction to the initiative outweighed any potential loss of in-store sales.

Shell has found that the customer is not the only beneficiary of the technology. The company is now able to quickly gather information about when and where its customers purchase gasoline in much the same way the marathon and other races can track precisely when runners have crossed the various kilometre markers. Also, because fill-ups are faster, the company can increase the effective capacity of its gas stations.

Questions

1. Can Shell Canada use RFID technology to achieve a sustainable competitive advantage?
2. What other applications can you think of for RFID technologies?

Source: Adapted from Jonathan Copulsky and Mark Whitmore, "Giving Time Back to Your Customers," IT World Canada (November 1, 2002).

Additionally, inventory management systems may monitor transaction activity and use this information to manage inventory reordering. This is an example of the output from a TPS being the input to another system.

Management Information Systems

Management information system (MIS) is a term with two meanings. It describes the field of study that encompasses the development, use, management, and study of computer-based information systems in organizations. It also refers to a specific type of organizational information system. An MIS is used to produce scheduled and ad hoc reports to support the ongoing, recurring decision-making activities associated with managing an entire business or a functional area within a business. Consequently, an MIS often resides at the managerial level of the organization, as shown in Figure 6.11. We will discuss the reports produced by an MIS later in this section.

Whereas TPSs automate repetitive information-processing activities to increase efficiency, an MIS helps midlevel managers to make more effective decisions. Management information systems are designed to get the right information to the right people in the right format at the right time to help them make better decisions. MISs can be found throughout the organization. For example, a marketing manager for Nike may have an MIS that contrasts sales revenue and marketing expenses by geographic region so that he can better understand how regional marketing for the "Tiger Woods Golf" promotion is performing. Examples of the types of activities supported by MISs include

- Sales forecasting
- Financial management and forecasting
- Manufacturing planning and scheduling
- Inventory management and planning
- Advertising and product pricing

Architecture of a Management Information System

The basic architecture of an MIS is shown in Figure 6.12. At regular intervals, managers need to review summary information of some organizational activity. For example, a sales manager at a Ford dealership may review the weekly performance of all his sales staff. To aid his review, an MIS summarizes the total sales volume of each salesperson in a report. This report may provide a plethora of information about each person, including the following:

- What are this salesperson's year-to-date sales totals?
- How do this year's sales figures compare with last year's?
- What is the average amount per sale?
- How do sales change by the day of the week?

Imagine the difficulty of producing these weekly reports manually for an organization that has 50 salespeople, 500 salespeople, or even 5000 salespeople! It would be very difficult, if not impossible, to create these detailed reports on each salesperson without an MIS.

An MIS combines information from multiple data sources into a structured report that allows managers to monitor and manage the organization better. Reports produced at predefined intervals—daily, weekly, or monthly—to support the routine informational needs of managerial-

Figure 6.11 Management information systems are used to improve managerial-level decision making.

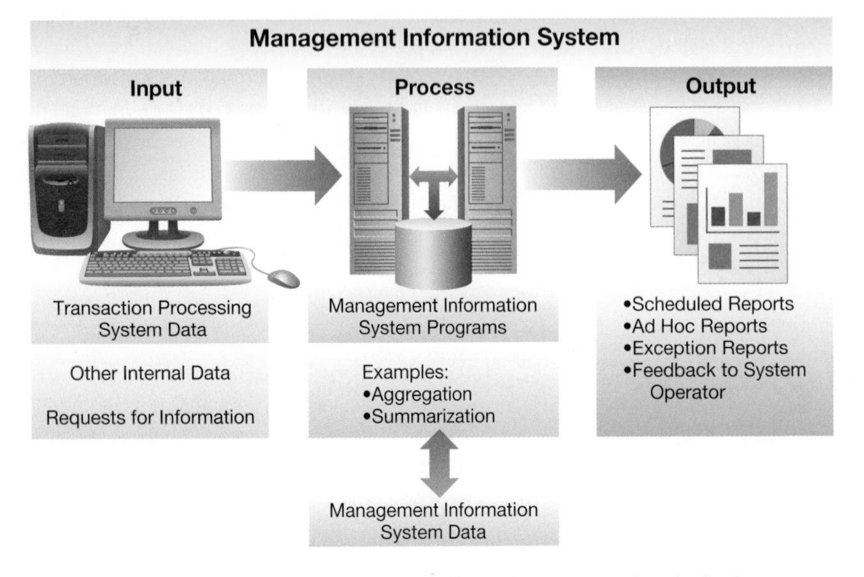

Figure 6.12 Architecture of a management information system using the basic systems model.

level decision making are called ***scheduled reports*** (e.g., a weekly inventory level report). These reports can provide summaries of all types of information but most often provide information related to key indicators. A ***key-indicator report*** provides a summary of critical information on a recurring schedule. Key-indicator reports provide high-level summaries so that a manager can quickly see if all important activities are operating as planned. Management information systems can also be used to produce ***exception reports*** that highlight situations that are out of the normal range. For example, a manager with a large number of sales personnel can produce an exception report highlighting those not achieving minimum sales goals. By focusing the manager's attention on specific information, the MIS helps the organization take a first step in making better decisions. When managers want greater detail as to why a key indicator or exception is not at an appropriate level, they request that a ***drill-down report*** be produced. In essence, drill-down reports provide details behind the summary values on a key-indicator or exception report.

Managers can also use an MIS to make ad hoc requests for information. ***Ad hoc reports*** refer to unplanned information requests in which information is gathered to support a nonroutine decision (e.g., world events precipitate an unforeseen demand for a product). For example, if a particular product at the dealership, such as the Ford Escape, is not selling as well as forecasts predicted, then the manager can request a report showing which salespeople are selling the product effectively and which are not. The manager could use this information to examine reasons that this is occurring and investigate ways to intervene before the problem gets out of hand.

The characteristics of an MIS are summarized in Table 6.3. In general, inputs to an MIS are transaction processing data produced by a TPS, other internal data, such as sales promotion expenses, and ad hoc requests for special reports or summaries. The processing aspect of an MIS system focuses on data aggregation and summary. Outputs are formatted reports that provide scheduled and nonrecurring information to a midlevel manager. For example, a store manager can use an MIS to review sales information to identify products that are not selling and are in need of special promotion.

Executive Information Systems

In addition to operational personnel and midlevel managers, top-level managers or executives can use information technology to support day-to-day activities such as cash and investment management, resource allocation, and contract negotiation. Information systems designed to support the highest organizational managers are called ***executive information systems (EISs)***. An EIS (sometimes referred to as an *executive support system*—ESS) consists of technology (hardware, software, data, and procedures) and the people needed to consolidate information and support users to assist executive-level decision making (Figure 6.13). An EIS provides information to executives in a very highly aggregated form so that they can scan information quickly for trends and anomalies. For example, executives may track various market conditions—such as the Dow Jones Industrial Average—to assist in making investment decisions. Although EISs are not as widely used as other types of information systems, this trend

Table 6.3 ***Characteristics of a management information system.***

Inputs	Transaction processing data and other internal data; scheduled and ad hoc requests for information
Processing	Aggregation and summary of data
Outputs	Scheduled and exception reports; feedback to system operator
Typical Users	Midlevel managers

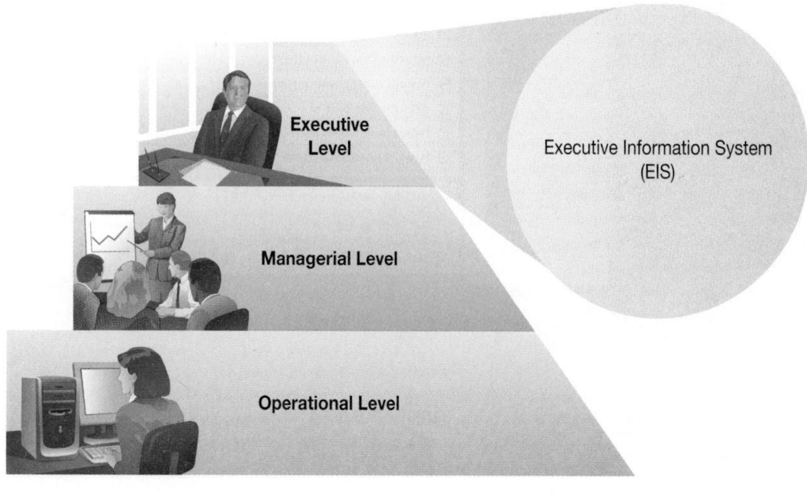

Figure 6.13 Executive information systems are used to improve executive-level decision making.

Web Search

Go to Globeinvestor, **www.globeinvestor.com**, to track a basket of stocks and mutual funds for the past 30 days.

is rapidly changing, because more and more executives are becoming comfortable with information technology and because an EIS can provide substantial benefits to the executive. Activities supported by an EIS include

- Executive-level decision making
- Long-range and strategic planning
- Monitoring of internal and external events and resources
- Crisis management
- Staffing and labor relations

An EIS can deliver both "soft" and "hard" data to the executive decision maker. ***Soft data*** include textual news stories or other nonanalytical information. ***Hard data*** include facts and numbers. Lower-level TPSs and MISs generate much of the hard data provided by an EIS. Providing timely soft information to executive decision makers has been much more of a challenge. For example, deciding how to get the late-breaking news stories and information to the system in a format consistent with the EIS philosophy was a significant challenge to organizations. Many investment organizations, for example, subscribe to online services such as Dow Jones as a source for their stock market data. However, executives typically want to view only data that are aggregated and summarized in a user-friendly format. To get the right information into the hands of the executives, personnel or specially designed systems select appropriate information and translate the information into a user-friendly format.

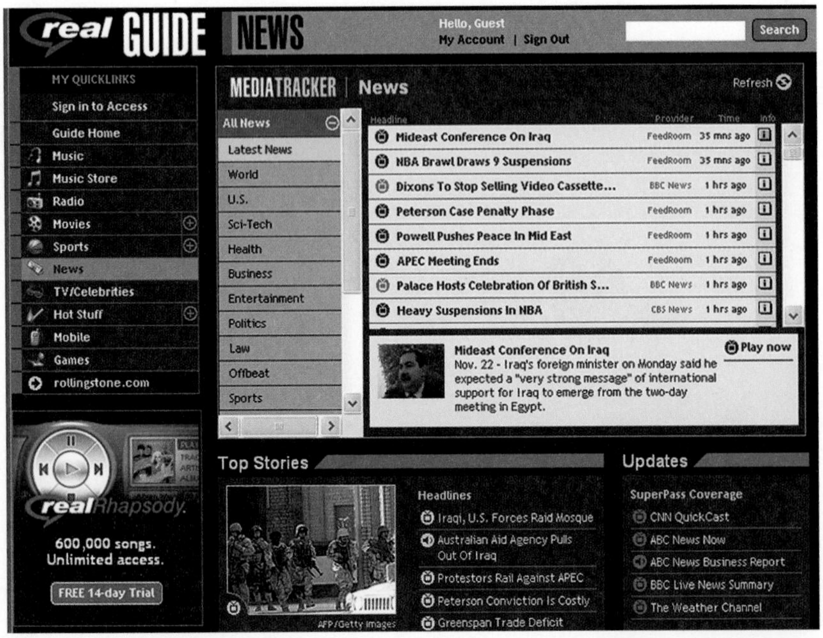

The Internet has made it much easier to gather soft data to support executive decision making. The use of numerous web-based news portals such as Canada.com, CNN.com, and canoe.ca allows users to easily customize news content so that assistants can quickly summarize and evaluate information for viewing by executives. In addition, online streaming media—video and audio—is radically changing how many executives gain soft information. Various subscription-based services from RealNetworks, Yahoo!, CNN, and others provide customized content on almost any subject or industry, virtually as it hits the news wires. Figure 6.14 shows an example of the range of content available from RealNetworks. Two very powerful features of these services make it particularly attractive for gathering soft data. First, these services can be customized to filter information so that they deliver only the information deemed relevant to the executive. For example, if an executive is interested in the software, Internet/online, and telecommunications industries, then these industries can be specifically tracked. Second, these services will deliver this information to virtually any device, literally tracking you until you receive the message. For example, they can be customized so that important information is sent to a computer (using e-mail, instant messaging, or a web link), a cell phone, or even a pager. The goal is to get the right information to a customer, using the most convenient medium.

Figure 6.14 RealNetworks provides a broad range of content that can be integrated into applications or sent to a variety of devices.

Architecture of an Executive Information System

The architecture of an EIS is shown in Figure 6.15. Inputs to an EIS are all internal data sources and systems as well as external data sources such as Dow Jones and CNN that contain information on competitors, financial markets, news (local, national, and international), and any other information the executive deems important in making day-to-day decisions. An EIS could "overload" the executive with too much information from too many sources. System designers use filtering software to customize the EIS so that only key information is provided, in its most effective form, to executives. Also, system designers provide output information to executives in a highly aggregated form, often using graphical icons to make selections and bar and line charts to summarize data, trends, and simula-

Table 6.4 ***Characteristics of an executive information system.***

Inputs	Aggregate internal and external data
Processing	Summarizing, graphical interpreting
Outputs	Summary reports, trends, and simulations; feedback to system operator
Typical Users	Executive-level managers

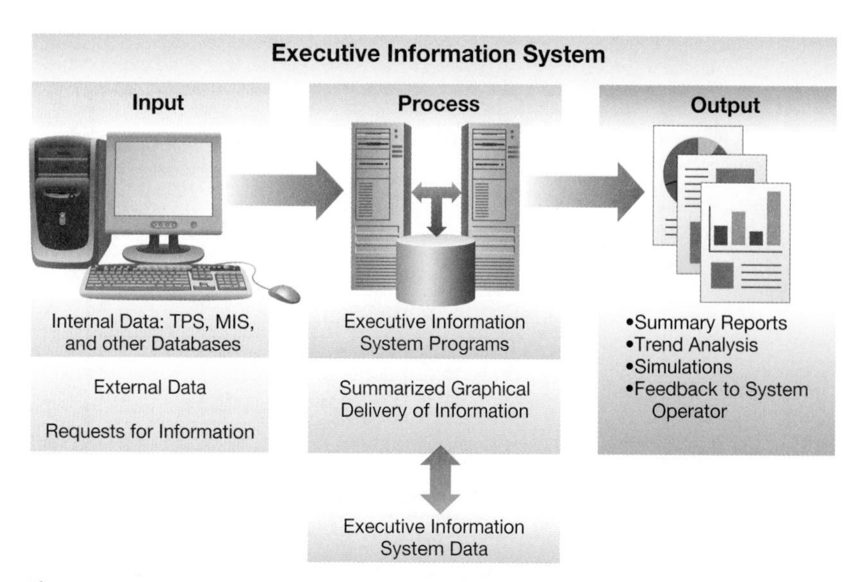

Figure 6.15 Architecture of an executive information system using the basic systems model.

tions. Large monitors are often used to display the information so that it is easier to view. The characteristics of an EIS are summarized in Table 6.4.

Although data are provided in a very highly aggregated form, the executive also has the capability to drill down and see the details if necessary. For example, suppose an EIS summarizes employee absenteeism, and the system shows that today's numbers are significantly higher than normal. The executive can see this information in a running line chart, as illustrated in Figure 6.16. If the executive wants to understand why absenteeism is so high, then a selection on the screen can provide the details behind the aggregate numbers, as shown in Figure 6.17. By drilling down into the data, the executive can see that the spike in absenteeism was centred in the manufacturing area. An EIS also can connect the data in the system to the organization's internal communication systems (e.g., e-mail or voice mail) so that the executive can quickly send a message to the appropriate managers to discuss solutions to the problem she discovered in the drill down.

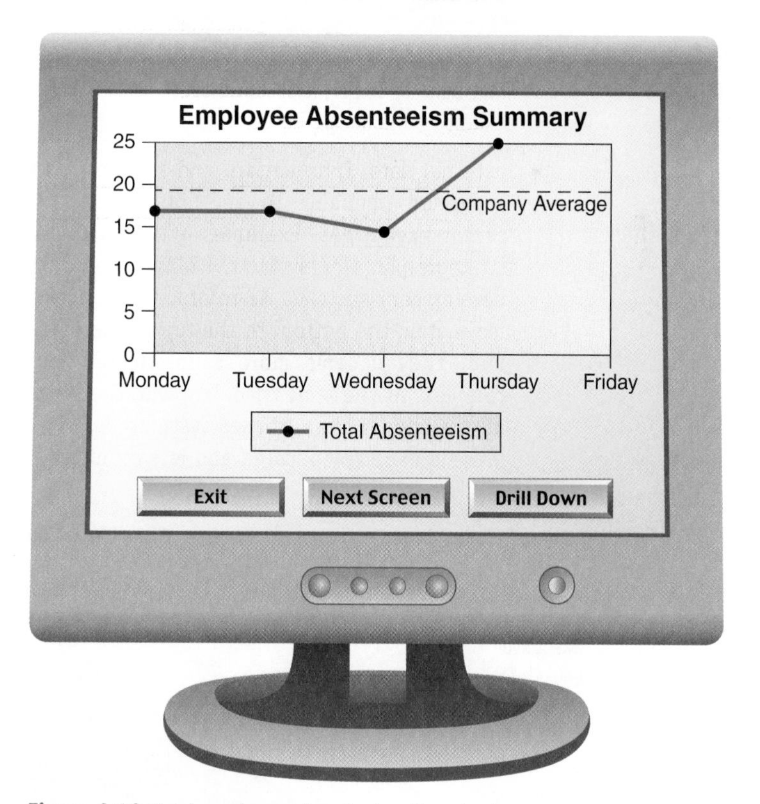

Figure 6.16 Total employee absenteeism line chart.

The Relationship Among Types of Information Systems

Figure 6.18 shows the relationship among operational, managerial, and executive levels of decision making in the form of a pyramid. The operational level is shown at the base of the pyramid. Information systems at this level include TPSs such as accounting and cash management systems. Transaction processing systems typically account for the largest and most costly component of an organization's IT infrastructure. The managerial level is shown in the middle of the pyramid. Information systems operating at this level analyze, aggregate, and summarize data from the operational level and thus transform raw data into information useful for decision making. Management information systems include budgeting systems and production scheduling systems. The top of the pyramid is occupied by the executive level. Information systems at this level aggregate and present internal and

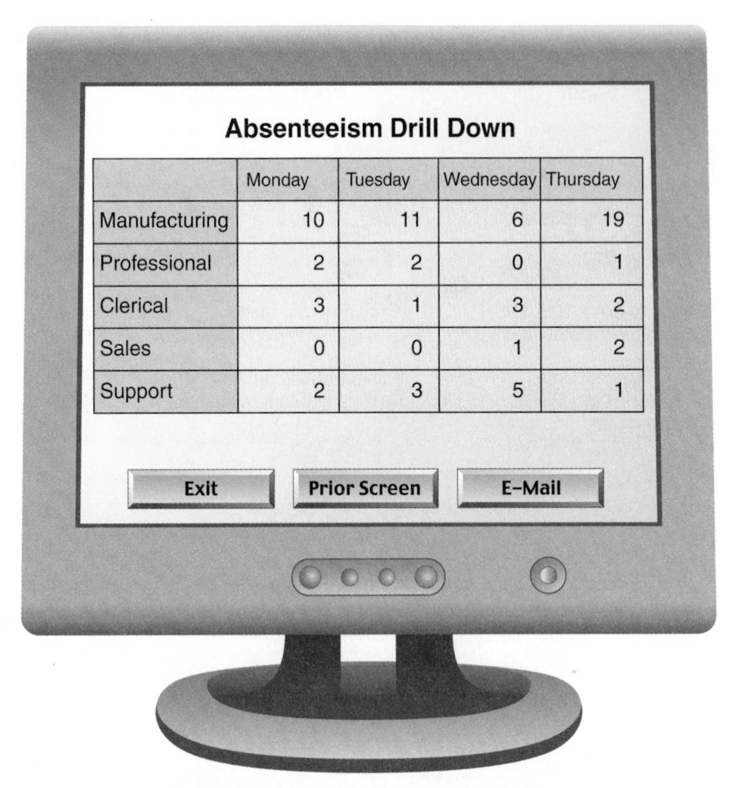

Figure 6.17 Drill-down numbers for employee absenteeism.

external data, information, and knowledge in a format amenable to decision making by senior executives. Examples of EISs include strategic planning systems, R&D, and product development systems. As information systems move from the bottom to the top of the pyramid, they become more sophisticated and complex. At the same time, however, the types of decisions that these systems support become more complicated and less structured. Thus, despite their sophistication, information systems at the executive level are comparatively less effective at supporting executive decisions than TPSs are at supporting operational decisions.

INFORMATION SYSTEMS THAT SPAN ORGANIZATIONAL BOUNDARIES

The preceding section examined three general classes of information systems within specific hierarchical levels in the organization. There are also systems that span all levels of the organization (Figure 6.19). Six types of boundary-spanning systems are

- Decision support systems
- Expert systems
- Office automation systems
- Collaboration technologies
- Functional area information systems
- Global information systems

This section describes each of these in more detail. One additional form of organizational-spanning system, enterprise-wide information systems, is discussed in Chapter 7.

Decision Support Systems

Decision support systems (DSSs) are special-purpose information systems designed to support organizational decision making. A DSS is designed to support the decision making related to a particular recurring problem in the organization through the combination of hardware, software, data, and procedures. DSSs are

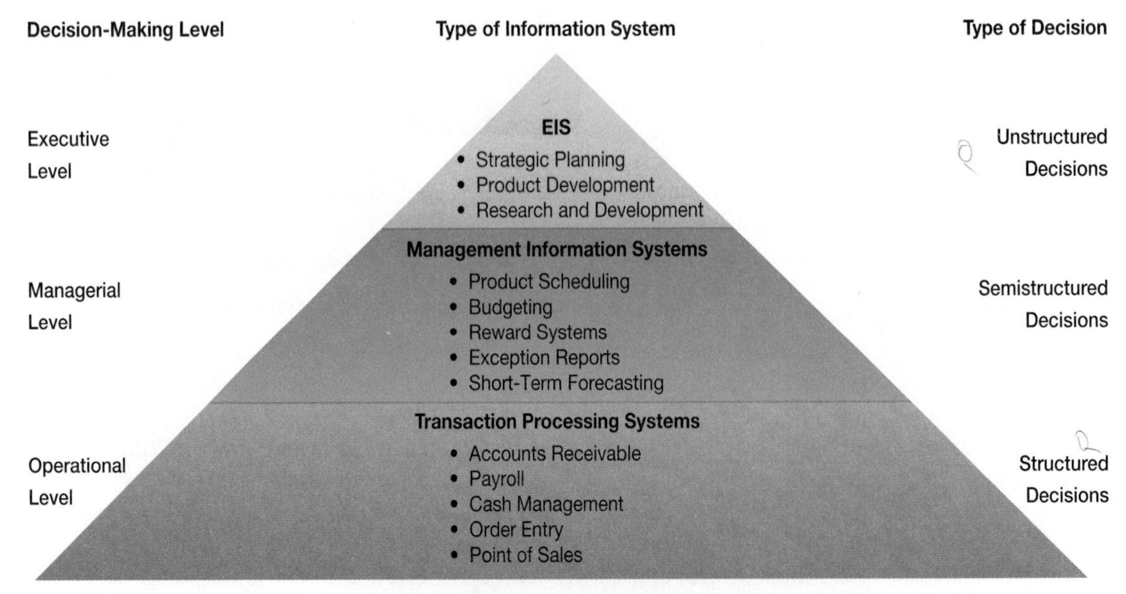

Figure 6.18 Examples of information systems at each organizational level.

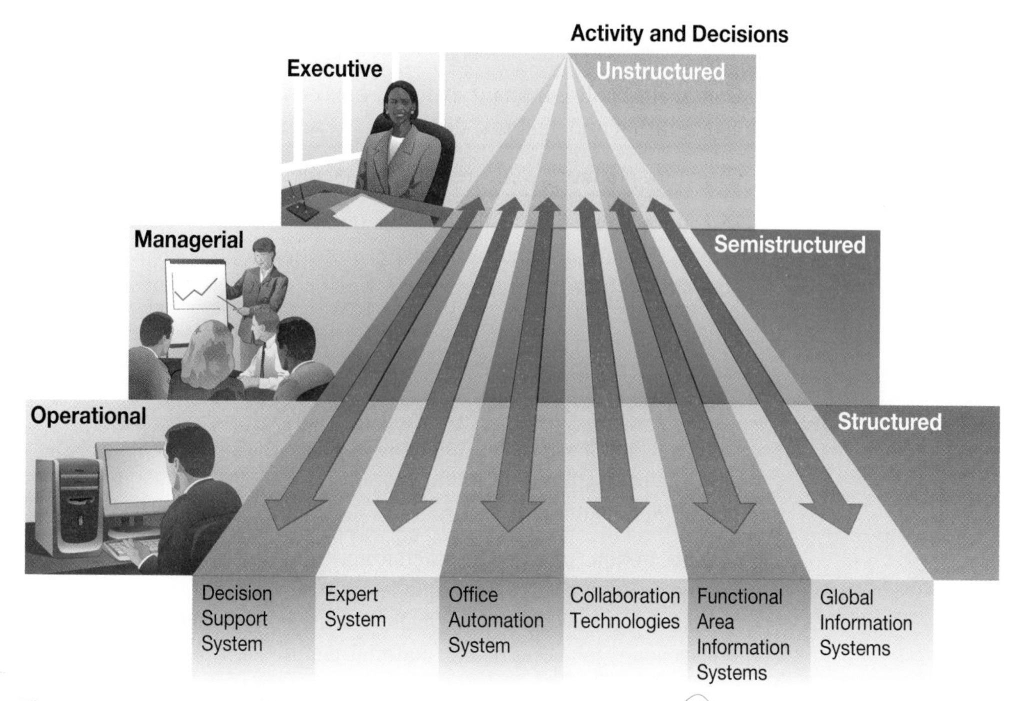

Figure 6.19 Organizational boundary-spanning information systems.

typically used by managerial-level employees to help them solve semistructured problems such as sales and resource forecasting, yet a DSS can be used to support decisions at virtually all levels of the organization. With a DSS, the manager uses decision analysis tools such as Microsoft Excel—the most commonly used DSS environment—to either analyze or create meaningful data to support the decision making related to nonroutine problems. A DSS is designed to be an "interactive" decision aid, whereas people use the systems described previously—TPS, MIS, and EIS—primarily in a passive way by simply reviewing the output from the system.

A DSS augments human decision-making performance and problem solving by enabling users to examine alternative solutions to a problem through "what-if" analyses. ***What-if analysis*** allows you to make hypothetical changes to the data associated with a problem (e.g., loan duration and interest rate) and observe how these changes influence the results. For example, a cash manager for a bank could examine what-if scenarios of the effect of various interest rates on cash availability. Results are displayed in both textual and graphical formats.

Architecture of a Decision Support System

Like the architecture of all systems, a DSS consists of input, process, and output components as illustrated in Figure 6.20 (Sprage, 1980). Within the process component, models and data are utilized. The DSS uses ***models*** to manipulate data. For example, if you have some historic sales data, then you can use many different types of models to create a forecast of future sales. One technique is to take an average of the past sales. The formula you would use to calculate the average is the model. A more complicated forecasting model might use time-series analysis or linear regression. Adidas–Salomon Canada used a new warehouse management system to support more accurate forecasting and decision making after

Web Search

Many life insurance companies need to examine their level of risk when providing you with insurance. Go to **http://moneycentral.msn.com/investor/calcs/n_expect/main.asp** and examine your life expectancy using an online decision support system.

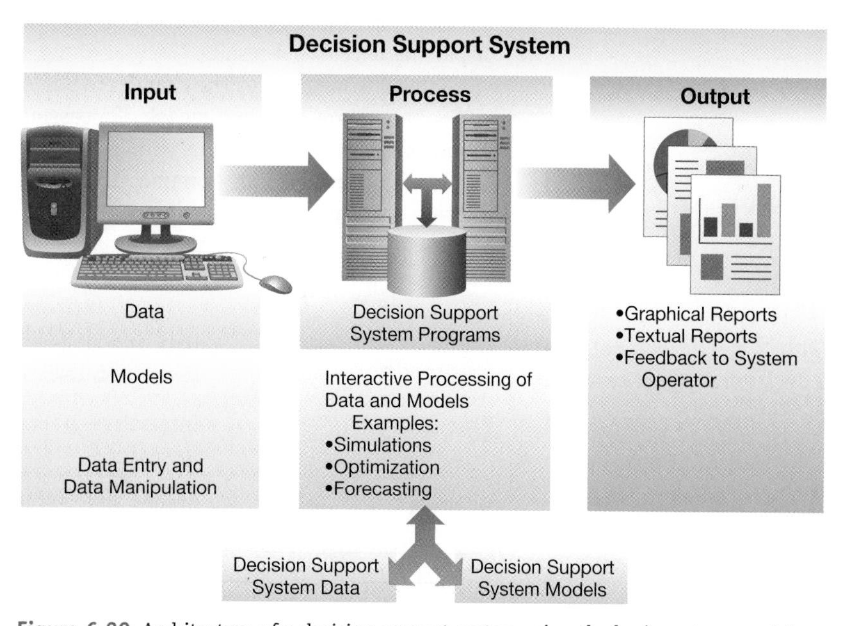

Figure 6.20 Architecture of a decision support system using the basic systems model.

Table 6.5 ***Common DSS models for specific organizational areas.***

Area	Common DSS Models
Accounting	Cost analysis, discriminant analysis, break-even analysis, auditing, tax computation and analysis, depreciation methods, budgeting
Corporate Level	Corporate planning, venture analysis, mergers and acquisitions
Finance	Discounted cash flow analysis, return on investment, buy or lease, capital budgeting, bond refinancing, stock portfolio management, compound interest, after-tax yield, foreign exchange values
Marketing	Product demand forecast, advertising strategy analysis, pricing strategies, market share analysis, sales growth evaluation, sales performance
Personnel	Labour negotiations, labour market analysis, personnel skills assessment, employee business expense, fringe benefit computations, payroll and deductions
Production	Product design, production scheduling, transportation analysis, product-mix inventory level, quality control, learning curve, plant location, material allocation, maintenance analysis, machine replacement, job assignment, material requirement planning
Management Science	Linear programming, decision trees, simulation, project evaluation and planning, queuing, dynamic programming, network analysis
Statistics	Regression and correlation analysis, exponential smoothing, sampling, time-series analysis, hypothesis testing

doubling the size of its Canadian operations through a series of acquisitions (see the Brief Case: Forecasting to Meet Changing Demand: Using a Decision Support System at Adidas-Salomon Canada). See Table 6.5 for a summary of the models used to support decision making in organizations. Data for the DSS can come from many sources, including a TPS or an MIS. The user interface is the way in which the DSS interacts with the user by collecting inputs and displaying output and results.

Table 6.6 summarizes the characteristics of a DSS. Inputs are data and models. Processing supports the merging of data with models so that decision makers can examine alternative solution scenarios. Outputs are graphs and textual reports. The next section discusses an example of a DSS that you might use at home.

Using a Decision Support System to Buy a Car

When you buy a new car, you must decide how to pay for it. Will you pay cash? Will you finance most or part of the purchase price? Organizations face the same decisions every day when purchasing supplies, raw materials, and capital equipment: Should they pay cash or finance these purchases? What information do they need to make this decision? The tools that organizations use are relatively simple and readily available to you. After going through the car purchasing example, you will have a better understanding of how organizations use decision support technology to help their employees make day-to-day decisions.

Table 6.6 ***Characteristics of a decision support system.***

Inputs	Data and models; data entry and data manipulation commands (via user interface)
Processing	Interactive processing of data and models; simulations, optimization, forecasts
Outputs	Graphs and textual reports; feedback to system operator (via user interface)
Typical Users	Midlevel managers (although a DSS could be used at any level of the organization)

Table 6.7 ***Interest rates and loan duration.***

Interest Rate	Loan Duration
4% per year	3 years
6% per year	4 years
8% per year	5 years

Assume that the selling price of the car you decide to purchase is $20 000 and that you make a $2500 down payment, leaving you with a monthly payment of about $400. You want to see how different financing options from your credit union might influence your monthly payments. As you can see from Table 6.7, interest rates vary depending upon the duration of your loan—lower rates for a shorter duration and higher rates for a longer duration. You now have all the information you need to analyze your financing options.

To conduct this analysis, you can use Microsoft Excel's loan analysis template (Excel uses the term "template" to refer to models). In this template, you enter the loan amount, annual interest rate, and length of the loan, as shown in Figure 6.21. With this information, the loan analysis DSS automatically calculates your monthly payment, the total amount paid, and the amount of interest paid over the life of the loan. You can change any of the input amounts to examine what-if scenarios—"What if I finance the loan over 4 years rather than 5?" This is exactly how your college or university examines its financing options when it makes capital equipment purchases. Using this DSS tool, you decide to purchase your new vehicle over 5 years (see Table 6.8 for a loan analysis summary). The next section discusses expert systems, a type of organizational information system that is closely related to DSSs.

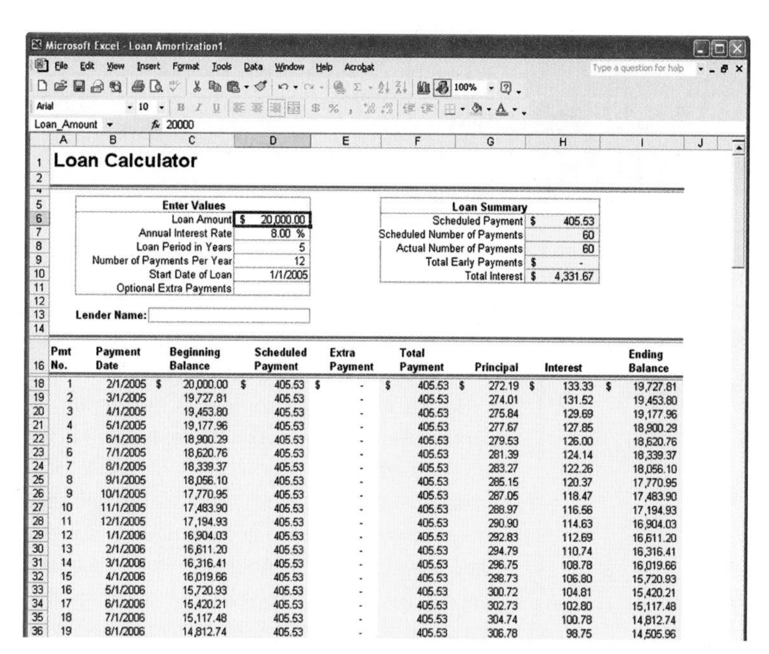

Pmt No.	Payment Date	Beginning Balance	Scheduled Payment	Extra Payment	Total Payment	Principal	Interest	Ending Balance
1	2/1/2005	$ 20,000.00	$ 405.53	$ -	$ 405.53	$ 272.19	$ 133.33	$ 19,727.81
2	3/1/2005	19,727.81	405.53	-	405.53	274.01	131.52	19,453.80
3	4/1/2005	19,453.80	405.53	-	405.53	275.84	129.69	19,177.96
4	5/1/2005	19,177.96	405.53	-	405.53	277.67	127.85	18,900.29
5	6/1/2005	18,900.29	405.53	-	405.53	279.53	126.00	18,620.76
6	7/1/2005	18,620.76	405.53	-	405.53	281.39	124.14	18,339.37
7	8/1/2005	18,339.37	405.53	-	405.53	283.27	122.26	18,056.10
8	9/1/2005	18,056.10	405.53	-	405.53	285.15	120.37	17,770.95
9	10/1/2005	17,770.95	405.53	-	405.53	287.05	118.47	17,483.90
10	11/1/2005	17,483.90	405.53	-	405.53	288.97	116.56	17,194.93
11	12/1/2005	17,194.93	405.53	-	405.53	290.90	114.63	16,904.03
12	1/1/2006	16,904.03	405.53	-	405.53	292.83	112.69	16,611.20
13	2/1/2006	16,611.20	405.53	-	405.53	294.79	110.74	16,316.41
14	3/1/2006	16,316.41	405.53	-	405.53	296.75	108.78	16,019.66
15	4/1/2006	16,019.66	405.53	-	405.53	298.73	106.80	15,720.93
16	5/1/2006	15,720.93	405.53	-	405.53	300.72	104.81	15,420.21
17	6/1/2006	15,420.21	405.53	-	405.53	302.73	102.80	15,117.48
18	7/1/2006	15,117.48	405.53	-	405.53	304.74	100.78	14,812.74
19	8/1/2006	14,812.74	405.53	-	405.53	306.78	98.75	14,505.96

Figure 6.21 Loan analysis template in Microsoft Excel.

Expert Systems

An ***expert system (ES)*** is a special type of information system that uses reasoning methods based on knowledge about a specific problem domain to provide advice, much like a human expert. Expert systems are used to mimic human expertise by manipulating knowledge (understanding acquired through experience and extensive learning) rather than simply manipulating information (see Turban, Aronson, and Liang, 2005, for more information). Human knowledge can be represented in an ES by facts and rules about a problem coded in a form that can be manipulated by a computer. When you use an ES, the system asks you a series of questions, much as a human expert would. It continues to ask questions, and each new question is determined by your response to the preceding question. The ES matches the responses with the defined facts and rules until the responses point the system to a solution. A ***rule*** is a way of encoding knowledge, such as a recommendation, after collecting information from a user. Rules are typically expressed using an "IF–THEN" format. For example, a rule in an ES for assisting with decisions related to the approval of automobile loans for individuals could be represented as follows:

IF personal income is $50 000 or more, THEN approve the loan.

Table 6.8 ***Loan analysis summary.***

Interest Rate	Loan Duration	Monthly Payment	Total Paid	Total Interest	Feasible Payment
4% per year	3 years	$590.48	21 257.27	$1 257.27	No
6% per year	4 years	$488.26	$23 436.41	$3 436.41	No
8% per year	5 years	$405.53	$24 331.67	$4 331.67	Yes

BRIEF CASE

Forecasting to Meet Changing Demand: Using a Decision Support System at Adidas–Salomon Canada

Adidas–Salomon is a global leader in the sporting goods industry. Some well-known brands under the Adidas–Salomon name include Adidas, Salomon, Taylor Made, and MAXFLI. Adidas–Salomon Canada Ltd. is based in Concord, Ontario, and operates a distribution centre in Brantford, Ontario.

Before the parent company's acquisition of Salomon/Bonfire and Taylor Made, leaders in the winter sports and golf industries respectively, Adidas–Salomon Canada relied on an inefficient paper-based warehouse and distribution system. After the acquisitions, Adidas–Salomon Canada was not only faced with updating this system and moving to a new automated facility but also suddenly faced with moving far more inventory—2.5 times more in the Adidas line alone—at a time when customer demand for turnaround, accuracy, and accountability was reaching new heights.

Adidas–Salomon Canada needed a forecasting and DSS that could handle this increased demand. The company chose a warehouse management and RF system that could work to integrate two different order management systems, one handling Adidas products from the Canadian headquarters in Concord and the other handling Salomon and Taylor Made orders from Portland, Oregon.

The company implemented a warehouse management system that supported 50 wireless handheld and vehicle-mounted scanning devices. With the new system in place, Adidas–Salomon knew precisely what was in its distribution centre and supply chain from the time a shipment was received at the loading dock until the time it left the warehouse. The new system also allowed Adidas–Salomon to better audit and record goods received from global factories and report discrepancies as they arrived. Finally, the new wireless technology allowed inventory to be counted while all other distribution centre activities were going on. The previous system required a complete 2-week shutdown to perform two semiannual inventory counts. Because of the new system, Adidas–Salomon Canada was able to cut its distribution costs in half and radically improve order accuracy. Since decision makers had access to more timely and accurate information, they could make better decisions.

Questions

1. Think of three decisions that are made easier because of the DSS in place at Adidas–Salomon Canada.
2. It has been said that information systems become less effective as decisions become more complex. Do you agree or disagree with this statement? Why or why not?

Source: Adapted from Adidas–Salomon Canada, "Increasing Efficiency Through Wireless Technology," Canadian Information Productivity Awards, 2005.

Web Search

Explore an online health expert system for common aliments at **http://easydiagnosis.com.**

The most difficult part of building an ES is acquiring the knowledge from the expert and gathering and compiling it into a consistent and complete form capable of making recommendations. Expert systems are used when expertise for a particular problem is rare or expensive, such as in the case of a complex machine repair or medical diagnosis. ESs are also used when knowledge about a problem will be incomplete—in other words, when judgment will be used to make a decision with incomplete information, such as designing an investment portfolio or troubleshooting a computer system. Examples of the types of activities that can be supported by expert systems include the following:

- Medical diagnosis
- Machine configuration
- Automobile diagnosis
- Financial planning
- Train and container loading
- Computer user help desk
- Software application assistance (e.g., Microsoft Help "Wizards")

Architecture of an Expert System

As with other information systems, the architecture of an expert system can be described using the basic systems model (Figure 6.22). Inputs to the system are questions and answers from the user. Processing is the matching of user questions and answers to information in the knowledge base. The processing in an ES is called ***inferencing***, which consists of matching facts and rules, determining the sequence of questions presented to the user, and drawing a conclusion. The output from an ES is a recommendation. For example, an ES is used by the

University of Victoria to determine which applicants to its School of Public Administration are likely to be accepted or rejected. Those in the middle go to human beings for further review. This ES is built by Victoria-based Acquired Intelligence Inc. (see profile in SME Success: Acquired Intelligence Inc.). The general characteristics of an ES are summarized in Table 6.9.

An Expert System on the Web

Historically, expert systems have been stand-alone applications that ran on PCs. With the advent of the Internet, EXSYS, a leading producer of ES technology, has provided an ES development environment that allows ESs to be delivered through the web. At the EXSYS website (**www.exsys.com**), you can test several demonstration

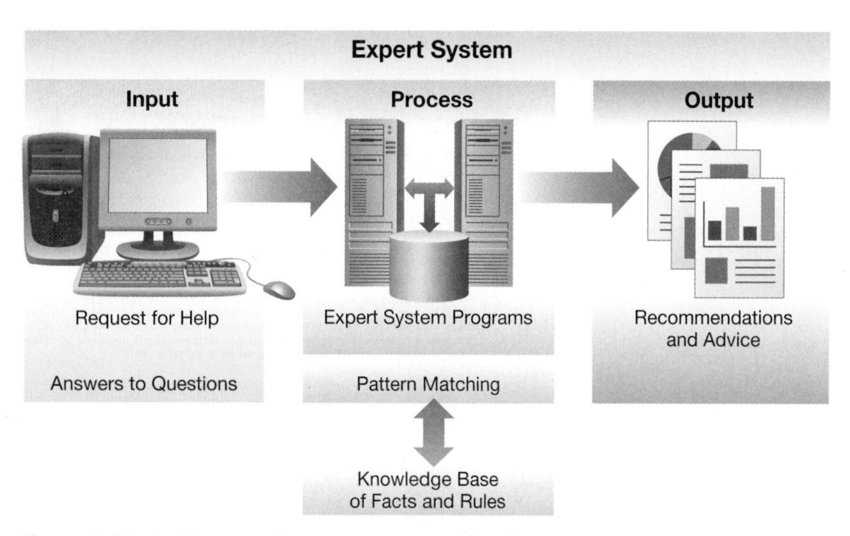

Figure 6.22 Architecture of an expert system using the basic systems model.

Inputs	Request for help, answers to questions
Processing	Pattern matching
Outputs	Recommendation or advice
Typical Users	Midlevel managers (although an expert system could be used at any level of the organization)

Table 6.9 ***Characteristics of an expert system.***

SME SUCCESS Acquired Intelligence Inc.

Every year, graduate schools receive many applications; in the case of business schools, these applications can number in the thousands. A subset of these applications can be ruled out quickly if they fail to meet certain basic requirements. However, in most schools, all the applications must be dealt with by hand. The process of screening these applications is time consuming and resource intensive. In addition, annual turnover of committee members leads to a problem in establishing a consistent selection procedure. Acquired Intelligence Inc. (**www.aiinc.ca**), based in Victoria, British Columbia, developed an ES for the University of Victoria's School of Public Administration to reduce the workload associated with graduate applications. The system was designed to screen applicants based on answers to a set of predefined questions. These questions were divided into three sections: university record, standard tests and rewards, and references. The system calculated a score based on the answers to these questions. This score was then used to compute a rating for the student. This rating was used to place the student into one of the three categories: "accept," "discuss," or "reject." As the number of applications was invariably greater than the number of available places, committee members met to consider only applications in the "accept" or "discuss" categories. This process saved committee members a substantial amount of time. A demo of this system is available at **www.aiinc.ca/demos/grad.shtml**.

Acquired Intelligence Inc. now sells its ES solutions to clients across Canada as well as Britain and the United States.

Questions

1. In which ways does this system address typical problems encountered by students, advisors, and faculty? Be specific.
2. Are there limits to the use of ESs? What types of decisions or situations are not appropriate for the use of ESs?

Figure 6.23 EXSYS web-based expert system.

ESs. One system, for example, provides advice on selecting the right camcorder; another system that helps to troubleshoot and repair the Cessna Citation airplane—lighting and engine starting—is a particularly sophisticated example (Figure 6.23). The system analyzes a user's response to several questions and presents specific repair or troubleshooting advice. This system also explains why it came to the conclusion that it did or why it is asking certain questions. This is a very powerful feature for training personnel and for helping users have confidence in the system's recommendation. Another site on the web, called Expert System Builder (**www.esbuilder.com**), allows users to download software that can be used to develop customized ESs.

Office Automation Systems

The ***office automation system (OAS)*** is the third type of system that spans organizational levels. Office automation systems are a collection of software and hardware for developing documents, scheduling resources, and communicating. Document development tools include word processing and desktop publishing software as well as the hardware for printing and producing documents. Scheduling tools include electronic calendars that help manage human and other resources, such as equipment and rooms. For example, "smart" electronic calendars can examine multiple schedules to find the first opportunity when all resources (people, rooms, and equipment) are available. Communication technologies include e-mail, voice mail, fax, videoconferencing, and groupware. Examples of the types of activities supported by an OAS include the following:

- Communication and scheduling
- Document preparation
- Analysis and merging of data
- The consolidation of information

Architecture of an Office Automation System

The architecture of an OAS is shown in Figure 6.24. The inputs to an OAS are documents, schedules, and data. The processing of this information involves storing, merging, calculating, and transporting these data. Outputs include messages, reports, and schedules. The general characteristics of an OAS are summarized in Table 6.10.

Automating Your Daily Calendar

A powerful tool for helping you get to class on time is Microsoft Outlook's Calendar. At the beginning of the semester, you can enter your class meeting times into the system. After they are entered, you can make these appointments recur automatically as long as you like, as illustrated in Figure 6.25.

Additionally, you can set an alarm to notify you that class will begin in a few minutes. You can also use the alarm feature to remind you of meetings or appointments. Busy executives use this reminder feature to make sure they stay on schedule and do not miss any important meetings.

Collaboration Technologies

To be competitive, organizations constantly need to bring together the right combinations of people who have the appropriate set of knowledge, skills, information, and authority to solve problems quickly and easily. Traditionally, organizations have used task forces, which are temporary work groups with a finite task and life cycle, to solve problems that cannot be solved well by existing work groups. Unfortunately, traditional task forces, like traditional organizational structures, cannot always solve problems quickly. Structure and logistical problems often get in the way of people trying to get things done quickly.

Organizations need flexible teams that can be assembled quickly and can solve problems effectively and efficiently. Time is of the essence. Membership on these ***virtual teams*** is fluid, with teams forming and disbanding as needed, with team size fluctuating as necessary, and with team members coming and going as they are needed.

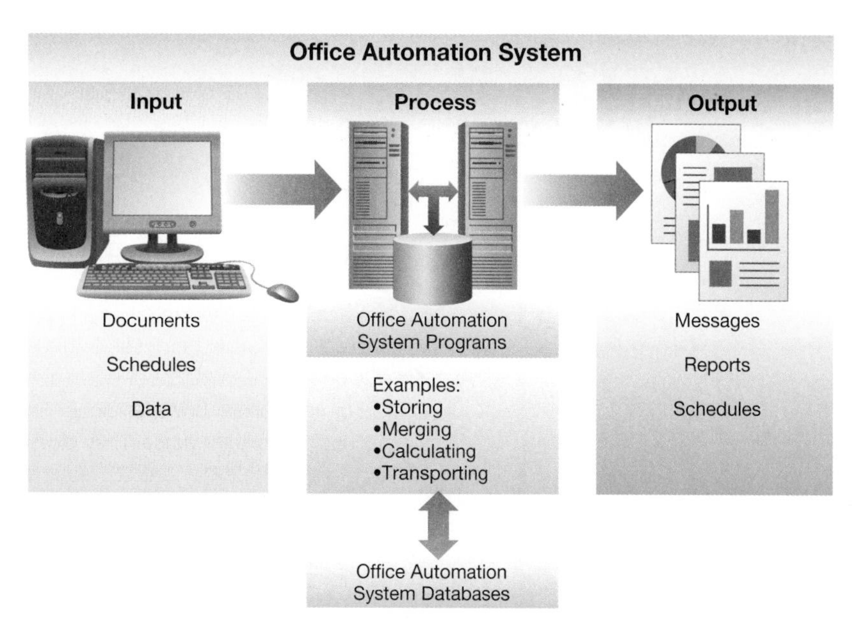

Figure 6.24 Architecture of an office automation system using the basic systems model.

Table 6.10 ***Characteristics of an office automation system.***

Inputs	Documents, schedules, data
Processing	Storing, merging, calculating, transporting
Outputs	Messages, reports, schedules
Typical Users	All organizational personnel

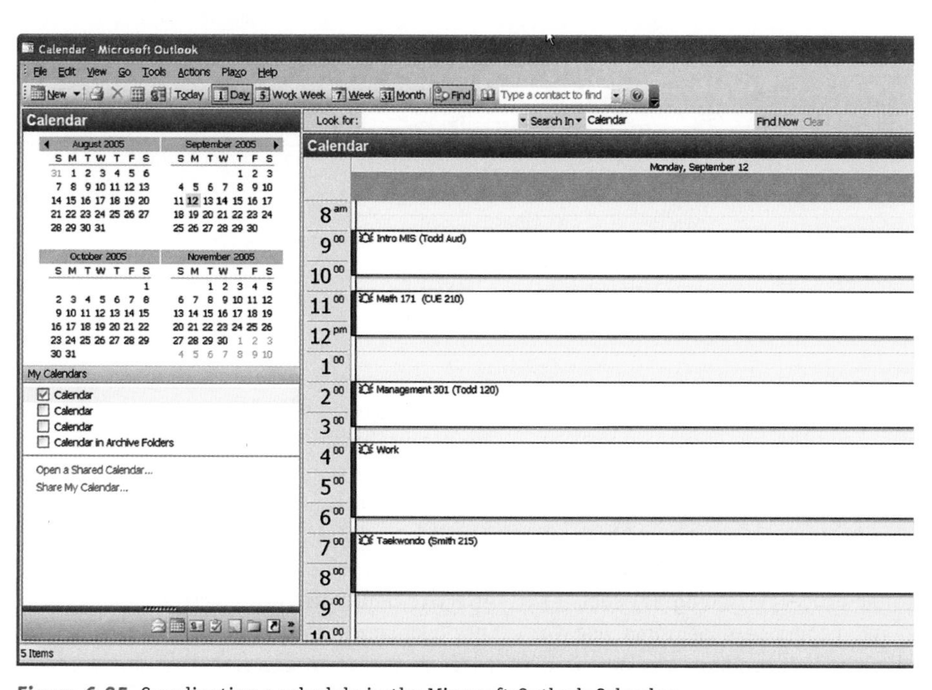

Figure 6.25 Coordinating a schedule in the Microsoft Outlook Calendar.

CANADIAN NETSTATS

The Cost of Spam

In 2004, nearly three-quarters of all e-mails in Canada were spam. If you are like most people, then you are probably getting increasingly tired of having to delete spam e-mails from your inbox. For example, Canadian Internet users received an average of 87 unsolicited e-mails per week in 2004. That number is up from 64 in 2002 but down from 134 in 2003. For companies, however, spam has become more than a mere annoyance. They lost an estimated $41 billion in 2004 due to reduced worker productivity and increased technology costs. Recent changes in legislation in Canada, the United States, and Europe are designed to reduce the amount of spam. Unfortunately, this seems not to have helped, especially in the United States, where most spam originates. Part of the problem is that much of the spam being sent today is routed through infected computers, unbeknownst to the user. Given the high proportion of Internet users—both at work and at home—with "always on" high-speed connections, as much as 30 percent of all spam messages are routed by infected machines.

Table 6.11 summarizes the categories of spam and the likely country of origin. An increasing challenge for organizations and society will be how to best combat this seemingly unstoppable plague on the Internet.

Source: **www.sophos.com/spaminfo/articles/dirtydozen.html**

Table 6.11 ***Categories of spam and countries most likely to send spam.***

Type of Spam	2004 Volume	Country of Origin	Percentage of Total
Products	22%	United States	56.74%
Financial	**20%**	**Canada**	**6.80%**
Adult	15%	China (& Hong Kong)	6.24%
Scams	8%	South Korea	5.77%
Other	7%	Netherlands	2.13%
Health	7%	Brazil	2.00%
Leisure	6%	Germany	1.83%
Internet	5%	France	1.50%
Fraud	4%	United Kingdom	1.31%
Political	2%	Australia	1.21%
Spiritual	2%	Mexico	1.19%
		Spain	1.05%
		Other	12.23%

Employees may, at times, find themselves on multiple teams, and the life of a team may be very short. In addition, team members must have easy, flexible access to other team members, meeting contexts, and information. Think of these virtual teams as dynamic task forces.

Traditional office technologies, such as telephones and pagers, are of some use to members of virtual teams but are not well suited to support the types of collaboration described previously. Telephones and pagers are not useful for rich, rapid, multiple-person team collaboration. This technology is best suited for person-to-person communication. E-mail is a useful technology for teams, but it does not provide the structure needed for effective multiperson interactive problem solving. Companies need technologies that enable team members to interact through a set of media either at the same place and time or at

Figure 6.26 Polycom's Executive Collection videoconferencing unit with dual 50-inch displays.

Source: Courtesy of Polycom, Inc. © 2004

different times and locations, with a structure to aid in interactive problem solving and access to software tools and information. A number of technologies, described in the following sections, fit the bill.

Videoconferencing

In the 1960s, at Disneyland and other theme parks and special events, the picturephone was first being demonstrated to large audiences. The picturephone company estimated that we would be able to see a live picture with our telephone calls in the near future. It took another 30 years, but that prediction has come true within many organizations. Many organizations are conducting ***videoconferencing***, and the demand for videoconferencing equipment is growing quickly. For example, sales for Polycom, a leading videoconferencing company, grew in total revenue from $39 million in 1996 to over $420 million in 2003. Dedicated videoconferencing systems can cost from a few thousand dollars to more than $60 000. For example, Polycom's top of the line "Executive Collection" videoconferencing unit comes with dual 50-inch plasma displays and has video quality similar to that of broadcast television (Figure 6.26).

Desktop Videoconferencing

Desktop videoconferencing represents a second generation of video communication that has been enabled by the growing power of processors powering PCs. A desktop system usually comprises a fast PC, a small camera (often with fixed focus, though zooming and panning features are available), a speaker telephone or separate microphone, videoconferencing software, and a special video board installed inside the computer. Using the Internet or a high-speed telephone line, desktop videoconferencing is a much less expensive option than stand-alone videoconferencing, but the quality of the video and audio is not as good. For example, for under $100, you can purchase one of the many cameras, such as a Logitech QuickCam, which plugs directly into the USB port on your PC (Figure 6.27). You can then use desktop videoconferencing software such as Microsoft's NetMeeting, Yahoo! Messenger, Windows

Figure 6.27 Logitech's popular QuickCam.

COMING ATTRACTIONS

Read My Lips—Using Face and Mouth Movements to Assist Speech Recognition

Speech recognition—using your voice to give commands to your computer or write essays without having to type them—offers a range of potential applications to increase productivity in homes and offices. With the advent of more and more powerful computers and the research work of many companies including Microsoft, Intel, and ScanSoft, it has actually become possible to obtain fairly accurate solutions; even standard software packages such as Windows XP and Office XP are already speech recognition enabled. However, if you have ever tried out this software, then you might have realized that both you and the computer need lots of training to obtain the desired accuracy. In addition to training, adjustment of microphones and background noise are important factors hindering accurate speech recognition, as the computer is in many cases not able to distinguish between the spoken words of the user and the noise of a truck passing by. For these reasons, it would at present not be feasible to have speech recognition–enabled ATMs or vending machines.

To deal with these shortcomings, computer giant Intel's Audio Visual Speech Recognition Team in Beijing, China, has recently developed a software that matches face and mouth movements with the user's speech. Falling prices for hardware such as microphones and cameras have helped to generate interest in such technologies. Although the software is still in the development phase, the researchers have already achieved increases in accuracy of up to 55 percent in noisy environments compared with conventional speech-recognition software. By making the source code of the software publicly available through open source, Intel hopes to increase the speed at which such technologies are developed and to enable this technology to be publicly available soon. With this technology, in the not-too-distant future, you might drive up to the ATM and ask the machine, "Could you please give me 200 bucks?"

Sources: Anonymous, "Teaching Computers to Read Lips," *Intel* (n.d.), **www.intel.com/labs/features/sw04034.htm**.
Michael Kanellos, "Intel's Sights on Lip-Reading Software," *News.com* (April 28, 2003), **http:// news.com.com/2100-1008-998576.html**.

Figure 6.28 The Sony Vaio TR Series notebook has an integrated camera built in for both still pictures and video images.

Messenger, and a variety of others to conduct desktop videoconferencing sessions with friends, family, and colleagues through the Internet. For the audio portion, you need a multimedia PC with a sound card and speakers. You speak into the microphone plugged into your sound card and hear other people through the speakers that are plugged into your sound card. Typically, the sound and video quality is not as good as that found on a stand-alone videoconferencing system.

Future of Desktop Videoconferencing

As computer components and fast connections to the Internet get less and less expensive, you can expect to see more desktop videoconferencing performed with your PC. In fact, some notebook computers are now manufactured and sold with video cameras built in (Figure 6.28). However, one of the most intriguing new technologies for desktop videoconferencing that we have seen is the omnidirectional camera. Developed at

Microsoft Research, the camera provides a 360° panoramic view as well as motion and sound sensing capabilities (Figure 6.29). This unit includes four tiny cameras and connects to a standard PC. Using a fast network connection, the unit can enable multiple people sitting around a table at one location to communicate with multiple people sitting around a table at another location. Each camera can sense sound and, if a person is talking, focus on that person. The camera can also detect motion and find and focus on that person's face, whether they are sitting at or standing around the table. This technology is in the research stage and is not currently being sold, although it works quite well. This type of videoconferencing unit opens up all kinds of possibilities and at a fraction of the cost of other videoconferencing units.

Figure 6.29 Microsoft Research has developed this omnidirectional, motion- and sound-detecting camera for desktop videoconferencing where multiple people are involved. Shown here are the camera unit, screen captures, and software interface.

"Viewing Meetings Captured by an Omni-Directional Camera," by Rui, Gupta, and Cadiz, Collaboration and Multimedia Systems Group, Microsoft Research, **http://www.research.microsoft.com/research/coet/Camera/chi2001/Omnidirectional/paper.doc**).

Groupware

The term ***groupware*** refers to a class of software that enables people to work together more effectively. As mentioned above, groupware and other collaboration technologies are often distinguished along two dimensions:

1. Whether the system supports groups working together at the same time—synchronous groupware—or at different times—asynchronous groupware.
2. Whether the system supports groups working together face-to-face or on a distributed basis.

Using these two dimensions, groupware systems can be categorized as being able to support four types of group interaction methods as shown in Figure 6.30. With the increased use of group-based problem solving and virtual teams, there are many potential benefits from utilizing groupware systems. These benefits are summarized in Table 6.12.

Asynchronous Groupware

A large number of asynchronous groupware tools are becoming commonplace in organizations, including e-mail, newsgroups and mailing lists, workflow automation systems, intranets, group calendars, and collaborative writing tools. One of the most popular groupware systems, and arguably the system that put groupware into the mainstream, appeared in 1989 when Lotus Development released its Notes software product (today, Lotus is owned by IBM). In recent years, many new

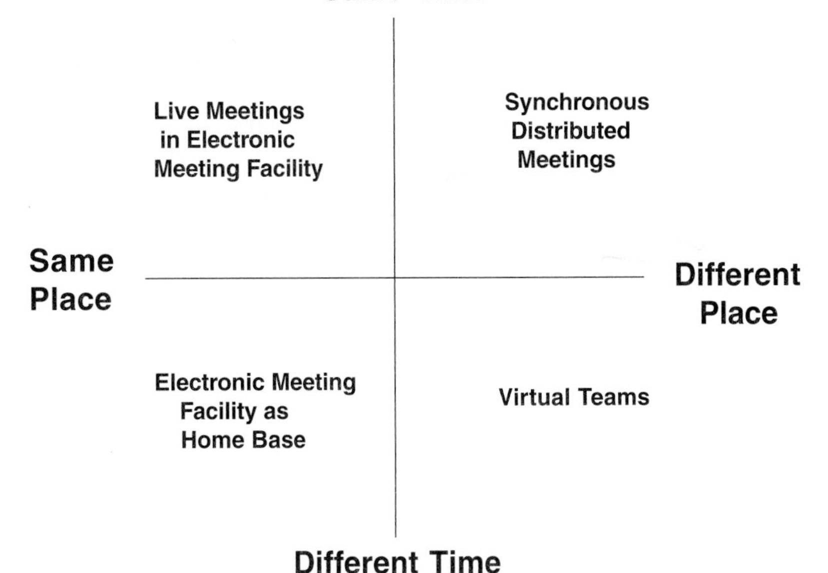

Figure 6.30 Groupware supports same and different time, as well as same and different place, group interaction.

Table 6.12 *Benefits of groupware.*

Benefits	Examples
Process structuring	Keeps the group on track and helps it avoid costly diversions (e.g., doesn't allow people to get off topic or the agenda)
Parallelism	Enables many people to speak and listen at the same time (e.g., everyone has an equal opportunity to participate)
Group size	Enables larger groups to participate (e.g., brings together broader perspectives, expertise, and participation)
Group memory	Automatically records member ideas, comments, votes (e.g., allows members to focus on content of discussions rather than on recording comments)
Access to external information	Can easily incorporate external electronic data and files (e.g., plans and proposal documents can be collected and easily distributed to all members)
Spanning time and space	Enables members to collaborate from different places at different times (e.g., reduces travel costs or allows people from remote locations to participate)
Anonymity	Member ideas, comments, and votes are not identified to others (if desired) (e.g., can make it easier to discuss controversial or sensitive topics without fear of identification or retribution)

groupware products have emerged, most of which work through or with the Internet. One of these products is Livelink, from Open Text Corporation, one of the Canada's leading IT firms (Figure 6.31).

Synchronous Groupware

Like asynchronous groupware, there are also many forms of synchronous groupware available to support a wide variety of activities including shared whiteboards, online chat, electronic meeting support systems, and, of course, video communication systems (discussed previously). Although many forms of groupware can be used to help groups work more effectively, one category of groupware focuses on helping groups have better meetings. These systems are commonly referred to as an ***electronic meeting system (EMS)***. An EMS is essentially a collection of PCs networked together with sophisticated software tools to help group members solve problems and make decisions through interactive, electronic idea generation, evaluation, and voting. Some typical uses for an EMS include strategic planning sessions, marketing focus groups, brainstorming sessions for system requirements definition, business process reengineering, and quality improvement. Electronic meeting systems have traditionally been housed within a dedicated meeting facility, as shown in Figure 6.32. However, EMSs are also being implemented with notebook computers so that the system can be taken on the road. Additionally, web-based implementations are supporting distributed meetings where group members access the EMS software from their computers in their offices or home. While EMS and related software have been around for quite some time, organizations are now beginning to discover how useful these tools can be to support e-meetings and other forms of teamwork (Figure 6.33).

Functional Area Information Systems

Functional area information systems are cross-organizational-level information systems designed to support a specific functional area (Figure 6.34). These systems may be any of the types described previously—TPS, MIS, EIS, DSS, ES, and OAS. A functional area represents a discrete area of an organization that focuses on a specific set of activities. For example, people in the marketing function focus on the activities that promote the organization and its products in a way that attracts and retains customers. People in

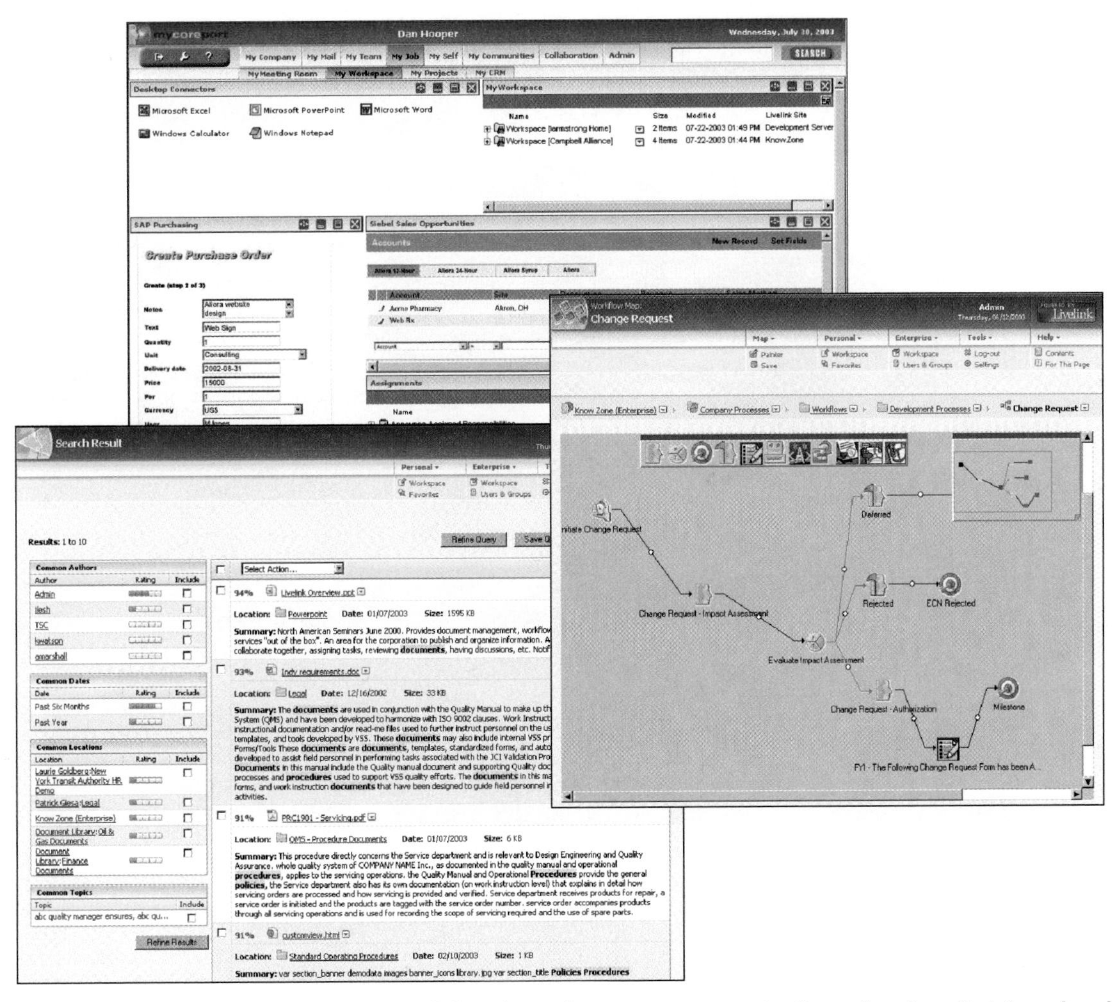

Figure 6.31 Livelink Enterprise Server® is collaboration and content management software from Open Text Corp., based in Waterloo, Ontario.

Source: Courtesy of Open Text

accounting and finance focus on managing and controlling capital assets and financial resources of the organization. Table 6.13 lists various organizational functions, describes the focus of each one, and lists examples of the types of information systems used in each functional area.

Global Information Systems

Organizations use a variety of system configurations to manage global operations more effectively. For example, Nestlé, one of the world's largest food producers, is considered to be one of the world's largest global companies, with over 500 factories and operations in more than 70 countries. Firms such as Nestlé, which are operating in multiple nations, can have five distinct types of global information systems: (1) international, (2) transnational, (3) multinational, (4) global, and (5) collaborative (Roche, 1992) (Table 6.14). We describe each in this section.

International information systems are a general class of information systems that support transactions that cross national boundaries. In other words, these systems support transactions that may originate in one nation and end in another nation. These types of systems can have either a centralized or a decentralized structure. Xerox Corporation uses a centralized information system that keeps track of all its copier machines that are placed in different customer locations around the world. This way it maintains strong control over all maintenance and billing issues regarding its copier machines. ***Transnational information systems***, on the other hand, are not specific to any country or any particular organization. They exist as separate entities and as an international "transactional" space allowing people from different parts of the world to conduct

Figure 6.32 A computer-supported meeting facility, complete with networked PCs and electronic meeting system software.

Source: Courtesy of Groupsystems.com

transactions simultaneously. An example of such an information system is the foreign exchange systems that allow traders from different parts of the world (connected through decentralized networks) to interact with each other.

Next are the ***multinational information systems,*** used often by multinational companies.

Figure 6.33 Meeting support software is becoming widely used and aggressively marketed.

Source: Phil Schofield/Time Life Pictures/Getty Images

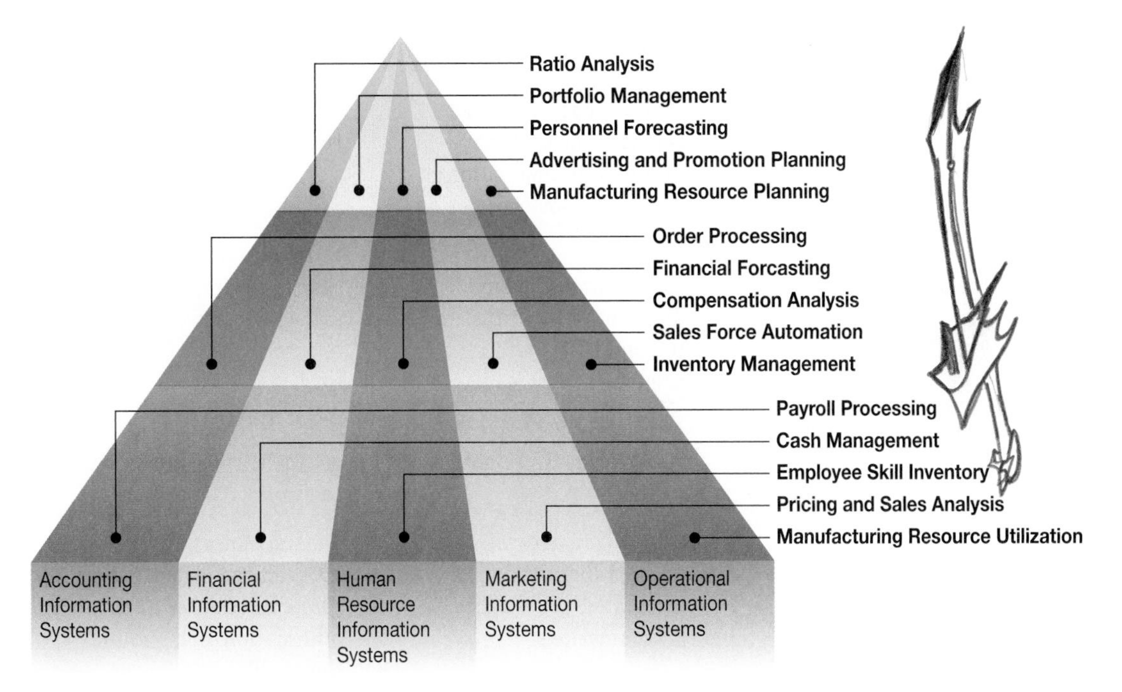

Figure 6.34 Functional area information systems.

These information systems act as a loose confederacy of various different local information systems. The existence of different types of rules and regulations on international data transfer and telecommunications has made this type of network very popular among multinational companies. This way, companies are able to retain the decentralized local data processing centres that are responsive to local needs and regulations and, at the same time, use information technology to

Table 6.13 ***Organizational functions and representative information systems.***

Functional Area	Information System	Examples of Typical Systems
Accounting and Finance	Systems used for managing, controlling, and auditing the financial resources of the organization	▮ Inventory management ▮ Accounts payable ▮ Expense accounts ▮ Cash management ▮ Payroll processing
Human Resources	Systems used for managing, controlling, and auditing the human resources of the organization	▮ Recruiting and hiring ▮ Education and training ▮ Benefits management ▮ Employee termination ▮ Workforce planning
Marketing	Systems used for managing new product development, distribution, pricing, promotional effectiveness, and sales forecasting of the products and services offered by the organization	▮ Market research and analysis ▮ New product development ▮ Promotion and advertising ▮ Pricing and sales analysis ▮ Product location analysis
Production and Operations	Systems used for managing, controlling, and auditing the production and operations resources of the organization	▮ Inventory management ▮ Cost and quality tracking ▮ Materials and resource planning ▮ Customer service tracking ▮ Customer problem tracking ▮ Job costing ▮ Resource utilization

Table 6.14 ***Types of global information systems.***

Type of Information System	Definition	Example
International Information System	System that supports transactions that may originate in one nation and end in another nation	Xerox's copier machine tracking system
Transnational Information System	International "transactional" space allowing people from different parts of the world to conduct transactions simultaneously	Foreign exchange systems that allow traders from different parts of the world to interact with each other
Multinational Information System	A loose confederacy of various local information systems	Nestlé's 140 financial systems used at different locations in the world
Global Information System	Centralized network with an even distribution of integrated applications to all the nations	General Motors global inventory management system that consolidates all inventory information from around the world
Collaborative Information System	System that integrates different applications but is not specific to any given user	The International Airline Reservation System funded jointly by many airline companies

integrate them loosely into the framework of the parent organization. Up until a few years ago, Nestlé had such an information system structure. It had over 140 financial systems that were being used around the world. However, the increasing globalization of the market and the recent advances in telecommunications and networks have caused a transition from multinational information systems to ***global information systems***. Such networks are used especially when a single transaction requires the input of data from multiple data centres located across more than one nation. These networks are usually centralized, and there is an even distribution of integrated applications to all the nations. As a result, data can be accessed irrespective of its location. After some major consolidation efforts, Nestlé has moved toward a global information system, namely through the implementation of an enterprise-wide information system (Chapter 7). It has cut down its number of financial systems to just a few, with the objective of relying on just one in the future.

Finally, there are the ***collaborative information systems*** that integrate different applications but are not specific to any given user. For example, international airline reservation systems such as Galileo or Apollo have been funded by different airline companies and allow a multitude of airlines and travel agents to execute transactions, irrespective of their geographic location. These systems support the operational collaboration of major airline companies and travel agents.

GLOBAL PERSPECTIVE

Managing Human Resources in a Global Organization

You can do several things to improve the management of human resources in global organizations. First, it is important to hire individuals who are experienced in working in cross-cultural teams, who can speak different languages, and who have the necessary cultural sensitivity to empathize with other cultures. In addition to the general IS staff, it is important to hire the proper IS leader or CIO. Global companies argue that the ideal quality required for a CIO is the ability both to understand the global strategies of the company and to be able to collaborate successfully with the regional offices to implement those global strategies.

Beyond personnel, the organizational reward system should be designed to reward individuals for their global initiatives rather than base rewards solely on the local information systems' goals within the organization. Additionally, the organizational culture needs to be modified to fit the needs of local employees. For example, Fujitsu is making a breakthrough in the international market (especially in Internet and multimedia products) after years of overseas failure. Forming joint ventures with international corporations such as Siemens, Fujitsu tries to enter new markets by utilizing the expertise and the brand names of its partners. To better deal with the new markets and business partners, Fujitsu has changed its culture significantly to fit the local needs. There has been a relaxation in the strict Japanese standards of dress and conduct, the introduction of flexible working hours, and the hiring of young, talented individuals representing a diverse set of cultures.

Figure 6.35 Computers can cause frustration in all cultures!

Finally, the organization as a whole should also be extremely sensitive to the various cultural issues and political problems that exist between people from different countries when they are involved in cross-cultural IS operations (see Figure 6.35). Such sensitivity and awareness can be developed through careful and in-depth research and also by having a diverse mix of employees representing different cultures.

Sources: Anonymous, "Fujitsu Siemens Computers Outperforms the European IT Market," Fujitsu Siemens Press Release (March 18, 2004), **www. fujitsu-siemens.com/aboutus/press/press_releases/index.html**.
Sanjima DeZoysa, "Japan and Europe—Worlds Apart?" *Telecommunications International* 36, no. 3 (March 2002): 38.

CAREER IMPLICATIONS

Organizational Information Systems

For Accounting and Finance

Accounting and finance professionals encounter a broad range of information systems at all levels of the organization, including systems for office automation and transaction processing as well as for managerial and executive decision support. For example, transaction processing is used to execute sales orders and employee payroll that can be aggregated by a decision support system to create payroll reports or inventory statistics for managers, whereas long-term financial forecasts could be compiled to support executives' strategic planning. Often, accounting and financial data serve as inputs into these systems.

For Operations Management

Operations management professionals use a variety of information systems to manage inventories; track costs, quality, and customer service or problems; and plan materials and resources. Historically, a lot of these activities have been performed using tedious calculations and methods, but the power of today's information systems tremendously streamlines these processes. Rather than spending time performing calculations and analysis, operations management professionals evaluate and review summary reports provided by a variety of organizational systems to track operational processes and to make decisions. Even though information systems perform the "dirty work" of making complex and tedious calculations, operations management professionals still have to make sense of a large number of complicated reports and analyses.

For Human Resources Management

Human resources managers use different types of organizational systems for performing their work; for example, at the operational level, information systems are used to keep an inventory of employees' skills or to process payroll. One level up in the organizational hierarchy, information systems are used to analyze compensation data and to determine how to reduce labour cost. At the executive level, information systems are used to forecast future personnel requirements and to plan long-term increases or reductions in workforce.

For Marketing

The marketing function in today's organizations can hardly exist without information systems. As sales forecasts are heavily based on past performance, information systems are used to make sense of this data at the different levels of the organizational hierarchy. Marketing professionals at the operational level use information systems to analyze pricing, sales, or product placement data to optimize returns. At the managerial level, information systems can be used to analyze sales force size and location; executives utilize information systems to plan long-term pricing and promotion campaigns.

For Information Systems

As different information systems are used at different levels of the organizational hierarchy, the level of support needed also differs widely. This means that information systems professionals have to support operational-, managerial-, and executive-level systems. Owing to limited resources, however, information systems managers often have to prioritize between the different users' support needs. Sometimes, transaction processing systems are mission critical, and support requests must be responded to immediately. Other times, the organizational hierarchy may dictate the priority of support—that is, executives are given priority, followed by managerial- and operational-level systems, respectively. Making sure the organizational systems are reliable and secure is a key aspect of the information systems function.

KEY POINTS REVIEW

1. **Describe the characteristics that differentiate the operational, managerial, and executive levels of an organization.** At the operational level of the firm, the routine day-to-day business processes and interaction with customers occur, and information systems are designed to automate repetitive activities, such as sales transaction processing. Operational-level managers such as foremen and supervisors make day-to-day decisions that are highly structured and recurring. At the managerial level of the organization, functional managers focus on monitoring and controlling operational-level activities and providing information to higher levels of the organization. Midlevel or functional managers focus on effectively utilizing and deploying organizational resources to achieve the organization's strategic objectives. At this level, the scope of the decision usually is contained within the business function, is moderately complex, and has a time horizon of a few days to a few months. At the executive level of the organization, decisions are often very complex problems with broad and long-term ramifications for the organization. Executive-level decisions are often referred to as being messy or ill-structured because executives must consider the ramifications of the overall organization.
2. **Explain the characteristics of the three information systems designed to support each of the unique levels of an organization: transaction processing systems, management information systems, and executive information systems.** Transaction processing systems are designed to process business events and transactions and reside close to customers at the operational level of the organization. These systems are used to automate repetitive information-processing activities to increase speed and accuracy and to lower the cost of processing each transaction—that is, to make the organization more efficient. Management information systems reside at the managerial level and are designed to produce regular and ad hoc reports to support the ongoing, recurring decision-making activities associated with managing an entire business or a functional area within a business. These systems are used to help midlevel managers make more effective decisions. Executive information systems are used to provide information to executives in a very highly aggregate form so that information can be scanned quickly for trends and anomalies. Executives use these systems to provide a one-stop shop for a lot of their informational needs.
3. **Describe the characteristics of the six information systems that span the organizational, managerial, and executive levels: decision support systems, expert systems, office automation systems, collaboration technologies, functional area information systems, and global information systems.** Decision support systems support organizational decision making and are typically designed to solve a particular recurring problem in the organization. DSSs are most commonly used to support semistructured problems that are addressed by managerial-level employees. A DSS is designed to be an interactive decision aid. An ES is a special type of information system that uses knowledge within some topic area to solve problems or provide advice. Expert systems are used to mimic human expertise by manipulating knowledge (understanding acquired through experience and extensive learning) rather than simply information. ESs are used when expertise for a particular problem is rare or expensive. In this way, organizations hope to replicate the human expertise more easily and inexpensively. Office automation systems are technologies for developing documents, scheduling resources, and communicating. Collaboration technologies such as videoconferencing, groupware, and EMSs are used to support the communication and teamwork of virtual teams. Functional areas represent discrete areas of organizations and typically include accounting and finance, human resource management, marketing, and production and operations management. Functional area information systems are designed to support the unique requirements of specific business functions. Finally, global information systems are used to support international activities of global organizations. There are five distinct types of global information systems: (1) international information systems, (2) transnational information systems, (3) multinational information systems, (4) global information systems, and (5) collaborative information systems. Each type of global information system has distinct characteristics to best support a given international information-processing situation.

KEY TERMS

REVIEW QUESTIONS

1. Compare and contrast the characteristics of the operational, managerial, and executive levels of an organization.
2. What is the difference between "hard" and "soft" data?
3. Describe the differences between online processing and batch processing. Give examples of each.
4. What are the three methods used for inputting data into a transaction processing system? Provide examples of each.
5. List three different types of reports and tell where or how the information from each is used.
6. How does a management information system differ from a transaction processing system in terms of purpose, target users, capabilities, and so forth?
7. Describe and give examples of two types of data entry.
8. How does an executive information system "drill down" into the data?
9. What are the three types of information systems that traditionally span the boundaries of organizational levels?
10. Explain the purpose of a model within a decision support system.
11. What is the difference between a decision support system and an expert system?
12. What is groupware, and what are the different types?
13. Compare and contrast stand-alone videoconferencing and desktop videoconferencing.
14. Provide some examples of functionally specific information systems and needs within an organization.
15. Define and contrast five types of global information systems.

SELF-STUDY QUESTIONS

Visit the Companion Website for this text for additional Self-Study Questions: **www.pearsoned.ca/jessup.**

1. At the __________ level of the organization, functional managers (e.g., marketing, finance, manufacturing, and human resources) focus on monitoring and controlling operational-level activities and providing information to higher levels of the organization.
   A. operational
   B. managerial
   C. organizational
   D. executive
2. Examples of the types of activities supported by management information systems include all of the following except __________.
   A. inventory management and planning
   B. manufacturing planning and scheduling
   C. financial management and forecasting
   D. sales and order processing
3. A __________ report provides a summary of critical information on a recurring schedule.
   A. scheduled
   B. exception
   C. key-indicator
   D. drill-down
4. Examples of the types of activities that can be supported by expert systems include all of the following except __________.
   A. payroll calculations
   B. financial planning
   C. machine configuration
   D. medical diagnosis
5. A supervisor having to decide when to reorder supplies or how best to allocate personnel for the completion of a project is an example of a __________ decision.
   A. structured
   B. unstructured
   C. automated
   D. delegated
6. The types of boundary-spanning systems include all of the following except __________.
   A. decision support systems
   B. resource planning systems
   C. office automation systems
   D. expert systems
7. __________ processing of transactions provides immediate results to the system operator or customer.
   A. Online
   B. Batch
   C. Fully automated
   D. Semiautomated
8. A marketing manager for Nike may have a(n) __________ system that contrasts sales revenue and marketing expenses by geographic region so that he can better understand how regional marketing for the "Tiger Woods Golf" promotions are performing.
   A. transaction
   B. expert
   C. office automated
   D. management information
9. In a(n) __________ data entry system, a data capture device such as a grocery store checkout scanner speeds the entry and processing of the transaction.
   A. manual
   B. semiautomated
   C. fully automated
   D. expert
10. A(n) __________ information system is defined as a loose confederacy of various different local information systems.
    A. international
    B. multinational
    C. collaborative
    D. transnational

PROBLEMS AND EXERCISES

1. Match the following terms with the appropriate definitions:

   _____ Operational level

   _____ Transactions

   _____ Virtual teams

   _____ Source document

   _____ Online processing

   _____ Management information system

   _____ Expert system

   _____ Inferencing

   _____ Transaction processing system

   _____ Decision support system

   a. An information system designed to process day-to-day business event data at the operational level of an organization
   b. A special-purpose information system designed to mimic human expertise by manipulating knowledge (understanding acquired through experience and extensive learning) rather than simply information
   c. The bottom level of an organization, where the routine day-to-day interaction with customers occurs
   d. A special-purpose information system designed to support organizational decision making primarily at the managerial level of an organization
   e. Processing of information immediately as it occurs
   f. Repetitive events in organizations that occur as a regular part of conducting day-to-day operations
   g. An information system designed to support the management of organizational functions at the managerial level of the organization
   h. A document created when a business event or transaction occurs
   i. The matching of facts and rules as well as determining the sequence of questions presented to the user and drawing a conclusion
   j. Teams forming and disbanding as needed, with team size fluctuating as necessary and with team members coming and going as they are needed

2. Visit **http://guide.real.com** on the web. RealNetworks provides information on almost any subject or industry, virtually as it hits the newswires. What types of "hard" and "soft" data can you find?

3. Do you feel that, as much as possible, TPSs should replace human roles and activities within organizations? Why or why not? How much cost savings will there be if these humans are still needed to run the systems? What if you were the person being replaced? Will all errors necessarily be eliminated? Why or why not?

4. Imagine that your boss has asked you to build an inventory transaction system that would enable the receiving and shipping clerks to enter inventory amounts for purchases and sales, respectively. Discuss the pros and cons of building this system as an online processing system versus a batch processing system. Which would you recommend to your boss?

5. The national sales manager for ABC Corp. is interested in purchasing a software package that will be capable of providing "accurate" sales forecasts for the short term and long term. She has asked you to recommend the best type of system for this purpose. What would you recommend? Do you have any reservations about such a system? Why or why not?

6. Visit MSN Money (**http://moneycentral.msn.com/investor/calcs/n_expect/main.asp**) on the web to determine your life expectancy, using a DSS. What did you learn? Is there a difference between life expectancies for different genders? If you browse MSN Money, what other interesting stuff do you find? Also check out **www.bigcharts.com**.

7. Interview a top-level executive within an organization with which you are familiar or within one of the companies from the Brief Cases. Determine the extent to which the organization utilizes EISs. Does this individual utilize an EIS in any way? Why or why not? Which executives do utilize an EIS?

8. Based on your experiences with TPSs (in everyday life and/or in the workplace), which ones use online processing and which use batch processing? Do these choices fit the system, the information, and the environment? Would you make any adjustments? Why or why not?

9. Using any program you choose, or using the website **www.moneycentral.com**, find or create a template that you could use in the future to determine monthly payments on car or home loans. Compare your template with the one at **http://carpoint.msn.com/LoanCalc**. Would you have categorized the program you used to create this template as a DSS before doing this exercise?

10. Describe your experiences with ESs, or look up **www.exsys.com** on the web. In what situations did you encounter ESs, and what is their future? Did you actually use the system, or did another individual use it on your behalf?

11. Choose an organization with which you are familiar that utilizes OASs. Which systems does it use? Which functions have been automated, and which have not been? Why have some functions not been automated? Who decides which OAS to implement?

12. Have you seen or used ad hoc, exception, key-indicator, and/or drill-down reports? What is the purpose of each report? Who produces, and who uses the reports? Do any of these reports look or sound familiar from your work experience?

13. Interview an IS manager within an organization at a university or workplace. Of the three categories of information systems—transaction processing, management, and executive—which do people utilize most in this organization? Why? Have any of these areas experienced an increase or decrease in the last few years? What predictions does this manager have regarding the future of traditional information systems? Do you agree? Prepare a 10-minute presentation to the class on your findings.

14. Describe how various systems described in this chapter might enable employees to work from home rather than at the company's office. What technologies in particular might these employees utilize and how? Will companies look favourably on this use of technology? Why or why not?

15. Interview an IS professional and ask about travel and assignments outside of Canada. Do global assignments contribute to promotion? What is the length of an average assignment?

APPLICATION EXERCISES

Note: The existing data files referenced in these exercises are available on the Companion Website: **www.pearsoned.ca/jessup**.

Spreadsheet Application: Calculating Loan Payments

You have recently been hired by the Springfield County Employees' Health and Wellness services. As the location of your new office is not in walking distance and you need a dependable means of transportation for the winter months, you have decided to take out a loan for a new car. You have already taken a look at several offers but are unsure whether you can afford the cars. Set up a spreadsheet to calculate the car payments per month for the following situations:

- Price: $12 000, percentage rate: 5.5, time: 3 years.
- Price: $12 000, percentage rate: 6.0, time: 4 years.
- Price: $12 000, percentage rate: 6.5, time: 5 years.
- Price: $14 000, percentage rate: 5.5, time: 3 years.
- Price: $14 000, percentage rate: 6.0, time: 4 years.
- Price: $14 000, percentage rate: 6.5, time: 5 years.

Once you have calculated the payments, calculate the total amount to be paid for each car as well as the total interest you would pay over the course of the loan. Make sure to use formulas for all calculations and print out a professionally formatted page displaying the results and a page displaying the formulas. Hint: in Microsoft Excel, use the "PMT" function in the category "Financial" to calculate the payments. Use ctrl + ' (grave accent) to switch between formula and data views.

Database Application: Tracking Student Enrollment

This summer, you found a job with the office of the registrar. The registrar wants to know which courses were most popular during the summer session and asks you to prepare several reports. In the file SummerSession.mdb you find information about the students, instructors, and courses. You are asked to generate the following reports (if you are using Microsoft Access, then you might use the report wizard):

- List of all enrolled students grouped by class (including total number of students per class).
- List of students for each instructor (grouped by class, including total number of students).
- Classes taken by each student (including total number of classes).

Make sure to include appropriate headers and footers, such as title, report date, and page number, before printing the reports. Hint: In Microsoft Access, set up the necessary queries using the wizard before creating the reports.

ANSWERS TO THE SELF-STUDY QUESTIONS

1. B, p. 192	2. D, p. 198	3. C, pp. 198–199	4. A, p. 205	5. A, p. 192
6. B, p. 202	7. A, p. 195	8. D, p. 198	9. B, p. 196	10. B, p. 216

Case *Canadian Specialty Photography Retailer Says It Will Develop a Clearer Picture of What Is Going on in Its Stores Through Business Intelligence Software*

Black Photo Corporation (Black's) is Canada's largest specialty photography retailer, with over 181 stores across the country. Most of these stores are small- or medium-sized retail outlets located in shopping malls. Each of these outlets generates sales data that must be aggregated and organized on a company-wide basis. To facilitate the aggregation of this data across the company, Black's rolled out a series of online analytical processing (OLAP) tools developed by Cognos Incorporated. Online analytical processing tools allow managers to access and analyze data in real time. In 2004, Black's implemented a series of OLAP cubes to facilitate basket analysis. OLAP cubes are multidimensional databases that hold data like a 3-D spreadsheet allowing different views of the data to be quickly displayed. Basket analysis is a process by which bundles of products purchased by customers (i.e., in a shopping basket) are analyzed for trends and patterns. This information can support decisions on product location, store layout, and shelf-space allocation. Basket analysis can also be used to help design in-store promotions. For example, if basket analysis shows that customers often purchase film and batteries together, then the two products might be bundled together at a special price or be placed near one another on a shelf.

The company was also hoping to track key performance indicators at the store level and roll out business intelligence for budgeting and planning to its finance department, according to Ron Short, Black's director of information systems and technology. Since it began using business intelligence to sort out its mass of data and provide more information to its vendor partners, Short says that Black's has seen a 2000-percent return on investment (ROI)—an achievement that raised eyebrows among its senior managers. "No one believed our return on investment (ROI)," Short says, adding that deployment help from a consulting firm resulted in a 60-day turnaround on the project. "They were like, 'Yeah, right.'"

Part of that ROI can be attributed to a strategy whereby Black's charged the vendors who stocked its stores with product, like Pentax and Nikon, to access OLAP cubes containing a week's worth of sales data as a special service. Black's had originally considered using the tools only for internal forecasting analysis, but it soon became clear that vendors, too, might be interested in the data. "The vendors paid for this product," Short says. Most of the photography vendors were surprised that Black's was willing to share its data, he adds, but the idea was to help all its business partners make better decisions in terms of product mix. Internally, Black's wanted to be able to offer its stores more timely access to reports, which previously took days or weeks to complete. There was also the issue of catering to individual report requests and customizing data, according to Short. The self-service capabilities of the OLAP cubes helped address that issue. Store managers could now access data at any time and organize it in any way they chose.

Online analytical processing tools, basket analysis, and business intelligence software are all information systems designed to extract value from everyday transaction data. Transaction processing systems generate massive amounts of data, most of which is never used by management. These tools allow managers at different levels in the organization to access and perform analysis on this data in real time. "If you have 10 people sitting around a boardroom waiting for information, they all want it in 10 different ways," Short says. "I don't even know what some of them do with the data, to be quite honest, but this puts it back on them." Black's was focused on providing a "single view of the truth" by extracting the most reliable data from the company's mainframe computer. "You'd flip through some green screen to green screen," he recounts. "The data was there, but you just couldn't slice it down to what you needed."

Source: Adapted from Shane Schick, "Black's Takes Snapshot of Store Performance," *EDGE* magazine (December 2003): 26–27.

Discussion Questions

1. What are some of the challenges that Black's faced in accessing and analyzing its transaction processing data?
2. What advantages did the new tools provide to Black's?
3. Of the different types of organizational information systems covered in this chapter, could any other type of information system solve Black's problems? Why or why not?
4. Which of the several advantages that the system provided was the most important? Why?

Log on to the Companion Website at www.pearsoned.ca/jessup for an additional case.

Running Case: Connexion by Boeing

Organizational Systems

For commercial airlines, maximizing operational efficiency and market presence can be the key for survival. As discussed in earlier cases, the Boeing Company has envisioned the e-Enabled Advantage, which uses integrated information and communications systems to improve the ways an airline can run its business, as a way to help airlines achieve this goal. Drawing on resources of the entire company, Boeing hoped to give the airline industry a future in which people, airplanes, assets, information systems, knowledge applications, and decision support tools work together seamlessly across an airline's functional areas and hierarchical levels. In the near future, Jeppesen Electronic Flight Bag (EFB), SBS International Crew Scheduling and Management software, Connexion by Boeing, and Boeing Airplane Health Management (AHM) will be integrated, and airborne and ground-based operations will be linked in real time to enable people to achieve the airline's goals. Connexion's systems greatly facilitate the integration by providing a medium to transfer tremendous amounts of data at high speeds between the aircraft and the airline's operations centre.

The infrastructure necessary to e-Enable a commercial airplane is a complex system of systems that channels the wealth of information generated by airplane avionics, the airline operations centres, airport and air traffic managers, weather services, and regulatory agencies directly to the people who use the information, at the instant when that information is most useful. In addition to integrating existing information systems, a new generation of visualization tools and decision aids is currently under development to create robust flight plans, revise and optimize schedules in real time, and all but eliminate unscheduled maintenance.

For any commercial airline, the most important revenue-generating business function is flight operations. To increase efficiency before, during, and after the flight, Boeing's subsidiary, Jeppesen, has developed a system that makes all features of a traditional paper-based flight bag available electronically to the pilot and the crew. This EFB is a software and data services solution that offers airlines advanced information management capabilities and delivers more accurate performance calculations, thus creating significant savings of time and money while increasing safety and streamlining the management of flight information. Using information technology, airlines can realize the "Paperless Cockpit," in which most paper documents are eliminated. Revisions to electronic documents are made electronically, and computations are rapid and more precise. In addition to reducing the paper trail associated with flight planning and execution, the EFB integrates security-relevant features, such as cabin video surveillance, which also helps an airline to comply with security mandates for video and EFB functionality in a single system. Finally, certain EFB applications, such as Taxi Position Awareness, can contribute to a reduction or elimination of runway incursions. Enhanced position awareness and decreased pilot workload mitigate one of the top safety concerns in aviation today while also helping to improve the efficiency of ground operations.

In contrast to traditional paper-based flight documentation, the EFB can increase efficiency and effectiveness by providing accurate and timely performance calculations, such as precise, real-time calculation of takeoff and landing performance, including maximum takeoff and landing weights and engine power settings. The paperless cockpit also helps to create cost savings, as the electronic distribution of information can directly reduce support costs associated with receiving, reviewing, and distributing paper documents such as electronic navigation charts, electronic airplane and flight operations manuals, and electronic aircraft logbooks. In addition to offering superior search and retrieval functions, these electronic documents help to reduce an aircraft's take-off weight due to the reduced need for bulky paper-based documents.

Crew scheduling is an important supporting function to sustain an airline's flight operations. To provide airlines with a seamlessly integrated solution, Boeing decided to acquire SBS International, a company specializing in crew management solutions. These software tools help an airline monitor crew assignments in real time and help increase efficient use of resources by providing timely and accurate information, which helps to optimize crew scheduling and avoid rule-violation penalties that can adversely affect an airline's operating costs. In addition to the mere scheduling, these systems were even designed to amend hotel and ground transportation arrangements to the schedules, maintain detailed master records, and communicate with payroll systems. Using the high-speed data transmission capabilities of Connexion, these systems can be accessed inflight, maximizing the potential for last-minute schedule or ground transportation or accommodation changes, if necessary. For the crew, this real-time access to the latest information means less uncertainty and can increase the crew's satisfaction with their jobs. At the same time, the real-time availability helps the employees at the managerial levels of an airline, as crew members can accept or decline schedule change requests in a timelier manner, which helps to reduce uncertainty and aids in the crew-scheduling process.

Another important support function for an airline's flight operation is aircraft maintenance. Boeing AHM is a system designed to reduce delays, cancellations, air turnbacks, and diversions through the innovative use of existing data. Made possible by advances in data processing, transmission, and analysis, AHM integrates remote collection, monitoring, and analysis of airplane data to determine the status of an airplane's current and future serviceability. These data are converted into information airlines can use to make the operational or fix-or-fly decisions that can make the difference between profit and loss, because minimizing aircraft downtime is a very important factor in reducing operating costs and improving profitability.

When a fault occurs inflight, AHM allows airlines to make operational decisions immediately, and if maintenance is required, to make arrangements for the people, parts, and equipment sooner rather than later. It is also designed to aid in forecasting and fixing problems before failure, a process referred to as "prognostics." Problems that might have initiated unplanned maintenance can be performed on a planned basis, which helps the employees on the managerial level to schedule the aircraft's availability. The real-time information availability enabled by Connexion's systems helps to reduce schedule interruptions and trim the number of delays by sending data directly from air to ground, so that repair teams can begin work on a solution before the plane lands. The ground maintenance crews can directly access the aircraft's systems and diagnose the problem, and mechanics can work on fixing the problem as soon as the aircraft arrives at the gate. This helps to get the aircraft back into the air as soon as possible, which in turn helps to minimize costs associated with delays, rescheduling, or flight cancellations.

For an airline, being e-Enabled can mean gaining double advantages in attracting passengers and sustaining passenger loyalty. For example, the same Connexion by Boeing technologies that link the airplane with the airline enterprise by providing solutions such as the EFB, crew scheduling, and AHM also deliver real-time, high-speed connectivity directly to the passenger. From the comfort of their seats, passengers can tune in to their favourite web-based radio and video programs, follow live sporting events, choose from a list of premium entertainment options, exchange e-mail and instant messages with family and associates, send and receive documents and files, play video games, or shop for gifts and souvenirs on the Internet. Travel plan alterations—whether because of flight delays or simple changes in passenger plans—are no longer a disruption when onboard and ground-based information systems interact, enabling passenger

service agents to arrange new itineraries and deliver new tickets en route to the destination. With all the arrangements settled before the airplane touches down, passengers can relax and enjoy the travel experience.

As for any other company, information is only as valuable as the ability to act upon it. The e-Enabled Advantage integrates powerful visualization tools and decision aids to help an airline incorporate the latest information from throughout the network into dynamic planning (see photo above). Using the e-Enabled Advantage's integrated systems, an airline can interrupt the cascade of unforeseen events before they become costly schedule disruptions. On the flight deck, the Jeppesen EFB gives flight crews a sharper strategic picture of where they are, where they are going, and what is waiting beyond the horizon. Connexion can keep planners and air traffic managers aware of the airplane's situation and capabilities. Connexion's onboard server—matched with Boeing's communication, navigation, and surveillance (CNS) and air traffic management (ATM) applications, crew management applications, and Boeing's Integrated Airline Operations Center project—will present managers and planners with prioritized alternatives for unforeseen developments, ushering in a new era of fully informed decision making.

Sources: **www.boeing.com/commercial/ams/mss/brochures/airplane_health_brochure.html**, **www.boeing.com/commercial/e-enabled/index.html**, **www.jeppesen.com**, **www.sbsint.com**

Discussion Questions

1. Briefly discuss the various features of Boeing's e-Enabled airplane vision. How could the systems mentioned in the case be integrated with the different systems in other business functions (e.g., accounting, finance, sales, and marketing) of an airline? Explain.
2. Which other features necessary to sustain an airline's flight operation could be integrated into the e-Enabled Advantage? Look up potential solutions at **www.boeing.com**.
3. How can the information generated at the operational and managerial level be used at the executive level of an airline?

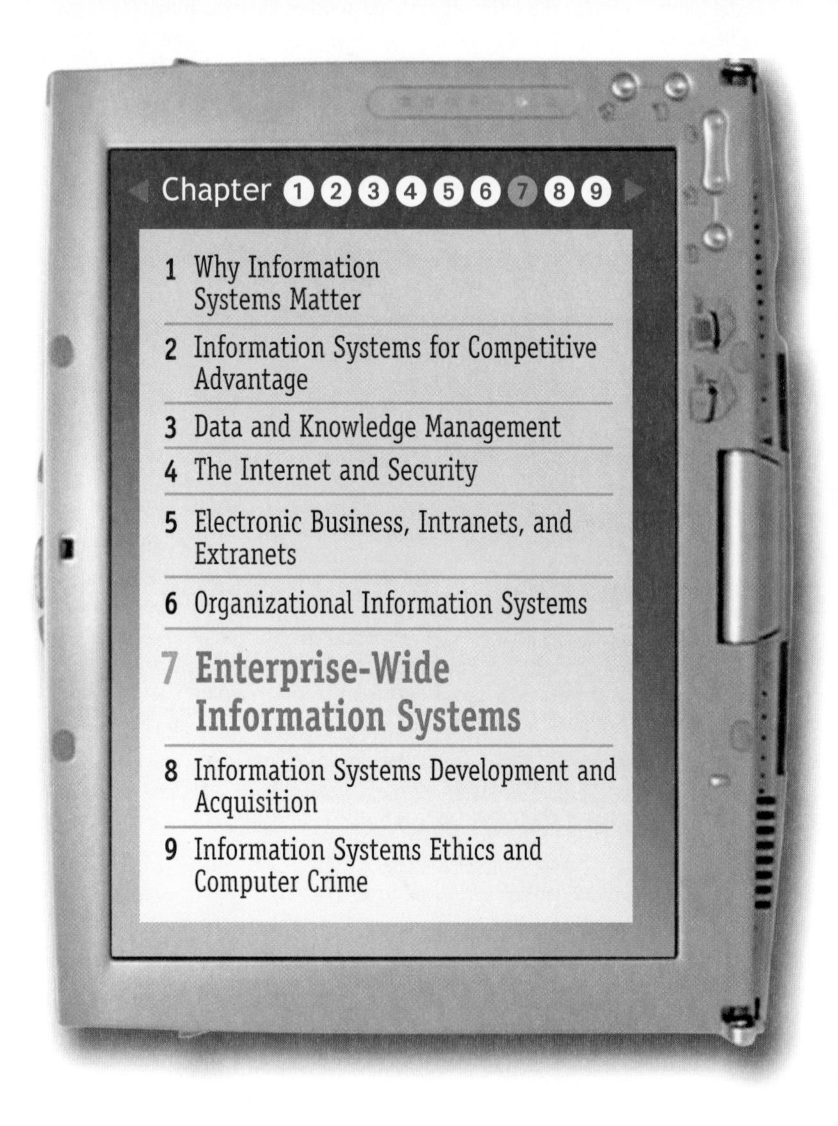

Preview

This chapter describes how companies are deploying enterprise-wide information systems to support and integrate their various business activities, to streamline and better manage interactions with customers, and to coordinate better with their suppliers to meet changing customer demands more efficiently and effectively. After reading this chapter you will be able to do the following:

1. Explain how organizations support business activities by using information technologies.
2. Describe what enterprise systems are and how they have evolved.
3. Explain the differences between internally and externally focused software applications.
4. Understand and utilize the keys to successfully implementing enterprise systems.

Canada Competes!

Nordia Inc. is a Canadian provider of multi-contact customer relationship management solutions. The company is based in Montreal and employs 2000 people in seven contact centres in Quebec and Ontario. Nordia also offers specialized programs such as directory assistance, relay services, and teleconferencing.

Nordia made a major step toward international expansion when it secured a large relay-service contract from the state of California in 2002. The contract required setting up a call centre in Canada to handle interactions from people with hearing and speech impediments. The call centre needed to handle calls relayed from U.S. callers using new technologies, including Internet protocol and wireless technologies as well as specialized technologies used by the hearing impaired and speech disabled. Experts from Nordia and its strategic partners, including Bell Canada and Nortel, developed and implemented a new technological platform integrating advanced call-management software. The system also permitted connection of relay services in several languages to U.S. clients through specialized Nordia agents in Canada.

Pierre Grimard, vice president of information technology for Nordia, put the work in perspective: "The creation of this new technological solution is unique and addresses quite a number of challenges. Our own expertise, combined with that of our partners, has enabled us to succeed in integrating communications using typed text, TTY (keyboard telephones), and voice over IP in one system, while at the same time establishing a connection between Canada and the US that permits relay-type calls to cross borders with all the necessary information."

The system enables the hearing-impaired and speech-disabled user to simulate a person-to-person call with the intervention of a relay-service agent. Management of relay-user preference profiles permits more efficient placement of calls to people frequently called by the user and quicker number dialling. The system developed by Nordia was deemed to be so successful that the state of California allocated additional call volumes to the company in 2005.

Source: Canadian Information Productivity Awards, 2005, **www.cipa.com/award_winners/winners_05/NordiaInc.html.**

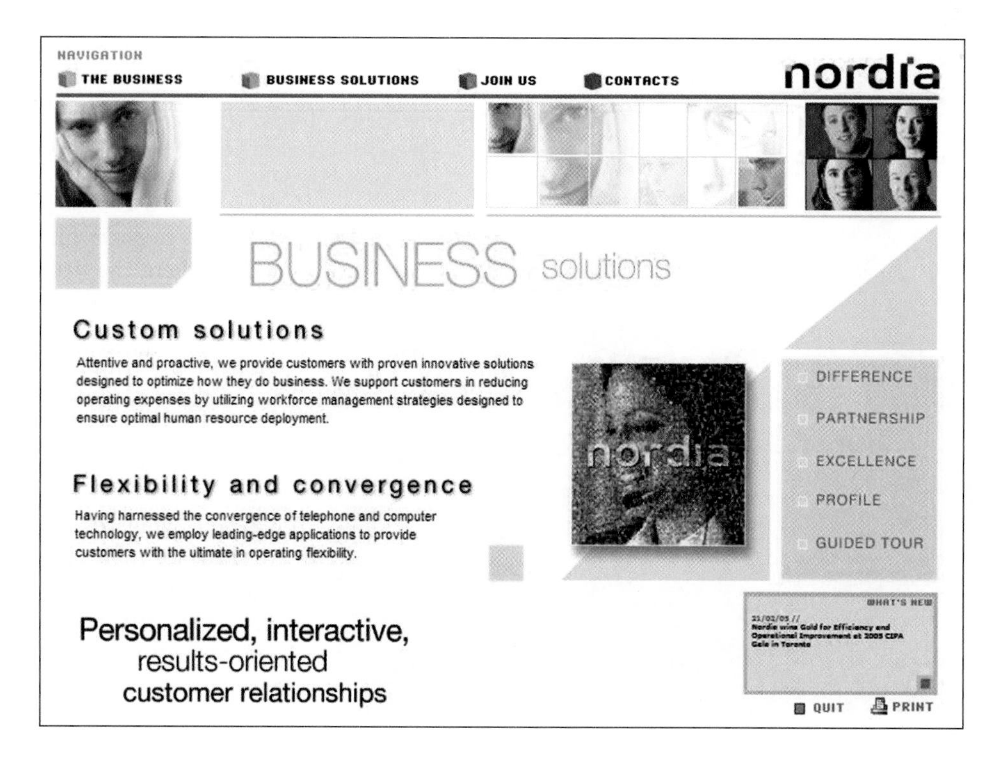

Source: Nordia. **www.nordia.com.**

Figure 7.1 People with enterprise systems skills are in high demand.

Source: Olivier Morin/APP/Getty Images

Large companies continue to find that they need systems that span their entire organization and tie everything together. As a result, an understanding of enterprise systems is critical to succeed in today's competitive and ever-changing world. People with enterprise systems skills (see Figure 7.1) are in high demand; therefore, the more you know about enterprise systems, the more you will be in demand in the employment marketplace.

Figure 7.2 Enterprise systems allow companies to integrate information across operations on a company-wide basis.

Source: © Lindsay Hebberd/CORBIS

ENTERPRISE SYSTEMS

Companies use information systems to support their various business processes and activities for internal operations such as manufacturing, order processing, and human resource management. Companies can also use information systems to support external interactions with customers, suppliers, and business partners. Businesses have leveraged information systems to support business processes and activities for decades, beginning with the installation of applications to assist companies with specific business tasks such as issuing paycheques. Oftentimes, these systems were built on different computing platforms, such as mainframes and minicomputers, each operating in unique hardware and software environments. Applications running on different computing platforms are difficult to integrate, as custom interfaces are required for one system to communicate with another.

Running different applications on separate computing platforms can create tremendous inefficiencies within organizations because data cannot readily be shared between the systems. Information must be reentered from one system to the next, and the same pieces of data may be stored in several versions throughout the organization. ***Enterprise-wide information systems (enterprise systems)***, thus, are information systems that allow companies to integrate information across operations on a company-wide basis (see Figure 7.2). Rather than storing information in separate places throughout the organization, enterprise systems provide a central repository common to all corporate users. This, along with a common user interface, allows personnel to share information seamlessly no matter where the data are located or who is using the application.

The emergence of the Internet and web has resulted in the globalization of customer and supplier networks, opening up new opportunities and methods to conduct business. Customers have an increasing number of options available to them, so they are demanding more sophisticated products that are customized to their unique needs. They also expect higher levels of customer service. If companies cannot keep their customers satisfied, the customers will not hesitate to do business with a competitor. Companies need to provide quality customer service and develop products faster and more efficiently to compete in global markets. Enterprise systems can be extended to streamline communications with customers and suppliers. Rather than focusing only on internal operations, these systems can also focus on business activities that occur outside organizational boundaries. Enterprise systems can help companies find innovative ways to increase accurate on-time shipments, avoid (or at least anticipate) surprises, minimize costs, and ultimately increase customer satisfaction and the overall profitability of the company.

Enterprise systems come in a variety of shapes and sizes, each providing a unique set of features and functionality. When deciding to implement enterprise solutions, managers need to be aware of many issues. One of the most important involves selecting and implementing applications that meet the requirements of the business as well as of its customers and suppliers. In the following sections, we examine the ways in which information systems can be leveraged to support business activities. This is followed by an in-depth analysis of how enterprise systems have evolved and how companies are using these systems to support their internal and external operations.

ENHANCING COMPETITIVE ADVANTAGE THROUGH THE SUPPORT OF BUSINESS ACTIVITIES

As discussed in Chapter 2, information systems can be used to increase competitive advantage by supporting and/or streamlining business activities (Porter and Millar, 1985). For example, an information system could be used to support a billing process in such a way that it reduces the use of paper and, more importantly, the handling of paper, thus reducing material and labour costs. This system can help managers keep track of that same billing process more effectively because they will have more accurate, up-to-date information about the process, enabling them to make smart, timely business decisions.

Information systems can be used to support either internally or externally focused business processes. Internally focused systems support functional areas, processes, or activities within the organization. These activities can be viewed as a series of links in a chain along which information flows within the organization. At each stage (or link) in the process,

CANADIAN NETSTATS

ICT Manufacturing Drops as ICT Services Expand

The ICT sector has always been important to the Canadian economy. However, the relative makeup of this industry sector has changed substantially over the past few years. Fuelled by the tech boom of the early 2000s, firms like Nortel produced huge quantities of ICT hardware. In the year 2000, ICT manufacturing comprised over 30 percent of the total ICT sector. As the boom became a bust, ICT manufacturing contracted until by 2002 it comprised only 16 percent of the ICT sector. Quebec and Ontario, with over 85 percent of Canadian ICT manufacturing, bore the brunt of this trend. However, the fall in manufacturing was offset by a steady rise in ICT services. This rise has been so large, in fact, that the total Canadian ICT sector grew each year from 2001 to 2004 (see Table 7.1).

Table 7.1 ***Canadian ICT sector growth from 2000 to 2004.***

ICT Sector	Unit	2000	2001	2002	2003	2004
ICT manufacturing	$Million	17 070	11 069	8889	8871	9949
% of total ICT	%	31	21	16	16	17
ICT Services	$Million	38 316	42 349	45 016	46 093	47 465
% of total ICT	%	69	79	84	84	83
Total ICT	$Million	55 176	53 857	54 608	55 698	58 112
ICT % of economy	%	5.8	5.6	5.5	5.5	5.6

Source: Statistics Canada

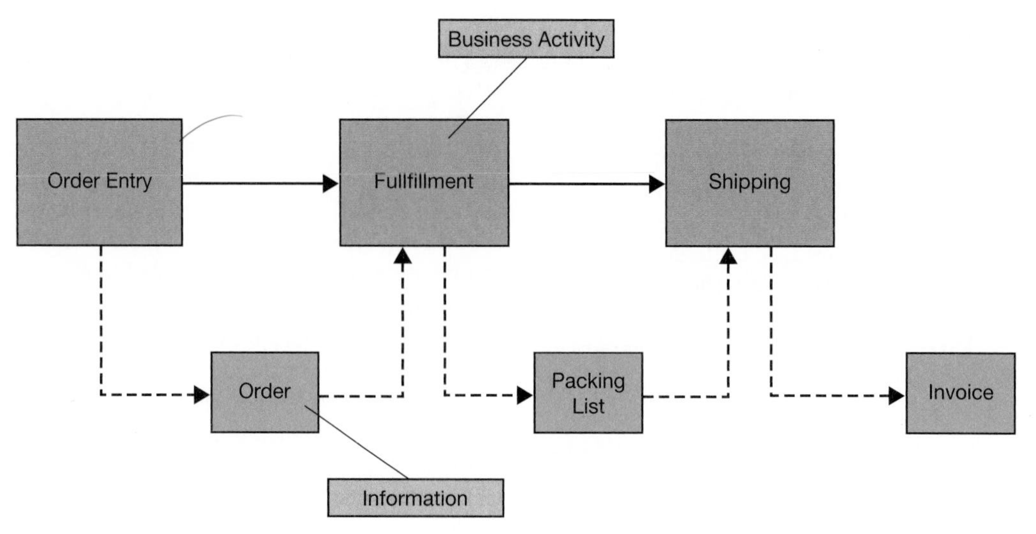

Figure 7.3 Information flow for a typical order.

value is added in the form of the work performed by people associated with that process, and new, useful information is generated. Information begins to accumulate at the point of entry and flows through the various links, or processes within the organization, progressing through the organization with new, useful information being added every step of the way. For example, when a customer places an order, the order is entered into an order-entry application. The information containing the order is sent to the fulfillment department, which picks the items from inventory, packages them for distribution, and produces an additional piece of information called a packing list, which specifies the items contained within the package. The package, along with the packing list, is forwarded to the shipping department, which coordinates the shipment, produces an additional piece of information in the form of an invoice, and sends the package with its associated invoice to the customer. Each link in the process has a unique set of information inputs and outputs, as depicted in Figure 7.3.

In contrast to internally focused applications, which coordinate functions inside organizational boundaries, externally focused systems coordinate business activities with customers, suppliers, business partners, and others who operate outside the organization's boundaries. Systems that communicate across organizational boundaries are sometimes referred to as ***interorganizational systems (IOSs)*** (Kumar and Crook, 1999). The key purpose of an IOS is to streamline the flow of information from one company's operations to another company's. This type of application could be used, for example, to coordinate the flow of information from a company to its potential or existing customers who exist outside the organization, and vice versa.

Competitive advantage can be accomplished here by integrating multiple business processes in ways that enable a firm to meet a wide range of unique customer needs. Sharing information between organizations helps companies adapt more quickly to changing market conditions. For instance, should consumers demand that a component be added to a product, a company can gain this information from its information systems that support sales and pass it along to its component suppliers in real time. Information allows the company and its suppliers to satisfy the needs of customers efficiently because changes can be identified and managed immediately, creating a competitive advantage for companies that can respond quickly.

We can view processes and information flows across organizations just as we previously viewed the processes and information flows within an organization. At each stage (or link) in the process, value is added by the work performed, and new, useful information is generated and exchanged between organizations (see Figure 7.4). Using IOS, one company creates information and transmits it electronically to another company.

For example, when a company places an order for components with a supplier, the supplier processes the order as shown in Figure 7.4. The supplier performs the shipping activity, which results in the delivery of a physical package and the electronic transmission of the associated invoice to the customer. At this point, the information crosses corporate boundaries

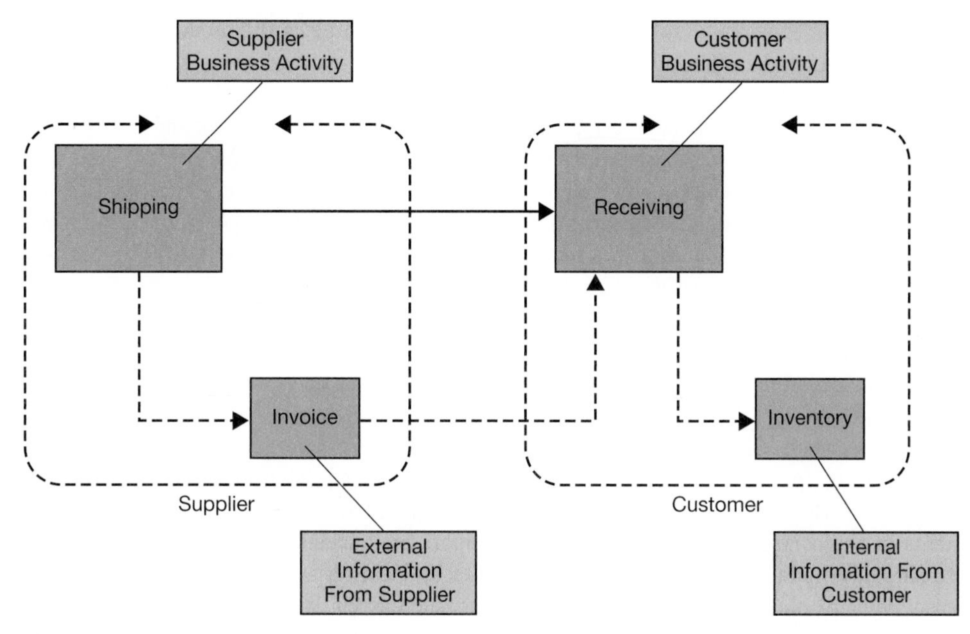

Figure 7.4 Information flow for a typical shipment across organizational boundaries.

from the supplier's organization to the customer's (the organization that ordered the component from the supplier). The customer's receiving department takes delivery of the supplier's package and verifies the invoice that was transmitted to ensure the order is complete. When the customer has accounted for the components, it stocks the items in inventory and updates inventory levels on its internal system accordingly.

Internally Focused Applications

As companies within certain industries operate their businesses differently, one of the first challenges an organization must face is to understand how it can use information systems to support its unique internal business activities. Generally, the flow of information through a set of business activities is referred to as a ***value chain*** (Porter and Millar, 1985), in which information and goods flow through functional areas that facilitate the internal activities of the business. Figure 7.5 depicts the value chain framework. In Chapter 2 we spoke of the strategic value of analyzing a value chain. We now show you how to use value chain analysis to implement enterprise systems.

Functional areas can be broken down into primary and support activities. Primary activities are functional areas within an organization that process inputs and produce outputs. Support activities are those activities that enable primary activities to take place. In the following sections, we focus on primary activities and then turn our attention to the support activities that make them possible.

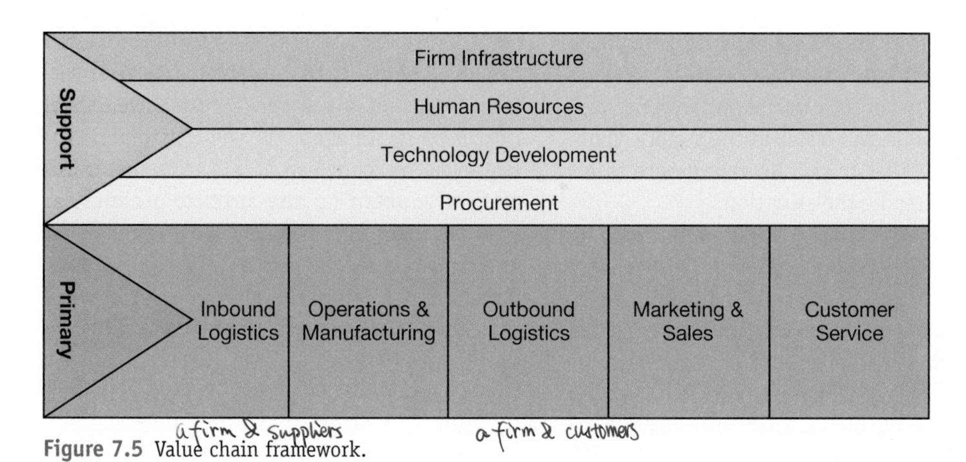

Figure 7.5 Value chain framework.

Porter and Millar, 1985.

Primary Activities

Primary activities include inbound logistics, operations and manufacturing, outbound logistics, marketing and sales, and customer service. These activities may differ widely based on the unique requirements of the industry in which a company operates, although the basic concepts hold in most organizations. Inbound logistics involves the business activities associated with receiving and stocking raw materials, parts, and products. For example, inbound logistics at Cisco Systems involves the receipt of electronic components that go into making their end products such as routers. Shippers deliver electronic components to Cisco, at which time employees unwrap the packages and stock the components in the company's inventory. Cisco can automatically update inventory levels at the point of delivery, allowing purchasing managers to access real-time information related to inventory levels and reorder points.

Once the components have been stocked in inventory, the functional area of operations takes over. Operations can involve such activities as order processing and/or manufacturing processes that transform raw materials and/or component parts into end products. As discussed in Chapter 5, Dell utilizes web-based information systems to allow customers to enter orders online. This information is used to coordinate the manufacturing of a customized personal computer, in which the component parts are gathered and assembled to create the end product. During this process, inventory levels from inbound logistics are verified; if the appropriate inventory exists, workers pick the components from existing supplies and build the product to the customer's specifications. When components are picked, items are deducted from inventory; once the product is assembled, inventory levels for the final product are updated. Canadian National Railways uses software from i2 Technologies to manage its vast inventory of rolling stock. The software forms the core of an information system used to forecast what will occur in the supply chain, then ensures that it has the appropriate assets in place to handle the situation.

The functional area of outbound logistics mirrors that of inbound logistics. Instead of involving the receipt of raw materials, parts, and products, outbound logistics focuses on the distribution of end products. For example, outbound logistics at Chapters.Indigo.ca involves the delivery of books that customers have ordered. Orders that have been processed by the operations area are forwarded to outbound logistics, which picks the products from inventory and coordinates delivery to the customer. At that point, items are packaged and deducted from the company's inventory, and an invoice is created that will be sent to the customer. Chapters.Indigo.ca can automatically update sales information at the point of distribution, allowing managers to view inventory and revenue information in real time.

The marketing and sales functional area facilitates the pre-sales (i.e., before the sale) activities of the company. These include such things as the creation of marketing literature, communication with potential and existing customers, and pricing of goods and services. As discussed in Chapter 5, many companies support the business activity of marketing and sales by creating an e-brochure. Other companies, such as Via Rail, use information systems to update pricing information and schedules. This information is entered directly into the pricing and scheduling systems, which allow the information to become immediately accessible throughout the organization and to end consumers through the corporation's website.

Whereas marketing and sales focus on pre-sales activities, the customer service functional area focuses on the post-sales (i.e., after the sale) activities of the company. Customers may have questions and need help from a customer service representative. Many companies, such as Hewlett-Packard (HP), are utilizing information systems to provide customer service. These applications allow customers to search for and download information related to the products they have purchased. For example, HP customers may need to install drivers for the printers they have just purchased. Rather than calling a customer service representative, customers can help themselves through a self-service customer support application.

Companies can use information systems to track service requests. When a customer calls in for repairs to a product, customer service representatives can access a wealth of information related to the customer. For instance, an agent can access technical information concerning the specific product, as well as review any problems the customer has encountered in the past. This enables customer service representatives to react quickly to customer concerns, improving the customer service experience.

Support Activities

Support activities are business activities that enable the primary activities to take place.

Support activities include infrastructure, human resources (HR), technology development, and procurement. Infrastructure refers to the hardware and software that must be implemented to support the applications that the primary activities use. An order entry application requires that employees who enter orders have a computer and the necessary software to accomplish their business objective. In turn, the computer must be connected through the network to a database containing the order information so that the order can be saved and recalled later for processing. Infrastructure provides the necessary components to facilitate the order entry process.

Human resources involves the business activities associated with employee management, such as hiring, interview scheduling, payroll, and benefits management. Human resources is classified as a support activity because the primary activities cannot be accomplished without the employees to perform them. In other words, all the primary activities use the human resources business activity. For example, if a company needs a new customer service representative to serve the growing volume of customers, the request is processed through the HR function, which creates the job description and locates the appropriate person to fill the job.

Technology includes the design and development of applications that support the primary business activities. If you are planning on pursuing a career in the management information systems field, the technology business activity is likely where you will find a job. Technology can involve a wide array of responsibilities, such as the selection of packaged software or the design and development of a custom application to meet a particular business need. Many companies are leveraging the technology business activity to build Internet, intranet, and extranet applications for these purposes. As seen in previous chapters, companies use these systems to support a wide variety of primary business activities.

Procurement refers to the purchasing of goods and services that are required as inputs to the primary activities. Allowing each functional area to send out purchase orders can create problems for companies, such as maintaining relationships with more suppliers than necessary and not taking advantage of volume discounts. The procurement business activity can leverage information systems by accumulating purchase orders from the different functional areas within the corporation. By having this information at their disposal, procurement personnel can combine multiple purchase orders containing the same item into a single purchase order. Ordering larger volumes from its suppliers means that the company can achieve dramatic cost savings through volume discounts. Procurement receives, approves, and processes requests for goods and services from the primary activities and coordinates the purchase of those items. This allows the primary activities to concentrate on running the business rather than adding to their workload. See Figure 7.6 for a sample of the Oracle iProcurement software application.

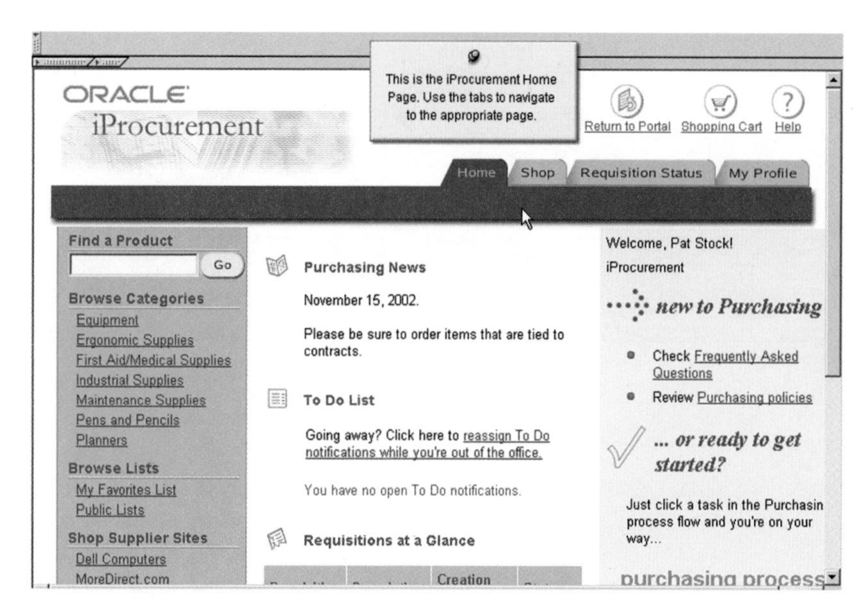

Figure 7.6 A sample of requisition management in Oracle's iProcurement software application.

Externally Focused Applications

The flow of information can be streamlined not only within a company but also outside organizational boundaries. A company can create additional value by integrating internal applications with suppliers, business partners, and customers. Companies accomplish this by connecting their internal value chains as a ***value system*** (Porter and Millar, 1985), in which information and goods flow from one company's value chain to another company's value chain. Figure 7.7 depicts the value system framework. In this diagram, three companies are aligning their value chains to form a value system. First, company A processes information through its value chain and forwards the information along to its customer, company B, which processes the information through its value chain and sends the information along to its customer, company C, which processes the

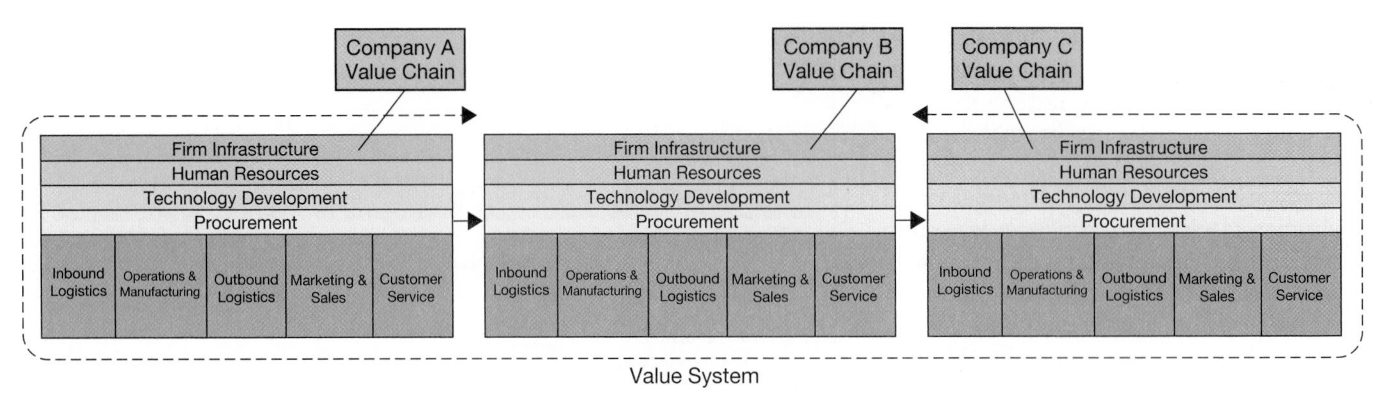

Figure 7.7 Value system framework.

Porter and Millar, 1985.

information through its value chain. Adding additional suppliers, business partners, and customers can create complex value systems. However, for our purposes, we simply view an organization's information systems as a value chain that interacts with the value chains of other organizations.

Externally focused systems can be used to coordinate a company's value chain with another company's value chain or with consumers (such as in business-to-consumer [B2C] electronic business). Any information that feeds into a company's value chain, whether its source is another company's value chain or an end consumer, is considered to be part of the value system. In other words, the value system for a particular organization acts like a vacuum cleaner, gathering information from the outside world.

The value system can be viewed as a river of information that flows from a source to an ultimate destination. Like a river, at any particular point there is a flow coming from ***upstream*** and progressing ***downstream***. Value systems comprise upstream and downstream information flows. An upstream information flow consists of information that is received from another organization, whereas a downstream information flow relates to the information that is produced by a company and sent along to another organization. For instance, using the value system depicted in Figure 7.7 as an example, the upstream and downstream information flows for company B become quite evident. In this case, company B receives information from its upstream supplier, processes the information through its internal value chain, and subsequently passes information downstream to its distributors and/or customers. These flows of external information into and from a company can be leveraged to create additional value and competitive advantage. Next, we will look at the enterprise systems used to support the processes and information flows we have talked about so far.

TYPES OF ENTERPRISE SYSTEMS

Enterprise systems come in two forms—packaged and custom. ***Packaged applications*** are software programs written by third-party vendors, whereas ***custom applications*** are software programs that are designed and developed by company personnel. Packaged applications that you are likely familiar with are Microsoft Money and Quicken, which allow users to purchase software off the shelf to help them with their financial matters. Packaged systems are highly useful for standardized, repetitive tasks such as making entries in a cheque register. They can be quite cost effective because the vendor that builds the software application can spread out development costs through selling to a large number of users.

Yet packaged applications may not be well suited for tasks that are unique to a particular business. In these cases, companies may prefer to develop (or have developed for them) custom applications that can accommodate their particular business needs. The development costs of custom systems are much higher than for packaged applications due to the time, money, and resources that are required to design and develop them. Furthermore, applications need to be maintained internally when changes are required. With packaged applications, the vendor makes the changes and distributes new versions to its customers. In all, there are tradeoffs when choosing between the packaged and custom application routes. Managers must consider whether packaged applications can meet the business requirements and, if not, conduct a cost-benefit analysis to ensure that taking the custom application approach will prove worthwhile to the company.

Figure 7.8 provides a high-level overview of how enterprise systems typically evolve. As companies begin to leverage information systems applications, they typically start out by fulfilling the needs of business activities in a particular department within the organization. Systems that focus on the specific needs of individual departments are not designed to communicate with other systems in the organization and are, therefore, referred to as ***stand-alone applications***. Stand-alone applications usually run on a variety of computing hardware platforms such as mainframes and minicomputers. Together, stand-alone applications and the computers they run on are often referred to as ***legacy systems***, given that they are typically older systems that are either fast approaching or beyond the end of their useful life within the organization. Legacy systems tend to require substantial resources to maintain them to accommodate emerging business needs (O'Leary, 2000).

Companies can gain several advantages by integrating and converting legacy systems so that information stored on separate computing platforms can be consolidated to provide a centralized point of access. The process of ***conversion*** transfers information stored on legacy systems to a new, integrated computing platform, which typically comes in the form of ***Enterprise Resource Planning (ERP)*** applications. The decision to adopt an ERP system must not be taken lightly, as such systems can create substantial organizational disruption, at least during the implementation period. For many large firms, however, the long-term benefits of ERP systems outweigh the short-term costs. After extensive research, Microsoft decided to implement an ERP application from SAP (see Brief Case: SAP Implementation at Microsoft). Although ERP applications do an excellent job of serving the needs of internal business operations on an organization-wide basis, they are not designed to completely accommodate the communication of information outside the organization's boundaries.

Systems that facilitate interorganizational communications focus on either the upstream or the downstream information flow. Because these systems coordinate business activities across organizational boundaries, they are classified as externally focused applications. ***Supply Chain Management (SCM)*** applications operate on the upstream information flows, integrating the value chains of a company and its suppliers. By contrast, ***Customer Relationship Management (CRM)*** applications concentrate on the downstream information flows, integrating the value chains of a company and its distributors. In some cases, companies deal directly with end consumers rather than selling products through distributors. Customer Relationship Management applications can also accommodate this scenario.

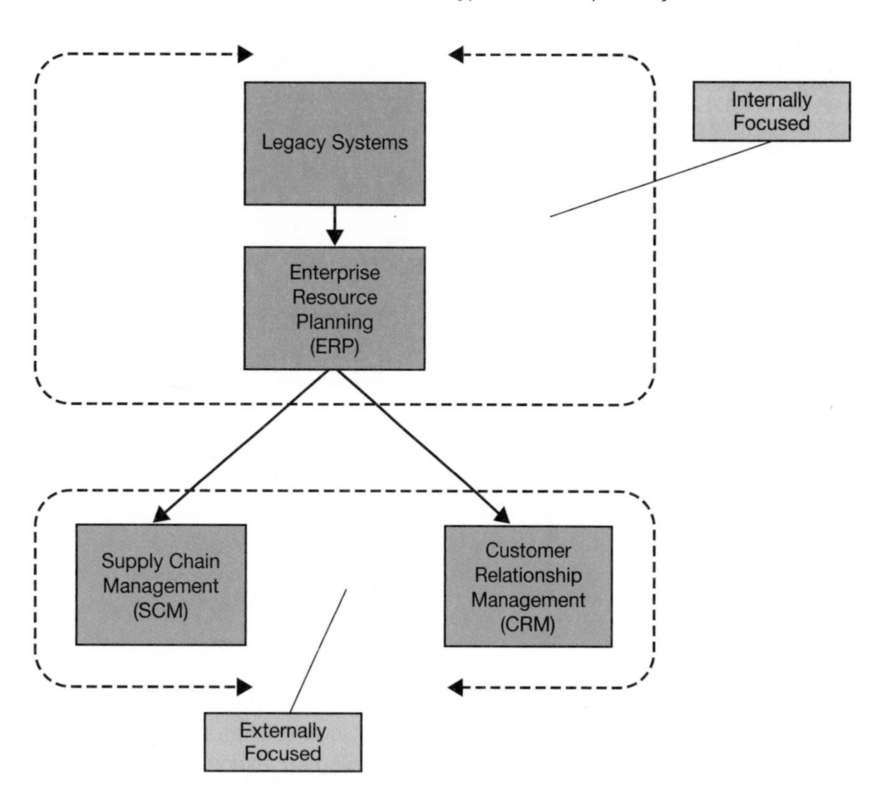

Figure 7.8 Stages of enterprise systems evolution.

Legacy Systems

When companies first use information systems to support business activities, they usually begin by implementing systems in various departments rather than starting with a single application that can accommodate all aspects of the business. Each department implements applications to assist it with its daily business activities, which are optimized for its unique needs and the manner in which personnel in a particular unit accomplish job tasks. These applications tend to be infrastructure-specific, meaning that they run on particular hardware and software platforms. As a result, each department normally has its own computing system that runs its necessary applications. Although departmental systems enable departments to conduct their daily business activities efficiently, these systems often are not very helpful when people from one part of the firm need information from another part of the firm (e.g., people in manufacturing need forecasts from sales).

BRIEF CASE SAP Implementation at Microsoft

Before implementing enterprise-wide information systems in the mid-1990s, Microsoft Corporation, the world's leading supplier of software applications, used a variety of legacy systems and stand-alone applications to support its internal operations. Some of these applications had been custom built internally, whereas others had been purchased as packaged software from outside vendors. All the applications ran on mainframe or midrange computing platforms. At the time, Microsoft maintained over 400 applications that used specialized user interfaces to access data from the various legacy systems. Integrating legacy systems in this way proved problematic for the company. As the applications grew more complex to accommodate the company's spectacular growth, integration became extremely difficult and expensive to maintain. Changes made to one legacy system commonly required extensive overhauls to the other legacy systems that were integrated with it. Furthermore, as the systems grew in complexity, the company found it more and more difficult to produce timely information to management, resulting in unacceptable delays during decision-making processes. Microsoft clearly needed an alternative approach to the manner in which it was supporting its internal business activities.

Seeing the need for an integrated, enterprise-wide solution, in 1992, Microsoft started to evaluate some enterprise system applications. During the next 2 years, the company proceeded further down the enterprise system path, yet did not have executive buy-in for the project, resulting in many delays. Management buy-in came in 1994, when the then vice-president of sales and support Steve Ballmer visited Wal-Mart, which was well respected in implementing information systems to support its internal business processes. Soon after, Microsoft selected SAP as its enterprise system vendor.

The first phase of the enterprise system implementation was to convert legacy systems supporting the company's financial activities to the new enterprise system environment. SAP's financial accounting (FI) module would be put to use to streamline Microsoft's financial processes, from initiating a transaction such as a purchase order to producing corporate financial statements. After realizing that some of its internal practices had become dated, the company decided to implement the FI module without customizations. This would require some reengineering of the company's financial business activities, but Microsoft wanted to experience the benefits of best practices that SAP had built into its software. Plus, by choosing not to customize the system, the company sidestepped many of the maintenance issues it had encountered with its custom legacy applications.

The implementation of the FI module was completed in 1996; it serves thousands of users at the company's headquarters in Redmond, Washington. Whereas it took Microsoft 3 weeks to put together its monthly financial statements when using its legacy systems, with the aid of the enterprise system package it took just 3 days to prepare the same statements. The time involved in processing payments to vendors was shortened dramatically, saving the company enormous sums of money while creating happy suppliers. Once the enterprise system was accepted at corporate headquarters, the system was rolled out over a 12-month period to thousands more financial users worldwide. Owing to the success of the SAP FI implementation, Microsoft decided to install SAP's HR module, and has, in addition to these, added modules for order management, sales and distribution/materials management, and SAP's Business Information Warehouse. Using SAP's enterprise system, Microsoft can better manage demand for its products and react more quickly to changes in demand; furthermore, in addition to increased revenue, Microsoft annually saves about $25 million due to the implementation of the enterprise system.

Questions

1. Why does a software giant like Microsoft rely on other companies to implement an enterprise system solution? Please be specific.
2. How does Microsoft benefit from implementing the system in different stages? If you have access to the Internet, read the full story and provide details from the case.

Source: Anonymous, "SAP: The Software That Drives Microsoft," *Case Study* (2001), **www.microsoft-sap.com/docs/Microsoft%2012pg%20Case%20Study.pdf**.

As previously described, given that these older systems are not designed to communicate with other applications beyond departmental boundaries, they are classified as "legacy" systems, or systems that operate within the confines of a particular business need. Legacy systems and their associated stand-alone applications can prove problematic when information from multiple departmental systems is required to make business decisions (as is often the case). For example, if the applications for inbound logistics and operations are not integrated, companies will lose valuable time in accessing information related to inventory levels. When an order is placed through operations, personnel need to verify that the components are available in inventory before the order can be processed.

If the inventory and order-entry systems are not integrated, personnel may have to access two separate applications. Furthermore, if these applications reside on different computing platforms, personnel must have two separate pieces of hardware on their desks to accomplish their duties. Figure 7.9 provides an example of how information flows through legacy systems within an organization.

As the diagram depicts, information is generated by the inbound logistics business activity, but it does not flow through to the next business activity, in this case operations. Because the inbound logistics and operations departments use different legacy systems, information cannot readily flow from one business activity to another. Understandably, this creates a highly inefficient process for operations personnel, who must have access to two systems to get both the order entry and the inventory information. For instance, if the inventory application is running on an IBM mainframe system and the order entry application is running on a UNIX-based minicomputer, operations personnel must have access to both the IBM mainframe and the UNIX systems. This may mean installing two separate terminals at an employee's desk so that the employee can view the information from both systems at the same time. In some cases, inventory information may be stored on both systems, creating the potential for inaccuracies. Should data be updated in one system but not in the other system, the data become outdated and inaccurate. In addition, there are further, unnecessary costs associated with entering, storing, and updating data redundantly.

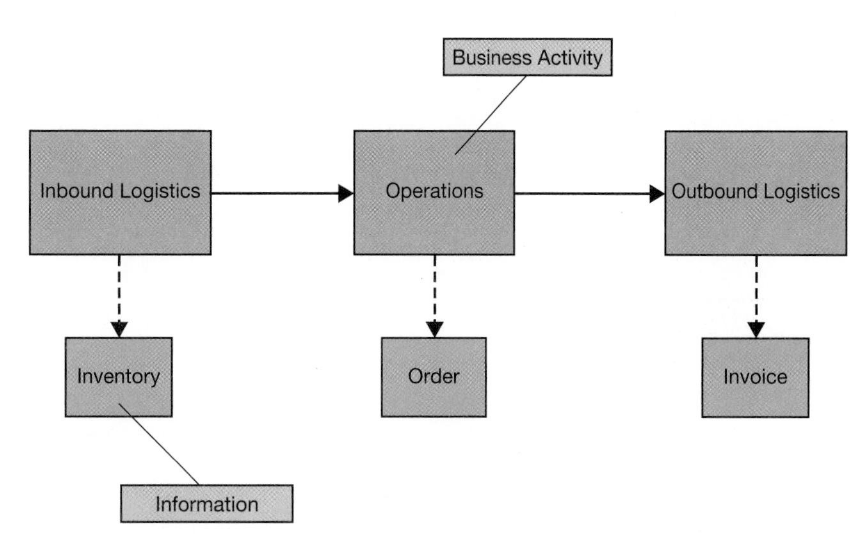

Figure 7.9 Information flow using legacy systems.

Enterprise Resource Planning

When companies realize that legacy systems can create dramatic inefficiencies within their organizations, the next step is to integrate legacy information on a company-wide basis. As previously described, applications that integrate business activities across departmental boundaries are often referred to as ERP systems. In the 1990s we witnessed companies' initial push to implement integrated applications, as exhibited by skyrocketing ERP sales at that time. Be aware that the terms "resource" and "planning" do not accurately describe the purpose of ERP, because these applications do very little in the way of planning or managing resources (Koch, Slater, and Baatz, 2000). The reason for the term "ERP" is that these systems evolved in part during the 1990s from Material Requirements Planning (MRP) packages. Do not get hung up on the words "resource" and "planning." The key word to remember from the acronym ERP is "enterprise."

Integrating Data to Integrate Applications

Enterprise Resource Planning takes stand-alone applications a step further by providing a common data warehouse and similar application interfaces that service the entire enterprise rather than portions of it. Information stored on legacy systems is converted into large, centralized data repositories known as data warehouses (see Chapter 3 for more information on data warehouses). Data warehouses are databases that store information related to the various business activities of an organization. Data warehouses alleviate the problems associated with multiple computing platforms by

Web Search

Visit the ERP jobs website at **www.erp-jobs.com** and see what types of career opportunities are currently available that are ERP-related. Which packages and skills do companies appear to be looking for? Prepare a short report about which ERP jobs are currently needed most.

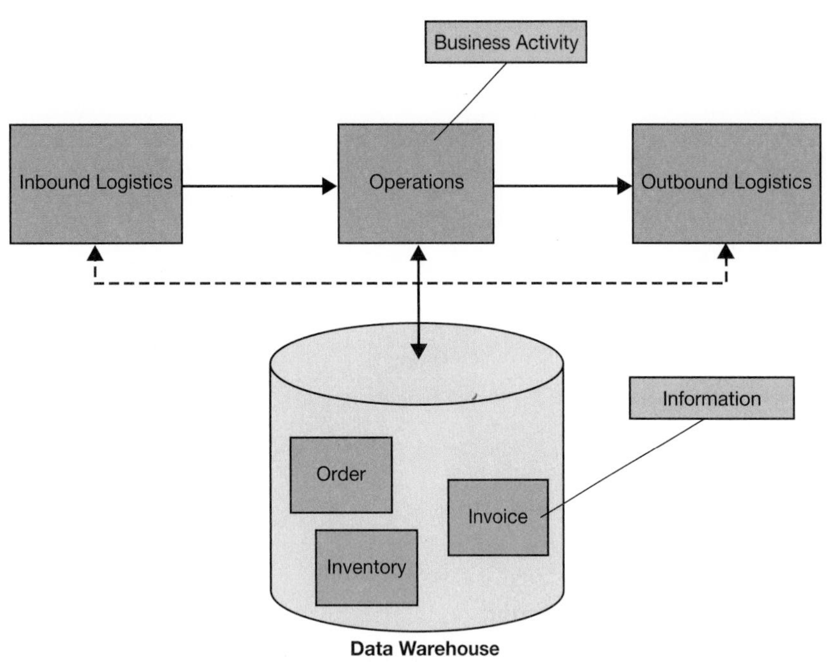

Figure 7.10 Information storage using an ERP solution.

providing a single place where all information relevant to the company and particular departments can be stored and accessed, as depicted in Figure 7.10.

In contrast to legacy systems, where it is difficult to share information between business activities, ERP applications make accessing information easier by providing a central information repository. Where an ERP solution is used, both inbound logistics and operations have access to inventory data because both business activities have access to the same pieces of information. Rather than information's flowing from one department to the next, data can be accessed and updated at will, meaning that the next business activity can access information in the data warehouse whenever it needs to. This gives personnel access to accurate, real-time information. The beauty of ERP lies in the fact that information can be shared throughout the organization. For example, inventory information is accessible not only to inbound logistics and operations, but also to accounting and customer service personnel. If a customer calls in wondering about the status of an order, customer service representatives can find out by accessing the data warehouse through the ERP application. Prior to the emergence of ERP, customer service representatives may have had to retrieve information from two or more separate computing systems, making their job extremely difficult while potentially resulting in dissatisfied customers. Storing data in a single place and making it available to everyone within the organization empowers everyone in the organization to be aware of the current state of business and to perform their jobs better.

Enterprise Resource Planning applications that access the data warehouse are designed to have the same look and feel, regardless of the unique needs of a particular department. Inbound logistics and operations personnel will use a common user interface to access the same pieces of information from the data warehouse. Although the inbound logistics screens and the operations screens will have different features tailored to the unique needs of the business activity, the screens will look comparable, with similar designs, screen layouts, menu options, and so on. The Microsoft Office products provide a useful analogy. Microsoft Word and Microsoft Excel are designed to serve separate functions (word processing and spreadsheets, respectively), but overall the products look and feel very similar to one another. Word and Excel have similar user interfaces and simply differ in the features and functionality that each application offers.

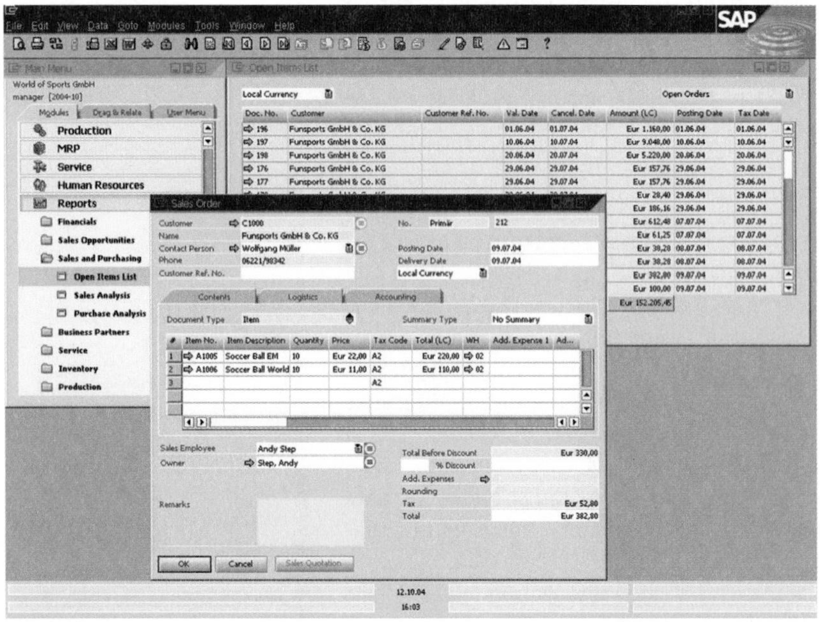

Figure 7.11 SAP is one of the most popular ERP products worldwide.

Source: SAP software **www.sap.com**

Choosing an Enterprise Resource Planning System

Enterprise Resource Planning systems are packaged applications that are purchased from software vendors. ERP vendors include SSA Baan, Oracle, Microsoft, and SAP among others. SAP (see Figure 7.11) continues to be the market leader in this segment and has become one of the largest software suppliers in the world, together with software behemoths Microsoft, Oracle, and Computer Associates. SAP now boasts 12 million users and 76 100 installations (see SAP website at **www.sap.com**). Are you interested in seeing what an ERP system actually looks like? SAP has a series on online demos of its growing line of ERP solutions for small and medium-sized businesses, called Business One (**www.sap.com/solutions/sme/businessone/demos/index.epx**).

Oracle, the world's second largest enterprise software supplier, started out in 1977 as a database vendor and grew into an ERP vendor by developing integrated applications that access information stored in the data warehouse. Interestingly, Oracle not only sells ERP software, but also continues to sell its popular database management software, which serves as the database engine underlying many of the other ERP products. In recent years, Oracle's share of the ERP market has grown with the acquisition of vendors such as PeopleSoft and J.D. Edwards.

Microsoft has traditionally been dominant in the desktop and small business computing market segments. However, for many years the company has set its sights on the lucrative midsize and enterprise application markets. Recently, the company consolidated many of its mid-market ERP products into a suite of products collectively called Microsoft Dynamics. At the same time that Microsoft is moving to the mid and enterprise-market levels, SAP is moving its product focus from the enterprise to the mid market, thus creating an interesting competitive landscape for ERP software.

When selecting an appropriate ERP application for a company, management needs to take many factors into careful consideration. Enterprise Resource Planning applications come as packaged software, which means a one-size-fits-all strategy. However, businesses have unique needs even within their own industries. In other words, like snowflakes, no two companies are exactly alike. Management must carefully select an ERP application that will meet the unique requirements of the particular company. Companies must consider some factors in the ERP selection. Among the most prevalent issues facing management are control, business requirements, and best practices (Ptak, 2000).

Control refers to the locus of control over the computing systems and decision making regarding these systems. Companies typically either opt for centralized control or allow particular business units to govern themselves. In the context of ERP, these decisions are based on the level of detail in the information that must be provided to management. Some corporations want to have as much detail as possible made available at the executive level, whereas other companies do not require such access. For instance, an accountant in one company may want the ability to view costs down to the level of individuals' transactions, whereas an accountant in another company may want only summary information. Another area related to control involves the consistency of policies and procedures. Some companies prefer that policies and procedures remain consistent throughout an organization. Other companies want to allow each business unit to develop its own policies and procedures to accommodate the unique ways that they do business. Enterprise Resource Planning applications vary widely in their allowance for control, typically assuming either a corporate or a business-unit locus of control. Some ERP applications allow users to select or customize the locus of control. In either case, management must consider the ERP's stance on control to ensure it will meet the business requirements of the company.

Owing to the fact that all companies are different, no packaged software application will exactly fit the unique requirements of a particular business. Enterprise Resource Planning applications come in a variety of shapes and sizes, each designed to accommodate certain transaction volumes and business activities. For example, Oracle and SAP ERP applications can potentially accommodate thousands of users if needed. As far as supporting various business activities is concerned, ERP systems can include a wide variety of features and functionality. Each function is classified as a component, and components are often bundled together to form software ***modules***. The ERP modules provided by each ERP vendor vary in the specific functions that they provide, as well as what they are called. Tables 7.2 and 7.3 outline the key SAP software tools and capabilities.

Table 7.2 ***Key components of the mySAP business suite.***

mySAP Customer Relationship Mgmt
mySAP ERP
mySAP Product Lifecycle Mgmt
mySAP Supplier Relationship Mgmt
mySAP Supply Chain Mgmt

Table 7.3 ***Key capabilities of mySAP ERP.***

Capability	Explanation
Business analysis	Enables you to evaluate your business performance by taking advantage of functionality for analyzing your workforce, operations, and supply chain.
Financial and management accounting	Allows you to manage corporate finance functions by automating financial supply chain management, financial accounting, and management accounting. This capability is enabled by mySAP ERP Financials.
Human capital management	Gives you the tools you need to maximize the profitability potential of your workforce, with functionality for employee transaction management and employee life-cycle management. This capability is enabled by mySAP ERP Human Capital Management.
Operations management	Empowers you to streamline operations with integrated functionality for managing end-to-end logistics processes—while expanding your collaborative capabilities in supply chain management, product life-cycle management, and supplier relationship management. This capability is enabled by mySAP ERP Operations.
Corporate services management	Allows you to optimize centralized and decentralized services for managing real estate, corporate travel, and incentives and commissions. This capability is enabled by mySAP ERP Corporate Services.
Self-services	Provides an employee-centric portal that enables both employees and managers to create, view, and modify key information. Uses a broad range of interaction technologies, including web browser, voice, and mobile devices, for easy access to internal and external business content, applications, and services.

As evidenced by Tables 7.2 and 7.3, it is critical for managers to understand the vendors' naming conventions and software modules to gain an understanding of how these features can be implemented to meet the requirements of the business's activities. The features and modules that the ERP comes with out of the box are referred to as the ***vanilla*** version. If the vanilla version does not support a certain business process, the software may require ***customizations*** to accommodate it. Customizations either provide additional software that is integrated with the ERP or direct changes to the vanilla ERP application itself. SAP, for example, includes literally thousands of elements in its ERP software that can be customized, and also offers many industry-specific versions of its software that have already been customized for a particular industry based on SAP's perceptions of the best way to do things in that industry (i.e., best practices). Companies must take special care when dealing with customization issues. Customizations can be costly, and maintaining and upgrading customizations can be troublesome. For example, a customization made to the vanilla version will need to be reprogrammed when a new release of the ERP is implemented. This is due to the fact that subsequent releases of the ERP do not contain the necessary logic embedded in the customizations. In other words, new vanilla versions must be continually upgraded to accommodate the customization. This process can involve a substantial investment of time and resources. Sometimes, the cost of these changes can be too much. London Drugs, based in Richmond, B.C., decided to drop its Peoplesoft ERP system (now part of Oracle) because the level of customization required became cost prohibitive. Instead, the firm decided to adopt a package specifically developed for the retail environment.

One of the major hurdles posed to companies that implement ERP applications involves changing business processes to accommodate the manner in which the software works. Enterprise Resource Planning implementations are often used as a catalyst for overall improvement of underlying business processes. ERP applications are designed to operate according to industry-standard business processes, known as ***best practices***. Many ERP vendors build best practices into their applications to provide guidelines for management to identify business activities within their organizations that need to be streamlined. Implementations typically go more smoothly when companies change their business practices to fit the way the ERP software operates.

Many organizations have spent many years developing business practices that provide them with a competitive advantage in the marketplace. Adopting their industry's best practices may force these companies to abandon their unique ways of doing business, putting them on par with their industry competitors. In other words, companies can potentially lose their competitive advantages by adapting the "best practices" within their industry. "Best practices" is an area that managers must carefully consider before selecting an ERP application. Some ERP vendors tightly integrate best practices into the software, and companies that reject best practices are in for a long and time-consuming implementation. Other vendors provide a series of options that companies select before implementing the software, allowing them some (but not complete) flexibility in changing their business processes to accommodate the ERP application. Given the importance and difficulty of changing business processes with ERP and other systems implementations, we describe business process change in more detail in the next section.

Business Process Reengineering

Business Process Reengineering (BPR) is a systematic, structured improvement approach by all or part of an organization whereby people critically examine, rethink, and redesign business processes in order to achieve dramatic improvements in one or more performance measures such as quality, cycle time, or cost. BPR was very popular in the early 1990s, when Michael Hammer and James Champy published their best selling book *Reengineering the Corporation*. In Table 7.4 we present a list of some related approaches for improving organizations.

Table 7.4 ***Some other terms closely related to Business Process Reengineering.***

Business Process Redesign
Business Process Improvement
Functional Process Improvement
Business Process Management (BPM)
Business Architecture Modernization (BAM)
Business Activity Modelling
Business Activity Monitoring
Workflow Management

Hammer and Champy and their proponents argued that radical redesign of an organization is sometimes necessary to lower costs and increase quality and that information technology is the key enabler for that radical change. The basic steps in reengineering can be summarized as follows:

- Develop a vision for the organization that specifies business objectives such as reducing costs, shortening the time it takes to take products to market, improving quality of products and/or services, and so on.
- Identify the critical processes that are to be redesigned.
- Understand and measure the existing processes as a baseline for future improvements.
- Identify ways that information technology can be used to improve processes.
- Design and implement a prototype of the new process(es).

Business Process Reengineering is like quality improvement approaches such as Total Quality Management and Continuous Process Improvement in that they are intended to be cross-functional approaches to improve an organization. BPR differs from these quality improvement approaches, however, in one fundamental way. Quality improvement approaches tend to focus on incremental change and gradual improvement of processes, whereas the intention behind reengineering is radical redesign and drastic improvement of processes.

Many BPR efforts were reported to have failed, and BPR gained the reputation of being a nice way of saying "downsizing." It is generally believed that these efforts failed because of lack of sustained management commitment and leadership, unrealistic scope and expectations, and resistance to change. Business Process Reengineering lives on and is still a relatively popular approach to improving organizations. The conditions that appear to lead to successful BPR implementations include support by senior management, shared vision, realistic expectations, participants empowered to reengineer, the right people participating, sound management practices, and appropriate funding. In any event, it is clear that business process change, in one form or another, continues to be necessary. Process reengineering and process management continue to thrive, led by vendors such as Savvion and consultants such as Accenture.

A growing useful body of research evidence on ERP implementations suggests that these BPR and related organizational issues are just as important as are the ERP technical implementation issues (Kumar and Van Hillegersberg, 2000; Markus and Tanis, 2000). Indeed, in order to be successful, in some situations managers must literally choose between either making the ERP system fit the organization or making the organization fit the ERP system (Soh, Sia, and Tay-Yap, 2000). Others have suggested that for the ERP system to help you transform the organization and gain new competitive capabilities, a full organizational and operational change process is required (Willcocks and Sykes, 2000). Finally, there is some evidence that, to be successful, managers must, in fact, first transform the organization and then implement the ERP system (Sarker and Lee, 2000). In any event, the evidence suggests that these organizational change issues are very important in the implementation of ERP and other enterprise-wide information systems.

WHEN THINGS GO WRONG

Ready to Sever: Sobeys Dumps SAP

Canadian grocery giant Sobeys said it has no plans to reconsider its decision to pull the plug on its year-old, SAP-powered ERP system. The Stellarton, Nova Scotia–based company claims the system caused its database to crash in early December 2000, leaving it unable to process the transactions moving through the stores' systems. Bill McEwan, Sobeys' chief executive, said the problem created a 5-week backlog just before the holiday shopping period.

The second largest supermarket chain in Canada, Sobeys has 400 company stores and 1000 franchise stores including IGA, Foodland, and Price Chopper outlets. On 24 January 2001, McEwan announced that the company was ditching the software because it couldn't handle its ordering and data processing needs for its stores in Ontario and Atlantic Canada. However, SAP officials said they only learned of the decision through a press release issued 2 days before a scheduled meeting with Sobeys brass.

"We're both surprised and disappointed by the announcement made by Sobeys," said William Wohl, spokesperson for SAP America in Philadelphia. "We've had such a good dialogue with Sobeys all along." Despite attempts by SAP to repair the relationship, Sobeys officials were adamant that the ERP project would be dismantled.

"It was a situation where we had a business disruption. We looked at an evaluation of our enterprise-wide software and that resulted in the decision, so I would be surprised if there was a change in conclusion," said Stewart Mahoney, vice-president of treasury and investor relations for Empire Company Ltd., which owns 62 percent of Sobeys.

"We indicated we plan to move ahead without SAP, and Mr. McEwan and the Sobeys' board of directors were quite clear in terms of Sobeys coming to that conclusion," he said. Mahoney added that the project would cost the company $89.1 million and that Sobeys was predicting the interruption of business would cut its quarterly operating profit by 16 cents a share. "We're through with that period. But there was an opportunity cost there because that's a busy period for us leading up to the Christmas rush," Mahoney said.

SAP had been working with the company before this project, implementing an HR and financial system. In fact, SAP and IBM were using Sobeys as an example of a satisfied customer.

"Overall, SAP has a good record of getting sizing performance right. But within the retail sector there have been projects which run into problems due to the very high volumes and narrow time windows involved," said Derek Prior, SAP research director with Stamford, Connecticut–based Gartner Group Inc. "You don't hear of these failures frequently. The successes are much higher, but successes aren't news."

Source: Adapted from Jennifer Brown, "Sobeys Fires SAP over ERP Debacle," *Computing Canada*, Vol. 27, No. 3 (February 9, 2001).

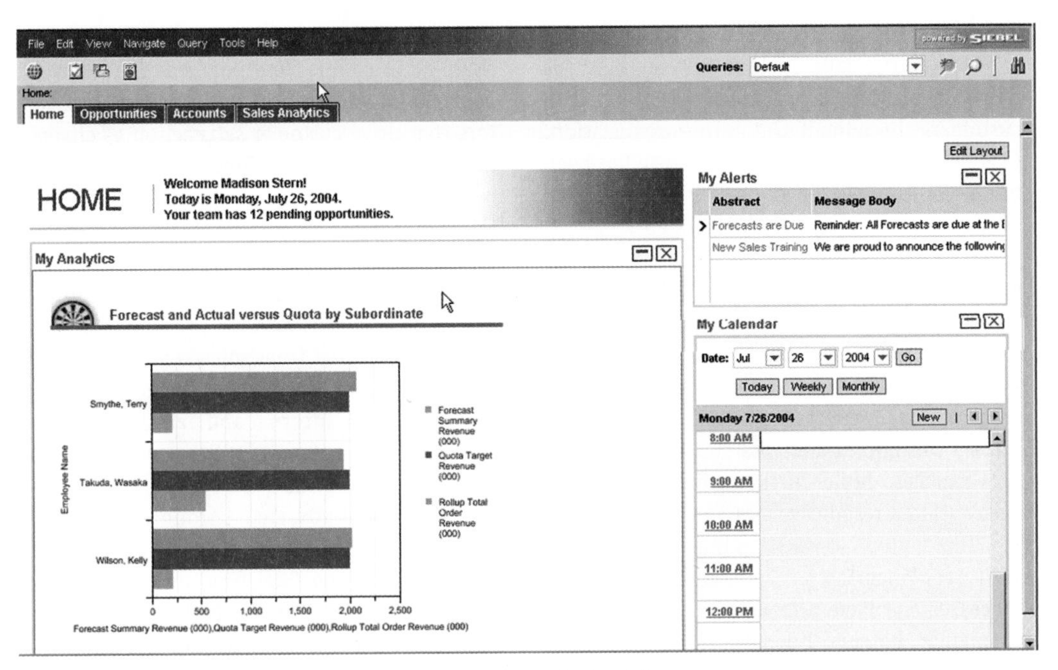

Figure 7.12 Sample screen from Siebel Marketing and Analytics Software.

While ERP helps companies to integrate systems across the organization, it falls short in communicating across organizational boundaries (Larson and Rogers, 1998). Because ERP applications are designed to service internal business activities, they tend not to be well suited for managing value system activities. Sometimes, ERP systems can even do more harm than good. For example, Halifax-based grocery chain Sobeys decided to pull out of an ERP implementation project with SAP after the software clashed with its internal legacy systems (see When Things Go Wrong: Ready to Sever: Sobeys Dumps SAP).

Companies wanting to integrate their value chains with the business activities of their suppliers, business partners, and customers typically choose to implement systems other than ERP to manage the upstream and/or downstream flow of information. These types of applications, designed to coordinate activities outside organizational boundaries, are discussed in the following sections.

Customer Relationship Management

With the changes introduced by the web, in most industries a company's competition is simply a mouse click away. It is increasingly important for companies not only to generate new business but also to attract repeat business. This means that to remain competitive, companies must keep their customers satisfied. In today's highly competitive markets, customers hold the balance of power because if they become dissatisfied with the levels of customer service they are receiving, they have many alternatives readily available. The global nature of the web has affected companies worldwide in virtually all industries. An economic transformation is taking place, shifting the emphasis from conducting business transactions to managing relationships. Vendors such as Oracle argue that the cost of trying to get back customers that have gone elsewhere can be up to 50–100 times as much as keeping a current one satisfied (see Figure 7.12 for a look at Oracle's Siebel CRM software). Companies are finding it imperative to develop and maintain customer satisfaction and develop deeper relationships with their customers to compete effectively in their markets.

How Customer Relationship Management Applications Work

Applications focusing on downstream information flows have two main objectives in mind—to attract potential customers and create customer loyalty. The process of attracting potential customers, or prospects, can be streamlined by implementing ***Sales Force Automation (SFA)*** applications, which mainly focus on contact management and scheduling. Sales Force Automation applications provide salespeople with computerized support tools to assist them in their daily routines. SFA focuses on pre-sales marketing and sales functions, whereas CRM applications go beyond SFA by offering post-sales support activities as well. Customer Relationship Management offers a completely integrated approach to customer management. CRM suites typically include SFA modules, as well as the ability to track activities related to customers throughout the entire organization. CRM helps close the loop once the sale has been made. For example, once a sale has been made, CRM can retrieve information related to a customer's order, such as identifying where the order is in the pipeline, whether it be in manufacturing, in the warehouse, or in the process of being shipped. CRM also integrates the multiple ways that companies interact with customers, such as e-mail and call centres. By providing exactly the information the customer requests, CRM can help build customer loyalty through demonstrated responsiveness.

The appropriate CRM technology combined with reengineering of sales-related business processes can have a tremendous impact on a company's bottom line. Oracle argues that improving customer satisfaction by 1 percent a year over a 5-year period can result in increases of more than 10 percent in return on investment over the period. To pursue customer satisfaction as a basis for achieving competitive advantage, organizations must be able to access information and track customer interactions throughout the organization, regardless of where, when, or how the interaction occurs. This means that companies need to have an integrated system that captures information from retail stores, websites, call centres, and various other ways that organizations communicate downstream within their value chain. More importantly, managers need the capability to monitor and analyze factors that drive customer satisfaction as changes occur according to prevailing market conditions.

Sources for Customer Relationship Management Applications

Customer Relationship Management applications come in the form of packaged software that is purchased from software vendors. CRM applications are commonly integrated with ERP to leverage internal and external information to serve customers. CRM vendors include E.piphany, Firepond (see Figure 7.13), Onyx Software, and Oracle, through its Siebel Systems brand. ERP vendors such as SAP are also entering the CRM fray, enhancing their enterprise solutions to include CRM. Like Enterprise Resource Planning, CRM applications come with various features and modules. Management must carefully select a CRM application that will meet the unique requirements of their particular company. In general, CRM applications are modularized along two lines—sales and service. Sales modules include SFA functions, which are designed to assist companies with the pre-sales aspects of the business activities, such as marketing and prospecting. Service modules help companies with the post-sales customer service aspects of their business.

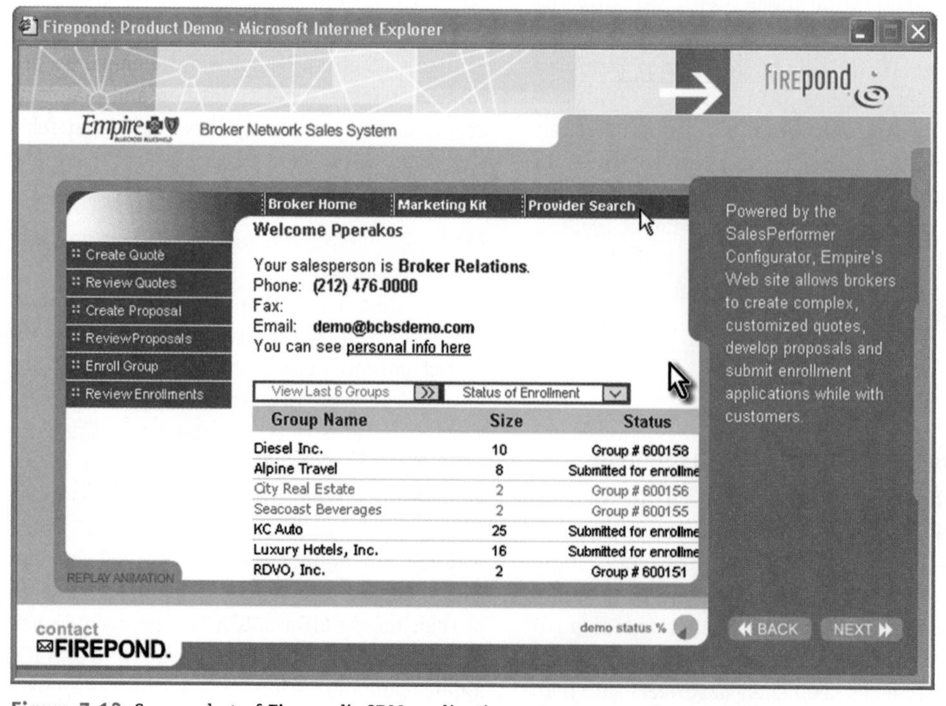

Figure 7.13 Screen shot of Firepond's CRM application.

Source: Firepond, 2001.

BRIEF CASE

Filling Cruise Ships Through E-Mail: CRM at Princess Cruises

The cruise ship industry is a multibillion-dollar industry; over the past years, both demand for and supply of cruises have increased rapidly. Unfortunately, the growing number of cruise liners has led to increased competition, and companies such as Princess Cruises have to fight harder than ever to keep their loyal customer base, especially due to slumps in the cruise ship sector after 11 September 2001 and the onset of the wars against terrorism. Princess Cruises, located in Miami, Florida, currently employs 12 000 people supporting the company's 12 cruise ships, which carry more than 1.1 million guests each year; another four ships are scheduled for delivery in 2007, increasing the company's capacity even more.

As long-term customers are often considered to be the most important type of guests for cruise lines or resort hotels, companies have to invest heavily in technology to retain these customers. E-mail provides a cost-effective way to target customers with up-to-date information about current offers and promotions or upcoming cruises. Traditionally, companies have used regular mail for this type of communications; however, customers are increasingly opting for receiving this news through e-mail. Setting up an e-mail solution for Princess Cruises meant that it had to be seamlessly integrated with its Siebel CRM and SFA solutions that were already in place. In addition to being able to handle periodic mailings on a very large scale, the system had to be able to send out last-minute campaigns to fill ships before they leave port. Therefore, Princess Cruises' marketing department had to be able to quickly locate potential guests for these cruises and target them with personalized e-mails.

To handle these requirements, Princess Cruises chose to implement Dynamic Messenger by Dynamics Direct. Because of the implementation of the system, Princess Cruises' e-mail marketing campaigns have increased by 210 percent. Furthermore, it is estimated that marketing employees spend about 50 percent less time in preparing these campaigns. In addition to these benefits, Princess Cruises' customers benefit from this solution, as they do not receive multiple messages about offers for trips they have declined or already signed up for.

Questions

1. How can e-mail of CRM help companies like Princess Cruises obtain a competitive advantage?
2. Many people are choosing to receive promotional e-mails to receive less junk mail in their postal mailbox; however, opting in to receive e-mails from many companies can lead to a flood of promotional e-mails in the e-mail inbox. Under which conditions can e-mails be used to effectively communicate offers and promotions to customers? Use details from the case to illustrate your points.

Sources: Anonymous, "Princess Cruises: Cruise Line Casts a Customized Net with New E-Mail Relationship Management Solution," *Microsoft Case Study* (August 13, 2003), **www.microsoft.com/resources/casestudies/CaseStudy.asp?CaseStudyID=14363**.

The service side of CRM brings with it many opportunities to gain competitive advantage by providing customized, individual attention to existing customers. However, facilitating premium customer service requires a great deal of coordination because customers can interact with a company across multiple channels and through different personnel within the organization. MGM Mirage, which operates the Mirage, MGM Grand, Bellagio, Treasure Island, Golden Nugget, and Beau Rivage casinos and resorts, has deployed CRM to help it design marketing campaigns, such as seasonal promotions and special events, for its existing customers. With the gaming industry growing exponentially, the market has become highly competitive, and MGM Mirage needed an advantage. Customer information—including gambling activities, lodging preferences, and purchase histories—from all of its properties can be consolidated, providing management with a comprehensive, real-time view of market conditions. With accurate, real-time information, management can make decisions more efficiently than their competitors and design targeted marketing campaigns that work. Similarly, American Airlines, one of the nation's largest commercial airline carriers, uses CRM to personalize products and services for its most loyal frequent flyers by giving them rewards for their patronage and increasing repeat business with its most profitable customers. Sony of Canada used mySAP CRM to manage its 2005 holiday marketing campaign.

The software allowed Sony of Canada to customize its marketing messages and focus on very precise consumer segments.

Marriott International, one of the world's largest hotel and resort corporations, built its marketing philosophy around creating a superior experience for its customers. The company implemented Oracle's Siebel CRM solution to accomplish just that. One way that Marriott achieved this goal was through the development of a program called Personal Planning Service, which allows the company to create personalized vacation itineraries for guests at the time a reservation is made. When a customer returns for a visit to any one of the Marriott's properties, an itinerary is built, based on customer requests and preference information stored in the CRM application. For example, when a customer arrives at one of Marriott's resorts, the company has scheduled client activities such as tee times, dinner reservations, and tours well in advance of the customer's stay. Marriott's CRM success has resulted in higher customer satisfaction and an increase of $100 per visitor in service revenues beyond the room rate.

Companies that have successfully implemented CRM can experience greater customer satisfaction and increase productivity in their sales and service personnel, translating into dramatic enhancements to the company's profitability. CRM allows organizations to focus on driving revenue as well as streamlining costs, as opposed to emphasizing cost cutting alone. Cost cutting tends to have a lower limit because there are only so many costs that companies can streamline, whereas revenue generation strategies are bound only by the size of the market itself. The National Quality Research Center estimates that a 1 percent increase in customer satisfaction can lead to a threefold increase in a company's market capitalization.

Supply Chain Management

In the previous section we looked downstream at CRM applications. Now we turn our attention upstream. Getting the raw materials and components that a company uses in its daily operations is an important key to business success. When deliveries from suppliers are accurate and timely, companies can convert them to finished products more efficiently. Coordinating this effort with suppliers has become a central part of companies' overall business strategies, as it can help them to reduce costs associated with inventory levels and to get new products to market more quickly. Ultimately, this helps companies drive profitability and improve their customer service, as they can react to changing market

ETHICAL DILEMMA

Targeting or Discriminating? Ethical Pitfalls of Customer Relationship Management

Customer Relationship Management—a marketer's dream. CRM systems promise companies the capability of getting to know their customers and maximizing the benefit gained from every customer. With the use of sophisticated tools, CRM software can help to analyze customer data and carve out even finer market segments. Once segmented, customers can be targeted with very specific "special offers" or promotions. For the company, this helps to reap the greatest returns from its marketing efforts, as only those customers are targeted who are likely to respond to the marketing campaign.

From a consumer's perspective, CRM systems seem like a good idea. Finally, you stop receiving advertisements for stuff that doesn't interest you. However, what if a company uses the CRM software in a more discriminating way? More sophisticated computer hardware and software allows companies to analyze more and more data about customers, which in turn helps to provide more individualized offers to each customer. Where do companies draw the line between offering certain clients customized deals and discriminating against others? What if companies use CRM tools in a less than ethical way? Consider the case of banks, which have the ability to segment their customers according to their credit worthiness and can use this data to target customers having a low credit rating. Although these customers are more risky for the banks, the higher fees and interest for credit make these customers especially lucrative. Would you call this a healthy relationship?

Sources: Alain Jourdier, "Too Close for Comfort," *CIO* (May 1, 2002), **www.cio.com/archive/050102/reality.html.**

GLOBAL PERSPECTIVE

CRM Sweeping Asia

With the opening of new markets such as China to Western companies, businesses in different industry sectors are trying to gain a foothold in these markets in an attempt to outpace their competitors. For example, companies in the automobile sector have already formed joint ventures with Chinese companies; as in their U.S. or European manufacturing plants, sophisticated Supply Chain Management (SCM) and ERP software tools are used to manage the production process. While software giants such as SAP or Oracle have so far provided SCM and ERP software to large, multinational companies in China, the market for small and medium businesses (SMEs) businesses with less than $250 million in revenue) has remained largely untapped.

As Chinese SMEs are starting to see the benefits of deploying enterprise software packages, neither international nor domestic software companies want to lose out on potentially huge revenues. A recent study has forecasted the supply-chain management market in China to grow by 10 percent per year until the year 2010. In tapping into this lucrative market, the international and domestic software companies face different challenges. A lack of expertise in building enterprise systems leads Chinese software companies to acquire European and North American companies that possess the necessary expertise. Recently, chinadotcom, a Chinese software company, acquired Ross Systems Inc. for $68.9 million to add SCM software to its portfolio of offerings. With this and other recent acquisitions, chinadotcom expects the annual revenues to more than double to $235–$300 million.

International software companies face a different problem, namely the prices of their software suites. Although revenues from doing business with Chinese SMEs still contribute only very little to the overall revenues of companies such as Oracle, SAP, or i2, these companies have to offer their products and services to Chinese businesses in order not to lose market share to their Chinese competitors. However, while Oracle's system tailored to the needs of SMEs costs about $75 000, Chinese companies can offer enterprise software at a much lower price by using cheaper domestic labour to program these systems; therefore, Oracle, i2, or SAP constantly must look for new ways to lower the costs of developing enterprise systems for these markets. No matter who wins the battle for the biggest market share, considering the predicted growth of the enterprise software market in China, fighting for it is likely to be well worth it.

Source: Laurie Sullivan, "Vendors Face Off in China," *InformationWeek* (April 26, 2004). **www.informationweek.com/story/showArticle.jhtml?articleID=19200109&pgno=1.**

conditions swiftly. Collaborating, or sharing information, with suppliers has become a strategic necessity for business success. By developing and maintaining stronger, more integrated relationships with suppliers, companies can more effectively compete in their markets through cost reductions and responsiveness to market demands.

The term ***supply chain*** is commonly used to refer to the producers of supplies that a company uses. Companies procure specific raw materials and components from many different suppliers. These suppliers, in turn, work with their suppliers to obtain goods; their suppliers work with additional suppliers, and so forth. The further out in the supply chain one looks, the more and more suppliers are involved. As a result, the term "chain" becomes somewhat of a misnomer as it implies one-to-one relationships facilitating a chain of events flowing from the first supplier to the second to the third, and so on. A more descriptive term to describe the flow of materials from suppliers to a company is ***supply network*** because multiple suppliers are involved in the process of servicing a single organization. Figure 7.14 depicts a typical supply network.

Several problems can arise when firms within a supply network do not collaborate effectively. Information can easily become distorted as it moves from one company down through the supply network, causing a great deal of inefficiency. Problems such as excessive inventories, inaccurate manufacturing capacity plans, and missed production schedules can run rampant. These issues can lead to degradations in profitability and poor customer service. Implementing software applications to manage a company's activities with its supply network can help alleviate these barriers to competitiveness.

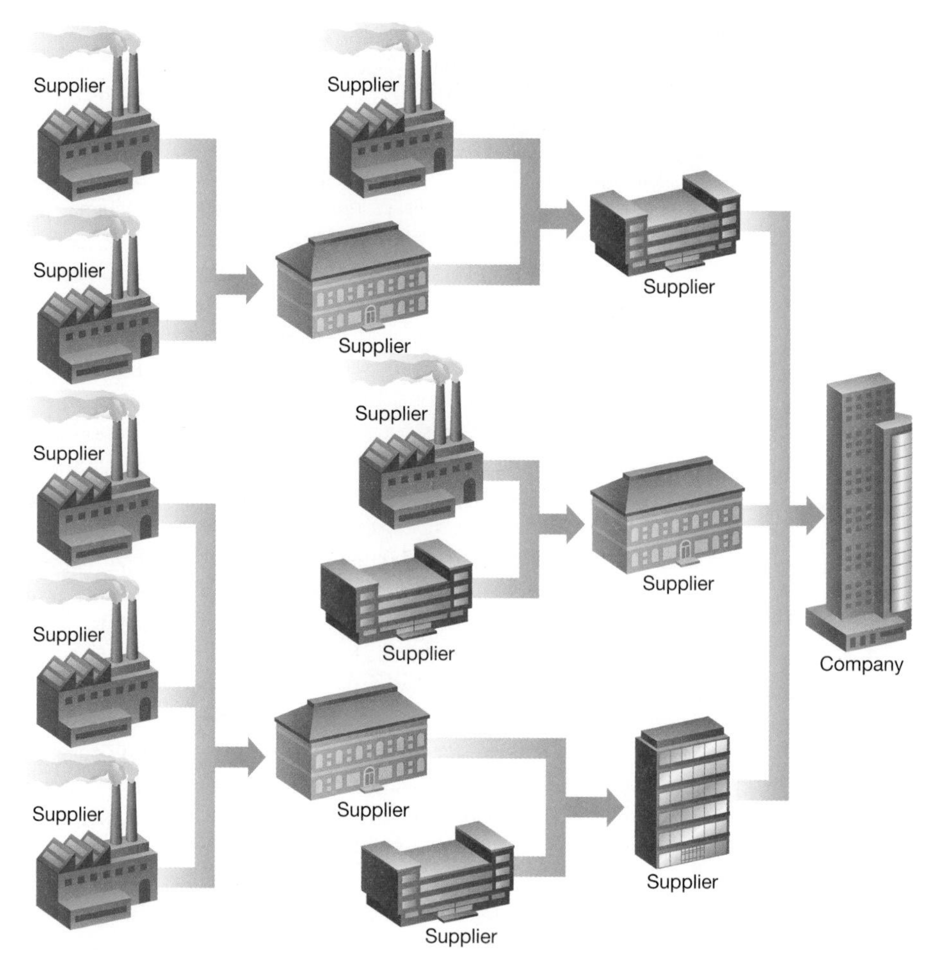

Figure 7.14 A typical supply network.

Applications focusing on upstream information flows have two main objectives in mind—to accelerate product development and to reduce costs associated with procuring raw materials, components, and services from suppliers. SCM applications are designed to assist companies in streamlining these areas. SCM applications are commonly integrated with ERP to leverage internal and external information to collaborate with suppliers. Most SCM applications come in the form of packaged software, which can be purchased from some of the leading SCM software vendors such as Agile Software, Ariba (see Figure 7.16), Commerce One, i2 Technologies, and Manugistics. ERP vendors including SSA Baan, Oracle, and SAP also offer SCM solutions that are integrated with their ERP applications.

Like ERP and CRM applications, SCM packages are delivered in the form of modules (see Table 7.5), which companies select and implement according to their business requirements.

The appropriate SCM technology, combined with the coordination of business processes with the supply network, can provide substantial paybacks for companies. SCM solutions help streamline work flow and enhance employee productivity. Companies can more efficiently manage business travel, time, and expenses, and collaborate with suppliers in real time. To pursue supplier collaboration as a basis for achieving competitive advantage, organizations must be able to access information and track activities throughout the supply network. This means that companies need to have an integrated system that captures information from the various methods they use to communicate upstream with their suppliers. More important, managers need the capability to monitor and analyze factors that drive supplier productivity to ensure they can meet demands based on prevailing market conditions.

Many companies utilize SCM applications to accelerate product development. The ability to swiftly react to changing market conditions can provide companies with the competitive advantage of bringing products to market more quickly than their competition.

COMING ATTRACTIONS

RFID Tags Revolutionize Supply Chain Management

Managing the flow of inventory throughout the supply chain has always been a cumbersome process for companies. In many cases, the inputs to the production process as well as the goods moving through the supply chain have to be tracked manually, which means packing and unpacking shipped or received goods, or counting and recording inventories. For the companies, be it the manufacturers, shipping companies, or retailers, this process is associated with tremendous costs (see Figure 7.15).

RFID tags offer the possibility of streamlining these processes, thereby enabling huge cost savings for the companies involved (for an extensive discussion of RFID, see Chapter 5). RFID tags can store product information in a chip that is connected to an antenna. With the appropriate hardware, the information stored in the chip can be read without having to open the package; unlike barcodes, which have to be passed close by the scanner, RFID data can be read from a distance of 10–20 feet. If the products are stored on pallets, they don't even have to be removed from the pallet to read each item's RFID information.

Retail giants such as Wal-Mart are currently in the process of requiring certain suppliers to equip their products with RFID tags to streamline SCM. ERP vendors such as SAP have recently integrated support for RFID data into their products to support these improvements in managing a business's supply chain; this way, the process of tracing the goods as they move through the supply chain can be improved tremendously, enabling companies to be more responsive when stock levels are getting low. Wouldn't it be nice not to face so many empty shelves at your favourite retailer?

Figure 7.15 Enterprise systems can increase data accuracy, efficiency, and reduce costs.

Sources: Anonymous, "Frequently Asked Questions," *RFID Journal*, **www.rfidjournal.com/article/articleview/207**. Information verified: October 24, 2004.
Anonymous, "SAP Launches First RFID Solution to Help Customers Automate RFID-Enabled Business Processes," SAP Press Release (January 12, 2004), **www.sap.com/solutions/scm/newsevents/index.asp?pressID=2609**.
Jay Wrolstad, "Wal Mart Launches RFID," *NewsFactor Network* (April 30, 2004), **www.newsfactor.com/story.xhtml?story_title=Wal_Mart_Launches_RFID&story_id=23904&category=entcmpt**.

The other major reason that SCM applications are becoming widely used is based on the fact that they can help companies streamline costs and create efficiencies across their supply networks. Dell uses Ariba's SCM application to automate its formerly paper-based purchasing process, shorten the time it takes to obtain goods and services from suppliers, and lower overall purchasing costs. Dell's SCM connected to its broad supplier network and integrated the company's purchasing activities with its existing ERP solution. Ariba SCM provides Dell with data to identify inefficiencies within its supply network and negotiate key contracts for goods and services, resulting in significant volume purchasing discounts. Ariba[1] showed that by automating and streamlining its procurement processes, Dell achieved over 60 percent reductions in procurement cycles and cost per purchase order.

Canadian National Railways (CN) adopted an SCM package from i2 Technologies. CN executives had difficulty analyzing the information coming in from the marketplace and could not utilize the company's many assets—tens of thousands of railcars, 1500 locomotives, and more than 25 000 kilometres of track—to meet customer demand. The

[1] See "Ariba Customer Success Stories" at **www.ariba.com**.

Web Search

Visit the Manugistics website at **www.manugistics.com** to see what the company is currently offering in the way of SCM capabilities. What other types of software and/or services does Manugistics offer? Explore how RFID tags can be used to improve SCM and prepare a brief presentation about the technology and its use in the context of SCM.

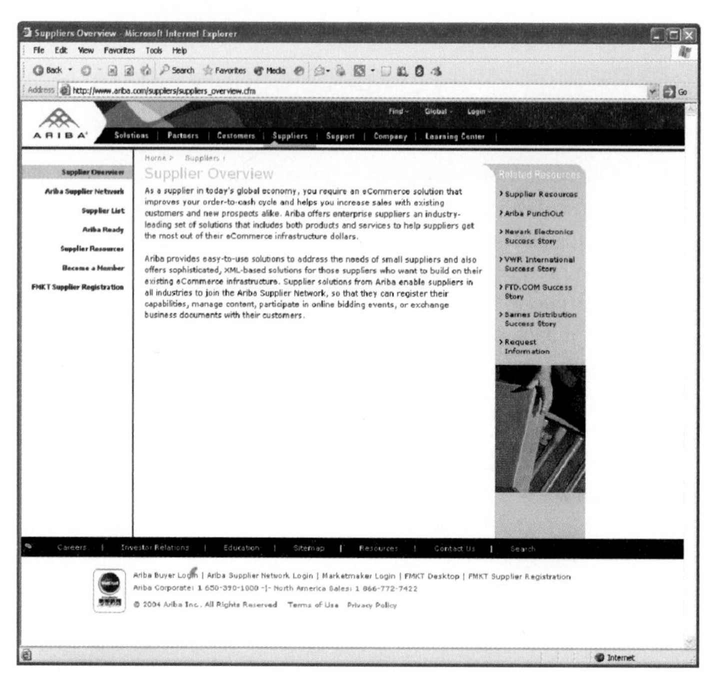

Figure 7.16 Ariba is a leader in supply chain management solutions.

Source: **www.ariba.com**

Table 7.5 ***Functions that optimize the supply network.***

Module	Key Uses
Supply chain collaboration	Share information and integrate processes up and down the supply chain Provide Internet-enabled processes such as collaborative planning, forecasting, and replenishment (CPFR) and vendor-managed inventory
Collaborative design	Streamline product design processes across supply chain partners to reduce time to market React quickly to changing market conditions, such as product launches and new customer segments
Collaborative fulfillment	Commit to delivery dates in real time Fulfill orders from channels on time with order management, transportation planning, and vehicle scheduling Support the entire logistics process, including picking, packing, shipping, and international activities
Collaborative demand and supply planning	Develop a one-number forecast of customer demand by sharing demand and supply forecasts instantaneously across multiple tiers Enable suppliers and vendors to use shared forecasts and real-time demand signals to replenish stock automatically
Collaborative procurement	Provide global visibility into direct material spending Allow partners to leverage buying clout and reduce ad hoc buying
Production planning	Support both discrete and process manufacturing Optimize plans and schedules while considering resource, material, and dependency constraints
Supply chain event management	Monitor every stage of the supply chain process, from price quotation to the moment the customer receives the product, and issue alerts when problems arise Capture data from carriers, vehicle on-board computers, GPS systems, and other sources
Supply chain exchange	Create an online supply chain community that enables partners to collaborate on design, procurement, demand and supply management, and other supply chain activities
Supply chain performance management	Report key measurements in the supply chain, such as filling management rates, order cycle times, and capacity use Integrate planning and execution functions with competitive information and market trends

Capability	Explanation
Planning	Enables you to model supply chains by providing comprehensive planning capabilities, including supply chain design, demand and supply planning, manufacturing planning, and transportation planning
Execution	Integrates planning, promising, logistics, and transactional systems through materials management, manufacturing execution, order promising, transportation execution, and warehouse management—augmented with radio frequency identification (RFID) technology
Coordination	Lets you monitor and analyze processes both within and outside your company by providing supply chain event management and supply chain performance management
Collaboration	Enables you to share information and set and achieve common supply chain goals through collaborative planning, forecasting, and replenishment (CPFR), support for vendor-managed inventory (VMI), and support for supplier-managed inventory (SMI)

Table 7.6 ***The primary capabilities of mySAP SCM.***

company used the SCM application to forecast its business opportunities as well as to integrate incoming market information. The solution allowed CN to recognize inconsistencies in its business system and find a solution to better manage its freight.

Where Is SAP Headed with SCM?

ERP leader SAP has been quickly gaining ground within the SCM software market as well with its powerful mySAP Supply Chain Management (mySAP SCM) software. Canada Post implemented mySAP SCM software to improve its package tracking capability. The system allows Canada Post not only to track shipments, but also to calculate precise cost data for each step in the collection and delivery process.

MySAP SCM is part of mySAP Business Suite and integrates seamlessly with all mySAP Business Suite solutions, as well as with non-SAP systems. In addition, together with other SAP solutions tightly integrated by the new SAP NetWeaver development platform, mySAP SCM can be used to support new product development and introduction processes. Table 7.6 outlines the primary capabilities of mySAP SCM.

SAP recently launched a new version of mySAP SCM that includes: (1) a fully automated replenishment process for products on a daily or sub-daily level, resulting in reduced inventory levels, shortened order cycle times, and improved customer satisfaction; (2) support for the use of RFID within warehouse and logistics processes so that firms can meet RFID mandates from government agencies as well as major retailers such as Wal-Mart and The Bay; (3) new and enhanced industry-specific functionality such as project manufacturing for the industrial machinery and components industry and store-level forecasting and replenishment for the retail industry; (4) automatic, adaptive forecasting and product life-cycle planning; (5) enhanced transportation planning and vehicle scheduling; (6) advanced shipping notice support and a built-in alert monitor; and (7) better web-based supplier collaboration tools. Given that SAP is now the 800-pound gorilla in the SCM market, it is worth watching where it is heading.

THE FORMULA FOR ENTERPRISE SYSTEM SUCCESS

To summarize, the main objective of enterprise systems is to create competitive advantage by streamlining business activities within and outside a company. However, many implementations are more costly and time consuming than originally envisioned. It is not uncommon to have projects that run over budget, meaning that identifying common problems and devising methods for dealing with these issues can prove invaluable to management. One survey suggested that 40–60 percent of companies that undertake enterprise system implementations do not fully realize the results that they had hoped for (Langenwalter, 2000). Companies that have successfully installed enterprise systems are found to follow a basic set of recommendations related to enterprise system implementations (Koch, Slater, and Baatz, 2000). Although the following list is not meant to be comprehensive, these recommendations will provide an understanding of some of the challenges involved in implementing enterprise systems:

Recommendation 1—Secure executive sponsorship.

Recommendation 2—Get help from outside experts.

Recommendation 3—Thoroughly train users.

Recommendation 4—Take a multidisciplinary approach to implementations.

Secure Executive Sponsorship

The primary reason that enterprise system implementations fail is believed to be a direct result of lack of top-level management support (O'Leary, 2000). Although executives do not necessarily need to make decisions concerning the enterprise system, it is critical that they buy into the decisions made by project managers. Many problems can arise if projects fail to grab the attention of top-level management. In most companies, executives have the ultimate authority regarding the availability and

SME SUCCESS: SAP Switches Focus from Big to Small in Canada

With a reputation for offering complex and highly expensive enterprise software, SAP AG is faced with a daunting task: can the company appeal to the global small- and medium-sized enterprise market? Growth in SAP's core business is slowing as most of the world's largest companies have already implemented some form of ERP system.

"For SAP to really grow, they have to expand into the mid-market," says Alan Pelz-Sharpe, vice-president, North America, for Ovum Consultants Inc. in Boston.

"For most smaller companies, they are going to be interested in Oracle, Accpac, or Microsoft. SAP just looks like a big, scary option." Branding, Pelz-Sharpe says, is one element SAP must address to change the perception with SMEs that its solutions are pricey and complex. "They're very good at the technology, but when it comes to pure advertising and brand management, they're not very good at it and they'll have to do a lot of work to address that."

SAP Canada acknowledged that an estimated 90 percent of business in Canada falls into the category of small- or medium-sized operations. To better address this market, SAP Canada refocused its marketing efforts and enlisted the assistance of regional partners. Companies with annual revenues of $20 million have the same problems to solve as companies with $100 million in revenues. To that end, SAP Canada offered tailored versions of its mySAP All-in-One and SAP Business One solutions through its channel partners nationwide. The strategy seems to have been successful. In 2005, SAP signed up 115 new customers in the SME segment.

SAP America CEO Bill McDermott also sounded off on the company's performance north of the 49th parallel. "Our business in Canada is doing very well," he said. "We are the enterprise application market leader and we think we can better serve our Canadian customers with our Business Suite and our NetWeaver architecture." McDermott said that Canada is a unique entity and will be treated as such. "Canada is a very special place, and we don't manage it as a region of the United States [the way] a lot of technology companies do. In fact, we believe it will be the growth engine of the North American market, if not all of SAP."

Georgetown, Ontario–based Mold-Masters Limited™, one of the world's largest suppliers of products to the plastic injection moulding industry, turned to SAP in 1999 as part of its Y2K preparations, says president Jonathon Fischer. Since then, the company has completed a number of projects using SAP technology, most recently a means of automating the design of its orders. An SAP-based application allows customers to feed requests into Mold-Masters' online business tool, called Merlin™, which sends orders directly to its plants. Approximately 25 percent of the company's orders are now processed online, Fischer says, and the company aims to have 50 percent of all orders handled through design automation by the end of this year.

McDermott says that 61 percent of all SAP projects are done in fewer than 9 months, and that Canadian customers have told him they managed to complete some projects in little more than 2 weeks. "Some of those projects [that went awry] were not managed very well, quite frankly," he says.

Source: Adapted from Liam Lahey, "Can SAP Rebrand to Penetrate Mid-Market?" *Computing Canada*, Vol. 29, No. 13 (July 4, 2003); and Shane Schick, "SAP Restructures Canadian Office at the Top Level," *Computing Canada*, Vol. 29, No. 21 (October 31, 2003).

distribution of resources within the organization. If executives do not understand the importance of the enterprise system, this will likely result in delays or stoppages because the necessary resources may not be available when they are needed.

A second problem that may arise deals with top-level management's ability to authorize changes to the way the company does business. When business processes need to be changed to incorporate best practices, these modifications need to be completed. Otherwise the company will have a piece of software on its hands that does not fit the way people accomplish their business tasks. Lack of executive sponsorship can also have a trickle-down effect within the organization. If users and midlevel management perceive the enterprise system to be unimportant, they are not likely to view it as a priority. Enterprise systems require a concentrated effort, and executive sponsorship can propel or stifle the implementation. Executive management can obliterate any obstacles that arise.

Get Help from Outside Experts

Enterprise systems are complex. Even the most talented information systems departments can struggle in coming to grips with ERP, CRM, and SCM applications. Costs can easily get out of hand as requirements change, and inevitable glitches arise that tie up valuable resources, time, and energy. Most vendors have trained project managers and consultants to assist companies with installing enterprise systems.

Vendors such as Oracle work with consulting firms such as Accenture and PricewaterhouseCoopers rather than maintaining a huge internal implementation division. Customers who are just starting with an enterprise implementation are often better off turning to these experts for help. Similarly, large organizations may already be using a suite of enterprise software solutions, including tools from SAP, Oracle, and IBM, and so may need to turn to a company such as iWay Software, which specializes in ***enterprise application integration*** and can tie all these disparate systems together. For example, it can help develop ***web services***, a standardized way of integrating web-based applications using open standards such as XML, SOAP, WSDL, and UDDI over the Internet.[2] Web services are used as a means for businesses to tie together their enterprise applications and help them to communicate with the enterprise applications of other businesses and with clients.

Consultants and specialized vendors offering these kinds of services can give a head start to companies that are just starting out, or save time for a company that is well down the road in using enterprise systems but needs help in taming their complex systems. These experts have experience in helping other companies implement the software, making them keenly aware of potential problem areas that may arise during the implementation. Many consulting organizations have developed tried and trusted methodologies that help companies develop an appropriate project plan to guide them through the installation process. These consultants have the advantage of ***economies of scale*** in that they are likely to be dealing with the same problem or task across dozens, if not hundreds, of firms and can afford to have full-time specialists to deal with specific problems, whereas one single organization cannot afford that luxury.

Using consultants tends to move companies through the implementation more quickly and tends to help companies train their personnel on the applications more effectively. However, companies should not rely too heavily on consultants and should plan for the consultants leaving once the implementation is complete. When consultants are physically present, company personnel tend to rely on them for assistance. Once the application goes live and the consultants are no longer there, users have to do the job themselves. A key focus should be facilitating user learning.

Thoroughly Train Users

Training is often the most overlooked, underestimated, and poorly budgeted expense involved in planning enterprise system implementations. Enterprise systems are much more complicated to learn than stand-alone systems. Learning a single application requires users to become accustomed to a new software interface, but enterprise system users regularly need to learn a new set of business processes as well. Once enterprise systems go live, many companies experience a dramatic drop-off in productivity. In a survey of 64 Fortune 500 companies that have implemented enterprise systems, 25 percent have experienced productivity problems after going live. The most common reason that performance problems arise is

[2] SOAP (Simple Object Access Protocol), WSDL (Web Services Description Language), and UDDI (Universal Description, Discovery, and Integration) are open standards for providing XML-based features and functionality.

CAREER IMPLICATIONS Enterprise-Wide Information Systems

For Accounting and Finance

Enterprise-wide information systems are heavily used by accounting and finance professionals. As ERP systems integrate different stand-alone applications and legacy systems into one platform, different modules can also serve the needs of the accounting and finance functions. For example, SAP's Financial Accounting module supports functions such as managing accounts receivable, accounts payable, or general ledgers. Similarly, Oracle's ERP system provides functions for managing accounts receivable and general ledgers and functions for cost management. Other applications provide tools for cash and investment management.

For Operations Management

Operations management professionals interact with enterprise-wide information systems on a daily basis. Given that many manufacturing companies have implemented ERP and SCM systems to manage their production and procurement processes, operations management professionals are at the heart of these systems within organizations. If you become an operations management professional, you likely will be working with these systems to streamline some aspect of the production process.

For Human Resources Management

Human resources management professionals will experience some challenging issues when their organization implements an enterprise-wide information system. For example, because these systems can be highly complex, HR management professionals will have to design comprehensive training strategies for employees working with the system. Likewise, when attempting to hire new employees who are proficient in working with the system, they may need new strategies to obtain qualified employees because of the scarcity of knowledgeable users. In some cases, current employees may resist the use of a newly implemented system, so creative strategies may be required to motivate the employees to stay with the organization and to work with the new system.

For Marketing

Many organizations are implementing CRM systems to support their sales and marketing activities. These systems provide sophisticated data mining tools to determine the most valuable customers. Additionally, SFA tools allow sales and marketing professionals to manage contacts, schedule salespeople, and assign territories. In many cases, CRM systems are integrated with the entire organization-wide ERP system; in other cases, companies choose to implement a stand-alone CRM. These systems are allowing organizations to get more out of their sales and marketing investments by allowing fewer professionals to effectively support more customers.

For Information Systems

Although most ERP systems can be implemented in a standard way, many organizations choose to customize the system to their specific needs. Consequently, there is a tremendous demand for information systems professionals who are skilled at ERP implementation and customization. Customization, however, makes ongoing system maintenance much more difficult because periodic off-the-shelf updates will not integrate seamlessly with customized modules. This means that information systems professionals have to routinely modify system updates to make them work with the current system.

that the applications and processes are different from the previous system (Shah, 2001). Users who have not mastered the new system will not be able to perform effectively. This issue can potentially lead to heightened levels of dissatisfaction among users, as they prefer to accomplish their business activities in a familiar manner rather than doing things in the new way. By training users before the system goes live and giving them sufficient opportunities to learn the new system, a company can allay fears and mitigate potential productivity issues.

Take a Multidisciplinary Approach to Implementations

Enterprise systems affect the entire organization; thus, companies should include personnel from different levels and departments in the implementation project (Kumar and Crook, 1999). In CRM and SCM environments in which other organizations are participating in the implementation, it is critical to enlist the support of personnel in their organizations as well. Project managers need to include the implementation personnels from midlevel management, the information systems department, external consultants, and most important, end users.

Failing to include the appropriate people in the day-to-day activities of the project can prove problematic in many areas. From a needs analysis standpoint, it is critical that all the business requirements be sufficiently captured before selection of an enterprise solution. As end users are involved in every aspect of daily business activities, their insights can be invaluable. For instance, an end user might make salient a feature that no one on the project team had thought of. Having an application that does not meet all the business's requirements can result in poorly fitting software or customizations. Another peril in leaving out key personnel is the threat of alienation. Departments and/or personnel who do not feel included may develop a sense of animosity toward the new system and view it in a negative light. In extreme cases, users will refuse to use the new application, resulting in conflicts and inefficiencies within the organization.

Although these expansive enterprise system implementations are often cumbersome and difficult, the potential payoff is huge. As a result, organizations are compelled to implement these systems. Furthermore, given the popularity and necessity of such systems, you are likely to find yourself involved in the implementation and/or use of such a system. We are confident that after reading this chapter you will be better able to understand and help with the development and use of such systems.

KEY POINTS REVIEW

1. **Explain how organizations support business activities by using information technologies.** Organizations use information systems to better perform all of the various business processes (and activities within these processes) throughout each of the functional areas of the firm. Whether taking an order for a product, manufacturing a product, securing supplies from another firm, shipping a product to a customer, or providing service after the sale, companies can use information systems to make each of these processes and activities more effective and efficient. More important, companies can use information systems to integrate these processes and activities and to accumulate and use wisely the information that is generated each step of the way.
2. **Describe what enterprise systems are and how they have evolved.** Enterprise systems are information systems that span the entire organization and can be used to integrate business processes, activities, and information across all the functional areas of a firm. Enterprise systems can be either prepackaged software or custom-made applications. One popular, powerful type of enterprise system is the Enterprise Resource Planning system, from vendors such as SAP and Oracle. These ERP packages evolved from "material requirements planning" systems during the 1990s and are, for the most part, used to support internal business processes. ERP implementations often involve business process reengineering, a systematic, structured improvement approach by all or part of an organization that critically examines, rethinks, and redesigns processes in order to achieve dramatic improvements in one or more performance measures, such as quality, cycle time, or cost.
3. **Explain the differences between internally and externally focused software applications.** Internally focused software applications are generally used to support business processes and activities that occur within the boundaries of a firm. Examples are the manufacturing of a product and the management of inventories. ERP packages are commonly used to support these types of processes and activities. External software applications are generally used to support business processes and activities that occur across organizational boundaries. Examples are taking product orders from customers and receiving supplies from other firms. Supply Chain Management packages, such as those from Manugistics, enable a firm to interact more effectively and efficiently with upstream business partners. Customer Relationship Management packages, such as those from Siebel Systems, enable a firm to interact more effectively and efficiently downstream with customers.
4. **List the keys to successfully implementing an enterprise system.** Experience with enterprise system implementations suggests that there are some common problems that can be avoided and/or should be managed carefully. These include (1) securing executive sponsorship, (2) getting necessary help from outside experts (i.e., specialized software vendors such as iWay or consultants such as Accenture), (3) thoroughly training users, and (4) taking a multidisciplinary approach to implementations. Key issues in current enterprise systems implementations include doing enterprise application integration and offering web services for enterprise applications using open standards such as XML.

KEY TERMS

best practices 243
Business Process Reengineering (BPR) 243
conversion 237
custom applications 236
Customer Relationship Management (CRM) 237
customizations 242
downstream 236
economies of scale 255
enterprise application integration 255
Enterprise Resource Planning (ERP) 237
enterprise systems 230
interorganizational systems (IOS) 232
legacy systems 237
modules 241
packaged application 236
Sales Force Automation (SFA) 245
stand-alone application 237
supply chain 249
Supply Chain Management (SCM) 237
supply network 249
upstream 236
value chain 233
value system 235
vanilla version 242
web services 255

REVIEW QUESTIONS

1. Describe what enterprise systems are and how they have evolved.
2. What are the advantages and disadvantages of enterprise systems?
3. What are the primary and support activities of a value chain?
4. Give an example of upstream and downstream information flows in a value system.
5. Compare and contrast customized and packaged applications.
6. How does Customer Relationship Management differ from Supply Chain Management?
7. Explain a data warehouse and the types of data that flow in and out of the warehouse.
8. Describe business process reengineering and give an example.
9. What are the four components of financial software modules?
10. What are the keys to successfully implementing an enterprise system?

SELF-STUDY QUESTIONS

Visit the Companion Website for this text for additional Self-Study Questions: **www.pearsoned.ca/jessup**.

1. __________ are information systems that allow companies to integrate information support operations on a company-wide basis.
   A. Customer Relationship Management systems
   B. Enterprise systems
   C. WANs
   D. Interorganizational systems
2. Which of the following is a primary activity according to the value chain model?
   A. firm infrastructure
   B. customer service
   C. human resources
   D. procurement
3. According to the value chain model, which of the following is a support function?
   A. technology development
   B. marketing and sales
   C. inbound logistics
   D. operations and manufacturing
4. All of the following are true about legacy systems except __________.
   A. they are stand-alone systems
   B. they are older software systems
   C. they are Enterprise Resource Planning systems
   D. they may be difficult to integrate into other systems
5. __________ is a component of the mySAP Business Suite.
   A. Customer Relationship Management
   B. Enterprise Resource Planning
   C. Supply Chain Management
   D. all of the above
6. Which of the following companies produces ERP systems?
   A. SSA Baan
   B. Oracle
   C. SAP
   D. all of the above
7. The __________ capability within SAP's ERP software allows you to manage corporate finance functions by automating financial Supply Chain Management, financial accounting, and management accounting.
   A. general ledger
   B. financial and management accounting
   C. accounts payable
   D. accounts receivable
8. Which of the following is commonly used to refer to the producers of supplies that a company uses?
   A. procurement
   B. sales force
   C. supply network
   D. customers

9. __________ is global visibility into direct material spending and allows partners to leverage buying clout and reduce ad hoc buying.
   A. Collaborative procurement
   B. Collaborative fulfillment
   C. Production planning
   D. Supply chain exchange

10. __________ is a systematic, structured improvement approach by all or part of an organization that critically examines, rethinks, and redesigns processes in order to achieve dramatic improvements in one or more performance measures such as quality, cycle time, or cost.
   A. Systems analysis
   B. Business Process Reengineering (BPR)
   C. Customer Relationship Management (CRM)
   D. Total Quality Management (TQM)

PROBLEMS AND EXERCISES

1. Match the following terms with the appropriate definitions:

   _____ Enterprise systems
   _____ Legacy systems
   _____ Web services
   _____ Supply chain
   _____ Customer Relationship Management
   _____ Value chain
   _____ Supply Chain Management
   _____ Business process reengineering
   _____ Collaborative design
   _____ Upstream information flow

   a. An information flow that consists of information received from another organization
   b. Older systems that are not designed to communicate with other applications beyond departmental boundaries
   c. Information systems that allow companies to integrate information support operations on a company-wide basis
   d. A standardized way of integrating web-based applications using open standards such as XML
   e. Applications that concentrate on downstream information flows, integrating the value chains of a company and its distributors
   f. Commonly used to refer to the producers of supplies that a company uses
   g. Streamlining product design processes across supply chain partners to reduce time to market and increase reaction time to changing market conditions, such as product launches and new customer segments
   h. The flow of information through a set of business activities
   i. Applications that operate on upstream information flows, integrating the value chains of a company and its suppliers
   j. Altering the way in which business processes are conducted

2. Find an organization that you are familiar with (or use one of the Brief Cases in the textbook), and determine how many software applications it is utilizing concurrently. Is the company's information system cohesive, or does it need updating and streamlining?

3. What part does training users in an ERP system play, and how important is it in software satisfaction? What productivity problems can result in an ERP implementation?

4. What are the payoffs in taking a multidisciplinary approach to an ERP implementation? What departments are affected, and what is the typical time frame? Research one of the Brief Cases in this chapter or find a company that has recently implemented an ERP system. What could the company have done better, and what did it do right?

5. Describe collaborative demand and supply planning, and find an example or two of companies applying this concept. What are the advantages and disadvantages? Is it cost effective? What were some of the challenges of implementation? What improvements could be made?

6. In the past few years, the ERP marketplace has become much less fragmented than it once was. Today, the market is dominated by two firms: SAP and Oracle. SAP is still the market leader, but with the acquisitions of J.D. Edwards, PeopleSoft, and Siebel Systems, Oracle moved into a close second. Check the websites of these two firms to see if either software firm has made any other announcements about future directions of their products and/or services, and check a web source of corporate financial performance information such as Yahoo! Finance (**http://finance.yahoo.com**) to see how these two firms are performing. How will the enterprise market spaces continue to be shaped and influenced by these two firms?

7. What companies are using data warehouses? Research this question, and determine the cost and size of a data warehouse. What are the advantages and disadvantages of data warehouses? What is the typical time frame for implementation?

8. In the Brief Case about Princess Cruises we wrote about their use of e-mail as a form of CRM. What else could Princess Cruises be doing to better utilize CRM capabilities? Think specifically about Oracle's Siebel CRM offerings and project how Princess Cruises might deploy a Siebel CRM solution and calculate a return on investment for it.

9. Based on your own experiences with applications, have you used customized or off-the-shelf applications? What is the difference, and how good was the system documentation?

10. Read the Brief Case in this chapter about SAP implementation at Microsoft. How many applications were combined into the ERP system? What was the time frame? Is there a disadvantage of this system, and, if so, what is it?

11. Go through the job ads in the newspaper or on the web and find a position that you would like to have in the future. Make an appointment to visit the company and ask questions of the human resources and information systems

departments. Determine who hires for this position and what the qualifications are for the position. Find out exactly what the daily duties of the position are. You might even consider investigating an internship. Prepare a brief report on your findings.

12. Choose an organization from one of the Brief Cases in the textbook or an organization with which you are familiar that utilizes Customer Relationship Management. Who within the organization is most involved in this process, and who benefits?

13. Search the web for recent articles on business process reengineering and related approaches for improving organizations. What is the current state-of-the-art for these approaches? To what extent are these "headlines" about information systems implementations?

14. Why are enterprise application integration and web services using open standards such as XML so important to enterprise system success? What key skills and related training would it require in order for someone to be proficient at fulfilling these types of needs?

APPLICATION EXERCISES

Note: The existing data files referenced in these exercises are available on the Companion Website: **www.pearsoned.ca/jessup.**

Spreadsheet Application: Choosing an ERP System at MountainSports

MountainSports is interested in integrating its business processes to streamline processes such as purchasing, sales, HR management, and CRM. Due to your success in implementing the e-commerce infrastructure, the director asks you for advice on what to do to streamline operations at MountainSports. Use the data provided in the file MountainSports.csv to make a recommendation about which ERP system to purchase. The file includes ratings of the different modules of the systems and the weights assigned to these ratings. You are asked to do the following:

- Determine the product with the highest overall rating. Hint: Use the SUMPRODUCT formula to multiply each vendor's scores with the respective weights and add the weighted scores.
- Prepare the necessary graphs to compare the products on the different dimensions and the overall score.

Please professionally format the graphs before printing them out.

Database Application: Managing Customer Relations at BlueSky Airlines

BlueSky Airlines, proudly serving central Europe since 1976, has recently implemented a frequent flyer program. As director of sales and marketing, you want to find out how to target these individuals better with promotions and special offers. In the file BlueSky.mdb you find travel data about the members of the frequent flyer program for the year 2004. Create the following reports:

- A report displaying all frequent flyers, sorted by distance travelled.
- A report displaying all frequent flyers, sorted by total amount spent.

Prepare professionally formatted printouts of all reports, including headers, footers, dates, etc. If you are using Microsoft Access, you might use the wizard to create the reports. Hint: Set up queries returning the sums of fares and distances before creating the reports.

ANSWERS TO THE SELF-STUDY QUESTIONS

1. B, p. 230	2. B, p. 234	3. A, p. 235	4. C, p. 237	5. D, p. 241
6. D, p. 240	7. B, p. 241	8. C, p. 249	9. A, p. 252	10. B, p. 243

Case *A Customer-Centric View at RBC Financial*

Royal Bank of Canada (RBC) Financial Group is Canada's largest financial services organization. A key part of RBC's success rests on its ability to assess and manage credit risk. There's the risk of lending money to the wrong person. Then there's the equally important risk of turning away potentially good clients who may not fit the profile of the ideal borrower. The trick is to know the difference between a good and a bad risk. Like most banks, RBC has been using automated tools for credit risk decisions for many years. However, like the rest of the industry, up until 2002 the company's approach was product based. Clients applied for credit products, and credit staff used specific product scorecards to evaluate their applications. These scorecards did not consider the individual's total relationship with the company. As a result, RBC was sometimes declining good customers—and losing their business to competitors.

RBC felt that it needed to build a client-centric rather than a product-centric risk assessment system. The fundamental goal of the system would be to reduce credit losses while improving customer service. RBC partnered with Experian UK, a software development firm, to build the new system, the core of which would be individual risk profiles for each of RBC's 11.5 million customers. When the system was launched in 2002, it made RBC the only financial institution in North America able to determine the credit risk of each customer based on their entire relationship with the bank.

A key challenge was to build a system that could interface with the company's enterprise data warehouse and CRM systems. With the new system, RBC no longer relies on product-based scores. It creates a single customer risk score that provides significantly higher predictive power and aligns with RBC's CRM capabilities. As a result, the company not only can make better lending decisions, it can better understand each individual customer. Clients who may have been turned down for loans in the past, based solely on RBC's product scorecard, now have a greater chance of being approved. Yet, the company has still been able to reduce its lending losses.

The system has resulted in a $180 million reduction in loan loss provision for credit losses, and an estimated 8 percent increase in credit product sales. It has also contributed to increased market share of mortgage, deposit, and personal credit products in Canada.

Today, RBC is one of only a few financial institutions in North America able to determine the credit risk of each of its customers based on their entire relationship with the company. Meanwhile, most of its competitors are still dependent on calculating risk on a per-product basis. "The powerful synergy between RBC Financial Group's retail banking strategy and the technology that supports it gives our company a distinct competitive advantage," says David McKay, Senior Vice President, Financing Products. "It also plays a key role in helping us maintain highly personalized, one-on-one relationships with 11.5 million people."

Source: The Canadian Information Productivity Awards, RBC Financial, **www.cipa.com/award winners/winners_04/RBCFinancial.html**.

Discussion Questions

1. Why is a customer-centric view superior to a product-centric view?
2. Do you think that RBC Financial can use its new system to create a competitive advantage as suggested in the case? If so, can that advantage be sustained?
3. Drawing on the RBC Financial case, describe three ways that a CRM system can improve profitability at a financial institution.

Log on to the Companion Website at www.pearsoned.ca/jessup for an additional case.

Running Case: Connexion by Boeing

Enterprise-Wide Information Systems

When Connexion by Boeing first envisioned providing high-speed Internet access to air travellers, many U.S. domestic and international airlines were highly interested in investing in Connexion by Boeing and offering this service aboard their aircraft. Unfortunately, the economic downturn of the past few years in the airline industry required most airlines to cut costs to survive. Consequently, the airlines' initial excitement vanished, and many of them decided to delay the implementation of broadband in-flight Internet access indefinitely. For Connexion, this meant an instant loss of many of its most promising customers, and much effort was expended to create additional services for the airlines. Even though many airlines decided not to implement Connexion's systems due to high initial setup costs, several airlines, such as Lufthansa and SAS, realized that providing in-flight Internet access could mean additional revenue, as market research has shown that 3 percent of U.S. frequent flyers would be willing to switch airlines to be able to stay in contact with their offices while aboard an aircraft. Furthermore, whenever airline passengers connect to the Internet while on the airplane, they are initially redirected to a portal site the airlines can use to offer services such as ticketing or reservation, or to sell duty-free products or other merchandise. This portal serves as an additional channel to sell the airline's products and services and generate revenue.

As well as the revenue generated by passengers using in-flight Internet services, Connexion's systems generate a wealth of additional data the airlines can use for their advantage. Connexion's executives viewed having access to this data as a unique selling point, so to capitalize on it they decided to offer an integrated CRM suite to the airlines to maximize the usefulness of the data generated. The Enterprise Operations Center and CRM applications were created to be used internally by Connexion and externally by the airlines (see figure on the next page).

To assist in analyzing customer usage data, Connexion created a data warehouse architecture allowing the airlines to determine relationships "hidden" in the data that could be translated into useful information. For example, hidden relationships might help to highlight additional opportunities for sales and marketing or allow the airline to monitor and manage customer satisfaction. The architecture consists primarily of Oracle and SQL Server 2000 databases, Oracle's CRM module, and Cognos data mining software, as well as a number of different systems for various functions, such as user management or flight visualization tools.

All site visitors connecting to the in-flight portal generate different types of information, such as how long they stay connected and what services they use.

The analysis of the portal data can help the airline to find out how the portal sales compare to sales from other channels, what parts of the portal are "sticky," which parts need improvement, and, most importantly, whether a person's behaviour on the portal site can predict whether he or she is a likely prospect. Other burning questions include how fast seat passengers are adopting Connexion services, how much revenue is being generated by customers per month, what the highest producers of margin are, what the indices that predict increased revenue and additional new sales are, and how the information can be modified to increase its value.

In addition to the analysis of portal visits and sales, airlines can benefit from the CRM ability to analyze customer satisfaction levels, to tell where the customers are coming from, and to tell what kind of customer support they receive. CRM analysis tools also help to compare forecasted versus actual in-flight Internet usage, find out which services are being used and what services are not being used and why, and find out how the services are performing. Emerging analysis metrics such as customer lifetime value, customer future value, customer return on investment, and customer loyalty are used to help create a seamless flow of information by individual customer, thereby enabling sales, marketing, and customer service to complete personalized campaigns unique to the customer's wants and needs.

While these tools were primarily developed for use by airlines, Connexion saw the opportunity to make extensive use of the system internally. Therefore, additional applications were developed. For example, it was decided to create an SFA system including lead and opportunity profile management, territory management, and sales forecasting. This system helps Connexion's sales force in the interaction with private, commercial, and governmental customers. For each sales lead and each customer, a detailed profile and customer history is created. This history helps to manage customer interactions and increase customer satisfaction, as all entities interacting with the customer have access to the customer profile and customer history. And the customer receives highly personalized service from the initial sales lead to follow-up sales support by Connexion's call centre.

In order to efficiently manage its services and after-sales support, Connexion integrated tools such as configuration and parts management into the Enterprise Operations Center. These tools track an installed configuration of parts and/or software for all sites, including aircraft, operation centres, and ground stations. By being able to assess individual and part type (or system) problems or history, the system's reliability, maintainability, and availability is greatly increased, which leads to increased customer satisfaction and thereby higher revenues for both Connexion and the private, governmental, and commercial customers. This system is accessible internally to Connexion, to the customers' maintenance facilities such as Lufthansa Technik, and to Connexion's service providers such as AT&T, Verestar Satellite Services (now part of SES Americom), and Sitel, the company managing Connexion's customer care centre.

As the information needs and the information systems platforms of the entities involved differ substantially, it was decided to provide a web-based interface for the interaction with the Enterprise Operations Center and the CRM system. The different internal and external customers can access the system through a portal site tailored to their respective information needs via a web browser. While being built on essentially the same site, the links provided on the CRM portal page were customized according to the user's access privileges. This way, it was

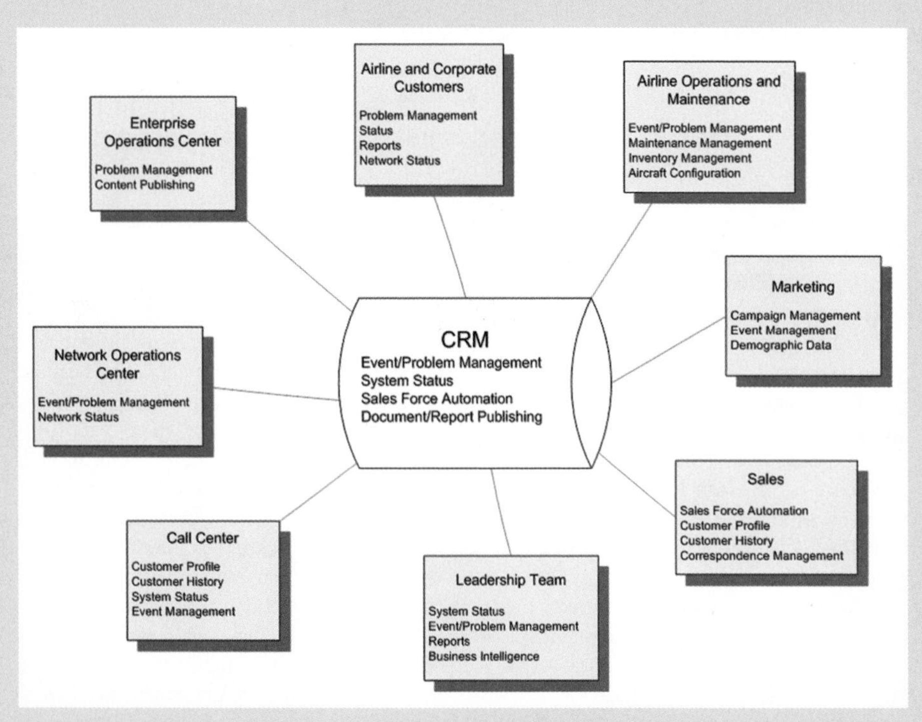

Internal and external users of the CRM system.

ensured that the individuals would have access to the information needed, while at the same time access to other parts of the system could be restricted. For example, an airline's maintenance employees can access the problem management module, but access to customer profiles or history is restricted.

For Connexion, the Enterprise Operations Center is seen as one of the most important features needed for providing in-flight Internet service as well as a tool offering additional value to its customers. By offering these capabilities, Connexion's executives hope to be able to expand Connexion's market penetration and increase the number of airlines implementing the system.

Discussion Questions

1. What are the main features of Connexion's Enterprise Operations Center/CRM system?
2. Do you see the internal or the external use of the system as more important for Connexion? Why?
3. Which additional types of enterprise systems could be integrated into Connexion's existing system?

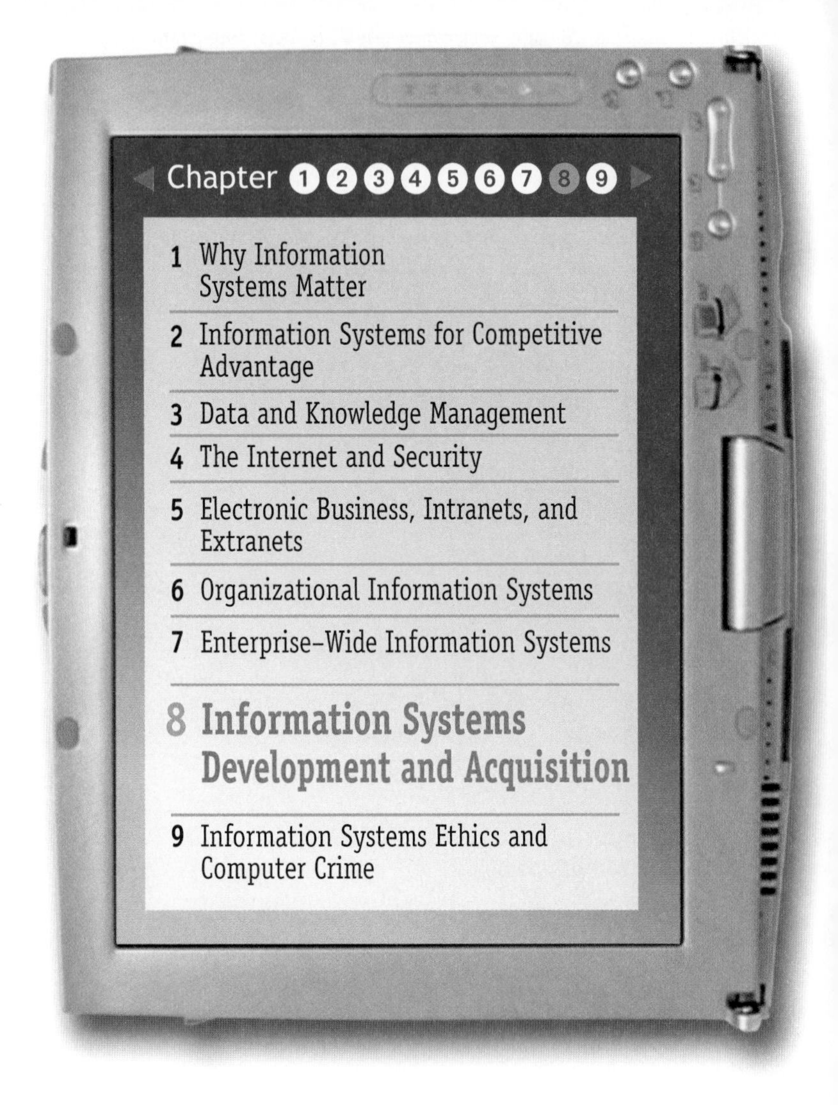

Preview

As you have read throughout this book and have experienced in your own life, information systems (IS) are of many different types, including decision support systems, executive IS, group support systems, and Internet commerce systems. Just as there are different types of systems, different approaches have been found to be more appropriate for developing some types of systems and less appropriate for others. Learning all the possible ways to develop or acquire a system, and more importantly, how to identify the optimal approach, takes years of study and experience. Toward this end, this chapter has several objectives. After reading this chapter, you will be able to do the following:

1. Understand the process used by organizations to manage the development of information systems.
2. Describe each major phase of the systems development life cycle (SDLC): systems identification, selection, and planning; system analysis; system design; system implementation; and system maintenance.
3. Describe prototyping, rapid application development (RAD), object-oriented analysis (OOA), and design methods of systems development, along with each approach's strengths and weaknesses.
4. Understand the factors involved in building a system in-house, along with situations in which it is not feasible.
5. Explain three alternative systems development options: external acquisition, outsourcing, and end-user development.

Information Systems Development and Acquisition

American Firm Chooses to "Nearsource" Information Technology in Halifax

In 2003, outsourcing firm Keane Inc. agreed to fill 175 information technology (IT) jobs over 3 years at its Halifax Advanced Development Centre. Headquartered in Boston, Keane works with large firms and government agencies to plan, build, and manage application software, primarily through outsourcing agreements.

Keane planned to hire about 50 people in Halifax in 2004, said Alaisdar Graham, managing director of the Nova Scotia facility, and the rest in 2005. Graham said that the Halifax operation, which employed more than 300 people, had seen 30-percent annual growth and that there was "no sign of it slacking off."

Keane's announcement is an example of nearshore outsourcing, in which U.S. companies shift IT work to Canada because of lower salary and infrastructure costs, proximity to the United States, similarity of culture, and quality of service. Nearshore outsourcing has become a bright spot for the Canadian IT industry, with companies such as Montreal-based CGI Group Inc., RIS Resource Information Systems Inc. of Toronto, and others providing software development and services to U.S. clients. In late 2003, EDS Canada announced plans for a Global Centre of Excellence based on Microsoft Corp.'s NET technology in Victoria. EDS said the centre would create 100 jobs.

Skills that Keane needed include Java, Perl, and COBOL programming and expertise with Unix, Sybase, and WebSphere, Graham said. The company hoped to fill many jobs locally but would also recruit from other provinces. The jobs would be of "huge" importance to the province, said Joe Gillis, a spokesman for Nova Scotia Business Inc., the provincial government agency that authorized the $1.5 million in rebates to Keane.

Nova Scotia's Economic Development Office gave Keane $2.5 million in funding to help it attain Capability Maturity Model Level 5 assessment from the Software Engineering Institute. Graham said his operation is the first Canadian nearshore outsourcing facility to obtain this designation for continuous process optimization, which he considers directly responsible for its growth. Graham said that Keane originally located in Halifax because of Nova Scotia's low cost of living and proximity to New England, where many of Keane's clients are located. The company also received grants from the provincial and federal governments when it established the operation.

Source: Adapted from Grant Buckler, "American Outsourcing Firm Expands Halifax Operation," *Computing Canada*, Vol. 29, No. 23 (November 28, 2003).

Boston-based Keane Inc. chooses "nearshore" outsourcing in Halifax over "offshore" outsourcing in Asia or Eastern Europe.

Source: Keane Inc.

If you are a typical business student, you might be wondering why we have a chapter on building and acquiring information systems. The answer is simple: No matter what area of an organization you are in—such as marketing, finance, accounting, human resources, or operations—you will be involved in the systems development process. In fact, research indicates that the IS spending in most organizations is controlled by specific business functions. What this means is that even if your career interests are in something other than IS, it is very likely that you will be involved in the IS development process. Understanding all available options is important to your future success.

THE NEED FOR STRUCTURED SYSTEMS DEVELOPMENT

The process of designing, building, and maintaining information systems is often referred to as ***systems analysis and design***. Likewise, the individual who performs this task is referred to as a ***systems analyst***. Because few organizations can survive without effectively utilizing information and computing technology, the demand for skilled systems analysts is very strong. Organizations want to hire systems analysts because they possess a unique blend of managerial and technical expertise—systems analysts are not just "techies." In fact, systems analysts remain in demand precisely because of this unique blend of abilities, but it was not always this way.

The Evolution of Information Systems Development

In the early days of computing, systems development was considered an art that only a few technical "gurus" could master. Unfortunately, the techniques used to construct systems varied greatly from individual to individual. This variation made it difficult to integrate large organizational IS. Furthermore, many systems were not easily maintainable after the original programmer left the organization. As a result, organizations were often left with systems that were very difficult and expensive to maintain. Many organizations, therefore, underutilized these technology investments and failed to realize all possible benefits from their systems.

To address this problem, IS professionals concluded that system development needed to become an engineering-like discipline (Nunamaker, 1992). Common methods, techniques, and tools had to be developed to create a disciplined approach for constructing IS. This evolution from an "art" to a "discipline" led to the use of the term ***software engineering*** to help define what systems analysts and programmers do. Transforming IS development into a formal discipline would provide numerous benefits. First, it would be much easier to train programmers and analysts if common techniques were widely used. In essence, if all systems analysts had similar training, it would make them more interchangeable and more skilled at working on the systems developed by other analysts. Second, systems built with commonly used techniques would be more maintainable. Both industry and academic researchers have pursued the quest for new and better approaches for building information systems.

Options for Obtaining Information Systems

Organizations can obtain new information systems in many ways. One option, of course, is for the members of the organization to build the IS themselves. Organizations can also buy a prepackaged system from a software development company or consulting firm. Some IS that are commonly used in many organizations can be purchased for much less money than what it would cost to build a new one. Purchasing a prepackaged system is a good option as long as its features meet the needs of the organization. A payroll system is an example of a prepackaged system that is often purchased rather than developed by an organization because tax laws, wage calculations, cheque printing, and accounting activities are highly standardized. Figure 8.1 outlines several sources for IS.

A third option is to have an outside organization or consultant custom-build a system to an organization's specifications. This is generally referred to as having the development outsourced. This is a good option when an organization does not have adequate systems development resources or expertise. A final option is to let individual users and departments build their own custom systems to support their individual needs. This is referred to as end-user development. Most organizations allow end-user development to be used to construct only a limited range of systems. For example, systems that span organizational boundaries or perform complex changes to corporate databases are typically not candidates for end-user development. Alternatively, a common application that might be constructed using end-user development is a data analysis system using a spreadsheet application such as Microsoft Excel. Regardless of the source of the new information system, the primary role of managers and users in the organization is to make sure that any new system will meet the organization's business needs. This means that managers and users must understand the systems development process to ensure that the system will meet their needs.

Information Systems Development in Action

The tools and techniques used to develop information systems are continually evolving with the rapid changes in IS hardware and software. As you will see, the IS development approach is a very structured process that moves from step to step. Systems analysts become adept at decomposing large, complex problems into many small, simple problems. They can then easily solve each simple problem by writing a relatively short computer program. The goal of the systems analyst is to build the final system by piecing together the many small programs into one comprehensive system. This process of decomposing a problem is outlined in Figure 8.3. An easy way to think about this is to think about using Lego blocks for building a model house. Each individual block is a small, simple piece that is nothing without the others. When together, the blocks can create a large and very complex design. When systems are built in this manner, they are much easier to design, program, and, most importantly, maintain.

The Role of Users in the Systems Development Process

Most organizations have a huge investment in transaction processing and management information systems. These systems are most often designed, constructed, and maintained by systems analysts within the organization, using a variety of methods. When building and maintaining IS, systems analysts rely on information provided by system users, who are involved in all phases of the system's development process. To effectively participate in the process, it is important for all members of the organization to understand what is meant by systems development and what activities occur. A close and mutually respectful working relationship between analysts and users is a key to project success. Now that you understand the history and need for systems development, it is time to consider some of the relevant techniques that are used in systems development.

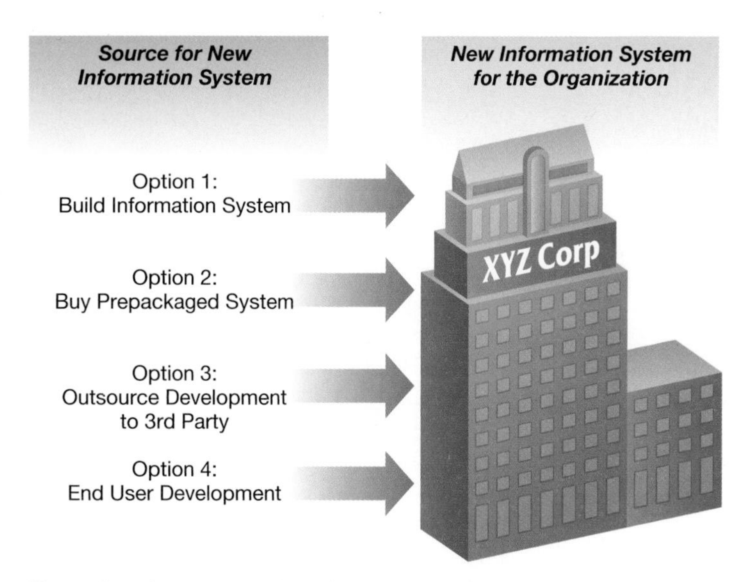

Figure 8.1 There are a variety of sources for information systems.

STEPS IN THE SYSTEMS DEVELOPMENT PROCESS

Just as the products that a firm produces and sells follow a life cycle, so do organizational information systems. For example, a new type of tennis shoe follows a life cycle of being introduced to the market, being accepted into the market, maturing, declining in popularity, and ultimately being retired. The term ***systems development life cycle (SDLC)*** describes the life of an information system from conception to retirement (Hoffer, George, and Valacich, 2005). The SDLC has five primary phases:

1. System identification, selection, and planning
2. System analysis
3. System design
4. System implementation
5. System maintenance

Figure 8.4 is a graphical representation of the SDLC. The SDLC is represented as four boxes connected by arrows. Within the SDLC, arrows flow in both directions from the top box (system identification, selection, and planning) to the bottom box (system implementation). Arrows flowing down represent that the flow of information produced in one phase is being used to seed the activities of the next. Arrows flowing up represent the possibility of returning to a prior phase, if needed. The system maintenance arrow connecting the last phase

WHEN THINGS GO WRONG

An Information Traffic Jam on the Autobahn

Being at the centre of the European Union, Germany's famous Autobahn system constantly has to deal with large amounts of transit traffic, in both north–south and east–west directions (and vice versa) (see Figure 8.2). In addition to vacationers overcrowding the Autobahns each summer, heavy truck traffic increases congestion and traffic jams throughout the year. To entice freight companies to use trains to move goods and to generate revenue for the maintenance of the Autobahns, the German government decided to build a satellite-based system to collect road tolls from heavy trucks. It was envisioned that the system would use Global Positioning System (GPS) data to calculate the exact distance travelled on the Autobahn by each truck and charge the trucking companies accordingly.

In June 2002, an industry consortium led by DaimlerChrysler and Deutsche Telekom won the bid to implement the system, which was supposed to be up and running by 31 August 2003. However, things did not quite work out according to the plan: political quarrelling and antitrust lawsuits caused major delays, resulting in the deadline being moved to 2 November 2003. Owing to technical difficulties, the industry consortium could not meet this deadline either, leading to €180 million in lost revenues per month for the government. Further political disputes finally led to a revised start date, 1 January 2005, by which time a partial solution was implemented.

This time, success seems far more likely because large parts of the system have been tested with positive results; yet, as the overly optimistic initial goals could not be met, the German government as well as the companies involved have had huge losses. In 2003, Deutsche Telekom lost €210 million on the project, and DaimlerChrysler had to write off €250 million. As you can see, being realistic about goals and planning for contingencies is of major importance in IS project planning.

Sources: Anonymous, "Maut-Debakel bringt Telekom Verluste," *Netzeitung.de* (March 10, 2004), **www.netzeitung.de/servlets/page?section=5&item=276808**.
Anonymous, "Pleiten, Pech und Pannen," *Sueddeutsche.de* (February 17, 2004), **www.sueddeutsche.de/wirtschaft/artikel/875/26849**.
Bret Okeson, "DaimlerChrysler's Schrempp Faces Renewed Shareholder Criticism," Bloomberg.com (April 5, 2004), **http://quote.bloomberg.com/apps/news?pid=10000101&sid=aUsNwCf4HOKO&refer= japan**.
www.toll-collect.de.

Figure 8.2 The German Autobahn.
Source: Fabrizio Bensch/Reuters/Corbis

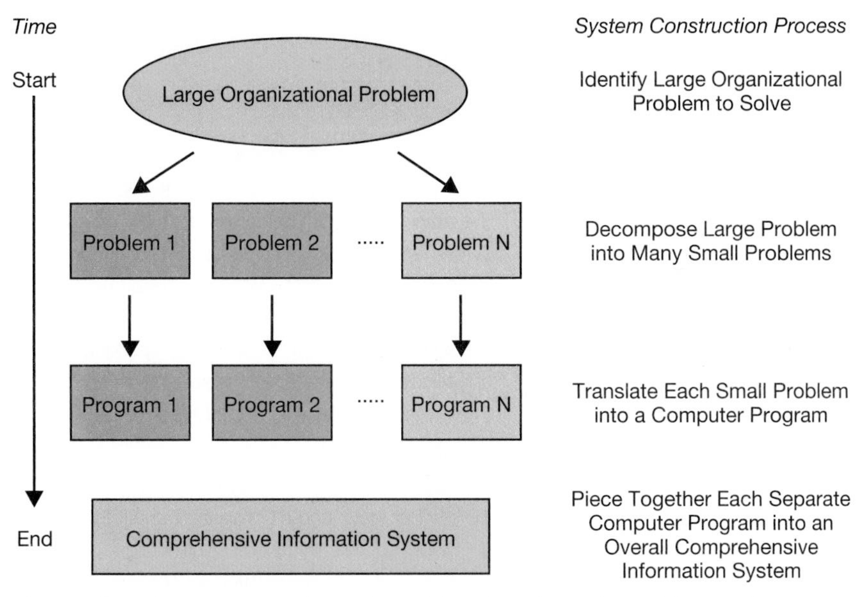

Figure 8.3 Problem decomposition makes solving big and complex problems easier.

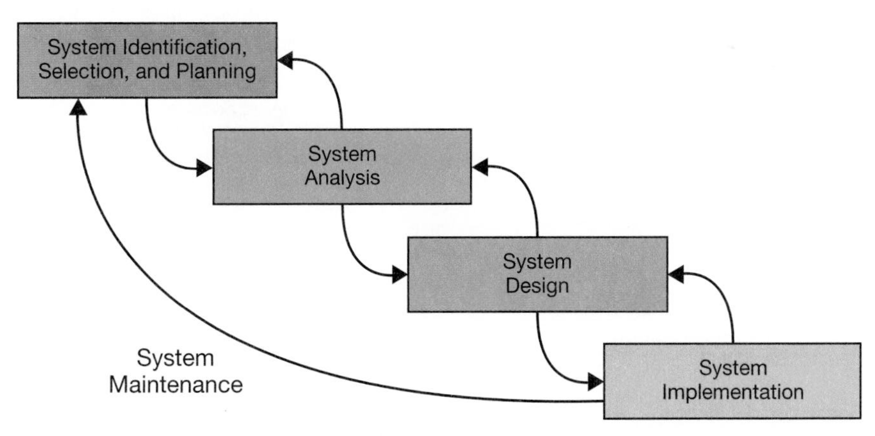

Figure 8.4 The systems development life cycle defines the typical process for building systems.

to the first is what makes the SDLC a cycle. The SDLC can be adapted to fit the requirements of different contexts and organizational environments. For example, the National Aeronautics and Space Administration (NASA) uses eight phases when developing its internal systems (see Brief Case: The Systems Development Life Cycle at NASA). However, most SDLC architectures, including NASA's, can be mapped onto the generic five-phase SDLC.

Phase 1: System Identification, Selection, and Planning

The first phase of the systems development life cycle is ***system identification, selection, and planning***, as shown in Figure 8.6. Understanding that it can work on only a limited number of projects at a given time due to limited resources, an organization must take care that only those projects that are critical in enabling the organization's mission, goals, and objectives are undertaken. Consequently, the goal of system identification and selection is simply to identify and select a development project from all possible projects that could be performed. Organizations differ in how they identify and select projects. Some organizations have a formal ***information systems planning*** process whereby a senior manager, a business group, an IS manager, or a steering committee identifies and assesses all possible systems development projects that an organization could undertake. Others follow a more ad hoc process for identifying potential projects or, in some cases, avoid planning altogether. Table 8.1 outlines some common excuses to avoid IS planning. Nonetheless, after all possible projects are identified, those deemed most likely to yield

BRIEF CASE

The Systems Development Life Cycle at NASA

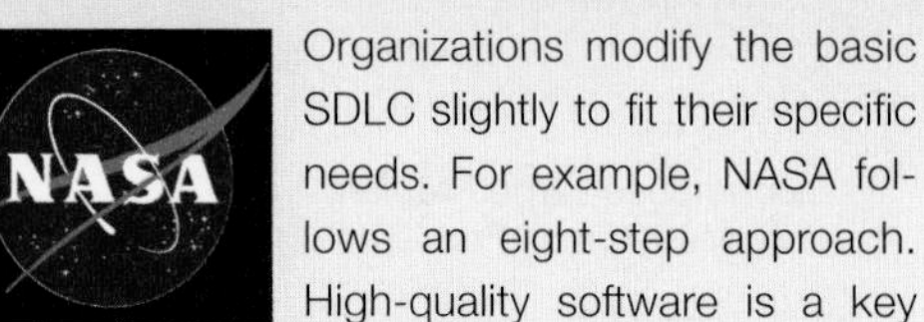

Organizations modify the basic SDLC slightly to fit their specific needs. For example, NASA follows an eight-step approach. High-quality software is a key component of NASA's success. The organization uses software to control countless earth-based systems such as those used to track, guide, and communicate with the space shuttles and space-based systems that control the functioning of orbiting satellites or even to find plankton in the world's oceans by analyzing the ocean colours (a system that has won NASA's Software of the Year Award in 2003). While the latter application is probably not mission critical, it is easy to imagine that a failure of the former systems could have catastrophic results. Consequently, NASA, like many other organizations, has chosen to follow a formal SDLC to help ensure software and system quality and, more importantly, to help protect the lives and safety of its astronauts. The value of having standard procedures and steps such as the SDLC when building software is that it not only speeds the development process but also ensures the creation of high-quality and reliable systems. As shown in Figure 8.5, the NASA SDLC comprises eight phases that are essentially the same as the five-step generic process described in this chapter. Within every step of the NASA SDLC, guidelines have been developed for accepting and ensuring the quality of work products created. These guidelines are used to make sure that all work products meet specifications and are error free before developers move to the next phase of the SDLC.

Questions

1. In what ways can a company benefit from an SDLC specifically tailored to the organization, as opposed to using the generic SDLC?
2. In which other ways could the SDLC be broken down for different industries? If you have access to the Internet, try to find examples of how the SDLC is modified for use in other industries.

Sources: Adapted from NASA, *Software Assurance Guidebook*, NASA-GB-A201, **http://satc.gsfc.nasa.gov/assure/agb.txt**. Anonymous, "NASA Honors Agency Software Development," *Spaceflight Now* (September 2, 2003), **www.spaceflightnow.com/news/n0309/02software**.

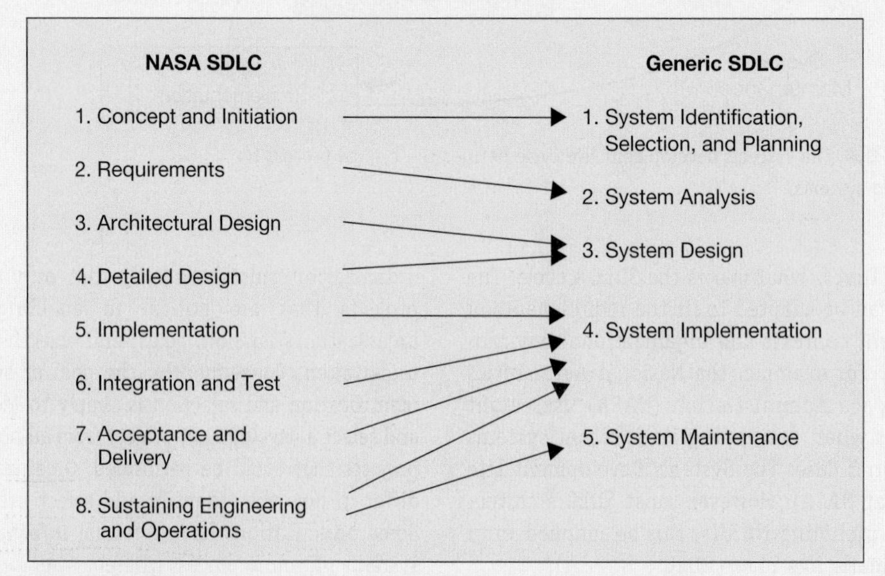

Figure 8.5 NASA's systems development life cycle as compared with the generic life cycle.

significant organizational benefits, given available resources, are selected for subsequent development activities.

It is important to note that different approaches for identifying and selecting projects are likely to yield different organizational outcomes (see Table 8.2). For example, projects identified by top management more often have a strategic organizational focus, and projects identified by steering committees more

Table 8.1 ***Common excuses to avoid IS planning.***

I have so little to spend on IT there is no point in planning.
We don't know anything about IT, so how can we plan?
Once you have chosen a vendor, they do the planning for you.
I don't have the staff or the time for a big planning exercise.
I have a friend who operates a similar company, so I just acquire what she has.

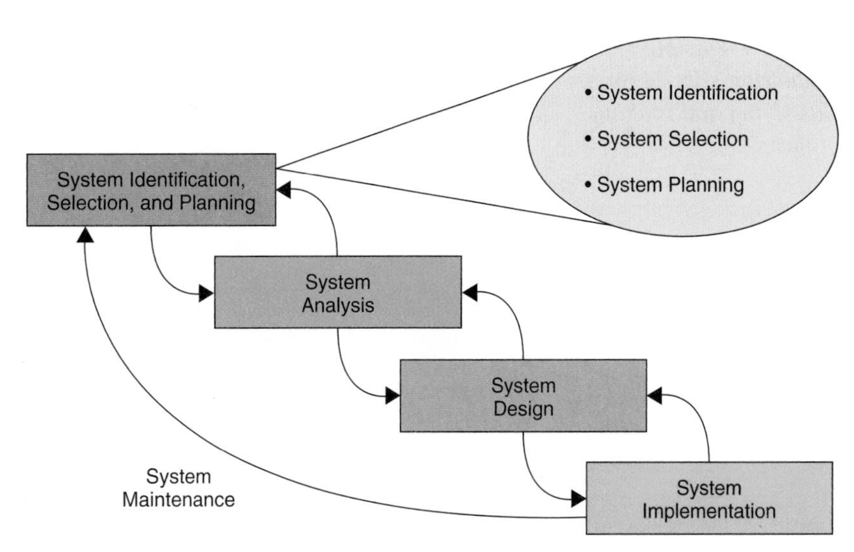

Figure 8.6 SDLC with Phase 1—system identification, selection, and planning—highlighted.

Table 8.2 ***Sources of systems development projects and their likely focus.***

Project Source	Primary Focus
Top management	Broad strategic focus
Steering committee	Cross-functional focus
Individual departments and business units	Narrow, tactical focus
Systems development group	Integration with existing information system focus

Adapted from McKeen, Guimaraes, and Wetherbe, 1994.

often reflect the diversity of the committee and therefore have a cross-functional focus. Projects identified by individual departments or business units most often have a narrow, tactical focus. Finally, the typical focus of projects identified by the development group is the ease with which existing hardware and systems can be integrated with the proposed project. Other factors—such as project cost, duration, complexity, and risk—are also influenced by the source of a given project. The source of projects has been found to be a key indicator of project focus and success.

Just as there are often differences in the source of systems projects within organizations, there are often different evaluation criteria used within organizations when classifying and ranking potential projects. During project planning, the analyst works with the customers—the potential users of the system and their managers—to collect a broad range of information to gain an understanding of the project size, potential benefits and costs, and other relevant factors. After collecting and analyzing this information, the analyst can bring it together into a summary planning document that can be reviewed and compared with other possible projects. Table 8.3 provides a sample of the criteria often used by organizations. When reviewing a potential development project, organizations may focus on a single criterion but most often examine multiple criteria to make a decision to accept or reject a project. If the organization accepts the project, system analysis begins.

Phase 2: System Analysis

The second phase of the systems development life cycle is called ***system analysis***, as highlighted in Figure 8.7. One purpose of the system analysis phase is for designers to gain a thorough understanding of an organization's current way of doing things in the area for which the new information system will be constructed. The process of conducting an analysis requires that many tasks, or subphases, be performed. The first subphase focuses on determining system requirements. To determine the requirements, an analyst works closely with users to determine what is needed from the proposed system. After collecting the requirements, analysts organize this information using data, process, and logic modelling tools. These elements will be illustrated and discussed later in the chapter (see Figure 8.11).

Collecting System Requirements

The collection and structuring of system requirements is arguably the most important activity in the systems development process

Web Search

One way to conduct interviews is over the telephone, using specially designed software. Visit **www.sawtooth.com** to get a feel for some of the services that are commercially available. If you try to look up "interviewing" in a web search engine, you will most likely find out a lot about how to have a successful job interview. This is a chance for you to practise your advanced web search skills (or to develop them) to find general information on interviewing for information systems requirements determination. What terms might you use other than "interviewing"? How might you qualify your search to find information more specific to your needs? Summarize your experiences in a two-page report to submit to your instructor.

Table 8.3 ***Possible evaluation criteria for classifying and ranking projects.***

Evaluation Criteria	Description
Strategic alignment 戰略聯盟	The extent to which the project is viewed as helping the organization achieve its strategic objectives and long-term goals.
Potential benefits	The extent to which the project is viewed as improving profits, customer service, and so forth, and the duration of these benefits.
Potential costs and resource availability	The number and types of resources the project requires and their availability.
Project size / duration	The number of individuals and the length of time needed to complete the project.
Technical difficulty / risks	The level of technical difficulty involved in successfully completing the project within a given time and resource constraint.

Hoffer, George, and Valacich, 2005.

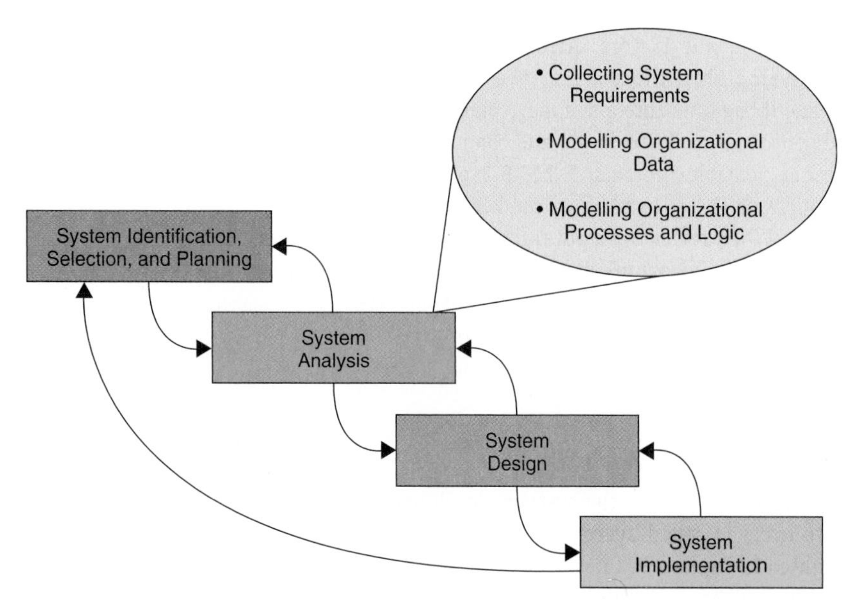

Figure 8.7 SDLC with Phase 2—system analysis—highlighted.

because how well the information system requirements are defined influences all subsequent activities. The old saying "garbage in, garbage out" very much applies to the system building process. ***Requirements collection*** is the process of gathering and organizing information from users, managers, business processes, and documents to understand how a proposed information system should function. Systems analysts use a variety of techniques for collecting system requirements, including (Hoffer, George, and Valacich, 2005)

- *Interviews.* Analysts interview people informed about the operation and issues of the current or proposed system.
- *Questionnaires.* Analysts design and administer surveys to gather opinions from people informed about the operation and issues of the current or proposed system.
- *Observations.* Analysts observe workers at selected times to see how data are handled and what information people need to do their jobs.
- *Document analysis.* Analysts study business documents to discover issues, policies, and rules as well as concrete examples of the use of data and information in the organization.

In addition to these techniques, there are contemporary approaches for collecting system requirements that include

- *Critical success factors (CSFs) methodology.* A CSF is something that must go well to ensure success for a manager, a department, a division, or an organization. To understand an organization's CSFs, a systems analyst interviews people throughout the organization and asks each person to define their own personal CSFs. After the analyst collects these individual CSFs, he or she can merge, consolidate, and refine them to identify a broad set of organization-wide CSFs, as shown in Figure 8.8. Table 8.4 summarizes the strengths and weaknesses of the CSF approach.
- *Joint application design (JAD).* A JAD is a special type of group meeting in which all (or most) users meet with the analyst at the same time. During this meeting, the users jointly define and agree upon system requirements or designs. This process has resulted in dramatic reductions in the

Table 8.4 ***Strengths and weaknesses of the CSF approach.***

Strengths	Weaknesses
Senior managers intuitively understand the approach and support its usage	High-level focus can lead to an oversimplification of a complex situation
Provides a method for understanding the information needs of the organization in order to make effective decisions	Difficulty in finding analysts trained to perform the CSF process that requires both understanding information systems and being able to communicate effectively with senior executives
	Method is not user-centred, but analyst focused

Boynton and Zmud, 1994.

length of time needed to collect requirements or specify designs. The JAD meeting can be held in a normal conference room or special-purpose JAD room (see Figure 8.9). Table 8.5 summarizes the strengths and weaknesses of the JAD approach.

Modelling Organizational Data

Data are facts that describe people, objects, or events. A lot of different facts can be used to describe a person: name, age, gender, race, and occupation, among others. To construct an information system, systems analysts must understand what data the IS needs to accomplish the intended tasks. To do this, they use data modelling tools to collect and describe the data to users to confirm that all needed data are known and presented to users as useful information. Figure 8.10 shows an entity-relationship diagram (ERD), a type of data model, describing students, classes, majors, and classrooms at a university. Each box in the diagram is referred to as a *data entity*. Each data entity may have one or more attributes that describe it. For example, a "student" entity may have attributes such as ID, name, and local address. Additionally, each data entity may be "related" to other data entities. For example, because students take classes, there is a relationship between students and classes: "Student Takes Class" and "Class Has Student." Relationships are represented in the diagram by lines drawn between related entities. Data modelling tools enable the systems analyst to represent data in a form that is easy for users to understand and critique. For more information on databases and data modelling, see Chapter 3, "Data and Knowledge Management."

Modelling Organizational Processes and Logic

As the name implies, ***data flows*** represent the movement of data through an organization or within an information system. For example, your registration for a class may be captured

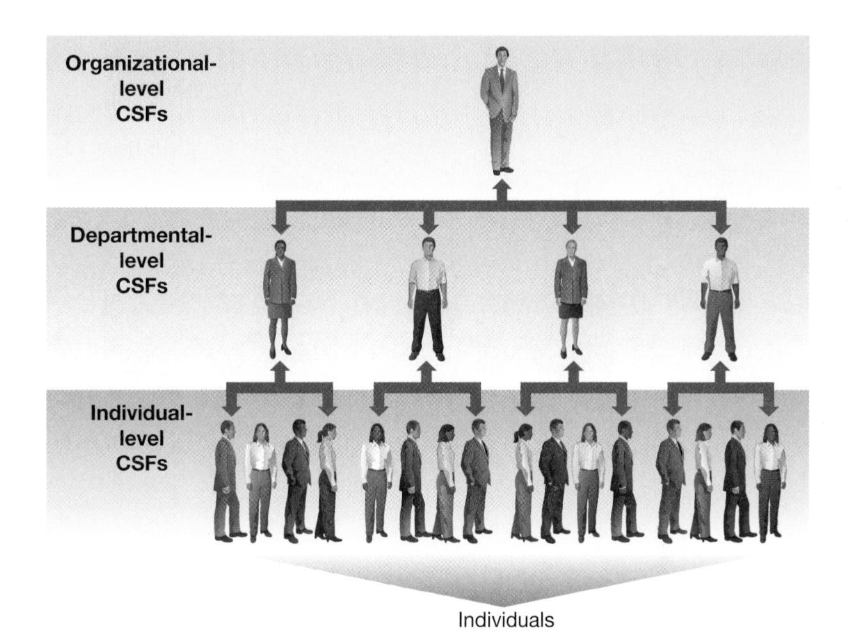

Figure 8.8 Merging individual CSFs to represent organization-wide CSFs.

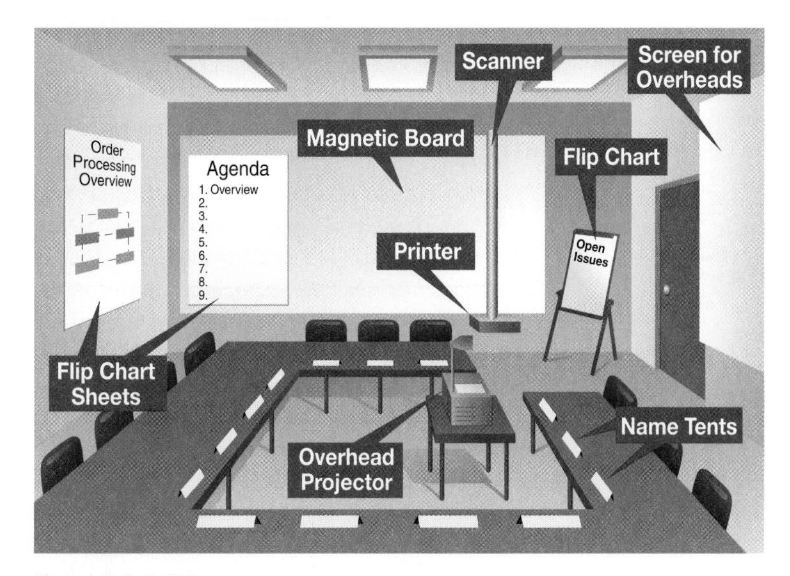

Figure 8.9 A JAD room.

Adapted from J. Wood and D. Silver, *Joint Application Design*, John Wiley & Sons. 1989.

Table 8.5 ***Strengths and weaknesses of the JAD approach.***

Strengths	Weaknesses
Group-based process enables more people to be involved in the development effort without adversely slowing the process	Very difficult to get all relevant users to the same place at the same time to hold a JAD meeting
Group-based process can lead to higher levels of system acceptance and quality	Requires high-level executive sponsor to ensure that adequate resources are available in order to allow widespread participation
Group involvement in the design and development process helps to ease implementation, user training, and ongoing support	

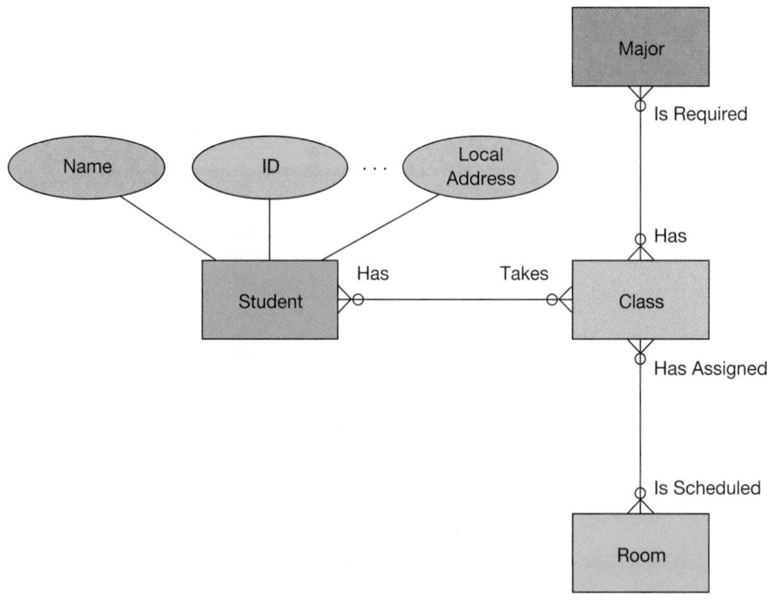

Figure 8.10 A sample ERD for students.

in a registration form on paper or on a computer terminal. After it is filled out, this form probably flows through several processes to validate and record the class registration, as shown as "Data Flows" in Figure 8.11. After all students have been registered, a repository of all registration information can be processed for developing class rosters or for generating student billing information, which is shown as "Data" in Figure 8.11. ***Processing logic*** represents the way in which data are transformed. For example, processing logic is used to calculate students' grade point averages (GPAs) at the conclusion of a term, as shown in the "Processing Logic" section in Figure 8.11.

After the data, data flow, and processing logic requirements for the proposed system have been identified, analysts develop one or many possible overall approaches—sometimes

ETHICAL DILEMMA

Protecting the Existing Structures—An Ethical Dilemma in IS Development

User input is one of the most important factors in successful information systems development; end users often have a good insight into what a new system should look like. Having worked extensively with the existing systems, the end users can point to features they would like to see added, changed, or dropped from the new system. For these reasons, the systems analyst usually seeks user input at different stages of the systems development life cycle.

Frequently, the different stakeholders of an IS development have divergent goals, especially in cases where existing business processes are radically changed. Consider Dave, the human resources manager of ACME Inc. in Regina, a company that is about to introduce a new payroll processing system (ACME and Dave are real people—the names have been changed to maintain confidentiality). Being a human resources manager, Dave has extensive input into the systems analysis and design process for the new system. The systems analyst has indicated that the addition of certain modules to the system would make several jobs redundant; owing to the good work climate, Dave has become a close friend with many of the employees who would face a layoff. As Dave knows that the additional modules would save the company a large amount of money due to staff reduction and error reduction, he feels obliged to support the installation of the additional modules. However, knowing that several of his employees would not be able to support their families after the layoff, he decides to find arguments against the installation of the modules. How would you have decided?

Requirements

Data

Name	Class	GPA
Suzanne Rivard	Senior	3.7
Lucas Yang	Grad	2.9
David Honsberger	Fresh	3.2

Data Flows

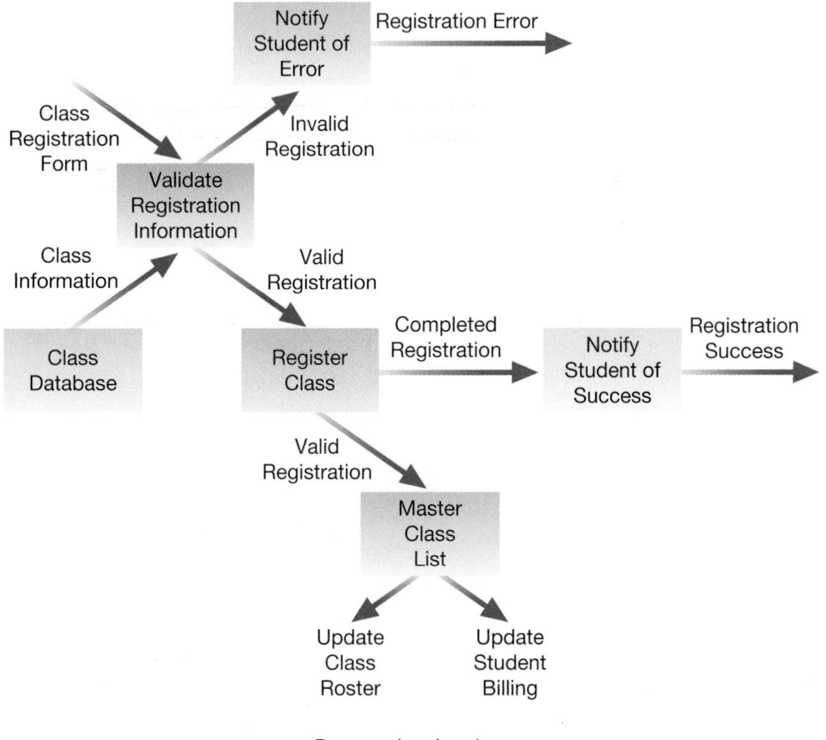

Processing Logic

```
i = read (number_of_classes)
total_hours = 0
total_grade = 0
total_gpa = 0
for j = 1 to i do
        begin
                read (course [ j ], hours [ j ], grade [ j ])
                total_hours = total_hours + hours [ j ]
                total_grade = total_grade + (hours [ j ] * grade [ j ])
        end
current_gpa = total_grade / total hours
```

Figure 8.11 Four key elements in the development of a system: Requirements, Data, Data Flows, and Processing Logic.

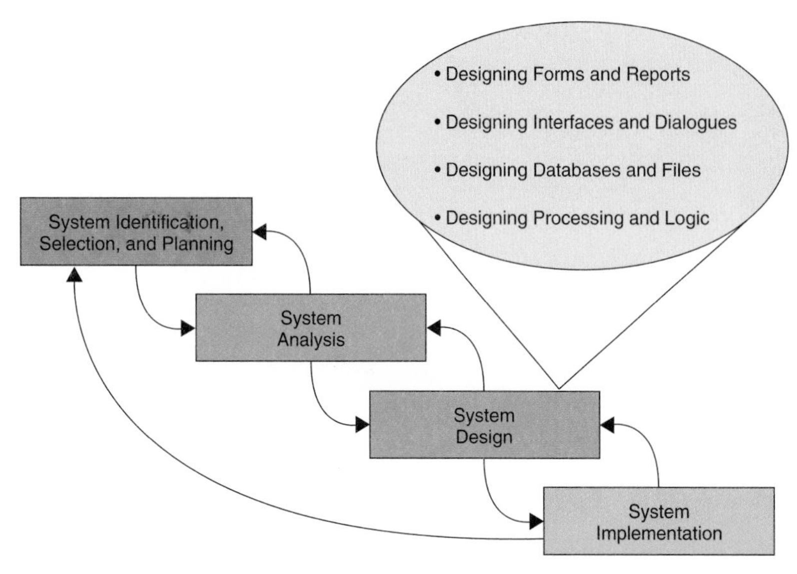

Figure 8.12 SDLC with Phase 3—system design—highlighted.

called designs—for the information system. For example, one approach for the system may possess only basic functionality but have the advantage of being relatively easy and inexpensive to build. An analyst might also propose a more elaborate approach for the system, but it may be more difficult and more costly to build. Analysts evaluate alternative system approaches with the knowledge that different solutions yield different benefits and different costs. After a system approach is selected, then details of that particular system approach can be defined.

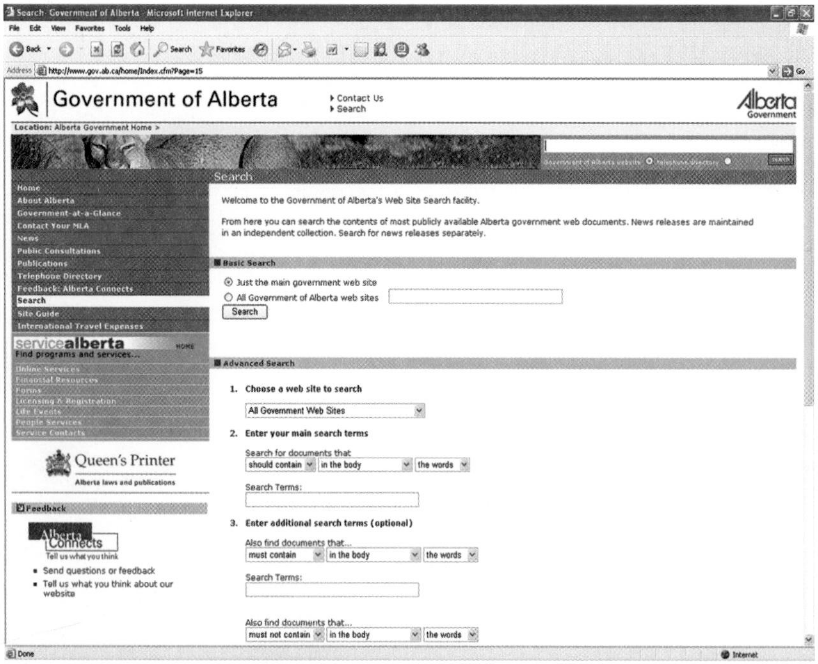

Figure 8.13 Government of Alberta advanced search form.

Source: © 1995–2006 Government of Alberta. Alberta Public Affairs Bureau.

Phase 3: System Design

The third phase of the systems development life cycle is ***system design***, as shown in Figure 8.12. As its name implies, it is during this phase that the proposed system is designed; that is, the details of the chosen approach are developed. As with analysis, many different activities must occur during system design. The elements that must be designed when building an information system include

- Forms and reports
- Interfaces and dialogues
- Databases and files
- Processing and logic

Designing Forms and Reports

A ***form*** is a business document containing some predefined data and often including some areas where additional data can be filled in. Figure 8.13 shows a computer-based form taken from a website of the Government of Alberta. Using this form, users can search for a wide variety of service information.

A ***report*** is a business document containing only predefined data. In other words, reports are static documents that are used to summarize information for reading or viewing. For example, Figure 8.14 shows a report summarizing regional sales performance for several salespeople.

Designing Interfaces and Dialogues

Just as people have different ways of interacting with other people, information systems can have different ways of interacting with people. A system interface might be text-based, communicating with you through text and forcing you to communicate with it the same way. Alternatively, a system interface could use graphics and colour as a way to interact with you, providing you with colour-coded windows and special icons. A system dialogue could be developed that does nothing and waits for you to type in a command. Or it could ask you questions to which you respond by typing in commands, or present you with a menu of choices from which you select your desired options. It could even do all these things. Over the past several years, standards for user interfaces and dialogues have emerged, making things easier for both designers and users. For example, both the Macintosh and the Windows operating systems are standards that are generally referred to as being a ***graphical user interface (GUI)***

Ascend Systems Incorporated
SALESPERSON ANNUAL SUMMARY REPORT 2006

REGION	SALESPERSON	SIN	QUARTERLY ACTUAL SALES FIRST	SECOND	THIRD	FOURTH
Nova Scotia						
	Park	123 456 789	16 500	18 600	24 300	18 000
	Angellotti	123 456 789	22 000	15 500	17 300	19 800
	Irving	123 456 789	19 000	12 500	22 000	28 000
New Brunswick						
	Doucet	123 456 789	14 000	16 000	19 000	21 000
	Fleury	123 456 789	7 500	16 600	10 000	8 000
	Bouquet	123 456 789	12 000	19 800	17 000	19 000
PEI						
	Clark	123 456 789	18 000	18 000	20 000	27 000
	Yim	123 456 789	28 000	29 000	19 000	31 000

Figure 8.14 Sales summary report.

Web Search

Some web-based forms are designed better than others. Go to the web and critique a form from one of your favourite websites, such as Sony (**www.sony.com**) or Roots (**www.roots.com/new_canada/html/index_canada.shtml**). Alternatively, an easy way to find such a form would be to go to any search engine—AltaVista or Google (**www.altavista.com, www.google.ca**)—and look at its "advanced" or "power" search form. Could any of these forms be improved? If so, how?

(Figure 8.15). (See Appendix B, "Information Systems Software," for more on GUIs.)

Designing Databases and Files

To design databases and files, a systems analyst must have a thorough understanding of an organization's data and informational needs. As described previously, a systems analyst often uses data modelling tools to first gain a comprehensive understanding of all the data used by a proposed system. After the conceptual data model has been completed, typically using an entity-relationship diagram, it can be easily translated into a physical data model in a database management system. For example, Figure 8.15 shows a physical data model to keep track of student information in Microsoft Access. The physical data model is more complete (shows more information about the student) and more detailed (shows how the information is formatted) than a conceptual data model. For example, contrast Figure 8.16 with the conceptual model in Figure 8.11 that contains student information.

Designing Processing and Logic

The processing and logic operations of an information system are the steps and procedures that transform raw data inputs into new or modified information. For example, when calculating your grade point average, your school needs to perform the following steps:

1. Obtain the prior GPA, credit hours earned, and list of prior courses.
2. Obtain the list of each current course, final grade, and course credit hours.
3. Combine the prior and current credit hours into aggregate sums.
4. Calculate the new GPA.

The logic and steps needed to make this calculation can be represented in many ways. One method, referred to as *writing pseudocode*—a textual notation for describing programming code—enables the systems analyst to describe the processing steps in a manner that is similar to how a programmer might implement the steps in an actual programming language. The "Processing Logic" in Figure 8.11 is an example of pseudocode. Other tools used by systems analysts during this activity include structure charts and decision trees. Converting pseudocode, structure charts, and decision trees into actual program code during system implementation is a very straightforward process.

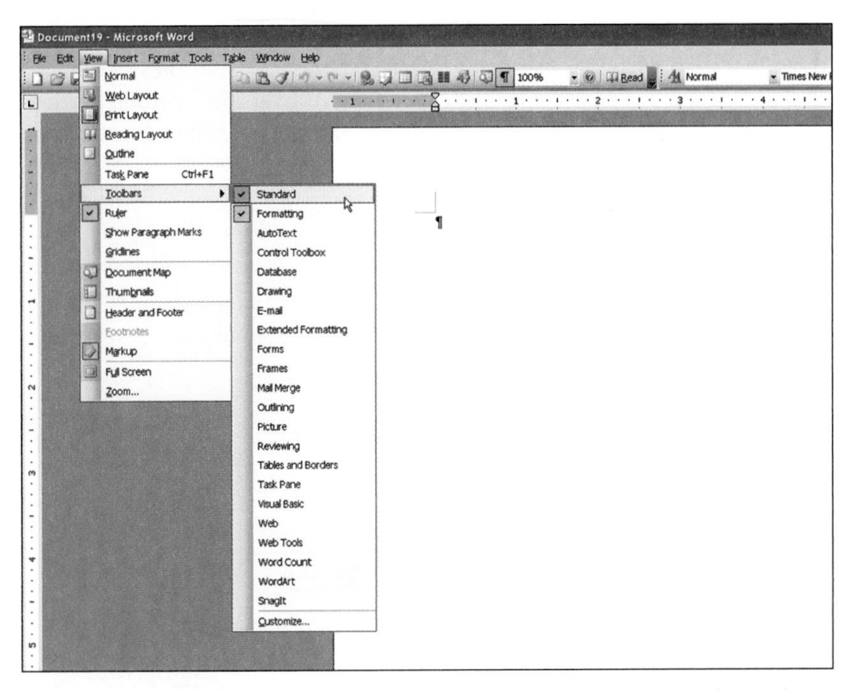

Figure 8.15 Most Windows-based programs follow a standard that governs the naming and placement of menus that makes it easier for users and for designers.

C:\MSOFFICCE\ACCESS\STUDENT.MDB — Sunday, June 23, 2006
Table: Students — Page: 1

Properties

Date Created:	6/23/06 10:35:41 PM	Def. Updatable:	Yes
Last Updated:	6/23/06 10:35:43 PM	Record Count:	0

Columns

Name	Type	Size
StudentID	Number (Long)	4
FirstName	Text	50
MiddleName	Text	30
LastName	Text	50
ParentsNames	Text	255
Address	Text	255
City	Text	50
Province	Text	50
Region	Text	50
PostalCode	Text	20
PhoneNumber	Text	30
EmailName	Text	50
Major	Text	50
Note	Memo	–

Figure 8.16 An Access database that shows the physical data model for student information.

Phase 4: System Implementation

Many separate activities occur during ***system implementation***, the fourth phase of the systems development life cycle, as highlighted in Figure 8.17. One group of activities focuses on transforming the system design into a working information system that can be used by the organization. These activities include software programming and testing. A second group of activities focuses on preparing the organization for using the new IS. These activities include system conversion, documentation, user training, and support. This section briefly describes what occurs during system implementation.

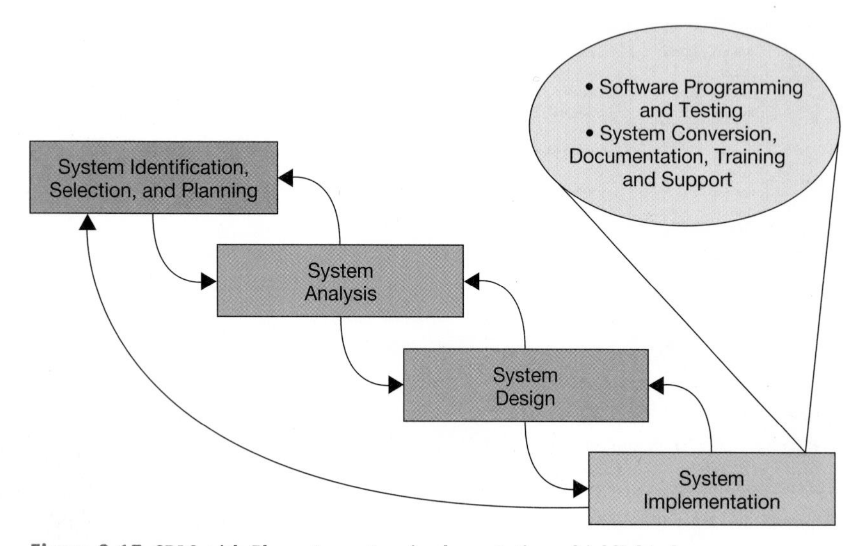

Figure 8.17 SDLC with Phase 4—system implementation—highlighted.

Software Programming and Testing

Programming is the process of transforming the system design into a working computer system. During this transformation, both processing and testing should occur in parallel. As you might expect, a broad range of tests are conducted before a system is complete, including developmental, alpha, and beta testing (see Table 8.6). In fact, software testing is a skill that is very much in demand in today's development environments (see Brief Case: Profile of a Software Tester).

System Conversion, Documentation, Training, and Support

System conversion is the process of decommissioning the current system (automated or manual) and installing the new system in the organization. Effective conversion of a system requires not only that the new software be installed but also that users be effectively trained and supported. System conversion can be performed in at least four ways, as shown in Figure 8.18.

Many types of documentation must be produced for an information system. Programmers develop system documentation that details the inner workings of the system to ease future maintenance. A second type of documentation is user-related documentation, which is not typically written by programmers or analysts but by users or professional technical writers. The range of documents can include the following:

- User and reference guides
- User training and tutorials
- Installation procedures and troubleshooting suggestions

In addition to documentation, users may also need training and ongoing support to use a new system effectively. Different types of training and support require different levels of investment by the organization. Self-paced training and tutorials are the least expensive options, and one-to-one training is the most expensive. Table 8.7 summarizes various user-training options.

In addition to training, providing ongoing education and problem-solving assistance for users is necessary. This is commonly referred to as ***system support***, which is often provided by a special group of people in the organization who make up an information centre (IC) or help desk. Support personnel must have strong

Testing Type	Focus	Performed by
Developmental	Testing the correctness of individual modules and the integration of multiple modules	Programmer
Alpha	Testing of overall system to see whether it meets design requirements	Software tester
Beta	Testing of the capabilities of the system in the user environment with actual data	Actual system users

Table 8.6 ***General testing types, their focus, and who performs them.***

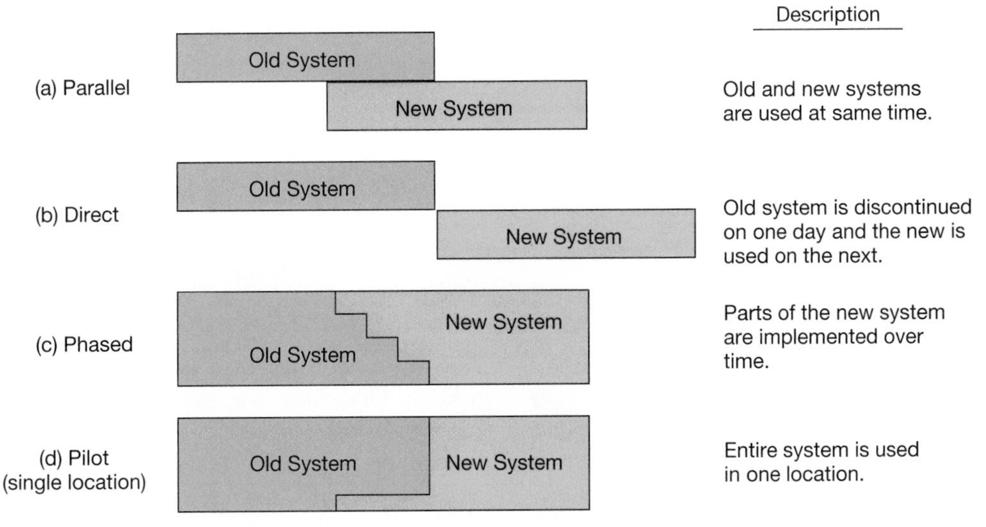

Figure 8.18 Software conversion strategies.

COMING ATTRACTIONS

Done with Your Work? Roll Up Your Screen and Take It Home!

In the coming years, it is predicted that electronic paper (e-paper) will revolutionize the way we're reading books or newspapers. E-paper offers the possibility to display black-and-white text and graphics on a flexible screen that can be rolled up after use and reused for reading the next day's edition of your favourite newspaper.

While e-paper has yet to hit the stores, scientists in Canada and the Netherlands are already working on flexible screens able to display moving images, which would make it possible to construct flexible e-paper or even flexible television screens. At the University of Toronto, a team of scientists has developed flexible screens using flexible organic light-emitting devices (FOLEDs), which can be produced at relatively low costs once they are ready to be produced on a large scale. Similarly, scientists at electronic giant Philips's research centre have developed a way to represent high-definition moving pictures on flexible screens using a technique called electrowetting, which promises the display of video content at movie speeds. Even though it still might take a few years for either of these two technologies to reach the market, aren't you looking forward to being able to unroll a flexible screen and use it with your cell phone to hold a videoconference with your friends?

Sources: Anonymous, "Catch a Flick on Flexible E-Paper," *Wired News* (September 24, 2003), **www.wired.com/news/technology/0,1282,60575,00.html**.
Anonymous, "Flexible E-Paper on Its Way," *Wired News* (May 7, 2003), **www.wired.com/news/technology/0,1282,58765,00.html**.
University of Toronto, "Flexible Screen Technology Ready to Roll," *ScienceDaily* (January 21, 2004), **www.sciencedaily.com/releases/2004/01/040121075325.htm**.

Table 8.7 ***User training options.***

Training Option	Description
Tutorial	One person taught at one time by a human or by paper-based exercises
Course	Several people taught at one time
Computer-aided instruction	One person taught at one time by the computer system
Interactive training manuals	Combination of tutorials and computer-aided instruction
Resident expert	Expert on call to assist users as needed
Software help components	Built-in system components designed to train and troubleshoot problems
External sources	Vendors, and training providers to provide tutorials, courses, and other training activities

BRIEF CASE

Profile of a Software Tester

A software tester spends most of his or her time trying to break software. Breaking software is referred to in the computer industry as "finding bugs." A bug is a programming error, design flaw, or anything else that results in the computer program not running as intended. Software testers spend countless hours trying to identify problems, typically long before the software is released to a widespread audience. Most software testers work, as you would guess, for software and computer companies such as Microsoft, IBM, or Netscape Communications. Software testers also work for companies in banking, insurance, and literally any other company devoted to developing high-quality software. For many companies, such as Scribe Software, a developer of data migration software, having the product certified for use with Microsoft products can be the key to successfully selling the software; therefore, companies such as VeriTest have specialized in offering software testing services for products to be compatible with Microsoft's software.

In most cases, software testers are not systems developers, but many know how to program. Organizations have discovered that testers find more errors if the people testing the software are separate from the development group. Companies often give cash bonuses to testers for each bug found to give them a strong motivation to find these pesky errors. Because testers must not only find errors but also describe them after they are found, software testers must also have good communication skills and be detail oriented, patient, self-motivated, and creative. In addition to looking for bugs, software testers are often assigned to provide customer support and training because of their intricate knowledge of how a new system works. Creating high-quality software requires a cooperative team of system designers, programmers, and testers. Good software testers are in high demand. So, if you like breaking things and getting paid for it, maybe you would be a good software tester.

Questions

1. Whereas some companies test their software thoroughly, others are trying to use a more reactive approach by first bringing the software to the market and then providing fixes and updates whenever problems come up. Under which circumstances would a company choose to use one approach over the other?
2. In the open source community, users are often "beta testers" of software products. Why do users do this "job" for free and offer their suggestions for improvement, if professional software testers can earn up to $75 000 for this?

Sources: Anonymous, "Scribe Hopes to Write Success Story with 'Verified For Microsoft CRM Status,'" ebizQ.net (May 10, 2004), **www.ebizq.net/news/4388.html**. Software Testing Institute, **www.softwaretestinginstitute.com.**

communication skills and be good problem solvers, in addition to being expert users of the system. An alternative option for a system not developed internally is to outsource support activities to a vendor specializing in technical system support and training. Regardless of how support is provided, it is an ongoing issue that must be managed effectively for the company to realize the maximum benefits of a system.

Phase 5: System Maintenance

After an information system is installed, it is essentially in the maintenance phase of the SDLC. In the maintenance phase, one person within the systems development group is responsible for collecting maintenance requests from system users. After they are collected, requests are analyzed so that the developer can better understand how the proposed change might alter the system and what business benefits and necessities might result from such a change. If the change request is approved, a system change is designed and then implemented. As with the initial development of the system, implemented changes are formally reviewed and tested before installation into operational systems. The ***system maintenance*** process parallels the process used for the initial development of the IS, as shown in Figure 8.19.

Interestingly, it is during system maintenance that the largest part of the system development effort occurs.

The question must be, then, why does all this maintenance occur? It is not as if software wears out in the physical manner that cars, buildings, or other physical objects do. Correct? Yes, but software must still be maintained. The types of maintenance are summarized in Table 8.8.

As with adaptive maintenance, both perfective and preventive maintenance are typically a much lower priority than corrective maintenance. Over the life of a system, corrective maintenance is most likely to occur after initial system installation or after major system changes. This means that adaptive, perfective, and preventive maintenance activities can lead to corrective maintenance activities if they are not carefully designed and implemented.

As you can see, there is more to system maintenance than you might think. Lots of time, effort, and money are spent in this final phase of a system's development, and it is important to follow prescribed, structured steps. In fact, the approach to systems development described in this chapter, from the initial phase of identifying, selecting, and planning for systems, to the final phase of system maintenance, is a very structured and systematic process. Each phase is fairly well prescribed and requires active involvement by systems people, users, and managers. It is likely that you will

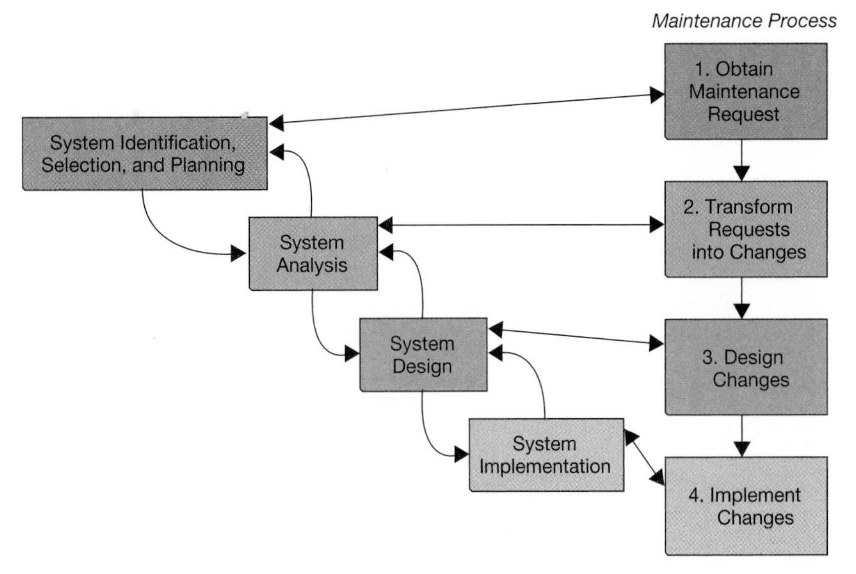

Figure 8.19 Mapping of maintenance to SDLC.

Table 8.8 ***Types of software maintenance.***

Maintenance Type	Description
Corrective maintenance	Making changes to an information system to repair flaws in the design, coding, or implementation
Adaptive maintenance	Making changes to an information system to evolve its functionality to accommodate changing business needs or to migrate it to a different operating environment
Perfective maintenance	Making enhancements to improve processing performance or interface usability, or adding desired, but not necessarily required, system features (in other words, "bells and whistles")
Preventive maintenance	Making changes to a system to reduce the chance of future system failure

have numerous opportunities to participate in the acquisition or development of a new system for an organization for which you currently work or will work in the future. Now that you have an understanding of the process, you should be better equipped to make a positive contribution to the success of any systems development project.

OTHER APPROACHES TO DESIGNING AND BUILDING SYSTEMS

The systems development life cycle is one approach to managing the development process and is a very good approach to follow when the requirements for the IS are highly structured and straightforward—for example, for a payroll or inventory system. Today, organizations need a broad variety of IS, not just payroll and inventory systems, for which requirements either are very hard to specify in advance or are constantly changing. For example, an organization's website is likely to be an information system with constantly changing requirements. How many websites have you visited in which the content or layout seemed to change almost every day? For this type of system, the SDLC might work as a development approach, but it would not be optimal. In this section, we describe three approaches for developing flexible information systems: prototyping, rapid application development, and object-oriented analysis and design.

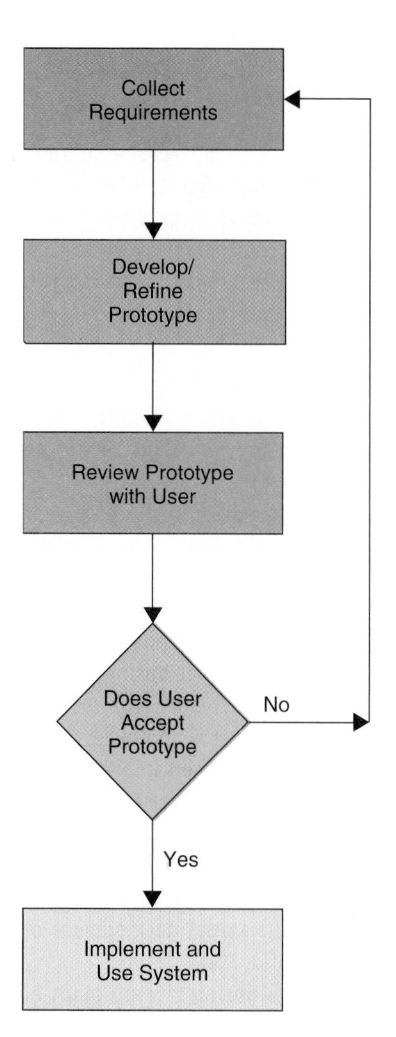

Figure 8.20 The prototyping process uses a trial-and-error approach to discovering how a system should operate.

Prototyping

Prototyping is a systems development methodology that uses a "trial and error" approach for discovering how a system should operate. You may think that this does not sound like a process at all; however, you probably use prototyping all the time in many of your day-to-day activities, but you just do not know it! For example, when you buy new clothes, you likely use prototyping—that is, trial and error—by trying on several shirts before making a selection.

Figure 8.20 diagrams the prototyping process when applied to identifying/determining system requirements. To begin the process, the system designer interviews one or several users of the system, either individually or as a group, using a JAD. After the designer gains a general understanding of what the users want, he or she develops a prototype of the new system as quickly as possible to share with the users. The users may like what they see or ask for changes. If the users request changes, the designer modifies the prototype and again shares it with them. This process of sharing and refinement continues until the users approve the functionality of the system.

Rapid Application Development

Rapid application development (RAD) is a four-phase systems development methodology that combines prototyping, computer-based development tools, special management practices, and close user involvement (Hoffer, George, and Valacich, 2005; McConnell, 1996; Martin, 1991). RAD has four phases: (1) requirements planning, (2) user design, (3) construction, and (4) the move to the new system. Phase 1, requirements planning, is similar to the first two phases of the SDLC, in which the system is planned and requirements are analyzed. To gain intensive user involvement, the RAD methodology encourages the use of JAD sessions to collect requirements.

Where RAD becomes radical is during phase 2, in which users of the IS become intensively involved in the design process. Computer-aided software engineering (CASE) and other advanced development tools (see Appendix B) are used to structure requirements and develop prototypes quickly. As prototypes are developed and refined, they are continually reviewed with users in additional JAD sessions. Like prototyping, RAD is a process in which requirements, designs, and the system itself are developed through iterative refinement, as shown in Figure 8.21. In a sense, with the RAD approach, the people building the system and the users of that system keep cycling back and forth between phase 2 (user design) and phase 3 (construction) until the system is finished. As a result, RAD requires close cooperation between users and designers to be successful. This means that management must actively support the development project and make it a priority for everyone involved. Table 8.9 illustrates the strengths and weaknesses of the three approaches to IS development discussed in this section.

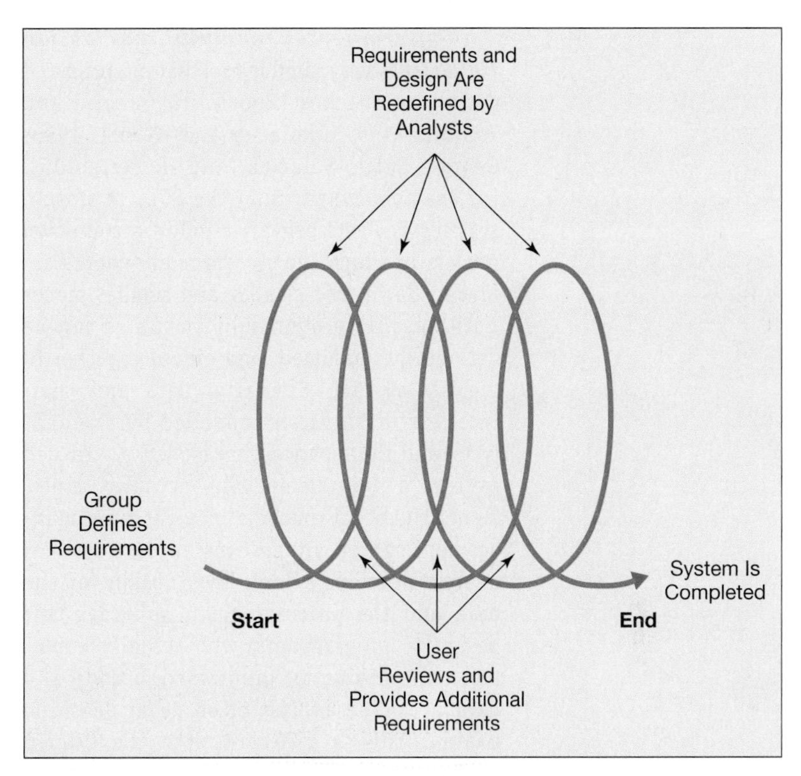

Figure 8.21 Iterative refinement is a key to the success of RAD.

Object-Oriented Analysis and Design

Object-oriented programming (OOP) is built around the idea that software can be made up of many interlinked objects. These objects can send, receive, and process data as well as communicate with other objects. As such, each object can be seen as a separate and independent component of a program. Objects can be recycled and reused in different programs. Thus, software does not need to be written from the ground up each time a new program is written, providing a way to develop programs at a reduced cost. The idea of OOP is quite different from traditional programming where software is thought of as a collection of procedures or instructions. Object-oriented programming has become very popular in software development and design. A more detailed discussion of OOP can be found in Appendix B.

Table 8.9 ***Strengths and weaknesses of prototyping, RAD, and object-oriented analysis and design approaches.***

Approach	Strengths	Weaknesses
Prototyping	Develops close working relationship between designer and users; works well for messy and hard-to-define problems	Not practical with a large number of users; system may be built too quickly, which could result in lower quality
Rapid Application Development	Active user involvement in design process; easier implementation due to user involvement	Systems are often narrowly focused—limits future evolution; system may be built too quickly, which could result in lower quality
Object-Oriented Analysis and Design	Integration of data and processing during design should lead to higher-quality systems; reuse of common modules makes development and maintenance easier	Very difficult to train analysts and programmers on the object-oriented approach; limited use of common modules

Object-oriented analysis and design (OOA&D) is very similar to other analysis and design approaches (Booch, 1990; Coad and Yourdon, 1991; Halladay and Wiebel, 1993; George, Batra, Valacich, and Hoffer, 2005). For example, when using the SDLC approach, systems analysts primarily follow a top-down process in which the system requirements are broken down into smaller and smaller pieces until specific programming modules can be defined, programmed, and pieced together to yield a system. Similarly, data and their interrelationships are modelled by the analysts, and these conceptual models are turned over to a programmer who actually implements these data models in a database management system. In most instances, a systems analyst develops a high-level design for the data and the processing and provides this design to programmers, who actually implement the design in programming code and databases. The analyst often never does any coding. This is different with the OOA&D approach, because of its tight coupling between the methods and data and between the conceptual model of the system and its actual implementation. OOA&D can turn every programmer into an analyst and every analyst into a programmer. What this means is that the analyst using an OOA&D approach can be thinking simultaneously right from the start about the "what" (the data) and the "how" (the operations to be performed) as he or she defines all the relevant objects that the system entails. Furthermore, if an object-oriented programming language is being used, it enables the design and implementation of the objects to happen quickly and simultaneously. In sum, OOA&D is a more integrative prototyping process than the SDLC approach, in which data and operations on the data are modelled separately and at a conceptual level and are later implemented and brought together in a subsequent phase of the systems development process.

This section has described other popular information systems development approaches beyond the SDLC. Additionally, there are even more approaches for designing and constructing IS beyond those discussed here (e.g., Agile Methodologies, EXtreme Programming). Each of these alternative methodologies focuses either on overcoming the limitations of the traditional SDLC or on finding ways to optimize some unique aspect of the development process (see Hoffer, George, and Valacich, 2005). Thus, the wise organization and skilled analyst often utilize multiple methods when developing a single system. What should be clear to you is that no approach is perfect and that all have strengths and weaknesses (see Table 8.9); a skilled systems developer, much like a skilled craftsperson, has many tools at his or her disposal. The skilled craftsperson chooses the most appropriate tool and approach for the task at hand. Using one systems development approach or tool for all systems and problems is akin to using only a hammer to build a house. Building a house with just a hammer might be possible, but it would probably be a strange-looking house!

NEED FOR ALTERNATIVES TO BUILDING SYSTEMS YOURSELF

Building systems in-house with the IS staff is always an option to consider. Many times, however, this is not a feasible solution. The following are four situations in which you might need to consider alternative development strategies.

Situation 1: Limited Information Systems Staff

Often, an organization does not have the capability to build a system itself. Perhaps its IS staff is small or deployed on other activities, such as maintaining a small network and helping users with problems on a day-to-day basis. This limited staff may simply not have the capability to take on an in-house development project without hiring several analysts or programmers, which is very expensive in today's labour market. For example, ADP Investor Communications provides a useful outsourced service to the financial services industry. Every time an investor purchases a mutual fund in Canada, the law requires that he or she receive a full prospectus of the fund within 48 hours. The process of collecting and mailing this information can be very cumbersome and expensive. ADP developed an outsourced solution that fulfills this requirement (see SME Success: ADP Develops Outsourced Service to Streamline the Distribution of Financial Information).

Situation 2: Information Systems Staff Has Limited Skill Set

In other situations, the IS staff may not have the skills needed to develop a particular kind of system. This has been especially true with the explosion of the web; many organizations are having outside groups manage their sites. For example, Walt Disney contracted the development and management of its website and the sites of many of its subsidiaries, including ABC News and ESPN, to a company called Starwave.com. Starwave was founded by Paul Allen, one of Bill Gates's initial partners at Microsoft and owner of the Portland Trailblazers, Seattle Seahawks, and numerous other companies (**www.paulallen.com**). This relationship continued until 1998, when Disney purchased Starwave and transformed it into the Walt Disney Internet Group (Court, 1998). In essence, Disney did not initially have the right set of skills to move onto the Internet, so it had an outside organization develop and manage its websites. Once it realized the strategic importance of the Internet, Disney purchased this expertise by buying Starwave. In sum, although the existing IS staff at Disney was highly skilled at producing and managing traditional applications, the sudden call for web-based systems required that Disney seek outside help. It is not as if the IS director can tell the CEO that Disney cannot build a new website because the IS staff does not have the necessary skills to build it! Fortunately, there are alternatives to having the IS staff build the system; the IS director can simply tap into specialized skills that are not present within the existing IS staff but that are available on the open market.

Situation 3: Information Systems Staff Is Overworked

In some organizations, the IS staff may simply not have the time to work on all the systems that the organization requires or wants. Obviously, the number of people dedicated to new development is not infinite. Therefore, you must have ways to prioritize development projects. In most cases, systems that are of strategic importance or that affect the whole organization are likely to receive a higher priority than those that offer only minor benefits or affect only one department or a couple of people in a department. Nonetheless, the IS manager must find a way to support all users, even when the IS staff may be tied up with other "higher-priority" projects.

Situation 4: Problems with Performance of Information Systems Staff

Earlier in this book, we discussed how and why systems development projects could sometimes be risky. Often the efforts of IS departments are derailed due to staff turnover, changing requirements, shifts in technology, or budget constraints. Regardless of the reason, the result is the same: another failed (or flawed) system. Given the large expenditures in staff time and training as well as the high risk associated with systems development efforts, the prudent manager tries to limit the risk of any project as much as possible. What if it were possible to see the completed system to know what it looked like before development began? Being able to see into the future would certainly help you learn more about the system and whether it would meet your needs, and it would help to lower the risk of a project. When building a system in-house, it is obviously not possible to see into the future. However, using some of the alternative methods described in this chapter, you can, in fact, see what a completed system might look like. These methods will enable you to know what you are buying, which greatly lowers the risk of a project.

COMMON ALTERNATIVES TO IN-HOUSE SYSTEMS DEVELOPMENT

Any project has at least four different systems development options. Previously, we discussed the first option: building the system in-house with your IS staff. The other options are

- External acquisition
- Outsourcing
- End-user development

The following sections examine each of these options in closer detail to see how one or more of them might fit the four situations described in the preceding section.

External Acquisition

Purchasing an existing system from an outside vendor such as IBM, EDS, or Accenture is referred to as ***external acquisition***. How does external acquisition of an IS work? Think about the process that you might use when buying a car. Do you simply walk into the first dealership you see, tell them you need a car, and see what they try to sell you? You had better not. Probably you have done some upfront analysis and know how much money you can afford to spend and what your needs are. If you have done your homework, you probably have an idea of what you want and

SME SUCCESS

ADP Develops Outsourced Service to Streamline the Distribution of Financial Information

ADP Investor Communications is a Mississauga, Ontario–based provider of outsourced transaction processing systems and investor communications services to the financial industry. ADP serves 14 000 North American public corporations on behalf of more than 100 financial institutions and mutual fund companies. The company provides corporate mailings and voting notices to security owners collected electronically from brokers, banks, trust companies, and their service bureaus.

When an investment dealer sells a mutual fund to a Canadian investor, securities regulations require that an up-to-date prospectus be sent within 48 hours to ensure that the investor has the information needed to understand the risks of investing in that fund. The traditional process of printing, stocking, picking, and distributing prospectuses has been done manually, using inventories of pre-printed, hard-copy documents. The system is inefficient, expensive, and the logistics can be a nightmare—with 40 000 independent financial advisers across the country, and a network of advisers and financial planners working for banks, brokerages, and securities firms, all able to sell funds and all needing to send prospectuses to investors.

ADP wanted to use technology to streamline the data collection and mailing process, but no technology existed that could manage the volume of information required by ADP. "For some time, the industry has been looking for a new way to streamline this process to make it faster and less expensive to send out up-to-date prospectus information—but not finding a sustainable technology solution to support it," said Sue Britton, senior vice-president at ADP Investor Communications.

In response to this market need, ADP developed Smart Prospectus, an outsourced service that offers investment and mutual fund dealers a more effective way to print and mail mutual fund prospectuses to Canadian investors. Smart Prospectus obtains prospectuses electronically from the System for Electronic Document Analysis & Retrieval (SEDAR), the standard industry repository to which all public companies and investment funds must send prospectuses and other regulatory documents. The prospectuses, which often contain information on many funds, are electronically disassembled by Smart Prospectus into fund-specific sections, and then re-assembled, digitally printed, and bound into a new personalized prospectus document containing only information relevant to the fund(s) the investor has purchased.

"In addition to providing confirmation of the investor's trades, the personalized prospectuses make relevant fund information more accessible, enabling more informed investment decisions," Britton says. By printing and sending prospectuses only as needed, the service eliminates requirements for a pre-printed document inventory, reducing paper and cost. Further savings in distribution and mailing are gained by consolidating prospectus information for multiple funds into a single document, along with trade confirmations.

Source: Canadian Information Productivity Awards: ADP Investor Communications, **www.cipa.com/award_winners/winners_05/ADPInvestorCommunications.html**.

which dealership can provide the type of car you desire (see Figure 8.22).

This upfront analysis of your needs can be extremely helpful in narrowing your options and can save you a lot of time. Understanding your needs can also help you sift through the salespeople's hype that you are likely to encounter from one dealer to the next as each tries to sell you on why their model is perfect for you. After getting some information, you may want to take a couple of promising models for a test drive, actually getting behind the wheel to see how well the car fits you and your driving habits. You might even talk to other people who have owned this type of car to see how they feel about it. Ultimately, you are the one who has to evaluate all the different cars to see which one is the best for you. They may all be good cars; however, one may fit your needs just a little better than the others.

The external acquisition of an information system is very similar to the purchase of a car. When you acquire an IS, you should do some analysis of your specific needs. For example, how much can you afford to spend, what basic functionality is required, and approximately how many people will use the system? Next, you can begin to "shop" for the new system by asking potential vendors to provide information about the systems they have to offer. After you evaluate this information, it may become clear that several vendors have systems that are worth considering. You may ask those vendors to come to your organization and set up their systems so that you and your colleagues are able to "test drive" them. Seeing how people react to the systems and seeing how each system performs in the organizational environment can help you "see" exactly what you are buying. By seeing the actual system and how it performs with real users, with real or simulated data, you can get a much clearer idea of whether that system fits your needs. When you take a car for a test drive, you learn how the car meets your needs. By seeing how the system meets your needs before you buy, you can greatly reduce the risk associated with acquiring that system.

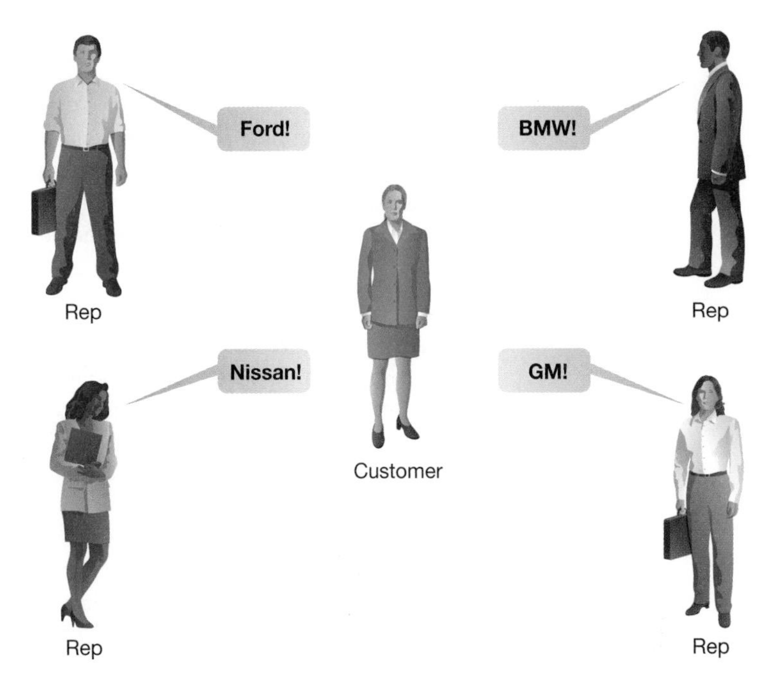

Figure 8.22 A prospective car buyer with a "wish list."

Steps in External Acquisition

In many cases, your organization will use a competitive bid process for making an external acquisition. In the competitive bid process, vendors are given an opportunity to propose systems that meet the organization's needs. The goal of the competitive process is to help the organization ensure that it gets the best system at the lowest possible price. Most competitive external acquisition processes have at least five general steps:

1. System identification, selection, and planning
2. Systems analysis
3. Development of a request for proposal (RFP)
4. Proposal evaluation
5. Vendor selection

You have already learned about the first two steps because they apply when you build a system yourself as well as when you purchase a system through an external vendor. Step 3, development of a RFP, is where the external acquisition process differs significantly from in-house development.

Development of a Request for Proposal

A ***request for proposal,*** or ***RFP***, is simply a report that is used to tell vendors what your requirements are and to invite them to provide information about how they might be able to meet those requirements (see Figure 8.23). An RFP is sent to vendors who might potentially be interested in providing hardware and/or software for the system.

Among the areas that may be covered in an RFP are

- A summary of existing systems and applications
- Reliability, backup, and service requirements
- Requirements for system performance and features
- The criteria that will be used to evaluate proposals
- Timetable and budget constraints (how much you can spend)

The RFP is then sent to prospective vendors along with an invitation to present their bids for the project. Eventually, you will likely receive many proposals to evaluate. If, on the other hand, you do not receive many proposals, it may be necessary to rethink the requirements—perhaps the requirements are greater than the

1. Summary of existing systems and applications
2. Reliability, backup, and service requirements
3. System performance and features
4. Evaluation criteria
5. Timetable
6. Budget

Figure 8.23 Sample RFP document for an information systems project.

budget limitations, or the timetable is too short. In some situations, you may first need to send out a preliminary request for information simply to gather information from prospective vendors. This will help you determine whether, indeed, the desired system is feasible or even possible. If you determine that it is, you can then send out an RFP.

Proposal Evaluation

The fourth step in external acquisition is to evaluate proposals received from vendors. This evaluation may include viewing system demonstrations, evaluating the performance of those systems, and examining criteria important to the organization and judging how the proposed systems "stack up" to those criteria. Demonstrations are a good way to get a feel for the different systems' capabilities. Just as you can go to the showroom to look over a new car and get a feel for whether it meets your needs, it is also possible to screen various systems through a demonstration from the vendor. During a demonstration, a sales team from the vendor gives an oral presentation about their system, its features, and cost, followed by a demonstration of the actual system. In some cases, this may take place at your location; other times, it may take place at the vendor's facility or at one of the vendor's clients, particularly when the system is not easily transportable. Although such demonstrations are often useful in helping you understand the features of different systems being proposed, they are rarely enough in and of themselves to warrant purchasing the system without further evaluation.

One of the ways you can better evaluate a proposed system is through ***systems benchmarking***. Benchmark programs are sample programs or jobs that simulate your computer workload. You can have benchmarks designed to test portions of the system that are most critical to your needs, based on your systems analysis. A benchmark might test how long it takes to calculate a set of numbers, how long it takes to access a set of records in a database, or how long it would take to access certain information given a certain number of concurrent users. Some common system benchmarks include

- Response time given a specified number of users
- Time to sort records
- Time to retrieve a set of records
- Time to produce a given report
- Time to read a set of data

In addition, vendors may supply benchmarks that you can use, although you should not rely solely on vendor information. For popular systems, you may be able to rely on system benchmarks published in computer trade journals such as *PC Magazine* or *PC Week*. However, in most cases, demos and benchmarks alone do not provide all the information you need to make a purchase. The systems analysis phase should have revealed some specific requirements for the new system. These requirements may be listed as criteria that the organization can use to further evaluate vendor proposals. Depending upon what you are purchasing—hardware, software, or both—the criteria you use will change. Table 8.10 provides examples of commonly used evaluation criteria.

Vendor Selection

In most cases, more than one system will meet your needs, just as more than one car will usually meet your needs. However, some probably "fit" better than others. In these cases, you should have a way of prioritizing or ranking competing proposals. One way of doing this is by devising a scoring system for each of the criteria and benchmarking results. For example, an organization might create a scoring

Table 8.10 ***Commonly used evaluation criteria.***

Hardware Criteria	Software Criteria	Other Criteria
Clock speed of CPU	Memory requirements	Installation
Memory requirements	Help features	Testing
Secondary storage (including capacity, access time, and so on)	Usability	Price
Video display size	Learnability	
Printer speed	Number of features supported	
	Training and documentation	
	Maintenance and repair	

system in which benchmarking results are worth 100 total points, whereas online help features are worth only 50 points. All the points for each criterion are then summed to give an overall score for each system. Then the system with the highest score (or one of the systems among several with the highest scores) is selected. Figure 8.24 shows an example of a form that could be used to evaluate systems and choose a vendor using this method.

In the example shown in Figure 8.24, system A looks like the best solution because it scored the highest. Using such an evaluation method, it is possible that scoring low on a given criterion might exclude otherwise outstanding systems from being purchased. You can see that systems B and C fared very poorly on the "Vendor Support" criterion. It is possible that those systems do not have very good vendor support. However, it is also possible that the vendor did not adequately communicate its commitment to support, perhaps because it did not realize it was such an important issue. Therefore, it is very important for you to communicate with vendors about the evaluation process and which criteria you value most highly.

Criterion	Max Points (or weight)	Systems Being Evaluated (Score)		
		A	B	C
Disk capacity	20	10	17	12
Compatibility	50	45	30	25
Usability	30	12	30	20
Vendor Support	35	27	16	5
Benchmark Results	50	40	28	30
(add as needed...)				
Total	185	134	121	92

Figure 8.24 Sample system evaluation form with subset of criteria.

Companies may use other less formalized approaches to evaluate vendors. Sometimes, they use simple checklists; other times, they use a more subjective process. Regardless of the mechanism, eventually a company completes the evaluation stage and selects a vendor, ending the external acquisition process.

Outsourcing

A related, but different, alternative to purchasing an existing system is outsourcing. With the external acquisition option, an organization typically purchases a single system

GLOBAL PERSPECTIVE

Computers for Africa—Bridging the Global Digital Divide

For most people in North America or Europe, computers and the Internet are regarded as ubiquitous—most people in Europe and America have access to a computer. The situation in Africa looks much different. Whereas in North America there are 511 computers per 1000 people, in sub-Saharan Africa in 2000, only 3 of 1000 people had access to a computer, putting these people at a huge disadvantage. Although every African country is connected to the Internet, Africa is estimated to have only 1 percent of the world's Internet connections. Realizing that each year in the United States alone an estimated 20 million computers become obsolete and end up in incinerators or landfills gives this problem a completely new dimension.

Charitable organizations such as "Computers for Africa" are attempting to fight this problem by providing U.S. companies with ways to donate used computer hardware to African social groups. Computers for Africa accepts donations from various different institutions such as banks, hospitals, and insurance companies; these computers are refurbished by student volunteers, loaded with free Linux operating systems and networking equipment, and then shipped as complete computer labs to the receivers in Africa. Not accepting individual donations ensures that the computer hardware of each computer lab is reasonably homogeneous, which helps to deal with support issues in the receiving organization; if a computer breaks down, working parts can still be used to support the remaining personal computers (PCs).

To increase the chances for job success of especially underprivileged groups, Computers for Africa primarily supports educational and training centres for youths, organizations that advance the status and well-being of women and girls, and organizations that share knowledge for social development. Even though approximately 700 computers shipped to Africa so far seem like a drop in the ocean, they will give about 10 000 people in East Africa access to a computer. After all, a small start to bridging the global digital divide is better than no start at all.

Source: Ed Royce, "Bridging the Information Technology Divide in Africa," *Digital Divide Network* (n.d.), **www.digitaldividenetwork.org/content/stories/index.cfm?key=140**. **www.computers4africa.org/index.htm**.

from an outside vendor. Outsourcing is the practice of turning over responsibility for some or all of an organization's IS development and operations to an outside firm. ***Outsourcing*** includes a variety of working relationships. The outside firm, or service provider, may develop your IS applications and house them within their organization, they may run your applications on their computers, or they may develop systems to run on existing computers within your organization. Anything is fair game in an outsourcing arrangement. Today, outsourcing has become a big business and is a very popular option for many Canadian organizations (see Canadian NetStats: Information System Outsourcing in Canada and the United States).

Why Outsourcing?

A firm might outsource some (or all) of its information systems services for many reasons. Some of these are old reasons, but some are new to today's environment (Applegate, Austin, and McFarlan, 2003):

- *Cost and quality concerns*: In many cases, it is possible to achieve higher-quality systems at a lower price through economies of scale, better management of hardware, lower labour costs, and better software licences on the part of a service provider.
- *Problems in IS performance*: IS departments may have problems meeting acceptable service standards due to cost overruns, delayed systems, underutilized systems, or poorly performing systems. In such cases, organization management may attempt to increase reliability through outsourcing.
- *Supplier pressures*: Perhaps not surprisingly, some of the largest service providers are also the largest suppliers of computer equipment: IBM, Hewlett-Packard, and Compaq. In some cases, the aggressive sales forces of these suppliers are able to convince senior managers at other organizations to outsource their IS functions.
- *Simplifying, downsizing, and reengineering*: Organizations under competitive pressure often attempt to focus on only their "core competencies." In many cases, organizations simply decide that running information systems is not one of their "core competencies" and decide to outsource this function to companies such as IBM and EDS, whose primary competency is developing and maintaining information systems.
- *Financial factors*: When firms turn over their information systems to a service provider, they can sometimes strengthen their balance sheets by liquidating their IT assets. Also, if users perceive that they are actually paying for their IT services rather than simply having them provided by an in-house staff, they may use those services more wisely and perceive them to be of greater value.
- *Organizational culture*: Political or organizational problems are often difficult for an IS group to overcome. However, an external service provider often brings enough clout, devoid of any organizational or functional ties, to streamline IS operations as needed.
- *Internal irritants*: Tension between end users and the IS staff is sometimes difficult to eliminate. At times, this tension can intrude on the daily operations of the organization, and the idea of a remote, external, relatively neutral IS group can be appealing. Whether the tension between users and the IS staff (or service provider) is really eliminated is open to question; however, simply having the IS group external to the organization can remove a lingering thorn in management's side.

Managing the Information Systems Outsourcing Relationship

There are many hidden costs of outsourcing. In fact, according to a study by the Gartner Group, half of all outsourcing contracts are labelled "losers" by senior executives. The total cost of an outsourcing relationship does not consist only of the cost on the contract. For example, vendor search and contract preparation costs typically add about 3 percent to the total cost of an outsourcing project. It is often complicated and time consuming to transfer internal operations to an outsourcing partner. Ongoing management of the outsourcing relationship can add 8 percent to the cost of a contract, or more if the outsourcing partner is located overseas. If unchecked, poor language skills, time zone differences, visa difficulties, high employee turnover, cultural differences, lack of domain knowledge, and internal conflict can all conspire to reduce the effectiveness of an outsourcing relationship. Finally, transitioning operations from the outsourcing partner back into the firm once the contract is complete can be costly and time consuming.

McFarlan and Nolan (1995) argue that the ongoing management of an outsourcing alliance is the single most important aspect of the outsourcing project's success. Their

Web Search

Outsourcing has become very popular. Many observers believe that outsourcing will continue to grow as a way for organizations to develop and operate their information systems. Search the websites of some popular IS trade magazines to find out the latest news and predictions about outsourcing. Start with **www.computerworld.com** and **www.itbusiness.ca**. Then you might want to look at **www.outsourcing-center.com** for a host of materials on outsourcing. Prepare a two-page report for your instructor on outsourcing that analyzes current outsourcing practices and provides forecasts for the future of outsourcing.

recommendations for the best management are as follows:

1. A strong, active CIO and staff should continually manage the legal and professional relationship with the outsourcing firm.
2. Clear, realistic performance measurements of the systems and of the outsourcing arrangement, such as tangible and intangible costs and benefits, should be developed.
3. The interface between the customer and the outsourcer should have multiple levels (e.g., links to deal with policy and relationship issues and links to deal with operational and tactical issues).

Managing outsourcing alliances in this way has important implications for the success of the relationship. For example, in addition to making sure a firm has a strong CIO and staff, McFarlan and Nolan recommend that firms assign full-time relationship managers and coordinating groups lower in the organization to "manage" the IS outsourcing project. This means that as people within the IS function are pulled away from traditional IS tasks such as systems development, they are moved toward new roles and organized into new groups. The structure and nature of the internal IS activities changes from exclusively building and managing systems to including managing relationships with outside firms that build and manage systems under legal contract.

Not All Outsourcing Relationships Are the Same

Most organizations no longer enter into a strictly legal contract with an outsourcing vendor but into a mutually beneficial relationship with a strategic partner. In such a relationship, the firm and the vendor are each concerned with, and perhaps have a direct stake in, the success of the other. Yet other types of relationships exist, which means that not all outsourcing agreements need to be structured the same way (Fryer, 1994). In fact, at least three different types of outsourcing relationships can be identified as

1. basic relationship
2. preferred relationship
3. strategic relationship

A basic relationship can best be thought of as a "cash and carry" relationship, in which you buy products and services on the basis of price and convenience. Organizations should try to have a few preferred relationships, in which the buyer and supplier set preferences and prices to the benefit of each other. For example, a supplier can provide preferred pricing to customers that do a specified volume of business. Most organizations have just a few strategic relationships, in which both sides share risks and rewards.

We have now discussed two systems development alternatives that rely on external organizations to alleviate, either completely or partially, the burden of managing IS development projects in-house. In some cases, however, it may not be possible or convenient to rely on agencies outside the organization for development. In these cases, organizations may rely on another option for systems development projects.

End-User Development

In many organizations, the growing sophistication of users within the organization offers IS managers a third alternative for systems development. This third alternative is ***end-user development***—having users develop their own applications. This means that the people who are actually going to use the systems are also those who will develop those systems. End-user development, then, is one way IS departments can speed up application development without relying on external entities such as vendors or service providers (see Figure 8.25). However, end-user development also has risks associated with it. This section outlines the benefits of having end users develop their own applications as well as some of the drawbacks of this approach.

"We've decided to make all our products open source, and replace everyone's salary with tip jars."

Figure 8.25 End-user development can be a cost-effective way to develop or modify information systems.

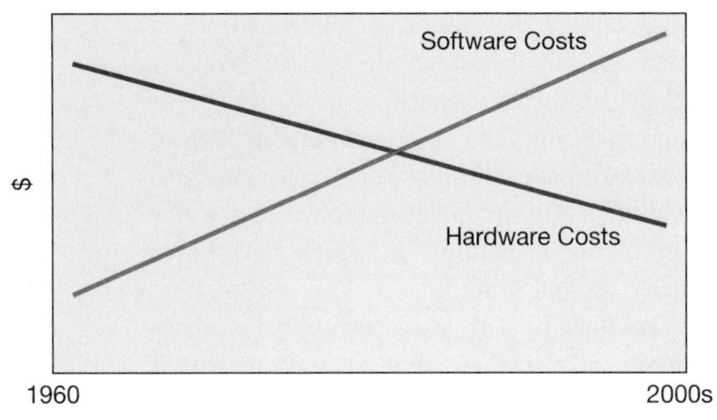

Figure 8.26 Rising software costs versus declining hardware costs.

Benefits of End-User Development

To help you better understand the benefits of end-user development, you should quickly review some of the problems with conventional development that are suggested by the four situations presented earlier in this chapter.

- *Cost of labour*: Conventional systems development is labour intensive. Over the past four decades, software costs have increased while hardware costs have declined, as shown in Figure 8.26. As you can see from the figure, it becomes much cheaper for IS managers to substitute hardware for labour by giving users their own equipment. An IS manager can significantly reduce the cost of application development simply by giving end users the tools they need and enabling them to develop their own applications. Better yet, the various departments within the organization can purchase their own equipment, and the IS staff can simply provide guidance and other services.
- *Long development time*: New systems can take months or even years to develop, depending on the scale and scope of the new system and the backlog of systems waiting to be developed. As a result, users' needs may significantly change between when a system is initially proposed and when it is actually implemented. In these cases, the system may be virtually obsolete before it has even been implemented. End user–developed systems can "skip" the queue of systems waiting to be developed by the IS organization, resulting in more rapidly developed systems.
- *Slow modification or updates of existing systems*: Related to the time it takes to develop new systems is the problem of maintaining existing systems. Often, updates to existing systems are given a lower priority than developing new systems. Unfortunately, this can result in systems that are unable to keep pace with changing business needs, becoming antiquated and underused. When end users develop their own systems, the users have the responsibility of maintaining and updating applications as needed. Also, when systems are implemented, they often cause changes to the underlying business processes. These changes may necessitate further change or modification to the application, as highlighted in Figure 8.27. Rather than rely on IS to make these changes, users are able to modify the application in a timely manner to reflect the changed business process.
- *Work overload*: One reason for long development times and slow modifications is that IS departments are often overloaded with work. When you leverage the talents of end-user developers, you can, in effect, increase the size of the development staff by shifting some of the workload normally handled by IS professionals to end users, as depicted in Figure 8.28.

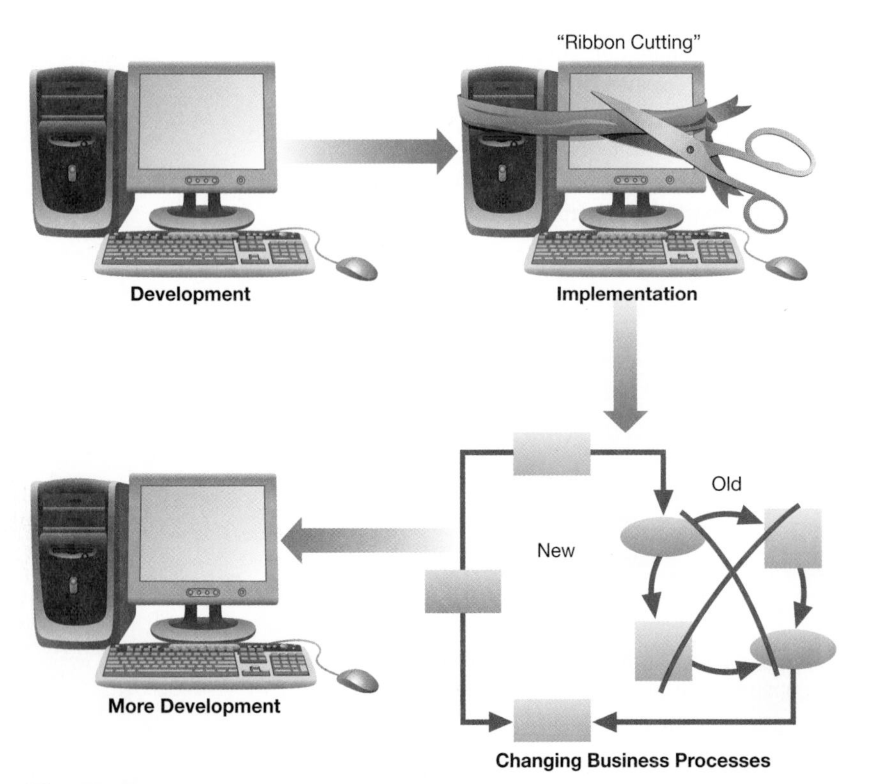

Figure 8.27 Continuous cycle of development: a system is developed and implemented. However, it eventually becomes inadequate, and new development takes place.

End-user development can radically decrease the development workload in the IS department. However, such a shift may cause other areas within IS, such as a help desk, for

CANADIAN NETSTATS

Information System Outsourcing in Canada and the United States

In recent years, outsourcing has become a very popular option for organizations. Canadian firms have entered into IT outsourcing contracts worth well over $1 billion per year over recent years (see Table 8.11). For example, in 2002, CIBC entered into a 7-year agreement with HP worth $2 billion. Large outsourcing agreements of this sort often involve asset transfers between a firm and its outsourcing partner. Information technology staff may also become employees of the outsourcing firm. For example, 175 employees of National Bank Financial transferred to IBM upon signing their outsourcing agreement, and 550 Caisses Desjardins staff moved to CGI as part of their agreement. The volume of IT outsourcing in Canada compares favourably with amounts in the United States.

Table 8.11 ***Selected outsourcing agreements in Canada and the United States.***

Company	Outsourcing Partner	Value of Outsourcing Contract	Year Contract Signed	Duration of Contract
CANADA				
CIBC	HP	$2B	2002	7 years
Casisses Desjardins	CGI	$1B	2000	10 years
B.C. Hydro	Accenture	$1B	2001	10 years
Air Canada	IBM	$908M	2001	7 years
Scotiabank	IBM	$900M	2001	7 years
TD Bank	IBM	$720M	2003	7 years
National Bank	Cognicase	$600M	2000	10 years
MDS	IBM	$293M	2003	7 years
CP Rail	IBM	$200M	2003	7 years
National Bank Financial	IBM	$200M	2003	9 years
ATB Financial	IBM	$90M	2003	5 years
UNITED STATES				
J.P. Morgan Chase	IBM	US$5B	2002	7 years
Bank of America	EDS	US$4.5B	2002	10 years
American Express	IBM	US$4B	2002	7 years
Procter & Gamble	HP	US$3B	2003	10 years
Visteon	IBM	US$2B	2003	10 years

Adapted in part from Larry Dignan, "Outsmarting Outsources," *Baseline Magazine,* 20 (July 2003).

example, to become flooded with requests for assistance. Nonetheless, end-user development can be an excellent option for organizations faced with some of the problems previously described.

Encouraging End-User Development

End-user development sounds great, but how can organizations encourage and enable users to develop their own systems? Fortunately, the availability of easy-to-use, fourth-generation development tools (see Appendix B) has enabled end-user development to become more practical today than in the early to mid-1980s. There are five categories of fourth-generation tools:

1. ***Personal computer tools***: Many users throughout an organization use PC tools,

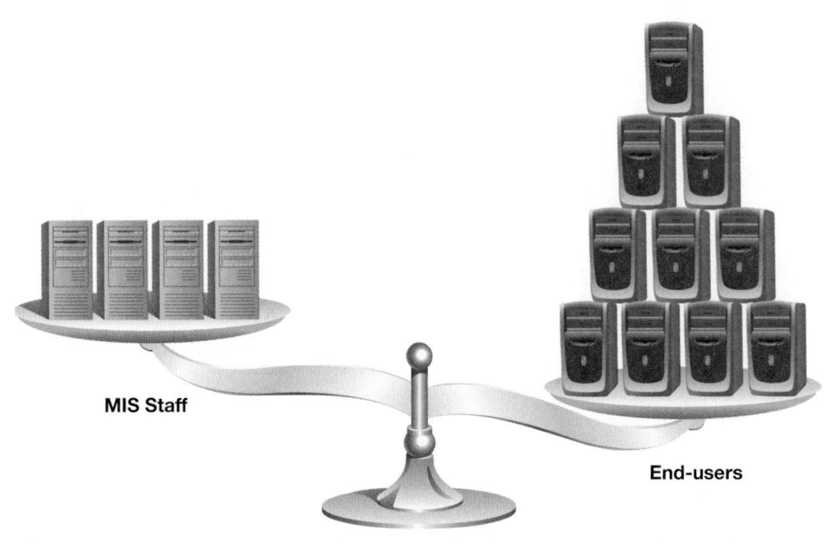

Figure 8.28 Shifting systems development workload as end-user development has become more prevalent.

including spreadsheets, database management systems, and graphics programs. Frequently, these tools enable users to build their own applications using macro languages or embedded tools within the software that are designed to enable users to customize their own systems.

2. ***Query languages/report generators***: These tools, usually associated with database systems, enable you to search a database by entering various search criteria. Structured Query Language (SQL) is the most common query language for this purpose. For example, you may say, "Give me the part numbers for any inventory that we have in stock whose quantity exceeds 30." A query language structures that query and presents the results of the query to the user. Report generators are similar to query languages and are designed to produce textual and tabular reports easily. Although users often use query languages independently, report generators may require some assistance from IS staff.
3. ***Graphics generators***: People can use these tools to extract relevant information from databases and convert that data to a graphic such as a pie chart, a line graph, or an area plot. As with report generators, users can specify many different formats.
4. ***Decision support or modelling tools***: Although spreadsheets can be used as decision support aids, dedicated decision support tools are often available for more complex, multidimensional models that may be too complicated to be handled easily in a spreadsheet. These tools can enable users to develop decision support systems to aid in making decisions.
5. ***Application generators***: Application generators are designed to automate much of the relatively tedious programming work associated with systems development. With these tools you can specify what you want to do, then the application generator decides how to accomplish that task and generates the program code. Application generators can be used to get prototypes up and running quickly, get feedback from other potential users, and make necessary changes. Computer-aided software engineering tools often include an application generator that end users or IS professionals can use.

End-User Development Pitfalls

This chapter has painted a pretty rosy picture of end-user development so far. However, it is important to understand that along with the benefits come some problems, as illustrated in Figure 8.29. The information systems and computer science professions have established software development standards and generally accepted practices that are used throughout different organizations and across different types of systems. Unfortunately, users may not be aware of these standards, such as the need for adequate documentation, built-in error checking, and testing procedures. In small, personal applications, not adhering to the standards may not present a problem. However, if the system manages or interconnects with important business data, then lack of adherence to sound principles can quickly become a big problem if data become corrupted.

Figure 8.29 End-user development can sometimes be problematic.

Another problem for end user–developed systems is a potential lack of continuity. Suppose Benjamin develops a new system that meets his needs perfectly. Benjamin understands the system and uses it every day. However, one day Benjamin is transferred and is replaced by Christopher, a new hire to the company. The system that was intuitive for Benjamin to use may not be so intuitive for Christopher. Christopher may quickly abandon Benjamin's system or may be forced to develop his own system. This example shows how end-user development can easily result in a lack of continuity among applications, leading to redundant development efforts and a lot of wasted productivity in the organization. In organizations where turnover is frequent, a lot of time can be lost "reinventing the wheel" simply because systems that are in place are undocumented and cannot easily be used by new employees.

A third potential problem with end-user development relates to security. End users may not be aware of security vulnerabilities that exist or are created by their efforts. Many data security failures in organizations have been traced back to specialized software developed or modified by end users. Often this software is created with good intentions, perhaps as a technical "workaround" to enhance workplace efficiency. However, without sufficient knowledge of the overall IS architecture, good intentions can lead to disastrous results.

Related to the continuity problem is the question of whether users and managers should be spending their time on IS development. That is, the organization has hired individuals to be financial managers, production managers, marketers, or salespeople. The organization expects these employees to add value to the organization based on the skills they have to offer. If their time and energy are diverted to developing new systems, then the organization loses out on the potential productivity these individuals have to offer in other ways. Also, individual motivation, morale, and performance might suffer if the employee is unable to concentrate on his or her area of expertise and instead spends too much of his or her time worrying about developing new systems.

Fortunately, organizations that have been successful in moving to end-user development are aware of many of these problems and have established some controls to avoid them. One control mechanism is an information centre (IC), which is charged with encouraging end users to develop their own applications while at the same time providing some management oversight. The IC staff can assist or train end users in proper development techniques or standards, prevent redundancy in application development, and ensure that systems are documented properly. The IC staff are often not functional-area experts but are typically experts in using the fourth-generation tools. Working together, end users and the IC staff can develop useful systems for an organization.

CAREER IMPLICATIONS

Information Systems Development and Acquisition

For Accounting and Finance

The accounting and finance departments play an important role in the IS development and acquisition process. For example, before the start of the project, a thorough cost-benefit analysis of the proposed system has to be performed where "make or buy or abandon" decisions are based on financial considerations. During the course of the project, accounting and finance professionals are called upon to update the financial analyses to ensure that costs and expected benefits are still within the predetermined boundaries.

For Operations Management

Enterprise Resource Planning (ERP) systems are often used in manufacturing companies to streamline the entire production process. As an operations management professional, you might be interacting with ERP systems on a daily basis. However, if you join a company that has not yet integrated its legacy systems, you might find yourself involved in the implementation of an ERP system. In this case, knowing about the benefits and drawbacks of such systems and about the different aspects to consider when implementing them will help you make an educated decision about which system to choose and how to best implement it.

For Human Resources Management

Organizations that need a new IS must always consider whether to make or buy the system. An organization that often builds new systems in-house might already have a large in-house IS department with many systems analysts, network specialists, database administrators, and programmers. Nevertheless, in some cases, such as when the new system requires cutting-edge expertise, additional staff may be needed to complete the project. Organizations are increasingly examining alternatives to hiring permanent development employees, such as global outsourcing and contract programming. How an organization chooses to build and acquire IS has important implications for the human resources management function.

For Marketing

Marketing professionals who are working in an organization that is launching a new informational or B2C e-commerce site may find themselves heavily involved in the development of such a system. For the system to look and perform properly, marketing professionals will work closely with IS professionals to design exactly the right system. It will, therefore, be beneficial to understand various systems development methodologies to best interact with developers so that the system satisfies the design criteria set by the marketing department.

For Information Systems

Information systems professionals often have to participate in the development of new systems for other organizational departments. Because of this, it is essential that IS professionals understand a variety of systems development methodologies and techniques to make this process most effective. Determining systems requirements, analyzing options, designing system modules, and implementing the system requires that IS professionals work very closely with people throughout the organization. Being skilled in a broad range of IS development and acquisition techniques is fundamental to career success. Recent evidence in Canada suggests that salaries of IS professionals with skills in IS development methodologies and project management are rising at between 13 and 15 percent per year.

KEY POINTS REVIEW

1. **Understand the process used by organizations to manage the development of information systems.** The development of information systems follows a process called the systems development life cycle (SDLC). The SDLC is a process that first identifies the need for a system and then defines the processes for designing, developing, and maintaining an IS. The process is very structured and formal and requires the active involvement of managers and users.
2. **Describe each major phase of the systems development life cycle: systems identification, selection, and planning; system analysis; system design; system implementation; and system maintenance.** The SDLC has five phases: systems identification, selection, and planning; system analysis; system design; system implementation; and system maintenance. Systems identification, selection, and planning is the first phase of the SDLC, in which potential projects are identified, selected, and planned. System analysis is the second phase of the SDLC, in which the current ways of doing business are studied and alternative replacement systems are proposed. System design is the third phase of the SDLC, in which all features of the proposed system are described. System implementation is the fourth phase of the SDLC, in which the IS is programmed, tested, installed, and supported. System maintenance is the fifth and final phase of the SDLC, in which an IS is systematically repaired and improved.
3. **Describe prototyping, rapid application development, and object-oriented analysis and design methods of systems development, along with each approach's strengths and weaknesses.** Prototyping is an iterative systems development process in which requirements are converted into a working system that is continually revised through a close working relationship between analysts and users. The strengths of prototyping are that it helps develop a close working relationship between designers and users and that it is a good approach for hard-to-define problems. Its weaknesses are that it is not a practical approach for a large number of users and that it can at times lead to a lower-quality system if the system is built too quickly. Rapid application development is a systems development methodology that combines prototyping, computer-based development tools, special management practices, and close user involvement. The strength of RAD is that users are actively involved in the design process, which makes system implementation much easier. The weaknesses of RAD are that systems are sometimes narrowly focused—which might limit future evolution—and that quality problems might result if a system is designed and built too quickly (as is the case with prototyping). Object-oriented analysis and design is a systems development approach that focuses on modelling objects—data and operations bundled together—rather than on modelling these separately. The strengths of OOA&D are the integration of data and processing during the design phase, which should lead to higher-quality systems, and the reuse of common modules, which should make development and maintenance easier. The weaknesses of OOA&D are that it is very difficult to train analysts and programmers in the object-oriented approach and that analysts often recreate common modules.
4. **Explain the factors involved in building a system in-house, along with situations in which it is not feasible.** It is not feasible for an organization to build a system in-house in at least four situations. First, some organizations have limited IS staffing and, therefore, do not have the capability to build a system themselves. Second, an organization may have IS staff with a limited skill set. Existing IS staff may be highly skilled at producing traditional applications but not have the skills to build new types of systems or systems that require emerging development tools. Third, in many organizations, the IS staff does not have the time to work on all the systems that the organization desires. Fourth, some organizations have performance problems with their IS staff, whereby staff turnover, changing requirements, shifts in technology, or budget constraints have led poor results. In any of these situations, it may be advantageous to an organization to consider an alternative to in-house systems development.
5. **Explain three alternative systems development options: external acquisition, outsourcing, and end-user development.** External acquisition is the process of purchasing an existing information system from an external organization or vendor. External acquisition is a five-step process. Step 1 is system identification, selection, and planning, which focuses on determining whether a proposed system is feasible. Step 2 is systems analysis, which focuses on determining the requirements for the system. Step 3 is the development of a request for proposal (RFP). An RFP is a communication tool indicating an organization's requirements for a given system and requesting information from potential vendors on their ability to deliver such a system. Step 4 is proposal evaluation, which focuses on evaluating proposals received from vendors. This evaluation may include viewing system demonstrations, evaluating the performance of those systems, and examining criteria important to the organization and the ways the proposed systems meet those criteria. Step 5 is vendor selection, which focuses on choosing the vendor to provide the system. Outsourcing refers to the turning over of partial or entire responsibility for IS development and management to an outside organization. End-user development is a systems development method whereby users in the organization develop, test, and maintain their own applications.

KEY TERMS

request for proposal (RFP) 287
requirements collection 272
software engineering 266
system analysis 271
system conversion 278
system design 276
system identification, selection, and planning 269
system implementation 278
system maintenance 281
system support 278
systems analysis and design 266
systems analyst 266
systems benchmarking 288
systems development life cycle (SDLC) 267

REVIEW QUESTIONS

1. What are the five phases of the systems development life cycle?
2. List and describe six techniques used in requirements collection.
3. What are the four major components/tasks of the system design phase of the SDLC?
4. What are the four options for system conversion? How do they differ from each other?
5. Compare and contrast the four types of system maintenance.
6. What are the three alternative approaches to the SDLC for designing and building systems?
7. What are the advantages and disadvantages of prototyping?
8. List and define the four phases of rapid application development.
9. What is object-oriented analysis and design, and what are its strengths and weaknesses?
10. Define outsourcing, and list three major types.
11. What is system benchmarking, and what are some common benchmarks?
12. What are some of the reasons outsourcing is more popular than ever?
13. What are the three recommendations made in this chapter for managing an outsourcing IS relationship?
14. Describe five categories of fourth-generation tools.
15. End-user developers have what advantages and disadvantages?

SELF-STUDY QUESTIONS

Visit the Companion Website for this text for additional Self-Study Questions: **www.pearsoned.ca/jessup**.

1. Which of the following is not one of the five phases of the systems development life cycle?
   A. system analysis
   B. system implementation
   C. system design
   D. systems resource acquisition
2. __________ is the process of gathering and organizing information from users, managers, business processes, and documents to understand how a proposed information system should function.
   A. Requirements collection
   B. Systems collection
   C. Systems analysis
   D. Records archiving
3. Which of the following is the correct order of phases in the systems development life cycle?
   A. maintenance, analysis, planning, design, implementation
   B. analysis, planning, design, implementation, maintenance
   C. planning, analysis, design, implementation, maintenance
   D. maintenance, planning, analysis, design, implementation
4. In the systems design phase, the elements that must be designed when building an IS include all of the following except __________.
   A. reports and forms
   B. questionnaires
   C. databases and files
   D. interfaces and dialogues
5. __________ maintenance involves making enhancements to improve processing performance or interface usability, or adding desired, but not necessarily required, system features (in other words, "bells and whistles").
   A. Preventive
   B. Perfective
   C. Corrective
   D. Adaptive
6. Which of the following is an alternative to building a system in-house?
   A. external acquisition
   B. end-user development
   C. outsourcing
   D. all of the above
7. A __________ is a report that an organization uses to tell vendors what its requirements are and to invite them to provide information about how they might be able to meet those requirements.
   A. request letter
   B. vendor request
   C. RFP
   D. payables request
8. Which of the following is not a type of outsourcing?
   A. basic
   B. elite
   C. strategic
   D. preferred
9. Which of the following factors is a good reason to outsource?
   A. problems in IS performance
   B. supplier pressures
   C. financial factors
   D. all of the above
10. Most competitive external acquisition processes have at least five general steps. Which of the following is not one of those steps?
    A. vendor selection
    B. proposal evaluation
    C. development of an RFP
    D. implementation

PROBLEMS AND EXERCISES

1. Match the following terms with the appropriate definitions:

_____ RFP

_____ Systems benchmarking

_____ Alpha testing

_____ Systems development life cycle

_____ End-user development

_____ Prototyping

_____ Pilot conversion

_____ Systems analysis

_____ Outsourcing

_____ External acquisition

_____ Data flows

_____ Requirements collection

a. The movement of data through an organization or within an IS
b. Term that describes the life of an IS from conception to retirement
c. The second phase of the SDLC
d. The process of gathering and organizing information from users, managers, business processes, and documents to understand how a proposed IS should function
e. Performed by software testers to assess whether the entire system meets the design requirements of the users
f. When the entire system is used in one location but not in the entire organization
g. A systems development methodology that uses a trial-and-error approach for discovering how a system should operate
h. The practice of turning over responsibility for some or all of an organization's IS development and operations to an outside firm
i. Users developing their own applications
j. Purchasing an existing system from an outside vendor
k. A way to evaluate a proposed system by testing a portion of it with the system workload
l. A report that is used to tell vendors what your requirements are and to invite them to provide information about how they might be able to meet those requirements

2. Explain the differences between data and data flows. How might systems analysts obtain the information they need to generate the data flows of a system? How are these data flows and the accompanying processing logic used in the system design phase of the life cycle? What happens when the data and data flows are modelled incorrectly?

3. When Microsoft posts a new version of Internet Explorer on its website and states that this is a beta version, what does it mean? Is this a final working version of the software, or is it still being tested? Who is doing the testing? Search the web to find other companies that have beta versions of their products available to the public. You might try Corel (**www.corel.com**) or Adobe (**www.adobe.com**). What other companies did you find?

4. Why is the system documentation of a new IS so important? What information does it contain? For whom is this information intended? When will the system documentation most likely be used?

5. Conduct a search on the web for "systems development life cycle," using any search engine. Check out some of the hits. Compare them with the SDLC outlined in this chapter. Do all these life cycles follow the same general path? How many phases do the ones you found on the web contain? Is the terminology the same or different? Prepare a 10-minute presentation to the class on your findings.

6. Choose an organization with which you are familiar that develops its own information systems. Does this organization follow a systems development life cycle? If not, why not? If so, how many phases does it have? Who developed this life cycle? Was it someone within the company or was the IS adopted from somewhere else?

7. Describe your experiences with information systems that were undergoing changes or updates. What kind of conversion procedure was being used? How did this affect your interaction with the system as a user? Who else was affected? If the system was down altogether, for how long was it down? Do you or any of your classmates have horror stories or were the situations not that bad?

8. Compare and contrast RAD and object-oriented methodologies. What are the strengths and weaknesses of each? Visit Object FAQ at **www.objectfaq.com/oofaq2**.

9. Conduct a search on the web for "object-oriented analysis and design" using any search engine you wish. Check out some of the hits. You should have found numerous articles regarding OOA&D's use by IS departments. Are these articles positive or negative regarding OOA&D? Do you agree with the articles? Prepare a 10-minute presentation to the class on your findings.

10. Interview an IS manager within an organization with which you are familiar. Determine whether the organization uses methodologies such as prototyping, RAD, and/or OOA&D for system projects. Who chooses the methodology? If the organization has not used a methodology, is it because of choice, or is it because of a lack of need, understanding, or capability of using the methodology?

11. Choose an organization with which you are familiar and determine whether it builds its applications in-house. How many IS staff members does the organization have, and how large is the organization they support?

12. Think about the requirements of a career in IS. Do IS positions generally require people to work 40 hours a week, or more if a project has a deadline? Do positions in the IS department require people skills? To find these answers, visit the IS department at your university, a local business, or an online clearing house of jobs such as **www.monster.ca** or **hotjobs.yahoo.com**.

13. Find an organization, on the Internet at **www.itbusiness.ca** or **www.itworldcanada.com** or a company you may want to work for in the future that outsources work. What are the managerial challenges of outsourcing, and why is this a popular alternative to hiring additional staff?

APPLICATION EXERCISES

Note: The existing data files referenced in these exercises are available on the Companion Website: **www.pearsoned.ca/jessup**.

Spreadsheet Application: Outsourcing Information Systems at BlueSky

BlueSky Airlines wants to increase its consumer focus and wants to be able to better serve its most valued customers. Many members of the frequent flyer program have requested the ability to check on the status of their membership online; furthermore, the frequent flyers would welcome the opportunity to book reward flights online. As you know that there are many companies specializing in building such transactional systems, you have decided to outsource the development of this system. The following weights are assigned to evaluate the different vendors' systems:

- Online booking capability: 20 percent.
- User friendliness: 25 percent.
- Maximum number of concurrent users: 20 percent.
- Integration with current systems: 10 percent.
- Vendor support: 10 percent.
- Price: 15 percent.

Modify the BlueSky.csv spreadsheet to reflect the weights and use formulas to calculate the total points for each vendor. Hint: Use the SUMPRODUCT formula to multiply each vendor's scores with the respective weights and add the weighted scores. Use conditional formatting to highlight all vendors falling below 60 percent and above 85 percent to facilitate the vendor selection.

Database Application: Building a Movie Database

Since you and your roommates own a large number of DVD movies, you decide to create a database of the DVD collection to better locate individual movies. To make the system as useful as possible for all, you need to design reports for the users to retrieve information about the movies. Your roommates would like to have a system that contains the following information about the movies:

- Title.
- Copyright date.
- Category.
- Owner.

Each movie belongs to at least one category (e.g., comedy, action) but can also belong to multiple categories. Each category can contain multiple movies. Also, each movie belongs to one owner, but different people can own copies of the same movie. After designing the database, please design three professionally formatted reports that (1) list the movies in alphabetical order, (2) list all movies that belong to the different categories, and (3) list all movies that belong to a particular owner. Hint: In Microsoft Access, you can create queries before preparing the reports. Enter a few sample data sets and print out the reports.

ANSWERS TO THE SELF-STUDY QUESTIONS

1. D, p. 267	2. A, p. 272	3. C, p. 267	4. B, p. 276	5. B, p. 281
6. D, pp. 285, 290, 291	7. C, p. 287	8. B, p. 291	9. D, p. 290	10. D, p. 287

Case *IT Outsourcing: A Mixed Blessing for Canada*

The offshore outsourcing of technology jobs will have a negative impact on the viability of the IT industry in Canada, according to most professionals surveyed by the Canadian Information Processing Society (CIPS). Of the 111 senior IT professionals polled, more than half told CIPS they have outsourced some IT functions or are considering it; 69.4 percent said they believed the trend does not bode well for the sector's overall health. Only 33 percent said they believed offshore outsourcing would help the Canadian economy.

The research reflects the growing fear among Canadian IT workers that their skills may be obsolete if lower-level programming work is moved to India, China, Romania, or elsewhere (see Table 8.12). From the employer's perspective, however, offshore outsourcing is simply a matter of dollars and sense. "What is the difference between sourcing a product offshore? We all have radios here, and I doubt many of them were made in Canada," said Gabor Takach, a lawyer who leads the technology group at Torys LLP. "This trend [offshore outsourcing] represents a concentration of expertise and a new and efficient way of delivering a service." Paul Harrington, a consultant for retail, small business, and marketing companies, says some IT workers may have reason to feel paranoid. "When an industry disappears—like buggy whips—they just disappear. Everybody in every industry has to take a look at what's happening in their industry. This is an industry that's in a great deal of turmoil at the moment."

Kevin Yan, CEO of global software development services firm Arackal Digital Solutions, says he looks at offshore outsourcing as a productivity tool because it allows companies to eliminate low-value coding tasks. "If you have a better way of doing business out there, why wouldn't you do it?" John Chettleburgh, a staffing industry consultant and former vice-president at CNC Global, points out that most offshore outsourcing is done by Canada's largest firms, which means some of the jobs may not disappear entirely. "It could mean a renaissance for these kinds of jobs in the SME market in Canada."

Table 8.12 *Canada compared to other outsourcing destinations.*

Country or Region	Outsource Industry Revenue (Millions)	Number of Outsource IT Professionals	IT Employee Cost per Year	Charge Rate per Hour
Canada	$3 780	45 000	$36 000	$42
India	$8 955	137 500	$8 000	$15
Ireland	$1 920	30 000	$28 000	$32
China	$1 040	26 000	$9 600	$20
Eastern Europe	$360	12 000	$7 000	$15
Russia	$165	5 500	$7 000	$15
Mexico	$120	4 000	$7 000	$15

Adapted from "Will Work for Rupees," *Wired Magazine* (February 2004).

While CIPS found that coding, testing, call centre work, and some back-office banking activities were the primary candidates for offshore outsourcing, Yan warns that some skill sets are best kept at home. "Business knowledge is not easily replicable," he notes, adding that the ability to analyze processes can be a strong complement to an IT background. "You're bound to introduce risk into projects if you don't also integrate some onshore resources. If you don't do that, I would say you're bound to fail." Chettleburgh agrees, adding that corporate enterprises have to do a better job of retraining employees potentially affected by offshore outsourcing and better capturing the knowledge they have learned about their organization.

Takach describes himself as part of a "last generation" of students who graduated with an engineering degree who might have qualified for a management position. Today, he says, the situation is greatly changed. "You can still study computer science, but not with a view to just turning out code." "We're culturally indoctrinated [in North America] to want to advance and move ahead to bigger projects," adds Yan. "In India, it's different. They like doing the same thing. They appreciate the stability of the job." Although some firms, like EDS, are creating "nearshore" outsourcing operations in Canada, Chettleburgh says that the high Canadian dollar could "obliterate" the economic benefits of that model.

Source: Adapted from Shane Schick, "The Opportunity Cost of Offshore," ITBusiness.ca (February 2, 2004), **www.itbusiness.ca/index.asp?theaction=61&sid=54499#.**

Discussion Questions

1. Compare this case to the chapter's opening case. Drawing on these opposing opinions, what impact do you think the global trend toward IT outsourcing will have on Canada?
2. How does offshore IT outsourcing affect how information systems is taught at Canadian colleges and universities?
3. What elements of IT management can be outsourced, and what elements should be kept in-house?
4. Should the Canadian government step in to stem the flow of IT jobs going offshore? If so, how?

Log on to the Companion Website at www.pearsoned.ca/jessup for an additional case.

Running Case: Connexion by Boeing

Information Systems Development and Acquisition

In the late 1990s, a vision to take broadband Internet access to the sky was formed. While the technologies to make this vision possible already existed, no company had taken on the challenge to integrate the wide variety of technologies necessary—satellite communications, state-of-the-art antenna technology, large-scale networking technology, and mobile communications—to provide high-speed Internet access to airplane passengers. In addition to overcoming various technical hurdles, the Boeing Company needed to clearly establish that indeed there was adequate demand for such a system.

To gain an understanding of market potential, research was conducted that found that 62 percent of U.S. frequent business travellers were either "extremely" or "very" interested in broadband services and that 18 percent of U.S.-based frequent flyers and nearly 20 percent of European-based frequent flyers would pay $35 per flight for high-speed Internet service. Of the U.S. frequent flyers surveyed, 3 percent said they were extremely likely to switch carriers for such a service. These numbers clearly demonstrated a huge market potential for the airlines, as an average increase of a single passenger per international flight is worth approximately $1 million in additional airline revenue annually. These promising numbers were seen as an excellent basis to form the business case for the proposed system. Throughout the project identification phase of the project, several rounds of revisions were made to the business case before getting the final approval by Boeing's executives to launch the Connexion by Boeing system.

To maximize the revenue-generating potential of this business idea, Connexion's systems analysts worked closely with its marketing unit to understand the system features that would be necessary to meet the needs of their potential customers. Having established the key features of the proposed system, Connexion's marketing and sales team engaged several major airlines to identify the mandatory versus the desired features of the system. For example, many airlines were concerned with the time needed for the installation of the system, as any hour an aircraft does not spend in the air directly translates into lost revenue. Similarly, many airlines were concerned with the cost of installing the communications equipment and the pricing of the service for customers. The requirements collection phase produced the marketing requirements document, which then became the top-level business and systems requirements document. This document became the blueprint the systems analysts used to develop their top-level specifications on how to design the final system.

Once the detailed system design and product service development was completed, Connexion's systems engineering team involved all the integrated product teams (which represented the different stakeholders of the project) to develop the lower-level subsystems necessary for providing onboard Internet access. With these specifications, the requirements could be determined down to the element level. To comply with aviation standards and to facilitate installation and maintenance of the system, they had to set up the components as line replaceable units (LRUs), which are components of communications systems that adhere to various specifications, allowing the entire system to be easily exchanged during routine maintenance. This ensured that costs and time needed for installation and maintenance would be kept low.

The initial phases of the project went very smoothly. However, many of the assumptions of the business case were suddenly challenged by several successive events, including the first Iraq war (Desert Storm), the 11 September 2001 terrorist attacks, SARS, and overall economic downturn. Together, these events contributed to a significant downturn within the travel industry that very negatively impacted most commercial airlines. As a result, many of the airlines that had initially been interested in installing the system were forced to withdraw their commitment due to increased costs to comply with new security standards and reduced demand for air travel. For Connexion, the withdrawal of the commercial airline market required that the business case be reexamined. Given these dramatic changes, Connexion shifted its focus to the governmental and private-jet market segments to keep the business case viable. Nevertheless, although the commercial airline market was not currently interested in installing the system, Connexion managed to continue to involve 16 of the world's leading airlines in the process to identify and refine system features and services.

The airlines' involvement, critiques, and clarified requirements proved invaluable for Connexion, as it helped to refine the system

Connexion One Test Equipment.

specifications to meet the airlines' evolving market situation. It also slowly provided the airlines with the opportunity to buy into the system they were helping to design and review. Today, industry partners continue to work closely with Connexion in the evaluation of new services and system features.

Having finished the design phase, Connexion then started initial testing of the system. Aboard the specially equipped Boeing 737—the Connexion One—airplane, systems engineers thoroughly tested the functionality of the system. Using the test equipment installed aboard this aircraft, Connexion's engineers demonstrated that both wired and wireless modes could be operated safely without harmful interference with the airplane's communications, avionics, and navigations systems (see Chapter 4 for a detailed description of the system). Consequently, Connexion received approval for the system from the U.S. Federal Aviation Administration (FAA), as well as the certification by regulatory authorities in the United Kingdom and Germany, which granted certifications to Boeing and Lufthansa Technik that will allow the use of wireless laptops and personal digital assistants (PDAs) on select flights during the initial testing aboard commercial airliners.

In early 2003, the first demonstrations of the technology aboard commercial aircraft started on a Lufthansa flight between Frankfurt and Washington, DC. For the next 3 months, passengers successfully used Connexion's services aboard certain scheduled Lufthansa and British Airways transatlantic flights. These demonstrations helped to increase the number of other airlines interested in the service. Following Lufthansa, for example, airlines such as SAS, Japan Airlines, and ANA signed definite agreements to equip all or parts of their fleets with Connexion's systems.

While the system has been proven to work in commercial airline operations, Connexion's systems engineers continue working on refining the system. Owing to the demand by international airlines, Connexion decided to extend the coverage of its services to the transpacific routes as well as to South America and Africa. As many long-range international flights use routes through Greenland or northern Siberia or Alaska, the need to develop a next generation antenna arose. Connexion's first-generation antenna worked very well on routes up to a certain latitude; however, airplanes flying farther north were not able to connect to the geostationary satellites orbiting around the equator. In cooperation with Mitsubishi Electric Corporation, Connexion developed the next generation antenna, which helped to overcome these shortcomings and enable broadband Internet access at an even greater number of routes.

During the systems analysis and design process Connexion experienced several setbacks, primarily due to major international events. But by refining the system specifications based on changing requirements, Connexion weathered these crises and rolled out high-speed in-flight Internet access across private, governmental, and commercial sectors.

Discussion Questions

1. Briefly describe the systems analysis and design process at Connexion.
2. In what ways did Connexion follow the standard SDLC process as described in the chapter? Where did Connexion deviate from this process?
3. How can a company such as Connexion deal with continuously changing user requirements?

Preview

Given that computers and information systems are now a fundamental part of doing business, opportunities for misusing and abusing information, computers, and systems now abound. This new wired world we live in causes us to ask some important new ethical questions. Who owns information, particularly information about us? Who is responsible for the accuracy of information? Should guidelines be set for how business organizations and business professionals use information, computers, and information systems, and if so, what should these guidelines be? What penalties should be assessed for computer crime and abuses? After reading this chapter you will be able to:

1. Describe the advent of the Information Age and how computer ethics impact the use of information systems.
2. Discuss the ethical concerns associated with information privacy, accuracy, property, and accessibility.
3. Define computer crime, and list several types of computer crime.
4. Contrast what is meant by the terms "computer virus," "worm," "Trojan horse," and "logic or time bomb."

Information Systems Ethics and Computer Crime

Canada Competes!

Radialpoint: A Zero-knowledge Renaissance

One of Canada's best known software companies during the dot-com boom was Montreal-based Zero-knowledge systems. Zero-knowledge was founded in 1997 by Hammie Hill and his two sons, Austin and Hamnett. The company got its start designing tools and strategies to protect the privacy of Internet users. The company's main product allowed individuals to browse the web and use Internet-based applications such as e-mail, instant messaging, and online shopping with complete anonymity. However, while the product was popular with individual Internet users, the company couldn't find an effective way to build a reliable revenue stream. Like many dot-com era services, people valued anonymity while it was free, but balked when they had to pay for it. Also, some governments and law enforcement agencies expressed concern that Zero-knowledge's anonymizing tools could be used by criminals and terrorists to communicate with each other without being detected.

In 2002, the company switched its focus to concentrate on the enterprise market. Zero-knowledge built on its expertise in anonymous online activity to design privacy management tools for businesses. The company also started to offer consulting services as well as software. Zero-knowledge's timing was perfect, as new legislation in Canada and elsewhere was starting to crack down on the privacy management practices of organizations. Soon, the company was offering additional services to clients, such as virus detection, anti-spyware tools, firewalls, and parental controls. For example, the company provided data protection tools to all of Bell Sympatico's customers.

The company was successful in the enterprise market, but felt that its progress was hampered by an association with the dot-com era, criminal activity, and individual-level web use. Thus, in May, 2005, the company changed its name to Radialpoint. Today, Radialpoint provides security software for 14 million Internet users globally. While its main focus is still in Canada, most of Radialpoint's recent growth has come in the United States and Western Europe. In the United Kingdom, for example, Radialpoint has a 45 percent share of the Internet security service market.

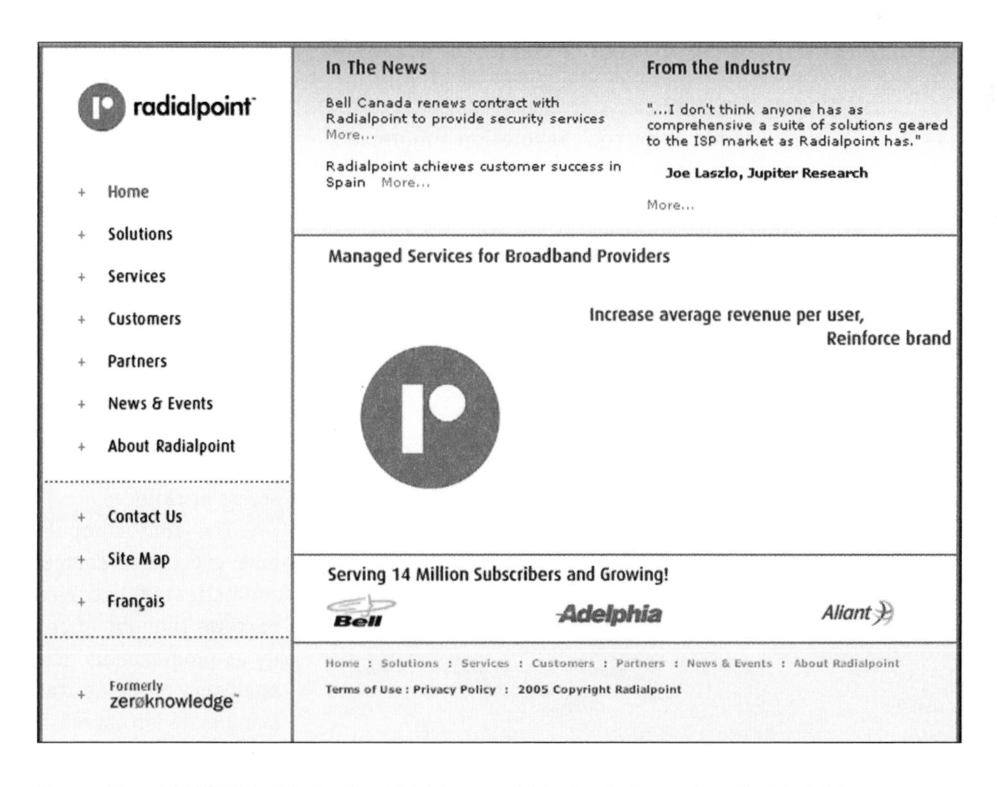

This chapter focuses on the last major topic related to why information systems matter to organizations, society, and you: specifically, various issues associated with information systems ethics and computer crime. Both topics are becoming increasingly important to successfully managing information systems and living our daily lives.

INFORMATION SYSTEMS ETHICS

In his book *The Third Wave*, futurist Alvin Toffler describes three distinct phases, or "waves of change," that have taken place in the past or are presently taking place within the world's civilizations (see Figure 9.1). The First Wave—a civilization based upon agriculture and handwork—was a comparatively primitive stage that began as civilizations formed and lasted for thousands of years. The Second Wave of change—the Industrial Revolution—overlapped the First Wave. The Industrial Revolution began in Great Britain toward the end of the eighteenth century and continued over the next 150 years, moving society from a predominantly agrarian culture to the urbanized machine age. Where once families supported themselves by working the land or handcrafting items for sale or trade, now mothers, fathers, and children left home to work in factories. Steel mills, textile factories, and eventually automobile assembly lines replaced farming and handwork as the principal source of family income.

As the Industrial Revolution progressed, not only did occupations change to accommodate the mechanized society, but so did educational, business, and social and religious institutions. On an individual level, now punctuality, obedience, and the ability to perform repetitive tasks were qualities to be instilled and valued in children in public schools and, ultimately, in workers.

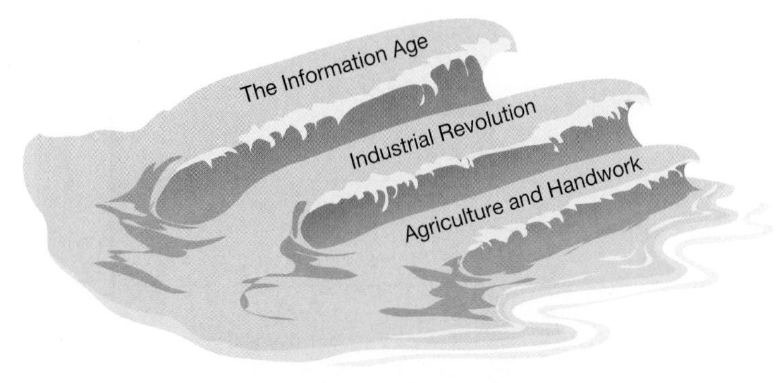

Figure 9.1 The Information Age is the biggest wave of change.

The Information Age Arrives

In a much shorter period of time than it took for civilization to progress past the First Wave, societies worldwide moved from the machine age into the ***Information Age***—a period of change Toffler has dubbed the "Third Wave." As the Third Wave gained speed, information became the currency of the realm. For thousands of years, from primitive times through the Middle Ages, information, or the body of knowledge known to that point, was limited. It was transmitted verbally, within families, clans, and villages, from person to person, generation to generation. Then came Johann Gutenberg's invention of the printing press with movable type in 1455, and a tremendous acceleration occurred in the amount and kind of information available to populations. Now knowledge could be imparted in written form, and sometimes came from distant locations. Information could be saved, absorbed, debated, and written about in publications, thus adding to the exploding data pool.

Computer Literacy and the Digital Divide

Most modern-day high school and university students have grown up in a computerized world. If by some chance they do not know how to operate a computer by the time they graduate from high school, they soon acquire computer skills, because in today's work world knowing how to use a computer—called ***computer literacy***—can mean the difference between being employed and being unemployed. Knowing how to use a computer can also open up myriad sources of information to those who have learned how to use the computer as a device to gather, store, organize, and otherwise process information. In fact, some fear that the Information Age will not provide the same advantages to "information haves"—those computer-literate individuals who have unlimited access to information—and "information have-nots"—those with limited or no access or skills.

The first computer-related occupations have evolved as computers have become more sophisticated and more widely used. Where once we thought of computer workers primarily as programmers, data entry clerks, systems analysts, or computer repairpersons, today many more job categories in virtually all industries (see Figure 9.2) involve the use of computers. In fact, today there are few occupations where computers are not somehow in use. Computers manage air traffic, perform medical

Figure 9.2 Computers are used in countless types of jobs and industries.

Sources: (9.2a) Benelux Press/© Getty Images, Inc. (9.2b) B. Busco/© Getty Images, Inc. (9.2c) Jean Louis Batt/© Getty Images, Inc. (9.2d) © Getty Images/Eye Wire, Inc.

tests, monitor investment portfolios, enable online shopping, and more. As they are especially adept at processing large amounts of data, they are used extensively by universities and public schools, in businesses of all sizes, and in all levels and departments of government. Engineers, architects, interior designers, and artists use special computer-aided design (CAD) programs. Musicians play computerized instruments, and they write and record songs with the help of computers. Not only do we use computers at work, we also use them in our personal lives. We teach our children on them, manage our finances, do our taxes, compose letters and term papers, create greeting cards, send and receive e-mail, surf the Internet, and play games on them.

Unfortunately, there are still many people in our society who are being left behind in the Information Age. The gap between those individuals in our society who are computer literate and have access to information resources like the Internet and those who do not is referred to as the digital divide. The ***digital divide*** is one of the major ethical challenges facing society today, when you consider the strong linkage between computer literacy and a person's ability to compete in the Information Age. For example, access to raw materials and money fuelled the Industrial Revolution, "but in the informational society, the fuel, the power, is knowledge," emphasized John Kenneth Galbraith, a Canadian-born economist specializing in emerging trends in the world economy. "One has now come to see a new class structure divided by those who have information and those who must function out of ignorance. This new class has its power not from money, not from land, but from knowledge."

The good news is that the digital divide in North America is rapidly shrinking, but there are still major challenges to overcome. In particular, people in rural communities, the elderly, people with disabilities, and minorities lag behind national averages for Internet access and computer literacy. Outside North America, the gap gets even wider and the obstacles much more difficult to overcome, particularly in the third world, where infrastructure and financial resources are lacking. Clearly, the digital divide is a major ethical concern facing the Information Age.

A broad range of ethical issues have emerged through the use and proliferation of computers. ***Computer ethics*** is used to describe the issues and standards of conduct as they pertain to the use of information systems. Ethics are now regarded as critical by many organizations. Some are even putting in place Chief Ethics Officers to oversee a company's ethical issues (see Brief Case: Creating an Ethically Managed Company). In 1986, Richard O. Mason wrote a classic article on the issues central to this debate—information privacy, accuracy, property, and accessibility—and these issues are still at the forefront of most ethical debates related to how information systems store and process information (see Figure 9.3). Next, we examine each of these issues.

BRIEF CASE Creating an Ethically Managed Company

The accounting scandals of the past years have left a lot of companies wondering what to do to create an ethically managed company. As chief ethics and compliance officer of Deloitte & Touche, LLP, Harold Tinkler proposed adherence to the three Cs—Culture, Control, and Consequences. While control (through checks and balances) and consequences (by creating responsibility) are important factors in creating an ethically managed company, the first C, culture, might be the most important one.

Creating a culture fostering ethical behaviour throughout the organization can be achieved by setting good examples throughout company leadership and by taking steps such as employing a chief ethics officer. In 2002, after having been charged with fraud for hiding more than $4 billion in costs, the global telecommunications player MCI WorldCom had to file for bankruptcy under Chapter 11. More than a year later, MCI slowly recovered; in an attempt to create a new ethical atmosphere throughout the organization and regain its stakeholders' confidence, it decided to hire Nancy Higgins as executive vice president of ethics and business conduct and chief ethics officer. Already, MCI has undertaken steps such as conducting ethics training for its more than 55 000 employees, establishing an official code of ethics, and setting up an ethics hotline to create an ethical culture throughout the company.

Questions

1. How can employing a chief ethics officer help a company create an ethical culture? Would you regard companies that do/don't have a chief ethics officer differently? Explain.
2. Do you know of other companies that have employed a chief ethics officer? If you have access to the Internet, research how other companies try to develop an ethical culture, and provide five specific examples.

Sources: Anonymous, "Deloitte Chief Ethics Officer Tinkler Outlines Three Critical Elements to Creating a Foundation for an Ethically Managed Company: Culture, Controls and Consequences Are the Core Requirements for Ethical Security," Deloitte Press Release (March 16, 2004), **www.deloitte.com/dtt/press_release/0,2309,sid%253D2281%2526cid%253D41724,00.html.**
Anonymous, "MCI Names Chief Ethics Officer," ITWorld.com (October 14, 2003), **www.itworld.com/Career/1909/031014mciethics/pfindex.html.**
Anonymous, "WorldCom Class Action Opt Out Deadline Has Been Extended," *Parker & Waichman* (n.d.), **www.worldcomstockfraud.com.**

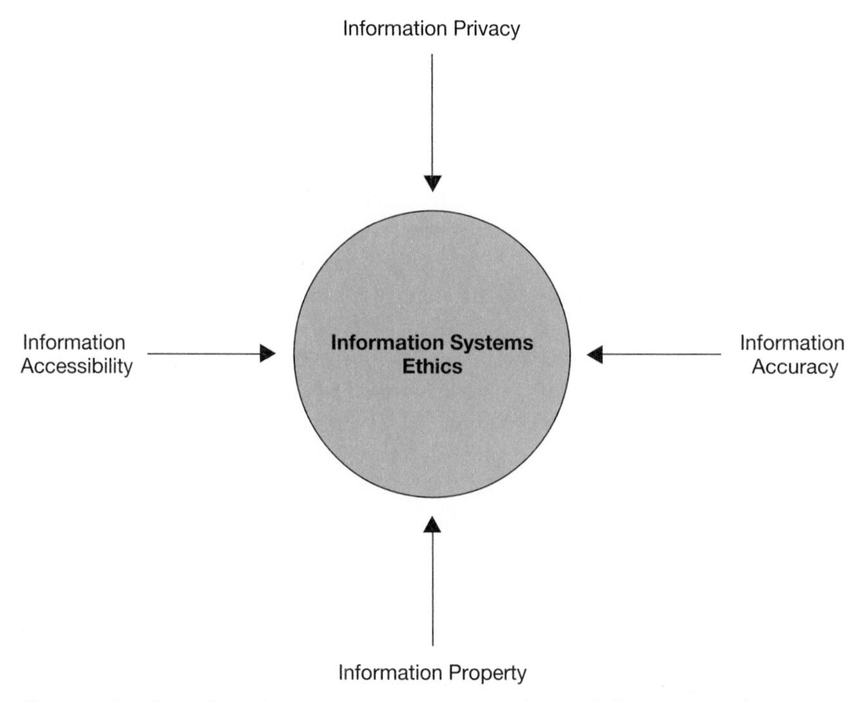

Figure 9.3 Information privacy, accuracy, property, and accessibility are central to most ethical concerns about information technology.

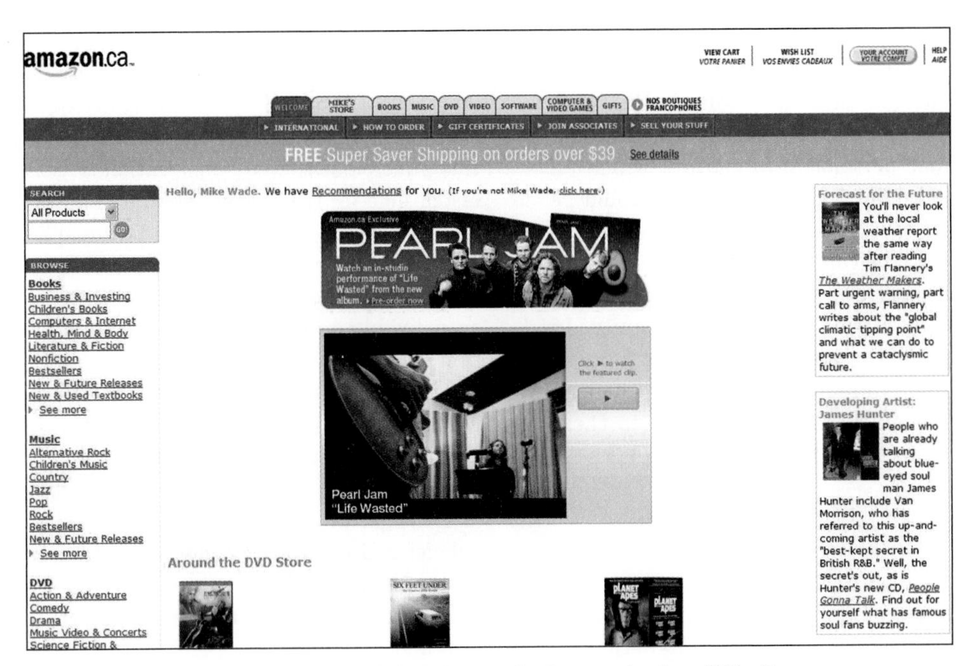

Figure 9.4 Remaining anonymous and shopping on the Internet is often difficult.

Source: www.amazon.ca

Information Privacy

If you use the Internet regularly, sending e-mail messages and visiting websites, you may have felt that your personal privacy is at risk. Several websites where you like to shop greet you by name and seem to know which products you are most likely to buy (see Figure 9.4). Every day the in-box in your browser's mail program is full to overflowing with messages urging you to buy something. As a result, you may feel as though eyes are upon you every time you log on to your ISP. ***Information privacy*** is concerned with what information an individual should have to reveal to others through the course of employment or through other transactions such as online shopping.

While the Information Age has brought widespread access to information, the downside is that others may now have access to personal information that you would prefer to keep private. Personal information, such as social insurance numbers, credit card numbers, medical histories, and even family histories, is now available on the Internet.

One of the fastest growing "information" crimes in recent years has been ***identity theft***. Identity theft is the stealing of another person's social insurance number, credit card number, and other personal information for the purpose of using the victim's credit rating to borrow money, buy merchandise, and otherwise run up debts that are never repaid. In some cases, thieves even withdraw money directly from victims' bank accounts. As many government and private organizations keep information about individuals in accessible databases, opportunities abound for thieves to retrieve it. Reclaiming one's identity and restoring a good credit rating can be frustrating and time consuming for victims.

The solution to identity theft lies in the government and private sector working together to change practices used to verify a person's identity. For example, a mother's maiden name and an individual's social insurance number are too easily obtained. Other methods of personal identification, such as biometrics and encryption, may need to be used if the problem is to be solved. Methods of information security—including biometrics and encryption—were discussed in Chapter 4, "The Internet and Security."

The widespread use of computers and the advent of the Internet have produced new concerns about privacy in Canada. The ease with which electronic information can be acquired, stored, searched, replicated, and transmitted has enormous implications for consumers who give personal information to a business. Even if the personal information is not given online, most businesses will still store information about their clients electronically. Why should governments, businesses, and consumers care about the trading of personal information? One reason is that personal information databases can become targets of illegal activity. Software can be hacked and hardware can be stolen. This means that sensitive information stored in databases could potentially fall into the wrong hands, with disastrous results for consumers. Another reason is that personal information, which an individual might find embarrassing, could be disclosed to others. Finally, many people believe that the continuing acquisition of personal information, particularly unauthorized acquisition, infringes on human dignity. In many parts of the world, the private sector has been largely unregulated. This has changed recently as governments responded to these new concerns about privacy.

Privacy Legislation in Canada

In Canada, the federal government enacted the Personal Information Protection and Electronic Documents Act (PIPEDA—the PIP rhymes with "dip," and EDA is pronounced like the last part of Canada), which became fully operative 1 January 2004. The objective of PIPEDA is to balance "the right of privacy of individuals with respect to their personal information and the need of organizations to collect, use or disclose personal information for purposes that a reasonable person would consider appropriate in the circumstances." The legislation applies to any organization in Canada that engages in "commercial activity." Not only does this include businesses in the private sector, but it may also include nonprofit organizations to the extent that they engage in commercial activities (e.g., fundraising). Any personal information that a business collects, uses, or discloses from its customers will fall under PIPEDA. In short, private-sector managers in Canada must be familiar with the main principles and rules of PIPEDA. The full legislation and accompanying commentary can be found at **www.privcom. gc.ca/legislation/02_06_01_e.asp.**

The portion of PIPEDA that deals with privacy was the result of negotiations among consumer advocates, businesses, and government during the mid-1990s. The result of these negotiations was the Canadian Standards Association's Model Code for the Protection of Personal Information, produced in 1996. The code stated that a balance must be struck between the desires of businesses to acquire personal information and the rights of consumers to the protection of their privacy. It set out 10 principles to guide businesses in the handling of personal information. This code was later adopted by Parliament when it drafted PIPEDA.

The following is a brief overview of the 10 principles found in PIPEDA:

- *Principle 1 Accountability:* The main point of this principle is that an organization is responsible for the personal information under its control and is obligated to comply with all the rules set out by PIPEDA. It also states that the organization shall designate an individual to ensure that the organization complies with these regulations. Compliance includes implementing procedures to protect personal information, establishing procedures to handle complaints, training staff, and developing information that will explain the organization's policies and practices. In addition, organizations must ensure that third parties who come into contact with personal information under the care of the organization provide comparable levels of protection for that information. This is especially important for businesses that outsource to third parties.
- *Principle 2 Identifying Purposes:* This principle requires that organizations identify the purpose for which personal information is collected. This information should be communicated to the individual when the information is collected. This principle is designed to operate in conjunction with the Consent, Limiting Collection, Openness, and Access principles noted below.
- *Principle 3 Consent:* This is perhaps the most important principle underlying PIPEDA. Quite simply, personal information should not be collected, used, or disclosed without the knowledge and consent of the individual. Parliament's view was that consent without knowledge (e.g., knowing the purpose of the collection) would be no consent at all. There are certain limited circumstances in which organizations may collect personal information without consent. The relevant exception is when the collection of the information is clearly in the best interests of the individual and consent cannot be obtained in a timely fashion. An organization may also use or disclose personal information in the case of an emergency that threatens the life, health, or security of an individual. If the organization identifies new purposes for the personal information in their possession, they must seek the consent of those individuals to use that information in that new way. Consent may be obtained in many ways: oral, written, a checkoff box, or even the signing of an application form that details

the collection, use, and disclosure of personal information. Finally, consent may be withdrawn at any time.

- *Principle 4 Limiting Collection:* This principle requires that organizations limit their collection of personal information to that which has been identified as necessary for its purposes. Personal information should not be collected indiscriminately. This is why identifying the purpose for which personal information is collected is so crucial. Without having identified the purpose for which personal information is collected, organizations can be in contravention of the act.
- *Principle 5 Limiting Use, Disclosure, and Retention:* This principle is similar to Limiting Collection in that it restricts the use and disclosure of personal information to that which has been identified as necessary for its purposes. However, there is a crucial addition that every manager needs to be aware of. Personal information that is no longer required to fulfill the organization's identified purpose must be destroyed, erased, or made anonymous. Furthermore, organizations must develop guidelines for this process.
- *Principle 6 Accuracy:* This principle has two components. The first is that personal information must be as accurate and up to date as is necessary for the purposes identified by the organization. The second is that an organization shall not routinely update personal information, unless it is necessary for the purposes identified for collecting the information.
- *Principle 7 Safeguards:* This principle is especially important for managers, even if they are not in charge of privacy protection at their organizations. This principle stipulates that organizations must safeguard the personal information that they collect. The more sensitive the personal information, the greater the safeguards required to protect it. Safeguards include physical measures (e.g., restricted offices), organizational measures (e.g., security clearances), and technological measures (e.g., passwords).
- *Principle 8 Openness:* This principle requires organizations to make information about their privacy procedures available to individuals. Specifically, individuals should not have to wait an unreasonable amount of time to receive this information. This is another reason why it is important for an organization to develop policies and procedures before it collects personal information.
- *Principle 9 Individual Access:* This principle, along with consent, represents the foundation of most modern privacy law. It stipulates that not only do individuals have a right to access their own personal information, but that they also have the right to challenge the accuracy of that information. For Canadian managers, this is important because they will need to arrange to store personal information in such a way that it can be readily accessed to accommodate this requirement. They will also have to provide information about third parties who have had access to this information. They will have 30 days from the receipt of the request to provide this information. This information is to be presented to the individual in such a way that it is easy to understand (e.g., no abbreviations or codes). One of the few exceptions to this principle is if access to an individual's personal information would in some way compromise the personal information of another.
- *Principle 10 Challenging Compliance:* This principle stipulates that an individual has a right to challenge an organization's compliance with these principles.

Many companies in Canada now post privacy policies in their offices, stores, and online (see Figure 9.5 for an information privacy statement

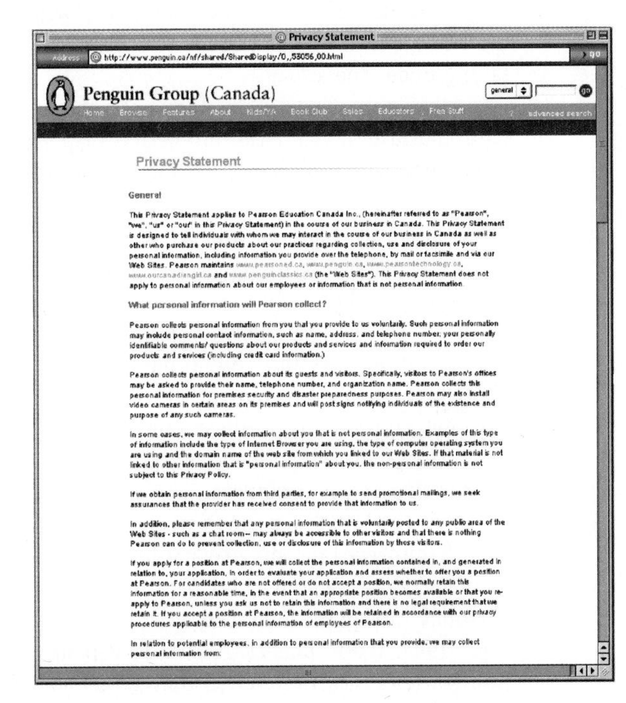

Privacy Statement

http://www.penguin.ca/nf/shared/SharedDisplay/0,,53056,00.html

Penguin Group (Canada)

Privacy Statement

General

This Privacy Statement applies to Pearson Education Canada Inc., (hereinafter referred to as "Pearson", "we", "us" or "our" in this Privacy Statement) in the course of our business in Canada. This Privacy Statement is designed to tell individuals with whom we may interact in the course of our business in Canada as well as other who purchase our products about our practices regarding collection, use and disclosure of your personal information, including information you provide over the telephone, by mail or facsimile and via our Web Sites. Pearson maintains www.pearsoned.ca, www.penguin.ca, www.pearsontechnology.ca, www.ourcanadiangirl.ca and www.penguinclassics.ca (the "Web Sites"). This Privacy Statement does not apply to personal information about our employees or information that is not personal information.

What personal information will Pearson collect?

Pearson collects personal information from you that you provide to us voluntarily. Such personal information may include personal contact information, such as name, address, and telephone number; your personally identifiable comments/ questions about our products and services and information required to order our products and services (including credit card information.)

Pearson collects personal information about its guests and visitors. Specifically, visitors to Pearson's offices may be asked to provide their name, telephone number, and organization name. Pearson collects this personal information for premises security and disaster preparedness purposes. Pearson may also install video cameras in certain areas on its premises and will post signs notifying individuals of the existence and purpose of any such cameras.

In some cases, we may collect information about you that is not personal information. Examples of this type of information include the type of Internet Browser you are using, the type of computer operating system you are using and the domain name of the web site from which you linked to our Web Sites. If that material is not linked to other information that is "personal information" about you, the non-personal information is not subject to this Privacy Policy.

If we obtain personal information from third parties, for example to send promotional mailings, we seek assurances that the provider has received consent to provide that information to us.

In addition, please remember that any personal information that is voluntarily posted to any public area of the Web Sites - such as a chat room-- may always be accessible to other visitors and that there is nothing Pearson can do to prevent collection, use or disclosure of this information by those visitors.

If you apply for a position at Pearson, we will collect the personal information contained in, and generated in relation to, your application, in order to evaluate your application and assess whether to offer you a position at Pearson. For candidates who are not offered or do not accept a position, we normally retain this information for a reasonable time, in the event that an appropriate position becomes available or that you re-apply to Pearson, unless you ask us not to retain this information and there is no legal requirement that we retain it. If you accept a position at Pearson, the information will be retained in accordance with our privacy procedures applicable to the personal information of employees of Pearson.

In relation to potential employees, in addition to personal information that you provide, we may collect personal information from:

Figure 9.5 Information privacy statement from Penguin Group.

from Penguin Group). Others are going a step further, requiring customers and employees to sign a privacy document or contract. If individuals are not satisfied with the handling of their personal information, PIPEDA stipulates that they may file a complaint with the Privacy Commissioner or go before the Federal Court to seek redress. Depending upon the size and seriousness of the violation, organizations could face steep fines for failing to protect personal information in their possession. Unfortunately, the precise protections, responsibilities, and stipulations contained within PIPEDA have proven difficult for many Canadian businesses to understand (see Brief Case: PIPEDA Creates Confusion for Businesses).

For example, the Privacy Commissioner recently released a decision involving data collection on the Internet. The case focused on whether a protocol called NETBIOS (Network Basic Input/Output System), which Microsoft uses to facilitate the sharing of printers and files on a local area network, could be considered personal information. Not only may NETBIOS contain personal information (e.g., username), but it may also compromise the security of Internet users. The commissioner found that NETBIOS constituted personal information under PIPEDA, because it could potentially contain personal information (although it normally would not). Because of the ruling, managers will have to consider all electronic interactions as falling under the act.

As we can see, PIPEDA does not set out hard and fast rules for the protection of personal information. Rather it sets out a series of general principles. It is important to understand that circumstances will dictate the type of actions necessary to comply with the law. The policies and procedures of a small business dealing with relatively general personal information will be very different from those of a larger organization dealing with very sensitive personal information. Managers must be prepared to match their privacy procedures with their business's circumstances.

Over the last few years, several provinces have begun working on privacy legislation. Quebec has had legislation regulating personal information in the private sector since 1994. On 1 January 2004, the Personal Information Protection Act (British Columbia) and the Personal Information Protection Act (Alberta) came into force. In addition, some provinces have freedom of information and protection (FOIP) acts that govern how Canadians can access information held by public bodies.

How do managers deal with many different privacy laws? Fortunately, the trend thus far seems to be that the provinces are passing legislation that is similar to PIPEDA, with the intent of producing similar regulatory regimes. The Privacy Commissioner of Canada has stated that if the provincial legislation is "substantively similar" to PIPEDA, then the provincial legislation will be applied to businesses that operate in that province. This was the case with the Quebec legislation, which the commissioner held was substantively similar to PIPEDA. "Substantively similar" means that the provincial law must contain, at a minimum, the 10 principles set out in PIPEDA. Canadian managers will have to follow both the federal and the provincial legislation.

Privacy Legislation in the United States

The United States lacks a comprehensive statute, such as PIPEDA, that regulates personal information in the private sector. Rather, the trend at the federal level is toward targeting particular consumers or certain types of personal information. One example of this is the Children's Online Privacy Protection Act (COPPA), which became fully operative in 2000. The legislation aims at protecting the personal information of children. IS managers operating in the United States will have to be familiar with COPPA because it applies not just to websites targeting children, but also to websites that receive visits from children. The Federal Trade Commission, which enforces COPPA, has developed guidelines for compliance. Firms must provide information on their websites about their collection polices, obtain "verifiable consent" from parents, provide a means for allowing parents to view their child's personal information, and establish internal security controls. Many of the FTC's guidelines are similar to the principles found in PIPEDA. Other legislation, such as the Gramm-Leach-Bliley Act (financial regulation), the Patriot Act, the Digital Millennium Copyright Act, and the Health Insurance Portability and Accountability Act (insurance regulation) have privacy components. Finally, the Sarbanes-Oxley Act contains stipulations that can result in public company executives being personally liable for the transgressions of the firms they manage. The threat of serious jail time can provide a powerful incentive to behave in a responsible manner.

BRIEF CASE PIPEDA Creates Confusion for Businesses

Experts point to a startling number of Canadian companies that don't know how to comply with the Personal Information Protection and Electronic Documents Act (PIPEDA), which became official for private firms on 1 January 2004. The legislation is proving to be a minefield for companies that don't understand the difference between the confidentiality of personal data and the collection of that data. "People are not aware of the depth, the breadth, the magnitude of it," says Ian Turnbull, executive director of the Canadian Privacy Institute, a consultancy that helps companies with privacy compliance. "A lot of people are turning to their lawyers, and their lawyers are giving them legal advice as opposed to practical advice. . . . They're not getting enough [information] and what they're getting is confusing."

A privacy tool developed by the Enterprise-Wide Privacy Task Force of the Canadian Institute of Chartered Accountants (CICA) and the American Institute of Certified Public Accountants (AICPA) aims to furnish Canadians with privacy information and put it in context. The 70-page best practices guide is designed to help companies comply with PIPEDA, as well as any relevant provincial and international privacy legislation. "It gives you the baseline best practices and then tells you where you have to supplement those to address unique specific requirements of one or more pieces of legislation," said Robert Parker, a partner with Deloitte's enterprise risk practice and one of the guide's contributors. Even companies that believe they are compliant with PIPEDA may only be paying it lip service, says Parker. There is a difference between writing a corporate-wide privacy policy and having not just your employees but also your back-office systems adhere to it.

Ontario's Information and Privacy Commissioner, Ann Cavoukian, has endorsed the CICA guide. "One thing that the commissioner has found as she's spoken to businesses is that [they] are looking for ways to help them comply with PIPEDA," says Brian Beamish, director of policy and compliance in the commissioner's office. "PIPEDA sets down some general principles for managing personal information, and it's sometimes difficult to transfer those general principles in what can be a complex business situation," he adds. Turnbull emphasizes the need for more practical solutions. "Organizations just don't have a good handle on the information they have," he says. "When the second hand swept by midnight on 31 December 2003, it started privacy for the whole country, and privacy is not going to go away."

Questions

1. What implications does PIPEDA have for a firm's IT function?
2. Do you think PIPEDA is good for Canadian businesses? Why, or why not?

Source: Adapted from Neil Sutton, "PIPEDA Confusion Sets In," ITBusiness.ca (March 29, 2004), **www.itbusiness.ca/it/client/en/Home/News.asp?id=4544&bSearch=True**.

Privacy Legislation in Europe

The regulation of personal information in the private sector in Europe is complex for two reasons. The first is that the European Union and its member states have a complex constitutional relationship. The second is that personal data protection in Europe is considered a fundamental human right ("Everyone has the right to the protection of personal data concerning him or her," Article 8 of the Charter of Fundamental Rights of the European Union).

The European Union implemented the General Data Protection directive (General Directive) in 1998. The directive applies to all member states, as well as to some non–EU members (Iceland, Liechtenstein, and Norway), which make up the European Free Trade Association. The General Directive has two aims: to ease information flow within the EU, and to provide a minimum level of data protection. Like PIPEDA, the General Directive has a series of guiding principles: legitimacy, finality, transparency, proportionality, confidentiality and security, and control. In addition to regulating member states, the General Directive forbids transferring personal data to third parties (i.e., countries that have not adopted the General Directive) that do not have a similar level of data protection. This means that companies based outside of Europe that wish to deal with the personal data of European citizens must reside in a country with comparable privacy laws. With PIPEDA, Canada qualifies for this standard, but many countries, including the United States, do not.

Web Search

Visit the Privacy Rights Clearinghouse, **www.privacyrights.org**, and learn more about how to protect your privacy. Review one of the site's numerous "fact sheets" on how to protect your privacy, and prepare a one-page report summarizing the fact sheet. Will reading these fact sheets influence your online shopping behaviour? If yes, what would you do differently? If not, how do you protect your privacy online?

Not only does each member state have its own method of administering the General Directive, but each may also have its own additional laws and regulatory schemes for personal information in the private sector. It is beyond the scope of this book to review data protection legislation in each of the EU member states. However, more information about privacy laws in the EU and around the world can be found at **www.epic.org/privacy or www.privacyrights.org**.

Before moving on, it is important to distinguish between unethical behaviour and a crime. Identity theft is clearly a crime. However, many "misuses" of computers and information may not be crimes but would be considered unethical by most people. As technology moves forward and allows humans to do things not possible before, existing laws often do not apply to these emerging situations. One of the ongoing debates regarding technological innovations revolves around the question: "Just because it is not a crime, does that make it okay to do it?"

How to Maintain Your Privacy Online

When you make web purchases in Canada, vendors are required by law to respect your privacy. However, the same levels of privacy protection do not exist in all jurisdictions. In the United States, for example, a vendor can track what pages you look at, what products you examine in detail, which products you choose to buy, what method of payment you choose to use, and where you have the product delivered. After collecting all that information, unscrupulous vendors can sell it to others, resulting in more direct-mail advertising, electronic spam in your e-mail inbox, or calls from telemarketers.

When surveyed about concerns related to online shopping, most consumers list issues of information privacy as a top concern. As a result, governments have pressured vendors to post their privacy policies on their websites. Unfortunately, these policies do not often protect the privacy of consumers. To protect yourself, you should always review the privacy policy of all companies you do business with and refuse to do business with those that do not have a clear policy. According to the Consumer Protection Working Group of the American Bar Association at safeshopping.org, a seller's privacy policy should at least indicate:

- What information the seller is gathering from you
- How the seller will use this information
- Whether and how you can "opt out" of these practices

To make sure your shopping experience is a good one, you can take a few additional steps to maintain your privacy.

- *Choose sites that are monitored by independent organizations.* Several independent organizations monitor the privacy and business practices of websites. Organizations such as **www.epubliceye.com** and **www.openratings.com** provide a valuable service for consumers by monitoring the business practices of sellers and requiring conformance to standard guidelines or giving consumers a rating of a seller's practices. Choosing sites that are independently evaluated by a reputable rating company is a good way to ensure your privacy.
- *Avoid having "cookies" left on your machine.* Many commercial websites are designed to leave a small file on your hard drive so that the owner of the site can monitor where you go and what you do on the site. It is possible that the site owner could obtain your e-mail address from the visit, potentially sending you unsolicited e-mail spam. Fortunately, most web browsers provide the ability to turn off cookies or to warn you that the site is trying to deposit a cookie on your hard drive; when configured to warn you, your browser will prompt you with a notification and ask you if you want to accept the cookie. In addition to using settings within your web browser, you can get special "cookie management" software to help better maintain your privacy (go to **www.cookiecentral.com** for more on cookie management options).
- *Visit sites anonymously.* There are ways to visit websites anonymously. Using services provided by companies such as Anonymizer (**www.anonymizer.com**), you have total privacy from marketers, identity thieves, or even coworkers when surfing the web. Their software blocks cookies, Java, and other tracking methods from being left on your computer; for sites that require cookies to be left on your machine in order for you to visit, the software allows cookies to be encrypted so that no one can trace your activity. Similarly, URL addresses are also encrypted so that anyone monitoring your activity cannot log a meaningful address.
- *Use caution when requesting confirming e-mail.* When you buy products online, many companies will send you a confirming e-mail message to let you know that the

order was received correctly. If you use a shared computer or buy online with a computer at work where your online activity can be monitored, you should take care to protect the privacy of your purchases. A good strategy is to have a separate e-mail account, such as one that is available for viewing via a web browser, which you use when making online purchases. For example, Hotmail, Yahoo!, Excite, and countless other web portals provide free e-mail services that can be accessed using a standard web browser. This allows you to keep your primary e-mail address private from unscrupulous sellers and keeps your correspondence private from anyone who has access to your computer.

Of course there are no guarantees that all your online experiences will be problem-free, but if you follow the advice provided here, you are likely to survive and thrive in the world of online electronic business.

Avoid Getting Conned in Cyberspace

"The Internet has changed the way consumers gather information, shop, and do business," U.S. Federal Trade Commission director of consumer protection Jodie Bernstein said in November 2000. Con artists and other lawbreakers have gone high-tech and are using the Internet to cheat consumers in a number of clever ways. The Federal Trade Commission has compiled advice on how not to get taken by crafty con artists on the Internet (**www.ftc.gov/bcp/conline/pubs/online/dotcons.htm**). Among the listed "dot-cons" were offers to let you see adult images in exchange for revealing your credit card number, auction cheats, charges for a "free" website appearing on telephone bills, and various investment, travel and vacation, business, and health care product scams. Table 9.1 summarizes the top ten cybercons being perpetrated on consumers using the Internet. Review this table so that you better understand what techniques con artists are using to separate you from your money. The best advice for doing business on the Internet is to follow the old adage, "if it is too good to be true, then it probably is."

Information Accuracy

The issue of information accuracy has become highly charged in today's wired world. ***Information accuracy*** is concerned with ensuring the authenticity and fidelity of information, as well as with identifying who is responsible for informational errors that harm people. With all the computerization that has taken place, people have come to expect to receive and retrieve information more easily and quickly than ever before. In addition, because computers "never make mistakes," we have come to expect this information to be accurate. A case in point is at the bank. The combination of automated teller machines, computerized record systems, and large, electronic client and transaction databases should provide customers with quick and accurate access to their account information. However, we continue to hear about and experience record-keeping errors at banks.

An error of a few dollars in your banking records does not seem significant. However, what if it were an error of hundreds or thousands of dollars in the bank's favour? What if the error caused one of your important payments (such as a home mortgage payment) to bounce, as was the case for many customers of the Royal Bank of Canada in May 2004? Bank errors can be quite important.

There are many stories of data accuracy problems with information systems, many of which have involved banks. For example, one such case occurred in Los Angeles but has surely been repeated many times around the world. The basic story is as follows. Louis and Eileen Marches had bought a house in the 1950s with financing through their local bank. Louis dutifully paid the monthly payments in person and made sure that his loan book was stamped "paid" every time, even after the bank's systems had been automated. Several years ago, the bank notified the Marches that their payments were in arrears. Louis went to the bank with his payment book, but because the account screen showed no payment, the teller, the head teller, and the bank manager refused to honour his stamped book. One month later the same thing happened again, and now 2 months were in arrears. The bank continued to refuse his proof of payment and based its decisions and actions solely on the computer system. Eventually, the bank foreclosed on the house, causing a near-fatal stroke for Eileen. After a long lawsuit, the Marches recovered $268 000 from the bank and the following apology: "Computers make mistakes. Banks make mistakes, too." Similar stories abound about people who have found that mistakes in their credit reports have led to disastrous results.

Table 9.1 ***Top ten list of dot-cons from the U.S. Federal Trade Commission and advice on how not to get conned.***

The Con	The Bait	The Switch	Advice
Internet auctions	Great deals on great products.	After sending money, consumers receive inferior item or nothing at all.	Investigate the seller carefully. Use a credit card or escrow service to pay.
Internet access service	Free money, simply for cashing a cheque.	After cashing the "free" cheque, consumers are locked into long-term web service with steep penalties for early cancellation.	Read both sides of the cheque, the fine print, or any documentation that comes with the cheque.
Credit card fraud	View online adult images for free, just for sharing your credit card number to "prove" you are over 18.	Fraudulent promoters run up unauthorized charges on consumers' cards.	Share your credit card numbers only when you are buying from a company you trust. Dispute unauthorized charges.
International modem dialling	Free access to adult material by downloading "viewer" or "dialler."	Exorbitant long-distance phone bills as the viewer or dialler reconnects to an international carrier.	Do not download programs providing "free" access without carefully reading all the fine print. Dispute unauthorized charges to your account.
Web cramming	Free custom-designed website for 30-day trial.	Telephone is billed even when consumers do not accept offer or agree to continue service.	Review phone bill carefully, and challenge all charges you do not recognize.
Multilevel marketing plans/pyramids	Make money selling products you sell as well as those sold by people you recruit to sell.	Consumers are required to recruit other distributors, but products sold to distributors do not qualify for commissions.	Avoid programs that require you to recruit distributors, buy expensive inventory, or commit to a minimum sales volume.
Travel/vacations	Great trips for bargain prices.	Low-quality accommodations and services, often with hidden charges.	Get references and the details of the trip in writing.
Business opportunities	Be your own boss, and earn a high salary.	Consumers invest in unproven or insecure ventures.	Talk with others who have made the same investment, get all promises in writing and study the contract carefully. Consult with a lawyer or accountant.
Investments	Realize huge investment returns.	Big profits always mean big risks.	Check with securities and commodities regulators; insist on talking with other investors.
Health-care products/services	Cure serious illness or fatal health problems.	Consumers put faith in unproven solutions and put off pursuing needed health care.	Consult with health professionals to evaluate cure-alls or promises to provide fast or easy cure.

Source: **www.ftc.gov/bcp/conline/pubs/online/dotcons.htm**

WHEN THINGS GO WRONG

The Canadian Revenue Agency Spills Personal Data

Canadian security experts lambasted the Canada Revenue Agency (CRA) over the lack of encryption to protect the personal data of more than 120 000 individuals that was lost when a server was stolen from a regional office. The CRA eventually admitted the breach weeks after its Quebec Tax Service office was broken into. One of the four stolen laptops, which acted as a server, contained a database with unencrypted information including names, dates of birth, social insurance numbers, and home addresses, but not personal income tax information, according to the CRA. In unscrupulous hands, this data could be used to apply for a driver's licence, credit card, or passport.

The database spanned records from 1999 to 2001. Approximately 94 000 of those affected were in the construction industry. The rest of the records contained information on employment insurance and Canada Pension Plan rulings on contract and independent workers. CCRA spokesman Dominique McNeely says it did not want to make the information public until it had contacted those affected by letter. "We had to check to make sure we were contacting the right clients," he says. "It did take us a while, but we had to make literally millions of calls and checks within our system."

McNeely says the servers were not contained in their usual locked room at the time of the theft. "They were in our office, which is protected by an alarm system, but most police agencies will concur it is practically impossible to stop a determined thief," he says. "We could talk about human error, but it's not like we left them on the front lawn." The CRA has put a 24-hour security guard on patrol at the office since the incident, McNeely says, and bars are being installed on the ground floor where a window was smashed. "Our servers aren't encrypted," he says. "They're only password-protected, because if our servers were encrypted, it would slow down our operations to a point where it just wouldn't be workable. That's why we keep them locked in a more secure room." Critics say there is no excuse in today's environment for claiming that reasonable encryption has a performance problem on IT equipment. "That's utter, unmitigated nonsense," says Mich Kabay, associate professor in the department of computer information systems at Norwich University in Northfield, Virginia. "You can use perfectly reasonable key lengths with off-the-shelf encryption software and do a reasonable job of interfering with all but a systematic, government-sponsored cracking attempt."

The incident marked the second time that a CRA office lost confidential information. In February 2003, a server, along with eight laptops containing information on 538 income assistance clients, was stolen from a two-storey building in Coquitlam, B.C.

Source: Adapted from Shane Schick, "CCRA Loses Data in Server Theft," *Computing Canada*, Vol. 29, No. 20 (October 27, 2003).

Now, imagine how significant a data accuracy error might be in other settings. Hospitals use similar automation and computer-intensive record keeping. Imagine what would happen if prescription information appeared incorrectly on a patient's chart and the patient became deathly ill as a result of the medicine that was mistakenly dispensed to him. The significance of such a data accuracy error could be tremendous. Furthermore, it would not be clear who was to blame. Would this be the fault of the doctor, the pharmacist, the programmer, the data entry clerk, or maybe some combination of errors by the system designer, the system analyst, the system programmer, the database administrator, and the vendor? It would be too easy simply to blame the computer; someone would need to be found at fault.

Computer-based information systems, and the data within those systems, are only as accurate and as useful as they have been made to be. The now infamous quote, "Computers make mistakes. Banks make mistakes, too" would be better restated as, "Computers never make mistakes; only humans make mistakes" (Mason, 1986). This reflects the need for better precautions and greater scrutiny when modern information systems are designed, built, and used. This means that everyone must be concerned with data integrity, from the design of the system, to the building of the system, to the person who actually enters data into the system, and to the people who use and manage the system. Perhaps more important, when data errors are found, people should not blame the

ETHICAL DILEMMA

Is It Acceptable to Use Technology to Check for Plagiarism?

A McGill University student successfully challenged the administration's requirement that students submit assignments to Turnitin.com, a California website monitoring plagiarism, or risk a zero grade. The second-year international development student had "an ethical and political problem" with Montreal based McGill's policy and refused to turn in his work, said Ian Boyko, national chairperson of the Canadian Federation of Students in Ottawa. "After some deliberation, the university realized it was on thin ice and agreed to mark his paper and not give him a zero."

The university student association noted several issues emerging from the incident. For one thing, many of its members are concerned that the decision to run papers through the site was made without consulting an "academic senate or university board of governors or department council," said Boyko. "But I think when a student writes an assignment, it's an original piece of work. It's the student's copyright, his or her intellectual property. For a student to have to submit that, without being compensated, so a website based in California can get richer, I think he took objection to that. Human beings have been detecting plagiarism for years. I don't see why that needs to all of a sudden come to an end right now."

Dave Chan, former president of the Graduate Business Council at York University, disagrees. "We discussed Turnitin with our students and they loved it. Plagiarism is a large and growing problem, and anything that can put a stop to it, or at least slow it down, is a good thing," he noted. "If a student has nothing to hide, then what's the problem?"

The McGill student's reluctance to participate in the program was the first such incident in the 6-year history of San Francisco–based Turnitin.com, said CEO Dr. John Barrie. The company said it has clients in more than 50 countries, receives more than 20 000 student term papers every day, and has never been sued. "If you just look at the odds, it was bound to happen at some point," he added. He said McGill has indicated no interest in cancelling its subscription.

Barrie seems unfazed by the episode at McGill. His company is on the verge of releasing a Canadian legal opinion stating that it's "100 percent in compliance with Canadian intellectual property and privacy laws. I have always thought that the claims by that particular student were without merit." Turnitin.com takes seriously the privacy rights of students and gives access to papers only to their instructors, he said.

Source: Adapted from Fawzia Sheikh, "Student Group Questions Ethics of Anti-Plagiarism Site," ITBusiness.ca (January 15, 2004), **www.itbusiness.ca/it/client/en/Home/News.asp?id=85&bSearch=True.**

computer. After all, people designed it, built it, and entered data into it in the first place.

Information Property

It happens to all of us. Nearly every day in the mail, we receive unwanted solicitations from credit card companies, department stores, magazines, or charitable organizations. Many of these envelopes are never opened. We ask the same question over and over again: "How did I get on another mailing list?" Your name, address, and other personal information were most likely sold from one company to another for use in mass mailings. You probably did not give anyone permission to buy or sell information about you, but that is not a legal issue, or a matter of concern, for some firms. ***Information property*** focuses on who owns information about individuals and how information can be sold and exchanged.

Intellectual property refers to property that is subject to copyright, trademark, or patent legislation. Intellectual property law has been around for centuries. The advent of personal computers and the Internet, however, has posed new challenges to intellectual property law in industrialized countries. For instance, any copyrighted material that exists in digital form can be endlessly replicated and transmitted. This is a double-edged sword for holders of copyright. On the one hand, it means that replication and distribution costs are low. But on the other hand, it makes it easy for others to violate that copyright.

Canada's Copyright Act grants a series of rights to the author of a work upon its completion. There are actually very few formal requirements for establishing **copyright** in Canada. One is that the author (whether a person or a corporation) must be a resident of Canada or a resident of a "treaty country"—which includes more than 150 countries around the world. The work must also be original and fall under the class of a literary, dramatic, musical, or artistic work. The courts will protect works in any form, including electronic. In Canada, computer software falls under the category of literary work. The most important right granted to the copyright holder is the right to reproduce a work and, by extension, the right to prevent others from reproducing it. Copyright issues have been thrust onto the world stage recently, primarily due to the ease with which digital information can be copied and distributed. For example, a litany of copyright issues has arisen from the extensive use of file-sharing networks. These networks became popular as a means to share digital music files but now are being used to distribute other digital products, including movies and software.

The legal implications of copyright for Canadian managers are extensive. The most common issue is dealing with software purchased from other companies. When a software program is purchased, most likely the company will not "own" that copy (as one might "own" a copy of a book that could be resold to a third party), but rather the company will have a licence to use that software program. That licence will be governed by the contract agreed to between the vendor and the purchaser.

The contract may restrict or limit the ways in which the IS manager can use or modify the program. Another copyright issue that managers may have to deal with relates to compiling databases. Courts in Canada and the United States have stated that the legitimate use of copyrighted material in one context does not necessarily mean that use in the compilation of a database will be legitimate.

Linking (through hyperlinks on one's website) to copyrighted material is another contentious issue. Copyright holders believe that such linking impairs the value of their work by making it easier for individuals to violate their copyright. In the United States, copyright holders have been aided by the passage of the Digital Millennium Copyright Act. The statute forbids offering, providing, or otherwise trading in copyrighted technology. Courts in the United States have used this legislation to force websites that provide links to copyrighted material to stop doing so. In Canada, the courts have drawn a distinction between hyperlinks that link to websites that offer copyrighted material (permissible) and embedded hyperlinks that automatically begin a transfer of information from another website (forbidden).

A **trademark** is a mark used by a firm for the purposes of distinguishing its goods and services from those of another firm. It therefore protects both firms and consumers. A trademark may be a design, word, phrase, slogan, colour, or sound. Because the purpose of the trademark is to distinguish one firm's goods and services from another's, it is imperative that the trademark be distinctive. The greater the distinctiveness of the trademark, the greater the protection it is afforded by the court. A trade name, which is used to identify a particular business, may be a trademark if it is also used to distinguish goods and services. In Canada, trademarks are established in one of two ways. The most common way is simply through the adoption and use of a trademark within Canada. The other way is registering the trademark under the federal Trade-marks Act.

A pressing trademark issue exists with domain names. Domain names are unique alphanumeric words that function as a stand-in for an Internet protocol address. In Canada and the United States, domain names are registered through approved registrars on a first-come, first-served basis. During the mid-1990s, many companies were slow to appreciate the economic potential of the Internet and failed to register appropriate domain names. This led to a phenomenon known as "cybersquatting," in which individuals and businesses essentially engaged in a kind of domain name arbitrage by registering the names of well-known companies and products. Rather than pay for those domain names, many companies decided to sue the holders of the domain name and the registrar for trademark violations.

It is important to note that domain name registration does not necessarily trump trademark law. In Canada, companies have had success in wresting away domain names on the basis of trademark violation. In the United States, trademark holders have been aided by the passage of the Anticybersquatting Consumer Protection Act in 1999. The act targets those who deliberately register a trademark as a domain name and allows the court to transfer the domain name to the trademark holder. Some cases are harder to arbitrate than others. For example, in 2004, Microsoft sued a young web designer in Victoria, B.C. The problem (from Microsoft's perspective) was that the young man's name was Mike Rowe, and he had created the domain name **www.mikerowesoft.com**.

In the end, Microsoft made an arrangement with Rowe, and he agreed to take the site down.

There are some other problems with current trademark law in the Information Age. Trademarks are generally considered in territorial terms. This means that trademarks are enforceable only in regions in which they are used. In other jurisdictions, it is possible for another company to use a similar trademark. Furthermore, it is possible for two different users to employ the same trademark in the same region so long as there is no risk of confusing consumers. For years, Canadian Airlines, an airline company, and Molson Canadian, a brewery, shared the trademark "Canadian." The problem is that domain names are unique. Different users simply cannot share them. Whose trademark takes precedence in such a circumstance? So far, there does not seem to be any clear guide. For instance, "Apple" is both a trade name and a trademark because it distinguishes the products and services of Apple Computers from those of its competitors. Interestingly, Apple the computer company is now being sued for trademark violations by Apple the record company over iTunes, the computer firm's foray into the music business.

A **patent** is a right to exclusively manufacture an invention for a specified time. In the United States, though not in Canada, patents have recently been extended to cover business methods. A business method patent can be gained by inventing a special technique for doing business. Most of these business methods relate to e-business. For instance, Priceline.com patented its reverse auction process. While Canadian companies have not been able to patent these business methods in Canada, they have registered patents in the United States. For instance, Royal Bank, a Canadian company, patented its automobile financing buy-back program in the United States.

Canadian managers should be aware that opportunities exist in the United States to patent such business methods and that pitfalls exist as well. Patent holders in the United States have shown that they are very much willing to sue those who they believe have infringed their patent. This is a lesson that Research in Motion (RIM), the Waterloo-based developer of the ubiquitous BlackBerry wireless device, learned the hard way. RIM was faced with a patent challenge to a key piece of software underlying its BlackBerry service. The firm suing RIM was a patent-holding company, in other words, a company whose sole function was to collect and then protect patents. RIM fought the lawsuit for years before eventually settling for more than $600 million. RIM proclaimed its innocence to the very end, but decided to settle the suit to avoid continued uncertainty over its future. Even smaller firms in Canada have had to pay more attention to the protection of their intellectual property (see SME Success: Unleashed Informatics Goes on the Offence to Protect Its Intellectual Property).

Spam, Cookies, and Spyware

In addition to the information you knowingly share with a website when purchasing a product, spam, cookies, and spyware are three ways that information property about individuals and organizations is being collected and (ab)used on the Internet. Spam, defined in Chapter 4, refers to unsolicited e-mail that promotes a product or service or makes some other type of solicitation. If you have ever signed up for a contest online, filled out a registration form for an Internet service, or even bought a book from Amazon.com (although not Amazon.ca due to PIPEDA in Canada), chances are your e-mail address was sold to e-marketers. Some spam consists of hoaxes, asking you to donate money to nonexistent causes or warning you of viruses and other Internet dangers that do not exist. Other times, spam includes attachments that carry destructive computer viruses. It is not advisable to ever reply to a spam message—even if it might feel good to do so at the moment—even if the message contains instructions for removing your e-mail address from the list. Replying to the message can actually be counterproductive because the spammer, or the person who sent the spam, may simply note that someone actually responded and mark your address for future mailings. In addition to e-mail-based spam, spam over Instant Messaging (IM)—called *spim*—is becoming increasingly common. Spim is particularly tricky because messages—typically a website link and some text saying how great the site is—are formatted to mimic communication in a chat session.

In addition to wasting people's time, spam (and spim) consumes a lot of network and computing resources. Although there are federal, provincial, and international laws related to spam, very little can be done to stop a motivated spammer (see **www.spamlaws.com** for more information). Consequently, most organizations utilize special-purpose spam-blocking software or hardware. These spam blockers are not perfect but are continuously improving. Additionally, a growing number of Internet service providers provide spam-filtering services

SME SUCCESS

Unleashed Informatics Goes on the Offence to Protect Its Intellectual Property

A company that started out as a life sciences IT project within a Canadian hospital has entered the commercial market by warning competitors to take their hands off its intellectual property. Unleashed Informatics has given an ultimatum to any for-profit firm that is selling a software product or service that falls under its patent, which is described as a "system for electronically managing, finding, and/or displaying biomolecular interactions."

Unleashed Informatics started out as a team of Mt. Sinai Hospital researchers in 2003. The team was using grid computing hardware and software from Sun Microsystems and others to create a web-accessible repository for all kinds of genomic and proteomic research. This system continues to exist, but changes in the funding for such projects by the Ontario government in 2004 forced the team to consider moving to Singapore and accelerated its plans to commercialize its technology. Unleashed Informatics was incorporated in 2004 and entered into an agreement with Mt. Sinai in 2005 for exclusive rights to the intellectual property, including a molecule database, manipulation software, and the data warehouse.

"We launched a lifeboat, and a handful of us got in," says Eric Andrade, Unleashed Informatics chief executive. "We did extensive survey work in terms of the competitive landscape in bioinformatics and it looked like there had been a massive forest fire. Anyone who was there was gone, or was on their last legs." As part of the agreement with Mt. Sinai, Unleashed Informatics continued to offer freely available versions of its data and software to academic researchers. But it also created a growing number of products that were offered via subscription fees.

Because the free versions of its software required registration, Andrade said that Unleashed Informatics knew its intellectual property was vulnerable. "We sit and watch these companies daily use our open access resources to market products that compete and infringe on the patent. It's a whole new world." Geoff Taber, a partner with Toronto-based Osler, Hoskin & Harcourt LLP, says that public sector institutions such as universities and hospitals are getting better at understanding the patent process and preparing their work for commercialization. "You need to do quite a bit of due diligence work," he notes.

Questions

1. The case suggests that intellectual property protection in North America is insufficient. Do you think it is about right, too strong, or not strong enough? Defend your position.
2. Unleashed Informatics is involved in publicly funded scientific research. Should its data be considered a public good, or do you think it should be allowed to protect its intellectual property?

Source: Shane Schick, "Life Science Project That Sprung from Mt. Sinai Hospital Puts Rivals on Notice," ITBusiness.ca (April 11, 2006), **www.itbusiness.ca/it/client/en/Home/News.asp?id=39023&bSearch=True**.

to limit the amount of spam deposited into individual mailboxes.

As described in Chapter 4, a cookie is a small text file on your computer that stores information about your web-browsing activity at a particular site. Every time you surf the web, tiny digital footprints about who you are, what sites you have visited, and other preferences such as the type of products you looked at can be stored on your computer—usually without your knowledge or consent. Organizations utilize cookies to collect information on who is visiting their websites in an attempt to better market and customize content. Unfortunately, the personal information you often provide a website when registering your name and contact information is often included in mailing lists that are sold to other e-marketers—and often those that send spam. Although you can choose to not accept the storage of cookies, you may not be able to visit the site, or it may not function properly. For example, to read *The New York Times* online, you must register by entering your name and other information. When you go through the registration process, cookies are stored on your machine. If you don't accept cookies or you delete the stored cookies, you are not allowed to access the online newspaper without reregistering. Although the use of cookies is a relatively well-known mechanism for "enhancing" your surfing experience, many privacy advocates believe that it is a form of spyware. If you like the personalized touch cookies can provide, you will have to decide if the subsequent loss of your information property is a fair trade-off.

Spyware is any technology that is used to collect information about a person or organization without their knowledge (see Chapter 4 for more on spyware). In other words, spyware is software that runs on a person's computer to collect information about the user and to transmit this information to some other party. This collected information is typically used for advertising purposes, although it can also be used for committing various types of computer crimes. For example, in addition to surfing preferences, spyware can be used to gather information about e-mail addresses, log-in names, passwords, and credit card numbers. Additionally, because spyware exists as an independent program—running hidden in the background—it has the ability to monitor keystrokes, scan files, record chat conversations or other applications, install other spyware programs, launch viruses, read cookies, and change default home pages on your browser.

Individuals and organizations that distribute spyware collect this information to use it for marketing, to sell it to "bulk" e-marketers (a nicer way to refer to "spammers"), or to commit a computer crime. A special type of spyware, called *adware*, collects information about a person to customize web browser banner advertisements. It is important to note that spyware is not currently illegal in Canada, although there is ongoing legislative hype about regulating it in some way. Unfortunately, most privacy advocates feel that it is unlikely that spyware will become illegal or heavily regulated any time soon.

Information Accessibility

With the rapid increase in online databases containing personal information and in the use of computer-based communication between individuals, the issue of who has the right to access and monitor this information has raised many ethical concerns. ***Information accessibility*** focuses on defining what information a person or organization has the right to obtain about others and how this information can be accessed and used.

For example, almost everyone sends and receives e-mail, whether or not they have a PC. All that is needed to participate is access to the Internet, whether through a home PC, a school's computer lab, wireless phone, handheld computer, or any of several other devices that provide Internet access. E-mail is one of the most popular software applications of all time, and projections are that its use will only continue to increase. That is why e-mail aficionados and privacy groups were worried

COMING ATTRACTIONS

She Loves Me, She Loves Me Not—Using Information Technology to Judge the Other's Sincerity

Have you ever wondered whether the person you're talking to is telling the truth? Using a lie detector might be one way to find out, apart from the fact that most people don't have access to lie detectors and that traditional lie detectors are fairly cumbersome to use. However, researchers in Israel have recently developed a lie detector that is small enough to fit in a pair of sunglasses and uses colour codes to indicate the confidence level of respondents' statements.

The lie-detecting glasses analyze the waveform of incoming speech to detect emotional patterns indicated by speed or pitch of the voice, compared to a conventional polygraph's analysis of body states such as sweating. As you might guess, this technology has first been developed for use by law enforcement officers. While the current results are highly promising, the equipment's deployment for these purposes still depends on a lengthy series of tests. As these tests are underway, the company has made the technology commercially available. V Entertainment's Love Detector combines indications of a speaker's emotion, concentration, anticipation, and embarrassment levels to a love index that tells you whether or not signs of love are detected in the analyzed part of the conversation. Before you think about taping the next conversation with your friend and running the test, ask yourself: would you like *your* calls to be scrutinized by a love (lie) detector?

Source: R. Colin Johnson, "Lie-Detector Glasses Offer Peek at Future of Security," *EE Times* (January 18, 2004), **www.eetimes.com/at/news/OEG20040116S0046**.

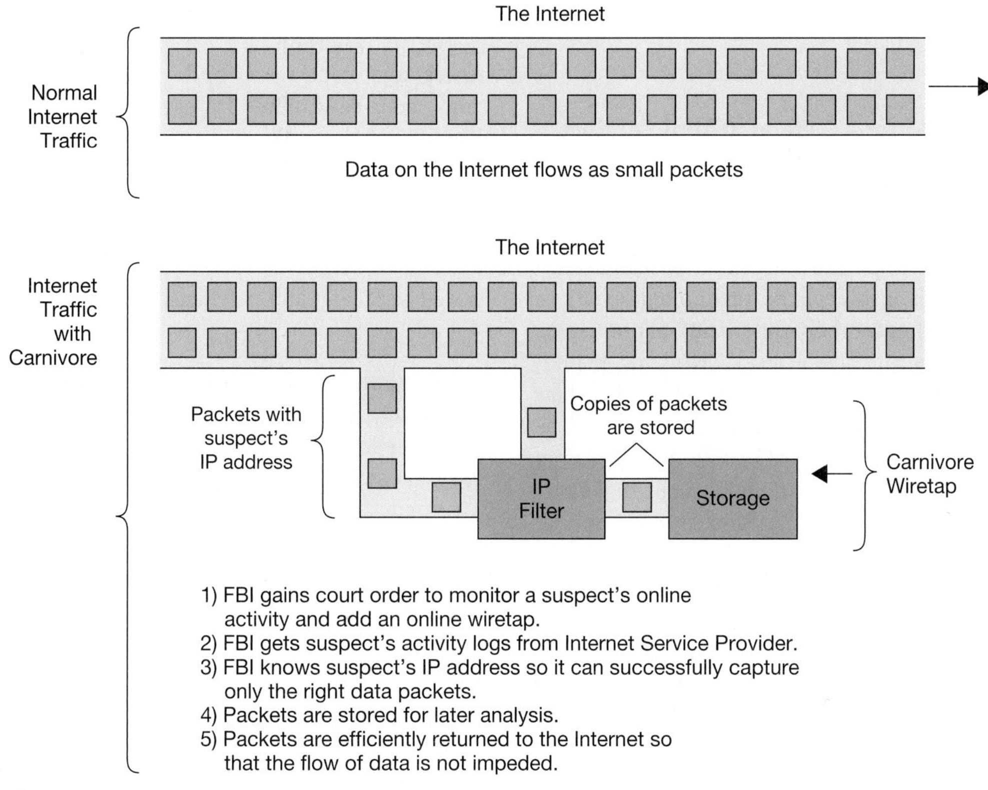

Figure 9.6 How Carnivore works.

when the FBI under the Clinton administration demonstrated a software application named Carnivore to telecommunications industry representatives. Carnivore, which was renamed DCS1000 after bad publicity in 2000, was designed to be connected to Internet service providers' computers, where it would lurk undetected by ISP subscribers, eavesdropping on all communications delivered by the ISP, including e-mail, instant messaging, chat rooms, and visits to Internet sites. If the FBI detected communications that it decided were threatening, as in, for example, activities of terrorists, members of organized crime groups, and hackers, it could unleash Carnivore (see Figure 9.6).

Carnivore provides the "surgical ability" to intercept and collect only those communications that are the subject of lawful wiretaps, explained FBI spokesman Paul Bresson in a *TechWeb* article (Mosquera, 2000). "There's a minimization factor built in [that] actually limits messages viewable to human eyes," he said. Despite built-in "minimization factors," Carnivore would sniff through a large percentage of ISP subscribers' activities on the Internet. "This is about the most intrusive form of search there is," countered Marc Totenberg, director of the Electronic Privacy Information Center (EPIC). Unlike police searches of cars and houses for drugs, Totenberg claimed, Carnivore would allow "dragnet fishing" while sifting through all traffic on an ISP.

After the September 11, 2001, terrorist attacks in the United States, government officials requested more leeway in deploying Carnivore in the government's ongoing fight against terrorism. Privacy groups are concerned that personal privacy might be eroded in a quest to provide heightened homeland security. Clearly, Carnivore and other eavesdropping technologies will be central to numerous ethical discussions.

Beyond the government's accessing information, recent court cases have not supported computer privacy for employee e-mail transmissions and Internet usage. For example, although most companies provide employees with access to the Internet and other outside e-mail systems, many periodically monitor the e-mail messages that employees send and receive. Monitoring employee behaviour is nothing new, and it was to many businesses a natural extension to monitor e-mail messages. As a case in point, several recent court case judgments have upheld corporations' rights to monitor their

Web Search

Cybersquatting is an ethical dilemma facing many famous people and companies. Use a search engine to investigate a popular entertainer who has an "official" website, and provide a list of domain names that are similar to those of the official site. Do these similar domain names provide appropriate services and information? Would you consider it unethical to use such a domain name for other purposes than, say, a fan page?

employees' e-mail messages and Internet activity.

The Need for a Code of Ethical Conduct

Not only has the Internet age found government playing catch-up to pass legislation pertaining to computer crime, privacy, and security, it has also created an ethical conundrum. For instance, the technology exists to rearrange and otherwise change photographs, but is the practice ethical? After all, if photographs no longer reflect absolute reality, how can we trust published images? It may not be illegal for you to "steal" computer time from your school or place of employment to do personal business, but most people would consider this unethical. Is it ethical for companies to compile information about your shopping habits, credit history, and other aspects of your life for the purpose of selling such data to others? Should guidelines be in place to dictate how businesses and others use information and computers? If so, what should the guidelines include, and who should write them? Should there be penalties imposed for those who violate established guidelines? If so, who should enforce such penalties?

Many businesses have devised guidelines for the ethical use of information technology and computer systems, and many computer-related professional groups have also published guidelines for their members. Such organizations include the Assistive Devices Industry Association of Canada, the Association for Computing Machinery, the Australian Computer Society, the Canadian Information Processing Society, the Data Processing Management Association, the Hong Kong Computer Society, the Institute of Electrical and Electronics Engineers, the International Federation for Information Processing, the International Programmers Guild, and the National Society of Professional Engineers.

Most universities and many public school systems have written guidelines for students, faculty, and employees about the ethical use of computers. EduCom, a nonprofit organization of colleges and universities, has developed a policy for ethics in information technology that many universities endorse. In part, the EduCom statement concerning software and intellectual rights says: "Because electronic information is volatile and easily reproduced, respect for the work and personal expression of others is especially critical in computer environments. Violations of authorial integrity, including plagiarism, invasion of privacy, unauthorized access, and trade secret and copyright violations, may be grounds for sanctions against members of the academic community."

Most organization and school guidelines encourage all system users to act responsibly, ethically, and legally when using computers and to follow accepted rules of online etiquette as well as federal and provincial laws.

Responsible Computer Use

The Computer Ethics Institute is a research, education, and policy study organization with members from the IT-related professions and from academic, corporate, and public policy communities. The group studies how advances in information technology have impacted ethics and corporate and public policy and has issued widely quoted guidelines for the ethical use of computers. The guidelines prohibit:

- Using a computer to harm others
- Interfering with other people's computer work
- Snooping in other people's files
- Using a computer to steal
- Using a computer to bear false witness
- Copying or using proprietary software without paying for it
- Using other people's computer resources without authorization or compensation
- Appropriating other people's intellectual output

The guidelines recommend:

- Thinking about social consequences of programs you write and systems you design
- Using a computer in ways that show consideration and respect for others

Responsible computer use in the Information Age includes avoiding the types of behaviour mentioned above. As a computer user, when in doubt, you should review the ethical guidelines published by your school, place of employment, and/or professional organization.

Some users bent on illegal or unethical behaviour are attracted by the anonymity they believe the Internet affords. But the fact is that we leave electronic tracks as we wander through the web, and some perpetrators have been traced and successfully prosecuted when they thought they had hidden their trails. Mafiaboy, the architect of a number of high-profile attacks, for example, was traced to a suburb of Montreal. The fact is, too, that if you post objectionable material on the Internet and people complain about it, your ISP can ask you to remove the material or remove yourself from the service.

COMPUTER CRIME

Computer crime is defined as the act of using a computer to commit an illegal act. The CRA incident mentioned in the When Things Go Wrong box in this chapter is an example of a computer crime. This broad definition of computer crime can include the following:

- Targeting a computer while committing an offence. For example, someone gains unauthorized entry to a computer system to cause damage to the system or to the data it contains.
- Using a computer to commit an offence. In such cases, computer users may steal credit card numbers from websites or a company's database, skim money from bank accounts, or make unauthorized electronic fund transfers from financial institutions.
- Using computers to support a criminal activity, despite the fact that the computers are not actually targeted. For example, drug dealers and other professional criminals may use computers to store records of their illegal transactions.

According to the Computer Security Institute (CSI), the overall trend for computer crime has been declining over the past several years (Gordon, Loeb, Lucyshyn, and Richardson, 2004). Nevertheless, the reported losses for organizations can be tremendous. For example, a recent CSI survey of 269 individuals from a variety of organizations estimated that the various computer crimes cost their organizations over US$140 million (see Figure 9.7). Note that this survey represents only a fraction of actual losses to the world economy, where worldwide losses for computer viruses alone were estimated to exceed US$55 billion in 2003. Many organizations do not report incidents of computer crime due to fear that negative publicity could hurt stock value or provide advantages to competitors. Thus, experts believe that many incidents are never reported. It is clear that computer crime is a fact of life. In this section, we briefly introduce this topic of growing importance.

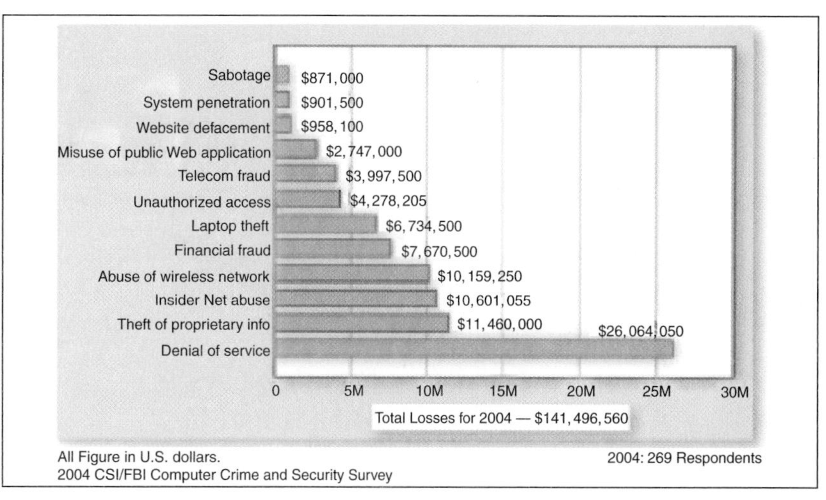

Figure 9.7 Type of computer crime and estimated financial losses for 269 respondents from a variety of organizations.

Computer Security Institute.

The Computer Access Debate

Traditionally, there have been two sides to the issue of computer access. On one side were liberal civil rights champions, the information industry, communications service providers, and expert computer users called hackers. This side prosecutes computer criminals under the law but does not prevent the free exchange of information.

On the opposing side of the computer access issue were privacy advocates, government agencies, law enforcement officials, and businesses that depend on the data stored in computers. Their point of view was much stricter, advocating the free exchange of information only among those with authorization for access. Anyone who breaks into a computer is trespassing, they said, and all intruders should be subject to penalties under the law.

In today's Information Age, however, the debate has expanded, and lines between the two sides may not be as clearly drawn. The global reach of computer networks has raised concern over copyrights, privacy, and security among all user groups. Most computer users now agree that ownership rights of those who create software and other copyrighted materials disseminated over networks must be protected. And when financial or health-related data is collected about individuals and stored on computers, that information should not be freely available to anyone who can retrieve it. Both sides of the information access argument agree that one of the major challenges of the Information Age will be to protect privacy and security while at the same time allowing authorized access to digitized information.

Unauthorized Computer Access

A person who gains unauthorized access to a computer system has committed a computer crime. ***Unauthorized access*** means that the

Figure 9.8 Unauthorized computer access is a crime.

Source: © Ted Goff

Web Search

The article at **www.cnn.com/TECH/specials/hackers/primer** describes three types of computer hackers; review this article, and prepare a short report that defines each of the three types.

person who has gained entry to a computer system has no authority to use such access (Figure 9.8). Here are a few examples from recent media reports:

- Employees steal time on company computers to do personal business.
- Intruders break into government websites and change the information displayed.
- Thieves steal credit card numbers and social security numbers from electronic databases, then use the stolen information to charge thousands of dollars in merchandise to victims.

Research conducted by the CSI has also found that the frequency of (successful) attacks on computer systems has been declining (see Figure 9.9). Of the 481 respondents, representing organizations large and small, from a variety of industries, "only" 53 percent reported unauthorized computer use in 2004—this is down from a high of 70 percent in 2000. Although computer crime has decreased somewhat, there is increasing demand for more and broader federal and provincial laws to expressly prohibit various crimes, given the widespread and increasing dependence on computer and networking technologies.

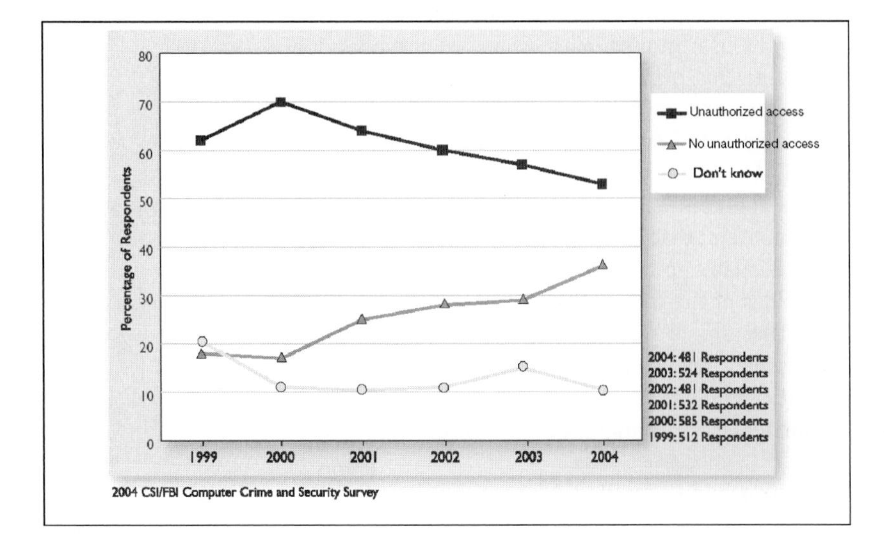

Figure 9.9 Unauthorized computer access has been on the decline.

Computer Security Institute.

Hacking and Cracking

Those individuals who are knowledgeable enough to gain access to computer systems without authorization have long been referred to as ***hackers***. The name was first used in the 1960s to describe expert computer users and programmers who were students at the Massachusetts Institute of Technology (MIT). They wrote programs for the mainframes they used and freely exchanged information, but they followed unwritten rules against damaging or stealing information belonging to others. They claimed that their motives for roaming freely through computer systems were based entirely on curiosity and the desire to learn as much as possible about computers.

As computer crime became more prevalent and damaging, true hackers—those motivated by curiosity and not by a desire to do harm—objected to use of the term to describe computer criminals. Today, those who break into computer systems with the intention of doing damage or committing a crime are usually called ***crackers***.

Types of Computer Criminals and Crimes

Computer crimes are almost as varied as the users who commit them (see Figure 9.10). Some involve the use of a computer to steal money or other assets, or to perpetrate a deception for money, such as advertising merchandise for sale on a web auction site, collecting orders and payment, then sending either inferior merchandise or no merchandise at all. Other computer crimes involve stealing or altering information. Some of those thieves who steal information or disrupt a computer system have demanded a ransom from victims in exchange for returning the information or repairing the damage. Cyberterrorists have planted destructive programs in computer systems, then threatened to activate them if a ransom is not paid

Figure 9.10 Computer crimes are as varied as the individuals who commit them.

Source: © Ted Goff

Figure 9.11 Many hackers have inside knowledge of organizational systems.

Source: © Ted Goff

(see more on cyberterrorism below). Crimes in the form of electronic vandalism cause damage when offenders plant viruses, cause computer systems to crash, or deny service on a website.

Use of the Internet has fostered other types of criminal activity, such as the stalking of minors and others by sexual predators through newsgroups and chat rooms. Those who buy and sell pornography have also found in the Internet a new medium for carrying on their activities.

Who Commits Computer Crimes?

When you hear the term "computer hacker," you might imagine a techno-geek, someone who sits in front of her computer all day and night attempting to break the ultra-super-secret security code of one of the most sophisticated computer systems in the world, perhaps a computer for the RCMP, a Swiss bank, or the CIA. While this fits the traditional profile of a computer hacker, there is no clear profile today. More and more people have the skills, the tools, and the motives to hack into a computer system. A modern-day hacker could be a disgruntled, middle-aged, white-collar worker sitting at a nice desk on the fourteenth floor of the headquarters building of a billion-dollar software manufacturer. Computer hackers have been around for decades. For the most part, we associate hackers with their pranks and crimes involving security systems and viruses. Hackers have caused the loss of billions of dollars' worth of stolen goods, repair bills, and lost goodwill with customers (see Brief Case: Computer Criminal Hall of Fame).

Surveys have shown that when businesses and other organizations are victimized, the perpetrators are most often employees or others inside the organization (see Figure 9.11). For example, in a 1998 survey of 1600 companies in 50 countries, cosponsored by PricewaterhouseCoopers and *InformationWeek*, 73 percent of the respondents reported some security breach or corporate espionage during a 1-year period. Intrusions and other attacks reported by survey respondents came from these groups (Figure 9.12), in order of frequency:

- Authorized employees—58 percent
- Employees who were not authorized to use a computer system—24 percent

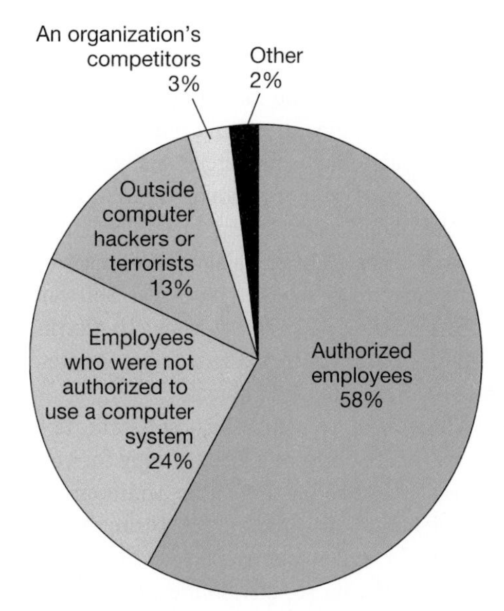

Figure 9.12 Who makes unlawful intrusions and other attacks into computer systems.

Table 9.2 ***Unauthorized computer access occurs from both inside and outside the organization.***

Incidents Number of Incidents	Total Incidents (by percentage)	Outside Incidents (by percentage)	Inside Incidents (by percentage)
1–5 incidents	47%	52%	52%
6–10 incidents	20%	9%	6%
> 10 incidents	12%	9%	8%
Don't Know?	22%	30%	34%

Gordon, Loeb, Lucyshyn, and Richardson, 2004.

- Outside computer hackers or terrorists—13 percent
- Organization's competitors—3 percent

In regard to unauthorized access intrusions, a 2004 survey reported by the CSI found that about half of all unauthorized access incidents were from within the organization (see Table 9.2). In sum, when an incident occurs, it most often is executed by an insider.

Data Diddling, Salami Slicing, and Other Techno-Crimes

As long as computers and the data they contain are an integral part of our daily lives, criminals will devise ways to take illegal advantage of the technology. Such crimes cost society billions of dollars annually. (The exact amount that companies lose as a result of computer crime can only be estimated since many businesses do not report crimes for fear of losing customers or devaluing the company's stock.) Over the years, colourful jargon has evolved to label the many types of computer crime, as summarized in Table 9.3.

Software Piracy

Software developers and marketers want you to buy as many copies of their products as you want, of course. But commercial software vendors do not want you or anyone else to buy one copy, then bootleg additional copies to sell or to give to others. Vendors also take a dim view of companies that buy one copy of a software application, then make many copies to distribute to employees. In fact, the practice is called ***software piracy***, and it is illegal.

When you buy commercial software, it is legal for you to make one backup copy for your own use. It is also legal to offer shareware or public domain software for free through bulletin boards and other websites. But warez peddling—offering stolen proprietary software for free over the Internet—is a crime. ("Warez" is the slang term for such stolen software.)

Software piracy has become a problem because it is so widespread, costing the commercial software industry billions of dollars a year. However, some governments, including Canada's, have started to get tough on piracy. The crime is difficult to trace, but a growing number of individuals and companies have been successfully prosecuted for pirating software. For example, in late 2006, Toronto construction consulting firm Curran, McCabe, Ravidran and Ross was fined $73 000 by the Canadian Alliance Against Software Theft for using pirated copies of Abobe, Autodesk, and Microsoft software.

Software Piracy Is a Global Business

A major international issue businesses deal with is the willingness (or unwillingness) of governments and individuals to recognize and enforce the ownership of intellectual property—in particular, software copyright. Piracy of software and other technologies is widespread internationally. The Business Software Alliance (BSA) points to countries such as Vietnam, China, Indonesia, Ukraine, and Russia as those with the highest percentages of illegal software (BSA, 2003). In these countries, more than 85 percent of the software used consists of illegal copies. Worldwide losses due to piracy exceeded US$13 billion in 2002! Because technology usage varies significantly by region, average piracy levels and dollar losses greatly differ across regions (see Table 9.4).

In addition to being a crime, is software piracy an ethical problem? Perhaps in part, but businesspeople must acknowledge and deal with other perspectives as well. In part, the problem stems from countries' differing concepts of ownership. Many of the ideas about intellectual property ownership are based on long-standing cultural traditions. For example, the concept of individual ownership of knowledge is traditionally a strange one in many Middle Eastern countries, where knowledge is

Table 9.3 *Types of computer crimes.*

Computer Crime	Description
Data diddling	The changing of data going into or out of a computer. For example, a student breaks into his university's grade-recording system and changes the grades he earned in last semester's classes, thus raising his grade point average.
Salami slicing	A form of data diddling that occurs when a person shaves small amounts from financial accounts and deposits them in a personal account. For example, a bank employee deposits a few pennies from each of thousands of accounts into an account set up in a fictitious name. The amounts are too small to raise flags, but over time the thief collects a substantial sum.
Phreaking	Crimes committed against telephone company computers with the goal of making free long distance calls, impersonating directory assistance or other operator services, diverting calls to numbers of the perpetrator's choice, or otherwise disrupting telephone service for subscribers.
Cloning	Cellular phone fraud in which scanners are used to steal the electronic serial numbers of cellular phones, which are used for billing purposes and are broadcast as calls are made. With stolen serial numbers, clones can be made to make "free" calls that are billed to the owner of the original cell phone.
Carding	Refers to the practice of stealing credit card numbers online, to be resold or used to charge merchandise against victims' accounts.
Piggybacking* or *shoulder-surfing	The act of simply standing in line behind a card user at an automated teller machine (ATM), looking over that person's shoulder, and memorizing the card's personal identification number (PIN). With the right equipment, the stolen numbers can then be placed on counterfeit access cards and used to withdraw cash from the victim's account.
Social engineering	Gaining information needed to access computers by means of tricking company employees by posing as a magazine journalist, telephone company employee, or forgetful coworker to persuade honest employees to reveal passwords and other information. The information is then used to break into a computer system or to steal company equipment and other contraband.
Dumpster diving	This approach requires no technical expertise, since it consists simply of going through dumpsters and garbage cans for company documents, credit card receipts, and other papers containing information that might be useful.
Spoofing/Phishing	A scam used to steal passwords for legitimate accounts on computers in which the "spoofer" uses a program that duplicates an organization's login screen. When legitimate users log on to the system, the counterfeit screen responds with an error message but secretly captures the user's ID and password. The swindle lets intruders pass as legitimate users, thus allowing them to steal computer time and resources. Phishing is similar to spoofing, in that unsuspecting users are tricked into divulging key information such as usernames, passwords, and credit card numbers. E-mail messages purporting to be from a legitimate source, such as eBay or Paypal, are used to lure people to a spoof of the genuine site.
Packet sniffing	Packet sniffing is the process of intercepting traffic passing over a digital network or part of a network. As data streams travel back and forth over the network, data packets are captured, decoded, and analyzed. The contents of those packets can then be used for malicious purposes.
Key logging	Also known by its full name of keystroke logging, key logging is a process of capturing a user's keystrokes. Key logging tools can be based on either software or hardware, both of which are widely available. Unlike some of the conduits for computer crime described here, key logging has legitimate uses. For example, it can be useful in determining sources of error in computer systems. Key logging systems are also frequently used by law enforcement to monitor illegal activity. Probably the most common application of key logging tools, however, is to screen for passwords or encryption keys.

BRIEF CASE

Computer Criminal Hall of Fame

A few individuals with expertise in hacking and phreaking used their skills to become well-known computer criminals:

- John Draper, aka "Cap'n Crunch," was a notorious phone phreak who operated in the late 1960s and early 1970s. Draper discovered that the whistle that came as a prize in boxes of Cap'n Crunch cereal perfectly duplicated the 2600-hertz tone used by the telephone company's switching system. He could blow the whistle into a telephone receiver and activate switches that allowed him to make free long distance calls. Draper was caught by the FBI and served a year and 4 months in prison in two separate convictions for wire fraud. Once released, Draper did not return to his old habits.
- Throughout his career as a phreak and cracker in the 1980s, Kevin Lee Poulsen's crimes ranged from setting up his own telephone wiretaps, to posing as a telephone directory assistance operator, to using computers to win cash and cars in radio giveaway contests. In 1990, he won a Porsche 944 after having taken over all phone lines going into L.A. to be the 102nd caller in a radio station's contest. Poulsen served nearly 5 years in prison. After his release in 1996, he became a computer security consultant.
- By 1995, Kevin Mitnick had been convicted 5 times of various telecommunications and computer crimes. He served time in a juvenile detention centre and in federal prison in California for stealing free long distance telephone service, breaking into Pentagon computers, stealing software online, and other techno-crimes. Mitnick violated terms of his probation and in 1992 was again on the run from the law. He continued to ply his trade, was captured in 1995, and was again sentenced to prison. Mitnick was released early in 2000 but was forbidden to use computers for 4 years after his release.
- The most famous Canadian hacker is probably Mafiaboy (his real name is protected by legislation covering young offenders), who admitted to 56 charges of mischief in January 2001. Mafiaboy was apparently responsible for initiating denial-of-service attacks that shut down a number of high-profile websites, including Yahoo!, CNN.com, Amazon.com, and eBay. For his crimes, Mafiaboy was sentenced to 8 months in a juvenile detention centre and fined $160. Estimates of the damage caused by Mafiaboy's actions range from US$7.5 million to US$1.7 billion.

Kevin Mitnick
Source: Dan Callister/Newsmakers/Getty Images

- In 2004, 18-year-old student Sven Jaschan from a small village in Germany created the Sasser worm, which purported to notify computer users of an update to fix a security hole in Microsoft's operating system; instead, it caused millions of computers all over the world to crash and reboot. Jaschan received a 21-month suspended sentence in July, 2005.

Questions

1. What do you think are the primary reasons for individuals to become hackers? While you might think that some of the actions performed did not do much harm, others might have caused great damage to the companies involved. How do you think hackers decide what/whom to target with their activities?
2. Many hackers, including some of the ones mentioned above, managed to be hired into high-paying jobs after the end of their hacking careers; some started their own businesses. Why do companies choose to hire former criminals, and sometimes pay them incredibly high salaries?

Sources: Anonymous, "New Sasser Version May Be Circulating," CNN.com (May 10, 2004), **www.cnn.com/2004/TECH/internet/05/10/computer.worm.ap/index.html**. **http://tlc.discovery.com/convergence/hackers/bio/bio.html.**

Table 9.4 ***Software piracy levels and dollar losses by region.***

Region	Piracy Levels	Dollar Loss ($M)
North America	23%	7 232
Western Europe	36%	9 600
Asia/Pacific	53%	7 553
Latin America	63%	1 273
Mid East/Africa	56%	1 026
Eastern Europe	71%	2 111

BSA, 2004.

meant to be shared. Plagiarism does not exist in a country where words belong to everyone. By the same token, piracy does not exist either. This view is gradually changing; the Saudi Arabia Patent Office granted its first patents several years ago, and their piracy rates have plummeted from 79 percent in 1996 to 50 percent in 2002.

In other cases, there are political, social, and economic reasons for piracy. In many other countries, software publishers are simply not catering to the needs of consumers, who often do not have the funds to purchase software legitimately. This is true in many areas of South America and other regions with low per capita income. It is particularly true of students and other members of university communities, whose needs are critical in some areas.

Other factors leading to piracy or infringement of intellectual property agreements throughout the world include lack of public awareness about the issue, lack of an industrial infrastructure that can produce legitimate software, and the increasingly high demand for computer and other technology products. The United States has repeatedly pressured and threatened other countries accused of pirating. It is interesting to note, however, that despite the fact that few of these cultural and economic explanations are valid in the United States, it leads the world in the sheer volume of illegal software in use. Businesses that operate in glass offices should surely not throw stones.

Computer Viruses and Other Destructive Code

Recently, Symantec, an antivirus and digital security firm, announced that it had identified "6784 new viruses attacking Windows machines in the first six months of 2006." ***Viruses*** are destructive programs that disrupt the normal functioning of computer systems. They differ from other types of malicious code in that they can reproduce themselves. Some viruses

GLOBAL PERSPECTIVE

Controlling Global Cybercrime

One of the difficulties in combating cybercrime is that the criminals often attack across international borders, making tracking, capturing, and punishing the culprits difficult or impossible. In late 2001, a controversial international treaty was finalized to combat cybercrime. The controversy surrounding the treaty centred on criticisms by privacy and human rights groups that believe it gives police and law enforcement agencies too much power, thereby infringing on personal privacy without adequate accountability and oversight. In addition, many Internet service providers are unhappy about some of the rules in the treaty; some of the new policies in the treaty require providers to retain user account information and other data, with no provisions for cost recovery. Another concern of privacy rights advocates is the "mutual assistance" clause, which legally binds the signatory countries to aid each other in international investigations. This might lead to a situation in which Canada or other signatory countries have to provide assistance to repressive regimes; countries with poor human rights could potentially ask Canada for help in investigating actions that are not considered unlawful in Canada, such as actions involving freedom of speech. Clearly, a treaty is needed to ensure secure global commerce, but designing and implementing the rules to fit the situations of all countries is proving to be quite difficult.

Sources: R. Perera, "Controversial Cybercrime Treaty Ready for Signatures," *Computerworld* (November 9, 2001), **www.computerworld.com.**
Kevin Poulsen, "U.S. Defends Cybercrime Treaty," *SecurityFocus* (April 23, 2004), **securityfocus.com/news/8529.**

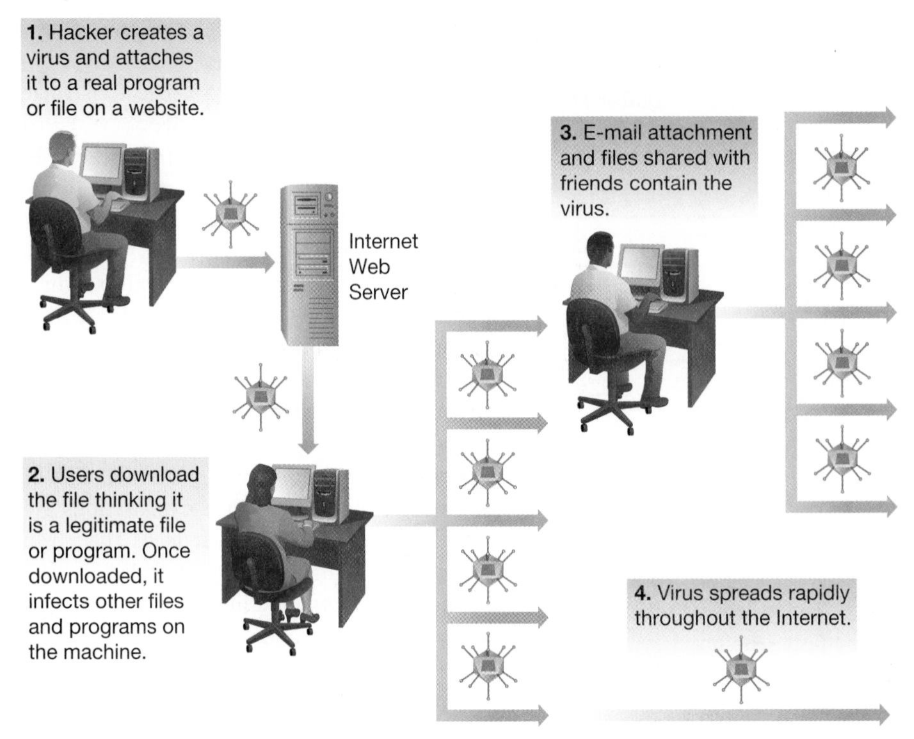

Figure 9.13 How a computer virus is spread.

are intended to be harmless pranks, but more often they do damage to a computer system by erasing files on the hard drive or by slowing computer processing or otherwise compromising the system.

Viruses are planted in host computers in a number of ways (Figure 9.13). Boot sector viruses attach themselves to that section of a hard or floppy disk that lets the user boot up or start the computer. They are most often spread through use of an infected floppy disk. File infector viruses attach themselves to files with certain extensions, such as .doc or .exe. Some viruses are a combination of boot sector and file infector viruses, and many of these can change to fool antivirus programs. Viruses transmitted through e-mail messages became popular in the late 1990s. When an unsuspecting recipient of an e-mail message opens the message or an attachment to the message, the virus is activated. Usually such e-mail viruses can then send copies of themselves to everyone in the victim's address book, thus spreading throughout networked computers at an alarming rate.

Worms, Trojan Horses, and Other Sinister Programs

Viruses are among the most virulent forms of computer infections, but other destructive code can also be damaging. A ***worm***, for example, usually does not destroy files, but, like a virus, it is designed to copy and send itself, spreading rapidly throughout networked computers. It eventually brings computers to a halt simply by clogging memory space with the outlaw code, thus preventing normal function.

Another destructive program is the ***Trojan horse***. Unlike a virus, the Trojan horse does not copy itself, but like viruses it can do much damage. When a Trojan horse is planted in a computer its instructions remain hidden. The computer appears to function normally, but in fact it is performing underlying functions dictated by the intrusive code. For example, under the pretext of playing chess with an unsuspecting systems operator, a cracker group installed a Trojan horse in a Canadian mainframe. While the game appeared to be proceeding normally, the Trojan horse program was sneakily establishing a powerful unauthorized account for the future use of the intruders.

Logic or time bombs are variations of Trojan horses. They also do not reproduce themselves and are designed to operate without disrupting normal computer function. Instead, they lie in wait for unsuspecting computer users to perform a triggering operation. Time bombs are set off by specific dates, such as the birthday of a famous person. Logic bombs are set off by certain types of

CANADIAN NETSTATS

Virus Epidemic

Can you remember all the viruses that made the news in the past months? In a typical month, over 1400 new viruses are added to a leading security software company's database (see Table 9.5). Handling the virus epidemic has become big business and a big headache for most organizations. According to a recent survey, 30 percent of large Canadian firms noted that internal breaches of network security was a huge issue, with 82 percent of large firms actually reporting a breach within the past 12 months. The figure was up from 67 percent in 2003. Each month it seems that virus threats increase, with new (and variations of old) viruses popping up throughout the Internet. Unfortunately, protecting computing resources will be an ongoing and constant challenge for all individuals and organizations.

Table 9.5 ***Top computer viruses in a recent month.***

Top Viruses February 2006

Ranking	Virus Name	Prevalence (%)
1	Email-Worm.Win32.Bagle.fj	4.76
2	Trojan-Spy.Win32.Banker.anv	2.2
3	Trojan-Spy.Win32.Banker.ark	2.04
4	Trojan-Spy.Win32.Bancos.ha	1.56
5	Worm.Win32.Feebs.gen	1.44

Source: **www.clickz.com/resources/email_reference/research_reports/article.php/3592386**.

operations, such as entering a specific password or adding or deleting names and other information to and from certain computer files. Disgruntled employees have planted logic and time bombs upon being fired, intending for the program to activate after they have left the company. In at least one instance in recent history, a former employee in Minnesota demanded money to deactivate the time bomb he had planted in company computers before it destroyed employee payroll records.

CAREER IMPLICATIONS

Information Systems Ethics and Computer Crime

For Accounting and Finance

Due to the accounting scandals of the past few years, accounting and finance professionals within organizations face increased responsibility for ethical reporting principles. In addition to providing accurate financial statements, companies have to provide outside examination of internal systems and demonstrate that controls are in place to prevent fraudulent actions. As much of the financial data flows through information systems, accounting and finance professionals have to be aware of how the different systems interact and whether the controls are working the way they should.

For Operations Management

Information systems offer many possibilities for organizations to obtain a competitive advantage over their rivals. In addition to using sophisticated Supply Chain Management software to streamline procurement and production processes, companies can decide to outsource work to foreign countries. Some companies use remote manufacturing technologies to produce their goods in countries with less stringent labour laws or environmental restrictions. In such cases, operations management professionals provide analyses regarding the tradeoffs associated with cutting costs via outsourcing to circumvent regulations versus staying at home and not laying off local workers.

For Human Resources Management

For the human resources management profession, ethics play an important role. In today's networked organizations, human resources policies focus on the appropriate use of information technologies in the workplace. For example, can employees use the Internet or e-mail for personal use? What about online chatting on systems like MSN, Skype, or Yahoo!? Human resources management professionals face the task of formulating and enforcing such policies while at the same time maintaining trusting relationships between employees and management.

For Marketing

For marketing professionals, the use of technologies such as B2C e-business sites or Customer Relationship Management (CRM) systems opens a wide variety of opportunities to collect data at various points of the interaction between the company and the customer. Information such as web surfing or purchasing behaviour can be analyzed in a variety of different ways to target customers most likely to react to marketing campaigns. While this can open up tremendous opportunities to increase sales, it may also provide insights into a person's lifestyle or behaviour. This information may infringe on privacy issues that some believe should be protected, thus creating added dilemmas for the marketing professional.

For Information Systems

Information systems professionals are increasingly being asked to strictly enforce the organizational polices on web surfing, personal e-mail usage, and online chatting. In some cases, you might also be asked to analyze the contents of an employee's computer to avoid theft of sensitive organizational data. Often an employee might not have done any harm to the organization, but nonetheless all files and information are carefully examined. While information systems professionals must ensure the security and integrity of the organization's systems and data, they also face the question of how ethical it is to monitor everyone's behaviour because of the wrongdoings of a handful of employees.

KEY POINTS REVIEW

1. **Describe the advent of the Information Age and how computer ethics impact the use of information systems.** The Information Age refers to a time in the history of civilization when information became the currency of the realm. To be successful in many careers today requires that people be computer literate, as the ability to access and effectively operate computing technology is a key part of many careers. A digital divide is said to exist between people who are computer literate and those who are not. Because computer literacy is so critical in the Information Age, a major ethical concern for society centres on who is computer literate and who is not.
2. **Discuss the ethical concerns associated with information privacy, accuracy, property, and accessibility.** Information privacy is concerned with what information an individual should have to reveal to others through the course of employment or through other transactions such as online shopping. Canada has enacted the Personal Information Protection and Electronic Documents Act to protect the rights of consumers in this country. Information accuracy is concerned with the authenticity and fidelity of information, as well as identifying who is responsible for informational errors that harm people. Information property focuses on who owns information about individuals and how information can be sold and exchanged. Information accessibility focuses on defining what information a person or organization has the right to obtain about others and how this information can be accessed and used. While the Information Age has brought widespread access to information, the downside is that others may now have access to your personal information that you would prefer to keep private. Because there are few safeguards for ensuring the accuracy of information, individuals and companies can be damaged by informational errors. Additionally, because information is so easy to exchange and modify, information ownership violations readily occur. Likewise, with the rapid increase in online databases containing personal information and the increase in the use of computer-based communication between individuals, the issue of who has the right to access and monitor this information has raised many ethical concerns.
3. **Define computer crime, and list several types of computer crime.** Computer crime is defined as the act of using a computer to commit an illegal act, such as targeting a computer while committing an offence, using a computer to commit an offence, or using computers in the course of a criminal activity. A person who gains unauthorized access to a computer system has also committed a computer crime. Those individuals who are knowledgeable enough to gain access to computer systems without authorization have long been referred to as hackers. Today, those who break into computer systems with the intention of doing damage or committing a crime are usually called crackers. Hackers and crackers can commit a wide variety of computer crimes, including data diddling, salami slicing, phreaking, cloning, carding, piggybacking or shoulder-surfing, social engineering, dumpster diving, and spoofing. Crackers are also associated with the making and distributing of computer viruses and other destructive codes. Finally, making illegal copies of software, a worldwide computer crime, is called software piracy.
4. **Contrast what is meant by the terms "computer virus," "worm," "Trojan horse," and "logic or time bomb."** Viruses are destructive programs that disrupt the normal functioning of computer systems. They differ from other types of malicious code in that they can reproduce themselves. Some viruses are intended to be harmless pranks, but more often they do damage to a computer system by erasing files on the hard drive or by slowing computer processing or otherwise compromising the system. A worm usually does not destroy files, but, like a virus, it is designed to copy and send itself, spreading rapidly throughout networked computers. It eventually brings computers to a halt simply by clogging memory space with the outlaw code, thus preventing normal functioning. Unlike a virus, the Trojan horse does not copy itself, but like viruses it can do much damage. When a Trojan horse is planted in a computer, its instructions remain hidden. The computer appears to function normally, but in fact it is performing underlying functions dictated by the intrusive code. Finally, logic or time bombs are variations of Trojan horses. They also do not reproduce themselves and are designed to operate without disrupting normal computer function. They lie in wait for unsuspecting computer users to perform a triggering operation. Time bombs are set off by specific dates, such as the birthday of a famous person; logic bombs are set off by certain types of operations, such as entering a specific password or adding or deleting names and other information to and from certain computer files.

KEY TERMS

REVIEW QUESTIONS

1. Describe the advent of the Information Age and how computer ethics impact the use of information systems.
2. What is the difference between the digital divide and computer literacy?
3. Compare and contrast information accuracy, information privacy, and information property.
4. Explain the purpose of PIPEDA.
5. Compare and contrast a worm, a virus, a Trojan horse, and a logic or time bomb.
6. List five dot-cons that you find interesting, and give the advice suggested for avoiding these traps.
7. What is identity theft, and what is the solution according to this chapter?
8. Define cybersquatting.
9. Define computer crime, and list several types of computer crime.
10. Define unauthorized access, and give several examples from recent media reports.
11. Viruses that are spread via e-mail transmitted over the Internet are also frequently in the news. What are five ways to prevent these viruses?

SELF-STUDY QUESTIONS

Visit the Companion website for this text for additional Self-Study Questions: **www.pearsoned.ca/jessup**.

1. Being __________, or knowing how to use the computer as a device to gather, store, organize, and process information, can open up myriad sources of information.
   - A. technology illiterate
   - B. digitally divided
   - C. computer literate
   - D. computer illiterate
2. A broad definition of computer crime includes all of the following except __________.
   - A. targeting a computer while committing an offence
   - B. using computers in the course of a criminal activity, despite the fact that the computers are not actually targeted
   - C. using a computer to commit a legal act
   - D. using a computer to commit an offence
3. __________ focuses on defining what information a person or organization has the right to obtain about others and how this information can be accessed and used.
   - A. Information accessibility
   - B. Information accuracy
   - C. Information privacy
   - D. Information property
4. The Computer Ethics Institute is a research, education, and policy study organization with members from the IT professions and from academic, corporate, and public policy communities. The guidelines prohibit all of the following except __________.
   - A. using a computer to harm others
   - B. using a computer to bear false witness
   - C. copying or using proprietary software without paying for it
   - D. using computer resources with authorization
5. In Canada, the federal law to protect privacy rights is called __________.
   - A. the Computer Fraud and Abuse Act
   - B. the Electronic Communications Privacy Act
   - C. the Personal Information Protection and Electronic Documents Act
   - D. the General Privacy Directive
6. Those individuals who break into computer systems with the intention of doing damage or committing a crime are usually called __________.
   - A. hackers
   - B. crackers
   - C. computer geniuses
   - D. computer operatives
7. Unauthorized access to a computer system is most likely to be committed by __________.
   - A. authorized employees
   - B. employees who were not authorized to use a computer system
   - C. outside computer hackers or terrorists
   - D. an organization's competitors
8. Crimes committed against telephone company computers with the goal of making free long distance calls, impersonating directory assistance or other operator services, diverting calls to numbers of the perpetrator's choice, or otherwise disrupting telephone service for subscribers is called __________.
   - A. phreaking
   - B. cloning
   - C. carding
   - D. data diddling

PROBLEMS AND EXERCISES

1. Match the following terms with the appropriate definitions:

   _____ Digital divide

   _____ Information privacy

   _____ Cyberwar

   _____ Information accuracy

   _____ Shoulder-surfing

   _____ Identity theft

   _____ Information accessibility

   _____ Worm

   _____ Computer ethics

   _____ Social engineering

   a. The stealing of another person's social insurance number, credit card number, and other personal information for the purpose of using the victim's credit rating to borrow money, buy merchandise, and otherwise run up debts that are never repaid
   b. An area concerned with what information an individual should have to reveal to others through the course of employment or through other transactions such as online shopping
   c. The gap between those individuals in our society who are computer literate and have access to information resources such as the Internet and those who do not
   d. Code that usually does not destroy files, but, like a virus, is designed to copy and send itself, spreading rapidly throughout networked computers and eventually bringing computers to a halt simply by clogging memory space with the outlaw code, thus preventing normal functioning
   e. An area concerned with ensuring the authenticity and fidelity of information, as well as identifying who is responsible for informational errors that harm people
   f. Focuses on defining what information a person or organization has the right to obtain about others and how this information can be accessed and used
   g. The issues and standards of conduct as they pertain to the use of information systems
   h. Gaining information needed to access computers by tricking company employees by means of posing as magazine journalists, telephone company employees, and forgetful coworkers to persuade honest employees to reveal passwords and other information
   i. The act of simply standing in line behind a card user at an automated teller machine (ATM), looking over that person's shoulder, and memorizing the card's personal identification number (PIN), then placing the stolen number on a counterfeit access card and using it to withdraw cash from the victim's account
   j. An organized attempt by a country's military to disrupt or destroy the information and communication systems of another country

2. The Electronic Frontier Foundation, **www.eff.org**, has a mission of protecting rights and promoting freedom in the "electronic frontier." The organization provides additional advice on how to protect your online privacy. Review its suggestions, and provide a summary of what you can do to protect yourself.

3. Do you consider yourself computer literate? Do you know of any friends or relatives who are not computer literate? What can you do to improve your computer literacy? Is computer literacy necessary in today's job market? Why or why not?

4. Look at the following websites for tips and articles on identity theft: **www.consumer.gov/idtheft** and **www.identitytheft.org**. Did you find anything that you think might help you in the future? Did you bookmark any of these tips or e-mail them to your classmates or friends?

5. Complete the computer ethics quiz at **web.cs.bgsu.edu/maner/xxicee/html/welcome.htm**, and visit **onlineethics.org/cases/robot/robot.html** for more issues on computer ethics and social implications of computing. Do ethical codes apply to all professions?

6. Find your school's guidelines for ethical computer use on the Internet and answer the following questions: Are there limitations as to the type of websites and material that can be viewed (i.e., pornography, etc.)? Are students allowed to change the programs on the hard drives of the lab computers or download software for their own use? Are there rules governing personal use of computers and e-mail?

7. Visit the Consumer Sentinel, **www.consumer.gov/sentinel**, to learn about how law enforcement agencies around the world work together to fight consumer fraud. The site contains statistics on consumer complaints and sorts this data in many interesting ways. Prepare a report using the most current data on the top five complaint categories.

8. Choose an organization with which you are familiar. Determine what the company's computer ethics policy is by obtaining a written copy and reviewing it. In addition, asking questions and observing several employees may provide insight into the actual application. Does this organization adhere to a strict or casual ethics policy? Prepare a 10-minute presentation to the rest of the class on your findings.

9. Visit **www.safeshopping.org** and prepare a summary of its top ten safe online shopping tips. Did you find these tips useful enough to share with a friend or classmate? Did you bookmark the site or e-mail it to a friend?

10. To learn more about protecting your privacy, visit **www.cookiecentral.com, www.privcom.gc.ca/index_e.asp,** and **www.ipc.on.ca**. Did you learn something that will help protect your privacy? Why is privacy more important than ever?

11. When you make a withdrawal or a deposit of funds at an ATM machine, do people stand back enough so they cannot watch you, or have you had someone hover over you? Are you careful to take any receipts with you and not leave any evidence of your access code and account number?

12. Should laws be passed to make spam a crime? How would such laws be enforced?

13. Do you think educational institutions should be allowed to monitor e-mail sent and received on school computers? Why or why not? Do you think that any e-mail messages sent or received

over a computer at work should be considered company property? Why or why not?

14. Do you feel the media generates too much hype regarding hackers and crackers? As companies such as Microsoft have been hacked into, are you concerned about your bank account or other sensitive information?

15. Review Table 9.1's list of dot-cons from the Federal Trade Commission. Have any suspicious groups contacted you or any of your friends or classmates?

16. Identity theft is a new type of theft. Visit **www.fraud.org** to find ways to protect yourself. Search the Internet for additional sources that provide information on identity theft, and make a list of other ways to safeguard against it. What are some of the losses in addition to stolen documents and additional bills to pay that may result from identity theft?

17. Search the Internet for information about the damaging effects of software piracy and/or look at the following website: **www.microsoft.com/piracy**. Is software piracy a global problem? What can you do to mitigate the problem? Prepare a short presentation to present to the class.

APPLICATION EXERCISES

Note: The existing data files referenced in these exercises are available on the Companion Website: **www.pearsoned.ca/jessup**.

Spreadsheet Application: Analyzing Ethical Concerns at MountainSports

Due to the employees' increased use of IT resources for private purposes at MountainSports, you have announced that a new IT use policy will be implemented. You have set up a website for the employees to provide feedback to the proposed changes; the results of this survey are stored in the file EthicsSurvey.csv. Your boss wants to use the survey results to find out what the greatest concerns in terms of ethical implications are for the employees, so you are asked to do the following:

- Complete the spreadsheet to include descriptive statistics (mean, standard deviation, mode, minimum, maximum, and range) for each survey item.
- Provide a graph highlighting means of the different items.

Use formulas to calculate all statistics for the responses to the individual questions. Hint: In Microsoft Excel, you can look up the necessary formulas in the category "Statistical." Make sure to professionally format the pages before printing them out.

Database Application: Tracking Software Licences at EasyTax

Recently, you have taken on the position of an IS manager at EasyTax, a small tax consulting firm in your home town. In your second week at work, you realize that many of the software licences are about to expire or have already expired. As you know about the legal and ethical implications of unlicensed software, you have decided to set up a system that lets you keep track of the software licences. You have already set up a database and stored some of the information, but you want to make the system more user friendly. Using the EasyTax.mdb database, please design a form to input the following information for new software products:

- Software title
- Installation location (office)
- Licence number
- Expiration date

Furthermore, please design a report displaying all software licences and expiration dates (sorted by expiration dates). If you are using Microsoft Access, you might use the wizards to design the forms and reports.

ANSWERS TO THE SELF-STUDY QUESTIONS

1. C, p. 306	2. C, p. 325	3. A, p. 322	4. D, p. 324
5. C, p. 310	6. B, p. 326	7. A, p. 327	8. A, p. 329

Case *The Ethics of IS Consulting*

Thousands of businesses, large and small, are actively participating in one of the fastest growing industry sectors of the modern world: information systems consulting services. Many large organizations, such as IBM, EDS, and Accenture, have long been successful in providing IS consulting services. New companies enter this industry on a daily basis.

As with other business endeavours, IS consulting services is an area of business that puts people into situations that test their ethics. One potentially problematic area that applies to all consulting—not just IS consulting—is the fundamental conflict of needing to secure consulting contracts to bring revenue into the consulting firm without over-promising what can be delivered and/or when it can be delivered. The pressure to bring in business to generate revenue is great. New business is, after all, the lifeblood of the consulting firm. There is natural pressure to secure a consulting contract even though it may not be absolutely clear that the firm can deliver exactly what the client wants or needs by the exact deadlines the client has set. For IS consultants, the pressure is great to promise that the job can be done quickly using "rapid" methodologies, especially given that these methodologies are in vogue. Of course, it is in the consulting firm's long-term interests not to over-promise, but the pressure is there nonetheless. Similarly, IS consultants might sometimes be tempted to sell their own or their partners' products to the clients even though it might not be in the client's best interest.

One other potential ethical dilemma facing IS consultants is the question of whom they work for and where their loyalties lie. With joint application design and the use of systems development teams in which IS consultants work closely with business users, it is sometimes difficult for consultants to determine exactly for whom they work—the client or the consulting firm. On the one hand, they are serving the client and must satisfy the client's needs. On the other hand, they work for the consulting firm. They may get pulled in two different directions, especially if the relationship between the client and the consulting firm deteriorates. The consulting firm might want the consultants to stick with the letter of the contract, to withhold certain services, or to keep their time with the client to a minimum. On the other hand, the consultants may want to go the extra distance to please the client. After all, with contemporary systems development approaches, the consultants probably spend more time with the client organization's personnel than with the consulting firm's personnel, and the client organization is likely to be doing the primary evaluation of the consultant's performance. In fact, in some cases, the consultants may be housed physically and semi-permanently within the client organization, may be paid directly by the client, and may enjoy other employee benefits provided by the client organization.

With increased use of joint application design and other approaches to partnering with business users comes one final, fundamental ethical dilemma that all consultants face daily. This dilemma is whether to solve problems for clients in such a way that the client learns how to solve the problems itself or to solve problems for clients in such a way that the client needs to ask the consultant to return to solve similar problems in the future. There is a natural pressure to do the latter to ensure future business.

A useful analogy for this ethical dilemma is the way that a barber cuts your hair. A barber who wants to ensure that you will have to come back again would give you the best possible haircut. In addition, the barber would have no mirrors in the shop so that you could not see what the barber was doing and would not answer any of your questions about how your hair was cut and styled. On the other hand, a barber who wanted you to become self-sustaining and empowered to take care of yourself would not only give you a good haircut, but would have mirrors all around so that you could see exactly what the barber was doing. The barber would explain exactly what he/she was doing at all times and answer any of your questions. Now, you would not necessarily be able to cut your own hair, but you would know how to do so and could explain this to another person, who could then cut your hair. You would not necessarily have to come back to that same barber. Good consultants do not try to generate more business for themselves the way the first barber does. They want you to ask them back because you want to have them back, not because you need to have them back.

Source: Rick Freedman, "Ethics of IT Consulting," *Consulting to Management* 15, no. 2 (2004): 19–21.

Discussion Questions

1. How would you deal with an IS manager who was pushing you to develop a system in a time frame that was too rapid to enable you to do a good job? What if it were the client who was pushing you?
2. To whom should an IS consultant ultimately be loyal, the client or the consulting firm? Why?
3. Should IS consultants strive not only to solve clients' problems but teach and enable them to solve their own problems in the future? Why or why not?
4. What, in your opinion, are some of the characteristics of a good consultant? How do you think a good consultant will ensure that a client will return in the future?

Log on to the Companion Website at www.pearsoned.ca/jessup for an additional case.

Running Case: Connexion by Boeing

Information Systems Ethics and Computer Crime

The terrorist attacks against New York's World Trade Center caused huge losses in terms of human lives as well as financial losses for all companies directly or indirectly affected by the events. For the airline industry, revenues dropped significantly in the aftermath of 9/11, as many of their most valued customers suddenly reduced air travel due to security concerns. Therefore, regaining the travellers' confidence was seen as a primary factor in many airlines' struggle for survival.

At the same time, the United States Department of Defense (DoD) and the newly created Department of Homeland Security started to combat the threat of terrorism in the United States and required the airlines to install advanced security measures aboard all commercial aircraft. One important way to minimize the threat of terrorism was to "engage terrorism abroad—to not let it cross borders—[through] preventative and proactive efforts to stop acts before they start," as one senior Boeing official stated. However, preventing terrorism from reaching the United States is a highly complex task due to the tremendous numbers of people, moving vehicles, and tons of freight that enter the

Table 9.6 *Cross-border traffic and commerce in the U.S.*

Number of trucks entering the United States each year	11.2 million
Miles of border the United States shares with Canada or Mexico	7500
Number of rail cars entering the United States each year	2.2 million
Number of foreign-flag ships making calls in U.S. ports each year	7500
Number of international flights each year	500 000
Number of calls at U.S. ports made each year by foreign-flag ships	51 000
Tons of freight brought into the United States by air each year	7.8 million
Number of different jurisdictions	About 87 000

Sources: **www.boeing.com/news/frontiers/archive/2004/march/cover1.html. www.boeing.com/ids/homeland_security/ourCapabilities1.htm. http://spacecom.grc.nasa.gov/icnsconf/docs/2002/03/Session_A2-5_Miller.pdf**.

United States each year. For example, 11.2 million trucks, 2.2 million rail cars, and 500 000 international flights enter the United States each year (see Table 9.6).

For companies such as Boeing, homeland security is a growth area, with an addressable market of $4–$6 billion a year from the U.S. Department of Homeland Security alone, along with opportunities from DoD and from abroad. Boeing also has an interest in ensuring the efficient flow of people and commerce—it is a leading U.S. exporter and one of the largest American importers, and relies on the aviation industry for about half its revenues in the United States. Boeing's homeland security–related projects include technological achievements such as the national missile defence and the Future Combat Systems (FCS), as well as numerous activities to increase aviation security by developing features such as reinforced cockpit doors for its aircraft. One of Boeing's subsidiaries working on homeland security-related projects is Connexion by Boeing, which is working on broadband and narrowband technology that can be used to improve communications to and from airplanes and between airplanes and air marshals. Air traffic management, the Boeing Commercial Airplanes Group, and Boeing's Integrated Defense Systems business unit of Space and Intelligence Systems also play a role in protecting the United States against terrorist threats.

A primary issue related to aviation security is that once an airplane has left the airport, it is largely disconnected from the rest of the world. During any flight, a variety of adverse conditions can occur, ranging from effects of extreme turbulence and medical emergencies to incidents of air rage, or, in the worst case, terrorist attacks or attempted hijackings. In case any of these events occur during a flight, the flight crew has to be able to handle the situation without being able to contact anyone for help. In most cases, it is not even possible to transmit detailed reports of the situation to the airline's operations centre, situation awareness centres, or FAA centres. The near-real-time data transmission capabilities offered by Connexion by Boeing help to deal with this issue. While the pilot and the rest of the crew will still have to handle the event on their own, Connexion's systems provide a way to enable data and voice communication between the aircraft and ground crews to exchange critical information about the event and to guide the aircraft's captain in decision making.

One application is real-time cabin surveillance. To enable this application, an aircraft needs to be equipped with several different cameras, such as cockpit door cameras or covert infrared or zoom-type cameras throughout the cabin. This system of cameras allows the crew at the flight deck to monitor any events occurring in the cabin during a flight, from the safety of the cockpit, without compromising security. The pilots can use specific software to remotely control the cameras' zoom or viewing angle to focus on certain parts of the aircraft's cabin. This video data, which is also stored in an onboard video recorder, can be accessed remotely by ground crews to improve collaborative decision making in response to threats or other non-normal events. The use of virtual private networks (VPN) ensures that only authorized users have access to this critical data. Furthermore, this video data can serve as evidence for law enforcement officers in cases of air rage or other passenger misbehaviour, such as theft or tampering. Redundant data storage (both airborne and on the ground) for most data flows is provided to support further non-real-time analysis. In addition to its serving as a threat deterrent if the airlines advertise its use onboard the airplane, the camera system may give the passengers a sense of security during the flight, which helps to strengthen the passengers' confidence in the safety of air travel.

Similarly, an aircraft's flight data can be monitored remotely, which helps the ground crews detect if there are any deviations from the airplane's regular flight path (see figures below). Used as a virtual cockpit voice recorder, the system can help to inform ground crews about whatever is happening on the flight deck, and can also serve as a backup for the physical black boxes installed aboard all commercial aircraft. At the same time, ground crews can query sensors throughout the aircraft, swhich help to detect any chemical, explosive, or biological threats. To help the situation awareness centres in assessing an event, flight information, data recorder, and GPS data are all simultaneously "live linked" over the Connexion broadband network.

Another key feature enabled by Connexion's system is the capacity to trigger silent alarms using small key-chain transmitters. This silent alarm feature allows the aircraft's captain, air marshals, and members of the cabin crew to covertly transmit signals to the airline's operations centre, FAA centres, and/or situation awareness centres. In cases where an aircraft has a situation or event that precludes normal communications, one or more crew members activate a silent alarm, which initiates an onboard sequence of events such as automatic cockpit or cabin video/audio capture. When these silent alarms are activated, the ground personnel attempts to contact the airplane using prearranged methods that the crew acknowledges using the onboard alarm system. If an onboard event alert is triggered and verified, the ground personnel can then execute a variety of response plans. As this can happen covertly, aggressive passengers or potential hijackers or terrorists remain unaware of the alarm being triggered, which can help in handling the situation.

In case all air traffic control communication between ground personnel and the aircraft is lost, Connexion's systems can serve as a backup communication link. As Connexion's systems use the same data link for the airline's internal communication and for the passengers' data communication, the internal communication can be given priority. This way, the entire bandwidth is available for the communication between the flight crew and the ground to handle critical situations.

These solutions, enabled by Connexion by Boeing's systems, can help improve the security of the international airspace and, at the same time, help the airlines regain the passengers' confidence in the security of air travel.

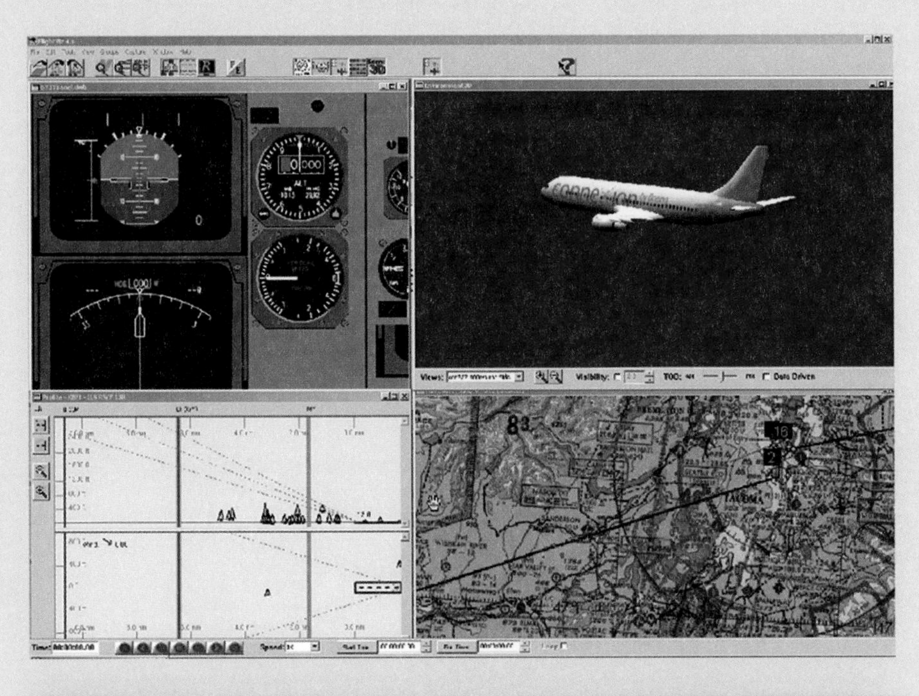

External monitoring of flight information.

Discussion Questions

1. In what other ways can Connexion's data transmission capabilities be used to increase aircraft security?
2. Do you see any ethical issues related to monitoring passengers during a flight? Why or why not?
3. In severe circumstances, the ground crews might end up in a situation in which they are able to watch the situation but are not able to react appropriately. How do you see the benefits of the systems in these cases? Can you see any ethical dilemmas arising from assessing a situation remotely and providing advice on somewhat limited information?

Appendix A: Information Systems Hardware

Preview

If you want to purchase a computer, you have a broad range of options. Over the years, hardware has become less expensive, making it possible for individuals and organizations of all sizes to take advantage of computer-based technologies. However, large computer systems can still cost more than a million dollars. Organizations must select the right hardware or risk making a costly mistake. To make an informed decision about information systems (IS) hardware, you must understand what IS hardware is and how it works. After reading this appendix, you will be able to do the following:

1. Describe key elements of information systems hardware.
2. List and describe the types of computers that are being used in organizations today.

Our approach in this appendix is not to bog you down with hardware facts and jargon but to provide you with an overview.

KEY ELEMENTS OF INFORMATION SYSTEMS HARDWARE

Information systems hardware is classified into three types: input, processing, and output devices (see Figure A.1). ***Input devices*** are used to enter information into a computer. ***Processing devices*** transform inputs into outputs. The ***central processing unit (CPU)***, with the help of several other closely related devices that store and recall information, is the most important processing element of a computer. We will discuss this in detail in this appendix. Finally, ***output devices***, such as a computer monitor and printer, deliver information to you in a usable format. This section describes each of these three key elements of information systems hardware. (For a more detailed discussion, see Keogh, 2002.)

Figure A.1 Input devices include the mouse and keyboard; output devices include the printer and monitor; the central processing unit transforms input into output.

Source: © Christina Kennedy/Photo Edit, Inc.

Input Devices

For information systems hardware to perform a task, data must be input into the system. Certain types of data can be entered more easily using one type of input device than another. For example, keyboards are currently the primary means to enter text and numbers. Alternatively, architects and engineers can use scanners to enter their designs and drawings into computers. Graphics tablets simulate the process of drawing or sketching on a sheet of paper. A great deal of research and development is conducted to identify optimal ways to input various types of information and to build and sell new input devices. To organize our discussion of input devices, we classify them into four general categories by the type of information being entered: entering text and numbers, pointing to and selecting information, entering batch data, and entering audio and video. Table A.1 summarizes the fundamental characteristics of each category.

Table A.1 ***Methods of providing input to an information system.***

Information Category	Representative Device(s)
Entering original text/numbers	Keyboard
Selecting and pointing	Mouse Trackball and joysticks Touch screen Light pen Touch pad
Entering batch data	Scanners Bar code/optical character readers
Entering audio and video	Microphones and speakers Video and digital cameras MIDI

Entering Text and Numbers

The primary device used to support the entry of text and numbers into a computer is the ***keyboard***. Used first as the input method on typewriters, keyboard data entry is a mainstay of the computer industry.

Ergonomics. One advance in keyboard technology is the ergonomically correct keyboard, which is designed to reduce the stress placed on the wrists, hands, and arms when typing. Figure A.2 shows a normal keyboard and the Microsoft Natural keyboard. When typing for long periods, some normal keyboard users develop aching, numbing, and tingling in their arms, wrists, or hands. These injuries are generally referred to as repetitive stress injuries. The broadened use of computers in the workplace and the associated injuries to workers, resulting in more sick days and insurance claims, has made the ***ergonomics***—the design of computer hardware and work environments that minimize health risks such as repetitive stress injuries—of keyboards and employees' workstations much more important to organizations. Other ways to reduce repetitive stress injuries include these:

- Have an ergonomically designed workplace—desk, chair, monitor size and angle, keyboard height and position.
- Take frequent breaks from typing. When your wrists and fingers start to ache, take a break.
- Maintain a straight wrist position when typing. Do not let your wrists bend up/down or left/right.
- Avoid resting on your wrists while typing. Keep your wrists elevated off the desk.
- Use a light touch on the keys. Do not press harder than you need to on the keyboard to enter information.
- Maintain good health habits, and exercise your arms, wrists, and hands.

Other keyboard innovations. Standard keyboards connect to the back of the system unit with a cord, but you can elect to purchase a cordless keyboard. Like television remote controls, battery-operated cordless keyboards use radio frequency waves to bounce signals to the computer. One drawback is that the keyboard must be proximate to the radio frequency receiver at all times for signals to be read correctly, and it will not respond if moved too far from the transmitter. An alternative wireless technology for connecting keyboards, mice, and other devices to a computer is Bluetooth—a short-range radio frequency that does not require line of sight. Bluetooth, which is becoming increasingly popular, will be discussed more thoroughly in Appendix C.

(a)

(b)

Figure A.2 Normal keyboard (a) versus the Microsoft Natural keyboard (b).

Source: Courtesy Apple Computer, Inc. [A.2b] Courtesy Apple Computer, Inc.

Pointing and Selecting Information

In addition to entering text and numbers, computer users use ***pointing devices*** to select items from menus, to point and to sketch or draw (see Figure A.3). You would probably have used a pointing device, such as a mouse, when using a graphical operating environment (such as Microsoft Windows) or when playing a video game. Several of the most popular types of pointing devices are listed in Table A.2.

Entering Batch Data

Another category of computer-based input is batch input. ***Batch input*** is used when a great deal of routine information needs to be entered into the computer. ***Scanners*** convert printed text and images into digital data.

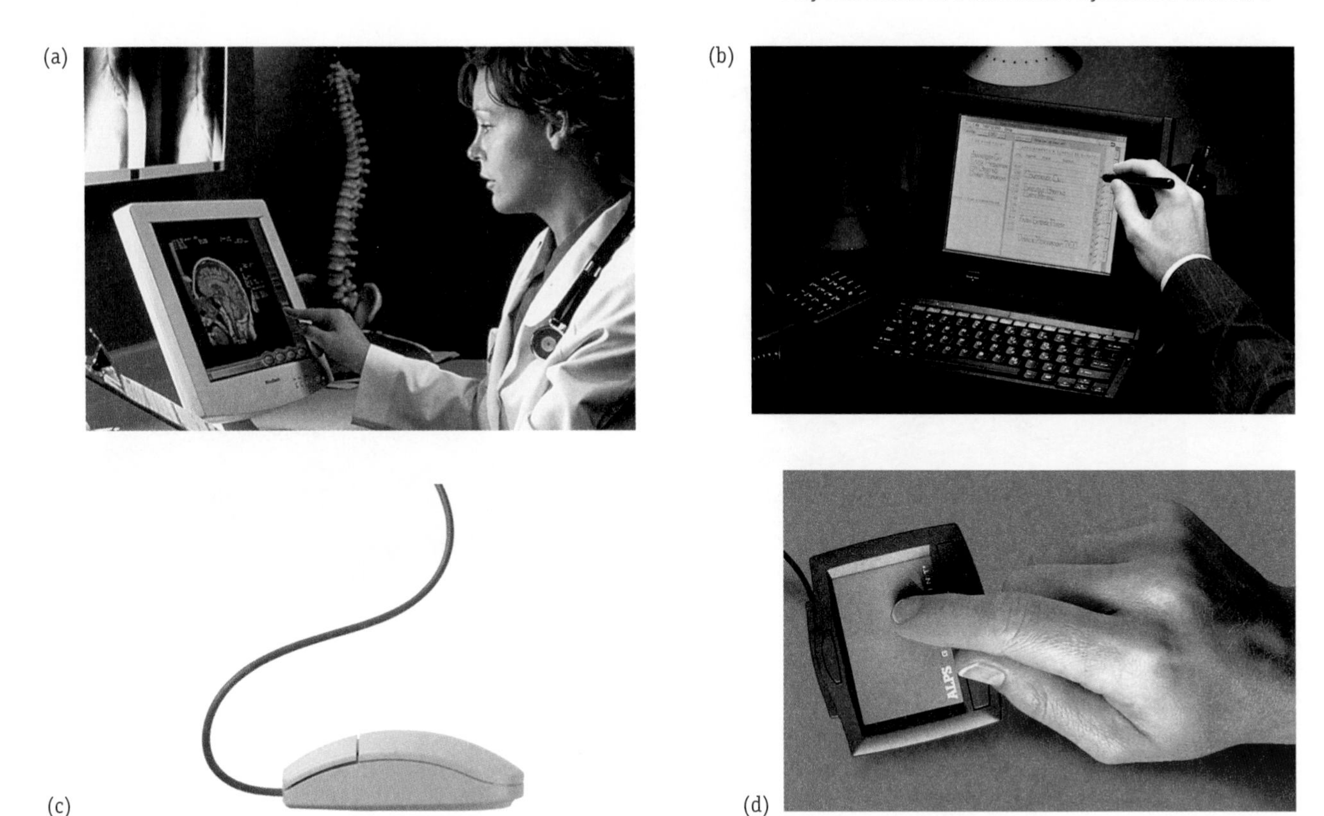

Figure A.3 Pointing devices: a touch screen (A.3a), a light pen (A.3b), a mouse (A.3c), and a touch pad (A.3d).

Sources: Getty Images, Inc. [A.3b] Courtesy Grid Systems Corporation. [A.3c] Getty Image, Inc. [A.3d] Apple Computer, Inc.

Table A.2 ***Selecting and pointing devices.***

Device	**Description**
Mouse	Pointing device that works by sliding a small box-like device on a flat surface; selections are made by pressing buttons on the mouse.
Trackball	Pointing device that works by rolling a ball that sits in a holder; selections are made by pressing buttons located near or on the holder.
Joystick	Pointing device that works by moving a small stick that sits in a holder; selections are made by pressing buttons located near or on the holder.
Touch screen	A method of input for which you use your finger; selections are made by touching the computer display.
Light pen	Pointing device that works by placing a pen-like device near a computer screen; selections are made by pressing the pen to the screen

Scanners range from a small handheld device that looks like a mouse to a large desktop box that resembles a personal photocopier, both of which are shown in Figure A.4. Rather than duplicating the image on another piece of paper, the computer translates the image into digital information that can be stored or manipulated by the computer. Special ***text-recognition software*** can convert handwritten text into the computer-based characters that form the original letters and words. Insurance companies, universities, and other organizations that routinely process large batches of forms and documents have applied scanner technology to increase employee productivity.

When the keyboard, mouse, and typical scanner cannot handle the job of transferring data to the computer, specialized scanners may be called for. These devices, which include optical mark recognition (OMR) devices, optical character recognition (OCR) devices, bar code

(a) 

(b) 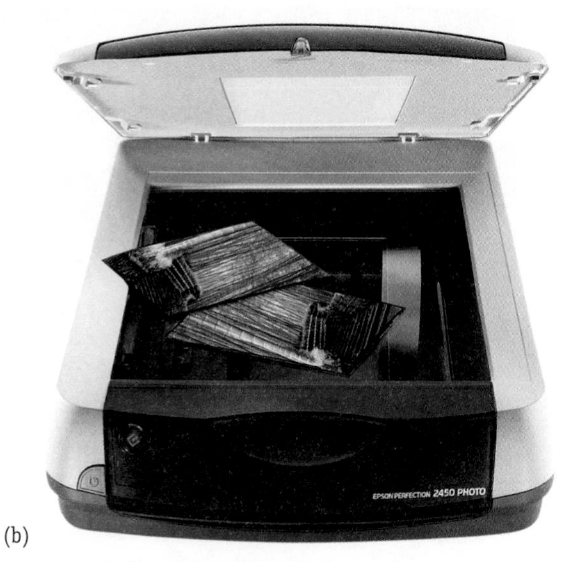

Figure A.4 Handheld (a) and flatbed (b) scanners are a type of batch input device.

Sources: [A.4a] Intermec Technologies Corporation. [A.4b] Courtesy of Epson America, Inc.

readers, and magnetic ink character readers, are summarized in Table A.3.

Smart Cards

Used in many European and Asian countries, as well as at many colleges and universities, ***smart cards*** are a special type of credit card with a magnetic strip, a microprocessor chip, and memory circuits. When issued by a school, smart cards are photo-identification cards that can also be used to unlock dormitory doors, make telephone calls, do laundry, make purchases from vending machines or student cafeterias and snack bars, and more. For making purchases, the cards are backed by funds deposited in a student account. Each time a user makes a purchase, the card keeps track of the balance remaining. Because of the microprocessor embedded in the smart card, it is much more resistant to tampering than current credit cards with magnetic strips.

Entering Audio and Video

Audio refers to sound that has been digitized for storage and replay on the computer. Audio input is helpful when a user's hands need to be free to do other tasks; it can be entered into computers through a microphone, radio, compact disk (CD), or other audio devices. ***Video*** refers to still and moving images that can be recorded, manipulated, and displayed. Video has become popular for assisting in security-related applications, such as room monitoring and employee verification. It has also gained popularity for videoconferencing and chatting on the Internet, and for using your personal computer (PC) and very inexpensive video cameras.

Table A.3 ***Specialized scanners for inputting information.***

Scanner	Description
Optical mark recognition (OMR)	Used to scan questionnaires and test answer forms where answer choices are circled or blocked in, using pencil or pen
Optical character recognition (OCR)	Used to read and digitize typewritten, computer-printed, and even hand-printed characters such as on sales tags on department store merchandise or patient information in hospitals
Bar code/optical character readers	Used in grocery stores and other retail businesses to record prices at the checkout counter; also used by libraries, banks, hospitals, utility companies, and so on
Magnetic ink character recognition (MICR)	Used by the banking industry to read data, account numbers, bank codes, and check numbers on preprinted cheques

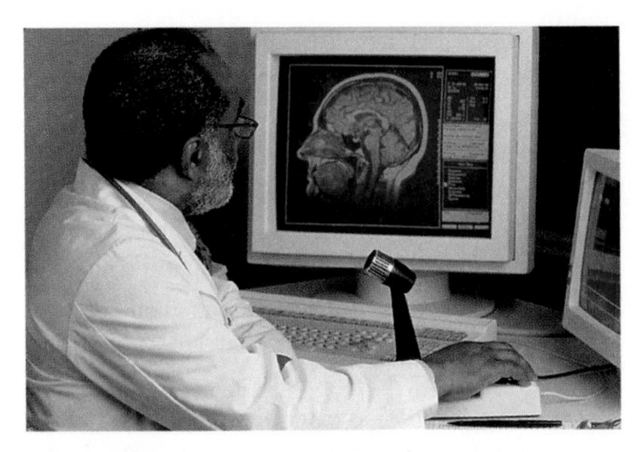

Figure A.5 Voice input is becoming an important way for many to interact with a computer.

Source: Peter Beck/Corbis/Stock Market

Voice input. Perhaps one of the easiest ways to enter data into a computer is simply to speak into a microphone. With the increased interest in such applications as Internet-based telephone calls and videoconferencing, microphones have become an important component of computer systems. A process called ***speech recognition*** also makes it possible for your computer to understand speech. The two-step process works like this. First, you speak into a microphone connected to a speech-recognition board installed in the system unit of your computer or plugged into a high-speed USB port (see Figure A.5). Then, special speech-recognition software digitizes your spoken words and displays them on the monitor screen. Speech-recognition technology is especially helpful for physicians and other medical professionals, people with disabilities, airplane cockpit personnel, factory workers whose hands get too dirty to use keyboards, and computer users who cannot type and do not want to learn. Drawbacks are that users must pause after each word, and computers do not always hear spoken words correctly.

Other audio inputs. Audio input devices let users enter sounds into the computer for processing. They can then analyze and manipulate the sounds through sound-editing software for output to audiotapes, CDs, or other media. Here are few examples of how audio input, other than spoken words, might be used:

- A musician connects an electronic keyboard to the computer in order to compose or manipulate music. Electronic keyboards or synthesizers are connected through a ***musical instrument digital interface (MIDI)*** port, which can also transfer sound to the computer. MIDI is a standard for connections and communications between your computer and digital musical instruments.
- A scientist studying the sounds made by whales enters those sounds into a computer to analyze pitch, volume, tone, and other patterns.
- Audiologists and other medical personnel enter sounds to be played back to patients during hearing tests or therapy.
- Forensic scientists use a computer to analyze a voice on a tape recorder for identification by a crime victim or witnesses.
- Filmmakers manipulate sounds to serve specific story purposes.

Video input. A final way in which information can be entered into a computer is through video input. Digital cameras record images, in digital form, on small, removable memory cards, rather than on film. Most cards can hold from 16 to 100 or more images. Card capacity depends upon the resolution you select and the preset capacity of the card you buy. When the camera's memory card is full, you can connect it to a port on a PC for downloading to the computer's memory. Accompanying software lets you clear the memory card for later use. Some digital cameras are portable and can be used at any location. Stationary digital cameras are attached to a video board inside the PC. They allow you to record digital photographs of yourself and others, documents, or products and other items. High-quality digital cameras are generally more expensive than film-based cameras, ranging in price from $250 to $10 000 or more. However, they offer two main advantages. You can store digital images without using a scanner, and you can take photographs without having the film developed. Presently, photographs taken with digital cameras are suitable for family albums, but for professional-quality photographs, traditional cameras are still the best choice.

Video cameras, VCRs, televisions, digital video disks (DVDs), and other video devices can provide video input to a computer. As huge digital files are created when video clips are put into the computer, storage requirements are demanding. That is why video segments run on PCs are usually short. A high-quality digital video camera is typically much more expensive than a comparable nondigital video recorder. These high-quality digital cameras are starting to be used in the motion picture industry and by manufacturing companies when performing quality control. For example, Ford Motor Company uses high-resolution video cameras to evaluate the quality of parts by comparing images of newly manufactured items with images stored in a database. If the images match, the part passes a quality control inspection. If the images do not match, the part can be rejected without human intervention.

However, there are also lower-quality cameras that are priced from $50 to $200 (see Figure A.6). These devices, often referred to as cams, have become very popular with people wanting to use the Internet for chatting with friends and family, using programs like Windows or Yahoo! Messenger. Unlike high-quality digital video cameras (see Figure A.7), these cams use ***streaming video***, in which the camera sends a sequence of moving images in a compressed form over the Internet; the images are displayed on the receiver's screen as they arrive. ***Streaming media*** is streaming video with sound. With streaming video or streaming media, a web user does not have to wait for the entire file to be downloaded before seeing the video or hearing the sound. Instead, the media are sent in a continuous stream that is played as it arrives. This is why streaming has become popular for real-time chatting, and it is how live broadcasts, like the news on CBC (**www.cbc.ca/newscast.html**), can be viewed on a computer over the Internet.

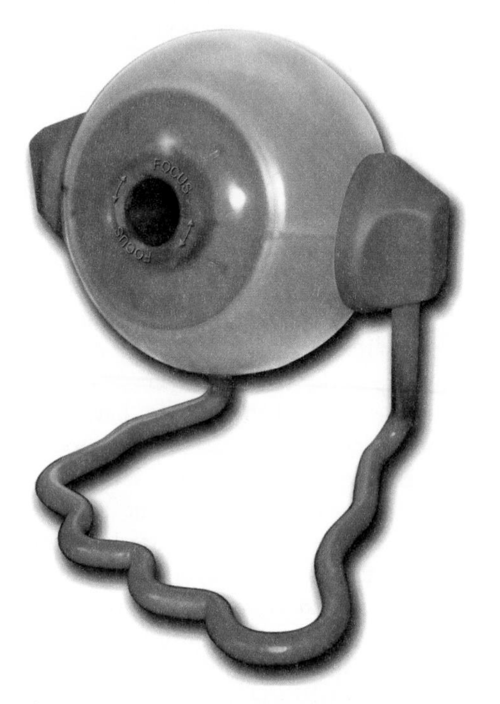

Figure A.6 Low-priced web cams are popular with people who like to chat over the Internet.

Source: © Orange Micro, Inc.

Figure A.7 High-quality digital video cameras can be connected directly to a computer for storing information as well as for editing and adding special effects.

Source: Courtesy of Sony Electronics, Inc.

Both audio and video are expected to increase in popularity as common input options. We have described numerous options for providing input to a computer. After information is entered into a computer, it can be processed, stored, and manipulated. In the next section, we describe the processing aspects of IS hardware.

Processing: Transforming Inputs into Outputs

In this section, we provide a brief overview of computer processing. To begin, we describe how data and information are represented within a computer. Next, we briefly describe the internal processing components of a desktop computer, focusing primarily on the central processing unit (CPU) and data storage technologies.

Binary Code

Your brain can readily process written words, photographs, music, an instructor's lecture (at least some of the time), videos, and much more. If you grew up speaking English, your brain will process incoming information in that language only. Similarly, computers can process incoming data, but only after the words, photographs, music, and other information have been translated into a language they can understand. The language that computers understand is called digital data or ***binary code***, which simply means that all incoming data must be translated into the 1s and 0s of binary math. Binary, or base-2 math (2, 4, 8, 16, 32, etc.), is used by computers instead of the more familiar base 10, because it simplifies the way a computer's hardware works.

Table A.4 ***Elements of computer storage.***

Measurement	No. of Bits	No. of Bytes	No. of Kilobytes	No. of Megabytes	No. of Gigabytes
Byte	8	1			
Kilobyte* (K)	8192	1024	1		
Megabyte (MB)	8 388 608	1 048 576	1024	1	
Gigabyte (GB)	8 589 934 592	1 073 741 824	1 048 576	1024	1
Terabyte (TB)	8 796 093 022 208	1 099 511 627 776	1 073 741 824	1 048 576	1024

*A kilobyte equals a little more than 1000 bytes, but the number is usually rounded to 1000. The same is true for the number of kilobytes in a megabyte, and so on.

Binary codes make up ***machine language***, the only language computers understand. The individual 1s and 0s that make up the code are called ***bits***—short for binary digits. Eight bits equal a ***byte*** or about one typed character, such as the letter "A" or the number "6" on the keyboard. You will often see computer storage and memory measurement terms. Table A.4 will help you make sense of them.

Future memory and storage capacities will also include petabytes (one quadrillion bytes), exabytes (one quintillion bytes), and brontobytes (one sextillion bytes). The bits in the binary code are the basic instruction units for all the work the computer does. The bits represent on/off commands for tiny electric switches inside the computer's processor. When a low-voltage current is applied to a switch, it is read as a 0, and the switch is closed. A high-voltage current is read as a 1, and the switch is opened. Similarly, positive and negative magnetized locations used to store data are represented in binary notation as 0s or 1s.

One of the biggest challenges for the computer industry has been to determine how to translate all the different types of information into digital data that a computer can understand. Early computers could not translate incoming data at all. They used paper cards on which strings of 1s and 0s were represented by punched holes. Later, computers received information from a keyboard, which was the first time a translation was made into 1s and 0s from text that computer users could understand. Today's computers can translate many types of data, including words, photographs, sound, and video, to binary code, then manipulate and store it. One of the main reasons why computers become so quickly outdated is that newer models keep coming out that can process more and more amounts and types of information.

Programs (applications) you run on your computer contain instructions. (This is software, covered in Appendix B.) Programs may tell the computer to open a specific file, move data from one location to another, open a new window on the monitor screen, add a column of figures, and so on. Before the computer can follow program instructions, however, those instructions must be converted to machine language. The CPU uses a special built-in program called a ***language translator*** to translate incoming data into binary code called machine language. After the processor converts incoming data to machine language, it organizes the bits into groups—for instance, 32-bit instructions—that represent specific operations and storage locations.

Once the computer receives instructions from a program, it processes the information into a form you, the computer user, can understand. In a word processing program, for example, the letters and numbers you type are displayed on the monitor, just as they would appear on a sheet of paper if you were using an old-fashioned typewriter. But, unlike on the typewriter, when you press the "L" key, for example, on the computer keyboard, the computer is actually receiving the information as a series of 1s and 0s, specifically "01001100." As you type a letter or a term paper, the data are processed, then displayed on the monitor in a form that makes sense to you. The binary code the computer actually uses is hidden from your view (see Figure A.8). You see words, lines, and

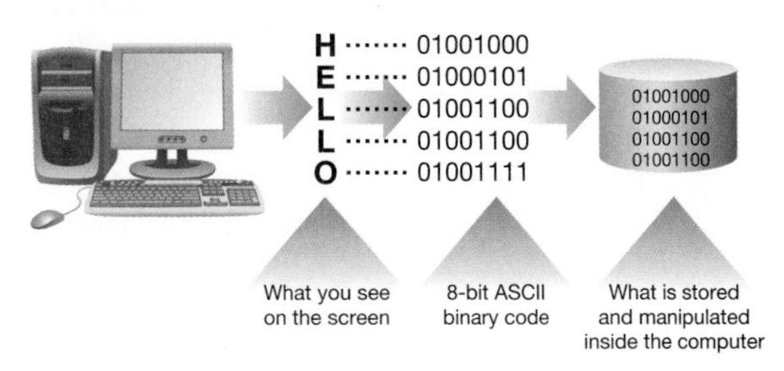

Figure A.8 How computers translate information into binary code so that the computer can store and manipulate the information.

Table A.5 ***ASCII codes for alphabet and numbers.***

Character	ASCII-8 Binary Code	Character	ASCII-8 Binary Code
A	0100 0001	S	0101 0011
B	0100 0010	T	0101 0100
C	0100 0011	U	0101 0101
D	0100 0100	V	0101 0110
E	0100 0101	W	0101 0111
F	0100 0110	X	0101 1000
G	0100 0111	Y	0101 1001
H	0100 1000	Z	0101 1010
I	0100 1001	0	0011 0000
J	0100 1010	1	0011 0001
K	0100 1011	2	0011 0010
L	0100 1100	3	0011 0011
M	0100 1101	4	0011 0100
N	0100 1110	5	0011 0101
O	0100 1111	6	0011 0110
P	0101 0000	7	0011 0111
Q	0101 0001	8	0011 1000
R	0101 0010	9	0011 1001

paragraphs. After you write a document, you can then print it out on paper, store it on the computer's hard disk, or even post it to an Internet website.

Other binary codes are used to relay data and instructions to and from the CPU. For example, fixed-length binary codes such as ***ASCII*** (American Standard Code for Information Interchange), ***extended ASCII***, and ***EBCDIC*** (Extended Binary-Coded Decimal Interchange Code) are used to represent numbers, letters, and other characters in a binary form. ASCII is the standard binary code adopted for data communications systems and is used by most microcomputers (see Table A.5). Then EBCDIC, developed by IBM, is used primarily on IBM mainframe computers. Both ASCII and EBCDIC use various eight-bit combinations to represent characters in the English language. Software translators are used to convert English characters in ASCII to characters in other languages such as Spanish, French, or German.

A third binary code, called ***Unicode***, is better suited than either ASCII or EBCDIC for representing the letters and characters in languages other than English. This is because Unicode uses 16 bits, instead of the 8 bits used by ASCII and EBCDIC, to represent characters. By using 16 bits, Unicode can represent more characters than ASCII and EBCDIC and can, therefore, encode most languages.

System Unit

A computer's ***system unit*** is the physical box that houses all the electronic components that do the work of the computer (see Figure A.9). Buttons on the outside, front surface of the system unit turn the machine on and off and reset the machine without turning the power off. Most PC system units include a CR–read-only memory (CD-ROM) drive and a diskette drive. Through ports at the back of the system unit you can connect peripheral hardware, such as a keyboard, a mouse, speakers, printers, and scanners.

The system unit contains the following:

- Motherboard, power supply, and fan
- Central processing unit
- Random-access memory (RAM) and Read-only memory (ROM)
- Hard drive, diskette drive, CD-ROM, or DVD-ROM drive
- Ports for plugging in peripherals and add-in slots for sound, video, internal modem, and other cards

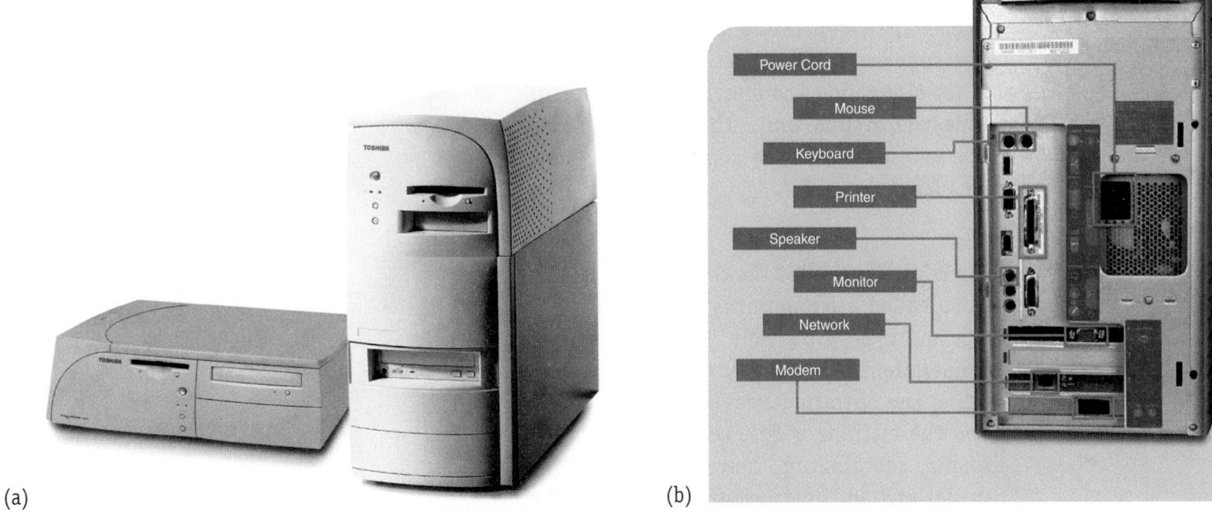

(a) (b)

Figure A.9 The system unit houses all the electronic components that do the work of the computer.

Source: Courtesy of Toshiba America Information Systems, Inc.

In all types and models of computers, the main circuit board or system board, most often called the motherboard, is the heart of the system unit.

Motherboard

The ***motherboard*** is aptly named because it contains all the components that do the actual processing work of the computer (see Figure A.10). It is a large printed plastic or fibreglass circuit board that holds or connects to all the computer's electronic components. Plugged into or otherwise connected to the motherboard are the CPU, often referred to as the computer's brain, RAM and ROM, hard disk, diskette, and CD-ROM drives, all expansion slots, ports for printers and other external devices, and the power supply.

The computer's ***power supply*** converts electricity from the wall socket to a lower voltage. Power can vary from 110 to 240 volts, depending upon where you are in the world, to lower voltages—5–12 volts DC—and the power supply adjusts voltage to prevent damage to the computer's components. The power supply also regulates the voltage to eliminate spikes and surges common in most electrical systems. For added protection against external power

Figure A.10 A computer's motherboard holds or connects to all the computer's electronic components.

Source: Peter Beck/Corbis/Stock Market

surges, most PC owners opt to connect their systems to a separately purchased voltage surge suppressor. The power supply includes a fan for air-cooling the electronic components inside the system unit. That low humming noise you hear while the computer is running is the fan.

Central Processing Unit

The CPU is often called the computer's brain. It is also called a microprocessor, processor, or chip, and it is responsible for performing all the operations of the computer. Its job includes loading the operating system (e.g., Windows) when the machine is first turned on and performing, coordinating, and managing all the calculations and instructions relayed to the CPU while the computer is running.

The CPU consists of two main sections: the ***arithmetic logic unit (ALU)*** and the ***control unit***. The ALU performs mathematics, including all forms of addition, subtraction, multiplication, and division. It also performs logical operations, which involve comparing packets of data, then executing appropriate instructions. Combined in various ways, these functions allow the computer to perform complicated operations rapidly. The control unit works closely with the ALU by performing four primary functions:

1. *Fetching* the next program instruction from the computer's memory.
2. *Decoding* instructions, so that the computer knows what to do next. The control unit uses separate registers (temporary storage locations inside the CPU) to store the instructions and to store information about storage location in memory.
3. *Retrieving* the necessary data from memory and telling the ALU to execute the required instructions. The control unit again uses registers to store retrieved data and the action performed.
4. *Storing* results of its computations in a register or in memory.

Both the ALU and the control unit use registers because they can access them more quickly than they can access main memory, thus adding to processing speed.

The CPU is composed of millions of tiny transistors arranged in complex patterns that allow it to interpret and manipulate data. The inner workings of a CPU are very complex. For most of us, it is easiest to think of a CPU as being a "black box" where all the processing occurs. The CPU is a small device made of

Figure A.11 The Intel Pentium IV microprocessor contains more than 55 million transistors.

Source: © Intel Corporation

silicon. For example, the Intel Pentium IV®CPU packs more than 55 million transistors into an area about the size of a dime! The Pentium IV, shown in Figure A.11, is packaged in a container that is bigger than a dime, because additional wiring is used to connect all these transistors of the CPU to the motherboard.

The general trend in computing is toward smaller, faster, and cheaper devices. But for how long can this trend continue? In the 1970s, Dr. Gordon Moore, then a researcher at Intel, hypothesized that computer processing performance would double every 18 months. When Moore made this bold prediction, he did not limit it to any specified time. This prediction became known as ***Moore's Law***. Interestingly, Moore has been basically correct so far. Feature size—the size of lines on the chip through which signals pass—has been reduced from about the width of a human hair in the 1960s (20 microns—a micron is equal to one millionth of a metre) to the size of a bacterium in the 1970s (5 microns) and to smaller than a virus today (13 microns—the feature size on an Intel Pentium IV). As feature size is reduced, a greater number and variety of circuits can be packed increasingly closer together. Both feature density and complexity have facilitated the continued performance increases that microprocessors have realized. Figure A.12 shows this trend. For more on Moore's Law, visit Intel's website (**http://www.intel.com/technology/mooreslaw/index.htm**); if you search on the web using the phrase "Moore's Law," you will get numerous interesting pages to review.

The number of transistors that can be packed into a modern CPU and the speed at which processing and other activities occur are remarkable. For example, the Intel Pentium IV can complete hundreds of millions of operations every second. To achieve these incredible speeds, the CPU must execute instructions very rapidly. In addition to the number of transistors on the CPU, three other factors greatly influence its speed—its system clock speed, registers, and cache memory—and these are described next.

Clock speed. Within the computer, an electronic circuit generates pulses at a rapid rate, setting the pace for processing events to take place, rather like a metronome marks time for a musician. This circuit is called the ***system clock***. A single pulse is a ***clock tick***, and in microcomputers, the processor's ***clock speed*** is measured in hertz (Hz). One megahertz (MHz) is one million clock ticks, or instruction cycles, per second. Microprocessor speeds are measured in different units, depending upon the type of computer. Personal computer speeds are most often measured in MHz or in gigahertz (GHz or one billion hertz). Microprocessor speeds improve so quickly that faster chips are on the market about every 6 months. Today, most new PCs operate at faster than 1 GHz. To give you an idea of how things have changed, the original IBM PC had a clock speed of 4.77 MHz.

See Table A.6 for a description of computer speeds. It takes a permanent storage device such as a hard disk about 10 ms (one thousandth of a second) to access information. Within a CPU, however, a single transistor can be changed from a 0 to a 1 in about 10 ps (one trillionth of a second). Changes inside the CPU occur about one billion times faster than they do in a fixed disk because the CPU operates only on electronic impulses, whereas the fixed disks perform both electronic and mechanical activities, such as spinning the disk and moving the read/write head. Mechanical activities are extremely slow relative to electronic activities.

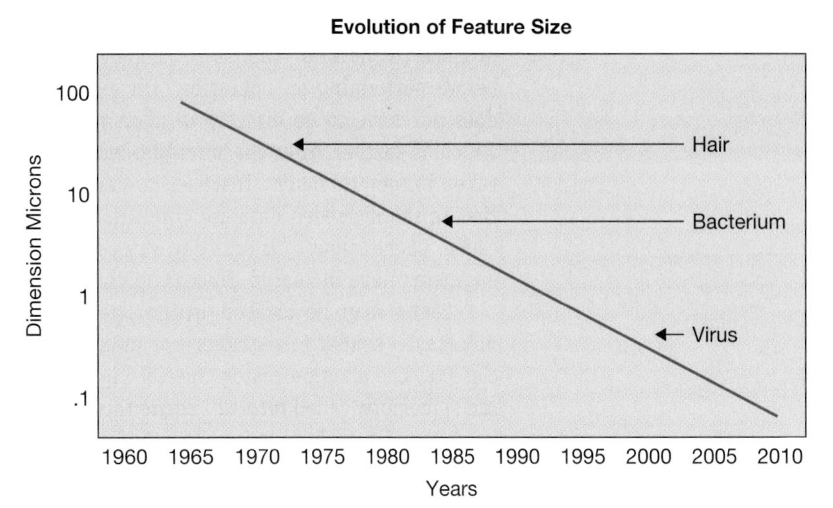

Figure A.12 Moore's Law predicted that computer processing performance would double every 18 months. To increase performance, feature size has had to shrink.

Registers. Within the CPU itself, ***registers*** provide temporary storage locations where data must reside while it is being processed or manipulated. For example, if two numbers are to be added together, both must reside in registers, with the result placed in a register. Consequently, one factor influencing the speed and power of a CPU is the number and size of the registers.

Cache memory. A ***cache*** (pronounced "cash") is a small block of memory used by processors to store those instructions most recently or most often used. Just as you might keep file folders you use most in a handy location on

Table A.6 ***Elements of computer time***

Name	Fraction of a Second	Description	Example
Millisecond	1/1000	One thousandth of a second	Fixed disks access information in about 10–20 milliseconds.
Microsecond	1/1 000 000	One millionth of a second	A 900MHz CPU executes approximately 900 million operations in a second—or about 900 operations every microsecond.
Nanosecond	1/1 000 000 000	One billionth of a second	Most types of RAM used in PCs have access times (the time needed to read information from the RAM to the CPU) from 5 to 70 nanoseconds (lower is better). Most cache memory has access times of less than 20 nanoseconds.
Picosecond	1/1 000 000 000 000	One trillionth of a second	Inside a CPU, the time it takes to switch a circuit from one state to another is in the range of 5–20 picoseconds.

your desktop, cache memory is located within or close to the CPU. Thanks to cache memory, before performing an operation, the processor does not have to go directly to main memory, which is farther from the microprocessor and takes longer to reach. Instead, it can check first to see if needed data are contained in the cache. Cache memory is another way computer engineers have increased processing speed.

Cache may be located inside the microprocessor—similar to registers—or outside, but close to, the microprocessor. Special high-speed cache memory, called ***internal cache*** (also called level 1 or L1 cache), is incorporated into the microprocessor's design. ***External or secondary cache*** (also called level 2 or L2 cache) is usually not built into the CPU but is located within easy reach of the CPU on the motherboard. The more cache available to a CPU, the better the overall system performs because more information is readily available.

The CPU translates input into binary data and binary data into information that can be understood by humans. To be used by the CPU, data must be stored either temporarily or permanently.

Primary Storage

Primary storage is for current information. Computers need temporary storage space for current calculations, and this type of memory, measured in bytes, provides it. In addition to registers and cache, described above, examples of primary storage are random-access memory (RAM) and read-only memory (ROM). RAM and ROM are made up of chips containing thousands of electronic circuits etched on silicon wafers. These memory chips are monolithic. That is, all the circuits found on one chip make up one inseparable unit of storage. Each circuit or switch is either conducting an electrical current (on) or not conducting an electrical current (off).

Random-Access Memory

Random-access memory is the computer's main or ***primary memory***. It consists of several chips mounted on a small circuit board called a ***double-inline memory module (DIMM)*** that plugs into the motherboard (see Figure A.13). RAM stores the programs and data currently in use. RAM is so named because data stored here can easily and quickly be accessed randomly by the CPU. RAM provides temporary storage of data for the CPU; because information is stored temporarily, it is referred to as ***volatile***. That is, instructions and work stored in RAM are lost when the power to the computer is turned off

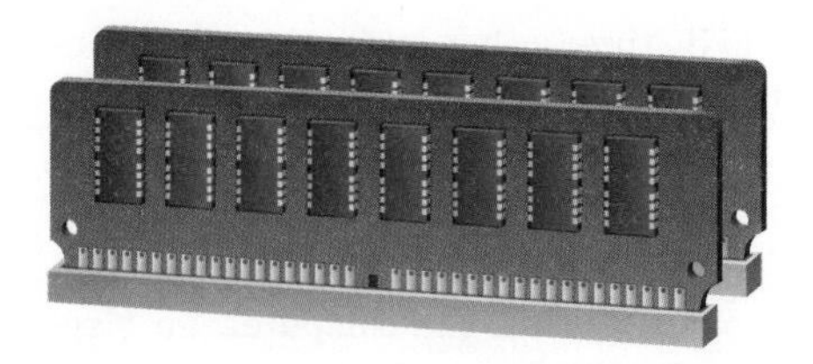

Figure A.13 Random-access memory (RAM) consists of several chips mounted on a small circuit board called a DIMM.

Beekman, *Computer Confluence* 5th ed., Prentice Hall, 2003.

or when new data are placed there. So if you have been working at your computer for hours on a research paper, do not trip over the power cord or otherwise accidentally turn off the power. If you do, unless you have saved your work in progress to your computer's hard disk or to a diskette (secondary storage), you will lose all your diligent work.

For the most efficient and speedy processing, the more RAM a computer has, the better. Today, the amount of RAM in microcomputers is measured in megabytes (MB) or gigabytes (GB). Most PC users consider 1 GB of RAM essential to run available software, and many routinely opt for 2 GB of RAM or more! Tomorrow's PC users will undoubtedly have some number of GB, or even terabytes, of RAM as an option.

Read-Only Memory

Read-only memory exists as a chip on the motherboard that can be read from but cannot be written to. That is, the CPU can read the information stored in ROM, but the computer user cannot change it. ROM is nonvolatile, which means that it does not lose its instructions when the power to the computer is turned off. ROM stores programs as instructions that are automatically loaded when the computer is turned on, such as the basic input/output system (BIOS).

A variation of ROM is erasable ROM, referred to as EEPROM (electrically erasable programmable ROM). You may have heard EEPROM referred to by a more user-friendly term, ***flash memory***. This type of memory can be repeatedly written to and erased like RAM, but, unlike RAM, it retains its information after power is turned off. Flash memory is the storage technology behind many popular consumer devices such as digital cameras, iPods and other MP3 players, and portable storage devices called ***flash drives*** (see Figure A.14). (Because a flash drive is a *removable* storage technology, it is both a primary and a secondary storage technology.)

(a)

(b)

(c)

Figure A.14 Flash memory is used as a storage technology in a variety of products.

Sources: (a) Phil Degginger/Color-Pic, Inc., (b) © Nicholas Eveleigh/Superstock, (c) photo by Business Wire via Getty Images

Secondary Storage

Secondary nonvolatile storage is for permanently storing data to a large-capacity storage component, such as hard disk, diskette, CD-ROM disk, magnetic tape, and, of course, flash drives (see Table A.7). Nonvolatile means that data are not lost from secondary storage when the computer's power is turned off. Hard disks and diskettes are magnetic media. That is, diskettes and the disks inside a hard disk drive are coated with a magnetic material. Reading data from the disks involves converting magnetized data to electrical impulses that can be understood by the processor. Writing to the disks is the reverse—converting electrical impulses to magnetized spots representing data.

Hard disk drives, diskette drives, and tapes are secondary storage devices with ***read/write heads*** that inscribe data to or retrieve data from hard disks, diskettes, and tapes. Hard disk, diskette, and tape drives are usually installed internally but may be externally located and attached through cables to ports on the back of the system unit. Diskettes

Type	Speed	Method of Data Access	Relative Cost/MB
Magnetic tape	Slow	Sequential	Low
Floppy disk	Slow	Direct	Low
Hard disk	Fast	Direct	Medium
Compact discs	Medium	Direct	Medium
Optical disks	Fast	Direct	Medium
Flash drive	Fast	Direct	High

Table A.7 ***Comparing methods of secondary storage.***

and tapes are removable secondary storage media. That is, they must be inserted into the appropriate drive (or tape reader) to be read from or written to and are removed when these tasks are accomplished.

Hard Drives

Most software run on a computer, including the operating system, is stored on the ***hard drive*** or ***hard disk***. The hard drive is a peripheral device usually located inside the system unit of a computer. It writes data and programs to a fixed disk. The storage capacity of the hard drives for today's microcomputers is now measured in GB or billions of bytes. It is not unusual for PCs currently on the market to come equipped with hard drives with 50–100 GB storage capacities. Modern supercomputers can have millions of GB of storage. Most microcomputers have one hard drive, but additional drives can usually be added, either internally or externally. To make sure critical data are not lost, some computers employ ***RAID (redundant array of independent disks)*** technology to store redundant copies of data on two or more hard drives. RAID is not typically used on an individual's computer but is very common for web servers and many business applications.

Hard drives consist of several disks, or platters, stacked on top of one another so that they do not touch (see Figure A.15). Each disk within a disk pack has an access arm with two read/write heads—one positioned close to the top surface of the disk and another positioned close to the bottom surface of the disk. (Both surfaces of each disk are used for data storage, usually with the exception of the top surface of the top disk and the bottom surface of the bottom disk.) The read/write heads do not actually touch either surface of the disks. In fact, a ***head crash*** occurs if the read/write head for some reason touches either surface of the disk. When this happens, data are lost. The disks inside the hard drive rotate as data are written to or read from them.

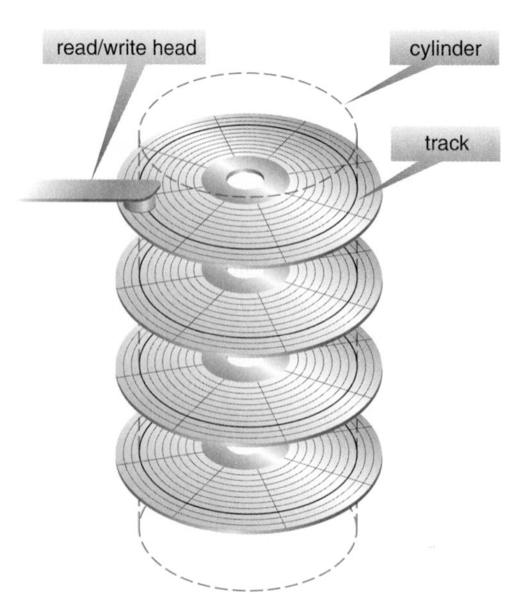

Figure A.15 A hard drive consists of several disks that are stacked on top of one another and read/write heads to read and write information.

Pfaffenberger/CIYF Brief 2003, Prentice Hall, 2003.

Diskette Drives and Diskettes

Most personal computers also contain diskette drives. They are separate from the hard drive, and the port for inserting diskettes is located on the outside of the system unit.

Diskettes (also called floppy disks) are 3.5-inch, round, flexible Mylar devices that record data as magnetized spots on tracks on the disk surface (see Figure A.16). The actual diskette is enclosed in a nonflexible plastic jacket that fits into the diskette drive on the computer so the diskette can be read or written to. Diskettes are small enough to be easily carried home in a purse or a pocket and can be used by more than one computer. The disadvantage to using diskettes for storage is that they may not have sufficient capacity to store large amounts of data. (Typically, one diskette can store 1.4 MB of data, although higher capacity diskettes are available.)

In addition to the standard internal hard disk, some microcomputers may also have a ***Zip drive***®, which is a high-capacity, removable diskette drive that uses 100, 250, or 750 MB zip disks or cartridges. Zip drives offer computer users easy-to-use additional data storage that is handy for backing up information and sharing stored data with other computers.

Although diskettes are still in use, flash memory–based flash drives are quickly replacing them as an inexpensive portable storage medium. In fact, Dell Computers and other manufacturers no longer include a diskette

Figure A.16 Diskettes provide low-capacity storage.

drive as standard equipment; diskette drives are included only as an option. Likewise, rewritable CDs (CD-RW) and DVDs (DVD-RW) are quickly replacing Zip drives as high capacity, inexpensive removable storage.

Optical Disk Storage

Optical disks, or those using laser beam technology, have become popular as storage requirements have increased. An ***optical disk***, coated with a metallic substance, is written to when a laser beam passing over the surface of the disk burns small spots into the disk surface, each one representing a data package. The data can be read when a laser scans the surface of the disk and a lens picks up various light reflections from the data spots. Some optical ***disks*** are read only. That is, information is entered on them by a manufacturer. The information cannot be changed, nor can new information be written to the disk by the computer user. One advantage to using optical disks for storage is that they can hold much more information than diskettes: one optical disk can record the information from at least a dozen diskettes. Optical disks have made possible the huge growth in multimedia software applications for PCs.

Magneto-Optical (MO) Disks. One type of optical disk, called the ***magneto-optical (MO) disk,*** can hold a large amount of information, as do other optical disks, but you can also write to the disk. The plastic surface of the disk contains tiny metallic crystals. To write information, a laser beam melts a small spot on the plastic surface of the disk. A magnet then rearranges the metallic crystals while the plastic is still hot and malleable. The crystals are arranged so that some reflect light while others do not. Those crystals that reflect light can later be read by a laser.

Compact Disks. The most popular type of optical disk storage is the ***CD-ROM (compact disc—read-only memory)***. A CD-ROM drive is now a standard equipment with most computer systems. As the name implies, CD-ROMs can only be read; they cannot be written to. Because the typical CD-ROM disk can store up to 660 MB, which is equal to about 400 diskettes, they can easily hold entire encyclopedias, plus audio and video clips, and more (see Figure A.17).

Another type of optical disk that data can be written to is the ***CD-R (compact disc—recordable)***. Using these disks requires special software and a CD-R drive, distinct from a CD-ROM drive. Once written to, however, CD-Rs can be read by any CD-ROM drive. One of the problems with a CD-R is that information can be written onto it only once. A ***CD-RW disk (compact disc—rewritable)*** allows the disk to be written onto multiple times. Most new computers come with a CD-RW drive so that users can store and back up large amounts of information on a reusable disk.

Figure A.17 CD-ROM is a popular storage method because it is inexpensive, reliable, and provides abundant storage capacity.

Source: © Corbis/Stock Market

Digital Video Disks (DVDs). Currently, a ***digital video disk-read only memory (DVD-ROM)*** has more storage space than a diskette or CD-ROM, because DVD-ROM (typically referred to as simply DVD) drives use a shorter-wavelength laser beam, which allows more optical pits to be deposited on the disk. Single-layered disks hold about 4.7 GB of information, and double-layered disks increase storage capacity to 17 GB. The huge storage capacity of DVDs makes them ideal for movie-quality videos with state-of-the-art sound. Experts predict that the DVD will eventually replace the CD-ROM because of its increased storage capacity. Like CD-ROMs, there are DVD-R and DVD-RW versions of this storage technology.

Magnetic Tapes

Magnetic tapes used for storage of computer information consist of narrow plastic tape coated with a magnetic substance. Storage tapes range from one-half-inch wide, wound on a reel, to one-fourth-inch wide, wound into a plastic cassette that looks much like a music cassette tape. As on other forms of magnetic storage, data are stored in tiny magnetic spots. Storage capacity of tape is expressed as ***density***, which equals the number of ***characters per inch (CPI)*** or ***bytes per inch (BPI)*** that can be stored on the tape. Mainframe computers use tape drives called stackers that wind tape from a supply reel to a take-up reel as data are read.

Magnetic tape is still used for storing large amounts of computer information, but it is gradually being replaced by high-capacity disk storage, as disk storage is equally reliable. In fact, information stored on disks is easier to locate, because computers must scan an entire tape to find a specific data file.

Ports

To use the full functionality of a computer, you need to be able to connect various types of devices, such as mice, printers, and cameras, to the system unit. A ***port*** provides a hardware interface—plugs and sockets—for connecting devices to computers. The characteristics of various types of ports are summarized in Table A.8.

Now that you understand how information is input into a computer and how it is processed, we can turn our attention to the third category of hardware—output technologies.

Output Devices

After information is input and processed, it must be presented to the user. Computers can display information on a screen, print it, or emit sound. The sections that follow discuss details about how each of these output devices operates.

Video Output

Monitors are used to display information from a computer. They consist of a cathode ray tube (CRT), which is similar to a television, but with much higher resolution. Many PCs and all notebooks use ***liquid crystal display (LCD)*** or plasma screens. The research and development of monitor technologies focuses on creating lightweight, low-cost, high-resolution devices. Because display monitors are embedded into a broad range of products and devices, such as automobiles, to display global positioning, route maps, and other relevant information, they must be sturdy, reliable, lightweight, and low in cost (see Figure A.18).

Printers and Plotters

Information can be printed in several different ways, as shown in Figure A.19. A plotter (Figure A.19a) is used for transferring engineering designs from the computer to drafting paper, which is often as big as 34 × 44". The plotter uses several pens as it draws

Table A.8 ***Common computer ports, their applications and description.***

Port Name	Used to Connect	Description
Serial	Modem, mice, keyboard, terminal display, MIDI	• Used to transfer one bit at a time • Slowest data transfer rates
Parallel	Printer	• Used to transfer several bits concurrently • Many times faster than serial
SCSI (pronounced "scuzzy")	Printer, scanner, external disk drives	• Very fast type of parallel communication • Up to 80 million bits per second • Daisy chain devices together
USB (Universal Serial Bus)	Printer, scanner, mice, keyboard, digital camera and camcorders, external disk drives	• A very high speed data transfer method • Up to 480 million bits per second • Up to 127 devices simultaneously connected
IEEE 1394 ("Fire Wire")	Digital camera and camcorders, external disk drives	• Extremely high speed data transfer method • Up to 800 million bits per second • Up to 63 devices simultaneously connected

(a) (b)

Figure A.18 Monitors display information from a computer: a CRT-type display (a) and an LCD-type display (b).

Source: Courtesy of View Sonic Corporation

each of the lines individually. ***Dot matrix printers*** (Figure A.19b) are older, electric typewriter-based technology for printing information on paper. Letters are formed using a series of small dots. Once the most commonly used type of printer, dot matrix printers are now mostly found printing voluminous batch information, such as periodic reports and forms. ***Ink-jet printers*** use a small cartridge to transfer ink onto paper. This process creates a typewriter-like image that can initially smear because the ink is

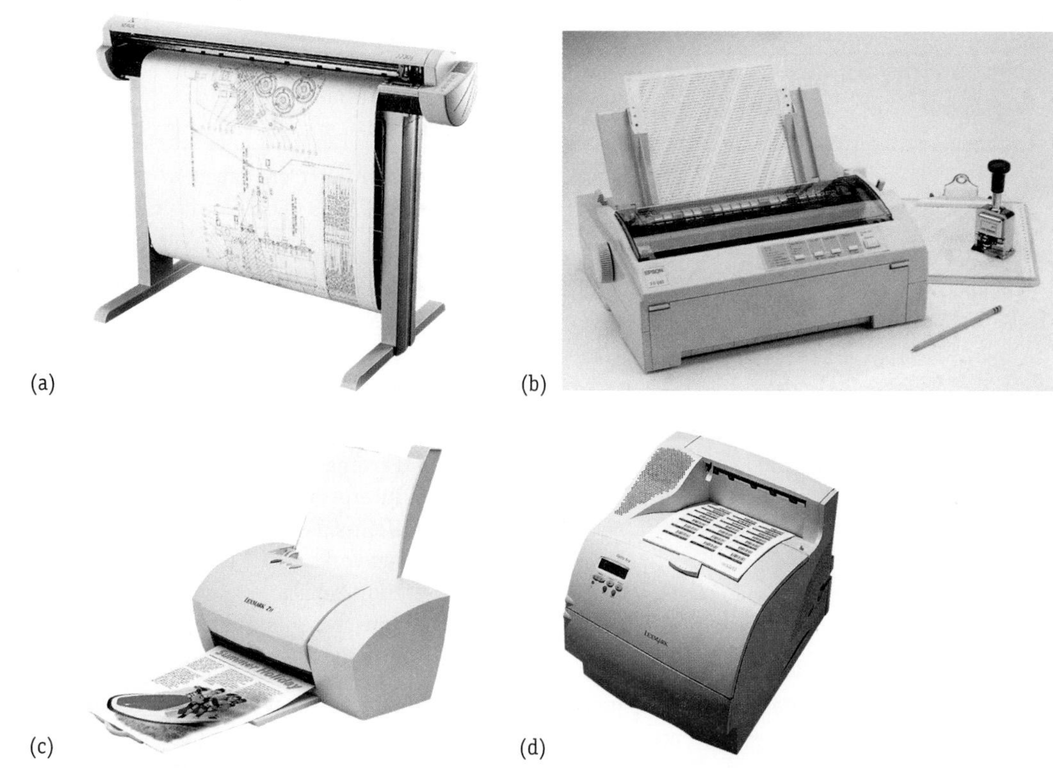

(a) (b) (c) (d)

Figure A.19 A plotter (a), a dot matrix printer (b), an ink-jet printer (c), and a laser printer (d),

Sources: [A.19a] Courtesy of Xerox Corporation, [A.19b] Courtesy of Epson America, Inc., [A.19c] Lexmark International, Inc., [A.19d] Lexmark International, Inc.

wet when it is sprayed onto the paper. Ink-jet printers (Figure A.19c) can be designed to print both black and white and colour. ***Laser printers*** are the most commonly used printers today. They use an electrostatic process to force ink onto the paper, literally "burning" the image onto the paper. The resulting high quality is considered necessary for almost all business letters and documents. Laser printers (Figure A.19d) can also produce colour images, but high-end colour laser printers can cost thousands of dollars.

Audio Output

In addition to transmitting text as output, a computer can transmit audio as output. With the use of small specialized speakers and a ***sound card***, a computer can produce stereo-quality sound. The computer translates digits into sound by sending data to a sound card that interprets these data into tones. The tones are then sent to the speakers for output. Musicians and composers often use this output to simulate a full orchestra when working on new or unfamiliar pieces of music.

Now that you understand how computer hardware works, we can discuss the types of computers that people and organizations typically use.

TYPES OF COMPUTERS

Over the last 60 years, IS hardware has gone through many radical changes. In the 1940s, almost all business and government IS consisted of file folders, filing cabinets, and document repositories. Huge rooms were dedicated to the storage of these records. Information was often difficult to find, and corporate knowledge and history were difficult to maintain. Only certain employees knew specific information. When these employees left the firm, so did all their corporate knowledge. The computer provided the solution to the information storage and retrieval problems facing organizations of the 1940s. Shifts in computing eras were facilitated by fundamental changes in the way computing technologies worked. Each of these fundamental changes is referred to as a distinct generation of computing. Table A.9 highlights the technology that defined the five generations of computing. We conclude by briefly describing the five general types of computers currently being used in organizations (see Table A.10).

Table A.9 ***Five generations of computing.***

Generation	Timeline	Major Event	Characteristics
1	1946–1958	Vacuum tubes	• Mainframe era begins • ENIAC and UNIVAC were developed
2	1958–1964	Transistors	• Mainframe era expands • UNIVAC is updated with transistors
3	1964–1990s	Integrated circuits	• Mainframe era ends • Personal computer era begins • IBM 360 with general purpose operating system • Microprocessor revolution: Intel, Microsoft, Apple, IBM PC, MS-DOS
4	1990s–2000	Multimedia and low cost PCs	• Personal computer era ends • Interpersonal computing era begins • High-speed microprocessor and networks • High-capacity storage • Low-cost, high-performance integrated video, audio, and data
5	2000–present	Widespread Internet accessibility	• Interpersonal computing era ends • Internetworking era begins • Ubiquitous access to Internet with a broad variety of devices • Prices continue to drop; performance continues to expand

Table A.10 *Characteristics of computers currently being used in organizations.*

Type of Computer	Number of Simultaneous Users	Physical Size	Typical Use	Memory	Typical Cost Range
Supercomputer	1-several	Like an automobile	Scientific research	2000+ GB	$1 000 000 to more than $20 000 000
Mainframe	1000+	Like a refrigerator	Large general-purpose business and government	Up to 100+ GB	$1 000 000 to more than $10 000 000
Midrange	4–200	Like a file cabinet	Midsize general-purpose business	Up to 10GB	$10 000 to more than $100 000
Workstation	1	Fits on a desktop	Engineering design	1GB to 4GB	$5000 to more than $50 000
Microcomputer	1	Handheld to fitting on a desktop	Personal productivity	512MB to 2GB	$500 to more than $5000

Supercomputers

The most powerful and expensive computers that exist today are called ***supercomputers***. Supercomputers are often used for scientific applications, solving massive computational problems that require large amounts of data. They can cost many millions of dollars. For example, Sandia National Laboratories uses a supercomputer to model the physics of nuclear explosions. This particular machine has several GB of RAM and the computational horsepower of more than 9000 Pentium processors. Pharmaceutical companies, such as Eli Lilly and Dow Chemical, use supercomputers to design and evaluate new combinations of chemical elements to quickly identify promising prescription drugs and treatments. IBM's "Blue Pacific" supercomputer operates 15 000 times faster than an average PC, with more than 5800 processors and 2.6 trillion bytes of memory. To achieve this incredible speed, supercomputers are equipped with numerous fast processors that work in parallel to execute several instructions simultaneously. An extensive staff is usually required to operate and maintain supercomputers and to support the researchers and scientists using them. Supercomputers often run only one application at a time in order to dedicate all processing capabilities to a single massive application. Figure A.20 shows a Cray supercomputer, one of the most popular computers in this class. In addition to Cray and IBM, leading producers of supercomputers are Hitachi, NEC, and Fujitsu.

Mainframes

The backbone of large corporate computing has historically been large, high-powered computers called ***mainframes***. These machines can be the size of a large refrigerator (and even larger), and they often cost several million dollars to purchase. Organizations normally use mainframe computers for processing large amounts of business data, and the machines are designed to support hundreds, or even thousands, of users simultaneously. In addition to businesses, many federal and state governments use mainframe computers to manage the massive amount of data generated by day-to-day governmental activities. Federal agencies, such as the Canada Revenue Agency (CRA), have several mainframe computers to handle the massive databases related to individual and corporate payroll and tax information. Large corporations, such as Avis, Air Canada, and Fairmont Hotels, use mainframes to perform repetitive tasks, such as processing

Figure A.20 The Cray supercomputer.

Source: Cray, Inc.

Figure A.21 IBM mainframe computer.

Source: Courtesy of IBM Corporate Archives

reservations. Unisys and IBM are the largest producers of mainframes (see Figure A.21).

Midrange Computers

Midrange computers, often referred to as minicomputers, are scaled-down versions of mainframes that were created for companies that did not have the budgets for mainframes and did not need that amount of computing power. In the last 10 years, the distinction between large midrange computers and small mainframes has blurred in both performance and price. Nonetheless, midrange computers have become integral to many smaller and midsized organizations and typically cost tens to hundreds of thousands of dollars, supporting from 4 to 200 users simultaneously. As with mainframes, IBM is a leader in the midrange computer market, with its AS/400 model. Manufacturers such as Hewlett-Packard also service this market. The midrange market as a whole has been declining as workstations and microcomputers have become faster and have absorbed some of the functionality once required of midrange and mainframe computers.

Figure A.22 A Sun workstation is typically used by engineers.

Source: © Getty Images, Inc.

Workstations

Workstations are a special class of microcomputer (as is your PC); they are designed for individuals and have the power of some midrange computers, but they fit on a desktop. Computer hardware companies such as Silicon Graphics, Sun Microsystems, and Hewlett-Packard are leaders in this market. Workstations have an extremely fast CPU (or multiple CPUs), large capacities of RAM and secondary storage, and high-quality video displays, and cost between \$5000 and \$50 000. Figure A.22 shows a Sun SPARCstation, one of the most popular computers in this class. Workstations are often used by engineers to design new products using processing-intensive applications, such as computer-aided design (CAD); by financial analysts modelling stock market fluctuations; and by researchers working with large, complex, computationally intensive applications. For example, researchers at NASA are using workstations to study the effects of global warming on ocean surface temperatures.

Microcomputers

Microcomputers, also referred to as ***personal computers (PCs)***, fit on desktops, generally cost between \$500 and \$5000, and are used in homes and offices (see Figure A.23). Microcomputers can be relatively stationary desktop models or portable, notebook-sized computers that weigh about 2.5 kg or less. High-end microcomputers can cost more than \$5000 and rival the power and speed of low-end workstations. High-end microcomputers are often used as network and web servers that manage shared resources such as printers and large databases or deliver content over the Internet. In the last 20 years the popularity of microcomputers has exploded. Within organizations, microcomputers

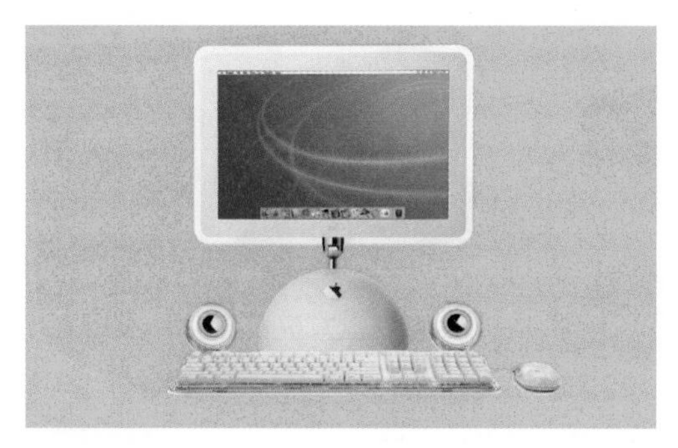

Figure A.23 A personal computer.

Source: Apple Computer, Inc.

are the most commonly used computing technology for knowledge workers, and they have become as commonplace as the telephone. In fact, more microcomputers than televisions are now sold in the United States each year. Let us delve a bit deeper into the development of microcomputers.

Network Computers

A ***network computer*** (sometimes called a *thin client*) is a microcomputer with minimal memory and storage, designed to connect to networks, especially the Internet, to use the resources provided by servers. The concept of network computing is to reduce the obsolescence and maintenance of PCs by allowing inexpensive machines to access servers that deploy resources—software programs, printers, and so on—to all machines on the network. Many feel that network computing is the wave of the future because the machines are less expensive than typical PCs and because they can be administered and updated from a central network server. Oracle and Sun Microsystems are two companies aggressively pushing the network-computing concept (see Figure A.24).

Figure A.24 A Sun Microsystems network computer.

Source: Chris LaGrand/Getty Images, Inc.

Portable Computers

When computers appeared that could fit on a desktop, users considered them the ultimate in lighter, smaller, and handier machines. Then came laptop computers you could carry, but the first models were heavy and bulky. Next on the portable computer scene were notebook computers that could fit in a backpack or briefcase. Today battery-powered laptop and notebook computers are popular for both business and personal use (see Table A.11 for a summary of tradeoffs between desktop and portable computers). The computers are equipped with a flat display panel, fold into a small, convenient carry case, and can weigh as little as 2.5 kg or less. With a portable computer, you can use a keyboard and a mouse, as well as a trackball, touch pad, or other built-in pointing device. Most portable computers come equipped with internal modems and USB ports and can connect to printers, scanners, or other peripherals. Many students, employees, and others now use a portable computer as their only PC rather than buying both a desktop and a portable machine. The two most popular forms of portable computers—notebooks and handhelds—are described below.

Notebook computers. Mobile computers once weighed 9 kg (20 lb) and were portable only in the sense that they could be moved—with difficulty—from one location to another. Fifteen years ago, machines evolved to what was referred to as a laptop, weighed around 4.5 kg (10 lb), and could be folded up and carried like

Table A.11 ***Tradeoffs between desktop and portable computers.***

Desktop Computer	Portable Computer
One location for use	Mobile—any location for use
Lower price	Higher price
Expandable	Very limited expandability
Better ergonomics—full size/high resolution colour screen, large keyboard, and so on	Cramped ergonomics—small screen, limited colour quality, small keyboard, awkward pointing device, and so on
Relatively easy to service/repair	Hard to service/repair

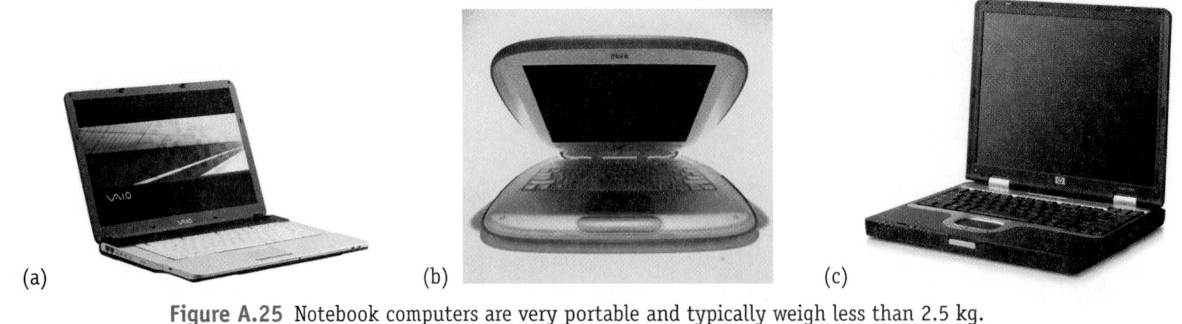

(a) (b) (c)

Figure A.25 Notebook computers are very portable and typically weigh less than 2.5 kg.

Sources: (a) © 2005 Sony Electronics Inc., (b) © Nicholas Eveleigh/Superstock, (c) photo supplied courtesy of HP

a briefcase. The trend has been toward smaller, lighter, yet ever more powerful ***notebook computers*** that weigh 2.5 kg (5 lb) or less and can be easily carried in a briefcase or backpack (see Figure A.25).

Tablet PCs. A ***tablet PC*** is a type of notebook computer that accepts input from an electronic pen (called a stylus) or a keyboard. There are two types of tablet PCs, slate and convertible (see Figure A.26). Slate models contain a variety of ports for plugging in external keyboards and other devices as needed. Typically, users interact with a slate tablet PC by using the stylus, using handwriting-recognition software to enter text and interpret commands. Slate models are particularly useful for applications where having a keyboard would be too bulky or it would be awkward to type. Alternatively, convertible models are quite similar to existing notebook computers but also have displays that swivel and fold flat to cover their keyboard. When *converted* into a tablet PC, they resemble a "fat" slate tablet PC.

Both slate and convertible models have a special type of screen that captures the movement of the stylus. Because tablet PCs have been designed to support mobile professionals in the work environment, all typically have built-in wireless Ethernet access for connecting to the Internet. To date, there are mixed reviews as to how effectively first-generation tablet PCs are performing in the workplace. Some feel that tablet PCs are still too heavy, that their batteries do not last long enough, and that the text-recognition capabilities are adequate at best. Nevertheless, experts feel that these limitations will be quickly overcome so that tablet PCs become a clear alternative to traditional notebook computers.

Handheld computers. The first handheld computers were introduced around 1994, but they failed to live up to expectations, perhaps because consumers had expected that they would replace PCs. Then in 1996, Palm introduced a handheld computer that was never

(a)

(b)

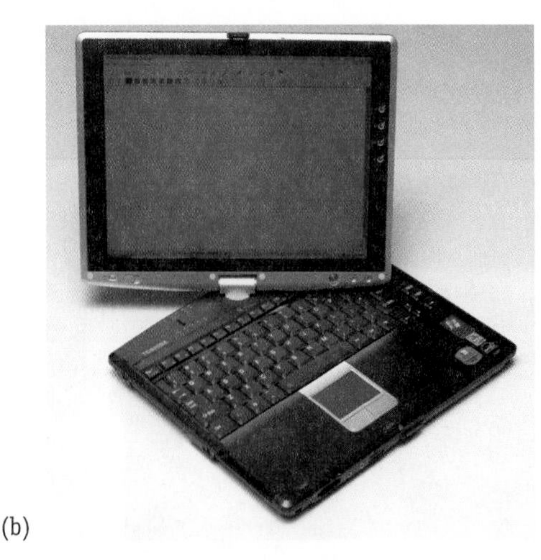

Figure A.26 Tablet PCs are designed to support mobile professionals.

Sources: (a) © James Leynse/CORBIS, (b) photo by Business Wire via Getty Images intended to replace the PC but performed some essential computing tasks so well that users could often leave their laptop and notebook computers at home. Since then, billed first as information appliances, then as ***personal digital assistants (PDAs)***, handheld computers have filled a niche in the portable computer market. Today, the capabilities of many PDAs are beginning to rival the functionality of desktop PCs. For example, Compaq's iPAQ Pocket PC allows users to send and receive e-mail, work on documents and spreadsheets, surf the web, and perform countless other activities (see Figure A.27).

As you can see, things have really evolved since the early mainframe days. In most organizations today, IS encompasses a diverse range of computing technologies, from supercomputers, mainframes, and midrange computers to workstations, PCs, and PDAs. For individuals, computers have become commonplace, with many families having several computers. Using history as a guide, it is a good bet that computing hardware will continue to evolve at a rapid pace, having some intended and unforeseen consequences for all of us.

(a)

(b)

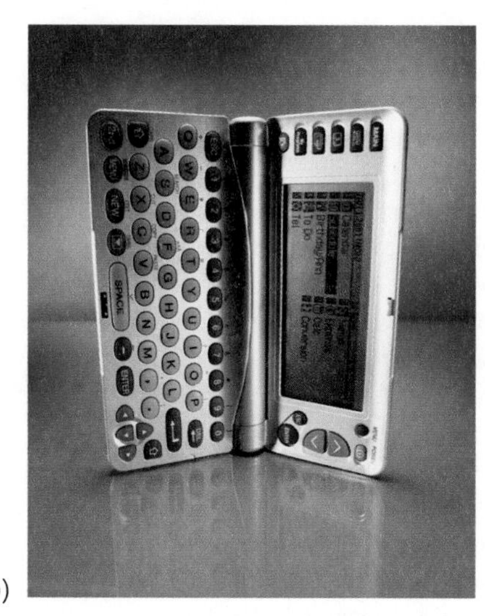

Figure A.27 Personal digital assistants allow you to have a very powerful computer in the palm of your hand.

Sources: (a) Photo by Stephen Chernin/Getty Images, (b) © Nicholas Eveleigh/Superstock

KEY POINTS REVIEW

1. **Describe key elements of information systems hardware.** Information systems hardware is classified into three types: input, processing, and output technologies. Input hardware consists of devices used to enter information into a computer. Processing hardware transforms inputs into outputs. The central processing unit (CPU) is the device that performs this transformation, with the help of several other closely related devices that store and recall information. Finally, output-related hardware focuses on delivering information in a usable format to users.
2. **List and describe the types of computers that are being used in organizations today.** Computers come in all shapes, sizes, degrees of power, and prices. The five general classes of computers are supercomputer, mainframe, midrange, workstation, and microcomputer. A supercomputer is the most expensive and most powerful kind of computer; it is primarily used to assist in solving massive research and scientific problems. A mainframe is a very large computer that is the main, central computing system for major corporations and governmental agencies. A midrange computer offers lower performance than mainframes but higher performance than microcomputers. Minicomputers are typically used for engineering and midsized business applications. A workstation is a very high-performance microcomputer, typically used to support individual engineers and analysts in solving highly computational problems. A microcomputer is used for personal computing, for small business computing, and as a workstation attached to large computers or to other small computers on a network. Portable computers—notebook computers, tablet PCs, and handheld computers—are a special type of microcomputer designed to support mobility.

KEY TERMS

arithmetic logic unit (ALU) 352
ASCII (American Standard Code for Information Interchange) 350
audio 346
batch input 344
binary code 348
bits 349
byte 349
bytes per inch (BPI) 358
cache 353
CD-R (compact disc—recordable) 357
CD-ROM (compact disc—read-only memory) 357
CD-RW (compact disc—rewritable) 357
central processing unit (CPU) 343
characters per inch (CPI) 358
clock speed 353
clock tick 353
control unit 352
density 358
diskettes 356
dot matrix printers 359
double-inline memory module (DIMM) 354
DVD-ROM (digital video disk—read-only memory) 357
EBCDIC (Extended Binary-Coded Decimal Interchange Code) 350
ergonomics 344
extended ASCII 350
external or secondary cache 354
flash drives 354
flash memory 354
hard disk 356
hard drives 356
head crash 356
ink-jet printers 359
input devices 343
internal cache 354
keyboard 344
language translator 349
laser printers 360
liquid crystal display (LCD) 358
machine language 349
magnetic tapes 358
magneto-optical (MO) disks 357
mainframes 361
microcomputers 362
midrange computers 362
monitors 358
Moore's Law 352
motherboard 351
musical instrument digital interface (MIDI) 347
network computer 363
notebook computer 364
optical disk 357
output devices 343
personal computers (PC) 362
personal digital assistants (PDA) 365
pointing devices 344
ports 358
power supply 351
primary memory 354
primary storage 354
processing devices 343
RAID (redundant array of independent disks) 356
random-access memory (RAM) 354
read-only memory (ROM) 354
read/write heads 355
registers 353
scanners 344
secondary nonvolatile storage 355
smart cards 346
sound card 360
speech recognition 347
streaming media 348
streaming video 348
supercomputers 361
system clock 353
system unit 350
tablet PC 364
text-recognition software 345
Unicode 350
video 346
volatile 354
workstation 362
Zip drives 356

REVIEW QUESTIONS

1. Information systems hardware is classified into what three major types?
2. Describe various methods for entering data into and interacting with a computer.
3. Define ergonomics, and give examples of how repetitive stress injuries could be reduced.
4. How do computers represent internal information, and how is this different from the ways in which humans typically communicate information to each other?
5. Describe the system unit and its key components.
6. What determines the speed of a CPU?
7. How do a computer's primary storage, secondary storage, ROM, and RAM interact?
8. Compare and contrast the different types of secondary data storage.
9. What are output devices? Describe various methods for providing computer output.
10. Describe the different types of computers and their key distinguishing characteristics.

SELF-STUDY QUESTIONS

Visit the Companion website for this text for additional Self-Study Questions: **www.pearsoned.ca/jessup**.

1. A system unit contains all of the following except __________.

A. CD-ROM
B. CPU
C. power supply
D. monitor

2. Which of the following is not an input device?

A. touch pad
B. touch screen
C. sound board
D. light pen

3. Which of the following is an example of hardware?

A. an operating system
B. Microsoft Suite
C. system software
D. CPU

4. Which of the following is an output device?

A. laser printer
B. touch screen
C. video camera
D. keyboard

5. Which of the following could be ergonomically designed?

A. keyboard
B. chair
C. monitor
D. all of the above

6. __________ can convert handwritten text into computer-based characters.

A. Scanners
B. Bar code/optical character readers
C. Text-recognition software
D. Audio video

7. A __________ card is a special credit card with a microprocessor chip and memory circuits.

A. smart
B. master
C. universal
D. proprietary

8. Which of the following has the largest storage, along with video capacity?

A. CD-ROM
B. floppy disk
C. DVD-ROM
D. cache memory

9. Which of the following types of computer is designed for personal and small business usage?

A. supercomputer
B. microcomputer
C. workstation
D. mainframe

10. A __________ is the most powerful and expensive computer today.

A. HAL
B. mainframe
C. personal digital assistant
D. supercomputer

PROBLEMS AND EXERCISES

1. Match the following terms with the appropriate definitions:

_____ Cache memory
_____ Batch input
_____ Smart card
_____ Ergonomics
_____ Audio
_____ DVD-ROM
_____ Motherboard
_____ Streaming video
_____ Network computer
_____ Flash memory

a. A special type of credit card with a magnetic strip that includes a microprocessor chip and memory circuits
b. A small block of memory used by the central processor to store those instructions most recently or most often used
c. An optical storage device that has more storage space than a diskette or CD-ROM and uses a shorter wavelength laser beam, which allows more optical pits to be deposited on the disk
d. A sequence of moving images, sent in a compressed form over the Internet and displayed on the receiver's screen as the images arrive
e. The design of computer hardware and work environments that minimize health risks such as repetitive stress injuries
f. A large printed plastic or fibreglass circuit board that contains all the components that do the actual processing work of the computer and holds or connects to all the computer's electronic components
g. A type of input for large amounts of routine information
h. A microcomputer with minimal memory and storage designed to connect to networks to use the resources provided by servers
i. Memory that can be repeatedly written to and erased like RAM, but unlike RAM it retains its information after power is turned off
j. Sound that has been digitized for storage and replay on the computer

2. Imagine that you have decided it is time to purchase a new computer. Analyze your purchase options with regard to using this computer for personal productivity versus business productivity. What differences might your potential usage make on your hardware choices? Why?

3. Imagine that you have just informed your supervisor that you will need to purchase new computers for yourself and three fellow employees. Your supervisor states that she has heard in the news that computer prices are dropping constantly, and she feels that you should wait a bit before making this purchase. She adds that you can still be 100 percent effective with your current computer and software. Develop a counterargument explaining why you should make the purchase now instead of waiting. Will this be a hard sell? Why or why not?

4. Go visit a computer shop or look on the web for mice or touch pads. What is new about how these input devices look or how they are used? What are some of the advantages and disadvantages of each device?

5. What types of printers are most common today? What is the cost of a colour printer versus a black-and-white one? Compare and contrast laser and ink-jet printers in terms of speed, cost, and quality output. What kind of printer would you buy or have you bought?

6. What happens when a computer runs out of RAM? Can more RAM be added? Is there a limit? How does cache memory relate to RAM? Why is RAM so important in today's modern IS world? Search the web for RAM retailers. Compare their prices and options.

7. Do you feel that floppy disks will be obsolete sometime in the near future? Why or why not? What storage and retrieval options are available in addition to CD-ROMs and floppy disks? What are you currently using, and what would you like to purchase?

8. Back in the 1970s, rockets were sent to the moon with the amount of computing power found in today's microcomputers. Now, these microcomputers seem to be outdating themselves every 2 years. Will this era of continuous improvement end? Why or why not? If so, when?

9. Do you have a Palm handheld or some other type of PDA, or know of someone who does? What functions do PDAs offer? Look on the web or go to the mall to shop for one. Are the prices decreasing? At what point do you plan to purchase one?

10. Interview an IS manager within an organization that you are familiar with. Determine what issues played a role in the latest IS hardware purchase this person made. Other than budget, what issues do you think should be considered?

11. Based on your experiences with different input devices, which do you like the best and least? Why? Are your preferences based on the devices' design or usability, or are they based on the integration of the device with the entire information system?

12. Visit a company that uses several different types of computers. Which types do they use? What categories of computers are used at this company (e.g., workstations)? Does the company have any plans to expand its computer usage to another category? Why or why not?

13. In simple language, explain what happens with the keystrokes that you type into a computer using a keyboard. Be sure to discuss memory, processing, and inputs. Draw any diagrams that may help you with this explanation.

14. Check the web for information on different types of Apple computers. What is new? What brands of Windows-compatible computers have you used or purchased? What are you currently using? What influences your computer purchasing decisions?

15. Choose a few of the computer hardware vendors that sell computers to the general public. These include Dell, Compaq, IBM, Gateway, Apple, and many lesser-known brands. Using each company's home page on the web, determine what options these vendors provide for input, processing, and output devices. Does it seem that this company has a broad range of choices for its customers? Is there something that you did not find available from this company? Present your findings in a 10-minute presentation to the rest of the class.

ANSWERS TO THE SELF-STUDY QUESTIONS

1. C, p. 350 2. C, p. 343 3. D, p. 343 4. A, p. 343 5. D, p. 344
6. C, p. 345 7. A, p. 346 8. C, p. 357 9. B, p. 362 10. D, p. 361

Appendix B: Information Systems Software

Preview

Software directs the functions of all computer hardware. Without software, the biggest, fastest, most powerful computer in the world is nothing more than a fancy paperweight. After reading this appendix, you will be able to do the following:

1. Describe the common functions of systems software.
2. Describe the various types of application software.
3. Describe the characteristics of various types of programming languages and application development environments.

If you use an ATM to withdraw money, word processing to prepare papers, or e-mail to communicate with your classmates and professors, you rely on software to execute instructions. Software is also intertwined with all types of products and services—toys, music, appliances, health care, and countless other products. As a result, the term "software" can be confusing because it is used in many different ways. We will unravel this confusion in the next section by describing the different types of software that are used in today's organizations.

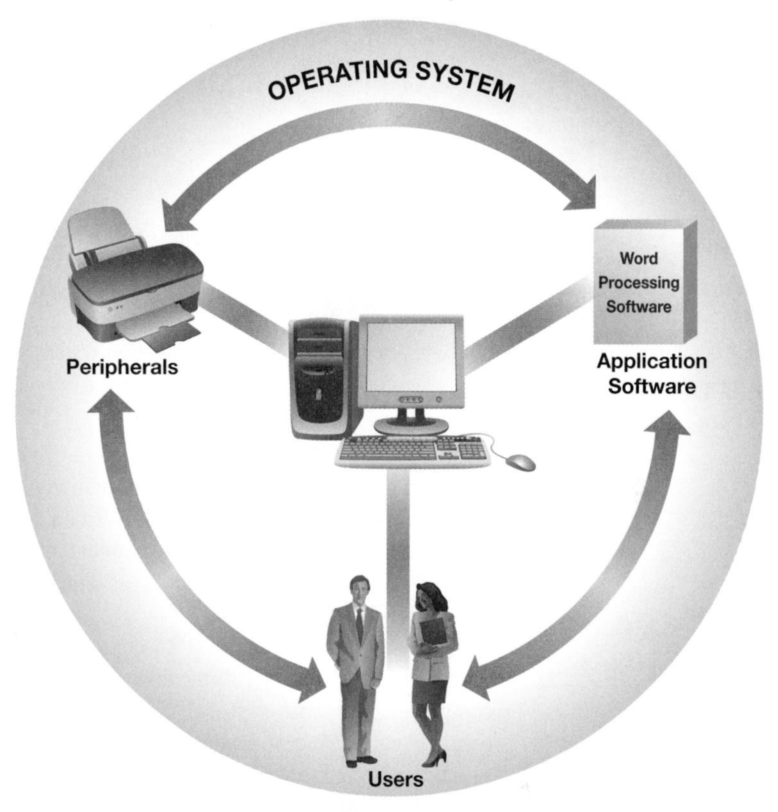

Figure B.1 Operating systems coordinate the interaction between users, application software, hardware, and peripherals.

KEY INFORMATION SYSTEMS SOFTWARE COMPONENTS

Software consists of programs, or sets of instructions, that tell the computer to perform certain processing functions. Software's job is to provide instructions that allow all the hardware components in your computer system to speak to each other. The two basic types of information systems software are systems software and application software. In the next section, we discuss systems software and how it supports the overall operation of the computer hardware.

Systems Software/Operating System

Systems software is the collection of programs that control the basic operations of computer hardware. A common form of systems software is an ***operating system***. Operating systems coordinate the interaction between hardware devices (e.g., the CPU and the monitor), peripherals (e.g., printers), application software (e.g., a word processing program), and users, as shown in Figure B.1.

Operating systems are often written in assembly language, a very low-level computer programming language that allows the computer to operate quickly and efficiently. The operating system is designed to insulate you from this low-level language and make computer operations unobtrusive. The operating system performs all the day-to-day operations that we often take for granted when using a computer, such as updating the system clock, printing documents, or saving information to a disk. Just as our brain and nervous system control our body's breathing, heartbeat, and senses without our conscious realization, the systems software controls the computer's basic operations transparently.

Common Systems Software Functions

Many tasks are common to almost all computers. These include getting input from a keyboard or mouse, reading and/or writing data

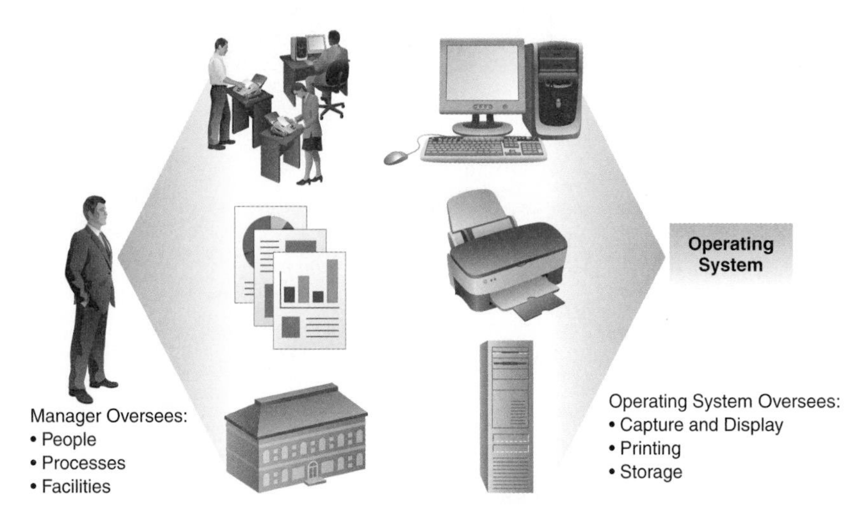

Figure B.2 A manager oversees organizational resources, whereas an operating system oversees computer resources.

from a storage device (such as a hard disk drive), and presenting information to you via a monitor. Each of these tasks is performed by the operating system, just as a manager of a firm oversees people and processes (as depicted in Figure B.2).

For example, if you want to copy a word processing file from a floppy disk onto your computer, operating systems make this very easy for you. Using an operating system such as Microsoft Windows, you simply use the mouse to point at a graphic icon of the word processing file on the floppy disk, then click and drag it onto an icon of your hard disk. That is all it takes to copy the file on the floppy disk to your hard drive. The operating system makes this process appear easy. However, underlying the icons and simple dragging operations is a complex set of coded instructions that tells the electronic components of the computer that you are transferring a set of bits and bytes located on the floppy disk to a location on your internal hard disk. Imagine if you had to program those sets of instructions every time you wanted to copy a file from one place to another. The operating system manages and executes these types of system operations so that you can spend your time on more important tasks.

Figure B.3 The Windows operating environment uses a graphical user interface.

The operating system performs many different tasks, including the following:

- Booting (or starting) your computer
- Reading programs into memory and managing memory allocation
- Managing where programs and files are located in secondary storage
- Maintaining the structure of directories and subdirectories
- Formatting disks
- Controlling the computer monitor
- Sending documents to the printer

Interfaces: Command Versus GUI

The operating system is stored on disk, and a portion of it is transferred into temporary memory when the computer boots up. After the operating system is in memory, it begins to manage the computer and provide an ***interface***. Different operating systems and application programs use different types of user interfaces, with the most typical being command, menu, or GUI. It is through this interface that you interact with the computer. The ***command-based interface*** requires that you type text commands into the computer to perform basic operations. You could type the command "DELETE File1" to erase the file with the name "File1." MS-DOS (Microsoft Disk Operating System) is an example of an operating system that uses a command-based user interface. A ***menu interface*** presents a list of options from which a user selects to invoke a command or system operation. Menus are popular because users only have to understand simple signposts and route options to navigate through a system.

The most common type of interface for the PC is called a ***graphical user interface (GUI)*** (see Figure B.3). The GUI uses pictures, icons, and menus to send instructions from the user to the computer system. GUIs eliminate the need for users to input arcane commands into the computer and are, therefore, a popular

Table B.1 ***Common operating systems.***

Operating System	Description
MVS/ESA (Multiple Virtual Storage/Enterprise Systems Architecture)	A highly reliable proprietary operating system developed in 1974 that is used on large IBM mainframe computers; it is being rapidly superseded by IBM's newer mainframe operating system, OS/390
UNIX	A multiuser, multitasking operating system that is available for a wide variety of computer platforms from vendors such as Sun Microsystems, Hewlett-Packard, and Silicon Graphics
MS-DOS (Microsoft Disk Operating System)	A command-based operating system used on IBM-compatible PCs that was first introduced in 1981
Windows	The most popular operating system in the world, operating on network servers, desktop PCs, notebooks, and handheld computers
OS/2	An operating system developed in 1988 by IBM for powerful PCs; can run applications written for OS/2, MS-DOS, Java, or Windows
Mac OS	The first commercially popular graphical-based operating system, making its debut in 1984, running on Apple Macintosh personal computers
Linux	A freely distributable operating system designed in 1991 by a Finnish university student, known for its security, low price, and adaptability to a variety of hardware platforms; by 2000, Linux powered 31 per cent of all web servers

interface. Examples of systems software using a GUI are the Windows and Macintosh operating systems.

Popular Operating Systems

Just as there are many kinds of computers, there are many different kinds of operating systems (see Table B.1). In general, operating systems—whether for large mainframe computers or for small notebook computers—perform similar operations. Obviously, large multiuser supercomputers are more complex than small desktop systems; therefore, the operating system must account for and manage that complexity. However, the basic purpose of all operating systems is the same.

Utilities

Another set of programs that fall under the umbrella of systems software are utilities. ***Utilities*** or ***utility programs*** are designed to manage computer resources and files. Some are included in operating systems software. Others must be purchased separately and installed on your computer. Table B.2 provides a sample of a few utility programs that are considered essential.

As mentioned earlier, systems software is only one type of software that is used to run a computer. In the next section, we discuss the second type, application software, that is used in today's information systems.

Application Software

Unlike systems software, which manages the operation of the computer, ***application software*** lets a user perform a specific task, such as writing a business letter, processing the payroll, managing a stock portfolio, or manipulating a series of forecasts to come up with the most efficient allocation of resources for a project. The application program interacts with the systems software, which, in turn, interacts with the computer hardware.

The two basic types of application software are the following:

- Customized, or proprietary, software—developed specifically by or for a particular organization
- Commercial software—purchased off the shelf and used by a variety of people and/or organizations to meet their specific needs

These two types of software will be discussed next.

Customized Application Software

Customized application software is developed to meet the specifications of an organization.

Table B.2 ***Common types of computer software utilities.***

Utility	Description
Backup	Archives files from the hard disk to a diskette or to tapes
File defragmentation	Converts a fragmented file stored on your hard disk (one not stored contiguously) into one that will load and be manipulated more rapidly
Disk and data recovery	Allows the recovery of damaged or erased information from hard and floppy disks
Data compression	Compresses data by substituting a short code for frequently repeated patterns of data, much like the machine shorthand used by court reporters, allowing more data to be stored on a disk
File conversion	Translates a file from one format to another, so it can be used by an application other than the one used to create it
Antivirus	Monitors and removes viruses—lines of code designed to disrupt the computer's operation and make your life miserable
Device drivers	Allows new hardware added to your computer system, such as a game controller, printer, scanner, and so on, to function with your operating system
Spam blockers	Monitors your incoming e-mail messages and filters or blocks the message from arriving
Spyware detection and removal	Monitors and removes spyware from your computer (see Chapters 4 and 9)
Media players	Allows music in formats such as MP3, WMA, or WAV or video in formats such as MPEG, AVI, ASF to be listened to or watched on a computer

This software may be developed in-house by the company's own information systems staff or it may be contracted, or outsourced, to a specialized vendor charged with developing the software to the company's contractual specifications. Customized application software has two primary advantages over commercial software:

1. Customizability—It can be tailored to meet unique user requirements. For example, suppose a retailer needs a kiosk in its store to help shoppers locate specific products. Many shoppers may not be familiar with computers and may be intimidated by operating a keyboard or a mouse. With customized software, the company could develop a touch screen input interface, with which users could simply point at objects in a catalogue. The computer could then process this information and tell the user that, for example, women's shoes are located on the first floor in the southeast corner and provide a map of the store.
2. Problem specificity—The company pays only for the features specifically required for its users. For example, company- or industry-specific terms or acronyms can be included in the program, as can unique types of required reports. Such specificity is not possible in off-the-shelf programs that are targeted to a general audience.

Off-the-Shelf Application Software

Although customized software has advantages, it is not automatically the best choice for an organization. ***Off-the-shelf application software*** is typically used to support common business processes that do not require any specific tailoring. Table B.3 summarizes advantages of the off-the-shelf application software.

Combining Customized and Off-the-Shelf Application Software

It is possible to combine the advantages of customized and off-the-shelf software. Companies can purchase off-the-shelf software and then modify it for their own use. For example, a retailer may want to purchase an off-the-shelf inventory management program and then modify it to account for the specific products, outlets, and reports it needs to conduct its day-to-day business. In some cases, the company selling the off-the-shelf software

Table B.3 ***Advantages of off-the-shelf application software.***

Advantage	Description
Low cost	Because off-the-shelf applications are developed for general markets, development costs are distributed across a large customer base.
Faster procurement	Customized software takes a notoriously long time to develop, whereas users can simply purchase off-the-shelf software and install it.
High quality	Because off-the-shelf software typically has a large customer base, developers continuously invest in refinement and testing.
Low risk	Off-the-shelf application software is relatively easy to evaluate through in-house testing, customer feedback, or software reviews in the popular and trade press.

makes these customized changes for a fee. Other vendors, however, do not allow their software to be modified.

Examples of Information Systems Application Software

Application software is categorized by its design and by the type of application or task it supports. The task-oriented categories for application software are (1) large business systems and office automation, and (2) personal productivity tools. Applications in the business category are purchased or developed by the organization to support the central, organization-wide operations of the company. Those in the office automation or personal productivity category are tools used to support the daily work activities of individuals and small groups. We will describe and provide examples of each type of application software in the following sections.

Business Information Systems

Business information systems are applications developed to perform organization-wide operations. For example, most organizations have payroll applications to process their payrolls. A payroll application may take as inputs individual time sheets. These time sheets can be fed through an optical scanner to create a file of time sheet data, organized by employee social security numbers. The application software can look at each employee's pay rate and hours worked to calculate a gross pay figure. The application software can also calculate the federal, provincial, and local taxes that must be deducted from the employee's gross pay. After calculating all deductions, the application arrives at a net pay owed each employee.

Once the application has taken all time sheets, organized and sorted them by employee, and calculated gross pay, deductions, and net pay for each employee, the figures form a payroll master file. The payroll application creates the payroll master file and backs it up, perhaps on a tape drive on a mainframe computer. To process cheques, the payroll application creates a cheque and register file that includes the date, the employee's name, the social security number, and the employee's net pay. The register file contains all the previous elements, along with the time period, gross pay, and deductions for that time period for the employee's records. The cheque file is sorted by department, and cheques are printed. Registers (a record of the cheques printed) are also sorted and printed for distribution to employees.

This payroll process may not seem to be complex to conduct for only two or three employees. However, consider a large governmental organization that must process and account for thousands of employees' cheques. Suddenly, a relatively simple process becomes a potential information-processing nightmare. Application software easily manages these very large data-intensive operations.

Mega-retailers such as Sears and Lands' End must manage millions of pieces of merchandise and millions of transactions on a daily basis (Figure B.4). These businesses rely on inventory management, order processing, billing, and shipping applications to conduct their operations. Without sophisticated, large-scale business application software, these businesses could not survive.

Office Automation/Personal Productivity Application Software

The second category of application software is called ***office automation*** or ***personal productivity software***. Individuals or groups who want to accomplish a wide range of tasks, from word processing to graphics to e-mail, use this type of software. Many of the large, well-known

Figure B.4 Large retailers manage millions of transactions per day.

Source: © Land's End, Inc. Used with permission.

software companies, including Microsoft, Corel, Netscape, and Lotus, produce office automation software. Table B.4 outlines several popular personal productivity tools. See Chapter 6 for more information on this topic.

Open Source Software

Open source software refers to systems software, applications, and programming languages in which the source code (the actual program code) is freely available to the general public for use and/or modification. Open source software is typically developed by a group of interested parties—individuals and organizations—who wish to improve and extend the software and share these changes with all interested parties. The open source concept has grown out of the broader technology community as a backlash to large software companies that dominate this industry. Nevertheless, many large mainstream software companies are actively involved in the open source community. For example, IBM is playing a leading role in evolving the Linux operating system. Likewise, Sun Microsystems is active in developing and extending the OpenOffice personal productivity software environment.

People and organizations that actively participate in the open source software communities have established a certification process, called the Open Source Initiative (OSI), that verifies that software meets a set of standards. To gain OSI certification, a piece of software must meet the following criteria:

- The author or holder of the licence of the source code cannot collect royalties on the distribution of the program.
- The distributed program must make the source code accessible to the user.
- The author must allow modifications and derivations of the work under the program's original name.
- No person, group, or field of endeavour can be denied access to the program.
- The rights attached to the program must not depend on the program's being part of a particular software distribution.
- The licensed software cannot place restrictions on other software that is distributed with it.

The primary goals of the OSI movement are to gain widespread participation from a broad range of programmers in order to more quickly evolve a piece of software's capabilities and to

Table B.4 ***Some examples of popular personal productivity tools.***

Tool	Examples
Word processor	Microsoft Word, Corel WordPerfect, Lotus Word Pro, Linux OpenOffice Writer
Spreadsheet	Microsoft Excel, Lotus 1-2-3, Linux OpenOffice Calc
Database management system	Borland Paradox, Microsoft Access, Borland dbase, Microsoft FoxPro, Lotus Approach, Linux OpenOffice Database Access
Presentation software	Microsoft PowerPoint, Software Publishing Corporation Harvard Graphics, Lotus Freelance Graphics, Linux OpenOffice Impress
E-mail	Microsoft Outlook and Outlook Express, Novell Groupwise, Lotus Notes
Web browser	Netscape Navigator, Microsoft Internet Explorer, Firefox, Opera
Chat	Window Messenger, Yahoo! Messenger, xchat, Trillian
Calendaring and contact management	Lotus Notes, Microsoft Outlook and Outlook Express

more readily find programming flaws. By having a broad and active community of programmers readily share and examine each other's work, proponents of this concept believe that improvements will happen at a faster pace. With the broad and growing success of Linux and OpenOffice, it is clear that open source software is becoming a clear alternative for individuals and organizations to consider when selecting a variety of software products.

PROGRAMMING LANGUAGES AND DEVELOPMENT ENVIRONMENTS

Each piece of application software we have discussed in this chapter is based on some programming language. A programming language is the computer language the software vendor uses to write application programs. For application software such as spreadsheets or database management systems, the underlying programming language is invisible to the user. However, programmers in an organization's information systems group and, in some instances, end users can use programming languages to develop their own specialized applications. Many different types of programming languages exist, each with its own strengths and weaknesses. Popular languages used in businesses and industry today are summarized in Table B.5.

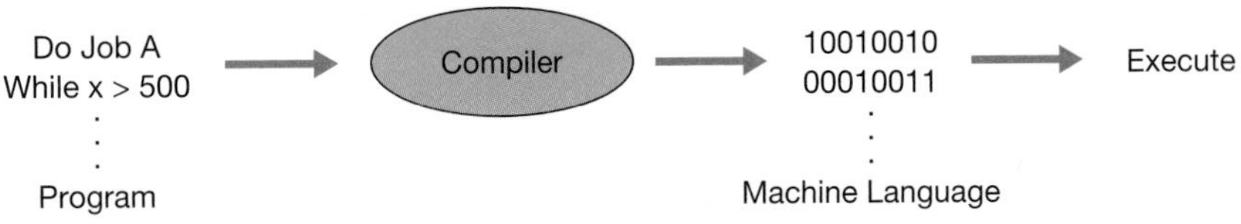

Figure B.5 A compiler translates the entire computer program into machine language, and then the CPU executes the machine language program.

Compilers and Interpreters

Programs created using programming languages must be translated into code—called assembly or ***machine language***—that the hardware can understand. Most programming languages are translated into machine languages through a program called a ***compiler***, as depicted in Figure B.5. The compiler takes an entire program written in a programming language, such as C, and converts it into a completely new program in machine language that can be read and executed directly by the computer. Use of a compiler is a two-stage process. First, the compiler translates the computer program into

Table B.5 ***Popular programming languages.***

Language	Application	Description
BASIC	General purpose	Beginner's All-Purpose Symbolic Interaction Code. An easy-to-learn language, BASIC works well on most PCs.
C/C++	General purpose	C++ is a newer version of C. Developed at AT&T Bell Labs. Complex languages used for a wide range of system and application programming.
COBOL	Business	Common Business-Oriented Language. Developed in 1960. It was the first language for developing business software. COBOL is used for most business transaction processing applications on mainframes.
FORTRAN	Scientific	FORmula TRANslator. The first commercial high-level language, developed by IBM in the 1950s. Designed for scientific, mathematical, and engineering applications.
Pascal	Teaching structured programming	Named after mathematician Blaise Pascal. Uses a building block approach to programming. Useful in developing large programs.
HTML	World Wide Web	Hypertext Markup Language. The most widely used language for developing web pages. Markup languages simplify pages for transmission by using symbols that tell what document elements should look like when displayed.
Java	World Wide Web	An object-oriented programming language developed at Sun Microsystems in the early 1990s. It is a popular programming language for the Internet because it is highly transportable from one make of computer to another.
LISP	Artificial intelligence	LISt Processor. Dates from the late 1950s. One of the main languages used to develop applications in artificial intelligence. Also the language for high-speed arcade graphics games.

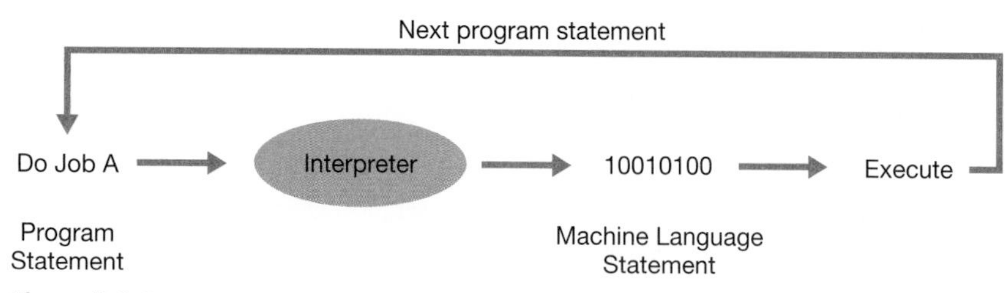

Figure B.6 Interpreters read, translate, and execute one line of source code at a time.

```
SELECT LAST FIRST
FROM CUSTOMER
WHERE CREDIT_LIMIT = 100
```

```
NEVO LIV
BROHMAN DAVID
BJERKAN HEIDI
JESSUP JAMIE
VALACICH JAMES
WADE CHRISTOPHER
```

Figure B.7 A 4GL query using SQL that requests that the LAST and FIRST name of those that have a CREDIT_LIMIT equal to $100 be displayed from a database called CUSTOMER.

machine language, and then the CPU executes the machine language program.

Some programming environments do not compile the entire program into machine language. Instead, each statement of the program is converted into machine language and executed one statement at a time, as depicted in Figure B.6. The type of program that does the conversion and execution is called an ***interpreter***. Programming languages can be either compiled or interpreted.

Programming Languages

Over the past few decades, software has evolved. In the early days of computing, programming languages were quite crude by today's standards. Initially used in the 1940s, the first generation of programming languages was called machine languages. Programmers wrote in binary code to instruct the computer exactly which circuits to turn on and which to turn off. As you might guess, machine language is very unsophisticated and therefore very difficult to write. Because it is so difficult, very few programs are actually written in machine language. Instead, programmers rely on higher-level languages. In the early 1950s, a more sophisticated method for programming was developed, in which the binary codes used in machine language were replaced by symbols, called symbolic languages, that were a lot easier for humans to understand. Programs written in symbolic language, or any higher-level language, still need to be converted into machine language to run.

In the mid 1950s, the first high-level programming language, called FORTRAN, was developed by IBM. The big innovation of high-level languages was that they used English-like words to instruct the computer. Consequently, high-level languages are much easier to program in than lower-level languages. Table B.5 indicates how some high-level languages are better suited for different applications. Programmers must fully understand the tasks that are to be accomplished when writing a new application in order to choose the best programming language for those tasks.

In the 1970s, several user-oriented languages called fourth-generation languages were created. These languages are more like English than third-generation languages in that they focus on the desired output instead of the procedures required to get that output. ***Fourth-generation languages (4GLs)***, also called outcome-oriented languages, are commonly used to write and execute queries of a database. For example, the widely used database query language called Structured Query Language (SQL) is a fourth-generation language (see Chapter 3 for more on SQL). See Figure B.7 for several lines of SQL displayed in a sentence-like statement requesting that the LAST and FIRST names of people in a database called CUSTOMER with credit limits equal to $100 be displayed.

More recently, ***fifth-generation languages (5GLs)*** have been developed for application within some expert system or artificial intelligence applications. 5GLs are called natural languages because they allow the user to communicate with the computer using true English sentences. For example, Hewlett-Packard and other software vendors have developed tools for document search and retrieval and database queries that let the user query the documents or database with English-like sentences. These sentences are then automatically converted into the appropriate commands (in some cases SQL) needed to query the documents or database and produce the result for the user. If the system does not understand exactly what the user wants, it can ask for clarification. The same code shown in Figure B.7 might appear as shown in Figure B.8 if a natural language were used. Although 5GLs are not common and are still being further developed, they have been used to forecast the performance of financial

BEGINNING WITH THE LAST NAME ON THE FOLLOWING LIST OF CUSTOMERS, FIND CUSTOMERS WHO HAVE A CREDIT LIMIT OF $100.

NEVO LIV
BROMHMAN DAVID
BJERKAN HEIDI
JESSUP JAMIE
VALACICH JAMES
WADE CHRISTOPHER

Figure B.8 A 5GL query using natural language to request the same information as the SQL query in Figure B.7.

portfolios, help diagnose medical problems, and estimate weather patterns.

Of course, programming languages continue to evolve. One new characteristic for describing programming languages is whether or not they are object-oriented. In addition, visual programming languages and web development languages are rapidly gaining popularity. Next, we discuss these.

Object-Oriented Languages

Object-oriented languages are the most recent in the progression of high-level programming languages. These languages allow programmers to group data and program instructions together into modules or ***objects*** that can be manipulated by the programmer. For example, an object might be student majors and grade point averages and a set of corresponding rules for calculating credits needed for graduation. The process of grouping pieces of data together is called ***encapsulation***. When pieces of data are encapsulated, they can be isolated from other parts of the program. The programmer can then make changes in various parts of the program without having to rewrite the entire code.

A second key characteristic of object-oriented languages is ***inheritance***. This means that when one class of objects is defined, all other objects with the same characteristics are automatically defined by the same terms. For example, if "student majors" is defined as an object for a search, then through inheritance, objects such as "English major," or "mathematics major" would fall under the same definition. Therefore, once an object is created, it can be plugged into several different applications. Programmers using object-oriented programming (OOP) can save time because they do not have to repeatedly write many lines of code to define the same or related objects.

In addition to being object-oriented, programs and programming languages can be ***event-driven***. Unlike a program written in a procedural programming language, a program written with the event-driven approach does not follow a sequential logic. The programmer does not determine the sequence of execution for the program. The user can press certain keys and click on various buttons and boxes that are presented. Each of these user actions can cause events to occur, which triggers a program procedure that the programmer has written. Object-oriented programming languages tend to be useful for designing event-driven applications. An example of an object-oriented environment that supports the development of event-driven applications is Microsoft Visual Basic. In addition, Visual Basic is also a visual programming language, which we will discuss next.

Visual Programming Languages

Just as you may have found it easier to use a computer operating system with a graphical user interface, such as Windows or Mac OS, programmers using ***visual programming languages*** may also take advantage of the GUI. For instance, programmers can easily add a command button to a screen with a few clicks of a mouse (see Figure B.9) instead of explaining pixel-by-pixel and using many lines of code. Visual Basic and Visual C++ are two popular examples of visual programming languages.

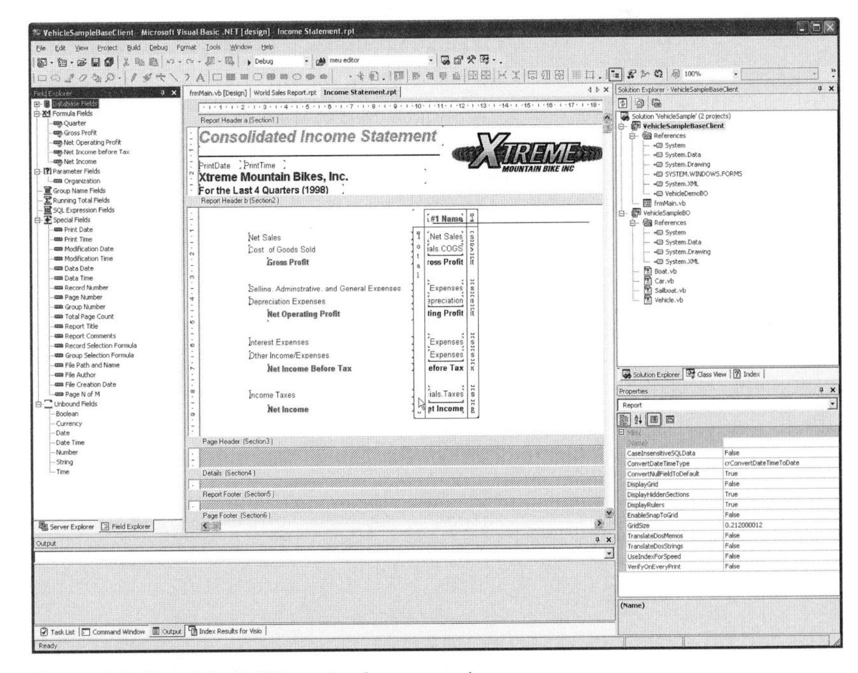

Figure B.9 Visual Basic.NET, a visual programming language, is used to create standard business forms.

Hoffer, George, and Valacich, *Modern Systems Analysis and Design*, 4th ed., Prentice Hall, 2005.

Web Development Languages

If you have been surfing the web for a while, you probably either already have a personal web page or have thought of posting one. In that event, you have some experience with using a programming language. The language you used to create your web page is called ***HyperText Markup Language (HTML)***. HTML is a text-based file format that uses a series of codes, or tags, to set up a document. Because HTML editing programs are visually oriented and easy to use, you do not need to memorize the language to set up a web page. The programs for creating web pages are called ***web page builders*** or ***HTML editors***, and there are many on the market, including Windows Notepad, most web browsers, and word processing programs such as Word and WordPerfect.

In HTML, the tags used to identify different elements on a page and to format the page are set apart from the text with angle brackets (<>). Specific tags are used to mark the beginning and the ending of an element or a formatting command. For example, if you want text to appear in bold type, the HTML tag to begin bolding is <b> and the tag to turn off bolding, at the end of the selected text, is </b>. The "href" command sets up a hyperlink from a word or image on the page to another HTML document. Tags also denote document formatting commands, such as text to be used as a title, sizes of text in headings, the ends of paragraphs, underlining, italics, bolding, and places to insert pictures and sound (see Table B.6).

A good way to learn HTML is to find a web page you like, then use the "View Source" command on your browser to see the hypertext that created the page (see Figure B.10). Once you have created your web page and saved it to disk, you can upload it to an Internet account you have created through your ISP.

XML

Extensible Markup Language (XML) was designed (1) to be used as a web page construction tool when users want to create their own markup tags and (2) to build database queries. XML is a powerful language that lets users create database fields for a number of different applications. XML makes it easy for web users to request and receive information from a variety of databases. To view documents created in XML, you need a browser that supports the language, commonly called an XML parser. The latest versions of Microsoft's Internet Explorer and Netscape Navigator can fill the bill.

Adding Dynamic Content to a Web Page

Markup languages such as HTML are for laying out or formatting web pages. If you want to add animated cartoons or other dynamic content, or have users interact with your web page other than by clicking on hypertext links, then you will need access to tools such as XML, Java, ActiveX, or a scripting language.

Java. ***Java*** is a programming language that was developed at Sun Microsystems in the early 1990s. It lets you spice up your web page by adding active content such as circles that whirl and change colours, hamsters marching to a tune, forms to help users calculate car payments at various interest rates, or any other such dynamic content (see Figure B.11). You can do this in one of two ways: by learning Java or a similar language and programming the content you want, or by downloading free general-purpose ***applets*** from the web. Applets are small programs that you can choose from to

Table B.6 ***Common HTML tags.***

Tag	Description
<html> . . . </html>	Creates an HTML document
<head> . . . </head>	Sets off the title and other information that is not displayed on the web page itself
<body> . . . </body>	Sets off the visible portion of the document
<b> . . . </b>	Creates bold text
<a href="URL"> . . . </a>	Creates a hyperlink
<a href="mailto:EMAIL"> . . . </a>	Creates a mailto link
<p> . . . </p>	Creates a new paragraph
<table> . . . </table>	Creates a table

gbc.schulich.yorku[1] - Notepad

File Edit Format View Help

```
<!DOCTYPE HTML PUBLIC "-//W3C//DTD HTML 4.01 Transitional//EN">
<html><!-- InstanceBegin template="/Templates/gbc_template.dwt" codeOutsideHTMLIsLocked="false" -->
<head>
<!-- InstanceBeginEditable name="doctitle" -->
<title>Graduate Business Council @ Schulich School of Business</title>
<!-- InstanceEndEditable -->
<meta http-equiv="Content-Type" content="text/html; charset=iso-8859-1">
<!-- InstanceBeginEditable name="head" -->
<meta name="Description" content="Graduate Business Council, Schulich School of Business, York University"
<meta name="Keywords" content="Graduate Business Council, Schulich School of Business, York University">
<!-- InstanceEndEditable -->
</head>

<body bgcolor="#787878" link="#0C3D91" vlink="#0C3D91" alink="#0C3D91" topmargin="0" marginwidth="0" margi
<!-- configure drop down menu -->
<!--     vqm__database='http://www.gbc.schulich.yorku.ca/gbc/gbc_new.nsf/';-->
  <script language="JavaScript1.2" vqm_id="http://www.paulfriesen.com/gbc_website.js">
        vqm__notice='Visual QuickMenu Pro, (c) 2004 OpenCube Inc., All Rights Reserved, Visit - www.opencu
        vqm__codebase='http://gbc.schulich.yorku.ca/';
        vqm__database='http://gbc.schulich.yorku.ca/';
</script>
  <script language="JavaScript1.2" src="http://gbc.schulich.yorku.ca/gbc_website.js"></script>
  <script language="JavaScript1.2" src="http://gbc.schulich.yorku.ca/tdqm_loader.js"></script>

<div align="center">
  <table width="750" border="0" cellspacing="5" cellpadding="0">
    <tr valign="bottom">
      <td width="50%" align="left"><font color="#FFFFFF" size="4" face="Verdana, Arial, Helvetica, sans-se
        Business Council</strong></font></td>
      <td width="50%" align="right"><font color="#FFFFFF" size="2" face="Verdana, Arial, Helvetica, sans-s
        416.736.2100 x66385<br>
        Email: </font><a href="mailto:gbc@schulich.yorku.ca"><font color="#FFFFFF" size="2" face="Verdana,
    </tr>
  </table>
  <table width="750" border="0" cellspacing="5" cellpadding="0">
    <tr>
      <td>
        <!-- insert drop down menu -->
        <script id="vqp_generate_mainitems" language="javascript1.2">generate_mainitems()</script>
      </td>
    </tr>
  </table>
  <table width="750" border="0" cellpadding="0" cellspacing="0" bgcolor="#FFFFFF">
    <tr>
```

Figure B.10 A web page (a) and the HTML commands used to create it (b).

Source: **Gbc.schulich.yorku.ca**

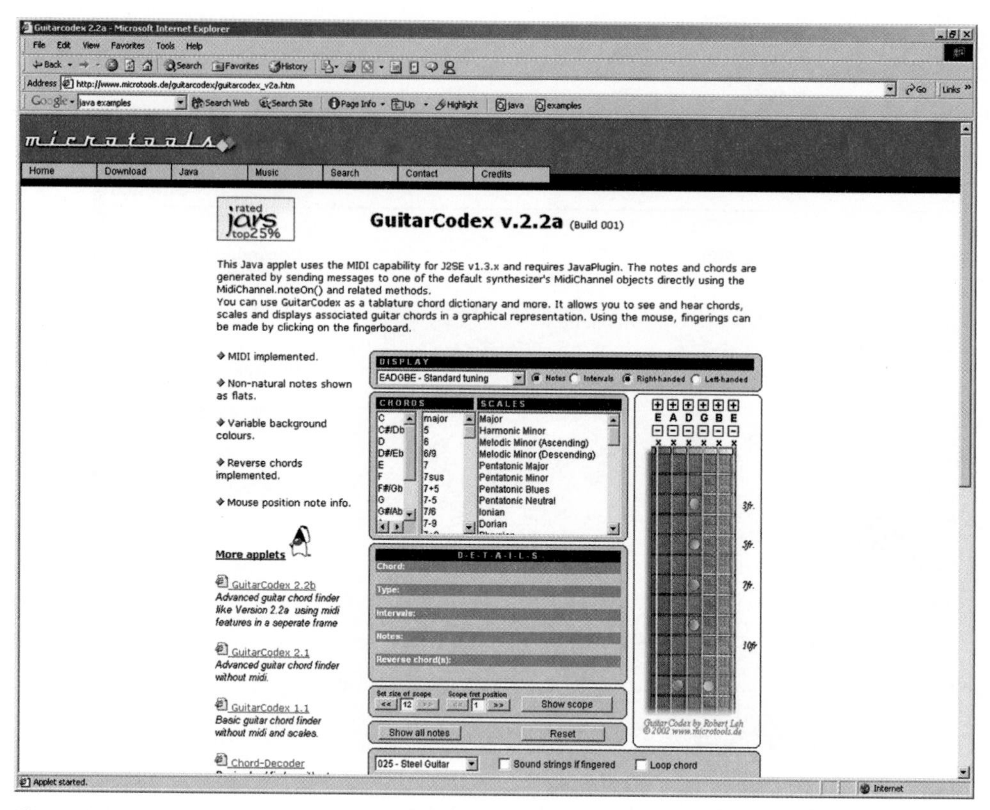

Figure B.11 Java helps to provide dynamic content to web pages.

provide the content you want on your web page. When a user accesses your web page, the applets you inserted are downloaded from the server with your web page to a Java-enabled browser running on a PC. Later, when the user leaves your web page, the web page and the applets disappear from his computer.

ActiveX. ***ActiveX*** was developed by Microsoft Corporation to perform the same function as Java. It, too, lets users program in or insert objects from any ActiveX-supported application or ActiveX-enabled web page. ActiveX differs from Java in that it was designed to run on Windows computers and is not always supported by other platforms.

Scripting languages. ***Scripting languages*** can also be used to supply interactive components to a web page. These languages let you build programs or scripts directly into HTML page code. Web page designers frequently use them to check the accuracy of user-entered information, such as names, addresses, and credit-card numbers. You can also use them to connect freestanding applets to your HTML-created web page. Two common scripting languages are Microsoft's VBScript and Netscape's JavaScript.

JavaScript. ***JavaScript***, created by Netscape, bears little resemblance to Java. The two are similar, however, in that both Java and JavaScript are useful component software tools for creating web pages. That is, both allow users to add or create applets that lend dynamic content to web pages. Both are also cross-platform programs, meaning that they can typically be used by computers running Windows, Linux, Mac OS, and other operating systems.

The development of programming languages is an ongoing process of change and innovation. These changes often result in more capable and complex systems for the user. The popularity of the Internet has spurred the creation of innovative and evolving software. From the pace of change that is occurring, it is clear that many more innovations are on the horizon.

Automated Development Environments

Over the years, the tools for developing information systems have increased both in variety and in power. In the early days of systems development, a developer was left to use a pencil and paper to sketch out design ideas and program code. Computers were cumbersome to use and slow to program, and most designers worked out on paper as much of the system design as they could before moving to the computer. Today, system developers have a vast array of powerful computer-based tools at their disposal. These tools have changed forever the ways in which systems are developed. ***Computer-aided software engineering (CASE)*** refers to automated software tools used by systems developers to design and implement information systems. Developers can use these tools to automate or support activities throughout the systems development process, with the objective of increasing productivity and improving the overall quality of systems. The capabilities of CASE tools are continually evolving and being integrated into a variety of development environments. Below we briefly review some of the interesting characteristics of CASE.

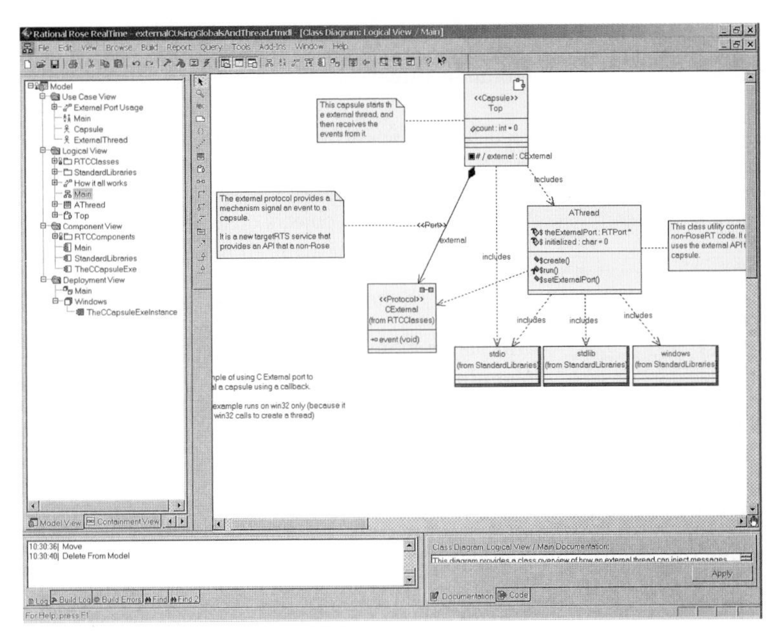

Figure B.12 High-level system design diagram from a CASE tool.

Hoffer, George, and Valacich, *Modern Systems Analysis and Design*, 4th ed., Prentice Hall, 2005.

Types of CASE Tools

Two of the primary activities in development of large-scale information systems are the creation of design documents and the management of information. Over the life of a project, thousands of documents need to be created—from screen prototypes to database content and structure to layouts of sample forms and reports. At the heart of all CASE environments is a repository for managing information.

CASE also helps developers represent business processes and information flows by using graphical diagramming tools. By providing standard symbols to represent business processes, information flows between processes, data storage, and the organizational entities that interact with the business process, CASE eases a very tedious and error-prone activity (see Figure B.12). The tools not only ease the drawing process but also ensure that the drawing conforms to development standards and is consistent with other design documents developed by other developers.

Another powerful capability of CASE is its ability to generate program source code automatically. CASE tools keep pace with contemporary programming languages and can automatically produce programming code directly from high-level designs in languages such as Java, COBOL, BASIC, and C. In addition to diagramming tools and code generators, a broad range of other tools assists in the systems development process. The general types of CASE tools used throughout the development process are summarized in Table B.7.

Table B.7 ***General types of CASE tools.***

CASE Tool	Description
Diagramming tools	Tools that enable system process, data, and control structures to be represented graphically.
Screen and report generators	Tools that help model how systems look and feel to users. Screen and report generators also make it easier for the systems analyst to identify data requirements and relationships.
Analysis tools	Tools that automatically check for incomplete, inconsistent, or incorrect specifications in diagrams, screens, and reports.
Repository	A tool that enables the integrated storage of specifications, diagrams, reports, and project management information.
Documentation generators	Tools that help produce both technical and user documentation in standard formats.
Code generators	Tools that enable the automatic generation of program and database definition code directly from the design documents, diagrams, screens, and reports.

Adapted from Hoffer, George, and Valacich, 2005. *Modern Systems Analysis and Design*, 4th ed., Upper Saddle River, NJ: Prentice Hall.

Table B.8 *Common impacts of CASE on individuals within organizations.*

Individuals	Common Impact
Systems analysts	CASE automates many routine tasks of the analyst, making the analyst's communication skills (rather than analytical skills) most critical.
Programmers	Will piece together objects created by code generators and fourth-generation languages. Their role will become more of maintaining designs than maintaining source code.
Users	Will be much more active in the systems development process through the use of upper CASE tools.
Top managers	Will play a more active role in setting priorities and strategic directions for IS by using CASE-based planning and through user-oriented system development methods.
Functional managers	Will play a greater role in leading development projects by using CASE to reengineer their business processes.
IS project managers	Will have greater control over development projects and resources.

Adapted from Chen and Norman, 1992.

The Influence of CASE on Individuals

CASE can be used to dramatically increase the speed of development and maintenance of a system, not to mention increasing the quality of the system. CASE also influences the culture of an organization in many significant ways. In fact, researchers have found that people with different career orientations have different attitudes toward CASE (Orlikowski, 1989). For example, those within the development group with a managerial orientation welcome CASE because they believe it helps reduce the risk and uncertainty in managing development projects. On the other hand, people with a more technical orientation tend to resist the use of CASE because they feel threatened by the technology's capability to replace some skills they have taken years to master. Table B.8 lists several possible impacts of CASE on the roles of individuals within organizations.

CASE is clearly a powerful technology that can have numerous and widespread impacts. Its adoption should be a well-thought-out and highly orchestrated activity.

KEY POINTS REVIEW

1. **Describe the common functions of systems software.** Systems software is the collection of programs that form the foundation for the basic operations of the computer hardware. Systems software, or the operating system, performs many different tasks. Some of these tasks include booting your computer, reading programs into memory, managing memory allocation to those programs, managing where programs and files are located in secondary storage, maintaining the structure of directories and subdirectories, formatting disks, controlling the computer monitor, and sending objects to the printer. The systems software manages the dialogue you can have with a computer using either a command-based or graphical interface. A command-based interface requires that text commands be typed into the computer, whereas a graphical user interface (GUI) uses pictures and icons as well as menus to send instructions back and forth between the user and the computer system.

2. **Describe the various types of application software.** You can find a large number of computer software applications. Customized application software is developed specifically for a single organization. This kind of software is tailored to an organization's unique requirements. Off-the-shelf application software is not customized to the unique needs of one organization but is written to operate within many organizations. In general, off-the-shelf software is less costly, faster to procure, of higher quality, and less risky than customized software. Business information systems are applications developed to perform a firm's organization-wide operations, such as payroll or inventory management. Office automation or personal productivity software is designed to support activities such as word processing and electronic mail.

3. **Describe the characteristics of various types of programming languages and application development environments.** A programming language is the computer language programmers use to write application programs. To run on a computer, programs must be translated into binary machine language. Programming languages are translated into machine languages through special types of programs called compilers and interpreters. Over the past several decades, software has evolved. Early software used machine language, which told the computer exactly which circuits to turn on and which to turn off. Next, symbolic languages used symbols to represent a series of binary statements. This was followed by the development of high-level languages, such as FORTRAN, COBOL, C, and Java. The difference between these high-level languages and earlier languages is that

the high-level languages use English-like words and commands, making it easier to write programs. Fourth-generation languages are called outcome-oriented languages because they contain even more English-like commands and tend to focus on what output is desired instead of the procedures required to get that output. Again, these languages made it even easier to program. Fifth-generation languages are called natural languages because they allow the user to communicate with the computer using true English sentences. In addition to this generational evolution, object-oriented programming, visual programming, and web development languages are relatively new enhancements to programming languages. Object-oriented languages group together data and their corresponding instructions into manipulable objects. Visual programming languages use a graphical interface to build graphical interfaces for other programs. Web development languages are a rapidly evolving set of tools designed for constructing Internet applications and web content. Together, object-oriented programming, visual programming, and web development languages are making it easier for programmers to develop today's complex software systems, especially for modern Internet-based systems. Finally, computer-aided software engineering environments help systems developers construct large-scale systems more rapidly and with higher quality.

KEY TERMS

ActiveX 380
applets 378
application software 371
business information systems 373
command-based interface 370
compilers 375
computer-aided software engineering (CASE) 381
customized application software 371
encapsulation 377
event-driven 377
Extensible Markup Language (XML) 378
fifth-generation languages (5GL) 376
fourth-generation languages (4GL) 376
graphical user interface (GUI) 370
HTML editors 378
HyperText Markup Language (HTML) 378
inheritance 377
interfaces 370
interpreter 376
Java 378
JavaScript 380
machine language 375
menu interface 370
object-oriented languages 377
objects 377
off-the-shelf application software 372
office automation software (OAS) 373
open source software 374
operating systems 369
personal productivity software 373
scripting languages 380
software 369
systems software 369
utilities 371
utility programs 371
visual programming languages 377
web page builders 378

REVIEW QUESTIONS

1. Define the term "software," and name several software packages and their uses.
2. Describe at least four different tasks performed by an operating system.
3. What is the difference between a command-based interface and a graphical user interface?
4. Describe the similarities and differences between at least two major operating systems in use today.
5. Name and describe four functions of utility programs.
6. Contrast using off-the-shelf application software with using customized application software.
7. Describe the evolution of programming languages as well as various contemporary programming languages in use today.
8. What is HTML, and why is it important?
9. Describe various options for adding dynamic content to a web page.
10. What is CASE, and how can it influence individuals within organizations?

SELF-STUDY QUESTIONS

Visit the Companion Website for this text for additional Self-Study Questions: **www.pearsoned.ca/jessup**.

1. Which of the following is an example of an operating system?
   A. Microsoft Access
   B. Microsoft Excel
   C. Microsoft Word
   D. Microsoft Windows
2. An operating system performs which of the following tasks?
   A. booting the computer
   B. managing where programs and files are stored
   C. sending documents to the printer
   D. all of the above
3. Which of the following is a popular operating system?
   A. Noodle
   B. Linux
   C. FORTRAN
   D. PowerEdge
4. Which is not an advantage of off-the-shelf application software?
   A. lower cost
   B. faster to obtain
   C. easier to use
   D. higher quality due to large customer base

5. Which is not an example of office automation or personal productivity software?
   A. payroll system
   B. database management system
   C. web browser
   D. word processing
6. Which of the following is not a tool for adding dynamic content to a web page?
   A. Hot Coffee
   B. ActiveX
   C. scripting languages
   D. Java
7. Automated software tools used to develop information systems that can improve the overall system quality and increase programmer productivity are called __________.
   A. computerized programming
   B. automated development
   C. computer-aided programming
   D. none of the above
8. A utility program may provide __________.
   A. antivirus protection
   B. file conversion capability
   C. file compression and defragmentation
   D. all of the above
9. Fifth-generation languages are also referred to as __________ languages.
   A. assembly
   B. natural
   C. high-level
   D. low-level
10. What were first generation programming languages called?
   A. natural language
   B. assembly language
   C. machine language
   D. none of the above

PROBLEMS AND EXERCISES

1. Match the following terms with the appropriate definitions:

   _____ Operating system

   _____ Applets

   _____ Visual programming languages

   _____ Graphical user interface

   _____ Object-oriented programming languages

   _____ Scripting language

   _____ Interpreter

   _____ Business information systems

   _____ Compiler

   _____ Customized application software

   a. Translates a computer program into machine language, which is then executed by the computer
   b. An interface that enables the user to use pictures, icons, and menus to send instructions to the computer
   c. Coordinates the interaction between users, applications, and hardware
   d. Applications developed to perform the organization-wide operations of a firm
   e. Programming languages that provide a GUI and are generally easier to use than non-GUI languages
   f. Small software programs that can be used to provide special features to a website
   g. Programming languages that group together data and their corresponding instructions into manipulable objects
   h. Software developed based on specifications provided by a particular organization
   i. Translates the computer program into machine language one statement at a time
   j. Used to supply interactive components to a web page by building programs or scripts directly into HTML page code
2. How do software programs affect your life? Give examples of software from areas other than desktop computers. Are the uses for software increasing over time?
3. In what situations would customized software be utilized? How does the cost compare with the benefit?
4. What are the implications for an organization of having more than one operating system? What might be the advantages? What are some of the disadvantages? Would you recommend such a situation? Can you find organizations using the World Wide Web that specifically mention their utilization of multiple operating systems in their information system architecture? Do these organizations comment on this arrangement or simply mention its existence? Prepare a 10-minute presentation to the rest of the class on your findings.
5. Imagine that you are in charge of procuring software applications for your division of a company. You are in need of a powerful business information systems software application that will control most of the accounting and bookkeeping functions. Based on your current knowledge of the intricacies of the accounting profession and its practices, would you be more likely to purchase this application as a customized software application or an off-the-shelf software application? Why did you select this choice? What would make you choose the other option?
6. What is a business information system, and what types of processing does it do? What do many companies' business systems track besides inventory? Why?
7. Based on the information within this appendix and within the chapters of this textbook, discuss the importance of a single decision to purchase one software application over another—for example, purchasing Microsoft Excel instead of Lotus 1-2-3. Who will be affected? How will they be affected? What changes might occur because of the purchase?
8. Based on your own experiences with computers and computer systems, what do you like and dislike about different operating systems that you have used? Were these uses on a professional

or a personal level, or both? Who made the decision to purchase that particular operating system? Did you have any say in the purchase decision?

9. Choose an organization that utilizes a variety of different software applications. Are these software applications customized applications, off-the-shelf applications, or a combination of both? Talk with some of the employees to determine how they feel about using customized versus off-the-shelf software applications.

10. Search the web for organizations that specialize in creating customized software applications for their clients. In what specific product categories do these organizations specialize, if any? Were you able to find any pricing information directly from their home pages?

11. Have the off-the-shelf software applications you have used met your requirements? Were you able to perform the functions and routines that you needed? Did the software meet your expectations? Would you have bought this type of software if you knew then what you know today?

12. Find an organization that does a lot of in-house programming and utilizes a variety of different programming languages. Determine the generation level of these languages. Are the same personnel programming in most (or all) of the languages, or are different personnel programming in each of the languages? Is this assignment of programmers intentional or unintentional?

13. Imagine that you and a friend are at a local ATM getting some cash from your account to pay for a movie. The ATM does not seem to be working. It is giving you an error message every time you press any button. Is this most likely a software-related problem or a hardware-related problem? Why? Use the information in this appendix and in the previous appendix to help you make your decision.

14. Describe how you would handle resistance to implementing CASE tools by those who feel they will be replaced by technology. From whom is this resistance most likely to come? Is this fear legitimate? Why or why not?

ANSWERS TO THE SELF-STUDY QUESTIONS

1. D, p. 370	2. D, p. 369	3. B, p. 371	4. C, p. 373	5. A, pp. 373–374
6. A, pp. 378–380	7. D, pp. 373–374	8. D, p. 371	9. B, p. 376	10. C, p. 375

Appendix C: Networking

Preview

The purpose of this appendix is to introduce key networking concepts, technologies, and applications. This discussion provides you with a solid foundation for understanding how computers are connected across a room or across the world. After reading this appendix, you will be able to do the following:

1. Describe the evolution of and types of computer networks.
2. Understand networking fundamentals, including network services and transmission media.
3. Describe network software and hardware, including media access control, network topologies, and protocols, as well as connectivity hardware for both local area and wide area networks.

Telecommunications and networking technologies, like those described throughout this book, are taking on more and more importance as organizations rely more on computer-based information systems. Understanding how the underlying networking technologies work and where these technologies are heading will help to complete your understanding of the "essential" elements of information systems. In this appendix we describe the enabling technologies underlying computer networks, how they are used together to form networks, and how these networks are used. The discussion begins with a description of the fundamental elements of computer networking.

EVOLUTION OF COMPUTER NETWORKING

Human communication involves the sharing of information and messages between senders and receivers. The sender of a message formulates the message in her brain and codes the message into a form that can be communicated to the receiver—through voice, for example. The message is then transmitted along a communication pathway to the receiver. The receiver, using his ears and brain, then attempts to decode the message, as shown in Figure C.1. This basic model of human communication helps us to understand telecommunications or computer networking.

Messages, Senders, and Receivers

Computer networking is the sharing of information or services. As with human communication, all computer networks require three things:

- Senders and receivers that have something to share
- A pathway or transmission medium, such as a cable, to send the message
- Rules or protocols dictating communication between senders and receivers

The easiest way to understand computer networking is through the human communication model. Suppose you are planning to study abroad in Europe for a semester. You need information about schools that accept exchange students. The first requirement for a network—information to share—has now been met. You start your search by writing a letter (coding your message) and faxing it to several schools. You have met the second requirement: a means of transmitting the coded message. The fax system is the pathway or transmission medium used to contact the receiver. Transmission media refer to the physical pathway—cable(s) and wireless—used to carry network information. At this point, you may run into some difficulties. Not all the receivers of your fax may understand what you have written—decode your message—because they speak other languages. Although you have contacted the receiver, you and the receiver of your message must meet the third requirement for a successful network: You must establish a language of communication—the

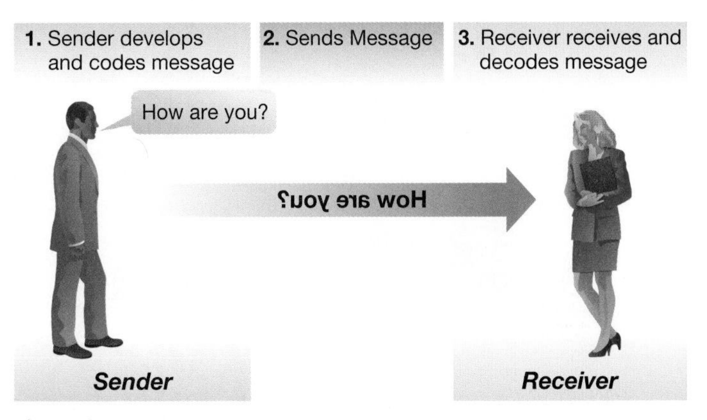

Figure C.1 Communication requires senders and receivers.

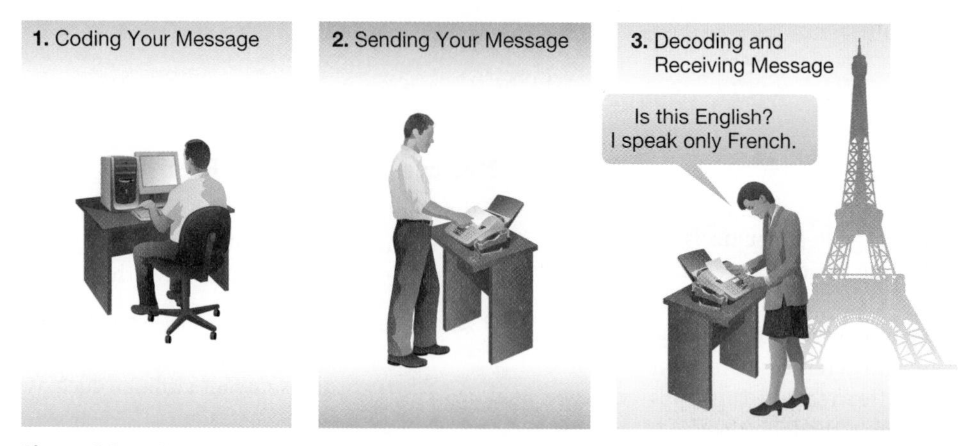

Figure C.2 Coding, sending, and decoding a message.

rules or protocols governing your communication. ***Protocols*** define the procedures that different computers follow when they transmit and receive data. You both might decide that one communication protocol will be that you communicate in English. This communication session is illustrated in Figure C.2.

Computer Networks

A fundamental difference between human and computer communication is that human communication consists of words, whereas computer communication consists of bits, the fundamental information units of computers, as depicted in Figure C.3. Virtually all types of information can be transmitted on a computer network—documents, art, music, and film—although each type of information has vastly different requirements for effective transmission. For example, a single screen of text is approximately 14 KB of data, whereas a photograph-quality picture could be larger than 200 MB of data (see Table C.1). The process of converting a photograph or a song into digital information, or bits, is called ***digitizing***. After information is converted into bits, it can travel across a network. To transmit either the screen of text or the picture in a timely manner from one location to another, adequate bandwidth is needed. For example, using a 56 kilobits per second (Kbps) modem—a modem that transmits approximately 56 000 bits of data in a second—a single screen of text would be transferred in under 1 second, while a high-quality photograph could take more than 4 seconds. Hence, different types of information have different communication bandwidth requirements.

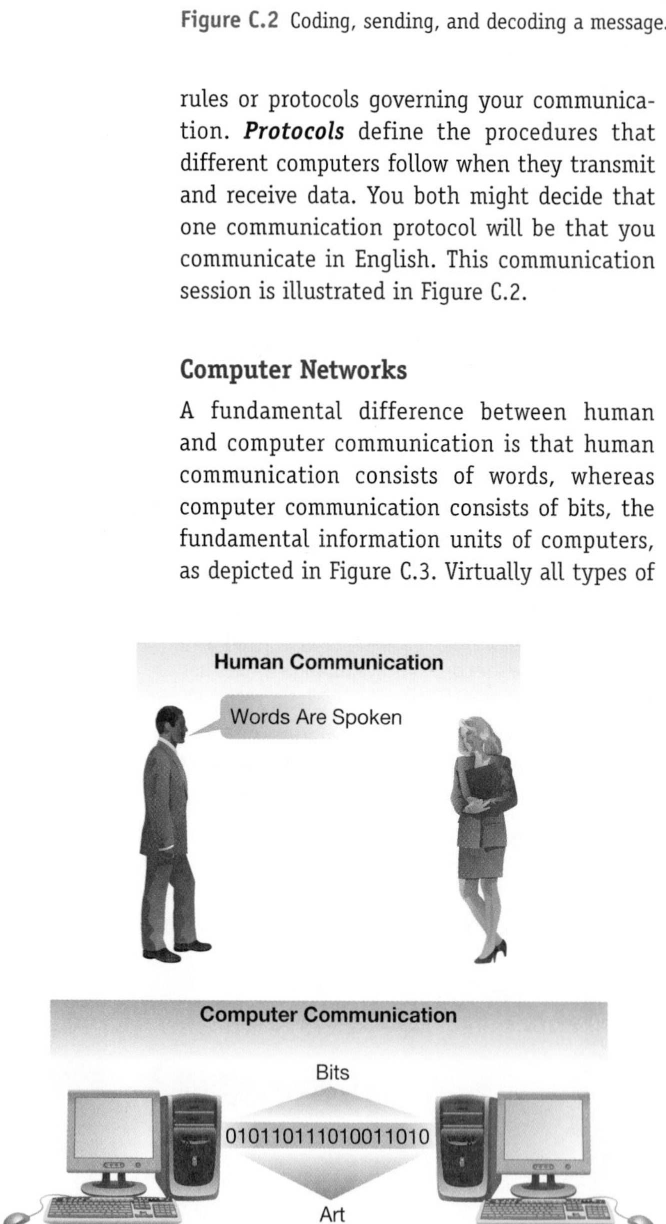

Now that you understand the basic elements of networks, we will talk about how they have evolved. Since the beginning of the Information Age in the 1950s, people and enterprises have used computers to process data and information. Over the years, however, computer networks have gotten better and better.

Figure C.3 In human communication, words are spoken and transmitted in the air. In computer communication, digital data are transmitted over some type of communication medium.

Centralized Computing

Centralized computing, depicted in Figure C.4, remained largely unchanged through the 1970s. In this model, large centralized computers, called mainframes, were used to process and store data. During the mainframe era (beginning in the 1940s), people entered data on mainframes through the use of local input devices called ***terminals***. These devices were

Type of Information	Raw Size	Compressed Size
Voice		
Telephone	64 KBps	16–32 KBps
Teleconference	96 KBps	32–64 KBps
Compact disc	1.41 MBps	63–128 KBps
Data		
Single screen of text	14.4 KB	4.8–7 KB
Typed page, single-spaced	28.8 KB	9.6–14.4 KB
Faxed page (low to high resolution)	1.68–3.36 MB	130–336 KB
Super VGA screen image	6.3 MB	315–630 KB
Digital X-ray	50.3 MB	16.8–25.1 MB
Publication-quality photograph	230.4 MB	23–46 MB
Video		
Video telephony	9.3 MBps	64–384 KBps
Video teleconferencing	37.3 MBps	384 KBps–1.92 MBps
CCITT multimedia	166 MBps	1.7 MBps
High definition television	1.33 GBps	20–50 MBps

Note: KB = Kilobytes, MB = Megabytes; KBps = kilobits per second; MBps = megabits per second; GBps = Gigabits per second.

Adapted from *Business Data Communications*, 2nd ed., by Stallings and VanSlyke. © 1997. Reprinted by permission of Prentice-Hall, Inc., Upper Saddle River, NJ.

Table C.1 ***Communication and storage/bandwidth requirements for different types of information.***

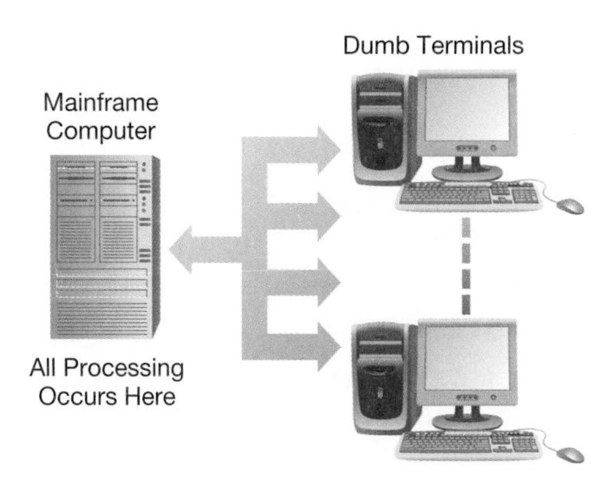

Figure C.4 In the centralized computing model, all processing occurs in one central mainframe.

called "dumb" terminals because they did not conduct any processing, or "smart" activities. The centralized computing model is not a true network because there is no sharing of information and capabilities. The mainframe provides all the capabilities, and the terminals are only input/output devices. Computer networks evolved in the 1980s when organizations needed separate, independent computers to communicate with each other.

Distributed Computing

The introduction of personal computers in the late 1970s and early 1980s gave individuals control over their own computing. Organizations also realized that they could use multiple small computers to achieve many of the same processing goals of a single large computer. People could work on subsets of tasks on separate computers rather than using one mainframe to perform all the processing. Achieving the goal of separate processing required computer networks so that information and services could be easily shared between these distributed computers. The 1980s were characterized by an evolution to a computing model called ***distributed computing***, shown in Figure C.5, in which multiple types of computers are networked together to share information and services.

Collaborative Computing

In the 1990s, a new computing model, called ***collaborative computing***, emerged. Collaborative computing is a synergistic form of distributed computing in which two or more networked computers are used to accomplish a common processing task. That is, in this model of computing, computers are not simply communicating data but are sharing processing capabilities. For example, one computer may be used to store a large employee database. A second computer may be used to process and update individual employee records selected from this database. The two computers collaborate to keep the company's employee records current, as depicted in Figure C.6.

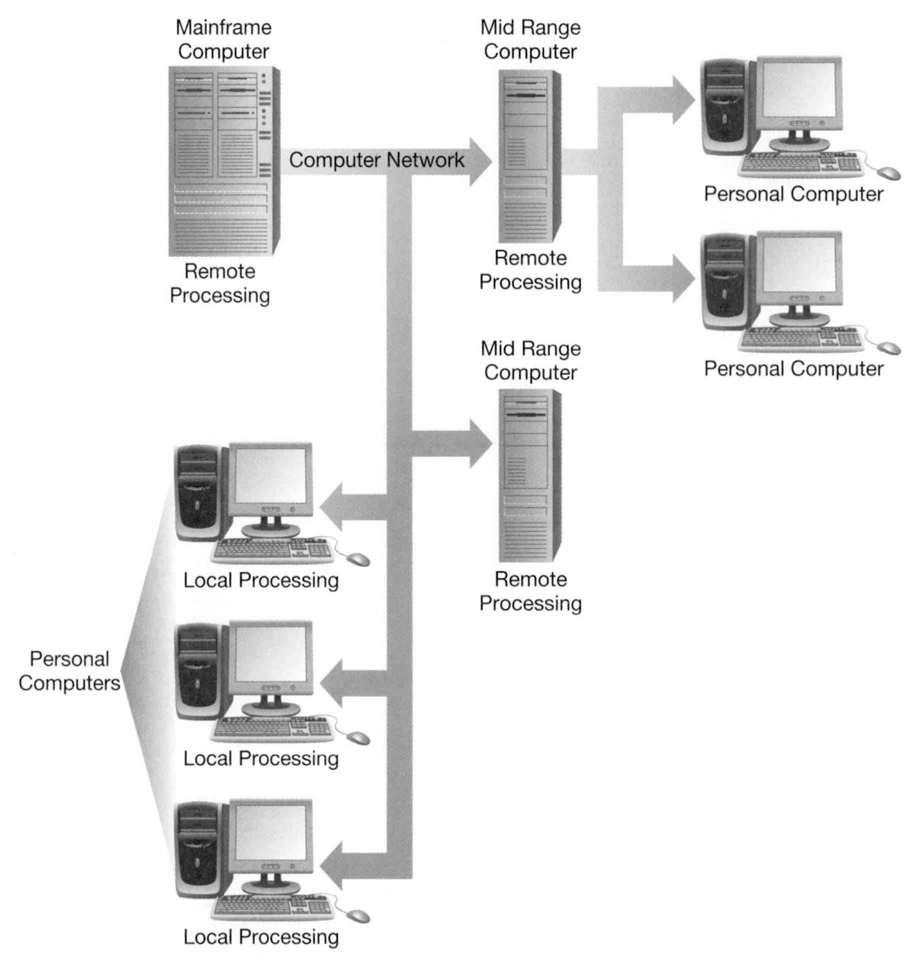

Figure C.5 In the distributed computing model, separate computers work on subsets of tasks and then pool their results by communicating over a network.

Types of Networks

Computing networks today include all three computing models: centralized, distributed, and collaborative. The emergence of new computing models did not mean that organizations completely discarded older technologies. Rather, a typical computer network includes mainframes, minicomputers, personal computers, and a variety of other devices. Computer networks are commonly classified by size, distance covered, and structure. The most commonly used classifications are a private branch exchange (PBX), local area network (LAN), wide area network (WAN), metropolitan area network (MAN), and personal area network (PAN). Each is described in the following sections.

Private Branch Exchange

A ***private branch exchange (PBX)*** is a telephone system that serves a particular location, such as a business (see Figure C.7). It connects one telephone extension to another within the system and connects the PBX to the outside

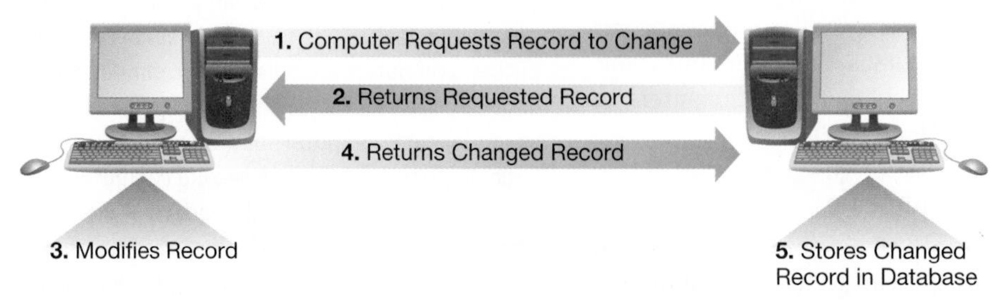

Figure C.6 In the collaborative computing model, two or more networked computers are used to accomplish a common processing task.

telephone network. It can also connect computers within the system to other PBX systems, to an outside network, or to various office devices such as fax machines or photocopiers. However, PBX networks are not normally used to transmit data. As they use ordinary telephone lines, PBX systems have limited bandwidth. This prevents them from transmitting such forms of information as interactive video, digital music, and high-resolution photos. Using PBX technology, a business requires few outside phone lines but has to purchase or lease the PBX equipment.

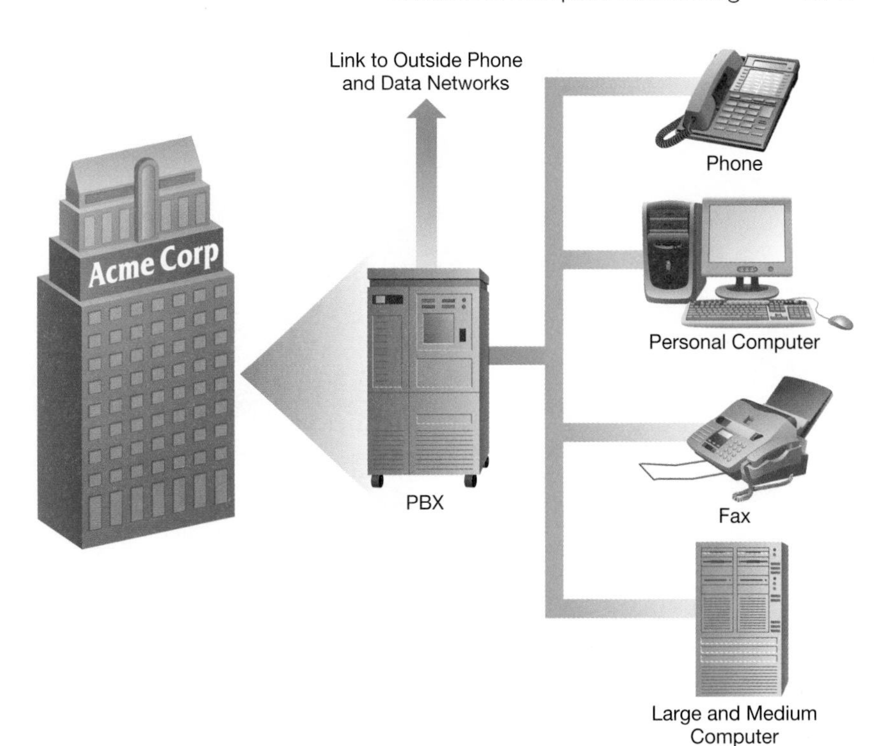

Figure C.7 A private branch exchange (PBX) supports local phone and data communications, as well as links to outside phone and data networks.

Local Area Network (LAN)

A ***local area network (LAN)***, shown in Figure C.8, is a computer network that spans a relatively small area, allowing all computer users to connect with each other to share information and peripheral devices, such as a printer. LAN-based communications may involve the sharing of data, software applications, and other resources between several users. LANs typically do not exceed tens of kilometres in size, and are typically contained within a single building or a limited geographical area. They typically use only one kind of transmission medium or cabling, such as twisted-pair wire or coaxial cable. There are also wireless local area network (WLAN) products available. These are very popular because they are relatively easy to set up and enable you to have a network without any network cables strewn around your home or office. WLANs will be discussed more thoroughly later.

Wide Area Network (WAN)

A ***wide area network (WAN)*** is a computer network that spans a relatively large geographical area. WANs are typically used to connect two or more LANs. Different hardware and transmission media are often used in WANs because they must cover large distances efficiently. Used by multinational companies, WANs transmit and receive information across cities and countries. A discussion follows of four specific types of WANs—global networks, enterprise networks, value-added networks, and metropolitan area networks.

Global Networks

A ***global network*** spans multiple countries and may include the networks of several organizations. The Internet is an example of a global network. The Internet is the world's largest computer network, consisting of thousands of individual networks supporting millions of computers and users in over 60 countries. We provide a detailed discussion of the Internet in Chapter 4.

Enterprise Networks

An ***enterprise network*** is a WAN that is the result of connecting disparate networks of a single organization into a single network (see Figure C.9).

Value-Added Networks

Medium-speed WANs, called ***value-added networks (VANs)***, are private, third-party-managed networks that are economical because

Figure C.8 A local area network (LAN) allows multiple computers located near each other to communicate directly with each other and to share peripheral devices, such as a printer.

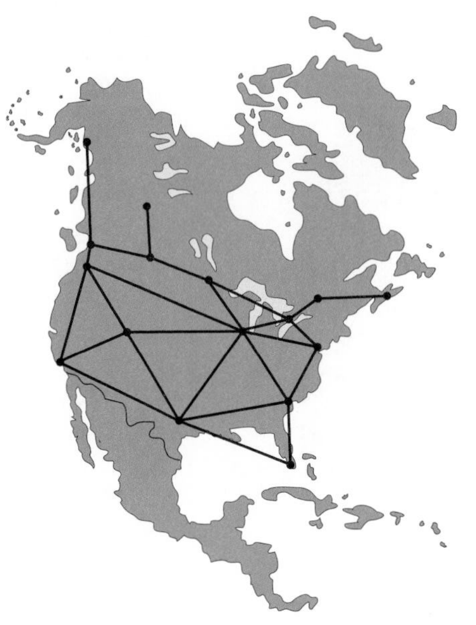

Figure C.9 An enterprise network allows an organization to connect distributed locations into a single network.

they are shared by multiple organizations. Customers lease communication lines rather than investing in dedicated network equipment. The "added value" provided by VANs can include network management, e-mail, EDI, security, and other special capabilities. Consequently, VANs can be more expensive than generic communication lines leased from a common telecommunication company like AT&T or Sprint, but they provide valuable services for customers.

Metropolitan Area Networks

A ***metropolitan area network (MAN)*** is a computer network of limited geographic scope, typically a city-wide area, that combines both LAN and high-speed fibre-optic technologies. MANs are attractive to organizations that need high-speed data transmission within a limited geographic area.

Personal Area Networks

A final type of computer network, called a ***personal area network (PAN)***, is an emerging technology that uses wireless communication to exchange data between computing devices using short-range radio communication, typically within an area of 10 metres. The enabling technology for PAN is called ***Bluetooth***, a specification for personal networking of desktop computers, peripheral devices, mobile phones, pagers, portable stereos, and other handheld devices. Bluetooth's founding members include Ericsson, IBM, Intel, Nokia, and Toshiba. Bluetooth is rapidly being integrated into a variety of personal devices to ease interoperability and information sharing (see Figure C.10).

Now that you have an understanding of the general types of networks, the next sections examine some of their fundamental components. This discussion is divided into two

Figure C.10 The Toyota Prius can be equipped with a Bluetooth network that allows drivers to operate their Bluetooth-enabled cellular phones, using hands-free operation through the car's onboard navigation system.

Source: Scott Halleran/Getty Images

areas: networking fundamentals and networking software and hardware. Together, these sections provide a foundation for understanding various types of networks.

NETWORKING FUNDAMENTALS

Telecommunications advances have enabled individual computer networks—constructed with a variety of hardware and software—to connect together in what appears to be a single network. Networks are increasingly being used to dynamically exchange relevant, value-adding knowledge and information throughout global organizations and institutions. The following sections take a closer look at the fundamental building blocks of these complex networks and the services they provide.

Servers, Clients, and Peers

A ***network*** consists of three separate components: servers, clients, and peers, as depicted in Figure C.11. A ***server*** is any computer on the network that makes access to files, printing, communications, and other services available to users of the network. Servers only provide services. A server typically has a more advanced microprocessor, more memory, a larger cache, and more disk storage than a single-user workstation. A ***client*** is any computer, such as a user's workstation or PC on the network, or any software application, such as a word processing application, that uses the services provided by the server.

Clients only request services. A client usually has only one user, whereas many different users share the server. A ***peer*** is any computer that may both request and provide services. Whether or not a particular computer or device on the network is considered a server, client, or peer depends on the operating system that is running. The trend in business is to use ***server-centric networks***, in which servers and clients have defined roles. However, ***peer-to-peer networks*** (often abbreviated as P2P) that enable any computer or device on the network to provide and request services can be found in small offices and homes. In P2P networks, all peers have equivalent capabilities and responsibilities; this is the network architecture behind popular file-sharing applications such as BitTorrent and KaZaA, where peers are able to connect directly to the hard drives of other peers on the Internet that are utilizing the software.

Figure C.11 A server is a computer on the network that enables multiple computers (or "clients") to access data. A peer is a computer that may both request and provide services.

Network Services

Network services are the capabilities that networked computers share through the multiple combinations of hardware and software. The most common network services are file services, print services, message services, and application services. ***File services*** are used to store, retrieve, and move data files in an efficient manner, as shown in Figure C.12a. An individual can use the file services of the network to move a customer file electronically to multiple recipients across the network. ***Print services*** are used to control and manage users' access to network printers and fax equipment, as shown in Figure C.12b. Sharing printers on a network reduces the number of printers an organization needs. ***Message services*** include the storing, accessing, and delivering of text, binary, graphic, digitized video, and audio data. These services are similar to file services, but they also deal with communication interactions between users and applications. Message services include e-mail or the transfer of messages between two or more networked computers, as shown in Figure C.12c. ***Application services*** run software for network clients and enable computers to share processing power, as shown in Figure C.12d. Application services highlight the concept of client/server computing, in which processing is distributed between the client and server. The servers store data and application programs and process clients' requests. For example, the physical search of database records may take place on the server, while a much smaller database application that handles the user-interface functions runs on the client.

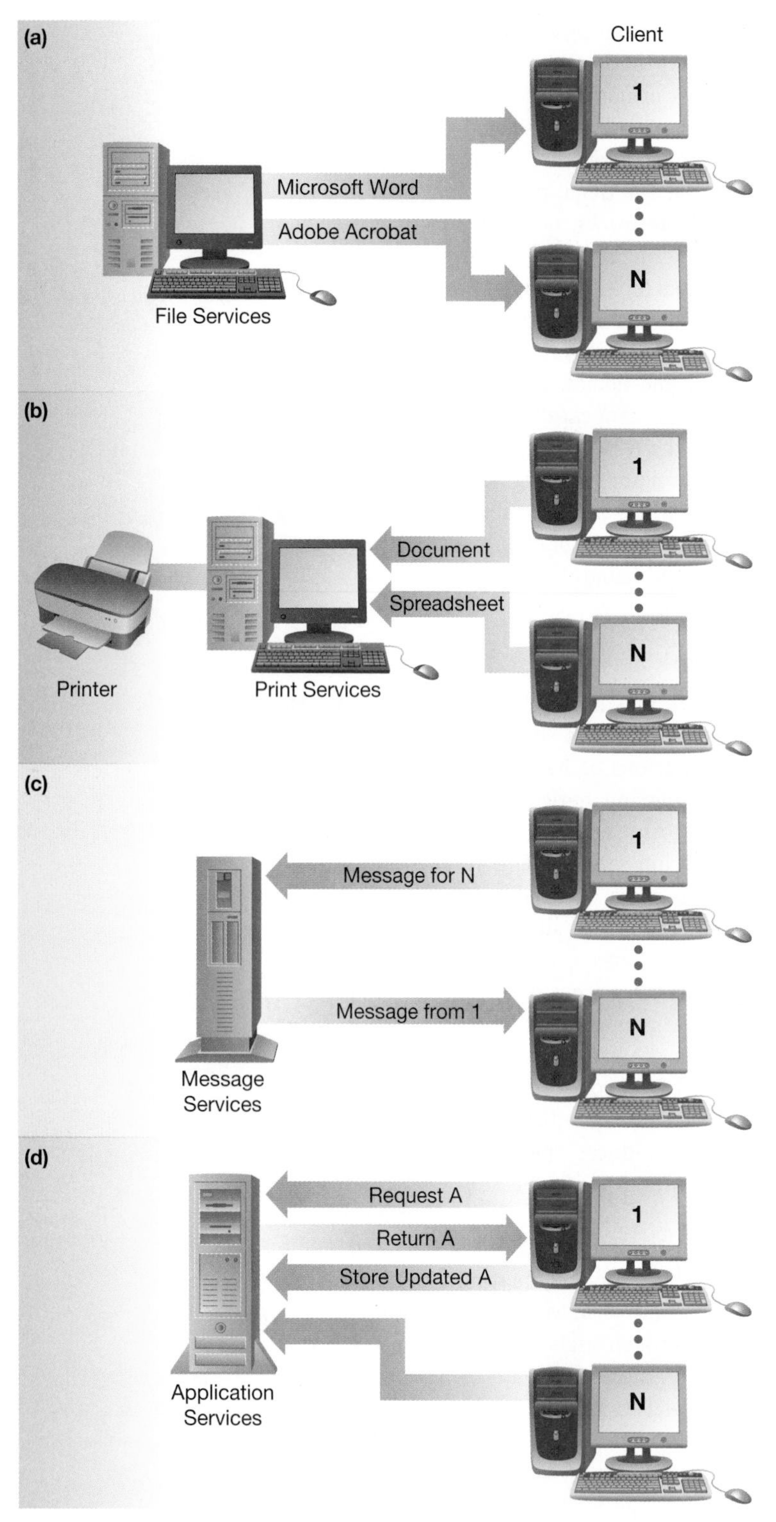

Figure C.12 Networks can provide file, print, message, and application services.

When an organization decides to network its computers and devices, it must decide what services will be provided and whether these services will be centralized (a server-centric approach), distributed (a peer-to-peer approach), or some combination of both. These decisions ultimately affect the choice of the network operating system. The ***network operating system (NOS)*** is system software that controls the network and enables computers to communicate with each other. In other words, the NOS enables network services. In most LAN environments, the NOS consists of two parts. The first and most complex part is the system software that runs on the file server. The system software coordinates many functions, including user accounts, access information, security, and resource sharing. The second and much smaller part of the NOS runs on each workstation connected to the network. In P2P networks, usually a piece of the NOS is installed on each attached workstation and runs on top of the local operating system. A recent trend is to integrate the NOS into the workstation operating system itself. Recent versions of Windows use this approach. Examples of NOSs are Novell NetWare, Microsoft Windows Server, and Converging Technologies LANtastic.

Transmission Media

Every network uses one or more types of ***transmission media***—the physical pathway to send data and information between two or more entities on a network. To send messages, computers send energy-based signals—electric currents using electromagnetic waves—to contact each other. These electromagnetic waves can be altered by semiconductor materials and are represented in two discrete, or binary, states—the 0s and 1s of a computer, known as bits. These bits are transmitted over physical pathways, or media, as computers communicate with each other.

When deciding which type of medium to use in a network, an organization should consider bandwidth, attenuation, immunity from electromagnetic interference and eavesdropping, the cost of the cable, and ease of installation, as summarized in Table C.2. Recall that ***bandwidth*** is the transmission capacity of a computer or communications channel, measured in megabits per second (Mbps), and represents how much binary data can be reliably transmitted over the medium in 1 second. Some networks have a bandwidth of 10 Mbps; others have 100 Mbps or more. To appreciate the importance of bandwidth for speed, consider how long it would take to transmit a document the length of this book (about two million characters or 16 million bits). It would take about 1.6 seconds at 10 Mbps and 16 seconds at

Medium	Key Benefit(s)	Drawback(s)
Twisted Pair	Inexpensive; easy to install and reconfigure	Highly susceptible to EMI, eavesdropping, and attenuation; unsuitable for high speeds
Coaxial	Higher bandwidth than twisted pair; lower susceptibility to EMI, eavesdropping, and attenuation than twisted pair	More expensive than twisted pair; more difficult to install, reconfigure, and manage attenuation than twisted pair; bulky
Fibre-Optic	Very high bandwidth; low attenuation and immune to EMI and eavesdropping	Expensive cable and hardware; complex installation and maintenance

Table C.2 ***Key benefits and drawbacks of different cable media.***

100 Mbps. In contrast, using a standard PC modem that transmits data at a rate of 56K bits per second (bps), it would take nearly 5 minutes to transmit the same document.

In addition to bandwidth, a second key issue to consider is transmission media's vulnerability to attenuation. ***Attenuation*** results when the power of an electric signal weakens as it is sent over increasing distance, as shown in Figure C.13. In a network, an important concern is how far a signal can travel and still maintain its original properties or meaning. ***EMI (electromagnetic interference)*** occurs when fluorescent lights, weather, or other electronic signals interfere with the original signal being sent. All media differ as to how immune they are to EMI, as we will see in the next sections.

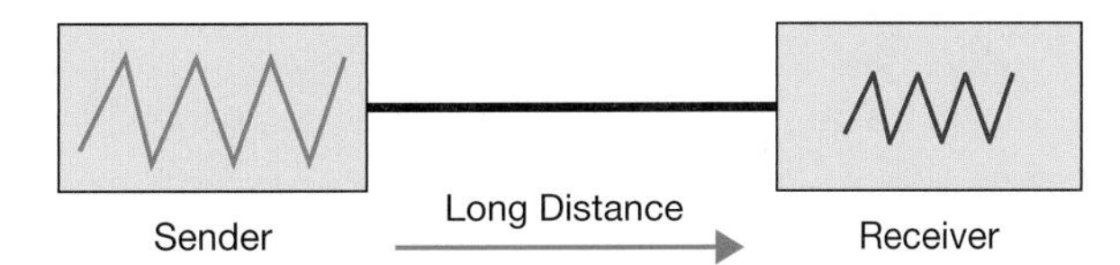

Figure C.13 Signals weaken when sent over increasing distances.

Two forms of media are used in networks: cable and wireless media. Although wireless data communication is being used increasingly, it is generally somewhat slower and less stable than wired cable media. Nevertheless, the capabilities of wireless media are rapidly improving, and wireless media have many useful applications. The following sections describe the characteristics of both cable and wireless media.

Cable Media

Cable media physically link computers and other devices in a network. The most common forms of cable media are twisted pair, coaxial, and fibre-optic.

Twisted Pair Cable

Twisted pair (TP) cable is made of two or more pairs of insulated copper wires twisted together (see Figure C.14). The cable may be unshielded (UTP) or shielded (STP). Telephone wire installations use UTP cabling. UTP is rated according to its quality; category 3 (Cat 3) and Cat 5 UTP are often used in network installations. Unshielded cable is cheap, easy to install, and has a capacity from 1 to 100 Mbps at distances up to 100 metres. However, like all copper wiring, it has rapid attenuation and is very sensitive to EMI and eavesdropping—the undetected capturing of network information. Shielded twisted cable is cable wrapped in an insulation that makes it less prone to EMI and eavesdropping. Shielded twisted cable is more expensive than unshielded twisted cable, and it is more difficult to install because it requires special grounding connectors to drain EMI. STP can support bandwidths up to 500 Mbps at distances up to 100 metres. However, it is most commonly used to support networks running at 16 Mbps.

Coaxial Cable

Coaxial (or "coax") cable contains a solid inner copper conductor, surrounded by plastic insulation and an outer braided copper or foil shield (see Figure C.15). Coax cable comes in a variety of thicknesses—thinnet coax and thicknet coax—based on resistance to EMI. Thinnet coax is less costly than STP or Cat 5 UTP; thicknet coax, however, is more expensive than STP or Cat 3 UTP. Coax is the simplest cable to install. The cable is cut, and a connector, called a T-connector, is attached to the cable and each device. Coax cable is most commonly used for cable television installations and for networks operating at 10 to 100 Mbps. Its attenuation is lower than twisted pair

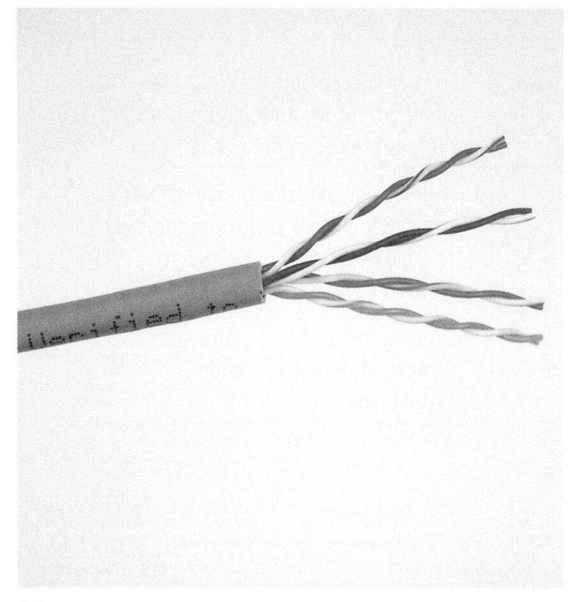

(a)

(b)

Figure C.14 At the top (C.14a) is a cable spliced open showing several twisted pairs, and below that (C.14b) is a sample network installation that utilizes many twisted pair cables at once.

Source: (C.14a) © Belkin Components, (C.14b) © Getty Images, Inc.

cable's, and it is moderately susceptible to EMI and eavesdropping.

Fibre-Optic Cable

Fibre-optic cable is made of a light-conducting glass or plastic core, surrounded by more glass, called cladding, and a tough outer sheath (see Figure C.16). The sheath protects the fibre from changes in temperature, as well as from bending or breaking. This technology uses

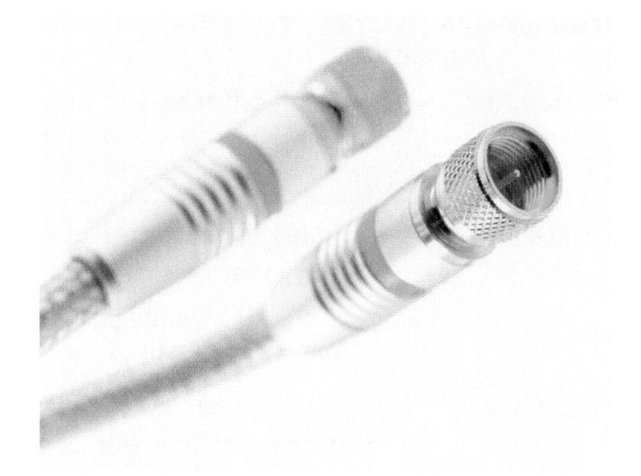

Figure C.15 These sample coaxial cables are ready to be connected to a computer or other device.

Source: © Getty Images, Inc.

pulses of light sent along the optical cable to transmit data. Fibre-optic cable transmits clear and secure data because it is immune to EMI and eavesdropping. Transmission signals do not break up because fibre-optic cable has low attenuation. It can support bandwidths from 100 Mbps to greater than 2 Gbps (gigabits per second) and distances from 2 to 25 kilometres. It can transmit video and sound. Fibre-optic cable is more expensive than copper wire because the cost and difficulties of installation and repair are higher for fibre-optic. Fibre-optic cables are used for high-speed ***backbones***—the high-speed central networks to which many smaller networks can be connected. A backbone may connect, for example, several different buildings in which other, smaller LANs reside. Table C.2 provides a comparison of benefits and drawbacks of the three different cable media that have been discussed.

Figure C.16 Fibre-optic cable consists of a light-conducting glass or plastic core, surrounded by more glass, called cladding, and a tough outer sheath.

Source: © Getty Images, Inc.

Protocol	Frequency	Bandwidth	Range	Typical Uses
Bluetooth	2.4 Ghz	1 Mbps	10 m	Headphones, keyboards, phones
Infrared	~100 Hz	~115 Kbps	5 m	Remote controls, PDAs
802.11b (Wi-Fi)	2.4 Ghz	11 Mbps	50 m	Office, home networks, laptops
802.11a	5 Ghz	54 Mbps	35 m	Office, home networks, laptops
802.11g	2.5 Ghz	22 Mbps	50 m	Office, home networks, laptops

Others: 802.11e (designed to support data streaming), 802.11i (includes advanced security features), 802.16e (WiMax fixed broadband wireless access), 802.20 (high-speed mobile broadband wireless access)

Table C.3 *Wireless protocols for data transmission*

Wireless Media

With the popularity of cellular phones and pagers, wireless media are rapidly gaining popularity. ***Wireless media*** transmit and receive electromagnetic signals using methods such as infrared line of sight, high-frequency radio, and microwave systems. Many home and corporate networks now use wireless media. In fact, networks based on wireless media are growing faster than all other types of networks put together. Unfortunately, the protocols and terminology surrounding wireless media can be confusing. Table C.3 compares some current and future wireless data transmission protocols.

Infrared Line of Sight

Infrared line of sight uses high-frequency light waves to transmit data on an unobstructed path between nodes—computers or some other device such as a printer—on a network, at a distance of up to 24.4 metres. The remote controls for most audio/visual equipment, such as your TV, stereo, and other consumer electronics equipment, use infrared light. Infrared systems may be configured as either point-to-point or broadcast. For example, when you use your TV remote control, you have to be in front of the TV to have successful communication. This is an example of point-to-point infrared. Many new printers and notebooks have the capability to transmit data using infrared communication, allowing these devices to be easily connected. With broadcast infrared communication, devices do not need to be positioned directly in front of each other, but simply have to be located within some distance of each other. Infrared equipment is relatively inexpensive, but point-to-point systems require strict line-of-sight positioning. Installation and maintenance focus on ensuring proper optical alignment between nodes on the network. Point-to-point infrared systems can support up to 16 Mbps at 1 kilometre, whereas broadcast systems support less than 1 Mbps. Attenuation and susceptibility to EMI and eavesdropping are problematic, particularly when objects obstruct the light path or when environmental conditions such as smoke or high-intensity light are prevalent.

High-Frequency Radio

High-frequency radio signals can transmit data at rates of up to 54 Mbps to network nodes from 12.2 up to approximately 40 kilometres apart, depending on the nature of any obstructions between them. The flexibility of the signal path makes high-frequency radio ideal for mobile transmissions. For example, most police departments use high-frequency radio signals that enable police vehicles to communicate with each other as well as with the dispatch office. This medium is expensive due to the cost of antenna towers and high-output transceivers. Installation is complex and often dangerous due to the high voltages. Although attenuation is fairly low, this medium is very susceptible to EMI and eavesdropping.

Three common applications of high-frequency radio communication are pagers, cellular phones, and wireless networks. A ***pager*** is a one-way, wireless messaging system. See Table C.4 for a summary of types of pagers and their advantages. In a business setting, there are countless uses for a pager. If you travel, your boss can easily contact you when you are away from the office. If you are on vacation, you can learn the outcome of an important business deal. Pagers are also popular with families for notifying others of changes in plans, notifying parents when kids need to be picked up from school, or notifying teenagers when it is time to come home!

Unlike pagers, a ***cellular phone*** provides two-way wireless communication. In a cellular system, for example, a city is divided into ***cells*** with a low-powered radio antenna/receiver in each cell; these cells are monitored and

Table C.4 ***Types of pagers.***

Pager Type	Description	Advantages
Tone-only	User is alerted with an audible tone to call a predetermined phone number for a message	Simple
Numeric display	User is alerted and number to call is displayed	Can use any phone number; phone number is stored; less chance of error or missing message
Alphanumeric display	User is alerted and reads alphanumeric message	Same as numeric display, plus complete, accurate text message
Tone and voice	User is alerted and receives a short voice message	User gets notification and message in single event; easier for caller and user

controlled by a central computer (see Figure C.17). Any given cellular network has a fixed number of radio frequencies. When a user initiates or receives a call, the mobile telephone switching office assigns the caller a unique frequency for the duration of the call. As a person travels within the network, the central computer at the switching office monitors the quality of the signal and automatically assigns the call to the closest cellular antenna.

Cellular phones can transmit information in either an analog or digital format. Digital format is the newer technology and is quickly replacing older analog phones and networks. Overall, digital formats improve call quality, have greater security, and allow users to use advanced data services such as mobile Internet access. Alternatively, analog provides better roaming coverage and is generally cheaper.

Cellular technology is quickly evolving. First-generation (1G) cellular used analog signals and was not capable of providing data services such as e-mail or web access. Second-generation (2G) cellular uses digital signals and allows voice and data services up to 9.6 Kbps; 2.5-generation cellular (2.5G) also uses digital signals and can transmit voice and data at rates as high as 115 Kbps. Third-generation (3G)—not currently available in the United States, but available in some parts of the world—uses digital signals and can transmit voice and data up to 384 Kbps when the device is moving at pedestrian speeds, 128 Kbps when moving in a car or train, and up to 2 Mbps when fixed to a permanent location. Clearly, as network coverage expands and worldwide standards solidify, 3G digital cellular networks will completely replace analog previous generation systems.

High-frequency radio-wave technology is increasingly being used to support ***wireless local area networks (WLANs)***. WLANs are also referred to as ***Wi-Fi (wireless fidelity)***

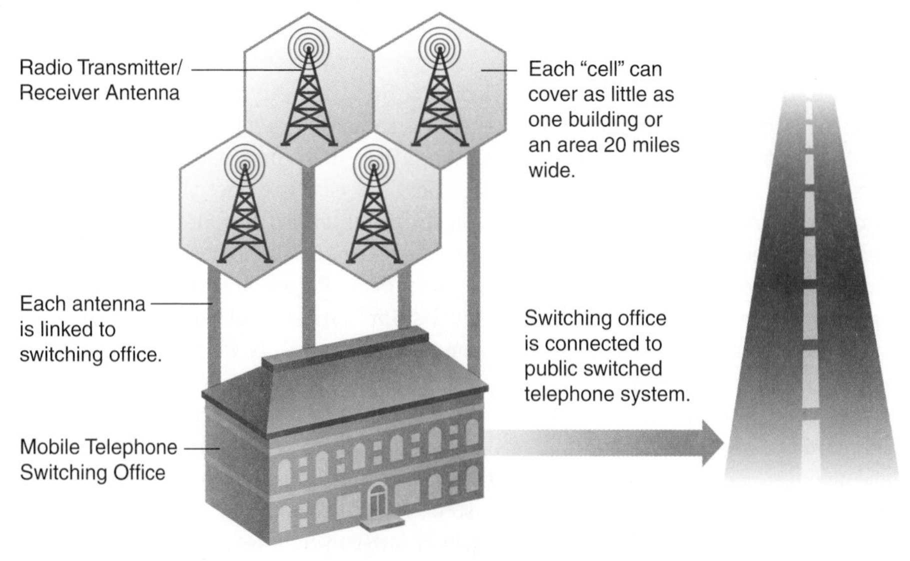

Figure C.17 A cellular network divides a geographic region into cells.

and are based on a standard called ***802.11***. The 802.11 standard has been universally adopted and has transmission speeds up to 54 Mbps. The ease of installation has made WLANs popular for business and home use. For example, some homes and many buildings have (or want) multiple computers and need to share Internet access, files, and peripheral devices. Unfortunately, many older buildings and homes do not have a wired infrastructure to easily connect computers and devices, making wireless networking particularly attractive. For example, Washington State University wanted to transform a traditional computer classroom—with obtrusive desktop computers sitting atop rows of desks that had wires and cables everywhere—into a flexible and comfortable team-learning environment where technology was present, but not overwhelming. With the help of the Boeing Company, Dell Computers, and Intel, students now sit in one of several comfortable learning stations using a variety of mobile wireless technologies (see Figure C.18). Through the use of wireless technologies, many organizations are transforming their work environments into better team collaboration environments.

The last example where high-frequency radio is being used is in the operation of personal area networks (PANs). As discussed previously, PANs use low-powered Bluetooth radio-wave technology. Using Bluetooth, PANs are becoming extremely popular to connect cell phones to headsets, MP3 players to music servers, automobiles to cell phones, and countless other applications. If you don't have a Bluetooth-enabled device yet, chances are that you soon will.

Figure C.18 The Boeing Wireless Classroom of the Future at Washington State University provides a flexible and comfortable learning environment for students.

Source: Courtesy of Boeing

Microwave

Microwave transmission is a high-frequency radio signal that is sent through the air using either terrestrial (Earth-based) systems or satellite systems. Both terrestrial and satellite microwave transmission require line-of-sight communications between the signal sender and the signal receiver. ***Terrestrial microwave***, shown in Figure C.19, uses antennae that require an unobstructed path or line-of-sight between nodes. Terrestrial microwave systems are used to cross inaccessible terrain or to connect buildings where cable installation would be expensive. The cost of a terrestrial microwave system depends on the distance to be covered. Typically, businesses lease access to these microwave systems from service providers rather than invest in antenna equipment. Data may be transmitted at up to 274 Mbps. Over short distances, attenuation is not a problem, but signals can be obstructed over longer distances by environmental conditions such as high winds and heavy rain. EMI and eavesdropping are significant problems with microwave communications.

Satellite microwave, shown in Figure C.20, uses a relay station that transfers signals between antennae located on Earth and satellites orbiting the Earth. In other words, a ***satellite*** is

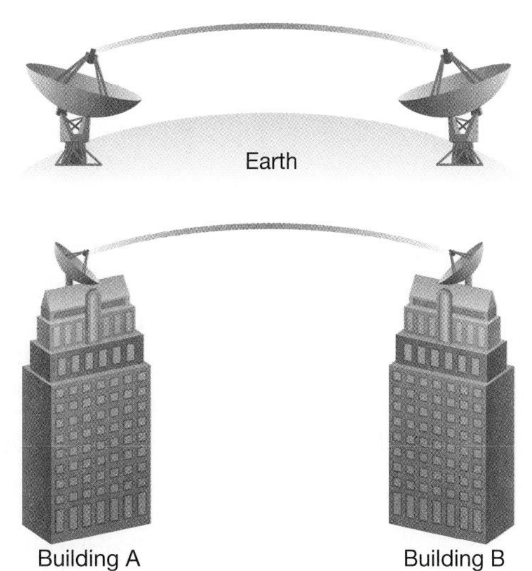

Figure C.19 Terrestrial microwave requires a line-of-sight path between a sender and a receiver.

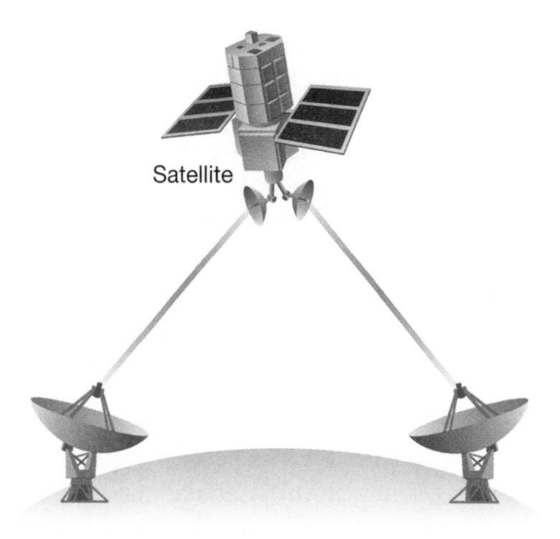

Figure C.20 Communications satellites are relay stations that receive signals from one Earth station and rebroadcast them to another.

a microwave station located in outer space. Satellite transmissions are delayed because of the distance signals must travel. Satellites orbit from 600 to 36 800 kilometres above the Earth and have different uses and characteristics (see Table C.5). Satellite communication's greatest strength is that it can be used to access very remote and undeveloped locations on the earth. Such systems are extremely costly because their use and installation depends on space technology. Companies such as AT&T sell satellite services with typical transmission rates ranging from <1 to 10 Mbps, but the rates can be as high as 90 Mbps. Like terrestrial microwave, satellite systems are prone to attenuation and susceptible to EMI and eavesdropping.

As with cable media, there are key differences between the types of wireless media. Table C.6 summarizes the key benefits and drawbacks of each wireless medium. Table C.7 compares wireless media across several criteria.

NETWORK SOFTWARE AND HARDWARE

Standards play a key role in creating networks. The physical elements of networks—adapters, cables, and connectors—are defined by a set of standards that have evolved since the early 1970s. Standards ensure the interoperability and compatibility of network devices. The Institute of Electrical and Electronics Engineers (IEEE) has established a number of telecommunications standards. The three major standards for LAN cabling and media access control are Ethernet, token ring, and ARCnet. See Table C.8 for a summary of LAN standards. Each standard combines a media access control technique, network topology, and media in different ways. Software is blended with hardware to implement protocols that allow different types of computers and networks to communicate successfully. Protocols are often implemented within a computer's operating system or within a special

Table C.5 ***Characteristics of satellites with different orbits.***

Name	Distance from Earth	Common Application
Low Earth Orbit (LEO) Satellite	600–1600 kms	• Not fixed in space in relation to the rotation of the Earth; circle the Earth several times per day. • Photography for mapping and locating mineral deposits; monitoring ice cap, coastline, volcanoes, and rainforests; research plant and crop changes; monitor wildlife and animal habitat and animal changes; search and rescue from downed aircraft or ships that are in trouble; research projects in astronomy and physics.
Medium Earth Orbit (MEO)	1600–36 800 kms	• Not fixed in space in relation to the rotation of the Earth; circle the Earth more than one time per day. • Primarily used in geographical positioning systems (GPS mapping) for navigation of ships at sea, spacecraft, airplanes, automobiles, and military weapons.
Geosynchronous Earth Orbit (GEO)	36 800 kms	• Fixed in space in relation to the rotation of the Earth; circle the Earth one time per day. • Because it is fixed in space, transmission is simplified. • Transmission of high-speed data for television, weather information, remote Internet connections, satellite digital radio, telecommunications (satellite phones).

Table C.6 ***Key benefits and drawbacks of different wireless media.***

Medium	Key Benefit(s)	Drawback(s)
Infrared line of sight	Easy to install and configure; inexpensive	Very limited bandwidth; line of sight required; environmental factors influence signal quality
High-frequency radio	Mobile stations; low attenuation	Frequency licensing; complex installation
Terrestrial microwave	Can access remote locations or congested areas; high bandwidth; low attenuation	Frequency licensing; complex installation; environmental factors influence signal quality
Satellite microwave	Can access remote locations; high bandwidth; Earth stations can be fixed or mobile	Frequency licensing; complex installation; environmental factors influence signal quality; propagation delays

Table C.7 ***Relative comparison of wireless media.***

Medium	Expense	Speed	Attenuation	EMI	Eavesdropping
Infrared line of sight	Low	Up to 16 Mbps	High	High	High
High-frequency radio	Moderate	Up to 54 Mbps	Low	High	High
Terrestrial microwave	Moderate	Up to 274 Mbps	Low	High	High
Satellite microwave	High	Up to 90 Mbps	Moderate	High	High

Key: Mbps = megabits per second.

Table C.8 ***Summary of major LAN standards.***

Network Standards	Access Control	Topology	Typical Media	Speed
Ethernet	CSMA/CD	Bus	Coax or twisted pair	10–100 Mbps
Token ring	Token passing	Ring	Twisted pair	4–100 Mbps
ARCnet	Token passing	Star or bus	Coax or twisted pair	2.5–20 Mbps

piece of software called a network operating system. Each of these topics is described more thoroughly below.

Media Access Control

Media access control is the set of rules that governs how a given node or workstation gains access to the network to send or receive information. There are two general types of access control: distributed and random access. With distributed control, only a single workstation at a time has authorization to transmit its data. This authorization is transferred sequentially from workstation to workstation. Under random control, any workstation can transmit its data by checking whether the medium is available. No specific permission is required. The following sections describe each type in more detail.

Distributed Access Control

The most commonly used method of distributed access control is called token passing. ***Token passing*** is an access method that uses a constantly circulating electronic token, a small packet of data, to prevent collisions and give all workstations equal access to the network. A collision occurs when two or more workstations simultaneously transmit messages onto the network. A workstation must possess the token before it can transmit a message onto the network.

A workstation that receives the token and wants to send a message marks the token as busy, appends a message to it, and transmits

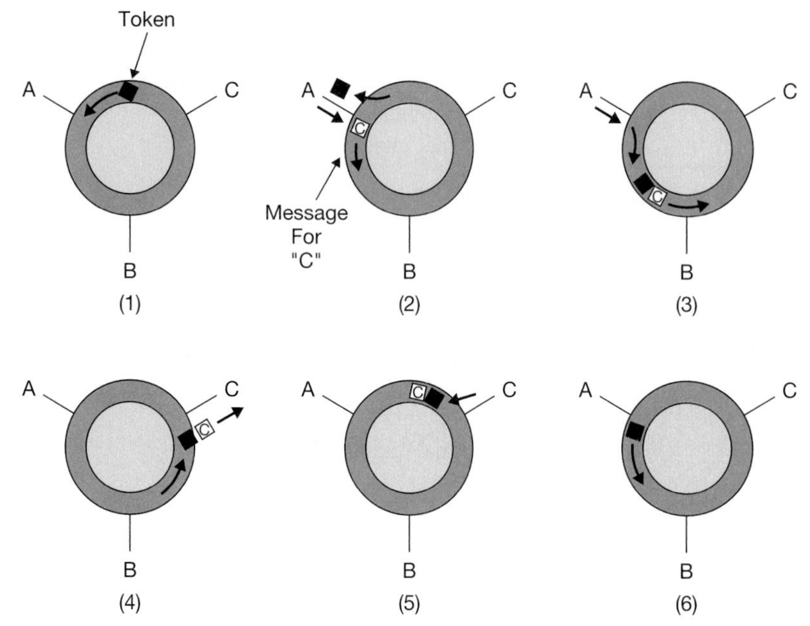

Figure C.21 Station A receives the token and adds a message for station C; C receives the message and token, then forwards both back to station A; station A removes the message and forwards the empty token on to the next station on the network.

both. The message and token are passed around the ring, as depicted in Figure C.21. Each workstation copies the message and retransmits the token/message combination. When it is received back at the originating workstation, the message is removed, the token is marked as free, and it is transmitted to the next workstation on the network.

Random Access Control

The most commonly used method of random access control is called ***CSMA/CD—carrier sense multiple access/collision detect.*** In CSMA/CD each workstation "listens" to the network to determine whether a message is being transmitted. If the network is quiet, the workstation sends its message; otherwise, it waits. When a workstation gains access to the medium and sends information onto the network, messages are sent to all workstations on the network; however, only the destination with the proper address is able to "open" the message. If two or more workstations try to send a message simultaneously, all workstations detect that a collision has occurred, and all sending is ceased. After a short random period of time, the workstations again try to send their messages. When network traffic is light, there are few collisions, and data are quickly transmitted. However, the speed of transmission deteriorates rapidly under heavy traffic conditions.

Network Topologies

Network topology refers to the shape of a network. The three common network topologies are star, ring, and bus.

Star Network

A ***star network*** is configured, as you might expect, in the shape of a star, as shown in Figure C.22a. That is, all nodes or workstations are connected to a central hub, or concentrator, through which all messages pass. Active hubs amplify transmission signals, so long cable lengths may be used. The workstations represent the points of the star. Star topologies are easy to lay out and modify. However, they are also the most costly because they require the largest amount of cabling. Although it is easy to diagnose problems at individual workstations, star networks are susceptible to a single point of failure at the hub, which would result in all workstations losing network access.

Ring Network

A ***ring network*** is configured in the shape of a closed loop or circle, with each node connecting to the next node, as shown in Figure C.22b. In ring networks, messages move in one direction around the circle. As a message moves around the circle, each workstation examines it to see whether the message is for that workstation. If not, the message is regenerated and passed on to the next node. This regeneration process enables ring networks to cover much larger distances than star or bus networks can. Relatively little cabling is required, but a failure of any node on the ring network can cause complete network failure. It is difficult to modify and reconfigure the network. Ring networks normally use some form of token-passing media access control method to regulate network traffic.

Bus Network

A ***bus network*** is in the shape of an open-ended line, as shown in Figure C.22c; as a result, it is the easiest network to extend and has the simplest wiring layout. This topology enables all network nodes to receive the same message through the network cable at the same time. However, it is difficult to diagnose and isolate network faults. Bus networks use CSMA/CD for media access control.

Protocols

In addition to media access control and network topologies, all networks employ protocols to

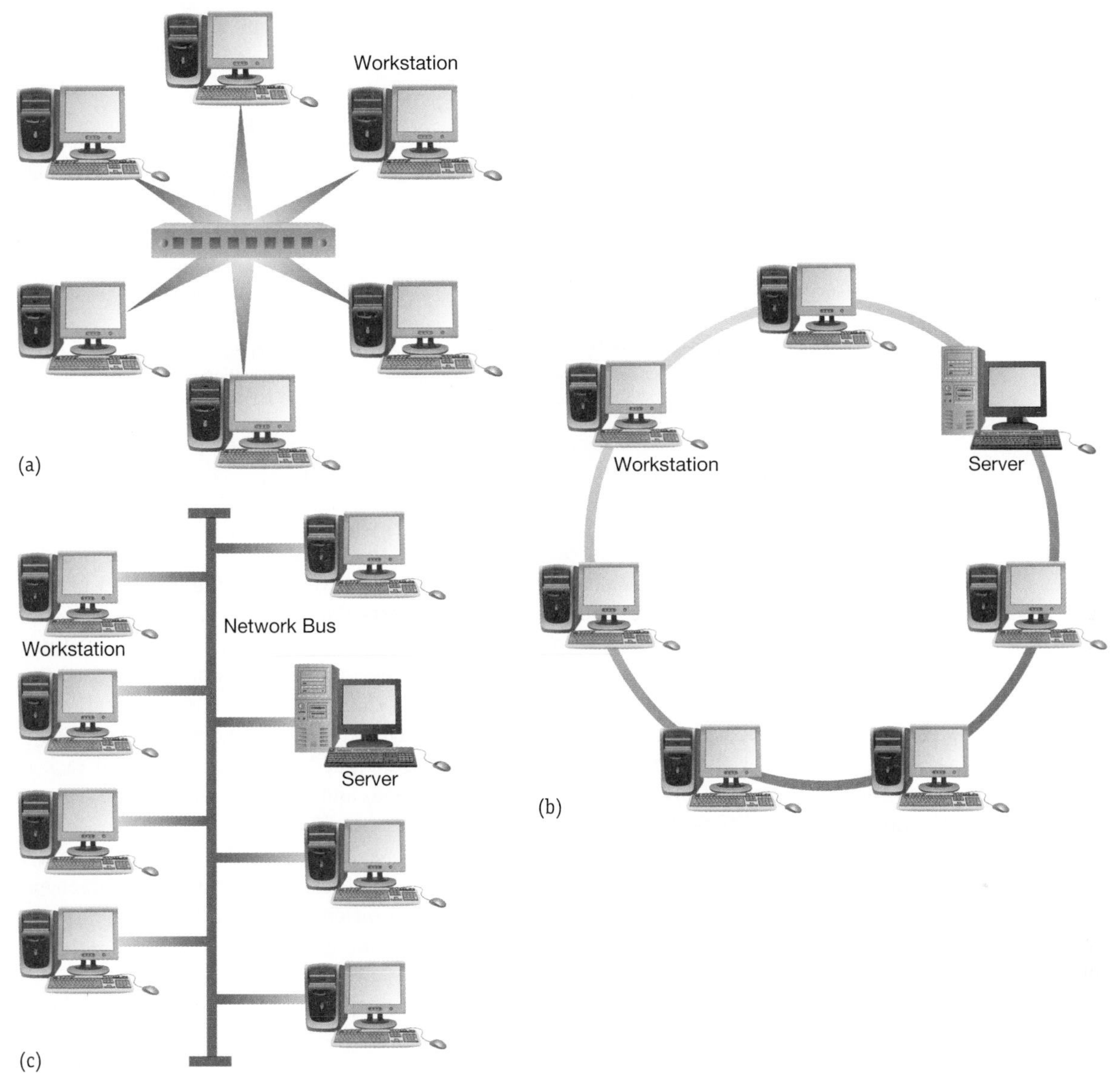

Figure C.22 (a) The star network has several workstations connected to a central hub. (b) The ring network is configured in a closed loop, with each workstation connected to another workstation. (c) The bus network is configured in the shape of an open-ended line where each workstation receives the same message simultaneously.

make sure communication between computers is successful. ***Protocols*** are agreed-upon formats for transmitting data between connected computers. They specify how computers should be connected to the network, how errors will be checked, what data compression method will be used, how a sending computer will signal that it has finished sending a message, and how a receiving computer will signal that it has received a message. Protocols allow packets to be correctly routed to and from their destinations. There are literally thousands of protocols for programmers to use, but a few are a lot more important than the others. In this section, we will first review the worldwide standard, called the OSI model, for implementing protocols. Next, we briefly review two of the more important network protocols: Ethernet and TCP/IP.

The OSI Model

The need of organizations to interconnect computers and networks that use different protocols has driven the industry to an open system architecture, in which different protocols can communicate with each other. The International Organization for Standardization (ISO) defined a networking model called the Open Systems Interconnection (OSI) that divides computer-to-computer communications into seven connected layers. The ***OSI model*** is a protocol that represents a group of specific

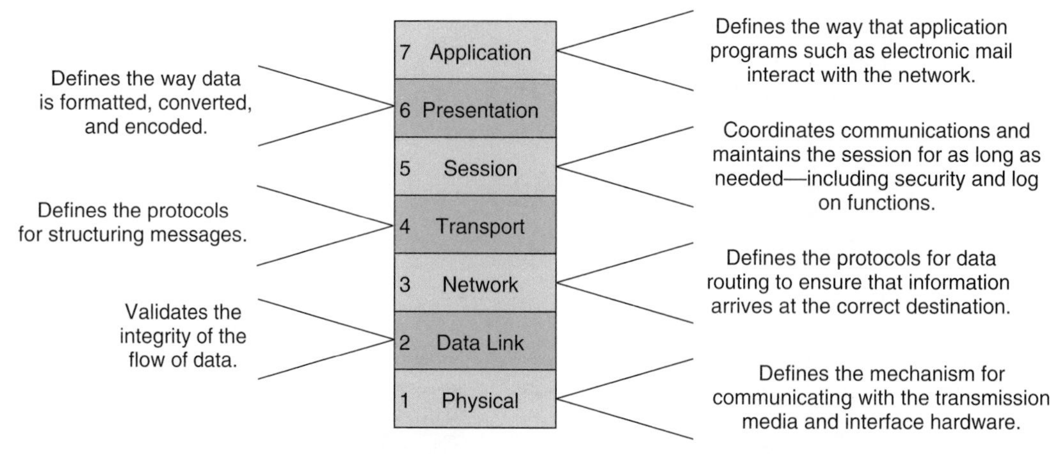

Figure C.23 The Open Systems Interconnection (OSI) model has seven layers and provides a framework for connecting different computers with different operating systems to a network.

tasks, represented in Figure C.23 as successive layers, that enable computers to communicate data. Each successively higher layer builds on the functions of the layers below. For example, suppose you are using a PC running Windows and are connected to the Internet, and you want to send a message to a friend who is connected to the Internet through a large workstation computer running UNIX—two different computers and two different operating systems. When you transmit your message, it is passed down from layer to layer in the Windows protocol environment of your system. At each layer, special bookkeeping information specific to the layer, called a header, is added to the data. Eventually, the data and headers are transferred from the Windows Layer 1 to UNIX's Layer 1 over some physical medium. Upon receipt, the message is passed up through the layers in the UNIX application. At each layer, the corresponding header information is stripped away, the requested task is performed, and the remaining data package is passed on until your message arrives as you sent it, as shown in Figure C.24. In other words, protocols represent an agreement between different parts of the network about how data are to be transferred.

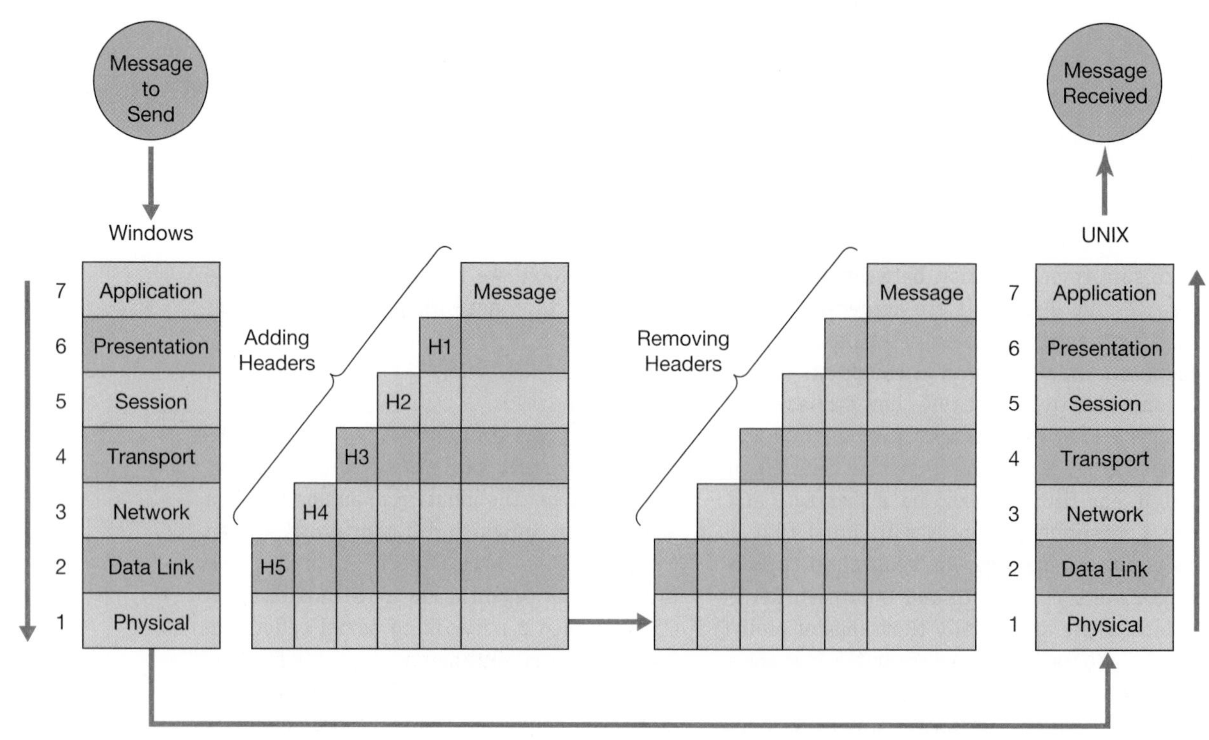

Figure C.24 Message passing between two different computers.

Ethernet

Ethernet is a local area network protocol developed by Xerox Corporation in 1976. It uses a bus or star network topology and uses random access control to send data. The original Ethernet supports data transfer rates of 10 Mbps. A later version, called 100Base-T or Fast Ethernet, supports transfer rates of 100 Mbps; the latest version, called Gigabit Ethernet, supports transfer rates of 1 gigabit, or 1000 megabits, per second. You need some type of Ethernet card installed in your computer to use this type of network connection.

TCP/IP

The Internet was based on the idea that individual networks could be separately designed and developed, yet still connect their users to the Internet by using their own unique interfaces. ***Transmission Control Protocol/Internet Protocol (TCP/IP)***, the protocol of the Internet, allows different interconnected networks to communicate using the same language. For example, TCP/IP allows IBM, Macintosh, and Dell users to communicate despite any system differences. Computer scientist Vinton Cerf and engineer Robert Kahn defined the Internet Protocol (IP), by which packets are sent from one computer to another on their way to a destination, as part of the DARPA project. TCP/IP was discussed more thoroughly in Chapter 4.

Connectivity Hardware

Stand-alone computers can be physically connected to create different types of networks. Transmission media connectors, network interface cards, and modems are used to connect computers or devices in a network. After individual devices are connected to the network, multiple segments of transmission media can be connected to form one large network. Repeaters, hubs, bridges, and multiplexers are used to extend the range and size of the network. These devices are described below.

Transmission Media Connectors

Transmission media connectors, or simply ***connectors***, are used to terminate cable in order to be plugged into a network interface card or into other network components. Connectors include T-connectors for coax cable and RJ-45 connectors (similar to a phone jack) for twisted pair cable.

Network Interface Cards

A ***network interface card (NIC)*** is a PC expansion board that plugs into a computer so that it can be connected to a network. Each NIC has a unique identifier (determined by the manufacturer) that is used to identify the address of the computer on the network.

Modems

A ***modem*** (MOdulator/DEModulator) enables computers to transmit data over telephone lines and thereby connect your PC with other PCs in a computer network. Because the dial-up telephone system was designed to pass the sound of voices in the form of analog signals, it cannot pass the electrical pulses—***digital signals***—that computers use. The only way to pass digital data over conventional voice telephone lines is to convert it to audio tones—***analog signals***—that the telephone lines can carry. Hence, a modem converts digital signals from a computer into analog signals so that telephone lines may be used as a transmission medium to send and receive electronic information. If you send an e-mail message from your university through the Internet to a friend at another university, the modem attached to your PC converts your digital message into audio tones. The message is transmitted over the telephone lines to your university, then travels through the Internet from your university to your friend's university. Your friend also uses a modem to dial into his/her university to read your message, as shown in Figure C.25.

Repeaters

A ***repeater*** is a network device used to regenerate or replicate a signal as it weakens when travelling on a network. A repeater also moves data from one media segment to another and effectively extends the size of the network.

Hubs

A ***hub*** is used as a central point of connection between media segments. Like repeaters, hubs enable the network to be extended to accommodate additional workstations. Hubs are commonly used in 10Base-T networks.

Bridges

A ***bridge*** is used to connect two different LANs or two segments of the same LAN by forwarding network traffic between network segments. However, unlike repeaters, bridges determine the physical location of the source and destination computers. They are typically used to divide an overloaded network into separate segments, helping to minimize inter-segment traffic. Bridges are also used to connect segments that use different wiring or network protocols.

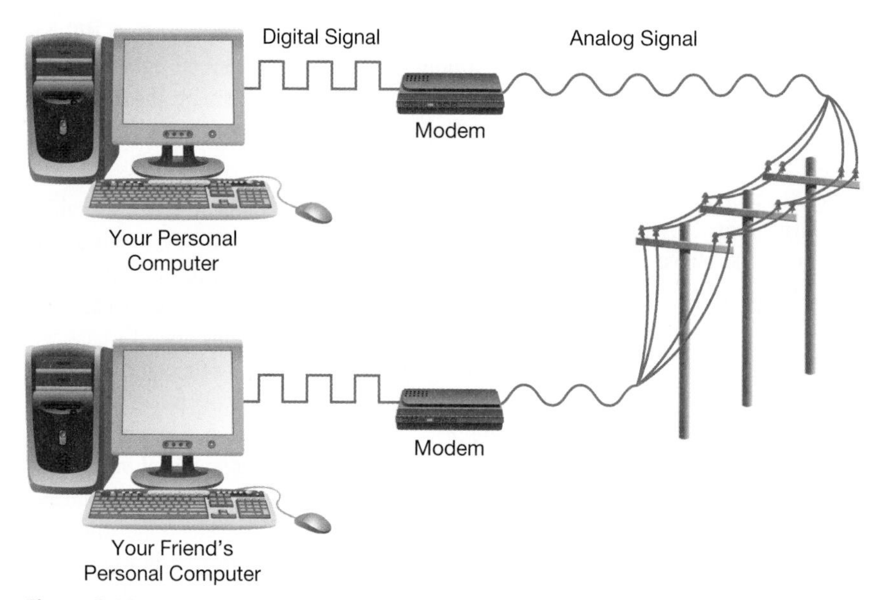

Figure C.25 Modems convert digital signals into analog and analog signals into digital.

Multiplexers

A ***multiplexer (MUX)*** is used to share a communications line or medium among a number of users. Sometimes the transmission medium provides more capacity than a single signal can occupy. To use the entire media bandwidth effectively, MUXs are used to transmit several signals over a single channel. MUXs convert and combine signals from multiple users for simultaneous transmission over a single line or medium.

Organizations use these components to construct a LAN by attaching individual computers and media segments into one network. Organizations today also want to connect users and/or networks in different geographical areas. Distributed LANs, interconnected by WANs, are needed to exchange data and information across an organization. The WAN, however, appears transparent to the user because information stored in a computer at another location appears to be locally available. ***Internetworking*** connectivity hardware—routers, brouters, CSUs (channel service units), and gateways—provides businesses with the freedom to locate their operations in different cities or countries, while at the same time running them as integrated units. These technologies will now be briefly described.

Switches

A ***switch*** is a device that channels incoming data from any of multiple input ports to the specific output port that will take the data toward its intended destination.

Routers

A ***router*** is an intelligent device used to connect two or more individual networks. When a router receives a signal, it looks at the network address and passes the signal or message on to the appropriate network. Unlike most switches, routers use software to predict the most efficient path through a large network, like the Internet.

Brouters

A ***brouter*** (pronounced brau-ter), short for bridge router, provides the capabilities of both a bridge and a router.

Channel Service Units

A ***channel service unit (CSU)*** is a device that acts as a "buffer" between a LAN and a public carrier's WAN. CSUs ensure that all signals placed on the public lines from the LAN are appropriately timed and formed for the public network.

Gateways

A ***gateway*** performs protocol conversion so that different networks can communicate even though they "speak" different languages. For example, communications between a LAN and a large system, such as a mainframe, whose protocols are different, require a gateway.

KEY POINTS REVIEW

1. **Describe the evolution of and types of computer networks.** Since the 1950s, three models of computing have been used. First, from the 1950s until the 1970s, the centralized computing model was dominant. In the centralized computing model, all processing occurs at a large central computer, and users interact with the system through the use of terminals. From the late 1970s until the late 1980s, a distributed computing model was dominant. In this model, separate computers work on subsets of tasks and then pool their results by communicating via a network. In the 1990s, the collaborative computing model emerged. In this model, two or more networked computers work together to accomplish a common processing task. There are several types of computer networks. A private branch exchange (PBX) is a private telephone exchange, located in a single facility, which provides both voice and data communication. A local area network (LAN) is a group of computers at one location that share hardware and software resources. A wide area network (WAN) refers to two or more LANs from different locations that are linked together. There are four general types of WANs: global networks, enterprise networks, value-added networks, and metropolitan area networks (MANs). A global network is a WAN that spans multiple countries and may include the networks of several organizations. An enterprise network is a WAN that connects all the LANs of a single location. Value-added networks are private, third-party-managed networks that are shared by multiple organizations. MANs span a limited geographic scope, typically a city-wide area with both LAN and high-speed fibre-optic technologies. A final type of computer network, called a personal area network (PAN), is an emerging technology that uses wireless communication to exchange data between computing devices using short-range radio communication, typically within an area of 10 metres.
2. **Understand networking fundamentals, including network services and transmission media.** In networking, a distinction is made between servers, clients, and peers. A server is a computer that stores information (programs and data) and provides services to users through a network. A client is any device or software application that makes use of the information or services provided by a server. Peers are two separate computers or devices on a network that request and provide services to each other. Servers and clients are combined to create server-centric networks. Peers are combined to create peer-to-peer networks. Networks provide file, print, message, and application services that extend the capabilities of stand-alone computers. The network operating system (NOS) is the major piece of software that controls the network. In a typical LAN, the NOS consists of two parts. The first and most complex is the system software that runs on the server. The NOS software coordinates many functions, including user accounts, access information, security, and resource sharing. The second and much smaller part of the NOS runs on each workstation connected to the LAN. Networks exchange information by using cable or wireless transmission media. Cable media include twisted pair, coaxial, and fibre-optic. Wireless media include infrared line of sight, high-frequency radio, and microwave.
3. **Describe network software and hardware, including media access control, network topologies, and protocols, as well as connectivity hardware for both LANs and WANs.** Network access control refers to the rules that govern how a given workstation gains access to the network. There are two general types: distributed and random access. With distributed access, only a single workstation at a time has authorization to transmit its data. Under random access control, any workstation can transmit its data by checking whether the medium is available. The shape of a network can vary; the three most common topologies are star, ring, and bus configurations. Protocols are agreed-upon formats for transmitting data between connected computers. The need of organizations to interconnect devices that use different protocols has driven the industry to an open system architecture, in which different protocols can communicate with each other. The International Organization for Standardization (ISO) defined a networking model called the Open Systems Interconnection (OSI) that divides computer-to-computer communications into seven connected layers. Each successively higher layer builds on the functions of the layers below. Hardware and software vendors can use networking standards such as OSI to build devices that can be more easily interconnected. Ethernet is an important protocol for LANs, whereas TCP/IP (Transmission Control Protocol/Internet Protocol) is most widely used for the world's largest WAN, the Internet. In a network, each device or computer must be connected to the medium or cable segment. To accomplish this, transmission media connectors, network interface cards, and modems are used. After individual devices are connected to the network, multiple segments of transmission media can be connected to form one large network. Repeaters, hubs, bridges, and multiplexers are used to extend the range and size of the network. Routers, brouters, CSUs (channel service units), and gateways are used to interconnect WANs.

KEY TERMS

analog signals 405
application services 393
attenuation 395
backbones 396
bandwidth 394
Bluetooth 392
bridges 405
brouter 406
bus network 402
cells 397
cellular phones 397
centralized computing 388
channel service unit (CSU) 406
client 393
coaxial (coax) cable 395
collaborative computing 389
connectors 405
CSMA/CD (carrier sense multiple access/ collision detect) 402
digital signals 405
digitizing 388
distributed computing 389
802.11 399
EMI (electromagnetic interference) 395
enterprise networks 391
Ethernet 405
fibre-optic cable 396
file services 393
gateway 406
global network 391

high-frequency radio 397
hub 405
infrared line of sight 397
internetworking 406
local area networks (LAN) 391
media access control 401
message services 393
metropolitan area network (MAN) 392
microwave transmission 399
modem 405
multiplexer (MUX) 406
network interface card (NIC) 405
network operating system (NOS) 394
network services 393
network topologies 402
networks 393
OSI model 403
pager 397
peer 393
peer-to-peer networks 393
personal area network (PAN) 392
print services 393
private branch exchange (PBX) 390
protocol 388, 403
repeaters 405
ring network 402
routers 406
satellite 399
satellite microwave 399
servers 393
server-centric networks 393
star network 402
switch 406
terminals 388
terrestrial microwave 399
token passing 401
Transmission Control Protocol/Internet Protocol (TCP/IP) 405
transmission media 394
twisted pair (TP) cable 395
value-added network (VAN) 391
Wi-Fi (wireless fidelity) 398
wide area network (WAN) 391
wireless local area networks (WLAN) 398
wireless media 397

REVIEW QUESTIONS

1. Compare and contrast centralized, distributed, and collaborative computing.
2. How are local area networks, wide area networks, enterprise networks, and global networks related to each other?
3. Explain the difference between servers, clients, and peers.
4. What are the major types of network services available?
5. What are three common types of transmission media that use cabling?
6. What are four common methods of wireless transmission media for networking, and how do they differ from each other?
7. What is a network topology? Describe the three common topologies that are used today.
8. What is the purpose of the OSI model?
9. What is Ethernet, and why is it so popular?
10. What is TCP/IP, and what roles does it play in the use of the Internet?
11. What are the various types of hardware used to connect computers together into networks?
12. What is a modem used for, and how does one work?

SELF-STUDY QUESTIONS

Visit the Companion Website for this text for additional Self-Study Questions: **www.pearsoned.ca/jessup.**

1. Which of the following is a type of computer on the network that makes access to files, printing, communications, and other services available to users of the network?
   A. server
   B. client
   C. peer
   D. pager
2. Which of the following is not a type of cable medium?
   A. twisted pair
   B. coaxial
   C. fibre optic
   D. tertiary groups
3. Which of the following is a type of wireless medium?
   A. fibre optic
   B. TCP/IP
   C. infrared
   D. microterminal
4. Which of the following are types of networks?
   A. star, ring, bus
   B. star, box, ring
   C. star, ring, triangle
   D. ring, bus, rectangle
5. All of the following are common applications of high-frequency radio communication except __________.
   A. pagers
   B. cellular phones
   C. wireless networks
   D. facsimiles
6. The International Organization for Standardization (ISO) defined a networking model called the __________ that divides computer-to-computer communications into seven connected layers.
   A. Network Allocation System (NAS)
   B. Open Systems Network (OSN)
   C. Open Systems Interconnection (OSI)
   D. Network Transfer System (NTS)
7. Which of the following is a type of LAN protocol developed by Xerox Corporation in 1976 that typically uses a bus or star network topology and uses random access control to send data?
   A. Ethernet
   B. bridge
   C. star
   D. gateway

Glossary

Abilene network backbone: The network that connects Internet2 universities by using regional network aggregation points called ***gigaPoPs*** and very high-speed network equipment and facilities.

Acceptable use policy: Computer and/or Internet use policy for people within an organization, with clearly spelled-out penalties for noncompliance.

ActiveX: Software components developed by Microsoft that provide dynamic content to a Web page in a manner similar to a Java applet.

Ad hoc reports: Reports created due to unplanned information requests in which information is gathered to support a nonroutine decision.

Adaptive maintenance: Making changes to an information system to make its functionality meet changing business needs or to migrate it to a different operating system.

Alpha testing: Testing performed by the development organization to assess whether the entire system meets the design requirements of the users.

Analog signals: Audio tones used to transmit data over conventional voice telephone lines.

Applet: A program designed to be executed within another application such as a Web page.

Application services: Processes that run software for network clients and enable computers to share processing power.

Application-level control: Level of control where a firewall might perform certain security measures only on specific applications, such as file transferring.

Application software: Software used to perform a specific task that the user needs to accomplish, such as writing a business letter, processing the payroll, managing a stock portfolio, or manipulating a series of forecasts to come up with the most efficient allocation of resources for a project.

Arithmetic logic unit (ALU): Part of the central processing unit (CPU) that performs mathematics, including all forms of addition, subtraction, multiplication, and division.

ARPANET: The Advanced Research Projects Agency Network, a large, wide area network that linked many universities and research centres.

ASCII (American Standard Code for Information Interchange): An eight-bit code for representing numbers, letters, and other characters in binary form.

Asymmetric digital subscriber line (ADSL): A data transfer format that enables large amounts of data to be sent relatively quickly over existing copper telephone lines with speeds ranging from 1.5 to 9 Mbps downstream and from 16 to 640 Kbps upstream.

Asynchronous transfer mode (ATM): A method of transmitting voice, video, and data over high-speed LANs at speeds of up to 2.2 Gbps.

Attenuation: The result when the power of an electric signal weakens as it is sent over increasing distance.

Attribute: Each record typically consists of many attributes, which are individual pieces of information. For example, a name and social insurance number are attributes about a person.

Audio: Sound that has been digitized for storage and replay on a computer.

Audit: A formal examination of an organization's security.

Authentication: The process of confirming the identity of a user who is attempting to access a system or Website.

Automating: Using information systems to do an activity faster or cheaper.

Backbone: A network that manages the bulk of network traffic and typically uses a higher-speed protocol than the individual LAN segments connected to it.

Backbone network: A network that manages the bulk of network traffic and typically uses a higher-speed protocol than the individual LAN segments connected to it.

Backup: Copies of critical systems and data, maintained on a regular basis.

Bandwidth: The transmission capacity of a computer or communications channel, often measured in megabits per second (Mbps); it represents how much binary data can be reliably transmitted over the medium in one second.

Batch input: Methods for rapidly entering large amounts of data into a computer.

Batch processing: The processing of transactions after some quantity of transactions are collected and then processed together as a "batch" at some later time.

Best-cost provider: An organization offering products or services of reasonably good quality at competitive prices.

Best practices: Procedures and processes from business organizations that are widely accepted as being among the most effective and/or efficient.

Beta testing: Testing performed by actual system users, who test the capabilities of the system with actual data in their work environment.

Binary code: Methods for representing digital data and information using sequences of zeros and ones.

Biometrics: A type of security that grants or denies access to a computer system through the analysis of fingerprints, retinal patterns in the eye, or other bodily characteristics.

Bits: The individual 1s and 0s that make up a byte.

Bluetooth: A wireless specification for personal area networking (PAN) of desktop computers, peripheral devices, mobile phones, pagers, portable stereos, and other handheld devices.

Bricks-and-clicks: Term used to identify firms doing traditional, physical business and doing business on the Internet as well.

Bricks-and-mortar: Term used to identify traditional firms doing business the old-fashioned way, from a physical storefront.

Bridge: Device used to connect two different LANs or two segments of the same LAN by forwarding network traffic between network segments; unlike repeaters, bridges determine the physical location of the source and destination computers.

Brouter: Short for ***bridge router*** (pronounced "brau-ter"); provides the capabilities of both a bridge and a router for managing network traffic.

Bus network: Network in the shape of an open-ended line; it is the easiest network to extend and has the simplest wiring layout.

Business information systems: Software applications that are developed to perform organization-wide operations.

Business model: A summary of how a company will generate revenue, identifying its product offering, value-added services, revenue sources and target customers.

Business process reengineering (BPR): Significant organizational change designed to improve the functioning of an organization as opposed to merely dropping in an information system with no attempts at changing and improving the organization.

Business rules: Rules included in data dictionaries to prevent illegal or illogical entries from entering the database.

Business-to-business (B2B): Electronic commerce that is used to conduct business with business partners such as suppliers and intermediaries.

Business-to-consumer (B2C): Electronic commerce used to conduct transactions between businesses and consumers.

Business-to-employee (B2E): Electronic commerce that occurs between businesses and their employees.

Byte: Typically eight bits, or about one typed character.

Bytes per inch (BPI): The number of bytes that can be stored on one inch of magnetic tape.

CA*net 4: Canada's high-speed network, similar to Internet2, that connects provincial research networks, universities, research centres, government research laboratories, schools, and other eligible sites.

Cable modem: A specialized piece of equipment that enables a computer to access Internet service designed to operate over cable TV lines.

Cache: Pronounced "cash," it is a small block of memory used by processors to store those instructions most recently or most often used.

Carding: Refers to the practice of stealing credit card numbers online, to be resold or used to charge merchandise against victims' accounts.

CD-R (compact disc—recordable): A type of optical disk to which data can be written.

CD-ROM (compact disc—read-only memory): A type of optical disk that cannot be written to, but can only be read.

CD-RW (compact disc—rewritable): A type of optical disk that can be written onto multiple times.

Cell: A geographical area containing a low-powered radio antenna/receiver for transmitting telecommunications signals within that area; monitored and controlled by a central computer.

Cellular phone: Mobile phone that uses a communications system that divides a geographic region into sections, called **cells**.

Central processing unit (CPU): Also called a microprocessor, processor, or chip, it is responsible for performing all of the operations of the computer.

Centralized computing: A system of large centralized computers, called mainframes, used to process and store data.

Certificate authority: A trusted intermediary between computers that verifies that a website is a trusted site and is used when implementing public key encryption on a large scale.

Channel service unit (CSU): A device that acts as a "buffer" between a LAN and a public carrier's WAN. CSUs ensure that all signals placed on the public lines from the LAN are appropriately timed and formed for the public network.

Characters per inch (CPI): The number of characters that can be stored on one inch of magnetic tape.

Chat messengers: Enable people to have real-time communication by entering text that appears on the other user's monitor.

Chief information officer (CIO): Title given to executive-level individuals who are responsible for leading the overall information systems component within their organizations and integrating new technologies into the organization's business strategy.

Circuit-level control: Prevention of unauthorized access to a private network by a firewall that detects when a certain type of connection or circuit has been made between specific users or systems on either side of the firewall.

Clicks-only company: Term used to identify firm doing business solely on the Internet, with no physical storefront.

Client: Any computer, such as a user's workstation or PC on the network, or any software application, such as a word processing application, that requests and uses the services provided by the server.

Clock speed: The speed of the system clock, typically measured in hertz (Hz).

Clock tick: A single pulse of the system clock.

Cloning: Cellular phone fraud in which scanners are used to steal the electronic serial numbers of cellular phones as calls are made.

Coaxial (coax) cable: Contains a solid inner copper conductor surrounded by plastic insulation and an outer braided copper or foil shield and is most commonly used for cable television installations and for networks operating at 10 Mbps. Its attenuation is lower than twisted pair cable, and it is moderately susceptible to EMI and eavesdropping.

Collaboration: Working together towards a common objective.

Collaboration system: An information system that enables people to communicate electronically with each other in order to solve problems, make decisions, and perform other forms of joint work.

Collaborative computing: A synergistic form of distributed computing, in which two or more networked computers are used to accomplish a common processing task.

Collaborative information system: A type of international information system that integrates different applications and data that can be shared by different companies in different countries.

Combination primary key: A combination of two or more attributes used to uniquely identify a row in an entity in a database.

Command-based interface: Computer interface that requires the user to enter text-based commands to instruct the computer to perform specific operations.

Competitive advantage: A firm's ability to do something better, faster, more cheaply, or uniquely when compared with rival firms in the market.

Compiler: A software program that translates a programming language into machine language.

Computer-aided design (CAD): Using high-powered computers to design very state-of-the-art, high-quality products.

Computer-aided design system: Using high-powered computers to design very state-of-the-art, high quality products.

Computer-aided software engineering (CASE): Software tools that provide automated support for some portion of the systems development process.

Computer-based information system: A combination of hardware, software, and telecommunications networks that people build and use to collect, create, and distribute data.

Computer crime: The act of using a computer to commit an illegal act.

Computer ethics: A broad range of issues and standards of conduct that have emerged through the use and proliferation of information systems.

Computer literacy: The knowledge of how to operate a computer.

Computer security: Precautions taken to keep computers and the information they contain safe from unauthorized access.

Connectors: Also called transmission media connectors; used to terminate cable in order to be plugged into a network interface card or into other network components. Connectors include T-connectors for coax cable and RJ-45 connectors (similar to a phone jack) for twisted pair cable.

Consumer-to-consumer (C2C): A form of electronic commerce that does not even involve business firms, such as an online textbook exchange service for students at a university or an online trading Website such as eBay.com.

Control unit: Part of the central processing unit (CPU) that works closely with the arithmetic logic unit (ALU) by fetching and decoding instructions, as well as retrieving and storing data.

Conversion: The process of transferring information from a legacy system to a new computing platform.

Cookie: A message passed to a web browser on a user's computer by a web server.

Copyright: A series of rights granted to an author of a work under the *Copyright Act.*

Corrective maintenance: Making changes to an information system to repair flaws in its design, coding, or implementation.

Cracker: An individual who breaks into computer systems with the intention of doing damage or committing a crime.

CSMA/CD (carrier sense multiple access/collision detect): A format in which each workstation "listens" to the network to determine whether a message is being transmitted. If the network is quiet, the workstation sends its message; otherwise, it waits. When a workstation gains access to the medium and sends information onto the network, messages are sent to all workstations on the network; however, only the destination with the proper address is able to "open" the message.

Custom applications: Software programs that are designed and developed by company personnel as opposed to being bought off-the-shelf.

Customer relationship management (CRM): The process of managing all aspects of the relationship with customers including finding them, marketing and selling to them, servicing their needs after the sale, and so on.

Customer relationship management system (CRMS): Information system to support interaction between the firm and its customers.

Customization: Modifying software so that it better suits user needs.

Customized application software: Software that is developed based on specifications provided by a particular organization.

Cyberterrorism: The use of computer and networking technologies against persons or property to intimidate or coerce governments, civilians, or any segment of society to attain political, religious, or ideological goals.

Cyberwar: An organized attempt by a country's military to disrupt or destroy the information and communication systems of another country.

Data: Recorded, unformatted information, such as words and numbers, that often has no meaning in and of itself.

Data dictionary: A document prepared by the database designers to describe the characteristics of all items in a database.

Data diddling: A type of computer crime where the data going into or out of a computer is altered.

Data flows: Data moving through an organization or within an information system.

Data mart: A data warehouse that is limited in scope and customized for the decision support applications of a particular end-user group.

Data mining: A method used by companies to sort and analyze information to better understand their customers, products, markets, or any other phase of their business for which data have been captured.

Data model: A map or diagram that represents the entities of a database and their relationships.

Data type: Each attribute in the database is a particular type such as text, number, or date.

Data warehouse: An integration of multiple, large databases and other information sources into a single repository or access point that is suitable for direct querying, analysis, or processing.

Database: A collection of related data organized in a way to facilitate data searches.

Database administrator (DBA): A person responsible for the development and management of the organization's databases.

Database management system (DBMS): A software application with which you create, store, organize, and retrieve data from a single database or several databases.

Decision support system (DSS): A special-purpose information system designed to support organizational decision making.

Defense Advanced Research Projects Agency (DARPA): A U.S. governmental agency that began to study ways to interconnect networks of various kinds, which led to the development of the ARPANET (Advanced Research Projects Agency Network).

Denial-of-service (DoS): Attack by unauthorized users that makes a computer systems unavailable or available with only a poor degree of service.

Density: The storage capacity of magnetic tape that is typically expressed in either characters per inch (CPI) or bytes per inch (BPI).

Desktop videoconferencing: The use of integrated computer, telephone, video recording, and playback technologies—typically by two people—to interact with each other using their desktop computers from remote sites.

Developmental testing: Testing performed by programmers to ensure that each module is error-free.

Differentiation strategy: An organization's strategy of providing better products or services than its competitors.

Digital divide: The gap between those individuals in our society who are computer literate and have access to information resources like the Internet and those who do not.

Digital signals: The electrical pulses that computers use to send information.

Digital subscriber line (DSL): Uses special modulation schemes to fit more data onto traditional copper phone wires; referred to as "last-mile" solutions because they are used only for connections from a telephone switching station to a home or office, and they generally are not used between telephone switching stations.

Digitization: A process that creates products without tangible features, which are commonly referred to as *virtual products.*

Digitizing: The process of converting a photograph or a song into digital information, or bits, which then can travel across a network.

Direct conversion: Changing from an old to a new system by beginning the new system and discontinuing the old system at the same time.

Disaster recovery plans: Plans created by organizations which spell out detailed procedures for recovering from systems-related disasters such as virus infections and other disasters (e.g., fire) that might strike critical information systems.

Disintermediation: The phenomenon of cutting out the intermediary and reaching customers more directly and efficiently.

Diskettes: Also called floppy disks, are 3½-inch, round, flexible Mylar devices that record data as magnetized spots on tracks on the disk surface.

Distance learning: The process of providing instruction to students who are physically separated from instructors through the use of communication technologies including videoconferencing, Internet chatting, and various Web-based tools.

Distributed computing: A model using separate computers to work on subsets of tasks and then pooling their results by communicating over a network.

Distribution portals: Enterprise portals that automate the business processes involved in selling or distributing products from a single supplier to multiple buyers.

Domain name: Used in uniform resource locators (URLs) to identify a source or host entity on the Internet.

Domain name system (DNS): A database used to associate Internet host names with their Internet IP addresses.

Dot matrix printer: A printing technology where characters and images are formed using a series of small dots; most commonly found in printing voluminous batch information, such as periodic reports and forms.

Double-inline memory module (DIMM): A small high capacity circuit board that can hold RAM chips, designed to replace the single-inline memory module (SIMM).

Downsizing: When companies slash costs, streamline operations, and/or let employees go.

Downstream: An information flow that relates to the information that is produced by a company and sent along to another organization such as a distributor.

Drill-down reports: Reports that provide details behind the summary values on a key-indicator or exception report.

Drive-by hacking: A new form of attack where an attacker accesses the network, intercepts data from it, and even uses network services and/or sends attack instructions to it, without entering the home, office, or organization that owns the network.

Dumpster diving: A type of computer crime where individuals go through dumpsters and garbage cans for company documents, credit card receipts, and other papers containing information that might be useful.

DVD-ROM (digital video disk—read-only memory): A type of optical disk that uses a shorter-wavelength laser beam that allows more information to be stored on a disk than a standard CD-ROM.

E-brochure: A web tool used to promote sales and marketing information.

E-business: The use of a variety of types of information technologies and systems to support every part of the business.

E-business innovation cycle: The time period and to what extent an organization derives value from a particular information technology.

E-information: The first stage of a website, in which information about a company and its product is disseminated globally to potential customers who have access to the Internet and a web browser.

E-integration: The second stage of a website, in which sites containing general information about a company and its product must be integrated with corporate databases to extract and display personal customer information necessary to achieve mass customization.

E-tailing: Electronic retailing.

E-transaction: This third stage of a website takes the e-integration stage one step further by adding the ability for customers to enter orders and payments online.

EBCDIC (Extended Binary-Coded Decimal Interchange Code): An eight-bit code for representing numbers, letters, and other characters in binary form; typically used on mainframe computers.

Economic opportunities: Opportunities that a firm finds for making more money and/or making money in new ways.

Economies of scale: A reduction in unit cost brought about by increased size of production facilities.

802.11: Universally adopted high-frequency radio-wave technology, with transmission speeds of up to 54 Mbps.

Electronic brochure: Using the web to disseminate sales and marketing information.

Electronic business (EB): How companies are conducting business electronically with their customers, business partners, and suppliers.

Electronic commerce: Exchanges of goods and services via the Internet among and between customers, firms, employees, business partners, suppliers, and so on.

Electronic data interchange (EDI): The digital, or electronic, transmission of business documents and related data between organizations via telecommunications networks that enables the online exchange and sale of goods and services between firms.

Electronic funds transfer (EFT): The process of transferring funds from one financial account to another via computer.

Electronic mail (e-mail): The transmission of messages over computer networks.

Electronic marketplace: Also called a trading exchange. A website built by a third party that allows buyers and sellers to come together, offering firms access to real-time trading with other companies in their vertical markets.

Electronic meeting system (EMS): A collection of personal computers networked together with sophisticated software tools to help group members solve problems and make decisions through interactive, electronic idea generation, evaluation, and voting.

EMI (electromagnetic interference): Occurs when fluorescent lights, weather, or other electronic signals interfere with the original signal being sent.

Enabling technologies: Information technologies that enable a firm to accomplish a task or goal or to gain or sustain competitive advantage in some way.

Encapsulation: The grouping of data and instructions into a single object in object-oriented programming languages.

Encryption: The process of encoding messages before they enter the network or airwaves, then decoding them at the receiving end of the transfer so that recipients can read or hear them.

End-user development: A systems development method whereby users in the organization develop, test, and maintain their own applications.

Enterprise application integration: Software encompassing a suite of enterprise solutions.

Enterprise network: A wide area network (WAN) that is the result of connecting disparate networks of a single organization into a single network.

Enterprise portal: Information system that provides a single point of access to secured, proprietary information, which may be dispersed throughout an organization.

Enterprise resource planning (ERP): Information system that supports and integrates all facets of the business, including planning, manufacturing, sales, marketing, and so on.

Enterprise systems: Information systems that support many or all of the various parts of the firm.

Entity: Things about which we collect data, such as people or classes.

Entity-relationship diagram (ERD): A diagramming technique that is commonly used when designing databases, especially when showing associations between entities.

Ergonomics: The design of computer hardware and work environments that minimize health risks.

Ethernet: A local area network protocol developed by Xerox Corporation in 1976. It uses a bus or star network topology and uses random access control to send data. The original Ethernet supports data transfer rates of 10 Mbps. A later version, called 100Base-T or Fast Ethernet, supports transfer rates of 100 Mbps, and the latest version, called Gigabit Ethernet, supports transfer rates of 1 gigabit, or 1,000 megabits, per second. You need some type of Ethernet card installed in your computer to use this type of network connection.

Ethics: The science of human duty that encompasses a system of principles and rules concerning duty. A broad range of ethical issues has emerged through the use and proliferation of computers.

Event-driven: Programming language characteristic that allows the development of programs to execute based on user-requested events rather than on a linear sequence through the program.

Exception report: Reports that highlight situations that are out of the normal operating range.

Executive information system (EIS): An information system designed to provide information in a very aggregate form so that managers at the executive level of the organization can quickly scan it for trends and anomalies.

Executive level: The top level of the organization, where executives focus on long-term strategic issues facing the organization.

Expert system (ES): A special-purpose information system designed to mimic human expertise by manipulating knowledge—understanding acquired through experience and extensive learning—rather than simply information.

Explicit knowledge assets: Knowledge assets which reflect anything that can be documented, archived, and codified, often with the help of information systems.

Extended ASCII: Character encoding system that includes characters common to many of the world's languages.

Extensible Business Reporting Lanuage (XBRL): An XML-based specification for publishing financial information, which makes it easier for companies to share information with each other, with industry analysts, and with shareholders.

Extensible markup language (XML): A web programming language that allows designers to create customized features that enable data to be more easily shared between applications and organizations.

External acquisition: The process of purchasing an existing information system from an external organization or vendor.

External or secondary cache: Special high-speed cache memory that is usually not built into the CPU, but is located within easy reach of the CPU on the motherboard.

Extranet: The use of the Internet by firms and companies for business-to-business interactions.

Facsimile: Machines that digitize images, such as letters, memos, newspaper and magazine articles, photos, contracts, even handwritten notes, so that they can be transmitted to other fax machines over telephone lines.

Fibre-optic cable: Made of a light-conducting glass or plastic core, surrounded by more glass, called cladding, and a tough outer sheath that protects the fibre from changes in temperature, as well as from bending or breaking; uses pulses of light sent along the optical cable to transmit video or sound data clearly and securely because it is immune to electromagnetic interference and eavesdropping; has low attenuation; can support bandwidths from 100 Mbps to greater than 2 Gbps (gigabits per second) and distances from 2 to 25 kilometres.

Fifth-generation language (5GL): Computer language developed for application within some expert system or artificial intelligence application, using English sentences.

File services: Processes used to store, retrieve, and move data files in an efficient manner; individuals can use the file services of the network to move a customer file electronically to multiple recipients across the network.

File transfer: The process of connecting to a remote computer in order to either upload (sending to the remote machine) or download (obtaining from the remote machine) files and data.

Firewall: Hardware or software designed to keep unauthorized users out of network systems.

Firewall architecture: The complexity and power of a firewall solution is tailored to a specific situation.

Fixed wireless: A wireless solution requiring that the user's computer be stationary rather than mobile.

Flash drive: A portable, removable data storage device.

Flash memory: A variation of ROM that can be repeatedly written to and erased like RAM, but, unlike RAM, it retains its information after power is turned off.

Foreign key: An attribute that appears as a nonprimary key attribute in one entity and as a primary key attribute (or part of a primary key) in another entity.

Form: 1. A collection of blank entry boxes, each representing a field, that is used to enter information into a database. 2. A business document that contains some predefined data and may include some areas where additional data is to be filled in, typically for a single record.

Fourth-generation language (4GL): Also called outcome oriented, a computer language commonly used to write and execute queries of a database.

Fully automated data entry: Data entry into an information system that does not require any human intervention.

Functional area information system: A cross-organizational-level information system designed to support a specific functional area.

Gateway: A connection between the internal computer systems and networks of a company and the Internet, enabling people to send electronic mail and other data or files over the Internet to and from nearly anywhere in the world.

Geostationary: A system of satellites that are placed in fixed positions above the Earth's surface and orbit along with the Earth (also called a geosynchronous orbit).

Geosynchronous: A system of satellites that are placed in fixed positions above the Earth's surface and orbit along with the Earth (also called a geostationary orbit).

GigaPoP: Regional network aggregation points used in connecting different systems within a network backbone, such as the Abilene network backbone.

Global information dissemination: A relatively economical medium for firms to market their products and services over vast distances.

Global information system: A type of international information system that is used when a single transaction requires the input of data from multiple centres located in more than one nation.

Global network: Spans multiple countries and may include the networks of several organizations. The Internet is an example of a global network.

Gopher: A text-based, menu-driven interface that enables users to access a large number of varied Internet resources as if they were in folders and menus on their own computers.

Graphical user interface (GUI): Computer interface that enables the user to select pictures, icons, and menus to send instructions to the computer.

Groupware: Software that enables people to work together more effectively.

Hacker: An individual who gains unauthorized access to computer systems.

Hard data: Facts and numbers that are typically generated by transaction processing systems and management information systems.

Hard drive or hard disk: A secondary storage device for storing data, usually located inside the system unit of a computer.

Hardware: Physical computer equipment, such as the computer monitor, central processing unit, or keyboard.

Head crash: A failure inside a hard disk when the read/write head touches the disk and results in the loss of the data and/or the operation of the hard disk.

High-frequency radio: Signals can transmit data at rates of up to 11 Mbps to network nodes from 12.2 to 39.6 kilometres apart.

Hub: Used as a central point of connection between media segments; like repeaters, hubs enable the network to be extended to accommodate additional workstations; commonly used in 10Base-T networks.

Hyperlink: A reference or link on a webpage to other documents that contain related information.

Hypermediation: A "pay by the click" pricing scheme in which the firm running the advertisement pays only when a web surfer actually clicks on the advertisement.

Hypertext: Text in a web document that is highlighted and, when clicked on by the user, evokes an embedded command that goes to another specified file or location and brings up that file or location on the user's screen.

Hypertext markup language (HTML): The standard method of specifying the format of webpages. Specific content within each webpage is enclosed within codes, or markup tags, which stipulate how the content should appear to the user.

Hypertext transfer protocol (HTTP): The process by which servers process user requests for webpages.

Identity theft: Stealing another person's social insurance number, credit card number, and other personal information for the purpose of using the victim's credit rating to borrow money, buy merchandise, and otherwise run up debts that are never repaid.

Inferencing: The matching of user questions and answers to information in a knowledge base within an expert system in order to make a recommendation.

Informating: The ability of information technology to provide information about the operation within a firm and/or about the underlying work process that the system supports.

Information: Data that has been formatted and/or organized in some way as to be useful to people.

Information accessibility: An ethical issue concerned with what information a person or organization has the right to obtain about others and how this information can be accessed and used.

Information accuracy: An ethical issue concerned with the authenticity and fidelity of information, as well as identifying who is responsible for informational errors that harm people.

Information Age: A period of time in society when information has become a valuable or dominant currency of the realm.

Information privacy: An ethical issue that is concerned with what information an individual should have to reveal to others through the course of employment or through other transactions such as online shopping.

Information property: An ethical issue that focuses on who owns information about individuals and how information can be sold and exchanged.

Information systems: Assumed to mean computer-based information systems, which are combinations of hardware, software, and telecommunications networks that people build and use to collect, create, and distribute useful data; this term is also used to represent the field in which people develop, use, manage, and study computer-based information systems in organizations.

Information systems access: Managing systems in order to control access to key computers, data, and networks.

Information systems planning: 1. A formal organizational process for assessing the information needs of an organization in which the systems, databases, and technologies for meeting those needs are identified.
2. Planning for the investment in the deployment of information systems. This planning helps people meet organizational strategies and objectives given the organization's resource constraints.

Information systems security: Refers to precautions taken to keep all aspects of information systems (e.g., all hardware, software, network equipment, and data) safe from unauthorized use or access.

Information technology (IT): Refers to machine technology that is controlled by or uses information.

Informational system: The systems designed to support decision making based on stable point-in-time or historical data.

Infrared line of sight: Uses high-frequency light waves to transmit data on an unobstructed path between nodes—computers or some other device such as a printer—on a network, at a distance of up to 24.4 metres.

Inheritance: A characteristic of object-oriented programming languages that requires lower-level objects, or "children", to inherit the characteristics of higher-level, or "parent", objects.

Ink-jet printer: A printing technology where characters and images are formed by transferring ink onto paper.

Input devices: Hardware that is used to enter information into a computer.

Instant messaging (IM): Having conversations with others in real time on the Internet.

Intangible benefits: A benefit of using a particular system or technology that is difficult to quantify. Examples of intangible benefits include faster turnaround on fulfilling orders and resulting improvements in customer service.

Intangible costs: A cost of using a particular system or technology that is difficult to quantify. Examples include the costs of reducing traditional sales, losing some customers that are not "Web ready," or losing customers if the web application is poorly designed or not on par with competitors' sites.

Integrated Services Digital Network (ISDN): A standard for worldwide digital communications that is intended to replace analog systems and uses existing twisted pair telephone wires to provide high speed data service.

Integration: The combination of two or more information systems, normally for a single purpose.

Interactive communication: Enables firms to build customer loyalty by providing immediate communication and feedback to and from customers, which can dramatically improve the firm's image through demonstrated responsiveness.

Interexchange carriers (IXC): Companies that sell long-distance services with circuits carrying service between the major telephone exchanges.

Interface: The way in which the user interacts with the computer.

Internal cache: Special high-speed cache memory that is incorporated into the microprocessor's design.

International information system: A general class of information systems that support transactions that cross national boundaries.

Internet: A term derived from the concept of internetworking, which means connecting host computers and their networks together to form even larger networks. The Internet is a large worldwide collection of networks that use a common protocol to communicate with each other.

Internet2: Developed in 1996 by leading universities as a faster, private alternative to the public Internet to be a testing-ground network to develop advanced Internet technologies and applications.

Internet backbone: The collection of main network connections and telecommunications lines that make up the Internet.

Internet commerce: Commercial activities occurring across the Internet.

Internet Corporation for Assigned Names and Numbers: Also called ICANN, a nonprofit corporation that assumed responsibility from InterNIC for managing IP addresses, domain names, and root server system management.

Internet over Satellite (IoS): Technologies that allow users to access the Internet via satellites that are placed in fixed positions above the Earth's surface in what is known as a geostationary or geosynchronous orbit (i.e., the satellite moves along with the Earth).

Internet Registry: A central repository for Internet-related information that provides central allocation of network system identifiers.

Internet relay chat (IRC): An application that allows typed conversations with others in real time on the Internet.

Internet service provider (ISP): An individual or organization that enables other individuals and organizations to connect to the Internet.

Internetworking: Connecting host computers and their networks together to form even larger networks.

InterNIC: A government-industry collaboration created by the NSF in 1993 to manage directory and database services, domain registration services, and other information services on the Internet.

InterNIC Registration Service: A service offered by InterNIC for assigning Internet addresses.

Interorganizational systems (IOS): Systems that communicate across organizational boundaries.

Interpreter: A software program that translates a programming language into machine language one statement at a time.

Intranet: An internal, private network using web technologies to facilitate the secured transmission of proprietary information within an organization, thereby limiting the viewing access to authorized users within the organization.

IP address: An Internet protocol address assigned to every computer and router to connect to the Internet; it serves as the destination address of that computer or device and enables the network to route messages to the proper destination.

IP datagram: A data packet that conforms to the IP specification.

IPv6: The latest version of the Internet protocol, also referred to as IPng, for IP next generation.

Java: An object-oriented programming language that was developed at Sun Microsystems in the early 1990s that is used in developing applications on the web and other environments.

JavaScript: A scripting language, created by Netscape, that allows developers to add dynamic content to websites.

Key-indicator report: Reports that provide a summary of critical information on a recurring schedule.

Keyboard: Input device for entering text and numbers into a computer.

Key logging: Also known as keystroke logging, it is the process of capturing a user's keystrokes, commonly used to screen for passwords or encryption keys.

Knowledge: A body of governing procedures, such as guidelines or rules, which are used to organize or manipulate data to make it suitable for a given task.

Knowledge assets: All the underlying skills, routines, practices, principles, formulas, methods, heuristics, and intuitions, whether explicit or tacit.

Knowledge management: Refers to the processes an organization uses to gain the greatest value from its knowledge assets.

Knowledge management system: A collection of technology-based tools that include communication technologies as well as information storage and retrieval systems to enable the generation, storage, sharing, and management of tacit knowledge assets.

Knowledge society: Term coined by Peter Drucker to refer to a society in which there is a relatively high proportion of knowledge workers, where these types of people have risen in importance and leadership, and where education is the cornerstone of the society.

Knowledge worker: Term coined by Peter Drucker to refer to professionals who are relatively well educated and who create, modify, and/or synthesize knowledge as a fundamental part of their jobs.

Language translator: A special built-in program in the CPU used to translate incoming data into binary code called machine language.

Laser printer: A printing technology where characters and images are formed by using a laser beam.

Learning organization: Described by David Garvin as an organization that is "skilled at creating, acquiring, and transferring knowledge, and at modifying its behaviour to reflect new knowledge and insights."

Legacy system: An older stand-alone computer system within an organization with older versions of applications that are either fast approaching or beyond the end of their useful life within the organization.

Liquid crystal display (LCD): A type of computer monitor that is most commonly used on notebook and portable computers.

Listserv: A mailing list that allows individual users to participate in group discussions via e-mail.

Local area network (LAN): A computer network that spans a relatively small area, allowing all computer users to connect with each other to share information and peripheral devices, such as a printer.

Logic (or time) bomb: A type of computer virus that lies in wait for unsuspecting computer users to perform a triggering operation or for a specific date before executing its instructions.

Low-cost leadership strategy: Strategy by which an organization offers the best prices in its industry on its goods and/or services.

M-commerce: Any electronic transaction or information interaction conducted using a wireless mobile device and mobile networks that leads to transfer of real or perceived value in exchange for information, services, or goods.

Machine language: A binary-level computer language that computer hardware understands.

Magnetic tape: A secondary storage method that consists of narrow plastic tape coated with a magnetic substance.

Magneto-optical (MO) disk: A type of optical disk that contains tiny metallic crystals where information is written to the disk using a laser beam to melt small spots on the plastic surface of the disk; once melted, a magnet then rearranges the magnetic crystals while the plastic is still hot and malleable to represent specific information.

Mailing lists: Also known as listservs; let you use e-mail to participate in discussion groups on topics of special interest to you.

Mainframe computer: A very large computer that is used as the main, central computing system for many major corporations and governmental agencies.

Making the business case: The process of identifying, quantifying, and presenting the value provided by an information system.

Management information system (MIS): 1. A field of study that encompasses the development, use, management, and study of computer-based information systems in organizations. 2. An information system designed to support the management of organizational functions at the managerial level of the organization.

Managerial level: The mid level of the organization, where functional managers focus on monitoring and controlling operational-level activities and providing information to higher levels of the organization.

Manual data entry: Having a person enter information by hand into an information system.

Mass customization: A web technology that helps firms tailor their products and services to meet a customer's particular needs.

Media access control: The rules that govern how a given node or workstation gains access to the network to send or receive information; there are two general types of access control: distributed and random access.

Menu-driven pricing: A pricing system in which companies set and present the prices that consumers pay for products; these prices are non-negotiable.

Menu interface: An interface which presents a list of options from which a user selects to invoke a command or system operation.

Message services: The storing, accessing, and delivering of text, binary, graphic, digitized video, and audio data; similar to file services, but they also deal with communication interactions between users and applications; include electronic mail or the transfer of messages between two or more networked computers.

Metropolitan area network (MAN): A computer network of limited geographic scope, typically a city-wide area, that combines both LAN and high-speed fibre-optic technologies. MANs are attractive to organizations that need high-speed data transmission within a limited geographic area.

Microcomputer: A category of computer that is generally used for personal computing, for small business computing, and as a workstation attached to large computers or to other small computers on a network.

Microwave transmission: A high-frequency radio signal sent through the air using either terrestrial (Earth-based) systems or satellite systems.

Midrange computers: Often referred to as minicomputers, these are computers whose performance is lower than that of mainframes, but higher than microcomputers.

Mobile wireless: Wireless approaches for connecting to the Internet where the computer or handheld device can be moved and will continue to connect.

Models: Conceptual, mathematical, logical, and analytical formulas used to represent or project business events or trends.

Modem: Short for modulator/demodulator; a modem is a device or program that enables a computer to transmit data over telephone lines.

Modules: In a software application, components (classified software functions) that are bundled together.

Monitor: A computer display screen.

Moore's Law: Hypothesis of Dr. Gordon Moore in the 1970s that computer processing performance would double every 18 months.

Motherboard: A large printed plastic or fibreglass circuit board that holds or connects to all of the computer's electronic components.

Multinational information system: A type of international information system that consists of a loose confederacy of various different local information systems.

Multiplexer (MUX): Used to share a communications line or medium among a number of users.

Musical Instrument Digital Interface (MIDI): A standard adopted by the electronic music industry for controlling and interconnecting musical devices and computers.

National Science Foundation: The organization in the U.S. that initiated the development of the NSFNET (National Science Foundation Network), which became a major component of the Internet.

National Science Foundation Network (NSFNET): A network developed by the U.S. in 1986 that became a major component of the Internet.

Nearly unlimited selection: A massive selection of products and/or services that includes both common and rare choices.

Network: A group of computers and associated peripheral devices connected by a communication channel capable of sharing information and other resources (e.g., a printer) among users.

Network access points(NAPs): Serve as access points for ISPs and are an exchange point for Internet traffic; these access points determine how traffic is routed and are often the points of most Internet congestion.

Network computer: A microcomputer with minimal memory and storage designed to connect to networks, especially the Internet, to use the resources provided by servers.

Network interface card (NIC): An expansion board that plugs into a computer so that it can be connected to a network.

Network operating system (NOS): System software that controls the network and enables computers to communicate with each other.

Network services: Capabilities of networked computers that enable them to share files, print, send, and receive messages, and to use shared software applications.

Network topology: The shape of a network; the three common network topologies are star, ring, and bus.

New economy: An economy in which information technology plays a significant role and that enables producers of both the tangible (computers, shoes, etc.) and intangible (services, ideas, etc.) to compete efficiently in global markets.

Newsgroups: Also called computer-based discussion groups; allow individuals and organizations to participate in discussions on almost any subject.

Newsreaders: Enable people with common interests to post and read messages categorized by topics.

Nonrecurring costs: One-time costs that are not expected to continue after the system is implemented.

Normalization: A technique for converting complex databases into ones that are simple and clear.

Notebook computer: A mobile microcomputer that weighs five pounds or less.

Object-oriented analysis and design (OOA&D): Systems development methodologies and techniques based on objects rather than on data and processes.

Object-oriented languages: Programming languages that group together data and its corresponding instructions into manipulatable objects.

Objects: The bundling of data and programming instructions for manipulating that data into a single module.

Off-the-shelf application software: Software designed and used to support general business processes that does not require any specific tailoring to meet the organization's needs.

Office automation or personal productivity software: Information systems that span organizational levels and are used for developing documents, scheduling resources, and communicating.

Office automation system (OAS): A collection of software and hardware for developing documents, scheduling resources, and communicating.

OLAP server: The chief component of an OLAP system that understands how data is organized in the database and has special functions for analyzing the data.

Online analytical processing (OLAP): Graphical software tools that provide complex analysis of data stored in a database.

Online customer service: Assistance for customers offered over the Internet.

Online ordering: Customers visiting a company's website to order and, in many cases, actually pay for products and services over the Internet.

Online processing: Processing of information as that information occurs.

Online transaction processing (OLTP): Immediate automated responses to the requests from multiple concurrent transactions from customers.

Open source software: Refers to systems software, applications and programming languages in which the source code is freely available to the general public for use and/or modification.

Operational level: The bottom level of an organization, where the routine, day-to-day business processes and interactions with customers occur.

Operational systems: The systems that are used to interact with customers and run a business in real time.

Operating system: Software that coordinates the interaction among hardware devices, peripherals, application software, and users.

Optical disk: A storage disk coated with a metallic substance that is written to (or read from) when a laser beam passes over the surface of the disk.

Organizational learning: The ability of an organization to learn from past behaviour and information and improve as a result.

Organizational strategy: A firm's plan to accomplish its mission and goals and to gain or sustain competitive advantage over rivals.

OSI model: Open Systems Interconnection; a protocol that represents a group of specific, successive tasks that enable computers to communicate with one another.

Output devices: Hardware devices that deliver information in a usable form.

Outsourcing: Turning over partial or entire responsibility for information systems development and management to an outside organization.

Packaged application: A software program written by third-party vendors.

Packet filter: Prevention of unauthorized access to a computer network by a firewall at the data packet level; data packets are accepted or rejected based on predefined rules.

Packet sniffing: The process of intercepting traffic passing over a digital network.

Packet switching: The process of breaking information into small chunks called data packets and then managing the transfer of those packets from computer to computer via the Internet.

Pager: A one-way, wireless messaging system.

Parallel conversion: Changing over from the old to a new system by running both at the same time until the organization is sure that the new system is error-free, that the users are adequately trained, and that the support procedures are in place.

Patent: A right to exclusively manufacture an invention for a specified time.

Peer: Any computer that may both request and provide services.

Peer-to-peer networks: Networks that enable any computer or device on the network to provide and request services.

Perfective maintenance: Making enhancements to improve processing performance, to improve interface usability, or to add desired, but not necessarily required, system features.

Personal area network (PAN): An emerging technology that uses wireless communication to exchange data between computing devices using short-range radio communication, typically within an area of 10 metres.

Personal computer (PC): A class of computers that fit on desktops and are used in homes and offices.

Personal digital assistant (PDA): A handheld microcomputer that has somewhat limited processing and storage capabilities.

Phased conversion: Change over from the old to a new system by utilizing parts of the new system and adding new modules and features to that new system as each part is validated as working properly. This process continues until the entire system is operating and the old system is replaced.

Phishing: A scam where unsuspecting users are tricked into divulging key information, such as usernames, passwords, and credit card numbers.

Phreaking: Crimes committed against telephone company computers with the goal of making free long-distance calls, impersonating directory assistance or other operator services, diverting calls to numbers of the perpetrator's choice, or otherwise disrupting telephone service for subscribers.

Piggybacking or shoulder-surfing: The act of simply standing in line behind a card user at an automated teller machine (ATM), looking over that person's shoulder, and memorizing the card's personal identification number (PIN).

Pilot conversion: Changing over from the old to a new system by running the entire system in one location until it is validated as operating properly and then diffusing the system into the entire organization.

Plain old telephone service (POTS): Standard telephone lines with a speed, or bandwidth, that is generally about 52 Kbps (52,000 bits per second); also called the public switched telephone network (PSTN).

Podcasting: Web feeding of audio or video files placed on the Internet and available for subscription or free download.

Pointing devices: Input devices for pointing at items and selecting menu items on a computer.

Port: Provides a hardware interface (plugs and sockets) for connecting devices to computers.

Portals: In the context of B2B electronic commerce, defined as access points (or front doors) through which a business partner accesses secured, proprietary information from an organization.

Power supply: A device that converts electricity from the wall socket to a lower voltage appropriate for computer components and regulates the voltage to eliminate surges common in most electrical systems.

Preventive maintenance: Making changes to a system to reduce the chance of future system failure.

Primary key: A field included in a database that ensures that each instance of an entity is stored or retrieved accurately.

Primary memory: The computer's main or random access memory (RAM).

Primary storage: Temporary storage that is also referred to as random access memory (RAM) and read-only memory (ROM).

Print services: Used to control and manage users' access to network printers and fax equipment.

Private branch exchange (PBX): A telephone system that serves a particular location, such as a business, connecting one telephone extension to another within the system and connecting the PBX to the outside telephone network.

Processing devices: Computer hardware that transforms inputs into outputs.

Processing logic: The steps by which data is transformed or moved, as well as a description of the events that trigger these steps.

Procurement portals: Enterprise portals that automate the business processes involved in purchasing, or procuring, products between a single buyer and multiple suppliers.

Protocols: Rules dictating communication between senders and receivers within a network.

Prototyping: An iteractive systems development process in which requirements are converted into a working system that is continually revised through close work between analysts and users.

Proxy server: A firewall that serves as, or creates the appearance of, an alternative server that intercepts all messages entering and leaving a network, effectively hiding the true network addresses.

Proxy variables: A measurement of changes as a result of systems implementation in terms of their perceived value to the organization, particularly where it is difficult to determine and measure direct effects from a system.

Public key: A data encryption technique that uses two keys—a private key and a public key—to encrypt and decode messages.

Public switched telephone network (PSTN): Also called plain old telephone service (POTS), it is a network of standard telephone lines with a speed, or bandwidth, that is generally about 52 Kbps (52,000 bits per second).

Pull marketing: A strategy by which companies must draw, or pull, visitors to their websites.

Push marketing: An active strategy in which the company pushes its information at the consumer whether it is wanted or not (e.g., television commercials).

Query: Method used to request information from a database.

Query by example (QBE): A capability of a DBMS that enables data to be requested by providing a sample or a description of the types of data we would like to see.

RAID (redundant array of independent disks): A secondary storage technology that makes redundant copies of data on two or more hard drives.

Radio frequency identification (RFID): The use of electromagnetic or electrostatic coupling in the FR portion of the electromagnetic spectrum in order to transmit signals; an RFID system uses a transceiver and antenna to transfer information to a processing device, or RFID tag.

Random-access memory (RAM): A type of primary storage that is volatile and can be accessed randomly by the CPU.

Rapid application development (RAD): A systems development methodology that combines prototyping, computer-based development tools, special management practices, and close user involvement.

Read-only memory (ROM): A type of primary storage on which data has been prerecorded and is nonvolatile.

Read/write heads: Components that inscribe data to or retrieve data from hard disks, diskettes, and tapes.

Record: A collection of related attributes about a single entity.

Recurring costs: Ongoing costs that occur throughout the life cycle of systems development, implementation, and maintenance.

Registers: Temporary storage locations inside the CPU where data must reside while it is being processed or manipulated.

Relational database model: The most common DBMS approach in which entities are presented as two-dimensional tables, with records as rows and attributes as columns.

Repeater: A network device used to regenerate or replicate a signal as it weakens when travelling on a network; also moves data from one media segment to another and effectively extends the size of the network.

Report: 1. A compilation of data from the database that is organized and produced in printed format. 2. A business document that contains only predefined data used for reading and viewing, typically for multiple records.

Report generators: Software tools for retrieving data from a database and manipulating (aggregate, transform, or group) and displaying it in a useful format.

Request for Proposal (RFP): A communication tool indicating buyer requirements for a given system and requesting information from potential vendors.

Requirements collection: The process of gathering and organizing information from users, managers, business processes, and documents to understand how a proposed information system should function.

Revenue model: A description of how the firm will earn revenue, generate profits, and produce a superior return on invested capital.

Reverse pricing: A pricing system in which customers specify the product they are looking for and how much they are willing to pay for it; this information is routed to appropriate companies, which either accept or reject the consumer's offer.

RFID tag: An object that can be attached to, or incorporated into, a product, for the purpose of identification using radio waves (see Radio frequency identification).

Ring network: A network that is configured in the shape of a closed loop or circle, with each node connecting to the next node.

Risk acceptance: Implementing no countermeasures and simply absorbing any damages that occur.

Risk analysis: The process in which you assess the value of the assets being protected, determine their likelihood of being compromised, and compare the probable costs of their being compromised with the estimated costs of whatever protections you might have to take.

Risk reduction: Taking active countermeasures to protect your systems, such as installing firewalls.

Risk transference: Having someone else absorb the risk, such as by investing in insurance.

Router: An intelligent device used to connect and route data traffic across two or more individual networks.

Rule: A way of encoding knowledge, typically expressed using an IF-THEN format, within an expert system.

Salami slicing: A form of data diddling that occurs when a person shaves small amounts from financial accounts and deposits them in a personal account.

Sales force automation (SFA): The system of applications that focus mainly on contact management and scheduling.

Satellite: A device launched to orbit Earth and enable network communication.

Satellite microwave: The process of using relay stations that transfer high-frequency radio signals between antennas located on Earth and satellites orbiting the Earth.

Scanners: Input devices that convert printed text and images into digital data.

Scheduled reports: Reports produced at predefined intervals—daily, weekly, or monthly—to support the routine informational needs of managerial-level decision making.

Scripting languages: A programming technique for providing interactive components to a web page.

Secondary key: Attributes not used as the primary key that can be used to identify one or more records within a table that share a common value.

Secondary nonvolatile storage: Methods for permanently storing data to a large-capacity storage component, such as a hard disk, diskette, CD-ROM disk, or tape.

Secure sockets layer (SSL): A popular public key encryption method used on the Internet.

Semiautomated data entry: Data entry into an information system using some type of data capture device such as a grocery store checkout scanner.

Semistructured decisions: Managerial-level decision making where solutions and problems are not clear cut and often require judgment and expertise.

Server: Any computer on the network that enables access to files, printing, communications, and other services available to users of the network; it typically has a more advanced microprocessor, more memory, a larger cache, and more disk storage than a single-user workstation.

Server-centric networks: Networks in which servers and clients have defined roles.

Service mentality: The belief among information systems personnel that their chief goal is satisfying their systems customers within the firm while fundamentally believing that the customers, not the systems personnel, own the technology and the information.

Single in-line memory module (SIMM): A small circuit board that can hold RAM chips.

Smart card: A special type of credit card with a magnetic strip, a microprocessor chip, and memory circuits.

Smartphone: A mobile phone with advanced functionality such as high speed data transfer capabilities, and 'always on' connectivity.

Social engineering: Gaining information needed to access computers by posing as a magazine journalist, telephone company employee, or forgetful co-worker in order to persuade honest employees to reveal passwords and other information.

Soft data: Textual news stories or other nonanalytical information.

Software: A program or set of programs that tell the computer to perform certain processing functions.

Software engineering: A disciplined approach for constructing information systems through the use of common methods, techniques, or tools.

Software piracy: A type of computer crime where individuals make illegal copies of software protected by copyright laws.

Sound card: A specialized circuit board that supports the ability to convert digital information into sounds that can be listened to on speakers or headphones plugged into the card; a microphone can also be plugged into the card for capturing audio for storage or processing.

Source documents: Documents describing a transaction that serve as a stimulus to a transaction processing system from some external source.

Spam: Electronic junk mail or junk newsgroup postings, usually for the purpose of advertising for some product and/or service.

Speech recognition: Software and hardware used to convert spoken words into commands and data.

Spoofing: A scam used to steal passwords from legitimate accounts by using phony login screens.

Spyware: Any software that covertly gathers information about a user without the user's knowledge through an Internet connection.

Stand-alone application: Systems that focus on the specific needs of individual departments and are not designed to communicate with other systems in the organization.

Star network: A network with several workstations connected to a central hub.

Strategic: A way of thinking in which a complex plan of action is made in order to achieve a specific goal.

Strategic planning: The process of forming a vision of where the organization needs to head, converting that vision into measurable objectives and performance targets, and crafting a plan to achieve the desired results.

Streaming media: Streaming video with sound.

Streaming video: A sequence of compressed moving images that are sent over the Internet.

Structured decisions: Decisions where the procedures to follow for a given situation can be specified in advance.

Structured Query Language (SQL): The most common language used to interface with databases.

Supercomputer: The most expensive and most powerful category of computers. It is primarily used to assist in solving massive research and scientific problems.

Supply chain: The network producers of supplies that a company uses.

Supply chain management (SCM): Management of the network of suppliers and subsuppliers that a company interacts with.

Supply network: The flow of materials from multiple suppliers involved in the process of servicing a single organization.

Switch: A device that channels incoming data from any of multiple input ports to the specific output port that will take the data toward its intended destination.

Symmetric digital subscriber line (SDSL): A data transfer format that enables large amounts of data to be sent relatively quickly over existing copper telephone lines; said to be symmetric because it supports the same data rates (up to 3 Mbps) for upstream and downstream traffic; works by sending digital pulses in the high-frequency area of telephone wires.

Symmetric secret key system: An encryption system where both the sender and recipient use the same key for encoding (scrambling) and decoding the message.

System analysis: The second phase of the systems development life cycle, in which the current ways of doing business are studied and alternative replacement systems are proposed.

System clock: An electronic circuit inside a computer that generates pulses at a rapid rate for setting the pace of processing events.

System conversion: The process of decommissioning the current system and installing a new system into the organization.

System design: The third phase of the systems development life cycle, in which all features of the proposed system are described.

System effectiveness: The extent to which a system enables people and/or the firm to accomplish goals or tasks well.

System efficiency: The extent to which a system enables people and/or the firm to do things faster, at lower cost, or with relatively little time and effort.

System identification, selection, and planning: The first phase of the systems development life cycle, in which potential projects are identified, selected, and planned.

System implementation: The fourth phase of the systems development life cycle, in which the information system is programmed, tested, installed, and supported.

System maintenance: The fifth (and final) phase of the systems development life cycle, in which an information system is systematically repaired and/or improved.

System support: Ongoing education and problem-solving assistance for users, often provided by a special group of people in the organization who make up an information centre (IC) or help desk.

System unit: The physical box that houses all of the electronic components that do the work of the computer.

Systems analysis and design: The process of designing, building, and maintaining information systems.

Systems analyst: The primary person responsible for performing systems analysis and design activities.

Systems benchmarking: A standardized set of performance tests designed to facilitate comparison between systems.

Systems development life cycle (SDLC): The process of identifying the need for, as well as designing, developing, and maintaining contemporary types of information systems.

Systems integration: Enabling two information systems to work together and/or to exchange data more seamlessly with each other.

Systems software: The collection of programs that controls the basic operations of computer hardware.

T1 line: Developed by AT&T as a dedicated digital transmission line that can carry 1.544 Mbps of information.

T3 line: A digital transmission line that provides about 45 Mbps of service at about 10 times the cost of leasing a T1 line.

Table: A collection of related records where each row is a record and each column is an attribute.

Tablet PC: A type of notebook computer that accepts input from an electronic pen (called a stylus) or a keyboard.

Tacit knowledge assets: Reflect the processes and procedures that are located in a person's mind on how to effectively perform a particular task.

Tag: A command that is inserted in a document to specify how the document, or a portion of the document, should be formatted and/or used.

Tangible benefit: A benefit of using a particular system or technology that can be quantified.

Tangible cost: A cost of using a particular system of technology that is quantifiable.

Technology: Any mechanical and/or electrical means to supplement, extend, or replace human, manual operations or devices.

Telecommunications: Refers to the transmission of all forms of information, including digital data, voice, fax, sound, and video, from one location to another over some type of network.

Telecommunications network: A group of two or more computer systems linked together with communications equipment.

Telecommuting: The process of working at home or at another remote location and "commuting" to the office via computing and networking technologies.

Telemedicine: The exchange of medical information from one location to another via a computer network.

Telnet: Enables users to connect, or log in, to any computer on the Internet.

Terminals: Local input devices used to enter data onto mainframes in centralized computing systems.

Terrestrial microwave: The process of using Earth-based antennas that require an unobstructed path or line of sight between nodes; often used to cross inaccessible terrain or to connect buildings where cable installation would be expensive.

Text-recognition software: Software designed to convert handwritten text into computer-based characters.

Token passing: An access method that uses a constantly circulating electronic token, a small packet of data, to prevent collisions and give all workstations equal access to the network.

Top-level domain: Categories of Internet domain names as indicated by their suffix (e.g.,.com,.edu, or.org).

Total quality management (TQM): A management system in which people within the organization are constantly monitoring what they do to find ways to improve the quality of operations, products, services, and everything else about the firm.

Trading exchange: A website where multiple buyers and sellers come together to conduct business; also called an electronic marketplace.

Transaction processing system : An information system designed to process day-to-day business event data at the operational level of the organization.

Transaction support: Compatibility between a system at the transaction or function that it is designed to support.

Transactions: Repetitive events in organizations that occur as a regular part of conducting day-to-day operations.

Transmission Control Protocol/ Internet Protocol (TCP/IP): The protocol of the Internet, which allows different interconnected networks to communicate using the same language.

Transmission media: The physical pathway to send data and information between two or more entities on a network.

Transnational information system: A type of international information system that is not specific to any country or any particular organization.

Trojan horse: A destructive computer code whose instructions remain hidden to the user because the computer appears to function normally, but in fact it is performing underlying functions dictated by the intrusive code.

Tunnelling: A technology used by VPNs to encapsulate, encrypt, and transmit data over the Internet infrastructure, enabling business partners to exchange information in a secured, private manner between organizational firewalls.

Twisted pair (TP) cable: Cable made of two or more pairs of insulated copper wires twisted together.

Unauthorized access: Occurs when a person gains access to a computer system without the authority to do so.

Unicode: A 16-bit code used for representing numbers, letters, and other characters in binary form.

Uniform resource locator: The unique Internet address for a website and specific web pages within sites.

Unstructured decisions: Decisions for which few or no procedures to follow can be specified in advance.

Upstream: An information flow consisting of information received from another organization, such as from a supplier.

Usenet: Enables groups of people with common interests to send messages or other binary information to each other. Unlike listserv, Usenet has no master list of subscribers. Rather, anyone with access to Usenet may use a newsreader program to post and read articles from the group.

Utilities or utility programs: Software designed to manage computer resources and files.

Value-added network (VAN): Medium-speed WANs that are private, third-party-managed networks and are economical because they are shared by multiple organizations.

Value chain: The process of adding value throughout each of the functions within the organization.

Value chain analysis: The process of analyzing an organization's activities to determine where value is added to products and/or services and the costs that are incurred in doing so.

Value system: A collection of interlocking company value chains.

Vanilla version: The features and modules that the ERP comes with out of the box.

Vertical market: A market comprising firms within a specific industry sector.

Video: Still and moving images that can be recorded, manipulated, and displayed on a computer.

Videoconferencing: The use of integrated telephone, video recording, and playback technologies by two or more people to interact with each other from remote sites.

Virtual company: A firm that exists either on paper or on the Internet but has few or no physical components or attributes.

Virtual private network (VPN): A secure network that utilizes telecommunications lines from a telephone service provider and enables a connection to be created when a transmission needs to take place and terminated once the transmission has been completed, and enables the user to scale bandwidth up and down as needed.

Virtual product: A product without tangible features created through the process of digitization.

Virtual teams: Work teams that are composed of members that may be from different organizations and different locations that form and disband as needed.

Virus prevention: A set of activities for detecting and preventing computer viruses, which has become a full time, important task for information systems within organizations and for all or us with our personal computers.

Viruses: Destructive programs that disrupt the normal functioning of computer systems.

Visual programming languages: Programming languages that have a graphical user interface (GUI) for the programmer and are designed for programming applications that will have a GUI.

Voice mail: Telecommunication technology that allows callers to leave voice messages in a voice mailbox, much like leaving a message on an answering machine.

Voice over IP (VoIP): A collection of hardware and software that enables the use of the Internet as the transmission medium for telephone calls.

Volatile: Memory that loses its contents when the power is turned off.

WAIS (wide area information server): Internet tool that enables users to locate information by indexing electronic data using standard keywords.

Watermarked: The process of marking products so that they can be traced to the original purchaser.

Web browser: A software application that can be used to locate and display web pages including text, graphics, and multimedia content.

Web browsing: How users view and interact with webpages on the World Wide Web.

Web commerce: The component of Internet commerce conducted strictly over the World Wide Web.

Webpage: A hypertext document that contains not only information, but also references or links to other documents that contain related information.

Webpage builders or HTML editors: Programs for assisting in the creation and maintenance of Webpages.

Web server: A computer used to host websites.

Web services: A standardized way of integrating web-based applications using open standards such as XML, SOAP, WSDL, and UDDI over the Internet.

Website: A collection of interlinked webpages created by the same author.

What-if analysis: A capability of some information systems (e.g., a decision support system) that allows a user to make hypothetical changes to the data associated with a problem and to observe how these changes influence the results.

Wide area network (WAN): A computer network that spans a relatively large geographical area; typically used to connect two or more LANs.

Wi-Fi (wireless fidelity): Wireless local area network protocol, based on the 802.11b standard, that normally supports transfer speeds of up to 11 Mbps.

Wireless local area network (WLAN): Local area network using a wireless transmission protocol.

Wireless media: The tools used to transmit and receive electromagnetic signals using methods such as infrared line of sight, high-frequency radio, and microwave systems.

Wisdom: Accumulated knowledge, gained through a combination of academic study and personal experience, that goes beyond knowledge by representing broader, more generalized rules and schemas for understanding a specific domain or domains; wisdom allows you to understand how to apply concepts from one domain to new situations or problems.

Work profile matrix: A chart that consists of job categories and work categories and shows how much time is spent on each of the job categories and each of the different types of work.

Workstation: A special class of microcomputer designed for individuals that has the power of some midrange computers but fits on a desktop.

World Wide Web (WWW): A system of Internet servers that support documents formatted in HTML, which supports links to other documents, as well as graphics, audio, and video files.

Worm: Destructive computer code that is designed to copy and send itself throughout networked computers.

Zip drive: A high-capacity, removable diskette drive that typically uses 100 MB Zip disks or cartridges.

References

CHAPTER 1

Porter, M. 1985. "Technology and Competitive Advantage," *Journal of Business Strategy* 5(3): 60–78.

Porter, M. and V. Millar. 1985. "How Information Gives You Competitive Advantage," *Harvard Business Review* 63(4): 149–161.

Stevens, D. 1994. "Reinvent IS or Jane Will." *Datamation* (December 15, 1994): 84.

Todd, P., J. McKeen, and R. Gallupe. 1995. "The Evolution of IS Job Skills: A Content Analysis of IS Jobs," *MIS Quarterly* 19(1): 1–27.

CHAPTER 2

Bakos, J. Y. and M. E. Treacy. 1986. "Information Technology and Corporate Strategy: A Research Perspective," *MIS Quarterly* 10(2): 107–120.

Brynjolfsson, E. 1993. "The Productivity Paradox of Information Technology," *Communications of the ACM* 36(12): 66–76.

Hagendorf, J. 1998. "Trying to Keep Pace—IS Spending Climbs, Along with Needs, Costs," *Computer Reseller News*. Information from: **www.techweb.com**. Information verified: April 29, 1998.

Harris, S. E. and J. L. Katz. 1991. "Organizational Performance and Information Technology Investment Intensity in the Insurance Industry." *Organization Science* 2(3): 263–295.

Leibs, S. and K. M. Carrillo. 1997. "Research Productivity—Replacing Workers with IS Doesn't Guarantee Maximum Gains, Finds a New Study from Harvard: What Does? You May Be Surprised," *InformationWeek*. Information from: **www.techweb.com**. Information verified: April 29, 1998.

Porter, M. E. 1979. "How Competitive Forces Shape Strategy." *Harvard Business Review* 57 (March–April 1979): 137–145.

Porter, M. E. 1985. *Competitive Advantage: Creating and Sustaining Superior Performance*. New York: The Free Press.

Porter, M. E. 2001. "Strategy and the Internet," *Harvard Business Review* 79(3): 62–78.

Shank, J. and V. Govindarajan. 1993. *Strategic Cost Management: Three Key Themes for Managing Costs Effectively*. New York: The Free Press.

Wheeler, B. C. 2002a. "Making the Business Case for IT Investments Through Facts, Faith, and Fear," ISWorld.net Online Teaching Case and Teaching Note. **www.coba.usf.edu/departments/isds/faculty/abhatt/cases/TN-ITInvestments**.doc.

Wheeler, B. C. 2002b. "NeBIC: A Dynamic Capabilities Theory for Assessing Net-Enablement." *Information Systems Research* 13(2).

Zuboff, S. 1988. *In the Age of the Smart Machine: The Future of Work and Power*. New York: Basic Books.

CHAPTER 3

Boar, B. 1998. "Understanding Data Warehousing Strategically." White paper, NCR. **www.ncr.com**.

Fox, P. (2004). Using IT to Tap Experts' Know-how. *ComputerWorld*. March 15. **www.computerworld.com/ softwaretopics/software/story/0,10801,91174,00.html**.

Hoffer, J. A., M. B. Prescott, and F. R. McFadden, 2002. *Modern Database Management*, 6th ed. Upper Saddle River, NJ: Pearson Education.

Malhotra, Y. 2004. Integrating Knowledge Management Technologies in Organizational Business Processes: Getting Real Time Enterprises to Deliver Real Business Performance. *Journal of Knowledge Management* (forthcoming).

Santosus, M., and J. Surmacz. 2001. The ABCs of Knowledge Management. *CIO* May 23. **www.cio.com/research/knowledge/edit/kmabcs.html**.

Winter, S. G. (2001). *Framing the Issues: Knowledge Asset Strategies. The Conference of Managing Knowledge Assets: Changing Rules and Emerging Strategies.* http://emertech.wharton.upenn.edu/ConfRpts_Folder/WhartonKnowledgeAssets_Report.pdf.

CHAPTER 4

Anonymous. America Online Blocks Half a Million Virus-Infected Emails from Reaching Its Members. http://us.mcafee.com/root/genericURL_genericLeftNav.asp?genericURL=/common/pressIncludes/Nov72003_1.asp&genericLeftNav=/common/en-us/html_files/aboutUs_nav.asp. Information verified: November 6, 2003.

Berghel, H. 1996. U.S. Technology Policy in the Information Age. *Communications of the ACM* 39(6): 15–18.

Looney, C. A., and D. Chatterjee. 2002. Web Enabled Transformation of the Brokerage Industry: An Analysis of Emerging Business Models. *Communications of the ACM* 45(8), 75–81.

Panko, R. 2004. *Corporate Computer and Network Security*. Upper Saddle River, NJ: Pearson Prentice Hall.

Volonino, L., and S. R. Robinson. 2004. *Principles and Practice of Information Security*. Upper Saddle River, NJ: Prentice Hall.

CHAPTER 5

Alexander, M. 2001. "IBM Web Site to Drive ASIC Design Collaboration," Information from: **www. internetweek.com/story/INW20010308S0004**. Information verified: July 27, 2001.

Bowman, R. J. 2003. From Public to Private: Trading Exchanges Change with the Times. *SupplyChainBrain.com*. December 30, 2003. **www.glscs.com/archives/12.03.exchanges.htm?adcode=10**.

Carr, N. G. 2000. Hypermediation: Commerce as Clickstream. *Harvard Business Review* (January–February): 10–11.

ChangeWave Research. 2004. ChangeWave Glossary. *ChangeWave.com.* **www.changewave.com/Glossary.html.**

Chatterjee, D. and V. Sambamurthy. 1999. "Business Implications of Web Technology: An Insight into Usage of the World Wide Web by U.S. Companies," *Electronic Markets—International Journal of Electronic Commerce & Business Media* 9(2) (Spring 1999).

Christensen, C. M. and R. S. Tedlow. 2000. "Patterns of Disruption in Retailing," *Harvard Business Review* (January–February 2000): 6–9.

CIO. 2004. Extensible Markup Language (HML). **www.cio.com/research/current/xml.html.**

Couzin, J. 2000. Analysis: EBay Fraud Lawsuit Raises Questions. *CNN.com.* Information from: **www.cnn.com/2000/TECH/computing/11/07/suing.ebay.idg.** Information verified: July 30, 2001.

Dell 2004. Information from **www.dell.com.** July 2004.

Edwards, J. 2003. Emerging Technology: Tag, You're It. *CIO* February 15. **www.cio.com/archive/021503/et_article.html.**

Kalakota, R., R. A. Oliva, and E. Donath. 1999. "Move Over, E-Commerce," *Marketing Management* 8(3) (Fall 1999): 23–32.

Looney, C. A. and D. Chatterjee. 2002. "Web-Enabled Transformation of the Brokerage Industry: An Analysis of Emerging Business Models," *Communications of the ACM* 45(8): 75–81.

Looney, C., L. Jessup, and J. Valacich. Emerging Business Models for Mobile Brokerage Services. *Communications of the ACM,* 47(6), 71–77.

Laudon, K. and C. Guercio-Traver. 2003. *E-Commerce: Business, Technology, Society.* New York: Pearson Addison Wesley.

Microsoft Corporation. 2001. "Microsoft Business Case Studies," Web.microsoft.com/business/casestudies/default.asp (June 2001).

MobileInfo. 2004. M-Commerce. *MobileInfo.com.* **www.mobileinfo.com/Mcommerce/index.htm.**

Prentice Hall. 2004. Glossary. http://wps.prenhall.com/wps/media/objects/505/517554/glossary.html.

Priceline.com. Information from **www.priceline.com.** July 2004.

Quelch, J. A. and L. R. Klein. 1996. "The Internet and Internal Marketing," *Sloan Management Review* 63 (Spring): 60–75.

Rebello, K. 1996. "Italian Sausage that Sizzles in Cyberspace," *BusinessWeek* (September 23, 1996): 118.

SciQuest. 2001. "SciQuest Corporate Page," Information from: **www.sciquest.com.** Information verified: August 1, 2001.

Stafford, T. F., and M. L. Gillensen. 2003. Mobile Commerce: What It Is and What It Could Be. *Communications of the ACM* 46(12): 35–40.

Szuprowicz, B. 1998. *Extranet and Intranet: E-commerce Business Strategies for the Future.* Charleston, SC: Computer Technology Research Corporation.

Turban, E., D. King, D., J. K. Lee, and D. Viehland, D. *Electronic Commerce 2004: A Managerial Perspective.* 3rd ed. Upper Saddle River, NJ: Pearson Education.

CHAPTER 6

Checkland, P. B. 1981. *Systems Thinking, Systems Practice.* Chichester, UK: John Wiley.

Roche, E. M. 1992. *Managing Information Technology in Multinational Corporations.* New York: Macmillan.

Sprague, R. H., Jr. 1980. "A Framework for the Development of Decision Support Systems," *MIS Quarterly* 4(4): 1–26.

CHAPTER 7

Koch, C., D. Slater, and E. Baatz. 2000. "The ABCs of ERP," *CIO Magazine.* Information from: **www.cio.com.** Information verified: August 6, 2001.

Kumar, K. and J. Van Hillegersberg. 2000. "ERP Experiences and Evolution," *Communications of the ACM* 43(4): 23–26.

Kumar, R. L. and C. W. Crook. 1999. "A Multi-Disciplinary Framework for the Management of Interorganizational Systems," *The DATA BASE for Advances in Information Systems* 30(1): 22–36.

Langenwalter, G. A. 2000. *Enterprise Resources Planning and Beyond.* Boca Raton, FL: St. Lucie Press.

Larson, P. D. and D. S. Rogers. 1998. "Supply Chain Management: Definition, Growth, and Approaches," *Journal of Marketing Theory and Practice* 6(4): 1–5.

Manugistics. 2001. "Enterprise Profit Optimization," Information from: **www.manugistics.com.** Information verified: August 16, 2001.

Markus, M. L. and D. Tanis. 2000. "The Enterprise Systems Experience—From Adoption to Success." In *Framing the Domains of IT Research: Glimpsing the Future Through the Past,* edited by R. W. Zmud. Cincinnati, OH: Pinnaflex Educational Resources.

O'Leary, D. E. 2000. *Enterprise Resource Planning Systems: Systems, Life Cycle, Electronic Commerce, and Risk.* 1st ed. New York: Cambridge University Press.

Porter, M. E. and V. E. Millar. 1985. "How Information Gives You Competitive Advantage," *Harvard Business Review* (July–August): 149–160.

Ptak, C. A. 2000. *ERP Tools, Techniques, and Applications for Integrating the Supply Chain.* Boca Raton, FL: St. Lucie Press.

Sarker, S. and A. S. Lee. 2000. "Using a Case Study to Test the Role of Three Key Social Enablers in ERP Implementation," *Proceedings of the International Conference on Information Systems,* Brisbane, Australia: 414–425.

Soh, C., S. K. Sia, and J. Tay-Yap. 2000. "Cultural Fits and Misfits: Is ERP a Universal Solution?" *Communications of the ACM* 43(4): 47–51.

Willcocks, L. and R. Sykes. 2000. "The Role of the CIO and IT Function in ERP," *Communications of the ACM* 43(4): 32–38.

CHAPTER 8

Applegate, L. M., R. D. Austin, and F. W. McFarlan. 2003. *Corporate Information Strategy and Management.* 6th ed. Chicago: Irwin.

Booch, G. 1990. *Object Oriented Design with Applications.* Redwood City, CA: Benjamin/Cummings.

Boynton, A. C. and R. W. Zmud. 1994. "An Assessment of

Critical Success Factors." In *Management Information Systems*, 2nd ed., edited by Gray, King, McLean, and Watson. Fort Worth, TX: The Dryden Press.

Coad, P. and E. Yourdon. 1991. *Object-Oriented Design*. Englewood Cliffs, NJ: Prentice Hall.

Court, R. 1998. "Disney Buys Out Starwave," **www.wired.com**, *Wired Magazine* (April 30, 1991).

Fryer, B. 1994. "Outsourcing Support: Kudos and Caveats," **www. computerworld.com**, *Computerworld* (April 11, 1994).

George, J. F., D. Batra, J. S. Valacich, and J. A. Hoffer. 2005. *Object-Oriented Systems Analysis and Design*. Upper Saddle River, NJ: Prentice Hall.

Halladay, S. and M. Wiebel. 1993. *Object Oriented Software Engineering*. Englewood Cliffs, NJ: Prentice Hall.

Hoffer, J. A., J. F. George, and J. S. Valacich. 2002. *Modern Systems Analysis and Design*, 4th ed. Englewood Cliffs, NJ: Prentice Hall.

Martin, J. 1991. *Rapid Application Development*. New York: Macmillan.

McConnell, S. 1996. *Rapid Development*. Redmond, WA: Microsoft Press.

McFarlan, F. W. and R. L. Nolan. 1995. "How to Manage an IT Outsourcing Alliance," *Sloan Management Review* 36(2): 9–24.

McKeen, J. D., T. Guimaraes, and J. C. Wetherbe. 1994. A Comparative Analysis of MIS Project Selection Mechanisms." *Database* 25(2): 43–59.

Nunamaker, J. F., Jr. 1992. "Build and Learn, Evaluate and Learn," *Informatica* 1(1): 1–6.

CHAPTER 9

BSA. 2003. Eighth Annual BSA Global Software Piracy Study. *Business Software Alliance* (June). **www.bsa.org**.

Global Software Piracy Study," *Business Software Alliance* (May). **www.bsa.org**.

Gordon, L. A., M. P. Loeb, W. Lucyshyn, and R. Richardson. 2004. 2004 CSI/FBI Computer Crime and Security Survey. *Computer Security Institute*. **www.gosci.com**.

Mason, R. O. 1986. "Four Ethical Issues for the Information Age," *MIS Quarterly* (16): 423–433.

Mosquera, M. 2000. "FBI E-Mail Surveillance Raises Privacy Concerns."**www.techweb.com/wire/story/TWB20000713S0013**.

APPENDIX A

Keogh, J. 2002. *The Essential Guide to Computer Hardware*. Ridgefield Park, NJ: Prentice Hall.

APPENDIX B

Chen, M. and R. J. Norman. 1992. "Integrated Computer-Aided Software Engineering (CASE): Adoption, Implementation, and Impacts." In *Proceedings of the Hawaii International Conference on System Sciences* 3, ed. J. F. Nunamaker, Jr. Los Alamitos, CA: IEEE Computer Society Press: 362–373.

Name Index

Organization Index

A

B

C

Subject Index

NOTE: Key terms and the page(s) on which they are defined appear in boldface.

A

B

C

F

J

K

L

M

T

Syed
9-840 2136
05 Accord
43 Knightswood Cres
Sandalwood Cres / McLaughlin